New Edition

Viewfinder Special

Lese- und Arbeitsbuch
für die gymnasiale Oberstufe

Langenscheidt

Berlin · München · Wien · Zürich · New York

Viewfinder Special

Herausgeber:
Prof. em. Dr. Dr. h.c. Dr. h.c. Peter Freese

Projekt-Team:
Dr. Martin Arndt, Münster
Prof. Dr. Mita Banerjee, Siegen
David Beal, M. A., Bochum
Cornelia Becker, Bremen
Dr. Peter Dines, Cert. Ed., Ludwigsburg
Prof. i.R. Dr. Hanspeter Dörfel, Ludwigsburg
Prof. Dr. Sabine Doff, Frankfurt/Main
OStR Dieter Düwel, Castrop-Rauxel
Prof. em. Dr. Dr. h.c. Dr. h.c. Peter Freese, Paderborn
Jennifer von der Grün, B. A., Dortmund
OStR Ulrich Imig, Wildeshausen
OStR Reimer Jansen, Oyten-Sagehorn
Dr. Michael Mitchell, M. A., Reken und Warwick
StD Dr. Peter-J. Rekowski, Kirchhain
OStR i.K. Peter Ringeisen, M. A., Amberg
Karl Sassenberg, Münster
StD Dr. Annegret Schrick, Essen
StR Susanne Stadler, Wiesbaden
Prof. Dr. Merle Tönnies, Paderborn
Prof. Dr. Laurenz Volkmann, Jena

Verlagsredaktion: Dr. Beatrix Finke

Visuelles Konzept: Barbara Slowik, Atelier S., München

Satz und Produktion: kaltnermedia GmbH, Bobingen

Umwelthinweis: Gedruckt auf chlorfrei gebleichtem Papier.

1. Auflage 2007

Druck: Stürtz GmbH, Würzburg
Printed in Germany
ISBN 978-3-526-51050-5

1 2 3 4 5 / 11 10 09 08 07

Contents

* Titles provided by the editors

1 The Media

Manchester Evening News

Final

30p

Wood's on fire

Meet the hunk who makes history come alive

Curly on his way back to the Street

£1m TO RIDE

Police want a huge rise in fees for Metro squad

EXCLUSIVE

WEATHER 6 BMDs 12 PUZZLES 29 DIARY 22 POSTBAG 23 TV 26-27 BUSINESS: 8 PAGES

EastEnders

family mis-fortunes

There's nothing but woe in Walford for the di Marco clan. Marc Bannerman explains why...

Sisterly love

MARQUIS
FOREVER TANGO

THE TIMES
MONDAY 30p
England stands up to the test
Genetics nature and nurture in the ring
How to spend £20,000 on Haute Couture
Blair to sack ten ministers in major reshuffle
Blériot Mark 2's Channel bid ends in the drink
Cook to shake-up Foreign Office after arms affair
'Tiny' Rowland lost will to live
England cash in on a testing time for umpires
0870 6 000 000
easyJet

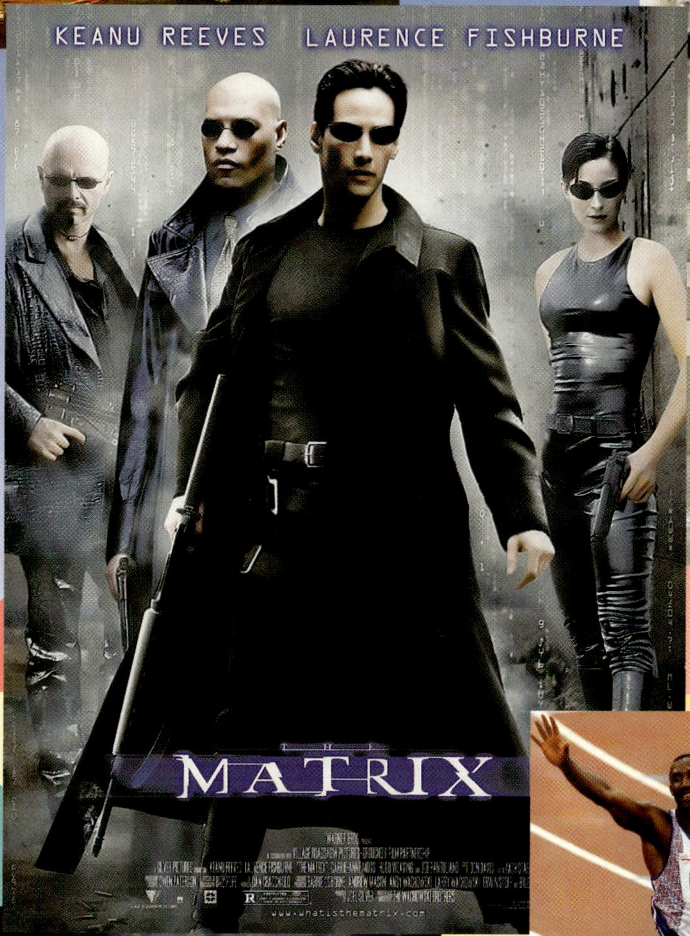
KEANU REEVES LAURENCE FISHBURNE
THE MATRIX
www.whatisthematrix.com

695

WHO WANTS TO BE A
MILLIONAIRE

1

"Private lives that even the tabloids cannot reach"

As a result of the intrusive behaviour of many representatives of the media world, voices have been raised and legal measures have been taken to protect the private spheres of celebrities. This means that newspaper editors are often in a dilemma, not knowing what they can legally publish and when they will have to fear the celebrities' lawyers. – Bill Hagerty, *The Independent on Sunday*, 17 August 2005.

THE RESIDENTS OF SOHAN ARE BEGGING FOR PRIVACY ...GET IT ON PAGES THREE FOUR SIX AND EIGHT AND I WANT **PICTURES!**

Celebrity coverage is now a legal minefield, and papers simply don't know what they can say.

The astonishing case of the actress who may or may not be pregnant has confirmed what everyone in the newspaper industry has believed for some time: celebrity requirements for protection of privacy are spinning out of control.

A most peculiar apology in Friday's *Daily Star* – it neglected to mention the reason why it was saying sorry – was the result of a flurry of legal activity following a story the previous day about Sienna Miller, whose recent exposure in the press has been concentrated on the escapades of errant fiancé Jude Law, rather than the actress's current success on the West End stage.

On the same day, *The Sun* had posed the question: was

Ms Miller expecting a child? The *Star* had no doubts. Neither did the American magazine that ran the story the previous day. It was soon all over the web. ITV's *This Morning* mentioned it. As a secret, the possible pregnancy of Ms Miller, whose very public private life had been in turmoil since Law cheated on her with his children's nanny, was about as watertight as a sieve.

Yet representations by her lawyers caused the *Star* to back off and agree to a form of words in apology that must have totally perplexed anyone who had missed the original story. As one lawyer put it: "The whole privacy situation has gone barmy."

Those toiling in the legal departments of national newspapers are now scratching their heads and contemplating the suggestion that a normal pregnancy can be considered a confidential matter. The rash of privacy actions brought or threatened and the demands being made of newspapers by celebrities are, they contend, making the truth a frequent casualty in what has become a battle to keep readers informed of the news, big and small, momentous and trivial.

Cases involving first Naomi Campbell and then Michael Douglas and Catherine Zeta-Jones were landmarks in the history of the press and privacy. What can be said now is that the conflicting interpretations of what should and shouldn't remain private make the subject a minefield for the press. This and the growth of "no win, no fee" legal representation have resulted in considerable growth in the privacy-based traffic heading for the office of a newspaper's lawyers.

Sienna Miller's grievance is not part of this scenario. Neither was the successful move by lawyers to prevent disclosure of the accurate and sad story concerning *Countdown* host Richard Whiteley's serious heart condition (he died the following day). But other demands in the name of privacy, often fuelled by greed as well as precedent, are of increasing concern.

The much-quoted article 8 of the European Convention of Human Rights declares that respect must be paid to private and family life, home and correspondence. The Press Complaints Commission adopted the same guidelines and requires editors to justify intrusions into any individual's private life as being in the public interest. So far, so good. And judges do back public interest arguments – David and Victoria Beckham last week won their libel action against *The People* for suggesting that he had mounted a hate campaign against their former nanny, but they had previously failed to obtain an injunction preventing the *News of the World* from publishing the nanny's disclosures about their marriage. Yet obtaining such judgements is a lottery for which some newspapers are becoming less inclined to buy a ticket.

A senior newspaper lawyer told me: "It's a celebrity age and readers demand vast amounts of celebrity content. Popular newspapers live on it. But now celebrities have solicitors buzzing around them and the question of privacy has become a milch cow.

"You wouldn't believe the number of complaints that come in from footballers when the paper gets something wrong, no matter how slight. They demand apologies and damages and often they've got agents as well as 'no win, no fee' lawyers egging them on."

It is some years since former PCC chairman Lord Wakeham warned that privacy would cease to be an issue only if "a once-free press had been subjected to such stringent laws and penalties that it no longer dare to report on matters of legitimate public interest", or the public loses "all interest in casting the odd glimpse into the secret world of those in the news". The first proviso has been taken care of by muddle and by "no win, no fee" assistance. The second seems unlikely in a climate where every cough and splutter of *Big Brother* contestants, let alone less savoury bodily functions, are devoured with the morning cornflakes.

There are signs that the truth may become even more elusive. In Ireland, where, as here, growing numbers of celebrities have complained about press intrusion into their private lives, privacy legislation is again being seriously considered.

The Irish Times reported: "Ministers have complained that journalists from tabloid newspapers have photographed them on private occasions ... and have on occasion sought to link them romantically – and sometimes inaccurately – with various people." Don't you just love that "sometimes"?

"Twenty years ago most of the privacy complaints we get wouldn't have got it off the ground unless the information came from a confidential source, a doctor for example," reckons another harassed member of a national newspaper legal team.

Meanwhile, the legal year clattered to an end with the settlement of what seemed to be a vast number of libel actions – the Beckhams vs *The People*; Northern Ireland football international Keith Gillespie vs *News of the World*; movie star Cameron Diaz vs *The Sun*; a former girlfriend of *EastEnders'* star Steve McFadden vs *Sunday Sport*. Result: Celebrities (substitute: celebrity's friend) 4 – Press 0.

And in the wider newspaper world, Richard Desmond launched a gossip website, the Daily Snack, which promises "bite-sized news and gossip" prepared by one journalist who will collate content from the company's newspapers and magazines. It will be penetrating stuff, no doubt. Desmond, lest we forget, owns the *Daily Star*.

Vocabulary

1 celebrity (n.): famous living person - **6 requirement** (n.): s.th. that s.o. needs or asks for - **7 to spin** (v.): to turn around and around very quickly - **8 peculiar** (adj.): strange, unfamiliar, or a little surprising - **10 flurry** (n.): a time when there is suddenly a lot of activity - **13 errant** (adj.): behaving badly, usually by not obeying your parents or not being faithful to your husband or wife - **21 turmoil** (n.): a state of confusion, excitement, or anxiety - **22 sieve** /sɪv/ (n.): a round wire kitchen tool with a lot of small holes, used for separating solid food from liquid or small pieces of food from large pieces - **24 to back off** (v.) here: to stop supporting s.th., or decide not to do s.th. you were planning to do - **27 barmy** (adj.): slightly crazy - **28 to toil** (v.): to work very hard for a long period of time - **30 to contemplate** (v.): to think about s.th. that you might do in the future - **31 confidential** (adj.): spoken or written in secret and intended to be kept secret - **31 rash** (n.): a large number of unpleasant events, changes etc. within a short time - **34 to contend** (v.): to argue or state that s.th. is true - **34 casualty** (n.): s.o. or s.th. that suffers as a result of a particular event or situation - **36 momentous** (adj.): a momentous event, change, or decision is very important because it will have a great influence on the future - **46 grievance** (n.): a belief that you have been treated unfairly, or an unfair situation or event that affects and upsets you - **48 disclosure** (n.): a secret that s.o. tells people, or the act of telling this secret - **51 to fuel** (v.): to make s.th., especially s.th. bad, increase or become stronger - **52 precedent** (n.): /ˈpres$^{\text{I}}_{\text{ə}}$dənt/ an action or official decision that can be used to give support to later actions or decisions - **57 intrusion** (n.): when s.o. does s.th. or s.th. happens that affects your private life or activities in an unwanted way - **61 libel** (n.): /ˈlaɪbəl/ when s.o. writes or prints untrue statements about s.o. so that other people could have a bad opinion of them - **62 to mount** (v.) here: to plan, organize, and begin an event or a course of action - **64 injunction** (n.): an order given by a court which tells s.o. not to do s.th. - **68 to be inclined to do s.th.** (adj.): to be likely to do s.th. - **72 to buzz around**: to move quickly around a place - **73 milch cow** (n.): s.th. that provides a lot of money for s.th. else - **78 to egg somebody on**: to encourage s.o. to do s.th., especially s.th. that they do not want to do or should not do - **84 to cast a glimpse**: to look quickly in a particular direction - **86 proviso** (n.): /prəˈvaɪzəʊ/ a condition that you ask for before you will agree to s.th. - **87 muddle** (n.): confusion - **89 every cough and splutter**: every small movement or change - **90 savoury** (adj..): /ˈseɪvəri/ pleasant or morally acceptable - **90 to devour** (v.): to eat s.th. quickly because you are very hungry - **94 elusive**: an elusive idea or quality is difficult to describe or understand - **106 harassed** (adj.): /ˈhærəst/ anxious and tired because you have too many problems or things to do - **108 to clatter** (v.): to move quickly and noisily - **118 bite-sized** (adj.): small enough to put into your mouth to eat - **119 to collate** (v.): to gather information together, examine it carefully, and compare it with other information to find any differences - **120 penetrating** (adj.): here: intrusive - **121 lest** (conj.): in order to make sure that s.th. will not happen

Explanations

8 *Daily Star*: British daily popular newspaper - **11 Sienna Miller**: Sienna Rose Miller, model and actress, born in New York City in 1981; on Christmas Day of 2004 she became engaged to Jude Law, in October 2005 they ended their engagement - **13 Jude Law**: David Jude Law, British actor, born In Lewlsham, London In 1972 - **14 West End**: the western part of central London, where there are large shops, theatres, expensive hotels etc. - **15 *The Sun***: a British tabloid daily newspaper which generally supports rightwing and nationalist political ideas - **18 ITV**: Independent Television, a group of British television companies that are funded by advertising - **18 *This Morning***: TV breakfast show - **37 Naomi Campbell**: a British model and actress, born in Streatham, South London on May 22, 1970 - **38 Michael Douglas**: an Oscar winning American actor and producer, born in New Brunswick on September 25, 1944 - **38 Catherine Zeta-Jones**: an Oscar winning Welsh actress, born in Swansea, Wales, on September 25, 1969, married to Michael Douglas - **49 *Countdown***: a British game show presented by Richard Whiteley from 1982 to 2005 - **56 Press Complaints Commission**: a British organisation that has regulated printed newspapers and magazines since 1990; the commission is funded by the annual levy it charges; it has no legal powers; all newspapers and magazines voluntarily contribute to the costs of, and adhere to the rulings of, the commission, effectively making the industry self-regulating - **60 David Beckham**: English football star, born in Leytonstone, London on May 2, 1975 - **60 Victoria Beckham**: born Victoria Adams, April 17, 1974, an English popular music singer, who first came to prominence as a member of a girl band, the Spice Girls, married David Beckham in 1999 - **61 *The People***: a British tabloid newspaper sold every Sunday, which is known for printing shocking articles about famous people, especially about their relationships and their sexual experiences - **64 *News of the World***: a British tabloid newspaper sold every Sunday, which prints shocking articles about famous people, especially about their relationships and sexual experiences; it sells more copies than any other British newspaper - **97 *The Irish Times***: Irish newspaper, launched in the late 1850s, the paper is generally perceived as liberal, social democratic and neutral on Irish unity - **113 *EastEnders***: a popular British soap opera on television, which is about the working class people who live in Albert Square in the East End of London; it deals with common social problems in a realistic way - **114 *Sunday Sport***: a British newspaper, which established itself in 1986 as a tabloid; it has published plainly ludicrous stories, such as a double-decker London bus being found frozen in the Antarctic ice

Awareness

1 Have you read any reports about the personal lives of celebrities recently? If so, where did you read these stories? Did you read them by chance or do you regularly read such publications? Who or what were these stories about?
2 What aspects of celebrities' lives are generally reported on in the print media?
3 Have you ever heard about any reactions on the part of celebrities whose private lives have been dealt with in the press? What were these reactions?

Comprehension

4 Describe the topical example that moved Bill Hagerty to write this article at this point of time.
5 What changes have taken place that have caused a lawyer to say "The whole privacy situation has gone barmy" (ll. 26f.)?
6 What consequences do these changes involve for the British press?

Analysis

7 Identify the standpoint of the journalist on the issue of privacy. Prove your ideas with concrete examples from the text.
8 What rhetorical and structural devices (Reference Library, p. 311) does Bill Hagerty use to express his views on the subject? Explain to what extent these means make his arguments convincing.

Opinion

9 In ll. 69–71 a lawyer claims that we live in "a celebrity age and readers demand vast amounts of celebrity content. Popular newspapers live on it." To what extent do you share the lawyer's view? Can you envisage any aspects of a celebrity's life that should not be covered by the press?
10 Why do you think so many readers are interested in or even fascinated by the personal lives of celebrities?
11 Think of some recent examples of intrusion into celebrities' lives. How do you think you would feel/react in their position?

Projects

12 The Press Complaints Commission deals with complaints about the way journalists work. Write a letter (Reference Library, p. 300) for Sienna Miller to the commission expressing indignation about the manner in which the British press reported about her.
13 Find an article in the German press about a celebrity. Make notes (Reference Library, p. 304) on the important facts in the article and present them to your partner. Exchange your notes and then use your partner's notes to write an article on the same topic for a popular British newspaper.
14 In the discussion about the right of the individual to privacy and the right of the press to inform its readership, there are different standpoints. For example, some editors are against all restrictions, others are in favour of self-regulation by the press. But there are also people who demand tighter government legislation. In order to elucidate these different positions, you could hold a debate (Reference Library, p. 299) in class. To do this divide yourselves into three groups. Each group takes on the role of one representative of the three groups and writes a speech presenting that person's viewpoint. One member of each group should then hold the speech (Reference Library, p. 301) in front of the whole course. Remember that the aim of the speech is to convince the listeners of your views. After the three speeches have been delivered, a general discussion can ensue. Finally a vote is held as to whose arguments and rhetorical techniques are the most convincing.
15 The cartoon on p. 8 reveals something about the attitude of the press towards the privacy of individuals. Describe the cartoon and explain its message.

Internet Project

16 The website www.media-awareness.ca/english/resources/educational/lessons/secondary/Broadcast_news/you_be_the_editor.cfm offers you the opportunity to act as the editor of a newspaper/magazine and to take decisions on the publication of photos and articles. You will find various cases and options you can discuss. Consider the cases and give reasons for your final decision.

2 Soap scenes and issues

The popularity of soap operas is not only based on stereotypes but also on the recurrence of certain themes soap viewers expect to be confronted with. These issues range from general social problems to personal intimate affairs. The following three photos present scenes in which some typical soap themes can be recognized.

Ever the gent, Phil leaves Doctor Trueman to pick up the pieces

Soap scene A

Inside Soap, 2 March 2001

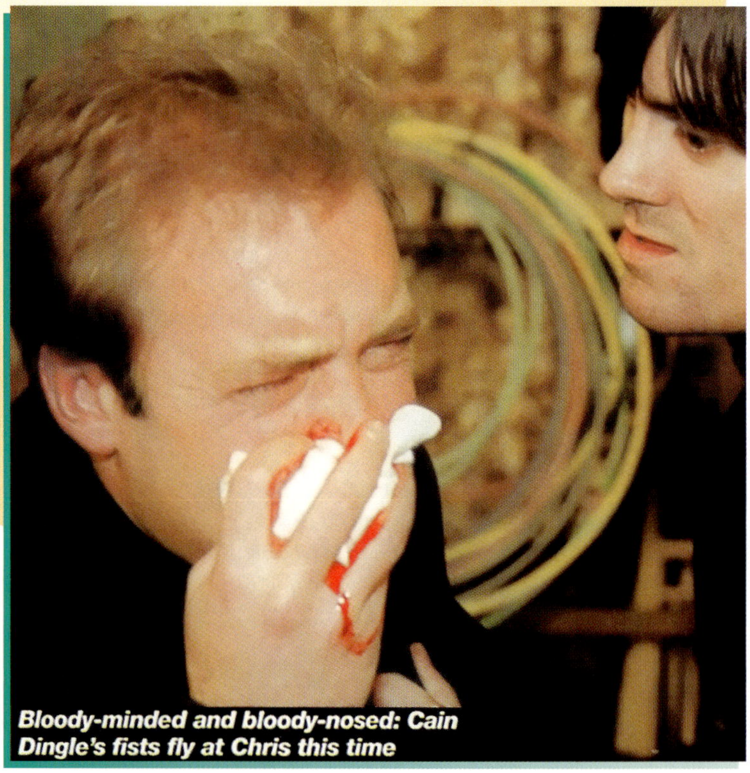

Bloody-minded and bloody-nosed: Cain Dingle's fists fly at Chris this time

Soap scene B

Soaplife, 10 May 2000

Soap
scene C

Inside Soap, 28 April 2000

Your cheatin' heart: will love rat Declan confess all to Gabby?

Explanation

Inside Soap: a British magazine that is published once a fortnight and gives information on all the current British soap operas: story-lines, news, gossip and behind the scenes information. It belongs to the Australian company PMP Communications.

AWARENESS

1 Drawing on your knowledge of soap operas, try to identify the themes that appear most frequently.

DESCRIPTION

2 Describe what is presented in each of these three pictures (Reference Library, p. 313).

ANALYSIS

3 From your observations of the pictures draw conclusions on what situations are presented. Which general themes are these situations based on?

OPINION

4 Why do you think stock themes play such an important role in soaps?
5 Some critics of soap opera claim that the realisation of these standard themes is to a large extent unrealistic. Would you share this view?

PROJECT

6 Watch an episode from a soap and report on it to your course taking the use of stereotype characters and stock themes into particular consideration.

3

"Cut! Why TV mustn't go soft on hard news"

Many people believe that the news broadcasts in general reflect reality in every detail. The journalist Martin Bell takes a critical look at the fact that some news programmes, especially those from war or battle zones, are 'filtered', supposedly for the benefit of the viewers. - *The Independent on Sunday,* 26 June 2005.

Television cameramen filming the distribution of goods to Iraqi people during the Iraq war

Broadcasters say that the time delay on live news announced last week would spare viewers' sensitivities. But should we really sanitise reports, asks Martin Bell.

This time, they've really done it. The BBC is the nations's premier news broadcaster – always in terms of quantity and more often than not in terms of quality. It has some of the best journalists around. It retains its grip, for most of the time, on a serious news agenda. It sets the standards by which others are judged. It has recovered from the Gilligan/Kelly/Hutton imbroglio, in which it was generally seen to be right, as the government was seen to be wrong. It lost that battle but won the war. Unlike the Government, it is widely trusted. It should be holding its positions on the high ground, not diving into the trenches. So why is it for ever running for cover without even the excuse of hostile fire? Under new editorial guidelines revealed last week it has committed itself to a time delay before broadcasting scenes of "sensitive and challenging events". This restriction, we are told, was brought on by last year's terrorist atrocity in Beslan in which 344 hostages died, half of them children. The scenes of terror and bloodshed were indeed distressing. They were broadcast around the world as they happened, not only by the BBC. But the BBC was, typically, the first to flinch from the consequences. It has now decided that, in future, it doesn't want to upset people with live and unedited images of real world violence. If a 9/11 were to happen tomorrow, the BBC would no longer be out there competing with its rivals. Instead it would avert its gaze from the news of the day and provide live coverage only of events that it deemed to be insensitive and unchallenging: Wimbledon perhaps, or the Eurovision Song Contest. Where will it end? With Terry Wogan reading the 10 o'clock news?

The length of the time delay is left unspecified. Minutes? Hours? Days? Even the shortest delay will have the viewers switching in droves to other, less neurotic and uncensored channels. It will leave them suspicious of the filtered version of reality on offer. And it will compromise the BBC's greatest asset, which is its global reputation as a trustworthy source of news. People will reasonably ask: if they are hiding this from us, what else are they hiding? [...]

The argument about televised violence is an old one. I was on the losing side of it for much of the 1990s, urging the editors to show the realities of the wars in Croatia and Bosnia: not all of them, of course, but enough to be truthful. Instead, we featured the outgoing fire but not the incoming, the militiamen blazing away in the ruins with their Kalashnikovs, but not the carnage and the casualties at the other end.

This was done, I was told, in the interests of good taste. But war is a bad-taste business. All that the censorship achieved, I believe, was to show it as an acceptable way of settling differences. No wonder that our present government, none of whose ministers know anything of warfare, is so addicted to it.

It remains one of life's small mysteries why the BBC should spend £50m on the little-watched News 24. Now eight years old, this enjoys the melancholy distinction of being the most frequently relaunched channel in broadcasting history. The BBC, like ITN, rushed into the rolling news business because it was there. They did it to compete with Sky, and without really thinking through the implications. As a result, we now have at least two more all-news channels than we need – indeed, in my view, three more.

The real charge against them is not that they upset people, but that they show so much more than they know. They put a premium on speed rather than accuracy. Time and again, with the mantra "Breaking news" they go to air with reports that turn out to be false or downright misleading. There was even a time when one news channel had on its screen savers the wonderfully revealing slogan "Never wrong for long". That should be the motto of rolling news – and, in an ideal world, its epitaph.

[...]

Journalists caught up in the whirligig of rolling news would do well to heed Kipling's wise advice to deliver their reports "soberly, and with what truth is possible". The proposal for a time delay on live coverage will do nothing to address the medium's fundamental shortcomings. It will merely add another layer of unbelievability.

Vocabulary

Title: to go soft: to avoid hurting s.o.'s feelings - **3 sensitivity** (n.): the quality or condition of being sensitive (responsive to external conditions or stimulation) - **3 to sanitise** (v.): to make more acceptable by removing unpleasant or offensive features - **9 agenda** (n.): a list or programme of things to be done or considered - **11 imbroglio** (n.): /ɪm'brəʊliəʊ/ difficult situation - **15 trench** (n.): a long narrow ditch embanked with its own soil and used for concealment and protection in warfare - **17 hostile** (adj.): relating to or characteristic of an enemy - **21 atrocity** (n.): an act of unusual cruelty - **23 distressing** (adj.): causing strain, anxiety, or suffering - **26 to flinch** (v.): to make a short backward movement when you are afraid of s.th. - **31 to avert** (v.): to turn away - **31 gaze** (n.): a steady, fixed look - **32 to deem** (v.): to regard, to consider - **38 in droves**: in large numbers - **41 asset** (n.): a valuable item that is owned - **42 trustworthy** (adj.): reliable - **50 militiaman** (n.): /m(ɪ/ə)'lɪʃəmən/ a man who is a member of a militia (an army composed of ordinary citizens rather than professional soldiers) - **50 to blaze** (v.): to fire, to shoot - **51 carnage** (n.): a massacre - **52 casualty** (n.): a person killed in an accident or in a war - **62 to relaunch** (v.): to reintroduce a product or brand to the market after changes or improvements have been made - **65 implication** (n.): consequence - **71 mantra** (n.): here: a commonly repeated word or phrase - **76 epitaph** (n.): an inscription on a tombstone in memory of the one buried there - **78 whirligig** (n.): here: a series of fast changes - **80 sober** (adj.): here: marked by seriousness

Explanations

21 Beslan: the Beslan school hostage crisis began when armed terrorists took hundreds of schoolchildren and adults hostage on September 1, 2004, at School Number One in the Russian town of Beslan in North Ossetia. On September 3, 2004, the third day of the standoff, shooting broke out between the hostage-takers and Russian security forces. According to official data, 344 civilians were killed, 186 of them children, and hundreds more wounded. The terrorist attacks were the responsibility of Chechen terrorist Shamil Basayev. - **28 9/11:** The terms "September 11", "11th September", and "9/11" have been widely used in the Western media as a shorthand for the September 11, 2001 attacks on the World Trade Center and The Pentagon in the United States of America. - **33 Wimbledon:** the All England Tennis Championships, commonly referred to as simply Wimbledon, is the oldest and most prestigious tennis tournament in the world. It takes place in the London suburb of Wimbledon every summer and is played on grass courts. - **33 Eurovision Song Contest:** an annual televised song contest with participants from numerous European countries, which has been running since 1956 - **34 Terry Wogan:** (born 3 August 1938) a popular radio and television broadcaster on the BBC - **47 the wars in Bosnia and Croatia:** the words refer to the Yugoslav wars, which were a series of violent conflicts in the territory of the former Yugoslavia and which took place between 1991 and 2001. They comprised two sets of successive wars affecting all of the six former Yugoslav republics. - **51 Kalashnikov:** an assault rifle designed by Mikhail Kalashnikov in 1947 - **79 Kipling:** Joseph Rudyard Kipling (December 30, 1865 - January 18, 1936) was a British author and poet, born in India. He is best known for the children's story *The Jungle Book* (1894).

Info

The Gilligan/Kelly/Hutton imbroglio

Andrew Paul Gilligan (born 22 November 1968) is a journalist best known for his report – while defence and diplomatic correspondent for BBC Radio 4's *The Today Programme* – about the British Government's dossier on weapons of mass destruction in Iraq. On May 29, 2003, back in Britain, Gilligan reported allegations that a dossier published by the British Government had deliberately exaggerated the military capabilities of Iraq in order to justify going to war with the country. In a subsequent newspaper article, Gilligan quoted a source as identifying Alastair Campbell, then the Prime Minister's Director of Communications and Strategy, as responsible for the exaggerations. Gilligan's source was one of the world's foremost biological weapons experts, Dr David Kelly, who committed suicide shortly after being identified as the source for the story. An inquiry, the Hutton Inquiry, was subsequently set up to investigate the circumstances leading up to Kelly's death.

Info

British Media

BBC: The British Broadcasting Corporation is the national broadcaster of the United Kingdom. It produces programmes and information services, broadcasting on television, radio, and the Internet. The BBC's main domestic services on television include BBC 1, BBC 2, BBC 3, BBC 4, the news channel BBC News 24, and the children's channels CBBC and CBeebies. The BBC also operates the UK's only dedicated politics channel, BBC Parliament, covering events in the British Houses of Parliament, Welsh Assembly, Scottish Parliament & European Parliament, as well as highlights of overseas legislatures such as the US Senate. National radio services include Radio 1, Radio 2, Radio 3, and Radio 4, and BBC Radio Five Live. In addition, the BBC operates the BBC World Service on radio, funded by and operated in cooperation with the Foreign and Commonwealth Office. The BBC produces a large body of programming for domestic and worldwide broadcast. Many programmes (especially documentaries) are sold to foreign television stations, and comedy, documentaries and historical drama productions are popular on the international DVD market. It is an autonomous corporation run by a board of governors appointed by the government for a term of four years (formerly five years). – **ITN**: Independent Television News, the main supplier of news broadcasts to two British television groups: ITV and Channel 4 – **Sky**: Sky News is Europe's first 24-hour television news channel, originally launched in February 1989. It is part of British Sky Broadcasting, a company that operates Sky Digital, the most popular subscription television service in the UK and Ireland.

Awareness

1 How important is it for you to hear/read the latest news? Where do you usually get your news from? Why do you make use of this particular source?

2 People are sometimes horrified by the presentation of violent scenes in the news. Can you think of any recent incidents whose coverage might have shocked viewers/readers? How do you feel about this problem?

Comprehension

3 The journalist's thesis appears in the headline and the subheading of the article. Explain his standpoint in your own words. What arguments for his view can you identify in the text?

4 As an expert in the field of news broadcasting Martin Bell expresses further criticism of recent developments in this area. What else does he criticize?

Analysis

5 Analyse the steps (Reference Library, pp. 312f.) in which Martin Bell proceeds to show his attitude towards recent trends in the presentation of news programmes.

6 What linguistic and stylistic devices (Reference Library, p. 311) does the journalist use to make his ideas convincing for the reader?

Opinion

7 In the subheading Martin Bell poses the question "But should we really sanitise reports?" How do you feel about this question? Write a personal comment.

8 Bell mentions a number of trends in news broadcasting in Great Britain. What developments have you observed in German news broadcasting? How do you see the future of news programmes on TV?

Projects

9 Try to find a news photo in a newspaper or magazine or on the Internet that can stand for a scene from a TV news programme and that could be considered to be distressing for some people. Use this photo as a basis for a discussion (Reference Library, p. 299) that could take place, e.g., at the BBC. One news editor is in favour of showing the scene in the next news broadcast, whereas his colleague is of the opinion that viewers should be spared such scenes. Write down the discussion between the two editors. You can also act it out.

10 Watch television news programmes regularly and record one programme in which you find scenes which may be deemed distressing. Present this programme to the class/course and comment on it. Your presentation should include comments on the choice of pictures, the way the film material is edited and the reporter's words. It will also be interesting to compare the presentation of the scene in the news programmes of various TV channels.

4

"Email me not. (But if you want to send a letter in a red envelope, that's different...)"

Written communication has undergone dramatic changes over recent years. Whereas not too long ago the traditional letter was the main form of written communication in all spheres of life, today e-mail contact is undermining this dominant position. Journalist Stephen Bayley examines various aspects of this phenomenon. - *The Independent on Sunday*, 15 December 2004.

This column is kept on track and arrives at its destination (here) only after painstaking and detailed discussions between the editor and me. In our transactions we cover the momentous cultural issues of the day and consider how we might best address them in respect of the delicate balance between insight, comment and critique which we like to think gives such point and style to the page.

A typical exchange goes like this:

Editor: "What you doing this week?"

Me: "Dunno. Call you later."

E-mail certainly has its advantages, but does not encourage felicity or elaboration. If our experience is anything to go by, literary correspondence will be an extinct genre within a few years. The letter will go the way of the post. Those fabulous exchanges where vanity was traded for advancement have been made redundant by electrons. The typewriter long since replaced pen, paper and ink, but now bit-spit has replaced the typewriter. Did you realise that there is nowhere on earth where a manual typewriter is manufactured? Not even for South American police forces to use in straight-to-video movies.

There is something inherent in e-mail that encourages crassness. This was noted by an early apologist, one J L R Licklader, who in a 1978 article (snappily called "Applications of Information Networks") promoted the medium's tolerance of bad typing and illiteracy as positive advantages. Single computers had been able to talk to one another since the early Sixties, but e-mail developed out of attempts to extend the computerisation of cross-country US air defence systems ("to prevent", in early Rumsfeldian, "technological surprise from enemies"). [...]

All communications technologies have an effect on their predecessors, but it is usually a cumulative rather than a destructive process. The invention of the telegraph and the telephone in the 19th century did not make letters redundant. Rather they liberated the epistolary medium from the banal tasks of making appointments or ordering stuff. If you can call to check a train time, why bother with a letter? In this sense the tele-media actually liberated letters from humdrum functionality and turned them into a self-conscious art form. In fact, the coming of the phone seems to have been a positive stimulus to literary

The need to write dozens of e-mails every day doesn't necessarily improve the style in which they are written.

correspondence: 11,000 of Forster's letters survive, and the edited correspondence of Virginia Woolf runs to six published volumes.

But e-mail is more culturally threatening. Deep in its architecture is the grim functionality of military communications and their preference for terse, spare language. A technology created so that air defence systems in Colorado and Arizona could simultaneously zap incoming Soviet ICBMs does not lend itself to fine expression. Yet its immediacy and efficiency are utterly addictive. An e-mail transaction has simultaneous benefits of speed and dissociation. Yes, you can get your message there instantly, but, no, you don't have to bother with the delaying or disabling social niceties of a phone call. And very few, save the impossibly anal, bother to save them. There will be no archives in future. As Frank Kermode, King Edward VII Professor of English at Cambridge, complained just two years after America went on-line, we are very unlikely to see *The Oxford Book of e-mails*.

So, whither the letter? Notwithstanding the imaginative efforts of Royal Mail to destroy its credibility, a version of mail remains, although it is a melancholy thing. Voltaire said that the arrival of the post is one of the "consolations of life". Voltaire had not seen my post-bag: today it contained press releases from five different car companies (there is a new Korean SUV upcoming), utility bills, catalogues of cardigans from a discount cashmere company in the Western Isles, some fliers from a pizzeria boasting a wood-fired oven, two books, a bogus Christmas card from an estate agent, a BBC contract for a pittance and an invitation to participate in the champagne launch of a block of flats in Knightsbridge. In short, not a single piece of correspondence generated by the human hand.

So I am encouraging a return to letter-writing. We reveal ourselves in our letters rather more than in our e-mails. […] There is something about the genteel pace of a letter that stimulates intimacy. Nancy Mitford thought air-mail was vulgar because it expressed an ungentlemanly urgency. In Venezuela, charmingly, they used to allow love letters to go at half-price, provided they were in red envelopes. We don't really have love e-mails, so something wonderful has been lost. The love-letter function has, of course, been taken over by SMS. David Beckham is its Laureate. But I do not think we will ever see *The Oxford Book of Text Messages*.

Vocabulary

2 painstaking (adj.): characterized by extreme care and great effort – **7 point** (n.): a quality or characteristic that is important or distinctive – **11 dunno**: (coll.) I don't know – **13 elaboration** (n.): the process of working out in detail by labour and study – **15 extinct** (adj.): no longer existing or living – **16 vanity** (n.): excessive pride in one's appearance or accomplishments – **19 bit-spit** (n.): 'bit' refers to computer bits, 'spit' to short expressions of emotion – **24 inherent** (adj.): occurring as a natural part or consequence – **25 crassness** (n.): lack of attention to detail – **25 apologist** (n.): a person who argues in defence or justification of s.th. – **28 illiteracy** (n.): the condition of being unable to read and write – **36 predecessor** (n.): a system that exists before the next is developed – **36 cumulative** (adj.): increasing or enlarging by successive addition – **39 epistolary** (adj.): being in the form of a letter – **43 humdrum** (adj.): lacking variety or excitement – **44 self-conscious art:** shows that the artist is paying too much attention to how the public will react – **51 terse** (adj.): brief and to the point – **54 to zap** (v.): to kill or destroy – **54 to lend o.s. to**: to be suitable for – **55 immediacy** (n.): directness – **57 dissociation** (n.): here: a lack of polite phrases – **61 anal** (adj.): here: showing too much concern for small details – **66 whither** (adj.): to what place, result, or condition – **66 notwithstanding** (prep.): in spite of – **70 consolation** (n.): s.o. or s.th. that makes you feel better when you are sad – **73 utility** (n.): here: a business that provides an essential service – **76 bogus** (adj.): not genuine – **77 pittance** (n.): a very small amount of money – **83 genteel** (adj.): marked by refinement in taste and manners – **91 laureate** (n.): one honoured or awarded a prize for great achievements

Explanations

33 Rumsfeldian: referring to Donald Rumsfeld (b. 1932), US Secretary of Defense 2001–2006 – **46 E.M. Forster**: Edward Morgan Forster (1879–1970), an English author – **47 Virginia Woolf**: (1882–1941), one of the foremost British authors and feminists of the 20th century – **54 ICBM:** Intercontinental Ballistic Missile: a very-long-range (greater than 5500 km) ballistic missile designed for nuclear weapons delivery – **67 Royal Mail**: the national postal service in the United Kingdom. – **69 Voltaire**: François-Marie Arouet (1694–1778), a French Enlightenment writer and philosopher – **72 SUV**: sport-utility vehicle – **74 Western Isles**: also called the Outer Hebrides, an island chain off the west coast of Scotland – **84 Nancy Mitford**: English novelist and biographer (1904–1973)

Awareness

1 What form of written communication do you use primarily? Do you still write letters? If so, on what occasions? Are there any situations in which you prefer writing e-mails?
2 E-mail writing has enjoyed tremendous popularity in recent years. Try to explain this development.

Comprehension

3 Characterize Bayley's attitude towards the two forms of written communication (letters/e-mails).
4 What arguments does the writer put forward to illustrate his views?

Analysis

5 What effect does the headline of this article have on the reader?
6 Analyse Bayley's line of argumentation (Reference Library, pp. 312f.). In what steps does he proceed?
7 What do the language and the style (Reference Library, p. 311) of the article reveal about the readership the text is aimed at?

Opinion

8 Towards the end of the text the writer states that "We reveal ourselves in our letters rather more than in our e-mails." (ll. 81f.). Comment on this statement.
9 How do you see the future of the letter? Do you think it will disappear completely in a few years?

Project

10 In lines 10f. the journalist presents a typical e-mail exchange between himself and his editor. If this exchange took place in letter form, it would most certainly be completely different. Write brief letters in which you consider the editor's and journalist's expectations and problems.

5 Caught in the web: Internet advertising for children

Various surveys have recently revealed that children have an increasing amount of money to spend and also strongly influence the purchasing habits of their parents. The advertising world, obviously aware of this, makes great efforts to target children through different media. Online advertising is the fastest growing marketing medium for reaching children at school and at home, which has become a major concern of some parents and teachers. Children are particularly vulnerable as they are not always in a position to distinguish between advertising and information.

AWARENESS

1 Taking into consideration the fact that children today have great spending power, describe to what extent the advertising world makes efforts to target the younger consumer generation.

2 What experiences do you have with online advertising? Would you say that it is difficult to distinguish between advertising and information?

DESCRIPTION

3 Explain what is the most conspicuous feature of this website.

4 Describe the various elements and the layout of this Internet page.

ANALYSIS

5 How do the designers of this website try to attract and maintain the children's attention?

OPINION

6 Would you consider this Internet page to be a potentially successful site? Explain your position.

7 Many parents are concerned about the influence of online advertising on their children. Do you think these worries are justified?

PROJECTS

8 The American Center for Media Education has claimed that "advertising practices are potentially very harmful to children." According to the CME these practices include:
- eliciting personal information from children through the use of prizes, games and surveys
- monitoring children's online activities and compiling detailed personal profiles
- designing personalized advertising aimed at individual children
- designing advertising environments to capture children's attention for extended periods of time
- seamlessly integrating advertising and content
- creating product "spokescharacters" to develop interactive relationships with children

Examine the websites of companies whose products may especially target children. To what extent can such harmful practices be found on Internet sites?

9 The competitive spirit of the advertising world has led to a number of competitions and awards for outstanding creativity. The Golden Marble Awards Best Online Ads, e.g., regularly presents the best Internet adverts.
Try to find as many advertising sites as possible that are aimed at children. Consider criteria such as animation, fun, games, information, etc., and decide which ads you would rate highest.

10 Choose a product that almost exclusively appeals to children. Using the criteria you have applied above, find a name and design a website for this brand.

6 Film poster: *Wall Street*

As a rule, shortly before a new film appears in the cinema posters for the film are published. They may appear outside the cinemas and copies may be printed in newspapers and magazines. The aim, of course, is to arouse curiosity in the general public and to encourage people to see the film. These posters have several features in common, i.e. they might allude to the topic of the film and they present the main actors or actresses as well as the director.

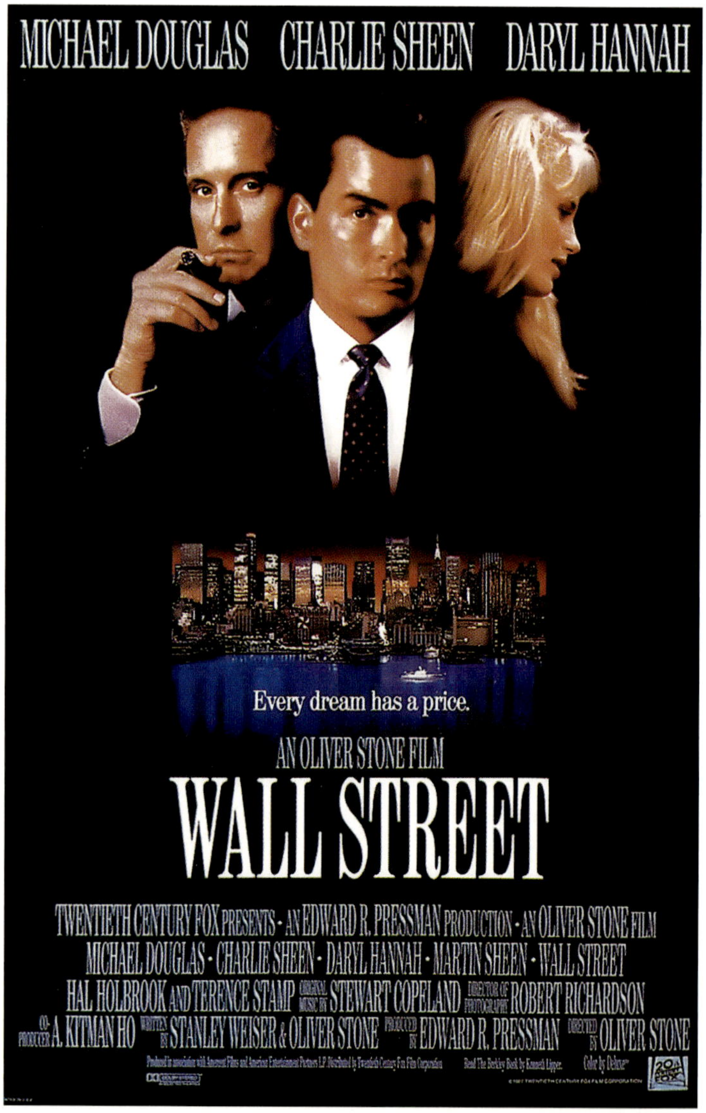

Explanation

Wall Street: (directed by Oliver Stone, 1987) The film revolves around Bud Fox (Charlie Sheen), a young and impatient Wall Street stockbroker, who is willing to do everything to get to the top. After meeting the highly successful but ruthless broker Gordon Gekko (Michael Douglas), whose motto is "Greed is good", Fox finds himself in a world of yuppies, dubious business deals and fast money. This world is completely at odds with his family and the way he was brought up.

Awareness

1 To what extent do you notice and closely look at film posters?

2 Can you remember any striking film poster that you have recently seen?
- Describe it to the course.
- What made it so impressive?

3 In how far are you influenced by film posters in your decision to watch a film? What other factors influence you in your choice of film?

Description

4 Describe the various elements of the poster on p. 20. Which do you consider to be the most striking feature?

Analysis

5 Examine the way the three persons are depicted. Take the following aspects into account:
- the constellation of the characters
- their facial expressions
- their appearance.

6 What impression do the smaller photo and the phrase create?

7 What do the various elements of this poster suggest about the content of the film?

Film poster for the satire The Truman Show, *starring Hollywood comedian Jim Carrey*

Opinion

8 How appealing do you think this poster is for the majority of people? Would it encourage you to go to see the film?

Project

9 Choose a film that you have recently seen in the cinema or on TV and design a poster for it. Consider which elements you would like to include and the amount of space each of them should cover.

10 A trailer for a film or a TV programme is a set of short extracts from it, which are shown or broadcast in order to advertise this film or programme. Record a number of trailers that appear on TV. Choose one of them that particularly appeals to you, present it to the course and explain why you find it so interesting.

11 There are several similarities between a film poster and a film trailer. Try to find the poster and the trailer for a film that has just been released. Present them to the course and ex-plain the similarities and differences between them.

Special Feature 1

The Arts

Frank Lloyd Wright, Guggenheim Museum, New York (1956–1959)

Nature is a revelation of God;
Art a revelation of man.
Henry Wadsworth Longfellow

Composing is like driving down a foggy road …
Benjamin Britten

Art, like morality, consists in drawing the line somewhere.
Gilbert K. Chesterton

Music can name the unnamable and communicate the unknowable.
Leonard Bernstein

Everything in the universe has rhythm.
Everything dances.
Maya Angelou

To give body and perfect form to your thought, this alone is what it is to be an artist.
Jacques-Louis David

Grant Wood, American Gothic *(1930)*

Sol LeWitt, Splotch No. 3 *(2000)*

William Turner, Rain, Steam and Speed *(1844)*

Art is the stored honey of the human soul, gathered on wings of misery and travail.
Theodore Dreiser

Good art is not what it looks like, but what it does to us.
Roy Adzak

The aim of art is to represent not the outward appearance of things but their inward significance.
Aristotle

St David's Cathedral, Rose Window (12th century)

Tasks and Project

1. Look at the works of art on this page. Does one of them appeal to you immediately? Why (not)? Try to explain.
2. Discuss the quotations about art and find out which of them convince you.
3. Project: Choose one of the artists and research his or her life and work.

The only way to do it is to do it.
Merce Cunningham

Architecture is inhabited sculpture.
Constantin Brancusi

The Puccini of Lowestoft

The classic themes of conscience and dissent breathe fresh life into Benjamin Britten's music

Hywel Williams (*The Guardian*, 5 December 2006)

Benjamin Britten's reputation as a composer stands as high as it has ever done, 30 years after his death in December 1976. In his case there has been hardly any of the negative "re-evaluation" so many popular artists suffer. Part of the reason is the extraordinary range of Britten's musical styles, and that variety reflects the extensive influences on him. Purcell's cadences and the choral traditions of the English cathedral; the Elizabethan melancholy of John Dowland's compositions for the lute; the continental experimentalism of Stravinsky, Mahler and Berg; the sounds of Japanese No drama: all went into the Britten mix at some stage during almost half a century of creative composition.

His fluently confident technique, however, stands at the point where virtuosity turns into genius. He absorbed and transmuted these influences so that his own subsequent compositions were no mere pastiches: they were invariably fresh, original and authentically Britten. (...) Britten's voice is always his own.

His eventual reputation as the patron saint of English music meant that Britten was garlanded with honours, including the Companion of Honour, the Order of Merit and, in his last months, a life peerage. But despite that establishment embrace, his career shows some of the difficulties of the artist in England.

Ralph Vaughan Williams, a professor at the Royal College of Music when Britten was a student there, was at the height of his influence during Britten's youth. The dead weight of Williams's ill-disciplined meanderings meant that a provincialising Victorian taste was having an artificially prolonged existence in English music. The early Britten, by contrast, was being influenced, through his teacher Frank Bridge, by Bela Bartok. But he was also quarrying deeper into his own national soil (...). *The Hymn to Saint Cecilia* (1942) recovered an English 17th-century sense of musical form while its libretto by Auden showed the same dazzling combination of a classical structure being interpreted by a modernist temperament.

Peter Grimes announced the arrival of a major Britten theme – that of the doomed and solitary outcast. The opera was first performed in 1945 and was part of the London cultural scene's post-war revival – showing Britten's ability to be part of a national consensus while standing aside from its triumphalism. This was, after all, an artist whose pacifism led him to leave England in 1939 as well as one whose ultimate loyalties impelled his return in 1942.

In the history of opera he is only rivalled by Puccini in his treatment of themes such as innocence and corruption, love's dependence and its betrayal.

The daily details of Britten's life were pretty dull. A dentist's son from Lowestoft and a cricket fan, he was a self-disciplined, middle-class professional type. But those qualities of application were placed at the service of genius. The recordings of his conducting and piano performances show some of Britten's scrupulous intensity. His own music retains its power to affect the ear and the mind because its themes are the classic ones of conscience and the individual voice of protest. Britten's very English dissent is also a major chapter in the history of the English sublime.

Vocabulary

subtitle: dissent (n.): refusal to agree with an accepted opinion – **23 transmute** (v.): change into s.th. else – **24 pastiche** (n.): a work of art that has been put together from various styles (imitating other works) – **28 garland** (v.): decorate – **36 ill-disciplined** (adj.): badly organized – **37 meandering** (n.): wandering aimlessly – **53 doomed** (adj.): certain to fail or be destroyed – **53 solitary** (adj.): lonely – **54 outcast** (n.): s.o. who is not accepted by the people they live among, or who has been forced out of their home – **62 impel** (v.): make s.o. feel an urgent duty to do s.th. – **73 scrupulous** (adj.): paying careful attention to all details – **78 sublime** (n.): s.th. that is so good or so beautiful that it deeply affects you

Tasks and Projects

1. What does this article tell you about Britten's links to the European tradition? Do you know any of the other composers?
2. Find out more about the composers mentioned in the text. Present your results to the class.
3. Have you heard of famous US-American composers? Do some research on Leonard Bernstein, Aaron Copland and Samuel Barber on the Internet.
4. Choose one of Britten's works and listen to it – perhaps your music teacher can lend you a CD. Talk about your reaction to it.

"But Is It Art?"*

Some people say modern art is hard to understand.

Marianne Macdonald, *The Independent*, 5 September 1995, p. 6.

The small boy was finding it hard to grasp what was going on. "Is she asleep, mummy?" he demanded. He peered up against the glass. "Is she Snow White? Is there a spell on her?"

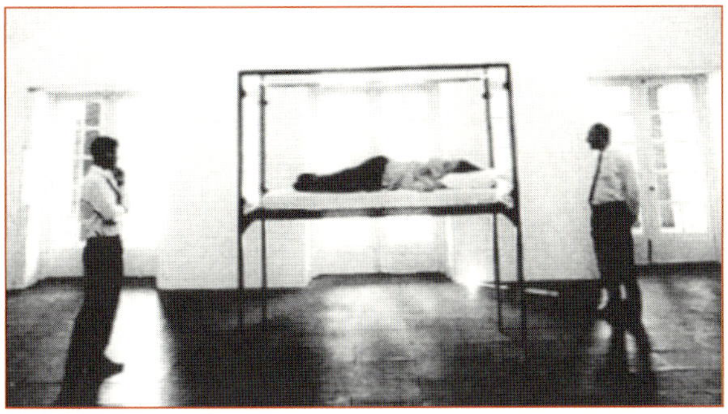

An art work?

"No, darling," whispered his mother. "It's an art work. She's lying there so we can look at her." The boy stuck his hands into his shorts and stared again at the unmoving form. "No," he said finally. "I don't think so. I think she's in a forest and she's waiting for a prince."

His confusion was not untypical of the 200 or so people who came into the Serpentine Gallery in Hyde Park yesterday to watch Tilda Swinton (...) sleeping in a glass tank in full view of the public. She was dressed simply for the occasion, just a cotton shirt, blue corduroys and a pair of canvas deck shoes. In front of her on the white mattress lay a pair of glasses, neatly folded, and behind her on the pillow streamed her red, unwashed hair.

She will lie in the tank from 10am until 6pm every day until Sunday, and yesterday, on day one, she showed no sign of nerves. In fact, she shows no signs at all. Her most notable movement came at 12.20pm, when she gave a deep sigh, lifted her left foot and turned dreamily on her back. Most of the time she lay on her left side, her arms wrapped around herself, her chin buried in the pillow and her eyes firmly closed. There were no embarrassing side-effects of sleep, such as dribbling or snoring.

"Do you think she can hear us?" a man with a goatee beard asked his friend. "I don't know, knock on the glass," his friend replied. They mooched over to the two security guards. "Does she move?" one asked. "Only occasionally," said the guard. "From one side to the other." Throughout the morning, the gallery-goers came and went in a reverential hush so as not to wake the actress. One man with a ponytail broke the silence by snorting loudly and walking out. He turned out to be a builder from Stornoway on the Outer Hebrides. "Call me a cynic, but I don't see the point," he said. But mostly the reception verged on rapturous. "It made my heart beat faster, I thought it was absolutely incredible," said Wolfgang, 31, a musician.

There was a sudden murmur. Tilda Swinton was moving. She stretched out her arms, turned her head, and sighed softly. Around her, the crowd stretched their necks and whispered eagerly to each other.

But is it art?

Vocabulary

27 to dribble (v.): to let liquid flow slowly out of the mouth – **29 goatee beard** (n.): small pointed beard – **30 to mooch** (v.): (infml.) to wander about with no purpose – **34 reverential** (adj.): full of respect – **34 hush** (n.): quiet, silence – **36 to snort** (v.): to make a rough noise through the nose – **39 to verge on** (v.): to be close to a harmful or extreme state

Explanations

3 Snow White: the princess in the famous Grimm fairy tale who is apparently killed by her stepmother and kept by the seven dwarfs in a glass case – **12 Tilda Swinton:** British actress (born 1960), known for both arthouse and mainstream films, e.g. the leading part in Sally Potter's *Orlando* (1992) and the part of the White Witch in *The Chronicles of Narnia* (2005, directed by Andrew Adamson). In 1995, she was part of artist Cornelia Parker's installation "The Maybe", where Swinton lay asleep in a glass case.

Tasks and Projects

1. What do you think about Tilda Swinton sleeping as art?
2. What do you think of the reactions from the people mentioned in the newspaper article?
3. Do you think art is important? Why?

2 Technology and the Environment

The Amazon rain forest intact and ...

"It's not Earth that's fragile: It's we who are fragile. Nature has withstood catastrophes far worse than what we've delivered. Nothing we do will destroy Nature. But we can destroy ourselves." – James Lovelock, one of the authors of the Gaia hypothesis.

... under assault

Global ecosystems and resources are simply not sufficient to sustain the current economies of the industrial West and at the same time bring more than 2 billion people into the global middle class through the same resource-intensive development model pioneered by North America and Europe. Limits on the ability to increase oil production, shortages of fresh water, and the economic impacts of damaged ecosystems and rapid climate change are among the factors that make it impossible to continue current patterns on such a vastly larger scale. Humanity is now on a collision course with the world's ecosystems and resources. In the coming decades, we will either find ways of meeting human needs based on new technologies, policies, and cultural values, or the global economy will begin to collapse.

Christopher Flavin and Gary Gardner, "China, India, and the New World Order", in Linda Starke (ed.): *State of the World 2006: Special Focus: China and India* (Washington: Worldwatch Institute, 2006), p. 4.

Prometheus Unleashed?

Over the past two and a half centuries technology has developed and spread at an ever-increasing rate. As a result, today, in the western world at least, we enjoy a higher standard of material comfort and social security than ever before. On average every second European has a car of his/her own; the average annual expenditure is about €30,000 per European household; statistically 80% of Europeans go away on holiday once a year, and 60% own their own house or apartment, two out of three Europeans has his/her mobile phone and every second European has access to the Internet. Their average life expectancy is about 78 years at birth. This material well-being has come about through technological and social developments that would have been inconceivable even a hundred years ago:

- the harnessing of natural and man-made energy resources
- the development of mass transportation
- the invention and production of highly effective and affordable electrical and electronic goods and devices at home and at work
- scientific and highly efficient methods of food production
- advances in medicine and health care

to name just a few.

Technology in the service of mankind

"I wonder which is more eco-friendly … buying a plastic Christmas tree or cutting down a real one."

"There ist nobody else. I'm afraid we've wiped out all of the other species."

But everything we do to improve our standard of living affects our social and natural environment, very often in ways that were not originally foreseen. Many of these "side-effects" have turned out to be very negative for the whole world; and while some effects may be positive for us in the short-term, they will have a disastrous impact on us in the longer perspective, especially for those parts of the world which are not as developed as we are.

Here are just some of them:

- an explosion in world population as a result of advances in medical science
- the accelerating growth of cities that in some places in the world goes unchecked, uncontrolled and in fact uncontrollable as a result of industrialisation
- the transformation of the natural world into a man-made environment
- the depletion of natural resources
- the degradation of the environment
- global warming and all its ramifications.

However, there is no going back. The question we face today is whether we shall be able to use technological advances to overcome the very damaging effects that these very advances have helped to create. Can we maintain our standard of living and preserve our natural environment? Or are we on a road to inevitable disaster that threatens not only our fragile way of life but life itself on the planet as we know it? The question is extremely complex and allows no easy answers. But answers must be found since our very survival on this planet is at stake.

Man, Nature and Technology

1

"The Industrial Revolution"

An understanding of the conflict between technological progress and ecological conservation presupposes some basic knowledge of how our technologically-shaped world came about. Some insights are provided by the following text, taken from *Encyclopaedia Britannica 2005 Deluxe Edition CD-ROM*, and the timeline on p. 30.

[The] Industrial Revolution in modern history [is] the process of change from an agrarian, handicraft economy to one dominated by industry and machine manufacture. This process began in England in the 18th century and from there spread to other parts of the world. Although used earlier by French writers, the term Industrial Revolution was first popularized by the English economic historian Arnold Toynbee (1852–83) to describe England's economic development from 1760 to 1840. Since Toynbee's time the term has been more broadly applied.

The main features involved in the Industrial Revolution were technological, socioeconomic, and cultural. The technological changes included the following: (1) the use of new basic materials, chiefly iron and steel, (2) the use of new energy sources, including both fuels and motive power, such as coal, the steam engine, electricity, petroleum, and the internal-combustion engine, (3) the invention of new machines, such as the spinning jenny and the power loom that permitted increased production with a smaller expenditure of human energy, (4) a new organization of work known as the factory system, which entailed increased division of labour and specialization of function, (5) important developments in transportation and communication, including the steam locomotive, steamship, automobile, airplane, telegraph, and radio, and (6) the increasing application of science to industry. These technological changes made possible a tremendously increased use of natural resources and the mass production of manufactured goods.

There were also many new developments in non-industrial spheres, including the following: – (1) agricultural improvements that made possible the provision of food for a larger non-agricultural population, (2) economic changes that resulted in a wider distribution of wealth, the decline of land as a source of wealth in the face of rising industrial production, and increased international trade, (3) political changes reflecting the shift in economic power, as well as new state policies corresponding to the needs of an industrialized society, (4) sweeping social changes, including the growth of cities, the development of working-class movements, and the emergence of new patterns of authority, and (5) cultural transformations of a broad order. The worker acquired new and distinctive skills, and his relation to his task shifted; instead of being a craftsman working with hand tools, he became a machine operator, subject to factory discipline. Finally, there was a psychological change: man's confidence in his ability to use resources and to master nature was heightened.

Vocabulary

2 agrarian (adj.): relating to farming or farmers – **17 motive power** (n.): the motive power or force for a machine, vehicle etc. makes it move – **18 petroleum** (n.): oil that is obtained from below the surface of the Earth and is used to make petrol – **21 expenditure** (n.): the action of spending or using time, money, energy etc. – **23 to entail** (v.): to involve s.th. as a necessary part or result – **36 distribution** (n.): the act of sharing things among a large group of people in a planned way – **40 shift** (n.): a change in the way people think about s.th.; in the way s.th. is done etc. – **42 sweeping** (adj.): affecting many things or making an important difference to s.th. – **45 of a broad order** (phr.): on a large scale – **51 to heighten** (v.): to increase or improve s.th.

Explanation

24 division of labour: the separation of a work process into a number of tasks, with each task performed by a separate person or group of persons. It is most often applied to systems of mass production and is one of the basic organizing principles of the assembly line. The reduction in production time and the ability to replace craftsmen with lower-paid, unskilled workers result in lower production costs and a less expensive final product. Contrary to popular belief, division of labour does not necessarily lead to a decrease in skills – known as proletarianization – among the working population. The Scottish economist Adam Smith saw this splitting of tasks as a key to economic progress by providing a cheaper and more efficient means of producing goods.

Awareness

1 Note down the associations that you have with the expressions "industrial" and "revolution". Share them with the rest of your class.

Comprehension

2 Explain in your own words what is meant by the term "Industrial Revolution", according to the extract from the Encyclopaedia. Give illustrative examples.

3 The introduction to the article mentions the three main features of the Industrial Revolution as being: technological, socioeconomic, and cultural. Which concrete examples would fit into these categories?

Analysis

4 Using a dictionary (Reference Library, pp. 304f.), find out the difference between "science" and "technology".

5 Analyse the logical relationship between the first and second paragraphs of the text.

6 What is the author's apparent attitude towards the developments s/he describes?

7 Looking at the timeline on p. 30, discuss the relationship between industrial inventions, agricultural improvements, improvements in transportation and population growth.

Opinion

8 On the basis of the information provided, discuss with your partner whether the Industrial Revolution was a positive or negative development. Look particularly at the effects on ordinary and poor people.

Project

9 The Industrial Revolution changed not only ways of life but significantly altered and expanded language. Some lexical terms modified their meaning while others had to be invented. Using an etymological dictionary (Reference Library, pp. 304f.) or the *Oxford English Dictionary* or *Webster's Third* look up the development in meaning of "manufacture", "engine", "machine", "automobile", "airplane", "industry" and any other industrial words and report back to the rest of your class.

Internet Projects

10 Using the Internet, find out why the Industrial Revolution started in England rather than elsewhere.

11 The article and the timeline refer to a number of inventions: the spinning jenny, the steam engine, the power loom, the internal-combustion engine etc.
Make a list and then, using the Internet, find out how at least three of these inventions function and report this to other members of your class. Also try to assess their impact on contemporary life.

12 Find out more details about the important inventors and improvers mentioned in the article and the time-flow chart.

Charles Dickens (1812–1870) is generally regarded as the greatest English novelist. In his works he addressed a wide readership and made appeal to the intellect, sentiments and humour of his readers. Most of his novels and stories present criticism of one or more aspects of Victorian society and attitudes. For example, in *A Christmas Carol* (1843) Dickens was particularly scathing of meanness and miserliness, such as revealed by Mr. Scrooge, while in *Bleak House* (1852–53) he satirized the inefficiency and corruption of the English legal system and, in *Oliver Twist* (1837–38), the inhuman treatment of the poor in general and children in particular. The tone of Dickens' works, particularly in his early career, was characterized by humour but in later life it became darker, more pessimistic and sarcastic. Dickens' childhood was insecure, since his father was imprisoned for debt and he was forced at an early age to work in a squalid factory. After serving as a solicitor's clerk, he worked as a reporter for London newspapers in the law courts and Parliament, with some success. These early experiences found their way later into Dickens' fiction. His career as a writer began in 1833 with short stories and articles for magazines. In 1837 his comic novel *The Pickwick Papers* (originally serialized in 20 monthly instalments) made Dickens the most popular novelist in England, a popularity which has continued up to the present day.

Vocabulary

Intro: unmitigated (adj.): complete – **detrimental** (adj.): /ˌdetr$^{ɪ}_{ə}$'mentl/ bad or harmful – **to be set** (v.): to take place – **fictitious** (adj.): /fɪk'tɪʃəs/ not existing in reality but invented – **3 as matters stand** (phr.): in reality; in actual fact – **5 savage** (n.): a wild or uncivilized person – **7 interminable** (adj.): /ɪn'tɜːm$^{ɪ}_{ə}$nəbəl/ never-ending – **7 serpent** (n.): snake – **7 to trail oneself** (v.): to make a track – **8 to uncoil** (v.): (usu. of a snake) to become untwisted; to straighten out – **10 ill** (adv.): here: unpleasant, foul – **10 dye** (n.) a substance used to colour material – **10 vast** (adj.): large – **10 pile** (n.): things placed on top of each other – **11 to rattle** (v.): to make a number of quick sharp noises – **11 to tremble** (v.): to shake uncontrollably with quick sharp movements – **12 piston** (n.): a part of an engine that moves up and down in a tube or cylinder – **13 monotonously** (adv.): /mə'nɒtənəsli/ in a tiring, dull way without change or variety – **15 to inhabit** (v.): to live in a place – **18 pavement** (n.): a path with a hard surface, usu. of stone, concrete or asphalt – **20 counterpart** (n.): a thing which is in the same or similar position as s.th. else – **24 shrouded** (adj.): covered or hidden – **24 haze** (n.): a light mist, smoke or smog – **25 impervious** (adj.): not allowing anything to pass through – **25 ray** (n.): a narrow beam or pencil of light – **27 bulky** (adj.): having great size – **27 blotch** (n.): a large irregular spot or mark – **27 prospect** (n.): a wide distant view – **28 blur** (n.): s.th. whose shape is not clearly seen – **28 soot** (n.): the black powder produced when s.th. is burnt – **28 confusedly** (adv.): in a disorderly manner – **29 to aspire** (v.): to direct one's hopes and efforts to some important aim – **29 vault** (n.): a high ceiling – **29 murkily** (adv.): in a dark and unpleasant way – **30 to creep** (v.): to move slowly close to the ground – **31 quarter** (n.): the direction from which s.th. comes – **31 dense** (adj.): difficult to penetrate or see through – **31 jumble** (n.): a disorderly mixture – **33 suggestive** (adj.): leading the mind into a particular way of thinking – **39 vapour** (n.): the gaslike form of a liquid – **40 to droop** (v.): to hang down – **42 stoker** (n.): a person who puts fuel (for example coal) into a furnace – **42 to emerge** (v.): to come out – **45 paling** (n.): a post or part of a fence – **46 swarthy** (adj.): dark – **46 visage** (n.): /'vɪzɪdʒ/ a face – **47 to contemplate** (v.): to look at s.th. thoughtfully – **49 to stifle** (v.): to stop s.o. from breathing properly – **52 story** (n.): any of the levels in a building – **53 to ooze** (v.): (of a thick liquid) to flow very slowly – **53 to trickle** (v.): to flow slowly in a thin stream – **56 to waste** (v.): to grow thinner and thinner and lose one's strength – **56 to toil** (v.): to work hard – **56 languidly** (adv.): without strength or any show of effort – **58 sane** (adj.): having a healthy mind – **58 wearisome** (adj.): tired – **60 foul** (adj.): (of weather) bad – **61 measured** (adj.): careful; exact; steady – **62 substitute** (n.): a replacement – **63 rustling** (adj.): making a sound like leaves in the wind – **63 hum** (n.): a continuous low sound – **65 whirr** (n.): a regular sound like s.th. beating against the air – **65 shaft** (n.): a bar which turns, or around which a belt or wheel turns, to pass on power, especially from an engine to s.th. driven by the engine

Explanations

55 simoom: a hot, dry sand-wind which blows through the African and Asiatic deserts

Factories from the inside c. 1830 ...

... at first sight, clean and bright ...

Awareness

1 You were born and bred in the country and as a young person come to a big industrial city for the first time. What do you see, hear, smell etc.? How do you react to these first, overwhelming impressions?

2 Imagine that you are a city planner. What would the modern city look like that you would design?

Comprehension

3 What does Dickens' "Coketown" look like? Describe it in your own words.

Analysis

4 Read the extra information on setting and atmosphere in the Reference Library, p. 309. What aspects of setting and atmosphere does Dickens concentrate on?

5 Analyse the stylistic and rhetorical means (for example, the use of adjectives, verbs, imagery, antithesis etc.) that Dickens employs to create the setting and atmosphere that make up his description of Coketown. (See the Reference Library, p. 311.)

6 Which aspects of industrialism are criticised in the text?

Opinion

7 Does Dickens' portrait of Coketown bear any resemblance to the industrial scene on p. 31? If so, in what respects?

8 In what ways have attitudes towards industrialism changed since the time of Dickens?

Project

9 Imagine that you are Charles Dickens and thoroughly disgusted with the working conditions in Coketown. Write a letter to a London newspaper (*The Times*, maybe) expressing your thoughts and feelings on the matter and calling for action from factory owners and the government.

Internet Projects

10 Not all of Dickens' contemporaries were critical of the Industrial Revolution. The Scottish chemist and philosopher Andrew Ure (1778–1857), for example, was particulary in favour. Find out as much as you can about Ure and his ideas from the Internet (e.g. http://www.fordham.edu/halsall/mod/1835ure.html) and present them to the rest of your class.

11 Using the Internet (for example, http://www.longwood.edu/staff/munsonjr/19europe/holley/holl2.htm or http://www.originsnetwork.com/help/about-gallery-employ.htm), find out as much as you can about working conditions for ordinary men, women and children in the Victorian age. Report back to the rest of your class or together with your group make a poster presentation of the topic including eye-witness accounts and illustrations.

12 Find out what measures were taken in the 19th century to improve conditions in factories in Britain.

3

Sinclair Lewis

Babbitt

One of the most important influences on our natural and social environment has been the automobile. In his novel, *Babbitt* (1922), Sinclair Lewis (1885–1951) describes attitudes to the car amongst members of the American provincial middle-class. The extract below describes a dinner-table conversation of the Babbitt family on the subject of buying a new car. - Sinclair Lewis, *Babbitt* (New York: Harcourt, Brace, and Co., 1950), pp. 73–75.

The roast of beef, roasted potatoes, and string beans were excellent this evening and, after an adequate sketch of the day's progressive weather-states, his four-hundred-and-fifty-dollar fee, his lunch with Paul Riesling, and the proven merits of the new cigar-lighter, he was moved to a benign, "Sort o' thinking about buying a new car. Don't believe we'll get one till next year, but still, we might."

Verona, the older daughter, cried, "Oh, Dad, if you do, why don't you get a sedan? That would be perfectly slick! A closed car is so much more comfy than an open one."

"Well now, I don't know about that. I kind of like an open car. You get more fresh air that way."

"Oh, shoot, that's just because you never tried a sedan. Let's get one. It's got a lot more class," said Ted.

"A closed car does keep the clothes nicer," from Mrs. Babbitt; "You don't get your hair blown all to pieces," from Verona; "It's a lot sportier," from Ted; and from Tinka, the youngest, "Oh, let's have a sedan! Mary Ellen's father has got one." Ted wound up, "Oh, everybody has got a closed car now, except us!"

Babbitt faced them: "I guess you got nothing very terrible to complain about! Anyway, I don't keep a car just to enable you children to look like millionaires! And I like an open car, so you can put the top down on summer evenings and go out for a drive and get some good fresh air. Besides – a closed car costs more money."

"Aw, gee whiz, if the Doppelbraus can afford a closed car, I guess we can!" prodded Ted.

"Humph! I make eight thousand a year to his seven! But I don't blow it all in and waste it and throw it around, the way he does! Don't believe in this business of going and spending a whole lot of money to show off and –"

They went, with ardor and some thoroughness, into the matters of streamline bodies, hill-climbing power, wire wheels, chrome steel, ignition systems, and body colors. It was much more than a study of transportation. It was an aspiration for knightly rank. In the city of Zenith, in the barbarous twentieth century, a family's motor indicated its social rank as precisely as the grades of the peerage determined the rank of an English family – indeed, more precisely, considering the opinion of old county families upon newly created brewery barons and woolen-mill viscounts. The details of precedence were never officially determined. There was no court to decide whether the second son of a Pierce Arrow limousine should go in to dinner before the first son of a Buick roadster, but of their respective social importance there was no doubt; and where Babbitt as a boy had aspired to the presidency, his son Ted aspired to a Packard twin-six and an established position in the motored gentry.

The favor which Babbitt had won from his family by speaking of a new car evaporated as they realized that he didn't intend to buy one this year. Ted lamented, "Oh, punk! The old boat looks as if it'd had fleas and been scratching its varnish off." Mrs. Babbitt said abstractedly, "Snoway talkcher father." Babbitt raged, "If you're too much of a high-class gentleman, and you belong to the *bon ton* and so on, why, you needn't take the car out this evening."

Both too expensive for Babbitt!

Sinclair Lewis (1885–1951) was born in Sauk Centre, Minnesota. As a boy he was a dreamer and at 13 unsuccessfully ran away from home to become a drummer boy in the Spanish-American war. He achieved wide recognition with the publication of *Main Street* in 1920. *Babbitt* (1922) and *Arrowsmith* (1925), for which he was awarded the Pulitzer Prize, are considered his best novels; *Elmer Gantry* (1927) and *Dodsworth* (1929) are also counted among his better novels. In 1930 Lewis received the Nobel Prize. He was the first American to be honored in this way. His lasting contribution to US-American literature is his ingenious and satirical portrayal of the mores and manners of the American middle-class in the 1920s.

Vocabulary

1 string bean (n.): a type of long thin green bean – **6 benign** (adj.): /bɪ'naɪn/: kind and gentle – **11 slick** (adj.): (coll.) good; swell – **11 comfy** (adj.): (coll.) comfortable – **15 shoot** (interj.): (euphemism for shit) used to express annoyance or surprise – **21 to wind up** (v.): to bring to an end – **29 gee whiz** (interj.): /'dʒiː'wɪz/ used as an introductory expletive or to express surprise or enthusiasm – **30 to prod** (v.): to urge; try to get a reaction from s.o. – **31 humph** (interj.): (a sound made with the lips closed to express a feeling of doubt or dissatisfaction) – **32 to blow s.th. in** (v.): to spend recklessly – **36 ardor** (n.): strong excitement or eagerness – **37 streamline body** (n.): (of a car) smoothly shaped frame and outer covering – **38 ignition** (n.): the means or apparatus for starting an engine (such as a car engine) by using electricity – **40 aspiration** (n.): strong desire to do s.th. or have s.th., esp. s.th. great or important – **40 knightly rank** (n.): membership of a high social class – **43 peerage** (n.): the rank of a peer (baron, viscount, earl, marquis, duke are the five noble ranks who in Britain (!) have the right to sit in the House of Lords) – **44 old county families** (n.): families belonging to the English gentry – **45 brewery barons** (n.): businessmen who have only recently become wealthy, brewing (producing), for example, beer and other malt liquors – **46 precedence** (n.): the right to be put or dealt with before others, esp. because of greater importance – **50 respective** (adj.): of or for each one; particular and separate – **51 to aspire** (v.): to direct one's hopes and efforts to some important aim – **55 to evaporate** (v.): to (cause to) change into steam and disappear – **57 punk** (n.): nonsense, foolishness – **58 varnish** (n.): a liquid which, when brushed onto articles made esp. of wood and allowed to dry, gives a clear hard bright surface – **59 snoway talkcher father:** That's no way to talk to your father – **61 bon ton** (n.): /'bɒn'tɒn/ the fashionable world; the upper classes

Explanations

4 his four-hundred-and-fifty-dollar fee: earlier in the book Babbitt made a real-estate transaction, his commission being $450.-. – **4 Paul Riesling**: a close friend of Babbitt's – **10 sedan**: an enclosed automobile body having two or four doors and seating four or more persons – **29 the Doppelbraus**: neighbors of the Babbitts – **41 Zenith**: name of the fictitious 'middletown' in the American Middle West in which the action of the novel takes place – **48ff. Pierce Arrow limousine; Buick roadster; Packard twin-six**: popular and prestigious automobiles in the 1920s – **53 motored gentry**: a comic allusion to the English class known as the "landed gentry": people from a high social class who own the land from which they obtain their income

Info

Automobiles in the USA

"Widespread adoption of the automobile did indeed reshape American lifeways. Patterns of courtship, residence, socialization of children, education, work habits, and use of leisure time were all radically altered by the adoption of the automobile. The rise of a standardized, middle-class national culture in the United States was greatly encouraged by the contributions of the motor vehicle to the decline of localism, ethnicity, and class differences. The modern industrial city with its residential suburbs is a product of automobility, as are most of the formidable problems for municipal and national government associated with the uncontrolled growth of megalopolis." (James Flink)

"After the Second World War, many factories converted from military production to automobile manufacturing. At the same time in North America, there was a great need for new housing. Urban development had traditionally focused upon public transit lines such as subways and trolleys or streetcars, but suddenly with the increased availability of the automobile, the first sprawling suburbs were built. The spread out nature of the suburbs made it difficult to travel by foot, bicycle or public transit and therefore North American cities slowly became dependent on the automobile." (Stuart Baird)

Vocabulary

Intro: issue (n.): /'ɪʃuː/ a subject to be talked about, argued about, decided – **to put into perspective** (v.): to present a problem, issue etc. in an objective way, usu. by considering all of its aspects, so that its importance is neither exaggerated nor underestimated – **environmentalist** (n.): a person who tries to prevent the environment from being harmed – **the humanities** (n.): studies such as ancient and modern literature, philosophy, history etc. – **3 doom story** (n.): a prediction about a future catastrophe which does not come true – **3 consequence** (n.): an effect – **3 to be upon s.o.** (v.): to affect s.o., usu. in a negative way – **5 vastly** (adv.): very much – **5 severity** (n.): here: great destructive power – **6 disruption** (n.): the act of causing disorder – **8 essence** (n.): the central or most important quality of a thing – **12 stately** (adj.): grand in style or size – **14 vulnerable** (adj.): easily harmed, hurt or damaged – **15 blight** (n.): a disease of plants that results in the drying up and dying of the diseased parts – **15 hiker** (n.): a person who goes on usu. long or difficult walks for pleasure – **17 to gather** (n.): here: to understand from s.th. said or done – **17 to the effect**: here: showing; indicating – **18 wrought** (adj.): made, done, brought about – **19 range** (n.): the limits within which variable amounts or qualities are included – **22 model** (n.): a simplified representation of a system etc., to assist calculations and predictions – **23 anxious** (adj.): worried and frightened – **23 despair** (n.): complete loss of hope or confidence – **26 motivator** (n.): s.th. which provides a person with a strong desire to do s.th. – **28 occasion** (n.): here: direct cause or reason – **33 reproduction** (n.): the process of producing a copy – **34 flaw** (n.): a fault or weakness that makes s.th. not perfect – **34 to account for** (v.): to cause; to be an explanation for – **35 substitute** (n.): a person or thing acting or used in place of another – **36 authentic** (adj.): genuine; real; not a substitute or copy – **36 humankind** (n.): the human race – **37 extension** (n.): the act of making s.th. longer, larger etc. – **43 accomplishment** (n.): an achievement; work finished completely and successfully – **44 leading edge** (n.): usu. the front part of a propeller or wing on an aircraft that cuts into the wind; here: s.th. which has the most advanced position in any course of development – **45 tip** (n.): usu. the pointed end of s.th. – **45 to be charged with** (v.): to be responsible for s.th. – **46 promotion** (n.): (successful) development – **48 to dissipate** (v.): to waste s.th.– **50 arcadian** (adj.): concerning simple, idealised country life – **50 pastoral** (adj.): concerning simple, peaceful country life – **51 to be doomed** (v.): to be certain to suffer unavoidable death or destruction – **53 to recover** (v.): to get or bring back s.th. which has been lost – **58 to loathe** (v.): to dislike very much – **61 solvable** (adj.): here: capable of being overcome – **62 sociology** (n.): a branch of knowledge concerned with societies and human behavior in groups – **63 fix** (n.): (coll.): the act of overcoming a difficulty or problem – **64 solution** (n.): the answer to a difficulty or problem – **64 humility** (n.): the quality of not being proud – **65 to originate** (v.): to have as an established starting point – **65 hubris** (v.): /'hjuːbrɪs/ great and unreasonable pride, often bringing great misfortune to the person who shows it – **66 central nervous system** (n.): the brain and the spinal cord – **67 cancer** (n.): a diseased growth in the body which may cause death – **71 to slaughter** (v.): to kill, usu. wrongly, cruelly and in great numbers – **74 to appoint** (v.): to choose for a position or job – **74 council meeting** (n.): a gathering of a group of people for the purpose of making laws, rules or decisions, or giving advice – **75 to overcome** (v.): to fight successfully against; to defeat

Explanations

2 the greenhouse effect: the process by which the sun's heat is trapped by the earth's atmosphere, leading to global warming – **6 ozone layer**: a part of the earth's atmosphere in which ozone is formed, preventing harmful radiation from the sun reaching the earth. Already in the 1970s depletion of the ozone layer caused by chlorofluorocarbons (CFCs), chemicals used in sprays, refrigerators etc. was noticed and in the 1980s and 1990s even large ozone holes. The main effect of ozone depletion is an increase in harmful ultra-violet rays reaching the earth's surface, leading to an increase in skin cancer amongst human beings and seriously damaging plants and animals (like plankton) that form important links in the food chain. Thanks to international cooperation the emission of CFCs has been greatly reduced and it is hoped that in about 50 years the ozone layer will have largely recovered. – **16 it is overwhelming**: the speaker means that the idea of this actually happening is impossible to comprehend or accept – **19 ecosphere**: the totality of living matter on earth and the environments in which it exists, seen as a complex interacting system – **21 on a random wave**: the speaker means that climatic developments are unpredictable or even chaotic when considered in the short-term but reveal a distinct pattern and regularity when looked at over a longer period of time. The phrase is taken from physics. – **33 inaccurate self-copying**: the system by which in nature living things produce young which are genetically similar to their parents but not identical. It is inaccurate self-copying which leads to developments and to differentiation between different members of a species. – **38 evolution**: the scientific idea of the gradual development of various types of plants, animals etc. from fewer and simpler forms – **39 genetic material**: all of the genes in a cell of a plant, animal or person. Genes control the development of the qualities of a living thing which have been passed on from its parents. – **39 species**: /spiːʃiːz/ a division of animal and plants which are alike in all important ways and can breed together to produce young of the same kind – **40 archive of evolutionary history**: a record of the past development of the genetic material of a species – **41 lost species**: a type of living thing which no longer exists and has become extinct – **52 divine drama**: the exciting and unusual set of events which God (or the gods) has (have) decided will shape the development of the universe – **53 ritual sense of evolution**: (probably) the feeling that evolutionary developments are a part of God's (religious) plan for the universe – **58 ironware technology:** the technology concerned with the production of large, heavy iron or steel objects – **68 Oneida Indians**: Iroquoian-speaking North American Indian tribe of what is now central New York State and one of the original five nations of the Iroquois League

James Lovelock (b. 1919) was born in Letchworth Garden City, England. He studied chemistry at the University of Manchester before taking up a Medical Research Council post at the Institute for Medical Research in London. In 1948 he received a Ph.D. in medicine at the London School of Hygiene and Tropical Medicine. Within the United States he has conducted research at Yale, Baylor University College of Medicine, and Harvard University. A lifelong inventor, Lovelock has created and developed many scientific instruments, some of which have been adopted by NASA in its program of planetary exploration. It was while working for NASA that Lovelock developed the Gaia Hypothesis. In early 1961, Lovelock was engaged by NASA to develop sensitive instruments for the analysis of extraterrestrial atmospheres and planetary surfaces. Lovelock also invented the Electron Capture Detector, which ultimately assisted in discoveries about the persistence of CFCs and their role in stratospheric ozone depletion. Lovelock is currently president of the Marine Biological Association, was elected a Fellow of the Royal Society in 1974, and in 1990 was awarded the first *Dr. A.H. Heineken Prize for the Environment* by the Royal Netherlands Academy of Arts and Sciences. An independent scientist, inventor, and author, Lovelock works out of a barn-turned-laboratory in Cornwall. In 2003 he was appointed a Companion of Honour (CH) by Queen Elizabeth II. From: http://en.wikipedia.org/wiki/James_Lovelock

Awareness

1 Imagine that you have been invited to participate in a symposium on environmental problems. Which aspects would you wish to discuss?

2 What specific contribution do you make to preserving the environment? Compare notes with your fellow students.

3 Find out as much as you can about tropical rain forests and the threats to their existence.

Comprehension

4 What do the respective speakers mean by the following expressions a) "reconstruct lost species" (l. 41), b) "arcadian or pastoral perfection" (l. 50)?

5 Summarize (Reference Library, pp. 302f.) the points of view put forward by a) B. Botkin, b) D. Foreman, c) J. Lovelock, d) F. Turner.

Analysis

6 Compare and contrast the comments of two of the speakers and the rhetorical means (Reference Library, p. 311) they use to put their ideas across.

Opinion

7 Which of the four speakers comes closest to your own view on man's future and that of the planet?

8 Discuss the implications of the cartoon on p. 39. Consider the situation of developing countries.

9 Do you agree with scientists and politicians who argue that atomic power is a remedy for global warming?

Projects

10 Devise a plan to help save the tropical rain forests. What can governments in the countries directly affected by rain forest depletion and in the West effectively do to a) stop the destruction b) repair the damage c) solve the economic, social and political conflicts leading to their destruction?

11 Write a report (Reference Library, p. 302) on some of the benefits of modern technology. Give examples.

12 Make suggestions as to how future technological developments could be influenced in such a way as to eliminate as many of the negative effects of technological progress as possible. What should a) governments/politicians, b) industry/industrialists, c) environmentalists, d) individuals DO?

13 Collect posters, brochures and other publicity material about a) environmental problems b) environmental movements c) environmental projects, and make an exhibition.

Internet Projects

14 Find out about environmental groups and their objectives; for example, Greenpeace, WWF, Friends of the Earth, or local environmental initiatives and report back to the rest of your class.

15 Find out more about Lovelock's Gaia hypothesis and the controversy surrounding it.

16 Read the predictions made by some famous Americans about the world in 2001 under: (http://www.popularmechanics.com/science/research/1281776.html?page=1&c=y). Choose three you agree with and three you disagree with. Explain why you dis/agree. Then make your own predictions and present them in the form of an essay, story or poem.

3 Education

A sculptor's vision of education – from the fine group by Albert Toft

College students in the USA

Newnham College Gardens, Cambridge

University of Illinois, campus

A comprehensive school in England

in Britain and the USA

Laurel and Hardy at school

The University of Cambridge, King's College

Students at a US university relax between classes

1 Look carefully at the buildings in the pictures and describe them. What do the tell you about what goes on in them and the people that use them?
2 Describe the sculpture by Albert Toft. What do you think it has to do with education?
3 Describe the people in the other pictures. What do they have in common and what differences can you make out?
4 Why is the picture of Laurel and Hardy funny? What does it tell us about education?

1 Comparing Education in Germany, England and the United States

	Germany	England/Wales	United States
Age at which school is started	6+	4+	6+
Time spent at primary school	4 years	6 years	5 years
Age at transfer to secondary school	10	11	11
Repeat a year if you fail	Yes	No	No
All-day schooling is the norm	No	Yes	Yes
Setting and streaming	No	Yes	Yes
Selective secondary education	Yes	No	No
External examinations at 16	No	Yes	No
External examinations at 18	No	Yes	No
Minimum school-leaving age	16	16	17
Students going into higher education	35%	40%	50%
Annual tuition fees for higher education	(variable)	€4,500*	$10,000**
Percentage of GDP spent on education	1.1%	1.1%	2.6%

* Maximum amount; the actual amount depends on parental income.
** At a public university for a resident of the state, but could be as high as $40,000 for a graduate programme.

Sources: Newsweek, *12 June 2006; en.wikipedia.org (Education in the USA); UK 2005 London: Office for National Statistics, 2005*

School System in England and Wales

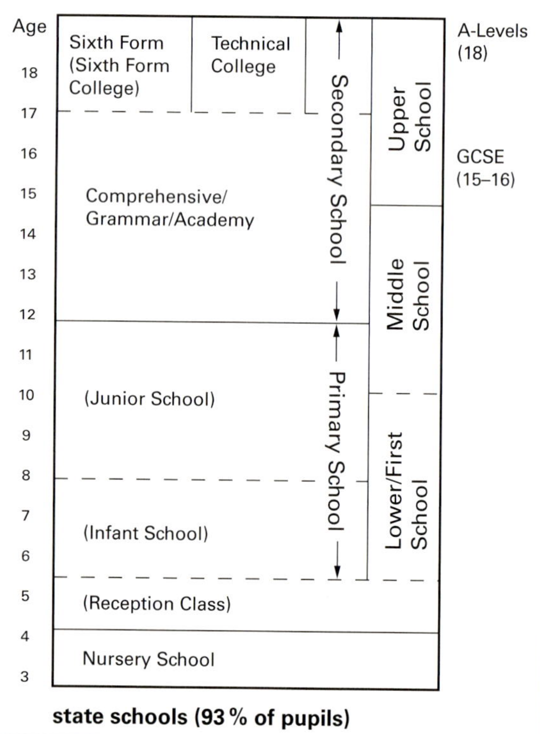

School System in the United States

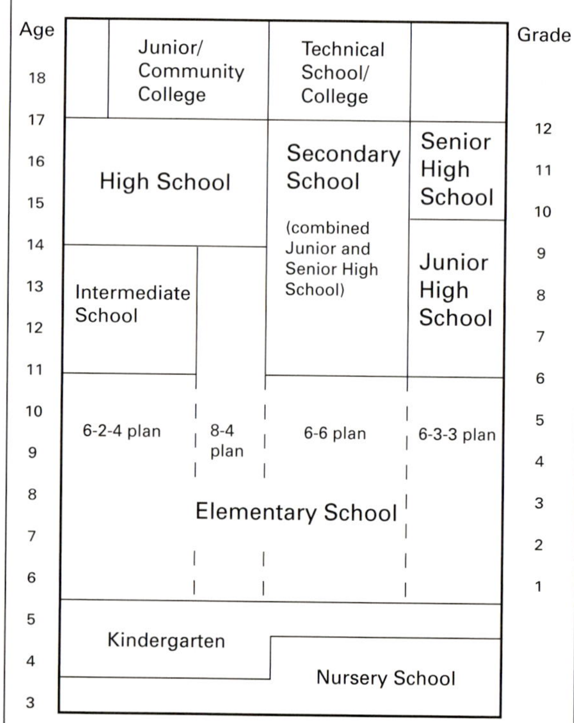

Explanations

setting: grouping students according to ability within a particular subject – **streaming:** BrE grouping students according to ability within whole classes (AmE tracking) – **GDP:** gross domestic product; the total value of all goods and services produced in a country in one year – **School System in England and Wales: GCSE:** General Certificate of Secondary Education; an examination in a range of subjects taken by students in schools in England and Wales at the age of 15 or 16. A good GCSE is a pass with grades A*, A, B or C. The other grades are: D, E, F, and G. – **A-level:** Advanced level; an examination that students usually take at the age of 18. Students usually take 3 or 4 subjects and courses last two years. Pass grades are A to E.

Opinion

1 What are the advantages and disadvantages of Germany's highly selective school system when compared with the comprehensive school systems of the US and England?
2 Compare the examination systems used in English and German schools. Which system do you think provides the better method of testing what has been learnt?
3 In general students in England and the US do not have to repeat a year if they fail any subjects. They move between sets and streams (AmE tracks) depending on their ability and achievement. Discuss (Reference Library, p. 299) whether streaming and setting or repeating a year are more effective.
4 What other features of the English and American education systems should or should not in your opinion be adopted in Germany? Justify your choices.

2 Francis Gilbert

"My First Ever Lesson"*

After studying English Literature at Sussex University and taking a Postgraduate Certificate in Education at Cambridge University, Francis Gilbert became a student teacher in a comprehensive school in Coventry. After observing a number of lessons the time came for Francis to teach his first lesson. A teacher's first lesson is usually a traumatic experience and Francis Gilbert's is no exception. Francis Gilbert, *I'm a Teacher, Get Me Out of Here* (London: Short Books, 2004), pp. 32–37.

Francis Gilbert's hilarious memoirs

This was Jesse's GCSE English class, the one which he had read articles about AIDS with, the class with the benighted, homophobic Daryl Jones. I was supposed to have another teacher in the class with me but Arthur hadn't arranged this. I was entirely on my own. I knew from observing a couple of other GCSE classes that everyone else in the English Department was reading *A Taste of Honey* by Shelagh Delaney and asking them to do a piece of coursework on it. The play was a bleak kitchen-sink drama written in the 1960s about a moaning teenage girl living in the poverty-stricken North who sleeps with a black man and gets pregnant. I liked the text although I was aware that it was very dated in its references. However, I hadn't had any time to prepare to teach it or even to think about whether I should teach it or not; it was the only suitable book I had seen in the stock cupboard and I pulled it out without a second thought.

Without any more ado, I handed out A *Taste of Honey*. Jesse's "fag hags", a group of pleasant girls with frizzy dyed blond hair and dressed in cheap pink and white shell suits, questioned me about what was going on.

"Where's Mr Stevens?" they asked.

"He's ill. Not here today," I said somewhat apologetically.

The girls nodded. Clearly they were used to such absences. "So what's happening, are you taking us from now on?"

"Maybe," I said hesitantly. I didn't want to hear them moaning about me, so I hedged my bets about telling them that as far as I was concerned I had them for the rest of the term.

"Now then," I said. "Could we have quiet please? I

need to see who is reading what role in this play. Could you put up your hand if you want to read?"

Everyone started shouting out that they wanted a role and then when I said they had a part they refused to take it. After ten minutes of trying to allocate roles, no one had a part. I remember feeling a sense of rising panic. What was I supposed to do? I was banking on reading the play for part of the lesson and then setting a written exercise, where they predicted what happened next, for the remainder of the lesson. But they hadn't read anything; how could they make a prediction from nothing?

These kids were laughing and jeering at me. I felt very vulnerable with my long ponytail. Sweat was beginning to seep through my shirt. I wandered around the class, trying to encourage kids on a one-to-one basis to take on a role. This worked a bit better because I managed to get a few of them to agree to read out aloud.

I succeeded in getting the play started with these readers. However, their faltering voices were virtually drowned out by the other kids who were still chatting very loudly. In particular, there was one kid, the surly, sunken-eyed Daryl Jones, who was pushing and shouting at the boy sitting next to him. He was by far the worst-behaved and noisiest kid in the class. I decided that I had to take him on if I was going to get anywhere. I wasn't going to wave my wrists limply at him or do my best to ignore him, as Jesse had done; I was going to confront him. I was a tough guy. I asked him to be quiet and to listen. He didn't respond – or rather he did by shoving his friend so hard that he fell off his seat. Everyone burst out laughing. As his friend picked himself off the floor, I approached Daryl Jones.

For the first time in the lesson, everyone was quiet. All eyes swivelled round to watch me as I stalked with a red and seething face towards Jones. He grinned at everyone and then let his head flop on to the desk with a soft thud. He appeared to shut his eyes.

I didn't know what to say to him because he wasn't being noisy any more. I picked up his book which had fallen on the floor and put it beside his tousled black hair; his face was still buried in his desk.

"You have to follow this," I said in an angry but calmish voice, as I pointed at a forlorn, dog-eared page of *A Taste of Honey*.

Jones didn't reply.

"Did you hear me?" I said.

Jones groaned in a pseudo-sleepy voice, "What, what did you say?"

The class tittered. They were still watching with avid attention.

"I said you need to follow this."

"Oh, fuck off, sir," said Jones, lifting his head slightly to show his hooded eyes. "I'm just trying to have a kip here."

An English lesson in a comprehensive school

There was an intake of breath and then an explosion of laughter from the class. I had been humiliated. This oily little runt had humiliated me. And I felt powerless. There was nothing I could do.

I soldiered on with the lesson. I backed away from Jones, leaving him slumped on the desk and, after the laughter has simmered down, carried on asking the few who wanted to read to read. And they did. I got to the end of the lesson. Jones didn't say another word but continued kipping. I left him well alone.

Although it wasn't a very pleasant experience, after I had recovered from my initial feelings of humiliation I began to reflect that it was all rather interesting.

Jones, for all his bolshiness, had been respectful. He'd said, "Fuck off, *sir*". His curious mixture of rebelliousness and servility struck me as odd but peculiarly comforting. I don't think anyone else in any other profession gets a rebuff like that; doctors, policemen, lawyers, civil servants are probably just told to fuck off, if at all. There was an aspect of gratitude and respect in Jones's insult which indicated that even when pupils are really wanting to make a teacher look like an idiot, they always have a degree of admiration for what they are trying to do.

Vocabulary

7 benighted (adj.): having no knowledge or understanding – **7 homophobic** (adj.): hating and fearing homosexuals – **22 coursework** (n.): work students do during a course of study rather than in examinations and that forms part of their final mark – **22 bleak** (adj.): without anything to make you feel hopeful or happy – **26 dated** (adj.): old-fashioned – **29 stock cupboard** (n.): a small room where books are kept – **31 without any more ado:** without wasting any more time – **33 frizzy** (adj.): with very tight curls – **34 shell suit** (n.): a light brightly coloured piece of clothing consisting of trousers and a jacket that fit tightly at the wrists and bottom of the trousers – **43 to hedge your bets:** to reduce your chances of s.th. bad happening by trying several different possibilities instead of one – **53 to bank on s.th.** (v.): to depend on s.th. happening – **59 to jeer** (v.): to laugh at s.o. in a way that shows you do not respect them – **60 vulnerable** (adj.): easily harmed or hurt – **61 to seep through** (v.): to flow slowly through – **67 faltering** (adj.): nervous and uncertain – **69 surly** (adj.): bad-tempered and unfriendly – **73 to take s.o. on** (v.): to start a fight or quarrel with s.o. – **74 to wave your wrists limply:** to behave in a weak and ineffective way – **78 to shove** (v.): /ʃʌv/ to push hard – **82 to swivel round** (v.): to turn round quickly – **82 to stalk** (v.): to walk in an angry way with long steps – **83 seething** (adj.): feeling so angry you are almost shaking – **88 tousled** (adj.): /'taʊzəld/ untidy looking – **91 forlorn** (adj.): here: in which no one is interested – **100 to titter** (v.): to laugh quietly in a high voice – **102 avid** (adj.): here: great – **109 hooded** (adj.): here: with lowered eyelids – **111 kip** (n.): informal sleep – **115 to humiliate** (v.): to make s.o. feel ashamed or stupid – **115 oily** (adj.): polite but in a way that people find unpleasant and insincere – **115 runt** (n.): a small unpleasant person – **117 to soldier on** (v.): to continue what you are doing in spite of difficulties – **118 slumped** (adj.): bent forward – **119 to simmer down** (v.): to become calm again – **126 bolshiness** (n.): being angry and not obeying people – **128 servility** (n.): being very eager to obey s.o. because you want to please them – **130 rebuff** (n.): an unfriendly answer to an offer of help – **131 civil servant** (n.) s.o. who works for the government

Explanations

Intro: Postgraduate Certificate in Education: the usual quali-fication for British graduates who want to become teachers; it involves one year of study at a University Department of Education and a term's teaching practice. – **1 Jesse:** Jesse Stevens, the teacher in charge of English teaching at the school; he is homosexual. – **2 GCSE:** General Certificate of Secondary Education; an examination in a range of subjects taken by students in schools in England and Wales at the age of 15 or 16. A good GCSE is a pass with grades A*, A, B or C. The other grades are: D, E, F, and G. – **5 AIDS:** acquired immune deficiency syndrome – **12 Arthur:** Arthur Digby, the Deputy Headteacher of the school – **20 English Department:** teaching in British schools is organised around depart-ments, each department dealing with one or more subjects (English, Modern Languages, Science, Mathe-matics, etc.) and having a teacher reponsible for that department, the Head of Department. – **20 *A Taste of Honey:*** written in 1958 by Shelagh Delany at the age of 19 and made into a film in 1961 (hence Gilbert's mistaken belief that the play was from the 1960s); the play and film were remarkable at the time for their realistic depiction of single motherhood, race and sexuality from a female point of view. – **22 kitchen-sink drama:** a serious play or film about problems that families have at home – **32 fag hag:** a girl or woman who likes to spend a lot of time with homosexual male friends (from "fag" slang for homosexual and "hag" an unattractive woman); these are girls who like the English teacher Jesse Stevens.

Awareness

1 Imagine you are going to teach your very first lesson. Choose a topic and prepare a short lesson of 15 minutes for your fellow pupils. After your lesson have a class discussion (Reference Library, p. 299) on why the lesson was successful or not.

Comprehension

2 Summarise (Reference Library, pp. 302f.) the sequence of events during Francis Gilbert's lesson.

Analysis

3 What was Francis Gilbert's lesson plan?
4 Why was the lesson not successful?
5 What insights do we gain about Francis Gilbert's attitudes to himself, his pupils and his subject, English?

Opinion

6 Imagine you had been observing Francis Gilbert's lesson. Write an assessment of it.
7 Imagine you had to teach a play or part of a play. How would you go about it? Write a short lesson plan for a play you know.
8 What do you think are the most important things for British students to learn in their English lessons and German students to learn in their German lessons? Write an outline of a possible syllabus for students aged 15–16.
9 Do you agree (Reference Library, p. 306) with Francis Gilbert's opinion on Daryl Jones's use of the word "sir"?
10 Rewrite the text from the point of view of one of the students in the class.

Project

11 Find out about the English comprehensive school: its history, the philosophy behind it and its present structure.

3 "Reforming England's Schools"

Faced with widespread dissatisfaction with England's comprehensive schools, attended by 88% of the country's children, the present Labour government has asked wealthy business people to finance so-called academies. These are also comprehensive but have greater financial resources and freedom than other schools. *The Sunday Times*, 10 December 2006, p. 1.16.

Unity Academy's futuristic building stands out in a landscape of council houses in Middlesborough. The school was one of the first of Blair's academies and its design was intended to signal that children in the area were to get a better deal.

Blair recently announced that the original plan for 200 academies – schools sponsored by wealthy businessmen – will be expanded to 400. Academies were intended to be beacons of excellence that would raise standards in deprived areas.

Unity has yet to match that vision, though others have done better. This year just 12% of 16-year-olds at Unity managed to get five good GCSEs that included English and maths – one of the worst results in the country. As well as the new building, pupils at Unity have £2,000 a year more spent on them than pupils in nearby schools.

Just four years on from the grand opening, Unity is a failing school. The government is paying the salary of David Triggs, the headmaster of a school in Essex, to turn it round.

"We are making progress, but it is a long haul," he said last week. "It is a very challenging environment. There are high levels of unemployment in the area, some of which is third generation."

Unity is not necessarily typical. Some parts of the education system have improved. In primary schools, more 11-year-olds now leave with levels of numeracy and literacy that allow them to make better progress than when Labour took office in 1997. Experts point out, however, that the biggest improvements occurred in the government's first three years, before the big increases in funding went in.

This year [2006 ed.] 120,000 11-year-olds left primary school without the reading and writing skills they needed for secondary school. Another 150,000 left with significant maths problems. Peter Tymms, the Durham University academic who analyses exam results as a service for schools, said: "Hardly any of Labour's initiatives have had any impact. The £500m spent on the literacy strategy in primary schools has barely raised standards. It has all been a lot of hot air."

At secondary level, a huge rise in funding has yet to bring significant improvements. This year only 45% of 16-year-olds managed to get five good GCSEs including English and maths. About 30,000 16-year-olds left school last year without a single GCSE.

The extra money has not prevented a sharp fall in science teaching [...]. Half of the top grades at A-level in physics are achieved by independent school pupils. About a quarter of 11–16 schools in the state sector do not have a qualified physics teacher and 12% have no qualified chemistry teacher.

It is not all bad news. Michelle Magrs, head teacher at Selly Park Technology College for Girls in Birmingham, believes extra money has been the major factor in improving the school's results.

The school's intake is 65% Asian, 10% white and 19% Afro-Caribbean. This year 85% of 16-year-olds got five good GCSEs. Ten years ago the figure was 27%. Last year, on the government's latest benchmark, which includes maths and English among the five GCSEs, the figure was 43%.

"The money has made a difference," says Magrs. "We have used it to attract specialists in maths and science."

But for every school that is getting better on the back of extra money, there are plenty of others that appear locked into a cycle of decline. Christopher Gilbert, the new chief inspector of schools, said recently that there are still too many schools that provide an inadequate education.

Of 6,000 schools inspected last year, 11% are outstanding, 48% are good, 34% are satisfactory and 8% are inadequate. At secondary level, just over one in eight were judged as inadequate. "I'm concerned about the gap between the best and worst provision," said Gilbert.

[...]

Vocabulary

3 council house (n.): a house that is provided by the local council – **14 beacon** (n.): an idea that guides or encourages you – **15 deprived** (adj.): not having the things that are necessary for a comfortable or happy life – **17 to match** (v.): to be equal to s.th. in value or quality – **27f. to turn s.th. round** (v.): to make s.th. be more successful – **35 numeracy** (n.): the ability to do calculations and understand simple mathematics – **36 literacy** (n.): the state of being able to read and write – **40 funding** (n.): money that is provided for a particular purpose – **76 benchmark** (n.): s.th. which is used as a standard by which other things can be judged – **82 on the back of** (prep.): after receiving – **92 provision** (n.): when you provide s.th. that s.o. needs now or in the future

Explanations

3f. Middlesborough: a port in northeast England, on the estuary of the River Tees; population 141,000 – **9 Blair:** Tony Blair; (b. 1953) British prime minister 1997–2007 and leader of the Labour Party since 1994 – **20 GCSE:** General Certificate of Secondary Education; an examination in a range of subjects taken by students in schools in England and Wales at the age of 15 or 16. A good GCSE is a pass with grades A*, A, B or C. The other grades are: D, E, F, and G. – **29 a long haul:** s.th. that takes a lot of time and effort – **63 A-level:** Advanced level; an examination that students usually take at the age of 18. Students usually take 3 or 4 subjects and courses last two years. Pass grades are A to E. – **64 independent school:** a school which is not owned or paid for by the government – **66 school in the state sector:** a school financed by the government

'Dad – can you read me my results?'

Awareness

1 Working in groups, write down what you know about schools in England. What are the main differences between schools in Germany and England? Use the following questions to structure your answer:
- When do children usually start school in England?
- What is the first type of school that children attend?
- What type of school do most children attend at the age of 11?
- What examinations are taken at English schools?
- When do students leave school?

Comprehension

2 What do we learn about Middlesborough from this article?

3 Why is Unity Academy described as a "failing school"?

4 How, according to the article, has government spending affected a) primary schools and b) secondary schools?

Analysis

5 Analyse the picture presented of England's schools in the article. In what areas has progress been made and where has there been no progress?

Opinion

6 What do you think of the idea that wealthy business people should sponsor and finance State schools?

7 Much of the article deals with the impact and importance of money spent on schools. Discuss (Reference Library, p. 299) how far a good education system depends on the amount of money invested in it and how far other factors may play an important role.

Project

8 Find out about the examinations used in English schools – GCSE and A-level – and compare them with the corresponding German examinations – *mittlere Reife* and *Abitur*. What are the advantages and disadvantages of the systems used in the two countries?

4

Tom Wolfe

I am Charlotte Simmons

Charlotte Simmons has just arrived at the prestigious Dupont University in Chester, Pennsylvania, a six hour drive from her home town of Sparta, North Carolina. After having driven her there and helping her to unpack, Charlotte's parents are saying farewell. Tom Wolfe, *I am Charlotte Simmons* (London: Vintage, 2005) pp. 87–92.

Charlotte lifted her head and looked at Momma.

"There's gon' be folks here wanting you to do thangs you don't hold with," said Momma. "So you jes' remember you come from mountain folks, on your daddy's side and my side, the Simmonses and the Pettigrews, and mountain folks got their faults, but letting theirselves git pushed into doing thangs iddn' one *uv*'m. We know how to be real stubborn. Can't nobody make us do a thang once we get hard set against it. And if anybody don't like that, you don't have to explain a thang to'm. All you got to say is, 'I'm Charlotte Simmons, and I don't hold with thangs like 'at. And they'll respect you for that." *They-at.* "I love you, little darling, and your daddy loves you, no matter whirr you're at in the whole wide world, you'll always be our good, good girl. "

Charlotte laid her head back on Momma's shoulder and sobbed softly. She could see her Daddy standing right there, and she took her tears to him and threw her arms around his neck, which clearly startled him. Daddy didn't hold with public displays of affection. Between sobs she whispered into his ear, "I love you, Daddy. You don't know how *much* I love you!"

"We love you, too," said Daddy.

He also didn't know how much it would have meant to her if he could have only brought himself to say *I*.

Charlotte kept waving, and Momma stuck her head out of the window and looked back and kept waving, until the poor, sad, brave pickup truck with the fiberglass camper top disappeared beyond the shade trees. Finally Charlotte turned around and headed back toward the stone fortress alone.

[...]

Beverly was already there when Charlotte reached room 516. They decided on who was going to have which side of the room – the two sides were identical, identically bare and spare – and they set about making up their beds and unpacking. What a lot of ... *things* ... Beverly had! She left her computer fax machine, television, refrigerator, microwave, and the rest of her electrical devices in their cartons, but she unpacked more pairs of shoes than Charlotte could even imagine one girl owning – at least a dozen – a dozen or more sweaters, most of them cashmere, skirts, skirts, skirts, shirts, shirts, shirts, camisoles, camisoles, camisoles, jeans, jeans, jeans ... Charlotte possessed not even the smallest of Beverly's various types of machines. For a computer, a necessity at Dupont, Charlotte was going to have to depend entirely on the so-called computer clusters in Dupont's main library. Rather than a dozen or more pairs of shoes, she had three: a pair of loafers, some sturdy leather sandals – "Jesus sandals," Regina Cox used to call them – and the pair of Keds she had on.

Beverly chatted with Charlotte in a dutiful fashion. Nothing she had to say bore even a hint of the excitement of a girl heading out with another girl, her new roommate, from another part of the country, on a four-year adventure at a great university. She spoke to Charlotte from an amicable distance. She spoke with the inflections of someone who was *showing an interest*. When Charlotte mentioned how fascinating

Campus of a US university

the French courses listed in the Dupont catalog sounded, Beverly's comment was that the French are *so* resentful of Americans these days you can like *feel* it in the air when you're around them. They were majorly boring, the French.

Beverly had only halfway squeezed her clothes into the closet and the bureau when it was time to go downstairs for the house meeting. The two hundred or so boys and girls at Edgerton House convened in what was known in Dupont (and British) parlance as the Common Room. [...]

Facing the assembly was a young woman in jeans and a man's-style button-down shirt. Charlotte was fascinated by her. She stood there in front of two hundred strangers with such an easy confidence. She was beautiful but casual, with an athletic figure – and such amazing blond hair! It was very curly but very long, wild, yet combed just so. She seemed the very essence of collegiate glamour. She identified herself as a senior and the R.A., the resident assistant, of Edgerton House. She was there to help them with any problems that came up. They should feel free to ring her up, e-mail her, or knock on her door at any time. Her name was Ashley Downes.

"The university no longer plays the role of parent," she was saying, "and certainly I don't. You're on your own. But there *are* some rules – not a lot, but some, and I'd be doing you a disservice if I wasn't frank about that. First of all, alcohol is prohibited in Edgerton and every other house on Little Yard. That doesn't just mean no drinking in public, but no alcohol in the building, period. It may not surprise you to learn that there *is* alcohol on the Dupont campus." She smiled, and many of the freshmen laughed knowingly. "But it's not gonna be here. Okay?" She smiled again. "In case you're worried, you're gonna discover this won't put an end to your social life."

Charlotte came close to letting her breath out audibly. What a relief! In Sparta she had been able to avoid the sodden, drunken milieu of the Channing Reeveses and the Regina Coxes simply by going home in the evenings and studying and ignoring the upside-down contempt she felt from them and their crowd. But here? It was well known that there was a lot of drinking in colleges, probably even at Dupont. At least she wouldn't have to deal with it in this building where she lived, thank God. If the R.A. could just reassure her about one other thing –

But in no time, it seemed, the meeting was over, and the freshmen departed the Common Room far more animated and vocal than when they arrived. They were already getting to know one another. Charlotte started to hang back, in hopes of having a word with Ashley Downes privately. But eight or ten freshmen were clustered about her, and Charlotte didn't want to ask her question in front of other people. She dawdled ... and dawdled ... for five minutes, ten minutes, before she finally gave up.

A graduate from a US university with her B.A. certificate

When she returned to the room, Beverly was there, standing in front of her bureau looking into a prop-up vanity mirror with tiny bulbs ablaze along the edges. She turned around. She was wearing black pants and a lavender silk shirt, sleeveless and open three or four buttonholes' worth in front. It showed off her suntan – but also her arms, which looked almost emaciated. She made Charlotte think of an all-dressed up stork. Her make-up did nothing for her nose and chin. They seemed even bigger somehow. She had put a peach-colored polish on her nails; it looked great on the tips of her perfectly tanned fingers.

"I'm meeting some friends at a restaurant," she explained, "and I'm late. I'll put away all that stuff when I come back." She gestured toward a mountain of bags and boxes piled this way and that.

Charlotte was astonished. The very first day wasn't even over, and Beverly was *going out to a restaurant.* Charlotte couldn't imagine such a thing. For a start, she didn't know a soul. And what if she did? She had a grand total of five hundred dollars to cover all outside expenses to the end of the first semester, four and a half months from now. She was going to have to eat every meal, seven days a week, in the university dining hall. That was provided for her by her scholarship. Unless someone took her to one, the Sizzlin' Skillet was the last restaurant she was going to eat in for a long time.

Beverly left. Charlotte sat on the edge of her bed, hunched over, hands clasped, thinking and thinking, glancing at Beverly's edifice of cartons, looking out the window at the dusk. She could hear people talking and occasionally laughing in the hall outside. Finally she worked up her nerve. Ashley, the R.A., had said they could knock on her door anytime. This would be pushing it perhaps, approaching her barely an hour after the meeting, but ... She stood up. Now was the time to do it, if she was going to do it at all.

The R.A.'s room was on the second floor. As Charlotte walked down the hall, she was startled to see a boy in cargo shorts, no shirt, emerge from a doorway and come dashing toward her. He was holding a small spiral notebook in one hand and glancing back over his shoulder and laughing in breathless bursts. As he hurtled past Charlotte, he said "Sorry!" – scarcely even looking at her. Now running toward Charlotte was a girl in a T-shirt and shorts, yelling, "Gimme that back, you little shit!" She wasn't laughing. Charlotte noticed that she was barefoot. She didn't say a thing as she ran by.

Charlotte hesitated in front of the R.A.'s door. Then she knocked. After a few seconds the door opened, and there was Ashley Downes, with her amazing mane of curly blond hair. She had changed into pants and a rather low-cut tank top. "Hi," she said in a puzzled fashion.

"Hi," said Charlotte. "I'm really sorry, Miz Downes – "

"Oh, come on, *please*, Ashley."

"I'm really sorry. I was just at the meeting, and I tried to get to talk to you afterward, but there were so many people." Blushing and lowering her chin: "You said come by anytime, but I know you didn't think *this* soon. I'm really sorry."

"Well – come on in," said the R.A. She smiled at Charlotte the way you might smile at a lost child. "What's your name?"

Charlotte told her and, once inside the room, stood there and began expounding, in an embarrassed way, upon how valuable the meeting had been and how much she thought she had gotten out of it, all the while noticing that this was a single room and a surprisingly messy one … bed unmade, clothes strewn on the floor, including a pair of dirty thong underpants. "But there was one thing …" Now that she had come to the point, she didn't know how to put it.

"Why don't you sit down," said the R.A. So Charlotte sat in a plain wooden chair, and Ashley Downes sat on the edge of her messy bed.

Charlotte struggled some more with her phrasing, finally saying, "But you didn't really talk about the coed dorm part. I mean you *did*, you certainly did talk about it, but there's one thing …" Words failed her again.

The R.A. now looked at her as if she were about six. She leaned forward and said quietly, "You mean … sex?"

Charlotte could feel herself nodding like a six-year-old. "Yes."

Ashley Downes leaned forward still further, resting her forearms on her knees, and intertwining her fingers. "Where are you from?"

"Sparta, North Carolina."

"Sparta, North Carolina. How big is Sparta?"

"About nine hundred people," said Charlotte. "It's up in the mountains." Just why she had added this bit of geographical intelligence, she couldn't have explained, not even to herself.

Ashley Downes averted her eyes and thought for a moment, then said, "Let me put your mind at ease. Yes, this is a coed dorm, and yes, there is sexual activity in coed dorms here at Dupont. What floor are you on?"

"Five."

"Okay. This is a coed dorm, but that doesn't mean boys are going to be running back and forth across the hall and jumping into bed with girls. Or for that matter, boys from any other part of Edgerton. In fact, if anything, it means they *won't*. There is no actual rule against it, but it's looked down upon. It's considered pathetic and dorky to be reduced to hooking up with someone from your own house. It's called dormcest."

"Dormcest?"

"Dormcest. You know, like incest. As a matter of fact, Edgerton always has a T-shirt for everybody at the end of the year listing all sorts of funny or stupid things that have happened in the house. Last year's had a line that said DORMCEST: THREE. That's three cases out of two hundred students. That's how dorky it is."

Now Charlotte could feel herself smiling like a six-year-old who has just stopped crying. She kept smiling and nodding and expressing her profound thanks, and she really hadn't meant to take up her time on the very first night.

Charlotte stood up, and Ashley stood up and put her arms around her shoulders as she walked her to the door. "I'm sorry, tell me your name again?"

"Charlotte Simmons."

"Well, Charlotte, I'll tell you something. This isn't Sparta, North Carolina, but I think you're gonna find it isn't Sodom and Gomorrah, either."

Tom Wolfe (1931-), born in Richmond, Virginia, is a best-selling American author and journalist. He graduated from Washington and Lee University, Lexington, Virginia, in 1951 and went on to take a Ph.D. in American Studies at Yale University in 1957. He then worked as a journalist for a number of well-known newspapers, including the *Washington Post* and the *New York Herald Tribune*. His best-known collections of journalism are *The Kandy-Kolored Tangerine-Flake Streamline Baby* (1965), *The Electric Kool-Aid Acid Test* (1968), *The Pumphouse Gang* (1968) and *Radical Chic and Mau-Mauing the Flak Catchers* (1970). His 1979 account of America's first astronauts, *The Right Stuff*, was made into a film in 1983. His first novel, *The Bonfire of the Vanities*, about the fall of a Wall Street bond trader, was published in 1987, and made into a film in 1990. A second novel, *A Man in Full*, followed in 1998. The novel *I am Charlotte Simmons*, published in 2004, chronicles the culture clash between a scholarship student from rural Appalachia and the class prejudice, sexual promiscuity and materialism she found at a prestigious American university.

Vocabulary

2 gon' (v.): coll. for going to – **2 thangs** (n.) dial. for things – **3 to not hold with** (v.): to not approve of or agree with – **3 jes'** (adv.): dial. for just – **7 git** (v.): dial. for get – **7 iddn':** dial. for isn't – **8 uv'm:** dial. for of them – **13 They-at** dial. for that – **14 whirr:** dial. for where – **18 to sob** (v.): to cry noisily while breathing in short sudden bursts – **56 camisole** (n.): a light piece of women's underwear that covers the chest down to the waist and has narrow bands over the shoulders – **61 cluster** (n.): a group of things of the same kind – **63 loafer** (n.): AmE a flat leather shoe that does not need to be fastened to your foot – **74 catalog** (n.): AmE (BrE catalogue) – **80 closet** (n.): AmE a cupboard built into the wall of a room from the floor to the ceiling (BrE wardrobe) – **80 bureau** (n.): AmE a piece of furniture with several drawers, used to keep clothes in (BrE chest of drawers) – **83 parlance** (n.): words used by a particular group of people – **93 senior** (n.): AmE a student in their last year of university – **105 period** (n.): AmE here used to emphasise that you have made a decision that cannot be changed (BrE full-stop) – **108 gonna** (v.) coll. for going to – **113 sodden** (adj.): very wet; here: from the use of alcoholic drinks – **129 to dawdle** (v.): here: to wait – **137 prop up** (adj.): here: a mirror that can be moved up and down – **138 vanity mirror** (n.): a mirror used when s.o. puts on make-up – **144 pants** (n.): AmE trousers – **151 emaciated** (adj.): /ɪ'meɪʃietᵻd/ extremely thin – **179 to push it** (v.): here: to do s.th. that is likely to annoy s.o. – **182 second floor:** AmE the floor above the ground floor (BrE first floor) – **184 cargo shorts** (n.): shorts with pockets at the side of the legs – **190 gimme** (v.): coll. for give me – **197 tank top** (n.): a piece of clothing like a T-shirt but with no sleeves – **198 Miz:** spoken form of Ms; used before a woman's family name when you do not want to indicate or do not know whether she is married or not – **211 gotten** (p.p.) AmE for BrE got – **214 thong underpants** (n.): underpants with a single string instead of a back part – **248 pathetic** (adj.): here: so stupid that it annoys you – **248 dorky** (adj.) AmE coll. stupid

Explanations

Intro: Dupont University: fictional university but loosely based on Duke University in North Carolina – **4 mountain folks:** people who live in the Appalachian and Alleghany mountains; they are considered to be poor and not well educated. – **64 Regina Cox:** a fellow-student of Charlotte's at her high school – **64 Keds:** an American brand of sports and casual shoes – **81 house:** some American universities, like many British public schools, are divided up into houses, i.e. students form groups and live in separate accommodation called houses. In many British state schools students continue to be divided into houses for the purpose of sports competitions. – **84 Common Room:** (also: common room) a room at a school or university where students can relax, read, and watch TV when they are not studying – **93 resident assistant:** an older student whose job is to supervise and help students living in a student dormitory (see coed dorm below) – **112 Sparta:** a small town in Alleghany County in the northern part of North Carolina – **113 Channing Reeves:** a fellow-student of Charlotte's at her high school – **170 scholarship:** a sum of money given to a student to help pay for their education – **170 Sizzlin' Skillet:** a fictional chain of restaurants; skillet AmE for BrE frying pan – **221f. coed dorm:** AmE coeducational dormitory; a large building at a university where students of both sexes live and sleep (BrE hall of residence)

Awareness

1 Imagine you are about to go to university. What are your expectations, hopes, and fears about your studies, your fellow-students, your financial situation, the teaching staff, and your future career?

Analysis

2 What kind of people are Charlotte's parents? How does the author make their social class clear?
3 What sacrifices did Charlotte have to make to gain entry to Dupont university?
4 Compare and contrast the social background and attitudes of Charlotte and Beverly.
5 The clothing and appearance of Beverly and Ashley make a great impression on Charlotte. Explain why this should be so.

Opinion

6 Charlotte is clearly worried at the prospect of living in a coed dorm. Would you share her worries? Explain your point of view on mixed dormitories.
7 Why should "dormcest" be considered so unacceptable?
8 Bearing in mind what you wrote in answer to question 5, discuss (Reference Library, p. 299) the influence of the peer group on the behaviour of you and your fellow-students. Is their influence in such matters as clothing, appearance, smoking and drinking, and leisure activities too great?

Project

9 Find out about the structure of the American system of higher education, how undergraduate courses are organised and what student life on campus is like.

5 "What Makes a High School Great?"

In Britain and the United States educationists are asking the same question: how can schools which cater for most of the population, the high school in the US and the comprehensive school in England, be made more responsive to the needs of its students and the rest of society? This article discusses some of the possibilities now being explored in the United States. *Newsweek,* 8 May 2006.

If you want to understand what's happening in some of America's most innovative public high schools, think back to your own experiences in that petri dish of adolescent social stratification known as the cafeteria. Were you a jock? A theater geek? A science whiz? Part of the arty crowd? Whatever your inclination, it defined where you sat. Now imagine that each of those tables was a school in itself – with a curriculum based on sports, drama, science or art and a student body with shared interests and common aptitudes. That radical idea is transforming thousands of high schools. A one-size-fits-all approach no longer works for everyone, the thinking goes; a more individualized experience is better. "We are changing the goal of high school and what it's possible to achieve there," says Tom Vander Ark, executive director of the Gates Foundation's education initiative, which has spent $1 billion in 1,600 high schools in 40 states plus the District of Columbia over the last six years.

For parents and students, these schools mean an often bewildering array of choices – small schools within larger schools, specialized charter and magnet schools for things ranging from fashion design to computer programming, even public boarding schools for budding physicists or artists. On the plus side, students get more adult attention and are less likely to be lost in the crowd. They can focus on subjects they really care about while still getting a grounding in the basics. But some educators think this boutique approach comes with a cost: the loss of a common experience that brings everyone together under one big roof. Maintaining quality is another major obstacle. "I think we're still flailing around," says James Anderson, a professor of educational policy studies at the University of Illinois. "A lot of this is more theater than substance." Vander Ark agrees that the new schools need to prove they're providing a markedly better alternative to regular public schools. "We want to make sure people raise the bar," he says.

[...]

Ask yourself, "What is high school really for?" Then look around at the options available to today's teenagers: diverse and compelling answers abound. Here are some of them.

Create Good Citizens

Everyone pays for public schools, so it makes sense that a primary mission should be teaching students to participate in the democratic process. A generation ago many schools required civics courses; far fewer do so today. "There is so much emphasis on preparing kids to survive economically," says Constancia Warren, senior program officer and director of urban-high-school initiatives for the Carnegie Corp. of New York. "As a result, are we really preparing kids for citizenship?"

In the past decade, many schools have started requiring community service. The César Chávez High School for Public Policy pushes that idea all the way to Capitol Hill, which, fortunately, is within walking distance. In addition to a rigorous college-prep curricu-

Reprinted courtesy Sidney Harris. © 1989

"Our core curriculum consists of the classics, math, science, and self-reliance in a competitive society. . . . You know, how to make a buck."

lum, students work as interns in Congress, at think tanks and advocacy groups in Washington. As seniors, they write a thesis on a public-policy issue and give a presentation before an audience that forces them to defend their stand.

[…]

Chávez now has 500 students, the majority from low-income families. They're budding activists like 17-year-old Eusevia Valdez, who had no idea what public policy was when she enrolled in the fledgling charter school as a freshman. Four years later, she not only understands public policy, she lives it. She wrote her senior thesis on flaws in immigration laws, something she understands from personal experience. Her parents are legal immigrants and she was born here, but the family has struggled to bring her older siblings to the United States from their native El Salvador. Her oldest sister was 21 before the paperwork was approved and, as a result, has been refused permission to immigrate. Her years at Chàvez, she says, "taught me to fight for what I believe in."

Celebrate Liberal Arts

Practical concerns – like helping kids figure out a career path – were not on the minds of the founders of Tempe Preparatory Academy in Arizona a decade ago. Instead, they created a charter school whose goal is to turn out students engaged in "the lifelong pursuit of truth, goodness and beauty," according to the school handbook. For 330 students in grades 7 to 12 that means providing a strong foundation in the arts, science and the humanities. The curriculum is based on the Great Books concept – the basis of Western Civilization, starting with the Greeks. "We don't want kids to specialize," says Daniel Scoggin, CEO of Great Hearts Preparatory Academies, the organization behind Tempe and two other similar schools in the Phoenix area. "We want them to get a broad, well-rounded education." All students take music, art, drama, math and science, languages (including Latin or Greek or a modern language), English and history. […]

Prepare for Work

Most high-paying jobs require some education beyond a high-school diploma, but kids from many families often struggle to get a college education. Early-college high schools can get them on track. By taking a combination of high-school and college courses over four or five years, students graduate with both a high-school diploma and an associate's degree – the equivalent of the first two years of college – at no additional cost. From there, they can enter the work force or finish the last two years of college.

In North Carolina, Gov. Mike Easley is trying to expand this concept to include students from all of the state's 100 counties by 2008 (there are just 13 of these schools now). North Carolina's Learn and Earn schools, Easley says, are based on the theory that if you learn more, you earn more. "In North Carolina, a lot of people grew up expecting to work in the textile mills, just like their parents did, and their grandparents did," says Easley. "But now, those jobs have gone to Asia." Education is the answer, he says: "We're trying to create the best work force in the world." […]

Emphasize Science and Technology

Competency in science and math are critical to the nation's economic strength, and districts around the country are looking for ways to get as many students as possible ready for technical careers. "High-school reform used to be the province of bleeding-heart liberals," says Van Schoales of the Colorado Children's Campaign. "Now it's different because the stakes are higher." That means teaching kids who might not have thought about science as a career. The Denver School of Science and Technology, an 18-month-old charter school, has attracted 229 students in grades 9 and 10 – about 60 percent minority and 45 percent from low-income families. The plan is to expand by a grade each year. With a sleek brick façade, the school looks more like it belongs to Silicon Valley than a Denver neighborhood in the midst of a redevelopment. Every student gets a tablet laptop for taking notes and the whole school has wireless access.

Help Boys and Girls Succeed – Separately

The first American public high school, established in Boston in 1821, was only for boys. But as the high-school movement spread, new schools quickly became coed, says David Tyack, an education historian at Stanford University. "Almost right from the beginning, society believed in integration by sex," he says. Now a small group of educators – bolstered by studies that show boys and girls learn differently – are turning to single-sex classrooms as a way to re-engage students, especially in low-income communities. One of the first to gain national attention was the Young Women's Leadership School in New York's East Harlem, now considered one of the best schools in the city. Research on the effect of single-sex schools is mixed, and there are no studies on single-sex classrooms in schools. Experts who study single-sex schools say there's considerable evidence that smaller class sizes would help just as much, especially for middle-class kids. But for boys from poor families, that extra attention and focus can make a difference, says Cornelius Riordan, a sociology professor at Providence College who is directing a study on single-sex schools for the U.S. Department of Education. […]

Vocabulary

3 petri dish (n.): /ˈpiːtri dɪʃ/ (also Petri) a small dish with a cover used by scientists to grow bacteria – **5 jock** (n.): AmE a student who plays a lot of sport and is often considered to be stupid – **5 geek** (n.): /giːk/ s.o. who is only interested in one thing and is therefore boring and unfashionable – **5 whiz** (n.): s.o. who is very skilled or intelligent in a particular activity – **6 arty** (adj.): knowing a lot about art, film or the theatre – **10 aptitude** (n.): natural ability or skill – **12 one-size-fits all** (adj.): designed to be suitable for everyone or every situation – **21 array** (n.): range; wide number of things – **24 boarding school:** a school where students live as well as study – **25 budding** (adj.): s.o. who is just starting – **32 grounding** (n.): a training in the basis parts of a skill – **41f. to flail around** (v.): here: to try lots of possibilities without having a clear idea of what you want – **49 markedly** (adv.): /ˈmɑːkɪ̵dli/ obviously; noticeably – **50 regular** (adj.): AmE normal – **55 compelling** (adj.): convincing; which makes you believe it must be true – **55 abound** (v.): to exist in very large numbers – **71 rigorous** (adj.): careful and thorough – **72 intern** (n.): AmE s.o., especially a student, who works for a short time in a particular job in order to gain experience – **72 think tank** (n.): a group of people with experience or knowledge of a particular subject, who work to produce ideas and give advice – **73 advocacy group** (n.): a group of people who try to persuade the government to do certain things – **73 senior** (n.): here: a student in their last year of high school – **74 thesis** (n.): a long piece of writing about a particular subject – **81 fledgling** (adj.): only recently formed and still developing – **82 freshman** (n.): AmE a student in their first year of high school – **84 flaw** (n.): fault – **87 sibling** (n.): brother or sister – **100 grade** (n.): AmE one of the 12 years that students are at school in the US school system; in grade 7 you are 12 years old. – **117 to be on track:** to be likely to achieve the result you want – **118 college** (n.): here: an educational institution attended after secondary school – **119 to graduate** (v.): AmE to complete your education at high school – **142 the stakes are high:** you risk losing a lot – **149 sleek** (adj.): smooth and attractive – **152 tablet** (adj.) here: small

Explanations

2 public high school: AmE a secondary school paid for by the local government – **16 Gates Foundation:** the Bill and Melissa Gates Foundation (www.gatesfoundation.org) has the aim of reducing inequalities in the US and around the world by focusing on improving health and education. – **19 District of Columbia:** a district of the US under the control of the federal government; it covers the same area as the city of Washington, the capital city of the United States. – **22f. charter school:** AmE a school which is publicly funded but has been freed from some of the rules and regulations which normally apply to public schools. In return for this freedom charter schools make themselves accountable to achieve certain results in student achievement as set out in a school "charter". – **22f. magnet school:** AmE a school which restricts entry either by competitive entrance tests or by a lottery system. This enables the school to have a wider range of students than would be possible in a neighbourhood school. Most magnet schools focus on a particular specialism such as science, engineering, languages, the humanities, the fine arts, or the performing arts. – **34 boutique approach:** here: choosing what you want to do from a range of options – **61 civics:** AmE a school subject dealing with the rights and duties of citizens and the way government works – **65 Carnegie Corp.:** The Carnegie Corporation of New York (www.carnegie.org) is a philanthropic organisation founded by the steel magnate Andrew Carnegie in 1911. It promotes "the advancement and diffusion of knowledge and understanding" (website p. 1) by providing financial help to all types of educational bodies, including libraries, in the US and the present and former countries of the British Commonwealth. – **68 César Chávez:** (1927-1992) an American farm worker, labour leader, and civil rights activist (www.cesarechavezfoundation.org) – **69 public policy:** all the actions of government, such as making laws, regulations and decisions in the areas of health, education, energy, the environment, defence, welfare, pensions, law and order, and foreign policy – **70 Capitol Hill:** general term for the whole of the US government (see Congress) – **71 college-prep:** designed to prepare students for college – **72 Congress:** the group of people elected to make laws in the US, consisting of the Senate (with 100 senators, two from each state) and the House of Representatives (with 435 members) – **93 liberal arts:** AmE the areas of learning which develop s.o.'s ability to think and increase their general knowledge rather than developing technical skills – **105 CEO:** Chief Executive Officer; the head of a large company – **108 Phoenix:** the state capital of Arizona – **115 high-school diploma:** AmE a document showing that a student has successfully completed their high school education – **124 Gov.:** Governor; the head of the government of a state in the USA – **140f. bleeding heart liberal:** s.o. who feels sympathy for poor people or criminals in a way you think is not helpful – **141f. Colorado Children's Campaign:** a group of parents and others who seek to improve the health, safety, education and economic security of children in the state of Colorado – **150 Silicon Valley:** the area between San Jose and Palo Alto in Santa Clara County, western California, noted for its computing and electronics industries

Awareness

1 What do you think are the qualities and attributes that make a good school? How, in particular, would it cater for your own personal needs? Compare your definition of a "good school" with those of your fellow students.

Comprehension

2 Explain the phrase "petri dish of adolescent social stratification".

Analysis

3 What are the arguments used to support the educational aims described under the headings: Create Good Citizens; Celebrate Liberal Arts; Prepare for Work Emphasize Science and Technology; Help Boys and Girls Succeed – Separately?

Opinion

4 Which of the educational aims listed in the article would you consider most important and which least important? Justify your choices.

5 Which of the educational aims listed in the article is emphasised most at your own school? Explain how it tries to achieve these aims and discuss how far it is successful. What would you like to be added to your school's curriculum?

6 Discuss the priority that should be given to the two conflicting approaches to education mentioned in the article: a) "the boutique approach", which offers a wide choice of types of school, and b) "a common experience", in which everyone learns together.

7 Some educationalists in Britain and the United States believe that secondary education can be improved by introducing single-sex schools. What, in your opinion, are the advantages and disadvantages of coeducation?

Project

8 Find out about the history of and philosophy behind the American high school.

A group of "jocks"?

4 Gender Roles

When we look at the world around us we see men and women, boys and girls, male and female, her and him, we see identity and otherness. It has been widely agreed in gender studies that gender is the social construction of male/female identity. Most people experience gender as "an emergent feature of social situations: as both an outcome of and a rationale for various social arrangements" (West/Zimmermann, 1991).[1] It can be seen as a set of ideas which influence male/female behaviour, a set of signs and symbols and a principle governing social organisation.

The term 'gender' itself is not very old. It came into existence in the course of the second-wave feminism beginning in the 1960s, in the wake of the Civil Rights Movement and world-wide protest marches. The theoretical concept was based on three principles. On the one hand the construct of gender is seen as flexible in contrast to the biological category of sex which is fixed. Secondly, both concepts presuppose the binary oppositions of male/female. And finally, there is a strong interaction between gender and other relevant categories such as race and class so much so that gender becomes the central criterion through which power structures can be explained.[2] But how is gender-specific behaviour projected on to the social being? The question has reopened the discussion about nature vs. nurture. Are behavioural differences the result of learning and conditioning or of emulation and imitation? How much of gender-specific behaviour can be attributed to people's genetic make-up and how much to their socialisation? Although on the surface level the characteristics associated with *male-ness* and *female-ness* give the impression of being 'natural' or biologically founded, they are – in fact – socially constructed and variable. Due to the fact that gender can only be understood in a social context the increasingly rapid change within this social context will have a decisive influence on the flexibility of gender roles in our modern world. To understand its essence we must first look at developments having

[1] West, Candace & Don H. Zimmermann (1991), "Doing Gender", in Susan Lorber & Judith Farell, eds., *The Social Construction of Gender,* Newbury Park – London – New Delhi: Sage Publications, 13-34. – [2] cf. von Rosenberg, Ingrid (2006), "Gender in der britischen Gesellschaft" in Hans Kastendiek et al., eds., *Länderbericht Großbritannien,* Berlin: Bundeszentrale für politische Bildung.

Equal but Different?

What are little boys made of?
What are little boys made of?
Frogs and snails
And puppy dog's tails.
That's what little boys are made of.
What are little girls made of?
What are little girls made of?
Sugar and spice
And all that's nice
That's what little girls are made of.

(Anonymous)

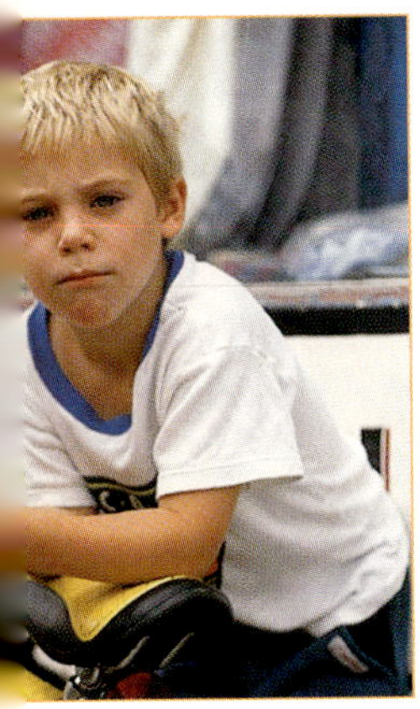

evolved over long periods of time. How can **the** male gender role be defined? Is it that of the cowboy roaming through the Wild West, of the New Super-dad or rather of metros like Robbie Williams and friends, cultivating their female side? What is the definition of **the** female gender role? Is it that of the suffragette on hunger strike, of the devoted mommy or of the "female chauvinist pig" of the 21st century? Or could it be that it is a little bit of everything and that not only have we become more tolerant, but also more flexible in our concept of gender roles, so flexible even that we can allow scope for playfulness and experiment? Could it be that the semiotics of behaviour, clothes and outward appearance are by no means as clear as they used to be, thus making their interpretation more complex, but more rewarding at the same time? Perhaps it will eventually help woman to get in touch with her 'inner man', and man with his 'inner woman'.

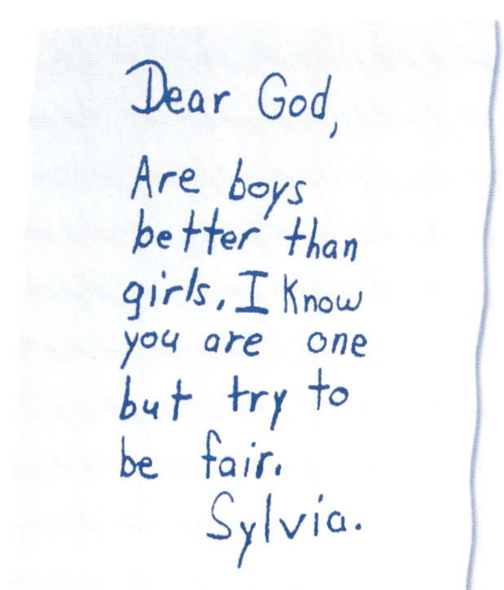

Dear God,

Are boys better than girls, I Know you are one but try to be fair.

Sylvia.

Child's letter from Children's Letters to God

1

"The Seneca Falls Convention"

The Seneca Falls Convention in 1848 marked the beginning of an organized women's movement in the U.S.A. Most of its members came from middle-class native-born families in small towns in the North and Midwest with strong reform movements. With the Declaration of Independence as their rhetorical model and ideological justification, the Declaration of Sentiments was approved by the convention and signed by 68 women and 32 men. – *The Feminist Papers: From Adams to de Beauvoir*, ed. by Alice Rossi (New York: Bantam, 1974), pp. 415–418.

When, in the course of human events, it becomes necessary for one portion of the family of man to assume among the people of the earth a position different from that which they have hitherto occupied, but one to which the laws of nature and of nature's God entitle them, a decent respect to the opinions of mankind requires that they should declare the causes that impel them to such a course.

We hold these truths to be self-evident: that all men and women are created equal; that they are endowed by their Creator with certain inalienable rights; that among these are life, liberty, and the pursuit of happiness; that to secure these rights governments are instituted, deriving their just powers from the consent of the governed. Whenever any form of government becomes destructive of these ends, it is the right of those who suffer from it to refuse allegiance to it, and to insist upon the institution of a new government, laying its foundation on such principles, and organizing its powers in such form, as to them shall seem most likely to effect their safety and happiness. [...]

The second class status of women (as well as other groups) is dramatized in this poster titled American Woman and Her Political Peers, *showing Frances Willard surrounded by a mentally handicapped man, a convict, a Native American, and an insane man.*

The history of mankind is a history of repeated injuries and usurpations on the part of man toward woman, having in direct object the establishment of an absolute tyranny over her. To prove this, let facts be submitted to a candid world.

He has never permitted her to exercise her inalienable right to the elective franchise.

He has compelled her to submit to laws, in the formation of which she had no voice.

He has withheld from her the rights which are given to the most ignorant and degraded men – both natives and foreigners.

Having deprived her of this first right of a citizen, the elective franchise, thereby leaving her without representation in the halls of legislation, he has oppressed her on all sides.

He has made her, if married, in the eye of the law, civilly dead.

He has taken from her all right in property, even to the wages she earns.

He has made her, morally, an irresponsible being, as she can commit many crimes with impunity, provided they be done in the presence of her husband. In the covenant of marriage, she is compelled to promise obedience to her husband, he becoming, to all intents and purposes, her master – the law giving him power to deprive her of her liberty, and to administer chastisement.

He has so framed the laws of divorce, as to what shall be the proper causes, and in case of separation, to whom the guardianship of the children shall be given, as to be wholly regardless of the happiness of women – the law, in all cases, going upon a false supposition of the supremacy of man, and giving all power into his hands.

After depriving her of all rights as a married woman, if single, and the owner of property, he has taxed her to support a government which recognizes her only when her property can be made profitable to it.

He has monopolized nearly all the profitable employments, and from those she is permitted to follow, she receives but a scanty remuneration. He closes against her all the avenues to wealth and distinction which he considers most honorable to himself. As a teacher of theology, medicine, or law, she is not known.

He has denied her the facilities for obtaining a thorough education, all colleges being closed against her.

He allows her in Church, as well as State, but a subordinate position, claiming Apostolic authority for her exclusion from the ministry, and, with some exceptions, from any public participation in the affairs of the Church.

He has created a false public sentiment by giving to the world a different code of morals for men and women, by which moral delinquencies which exclude women from society, are not only tolerated, but deemed of little account in man.

He has usurped the prerogative of Jehovah himself, claiming it as his right to assign for her a sphere of action, when that belongs to her conscience and to her God.

He has endeavored, in every way that he could, to destroy her confidence in her own powers, to lessen her self-respect, and to make her willing to lead a dependent and abject life.

Now, in view of this entire disfranchisement of one-half the people of this country, their social and religious degradation – in view of the unjust laws above mentioned, and because women do feel themselves aggrieved, oppressed, and fraudulently deprived of their most sacred rights, we insist that they have immediate admission to all the rights and privileges which belong to them as citizens of the United States.

[There follow a number of resolutions of which the following three may serve as examples:]

Resolved, That such laws as conflict, in any way, with the true and substantial happiness of woman, are contrary to the great precept of nature and of no validity, for this is "superior in obligation to any other."

Resolved, That all laws which prevent woman from occupying such a station in society as her conscience shall dictate, or which place her in a position inferior to that of man, are contrary to the great precept of nature, and therefore of no force or authority.

Resolved, That woman is man's equal – was intended to be so by the Creator, and the highest good of the race demands that she should be recognized as such.

Designed by the suffragettes in Britain, this peaceful propaganda poster alerts the public to the government's irrational stand against women.

Vocabulary

2 to assume (v.): to take or claim for o.s. - **4 hitherto** (adv.): formal for: up until now - **6 decent** (adj.): proper, socially acceptable - **7 to impel** (v.): to force - **12f. to be endowed with** (v.): to possess from time of birth - **14 inalienable rights** (n.): rights which cannot be taken away - **17 pursuit** (n.): /pə'sjuːt/ aim, effort towards s.th. - **18 to secure** (v.): to make certain that one gets s.th. - **27 allegiance** (n.): loyalty, faith, and dutiful support to a leader, country, idea, etc. - **38 usurpation** (n.): formal for the act of taking (power or position) for o.s. illegally or without having the right to do so - **41 object** (n.): purpose; aim - **42 to submit** (v.): to offer for consideration - **42 candid** (adj.): open, honest, and sincere in manner - **44 franchise** (n.): the right to vote in a public election, esp. one held to choose a parliament - **47 to withhold from** (v.): to keep back on purpose; to refuse to give - **48 degraded** (adj.): without self-respect or the good opinion of other people - **52 halls of legislation**: corridors of power, where laws are made - **56 civilly** (adv.): in accordance with civil law - **63 with impunity** (n.): without any danger of being punished - **66 covenant** (n.): a formal solemn agreement between two or more people or groups - **69f. to all intents and purposes**: in almost every way; very nearly - **74 to administer** (v.): fml. for: to give; dispense - **74 chastisement** (n.): /tʃæ'staɪzmənt/ punishment, esp. by beating - **79 separation** (n.): (law) a formal agreement by a husband and wife to live apart - **80 guardianship** (n.): the position of being responsible for s.o. else's child - **85 supremacy** (n.): the state of being supreme; having the highest position, in terms of power, importance, or influence - **93 but** (adv.): esp. literary for: only - **93 scanty** (adj.): hardly enough in size or quantity - **93 remuneration** (n.): formal for payment - **94 avenue** (n.): a means of reaching a desired result - **100f. subordinate** (adj.): of a lower rank or position - **101 apostolic** (adj.): of or concerning one of Christ's 12 apostles - **102 ministry** (n.): priests, considered as a group or profession - **107 delinquency** (n.): behaviour that is not in accordance with accepted social standards or the law - **108 to deem** (v.): fml. for: to consider - **109 account** (n.): importance - **110 to usurp** (v.): fml. for: to take (power or position) for o.s. illegally or without having the right to do so - **110 prerogative** (n.): a special right belonging to a particular person - **110 Jehovah** (n.): a name given to God in the Old Testament - **111 to assign** (v.): to give as a share or duty - **114 to endeavor** (v.): fml. for: to try - **117 abject** (adj.): fml. for: (of a condition) as low as possible; pitiful - **118 disfranchisement** (n.): state of having been deprived of the franchise - **122 aggrieved** (adj.): showing hurt, angry, and bitter feelings, esp. because one has been unfairly treated - **122 fraudulently** (adv.): deceitfully; got or done by fraud

Explanations

5 the laws of nature and of nature's God: *The Declaration* reflects the work of 17th and 18th century philosophers, particularly of John Locke (1632-1704). In 1690 he published *Two Treatises of Government*. In the first he refuted the divine right of kings and justified revolution. In the second he maintained that men have natural rights which government cannot interfere with or deprive them of because they are based on the unchangeable laws of nature or of God.

The first modern woman's rights convention, called through the initiative of **Lucretia Coffin Mott** (1793-1880) and Elizabeth Cady Stanton (1815-1902), was held in the Wesleyan Chapel at Seneca Falls, N.Y., on 19 and 20 July 1848. At the gathering a declaration of sentiments (modelled after the American Declaration of Independence) listing the many discriminations existing against women was read, and a series of eleven resolutions, one of them calling for woman suffrage, were adopted. Stanton was the leader of the American Women's Movement. Together with Susan B. Anthony (1820-1906) she demanded better education for women, a reformation of marriage laws, and legal equality. Between 1865 and 1893 she was president of the National Woman Suffrage Association; in 1888 she presided over the first International Women's Conference in Washington. The social reformers Mott, Stanton, and Anthony together were also called the invincible giants of early feminism. All three were agreed on the fact that that "the question of marriage was the foundation of all reforms for women".

Awareness

1 What motivated the American "Founding Fathers" to sign *The Declaration of Independence* in 1776?

2 Compare the two illustrations (pp. 60 and 61) and state common traits of the suffrage movements in Britain and the U.S.

Comprehension

3 What is meant by "one portion of the family of man" (l. 2) in the context of *The Declaration of Sentiments*?

4 What is the function of governments, according to the authors of *The Declaration of Sentiments*?

5 What is the right of those who are subject to a government?

6 How do the authors of *The Declaration of Sentiments* view the relation between men and women?

7 Re-write the 15 complaints starting with "He ..." (l. 43) in the form of demands.

Analysis

8 Analyse the use of language (Reference Library, p. 311) in the *Declaration* and classify the register.

9 Compare *The Declaration of Sentiments* to *The Declaration of Independence:* what are the similarities of the concerns reflected in the documents ?

10 One of the best-known quotations from *The Declaration of Independence* is that "all men are created equal". Compare the associations the Founding Fathers had with the word "men" with the associations of the early feminists and define the difference.

Opinion

11 Do you think it was a good idea to model *The Declaration of Sentiments* upon *The Declaration of Independence*? Give reasons for your opinion.

12 One spin-off of the Seneca Falls Convention was the women's suffrage movement. However, class and race differences made it difficult for women to unite. Working in groups, decide whether you would have joined the women's suffrage movement if you had been a black woman in the South or a female factory worker in the North.

Project

13 Design a pamphlet to be circulated by the press in which you propagate the most important of your demands (see task 7).

Internet Project

14 We have currently reached a phenomenon called Third Wave Feminism. Find out about its principles and policies. The following site might help you: http://womensissues.about.com/cs/feminism/f/thirdwave_p.htm.

2 "It is a truth universally acknowledged ...": Jane Austen and the Marriage Market*

For a long period of time the English novelist Jane Austen (1775-1817) had a small, but devoted following among academics, especially those who were interested in gender studies. In recent years there has been a Jane Austen "boom", which began with the first BBC film production of her novel *Pride and Prejudice* (first published in 1813); it has resulted in a number of film versions of her other novels and culminated in the recent new film version of *Pride and Prejudice* starring Keira Knightley, Judi Dench and Donald Sutherland, which had its German film debut in October 2005. The topic of young women of the landed gentry on the lookout for a husband, competing against each other in the process, seems rather old-fashioned, but the motivations and machinations of the literary characters have fascinated recent audiences and readers. - Jane Austen, *Pride and Prejudice* (Harmondsworth: Penguin, 1972).

Mr and Mrs Bennet with their five daughters

Plot Outline

"It is a truth universally acknowledged, that a single man in possession of a good fortune must be in want of a wife." The famous beginning of *Pride and Prejudice* is a truism which immediately plunges the reader into the marriage market of the novel. The problem arises from the necessity of attracting a likely candidate in the proper way or, failing that, in a way which may be taken to be proper by society. However, the problem becomes even more acute, if one looks at the disproportionate distribution of participants: 9 marrigeable young women are confronted with 4, more or less, eligible men. This shortage among the male domain makes it apparent to the reader/viewer how cruel the mechanisms of the market can be to any individual, whose personal likes and dislikes are hardly ever considered. A group of busybodies participating in the market are mothers like Mrs Bennet whose sole interest it is to have her five daughters married.

The following excerpt deals with the first proposal of Mr Darcy, a highly eligible man from Derbyshire, whose declaration of love seems rather offensive to Elizabeth Bennet, the second of the Bennet daughters and the most sensible one. Her rejection of the proposal does not only come as a shock to the suitor, but puts herself, from the market point of view, into a dicey situation, since she must fear to be left on the shelf owing to a lack of candidates.

A strained visit to Netherfield Park: Mr Bingley, his elegant sister Caroline and Mr Darcy are pretending to welcome female members of the Bennet family, while Elizabeth (on the left) is hoping not to be embarrassed by her relatives.

To understand the strained atmosphere and Elizabeth's rejection of Darcy it is necessary to review what has preceded this escalation. On his arrival at the marriage market of Meryton, Darcy is seen as a likely candidate for one of the eligible daughters, but since he refuses to play the game, public opinion turns against him and he is declared to be proud and distant.

In this episode Elizabeth still shares the prejudices of her social group, which is enhanced by the fact that at their first meeting Darcy offends her by refusing to dance with her, as "'She is tolerable, but not handsome enough to tempt [him].'" Elizabeth is determined to hate him.

As the plot develops, they are in each other's company for considerable lengths of time, which causes Darcy to mellow and to see some redeeming features in her intelligence and playfulness. Elizabeth, however, perceives everything about him in such a way that the prejudices she holds against him can only deepen. When she finds out that Darcy has discouraged his friend Bingley from being involved with Elizabeth's eldest sister Jane, she condemns him completely. Her dislike reaches its highest point, whereas Darcy cannot resist her charms and makes her an offer of marriage against his better judgement.

After a silence of several minutes he came towards her in an agitated manner and thus began.

'In vain have I struggled. It will not do. My feelings will not be repressed. You must allow me to tell you how ardently I admire and love you.'

Elizabeth's astonishment was beyond expression. She stared, coloured, doubted, and was silent. This he considered sufficient encouragement, and the avowal of all that he felt and had long felt for her, immediately followed. He spoke well, but there were feelings besides those of the heart to be detailed, and he was not more eloquent on the subject of tenderness than of pride. His sense of her inferiority - of its being a degradation - of the family obstacles which judgment had always opposed to inclination, were dwelt on with a warmth which seemed due to the consequence he was wounding, but was very unlikely to recommend his suit.

In spite of her deeply-rooted dislike, she could not be insensible to the compliment of such a man's affection, and though her intentions did not vary for an instant, she was at first sorry for the pain he was to receive; till, roused to resentment by his subsequent language, she lost all compassion in anger. She tried, however, to compose herself to answer him with patience, when he should have done. He concluded with representing to her the strength of that attachment which, in spite of all his endeavours, he had found impossible to conquer; and with expressing his hope that it would now be rewarded by her acceptance of his hand. As he said this, she could easily see that he had no doubt of a favourable answer. He spoke of apprehension and anxiety, but his countenance expressed real security. Such a circumstance could only exasperate farther, and when he ceased, the colour rose into her cheeks, and she said,

'In such cases as this, it is, I believe, the established mode to express a sense of obligation for the sentiments avowed, however unequally they may be returned. It is natural that obligation should be felt, and if I could feel gratitude, I would now thank you. But I cannot - I have never desired your good opinion, and you have certainly bestowed it most unwillingly. I am sorry to have occasioned pain to any one. It has been most unconsciously done, however, and I hope will be of short duration. The feelings which, you tell me, have long prevented the acknowledgment of your regard, can have little difficulty in overcoming it after this explanation.'

Mr Darcy, who was leaning against the mantle-piece with his eyes fixed on her face, seemed to catch her words with no less resentment than surprise. His complexion became pale with anger, and the disturbance of his mind was visible in every feature. He was struggling for the appearance of composure, and would not open his lips, till he believed himself to have attained it. The pause was to Elizabeth's feelings dreadful. At length, in a voice of forced calmness he said,

'And this is all the reply I have the honour of expecting! I might, perhaps, wish to be informed why, with so little endeavour at civility, I am thus rejected. But it is of small importance.'

'I might as well enquire,' replied she, 'why with so evident a design of offending and insulting me, you chose to tell me that you liked me against your will, against your reason, and even against your character? Was not this some excuse for incivility, if I was uncivil? [...]'

Jane Austen (1775–1817) was the daughter of a Hampshire clergyman. She always loved reading and started writing stories and burlesque novels at an early age. The first of her novels to be published was *Sense and Sensibility* (1811). Although Jane Austen led a very quiet life and never got married, her descriptions of contemporary society and of the relationships between women and men even today are widely acclaimed and loved by readers all over the world. The titles of her other novels, some of which were published posthumously, are *Mansfield Park, Emma, Northanger Abbey, Persuasion* and *Pride and Prejudice.*

Vocabulary

Intro: machinations (pl. n.): secret, clever, and often unfair methods used to achieve s.th. - **1 acknowledge** (v.): to admit or accept that s.th. is true - **2 fortune** (n.): a very large amount of money - **4 truism** (n.): statement that is clearly true - **10 acute** (adj.): very serious - **12 eligible** (adj.): good to marry - **39 suitor** (n.) (old use): a man who wants to marry a particular woman - **40 dicey** (adj.): slightly dangerous and uncertain - **85 ardent** (adj./literary): showing strong feelings of love - **87 colour** (v./literary): when s.o. colours, their face becomes redder because they are embarrassed - **88 avowal** (n.): /əˈvaʊəl/ a public statement about s.th. you believe in - **91 detail** (v.): to list things or give all the facts or information about s.th. - **93 degradation** (n.): here: change from a higher to a lower moral and social standard - **96 consequence** (n.): here: social importance - **102 resentment** (n.): a feeling of anger because s.th. has happened that you think is unfair – **102 subsequent** (adj.): happening or coming after s.th. else – **107 endeavour** (n.): an attempt to do s.th. new or difficult – **112 countenance** (n.): your face or your expression – **113 exasperate** (v.): to make s.o. very annoyed by continuing to do s.th. that upsets them – **116 obligation** (n.): a moral or legal duty to do s.th. – **121 bestow** (v.): to give s.o. s.th. of great value or importance – **122 occasion** (v.): to cause s.th. – **127 mantle-piece** (n.): (mod. BrE: mantelpiece) a wooden or stone shelf which is the top part of a frame surrounding a fireplace – **132 composure** (n.) the state of feeling or seeming calm – **138 civility** (n.) polite behaviour which most people consider normal

Awareness

1 A proverb says that marriages are made in heaven. Imagine that your dream partner "pops the question". What would the ambience be like? What would the wording of the proposal be?

2 Where in a person's life is etiquette of significance even in our modern world?

Comprehension

3 What compliments does Darcy verbalise?

4 In addition to the positive aspects he mentions what are his reservations about the match?

5 How does Elizabeth react
- a) to the situation in general
- b) to his mention of reservations?

6 Why does her reaction take Darcy by surprise?

7 How does the conversation end?

Analysis

8 Analyse the choice of words and the tone (Reference Library, pp. 311f.) in which the conversation takes place.

9 Make lists of positive and negative terms to describe appropriate and inappropriate social behaviour.

10 Analyse the non-verbal behaviour of both interlocutors.

Projects

11 Find out about life in Georgian England: in particular how society was structured, how marriages were arranged, what concept of etiquette prevailed, what social mobility meant for men and for women. You might find lots of hints about the facts of daily life in 19th-century England in the novels of Jane Austen herself and in Daniel Pool's *What Jane Austen ATE and Charles Dickens KNEW* (New York: 1993).

12 Design a film version of this episode.

Internet Projects

13 Check www.imdb.com and find out about the number and variety of film versions of Jane Austen's *Pride and Prejudice*. How can the attraction the material and plot still have on modern viewers be explained?

14 Choose two film versions and compare
- a) how characters and setting are rendered (Reference Library, p. 309).
- b) the cinematographic devices the producer uses. For ideas check the film glossary (pp. 49–55) in: *Viewfinder Topics Film, Soap and Photo* by D. Düwel and J. von der Grün.

Further Reading

15 Read the book that would have been more valuable to Mrs Bennet and at least one of her daughters than any book of etiquette: Rachel Greenwald, *The Program: How to Find a Husband After Thirty* (London: Timewarner 2004). According to the British newspaper *The Observer* this book is "the hottest thing to hit the dating scene since *Sex and the City*". The author uses not only the strategies but also the market technology she learned at Harvard Business School and turns the search for a husband into a business transaction. This is a modern version of the marriage market at the time of Jane Austen.

16 Read Karen Joy Fowler's novel *The Jane Austen Book Club* (London: Penguin 2004), which begins with the truism "Each of us has a private Jane Austen" (p. 1).

17 Read the following sequels to *Pride and Prejudice:*
Pemberley by Emma Tenant (London: Hodder and Stoughton, 1993)
Presumption by Julia Barrett (New York, 1993)
An Unequal Marriage or Pride and Prejudice Twenty Years Later by Emma Tennant (New York: St. Martin's Press, 1994)

3 "The myth of Super Dad"

From the new man of the 1980s via the smug dad to the super dad: how are male roles to be defined? Is this reality or simply a media hype? New Labour suddenly wants to be seen as the party of new fatherhood. It should take a reality check, says Dylan Jones, editor of *GQ magazine* and author of the following article. – *The Sunday Times,* 13 April 2003.

Last week saw the publication of two magazine interviews with the prime minister, both of which focused on his ability to juggle invading politically unstable Middle Eastern fiefdoms while looking at a rumbustious three-year-old. As Blair turns 50 he obviously feels the need to impress upon us the fact that he is a family man at heart.

In an interview with *She magazine,* Blair, posing for the pictures with Cherie in a crisp white shirt, offered some tantalising insights into his working day.

"You know what children are like," he said. "Kathryn's having a problem with her homework or Leo wants to play. One of the advantages of living above 'the shop' is that it's easy to pop up during the day. Or Leo comes down. I've got a fruit bowl in my office and he brings me fruit in a little trolley."

Tony Blair: Master of the Universe, New Man, Smug Dad, Super Dad – or just a dad who loves his children?

Apart from being a tremendous scoop on behalf of *She,* the magazine "for women who juggle their lives", this showed Blair trying to woo back waning female support for Labour.

A few days later, he was doing it again, this time in *Saga* magazine, which is aimed at older women. "Upstairs in Blair's office, I asked the prime minister if Leo keeps him young," writes the interviewer, Valerie Grove. "He certainly does," replies Blair, "especially when he wakes us up in the night, as he does rather frequently."

Who gets up to him? "Well, with our first three kids that was always my job. I'm afraid, especially recently, I have left it to Cherie." [...]

And then, to compound this onslaught of domesticity, 250,000 copies of a new trade department-funded magazine hits the news-stands and maternity wards: *Dad,* "the magazine for new fathers", designed to spread the word about recent paternity leave legislation and to make new dads better informed and more confident about their rights and responsibilities.

[...]

"Fathers have been left out of the family debate too long. There is a huge programme of support for mothers and rightly so," [Patricia Hewitt, the secretary for trade and industry] told The Sunday Times. "When you get pregnant there are antenatal classes, support networks, and then, when you actually have the baby as well as the direct support you're getting from the health service there's also a huge amount of information and advice, a bagful of products that you are given while you are still in the maternity ward. For men, for the fathers, there is almost nothing."

So why all this interest in modern fatherhood? Are we witnessing the return of the New Man? One can never put the appearance of interviews with the prime minister down to happenstance. Even if the readers of *She* and *Saga* have not been the victims of spin, one can't deny that Labour has brought the topic of fatherhood close to the top of its domestic agenda.

When it swept into power in 1997, the concept of the new dad seemed to be one of the (many) defining characteristics of the government's lifestyle manifesto. New Labour espoused modernity, egalitarianism and inclusivity, and a free tall skinny latte with every order.

Part of the manifesto determined that if you were a man it was okay to be the master of the universe as long as you spent serious quality time with the kids when you got home. But in terms of legislation, government policy focused far more on the rights of mothers (maternity leave, flexibility for working mums).

From this month, however, fathers have the right to two weeks' paid paternity leave – as long as they give three months' notice – and nearly 400,000 fathers each year are expected to take up this offer. Plus, fathers of young disabled children will get the right, like mothers, to work flexible hours.

"There are more and more surveys showing that fathers want to play a more active part in their children's lives than their own fathers did with them", Hewitt says. This may be true, but how many of them are able to? Even if they have the inclination, few British men have the time to play superdad.

British men work the longest hours in Europe; fewer than 15% of fathers with young children have flexible working hours; only 3% of all male workers have a jobshare; around one in eight working fathers work 60 or more hours a week, and over a third work more then 48 hours. Then there are the men who do not even have free access to their children: divorce rates have never been higher.

In many ways Labour is behind the curve in trying to encourage men to be a little more touchy-feely.

If one thinks back to the early 1990s, to a time when "yuppie"was officially a pejorative and when the all-new male consumer was beginning to tire of his mattblack designer home, and when advertisers were trying to find new ways in which to ensnare him, the New Man was born.

The new man, in case you have forgotten, was the caring-sharing type, the sort of guy who dressed in fancy designer clothes, who drove a souped-up Gti and who frequented fashionable riverside cocktail bars; but he was also the kind of guy who got up in the middle of the night to comfort his newborn baby, who wasn't afraid to push a pram through the park (Afraid! Ha! He loved it, looked forward to it!), who was quite willing to while away the hours discussing his feelings with his girlfriend's girlfriends as they all knocked back the Aqua Libra.

The advertising of this period reflects the new man, too: Armani, Gillette, Calvin Klein, Quorum and Next commissioned ads featuring well-groomed, well-dressed thirtysomething men with uncharacteristically serene babies.

Ah, this was the new "kinder, gentler", politically correct lifestyle made manifest. Glossy magazines soon followed suit, and these ads appeared opposite pages and pages devoted to media-savvy gadabouts pictured hugging offspring who seemed strangely intrigued to see their parents so close-up.

But the new man was an adland fantasy. Even the original new man poster boy, Mark Perry, turned out to be something of an unreconstructed lad. Perry, you may remember, was the male model who became famous as a pin-up of the early 1980s.

Looking not unlike James Dean, and stripped to the waist, Perry appeared in an astonishingly popular poster posing with a newborn baby.

The photograph was shot, oh-so tastefully, in black and white and became as popular as posters of Garfield or Adam Ant on female dormitory walls from St. Paul's to St. Mary's, Calne.

But Perry later wrote a book in which he claimed to have slept with more than 3,000 women between the ages of 15 and 33. Whether he was a lothario or a fantasist, he was hardly a new man. None of us was. He was a media creation, one which even the most cynical of us couldn't bring ourselves to buy into.

The prime minister himself isn't so much new man as Smug Dad, and while it would be unfair to say that Blair has exploited his family unit it won't have escaped anyone's notice that his family has helped enormously with his public image.

Smug Dads are those fathers who are overtly affectionate and extrava-

gantly show-offy about their children. "Smug Dad syndrome manifests itself in many ways, but the early telltale signs are fairly easy to spot," says one male friend of mine, a father of two who is himself something of a designer dad.

"Tick more than two of any of the following boxes and you can diagnose yourself with SDS, too. Do you insist on feeding/holding/ changing your baby's nappies in public/or at parties even though you might never go near it at home?"

"Do you play loud, ostentatious rough and tumble games in the park in close proximity to childless couples? Are you the owner of a nonsensical pavement-hogging off-road baby buggy imported from America via the web, which was bought simply for the reason that Tom Cruise has one?"

Smug Dads are everywhere. "I can't believe how tiredness has become such a furiously competitive game of one-upmanship with all the dads I know," said television presenter Johnny Vaughan last week.

"I was in a meeting the other morning and a dad I work with rolled in looking shattered. The conversation went something like this: 'How long did you get last night?' 'An hour and a half at most.' 'Really? Ours just sleeps for 20 minutes at a time at the moment. It's a nightmare.' Then, from the other side of the table another dad's voice piped up, 'Just the one is it? You wait until you've got two. That's when the real nightmares start'."

I must admit I was something of a smug dad when my first daughter was born, and I proudly stalked aound the office banging on about how little sleep I had had, how one of my arms was becoming longer than the other due to excessive midnight cradle rocking.

But soon I realized how facile this was. I wasn't really doing the work, I was just talking about it. I wasn't up all hours breastfeeding, I was trying to take the glory. I was just, after all, a typical man, not a new man at all, not even a new lad. And certainly not a superdad.

Justine Roberts, the founder of mumsnet.com, Britain's most popular parenting website where mothers swap advice on men and childcare, says superdads are few and far between.

"He's still definitely the exception and not the rule. We've recently conducted a survey on the state of modern motherhood and women are still doing the bulk of the childcaring. I wouldn't poohpooh these government initiatives ... but I don't know how much men are really interested. I think a lot of men still think of raising children as women's work."

Superdads are, like new men, simply mythical creatures. If one were a cynical person, one could imagine the conceit of the new government legislation and interest in fatherhood as simply a ploy to appeal, not to modern men, but to women voters.

[...]

Vocabulary

3 to juggle (v.): here: to try to fit two or more jobs, activities etc. into your life – **4 fiefdom** (n.): a feudal organisation – **4f. rumbustious** (adj.): full of energy, fun and noise – **10 tantalising** (adj.): making you feel a strong desire to have or do s.th. – **24 scoop** (n.): an important or exciting news story that is printed in one newspaper before any of the others know about it – **28 to woo** (v.): to try and persuade s.o. to do s.th. such as buy s.th. from you, vote for you, or work for you – **28 waning** (adj.): becoming gradually less strong or less important – **43 to compound** (v.): to make a difficult situation worse by adding more problems – **43 onslaught** (n.): /ɒnslɔːt/ the effect of s.th. that is unpleasant and could cause damage – **43 domesticity** (n.): life at home with your family – **45 maternity** (adj.): elating to a woman who is pregnant or who has just had a baby – **45 ward** (n.): a large room in a hospital where people who need medical treatment stay – **47 paternity leave** (n.): a period of time that the father of a new baby is allowed to stay away from work – **47 legislation** (n.): a law or a set of laws – **55 antenatal** (adj.): (BrE) /æntɪneɪtl/ relating to the medical care given to women who are going to have a baby – **73 happenstance** (n.): chance, or s.th. that happens by chance – **76 spin** (n.): the way s.o., especially a politician or business person, talks about information or a situation, especially in order to influence the way people think about it – **84 manifesto** (n.): a written statement by a political party, saying what they believe in and what they intend to do – **84 to espouse** (v.): (fml.) /ɪ'spaʊz/ to support an idea, belief etc, especially a political one – **85 egalitarianism** (n.): belief that everyone is equal and should have equal rights – **89 quality time** (n.): the time that you spend giving s.o. your full attention, especially time you spend with your children when you are not busy – **103 inclination** (n.): a feeling that makes you want to do s.th. – **114 touchy-feely** (adj.): too concerned with feelings and emotions, rather than with facts or actions – **116 pejorative** (adj.): (fml.) used to show disapproval or to insult s.o. – **119 to ensnare** (v.): (fml.) to trap s.o. in an unpleasant or illegal situation, from which they cannot escape – **123 souped-up** (adj.): used for a car that has been made more powerful – **129 to while away the hours**: to spend time in a pleasant and lazy way – **136 serene** (adj.): very calm or peaceful – **140 media-savvy** (adj.): s.o. who knows how to deal with the media – **140 gadabout** (n.): (infml.) s.o. who goes out a lot or travels a lot in order to enjoy themselves – **143 adland** (n.): the activity or business of advertising, considered as a whole – **207 to pipe up** (v.): (infml.) to suddenly say s.th. especially when you have been quiet until then – **230 mythical** (adj.): imagined or invented – **231 cynical** (adj.): unwilling to believe that people have good, honest, or sincere reasons for doing s.th. – **232 conceit** (n.): an attitude that shows you have too high an opinion of your own abilities or importance – **233 ploy** (n.): a clever and dishonest way of tricking s.o. so that you can get an advantage

Explanations

Intro: GQ: a magazine for men including news on lifestyle and fashion - **44 trade department-funded**: the money has been provided by the department of trade and industry; the secretary of state for trade and industry was Patricia Hewitt (later secretary of state for the health service) - **70 New Man**: a man who is considered to be very modern because he shares the work of looking after his children, cooking, cleaning the home etc. - **130 Aqua Libra**: trademark for a refreshing drink made with fruit juices and natural herbal extracts - **133 Armani, Gillette, Calvin Klein, Quorum, Next**: are all trademarks for various products which men associate with - **152 Garfield**: a cartoon cat - **153 Adam Ant**: lead singer of the pop group Adam and the Ants, famous in the early 1980s, before he started a solo career - **153 St. Paul's**: an independent boys' school in London - **154 St. Mary's, Calne**: an independent girls' school - **159 lothario** (n.): (literary or derog.) a man whose main interest is having as many female lovers as possible without having a serious relationship with any of them

Awareness

1 Try and remember who looked after you when you were a baby, a toddler or an infant.
2 Were there any differences in the nurture / care you got from your father or your mother?
3 Did your father change your nappies?

Comprehension

4 How does Tony Blair talk about his children and why does it surprise the reader?
5 What is meant by the Smug Dad Syndrome (II. 181f.) or SDS (I. 187) and how can one "diagnose" it?
6 What, according to the author, is the role of the media in the creation of the image of the Super Dad?
7 Explain why Mark Perry obviously did not qualify as the New Man.

Analysis

8 Characterise the following male figures:
- the Super Dad
- the New Man
- the Smug Dad.

9 Analyse the author's presentation of the topic and find out whose side he is on.
10 Outline the public image of Tony Blair that is evoked in this article.

Projects

11 Imagine you are a hard-working father of a toddler or of a teenager. How would you spend "quality time" with them? Work together in groups and design a schedule.
12 Play the role of a public relations expert who has to design the public image of celebrities. Design the public images of a male and a female celebrity, e.g. David Beckham and Leila Ali.

Internet Projects

13 Check http://www.mumsnet.com, which is supposed to be "Britain's most popular parenting website" (I. 220), and find out what topics are dealt with. Why do you think it is called "mumsnet", if it deals with parenting?
14 If you want to know e.g. how the New Man dresses for a summer's evening, go to http://men.style.com.

Further Reading

15 R. E. Page, "Cherie: Lawyer, Wife, Mum: Contradictory Patterns of Representation in Media Reports of Cherie Booth/Blair", *Discourse Society,* Sept. 1, 2003; 14(5); pp. 559-579.

4

"The new ladette or: Call my bluff?"*

Girls know how to have fun. Forget about sugar and spice! It's o.k. to be "a bit of a lad"! Or is it? Women are swilling lager and wolf-whistling with the best of them. David Thomas, the author of this article, happily relinquishes the male monopoly on blokish behaviour. – *The Sunday Times,* 19 February 1995.

Well, you can forget about that sugar-and-spice stuff, for a start. These days, girls are made of sterner stuff. A recent survey carried out by the AA showed that 54% of women questioned admitted acts of aggression on the road. The number of women jailed for motoring-related crimes has doubled in the past year. [...]

In general, women still commit far fewer crimes than men, but the rate at which their offences are increasing is much greater, so the gap is gradually narrowing. What makes young women act in this way? Well, one important factor in male crime is alcohol abuse, and here, too, the sexes are well on the road to equality.

The Brewers' & Licensed Retailers' Association predicts that by the year 2000 half of all pub-goers will be women. And they won't be sipping Babychams, either. Women make up one-third of all lager drinkers and one-sixth of ale buffs, according to a survey by the brewers Carlsberg-Tetley. There is an increasing number of all-girl drinking clubs, too. Especially on university campuses, such as Cambridge, for example. [...]

When the advertising agency Collett Dickenson Pearce compiled a marketing study called *A Portrait of Lads,* it found that 550,000 of the 2m young adults who fitted the criteria of being single, drinking more than eight pints a week, and having laddish attitudes, were female. So, is there a new generation of ladettes, or faux-blokes?

Sometimes it seems that way, as a slew of jeans and cola ads feature gangs of girls leering at cute young hunks or leaning out of windows to wolf-whistle beefy builders. At last year's Miss UK beauty competition, a Mr UK contest was introduced. When the male finalists paraded down the catwalk at London Grosvenor House Hotel, they were greeted with screams of appreciation and suggestive remarks from excited females in the audience. When the Misses' turn came, they were met by polite applause from the demure, bashful males in the room.

It is an increasingly typical pattern. According to Justine Frishmann, leadsinger with Elastica, her male fans tend to be friendly, shy, enthusiastic types. "I've certainly never felt like I'm being approached sexually." However, her boyfriend, Damon Albarn, leadsinger with Blur, finds that his fans are far more forward. "Girls can be a lot more obsessed about people in bands," says Frishmann. "I don't think it's very respectful for a boy to go up to a girl and just try it on with her, but it's more accepted if a girl does it to a bloke."

As if to prove that point, *Sky magazine* this month sent three female reporters off to a series of pubs and parties to try and pull men with naff male chat-up lines such as, "Cheer up, love, it may never happen". The resulting article was extremely funny, but its most revealing moments were the descriptions of the three writers themselves. "Babe One" was Sylvia, "the heat-seeking missile of the pulling world. Nigh-on insatiable, yet ruthlessly selective." Toni was "utterly powerless to resist the seduction of things she hasn't tried before". And Vicki was "possessed of a healthy sexual appetite. Better still, the concept of shame is meaningless to her."

These outrageously sexist and exploitative phrases were not the work of vile, male journo-pigs. They were produced, with tongues firmly placed in cheeks, by an editorial team, led by the magazine's editor, Angela Holden. They demonstrate that the upsurge of apparently laddish behaviour among

Hen behaving badly.

young women has not been accompanied by any desire to seem masculine or butch. Quite the contrary, the self-confessed babes and chicks who populate *Sky's* pages are unashamedly "gooey and giggly and girly".

Not so long ago, the very word "girl" was considered to be offensive by the right-on thought police. Those days are long gone, says Holden. "Young women are tired of being the standard-bearers for political correctness in the media. The idea that they are the long-suffering, wimpy victims of men's appalling behaviour is an annoying stereotype. You don't have to have a personality like a wet herbal tea bag."

Holden agrees that young women are acting in ways that were once reserved for men. "Men don't have the monopoly on fun. Once you accept that, all the other behaviour follows." However, she dismisses talk of faux-blokedom. "It's all about expressing your femaleness." Girls will call themselves babes or chicks for exactly the same reason gays call themselves queers: they are reclaiming sexist terms for themselves.

They are reclaiming sexist clothes, too. The Wonderbra phenomenon – based on a marketing campaign that was devised entirely by women – is a true sign of the times. The girls who wear these triumphs of mammary engineering are acting in an assertive, self-determined way that is traditionally masculine, while expressing their assertion in a manner that is undeniably feminine.

This is a difficult concept to grasp for those men still wedded to the notion of female victimisation. An increasing number of the complainants protesting to the Advertising Standards Authority over ads such as those for Wonderbra are men. It is no surprise: the idea that women are helpless pawns of a brutal patriarchy is deeply reassuring to the right-on male. He loves knowing that he could oppress women if he wasn't such a wonderful, caring guy.

Self-confident chicks who refuse to see themselves as anybody's victim are a very different matter. Personally, I think they are great, if only because their hearty commitments to bad behaviour destroys for once and for all the notion that there is something uniquely bestial about the male psyche.

In any case, we should not necessarily take the new ladettes at face value. Sarah Palmer is a market researcher who last year helped compile a survey on Wild Women for [an agency]. She found the young women she interviewed to be ultra-confident on the surface. But, she noted: "There is a lot of bluster beneath the confidence. There is enormous pressure to be sorted out, be cool, have a career, have a relationship. It's very difficult."

Any lad would understand. His cockiness, too, is all based on bluff or bluster. He is all mouth and no trousers. The ladette, meanwhile, is all mouth and no miniskirt. And what could be more equal than that?

Vocabulary

Title: to call s.o.'s bluff: to tell s.o. to do what they have threatened because you do not believe that they will really do it – **Intro/1 a bit of a lad**: (spoken) a man that people like even though he behaves rather badly – **Intro/2 to swill** (v.): (infml.) to drink s.th. in large amounts – **Intro/2 wolf-whistle** (v.): to whistle like men sometimes do to show that they think a woman is attractive – **Intro/3 to relinquish** (v.): to give up – **Intro/3 blokish** (adj.): if you do blokish things you behave in a traditionally male way – **2 be made of sterner stuff**: to have a strong character and be more determined than other people to succeed in a difficult situation – **5 to be jailed** (v.): to be sent to prison – **17 ale buff** (n.): s.o. who loves that type of beer and knows a lot about it – **34 faux** (adj.): artificial, but made to look real – **38 to leer** (v.): to look at s.o. in an unpleasant way that shows that you think they are sexually attractive – **39 hunk** (n.): (infml.) a sexually attractive man with a big strong body – **40 beefy** (adj.): big and strong – **47 appreciation** (n.): pleasure you feel when you realize that s.th. is good, useful, or well done – **38 demure** (adj.): /dimjuə/ quiet, serious and well-behaved; used esp. about women in the past – **50 bashful** (adj.): easily embarrassed – **60 to try it on with s.o.**: (BrE spoken) to attempt to start a sexual relationship with s.o. – **64 naff** (adj.): (BrE infml.) silly, here because it shows a lack of good taste – **64 chat-up line** (n.): (BrE) s.th. that s.o. says in order to start a conversation with s.o. they think is sexually attractive – **72 to pull** (v.): (BrE spoken) to attract s.o. in order to have sex with them or spend the evening with them – **72 nigh-on** (adv.): (old-fashioned) almost – **73 insatiable** (adj.): always wanting more and more of s.th. – **73 ruthless** (adj.): determined to get what you want – **84 vile** (adj.): extremely unpleasant or bad – **85 journo** (n.): sl. for journalist – **92 laddish** (adj.): (BrE) a young man who is laddish likes spending time with other men, drinking alcohol and enjoying things like sport, sex, and music – **94 butch** (adj.): (infml.) a woman who is butch looks, behaves, or dresses like a man; a man who is butch seems big and strong, and typically male – **95 babe** (n.): (spoken infml.) a word for an attractive young woman – **95 chick** (n.): (infml.) a word meaning a young woman, that some people think is offensive – **96 gooey** (adj.): showing your love for s.o. in a way that other people think is silly – **98 right-on** (adj.): (BrE infml.) s.o. who is right on supports social justice, equal rights, the protection of the environment etc.; often used to show disapproval because s.o. does this in an extreme (politically correct) way – **116 mammary** (adj.): (technical) connected with or relating to the breasts – **125 pawn** (n.): s.o. who is used by a more powerful person or group and has no control of the situation – **134 bestial** (adj.): (literary) behaving like an animal, esp. in a cruel way – **140 bluster** (n.): loud and angry speech that is not really impressive – **144 cockiness** (n.): too much confidence about yourself and your abilities, esp. in a way that annoys other people

Explanations

Intro/1 sugar and spice: refers to a nursery rhyme about the differences between girls and boys (see p. 59) – **3 AA**: Automobile Association; a British organisation which provides services for people who own cars – **13 The Brewers' and Licenced Retailers' Association**: this association published a beer and pub guide – **15 Babycham**: BrE, tdmk., a sweet, sparkling, alcoholic drink which comes in a small bottle. It is usually considered to be a woman's drink. – **18 Carlsberg-Tetley**: tdmk., famous beer brewery – **53 Elastica**: a punk band, famous on both sides of the Atlantic in 1995; they split up in 2001 – **57 Blur**: an equally famous Britpop band in the 1990s; Damon and Justine, who were often called the King and Queen of Britpop, have also split up – **82 sexist** (adj.): referring to the attitudes of s.o. who believes that one sex is weaker, less intelligent, or less important than the other – **100 political correctness**: a code of language, behaviour and attitudes that are carefully chosen not to offend or insult anyone – **113 Wonderbra**: tdmk. for a push-up bra – **123 Advertising Standards Authority (ASA)**: a British organisation which controls the activities of the advertising industry. If people think an advertisement is wrong or offensive, they can complain to this organisation, which may decide that the advertisement should not be used again.

Awareness

1 When you go out to a disco or pop concert next time, watch the behaviour of young women and young men and try to explain the differences.
2 When you go through some British (seaside) towns you will frequently find signs which declare an area to be an alcohol-free zone. Can you imagine why this is so? Do similar phenomena exist in your home country?
3 Make a list of adjectives that you think apply to men and another one that you think apply to women. Compare your lists in class.

Comprehension

4 What does the text say about the changing crime rates among women and men?
5 How does male/female behaviour differ when they are spectators at beauty competitions or listeners in the pop business?
6 To what extent has the behaviour of young women changed against the code of behaviour of young women in previous generations?
7 Why is the male author of the article glad about the changes?
8 Characterise the 'ladette'.

Analysis

9 Analyse examples of colloquial speech and slang in the text and what they contribute to the tone (Reference Library, p. 312) in which the article is presented.
10 Determine the text form (Reference Library, pp. 312f.) of this article.
11 Analyse to what extent it becomes obvious that the author of this article is a man.

Project

12 Work with your neighbour and imagine you have seen your dream man/dream woman. Design your chat-up line and then try it out in a roleplay.

Internet Projects

13 Check www.imdb.com and find out about "Britain's most successful sitcom of the 1990s" '(British) Men Behaving Badly' and how it can be related to the sociological concept that is called 'lad culture'.
14 Check www.imdb.com for ITV1's latest reality show "Ladettes to Ladies" in which "10 women compete to transform themselves (in Eliza Doolittle style) from ladettes to ladies".
15 The following advertisement was published in the Internet: "Notorious ladettes wanted for 2nd series at ITV's Finishing School – contact: michelle.woods@rdfmedia.com." Find out about the casting conditions.
Wikipedia quotes several links to investigate into lad culture:
"/wiki/Subculture"\
"/wiki/Britpop"\
"/wiki/Sitcom"\
"/wiki/Men_Behaving_Badly"\

Young People

They may be more involved than you think - and in ways that could change America's politics

by Scott Keeter | Pew Research Center for the People & the Press | 30 May 2006

Their "technological savvy" is what sets this generation

What's the new generation coming to? Are today's young people apathetic and politically inert, as the stereotypes suggest? Are they more reluctant to get involved in politics and public life than generations past? What will American politics be like when they are eventually in charge? The answers are not what you might think. Not only is there evidence of a reawakening of young people to public life, but today's youth are politically distinctive in many ways.

First, let's be clear who we are talking about. This is not "Generation X." The youngest GenXers are turning 30 this year, and some of them are over 40 now. Instead, we are focusing on the next generation – those in their teens and 20s today – who are sometimes labeled as "Millennials," "Gen Y," or "Gen Next." (We call) them the "DotNets," because of their technological savvy. Though there is no clear line dividing one generation from another, the boundary falls around 1976. Kids born after that year began coming of age in the 1990s and have experienced a very different social and political world than did Generation X, whose formative years were the 1980s.

It's true that over the past three decades, youth have been disengaging from conventional politics. In particular, electoral participation by America's youngest citizens has experienced a long, slow decline. In most elections since 18- to 20-year-olds were given the vote, voter turnout among younger Americans has fallen, and, indeed, has accounted for most of the drop in voter turnout overall in the United States during that period.

(... This) trend in falling voter turnout among young people was reversed in 2004. Among the voting age members of the DotNet cohort (ages 18–29), 49% voted, an increase of 9 percentage points from 2000. (...)

And electoral activity isn't the only story. Young people are active in public life in many other ways not reflected in the voting statistics. According to our 2002 study of 3,246 people – including 1,001 DotNets, many are engaged in volunteer activities and community problem-solving, and even more voice their opinions on public issues through the Internet and more conventional media.

About four-in-10 DotNets now say they have done some type of volunteer work in the past year, and 22% had volunteered regularly. These numbers were similar to those for all age groups. And UCLA's annual survey of college freshmen has documented a growing trend of volunteer activity over the past 15 years.

Young people also match their elders in working with others to solve community problems, and are active in fund raising for charitable causes as well. (...)

What values and opinions do today's youth bring to their public engagement? How are these views likely to affect American politics and public policy as the DotNet generation moves into positions of responsibility in government, business, education, and the non-profit world?

Today's younger Americans are more liberal than the country as a whole on many social issues. Thus it's worth considering what the future might look like when this group of younger Americans finally takes its turn running the country.

Young People More Liberal on Some, Not All Issues and Values

	All	18–29	30+
*Opinion about gay marriage^*	%	%	%
Favor	36	48	33
Oppose	53	48	54
Don't know	11	4	13
	100	100	100
*OK for black & whites to date**			
Completely agree	47	68	42
Mostly agree	30	23	32
Mostly disagree	10	3	12
Completely disagree	10	5	11
Don't know	3	1	3
	100	100	100
*Abortion should be ...**			
Generally available	35	31	37
More limited	20	24	19
Illegal except rape/ incest/save mother	31	30	31
Never permitted	11	13	10
Don't know	3	2	3
	100	100	100
*Government is ...^^*			
Wasteful and inefficient	47	32	52
Better than given credit for	45	64	40
Don't know	8	4	8
	100	100	100

Vocabulary

2 inert (adj.): not willing to do anything – **3 reluctant** (adj.): /ri'lʌktənt/ slow and unwilling – **17 savvy** (n.): (infml.) practical knowledge and ability – **29 turnout** (n.): the number of people who vote in an election – **35 cohort** (n.): (technical) a group of people of the same age, social class etc. – **48 UCLA:** The University of California at Los Angeles

Explanations

11 Generation X: the undefined generation, the unknown and unpredictable quantity; the term became popular through a 1991 novel, Douglas Coupland's *Generation X: Tales for an Accelerated Culture.*

UNICEF – VOICES OF YOUTH

Abigail in New York

"After arriving at the airport, I looked around with bright eyes and a big smile. I was hoping that when other people saw me, I could just bring out a glow in their faces. But I was quite frustrated! Maybe they were all exhausted because of the long flight. But an elderly Asian man smiled back at me and waved his hand a little and said, 'Hi.' Maybe he should join the UN Special Session or the Children's Forum. I really saw the child in him."
From Abigail's diary

When she was around 11 years old, Abigail began working with street children (children who live or work on the street) and those with special needs (children with disabilities or learning impairments). One motive was curiosity – she realized she d never gotten to know any street children well. But the curiosity was almost immediately replaced by an emotional connection.

Abigail was chosen as a delegate for the Children's Forum because of her volunteer work and her involvement with the Say Yes for Children campaign. She had already graduated from high school and was going on to study broadcast communications at the University of the Philippines.

Abigail had never left the Philippines before, so she was very excited about visiting New York. And getting a stranger to smile at her at an airport in one of the world's busiest and most worldly cities wasn't a bad start!

Abigail's special connection with street children

Abigail Manglicmot Fabrigas, 16, is from Olongapo City, a three-hour drive from Manila, the capital of the Philippines. Her father is an engineer, currently unemployed. Her mother teaches at a state school. Abigail is the eldest of three children - this, she says, has given her a strong feeling of responsibility for others.

As a member of her government's delegation to the Special Session, she says she wants to focus on the plight of street children, the inadequate investments in children's health and education, and the global problem of armed conflict. She plans to brainstorm with other children on how to make a real difference in the world.

"We the children are experts on being 8, 12 or 17 years old in the societies of today and to consult us would make your work more effective and give better results for children. My proposal is that you make us part of your team." Heidi Grande, 17, from Norway

The United Nations General Assembly Special Session on Children in New York City, from 8 to 10 May 2002, was another listening landmark. It was the first time that young people had played an official part in a meeting of the United Nations General Assembly: They came as official delegates from their governments and from non-governmental organizations (NGOs).

In the three days leading up to the Special Session, just over 400 children – 242 girls and 162 boys – from a total of 154 countries attended a related event: The Children's Forum. During the forum the young delegates' job was to explore ways to improve the rights of children and young people worldwide. They also came to discuss the many new challenges that have arisen since the 1990 World Summit for Children.

It was not only the young delegates themselves who had a chance to influence the Special Session. There had been a massive effort to consult children and young people beforehand. In all, UNICEF and its partners polled nearly 40,000 young people in 72 countries. Obviously, 40,000 young people don't all want the same things. But on some of the most crucial issues, there was a lot of agreement.

To start on a positive note, most young people said that they got on well with their parents and teachers and were generally happy. But most were also deeply worried about a range of problems, in particular:

- violence at home, at school or in the community
- discrimination against those who are poor, have disabilities, or minority children
- unemployment and poverty
- shortage of information about children's rights and about drugs, HIV/AIDS and sex
- lack of access to high-quality education
- the lack of opportunity to express opinions and have them taken into account

Tasks and Projects

1. Would you consider yourself a member of the "DotNet Generation"? In what context does it make sense to label people?
2. What does Scott Keeter expect of American politics in 2020? – Is there a similar development in your own country?
3. Do you think it is a good idea to have children as experts at the United Nations? What advantages/disadvantages can you see?
4. What is your opinion of Abigail and her cause? – Do you agree with her views?
5. Imagine your school was invited to name a delegate to a similar UN Special Session. Whom would you nominate and why? Discuss. – Would you like to go yourself? If so, what would you tell the politicians?

5 Britain in Europe

IDEAS

SPORTS

PEOPLE

ART AND LITERATURE

What do you know about Britain?

- What is the official name of Britain?
- Who gave Britain its name?
- What part of Britain is "Great" Britain?
- Which are the four national soccer teams that represent Britain?

What has Europe given to Britain?
What has Britain given to Europe?

INVENTIONS

FOOD AND DRINK

FASHION

What do you know about Europe?

- Where did Europe get its name?
- Which is the most densely populated European country?
- Which is the second largest European country after Russia?
- Where was the treaty signed that started the European Union?
- Which two countries have rejected membership of the European Union?
- Name the two European countries which each consist of one whole island.
- Which is the smallest European country?
- In which country is the geographical centre of Europe situated?

1

Stephen Clarke

An Englishman in Paris*

Paul West has, like many thousands of British people, moved to Europe to set up his own business, in his case an English tea shop. He is soon confronted with French bureaucracy and its many demands on employers and business people. One of them is the requirement that all business and advertising material should be written in French. – Stephen Clarke, *Merde Actually* (London: Bantam Press, 2005), pp. 276–281.

It was late, just before closing time, and I was resting my feet, reading the newspaper over a cup of Orange Pekoe. I didn't really pay any attention to the guy at first, except to do a double-take at his impeccable colour coordination. Sand-brown fleece, beige-and-green shirt, khaki chinos, light brown suede shoes. Even his hair matched, a kind of chestnut-and-grey flecked combination. Here, I felt, was a guy whose sock drawer was graded in a strict spectrum pattern.

I returned to reading the football pages. [...]

But my attention wandered back to the sock-drawer man again when I realized that he was arguing loudly with Benoît, who wasn't an arguing-loudly kind of guy.

'You must translate everything,' the sock-drawer guy was saying. 'Cup of tea, for example.'

'But every French person knows what a cup of tea is.'

'How do you know this? Perhaps I do not know this?'

'Don't you know what a cup of tea is?

'No.'

'Yes you do, you ordered one when you came in.'

'Perhaps I was just curious to know what this unknown thing was on the menu.'

I realized I had to intervene. Benoît was clearly up against a mind more fiendish than he could possibly imagine. A French bureaucratic mind.

I introduced myself and asked him what the problem was.

The guy didn't introduce himself. He simply snapped back a question, in French of course. 'What is a moog?'

'Moog?'

'Oui, moog of tea.'

'Ah, mug,' I corrected him.

'Oui, mag.'

'Mug.'

'Mog.'

'Mug.'

'Maaahg.'

'Oui, c'est ça,' I congratulated him. 'Un maaahhg est un grand coop.'

'Coop?'

'Cup.'

He snorted triumphantly. 'You see, even you do not know what a cup is. That is why you must translate it as tasse de thé. You must translate everything on your menu.'

He introduced himself as an inspector from the Ministère de la Francophonie, the government department that tries to protect the French language from attack by such invaders as 'le marketing', 'le Walkman' and, it seemed, 'le cup of tea'.

He flashed his ID card at a wide-eyed Benoît and me and informed us that it was illegal to have a menu that did not give French translations for every foreign ingredient or dish.

'What, even sandwich?' I asked. I pronounced it à la française; 'son-dweetch', though the French spell the word as in English.

'No, of course not.'

'OK, so if it is an English word that is used in French, or known by the French, I don't have to translate it.'

'English? But sandwich is French.' His cheeks flushed for a moment, but realized they were disrupting his colour scheme and quickly returned to their normal shade of grey-green.

'What? Sandwich is English.'

'Ho!' This was by no means a laugh. It was a cry of indignation. He appealed for support to Benoît, but by this time the poor lad was gaping at us mutely, stroking the tea urn for moral support. 'It is like les frites,' – French fries – the inspector went on. 'The whole world knows they are French, except the English who say they invented them. As do the Belgians, but who cares about them? We French have been eating sandwiches for much longer than you. The traditional baguette is the perfect bread for a sandwich.'

Apart from his wild rewriting of culinary history, he'd left himself open to attack here, and I darted in.

'No it's not. It's the worst bread in the world for a sandwich. You can't get it in your mouth.' I mimed the impossible task of closing your teeth on a baguette sandwich without first crushing it flat. 'And when you squeeze it, all the ingredients fall out the other end of the sandwich on to your trousers.'

His eyes narrowed at me. 'I thought we were having a linguistic conversation, Monsieur, not criticizing French table manners.' When a Frenchman uses 'Monsieur' at you in the middle of an argument, you know you've offended him badly.

'I wasn't criticizing French table manners,' I assured him. 'But sandwich really is an English word.'

'Nonsense. What is its meaning? Something to do with sand, no doubt?'

'It's the name of the man who invented it.'

'Ah oui. Monsieur Sandwich, a cousin of Monsieur Fish and Chips?' He bowed as if acknowledging polite applause at his rapier wit. Even Benoît accorded him a nod of appreciation.

I could see that I was rapidly sinking into the quicksand of an intellectual discussion that was only going to drag me under. This guy was a professional quibbler, after all. His clothes and his ID badge proved it.

And as everyone knows, once you're in quicksand, the last thing you should do is flail about and hope you can fight your way out.

Trouble is, some of us are just born flailers.

'Well, it's an English word so I'm going to translate it on my menu,' I told him.

'You will not translate it. It is French.'

'It is an English word and I demand the right to translate it.'

'I forbid you to translate it.' By this time we were practically nose to nose.

'I will translate it as "traditional English food with two slices of bread and, er, something between".' My French let me down at the end but the blow struck home.

'That would be a gross misrepresentation. The law forbids incorrect translations.'

'Oh yes? Well we shall see what Bruxelles says about that. Or Brussel as the Flemish residents call it. Bruxelles is just a bad translation, n'est-ce pas?'

The inspector took up the gauntlet and threw it back in my face. 'I will return, and if there is one mistake in the French translations on your menu, you will be obliged to reprint all of them, or face a heavy fine.'

No one throws gauntlets in my face and gets away with it, even if my face is the only part of me still sticking up out of the quicksand. 'Oh yes?' I replied. 'We will take the train together to Brussel to discuss the case.'

As the glass door clanged shut behind him, I'm sure both of us were feeling that peculiarly French sense of satisfaction at having created mutual outrage. Nothing at all had been resolved, but we'd had a damn good row and each of us had emerged feeling sure we were in the right. I was as exhilarated as a poodle strutting away after a damn good yapping match.

Vocabulary

4 to do a double-take (v.): to look at s.o. or s.th. again because you are very surprised by what you saw or heard – **4 impeccable** (adj.): without any faults – **6 chinos** (n. pl.) /'tʃiːnəʊz/: loose trousers made from strong woven cotton – **6 suede** (adj.) /sweɪd/: made of soft leather with a slightly rough surface – **23f. to be up against** (v.): to have to deal with – **24 fiendish** (adj.) /'fiːndɪʃ/: here: very clever in an unpleasant way – **28f. to snap back** (v.): here: answer quickly in an angry way – **42 to snort** (v.): to breathe air in a noisy way out through your nose, esp. to show you are annoyed or amused – **62 to flush** (v.): to become red in the face – **62 to disrupt** (v.): to prevent s.th. from continuing in its usual way – **68 to gape** (v.): to look at s.th. or s.o. for a long time with your mouth open because you are surprised or shocked – **68 mutely** (adv.): silently – **69 urn** (n.): a metal container that holds a large amount of tea or coffee – **77 to dart** (v.): to move suddenly and quickly – **95 to acknowledge** (v.): to show s.o. that you have noticed them – **96 rapier** (adj.): here: sharp – **96 to accord** (v.): here (fml.): to give – **99 quicksand** (n.): wet sand that is dangerous because you sink down into it if you try to walk on it – **100 to drag** (v.): here: to make s.o. feel unhappy – **101 quibbler** (n.): s.o. who argues about small unimportant details – **103 to flail about** (v.): to wave your arms in an uncontrolled way – **115 to let s.o. down** (v.): to make s.o. be less successful – **115 to strike home** (v.): to have the effect on s.o. you intended – **116 gross** (adj.): here: very wrong and unacceptable – **116 misrepresentation** (n.): a wrong description of a situation – **121 to take up the gauntlet** (v.): to accept the invitation to fight – **132 mutual** (adj.): mutual feelings are feelings that two or more people have for each other – **132 outrage** (n.): a feeling of great anger – **135 exhilarated** (adj.): feeling extemely happy – **135 to strut** (v.): to walk proudly with your head high and chest pushed forward – **136 yapping** (adj.): here: noisy like a dog barking

Franglais – a humorous mixture of French and English and a topic of several funny books, but no help in communicating with French officials

Explanations

13 Benoît: French waiter at Paul West's tea shop – **47 Ministère de la Francophonie:** the – fictional – French ministry responsible for seeing that French is used in France (see Info Box on p. 80) – **51 ID card:** document that shows your name and date of birth, usually with a photograph – **55 sandwich:** named after the 4th Earl of Sandwich, an English nobleman said to have eaten food within two slices of bread so as not to leave the gambling table

Info

"Ministère de la Francophonie"

In fact it is the Ministère de la Culture et de la Communication which is responsible for making laws to ensure that French is used in France and it was the law of 4 August 1994 which lays down policy for the use of French. The criteria for the use of so-called foreign words and their French equivalents – CRITER – can be found under: www.culture.gouv.fr/culturedglf/terminlogie/base-donnee.html. If the words sandwich and weekend are typed in, no French equivalent is given, whereas if the terms computer and monitor are typed in, the French equivalents *ordinateur* and *moniteur* are given. All French equivalents listed are, according to a decree of 3 July 1996, compulsory for use in state organisations.

Awareness

1 Discuss (Reference Library, p. 299) the type of business that you might be able to set up in another European country. What kinds of products or services could you offer?

Comprehension

2 Why has the French official come to Paul West's café?
3 What is it about the French official's appearance that Paul West finds particularly striking?
4 Why does the French official think that "sandwich" (l. 55) is a French word?

Analysis

5 Analyse the interaction between Paul West and the French official. Look at the following points: a) how they address each other; b) who asks questions and how the questions are expressed; c) how the questions are answered; d) how the two men express their French and English identities and respond to the identity of the other; e) show how the confrontation develops into a row.
6 What, seen from Paul West's point of view, is particularly French about the French official?
7 What, by implication, is particularly English about Paul West?
8 What role does the incorrect pronunciation of English words play in the text?

Opinion

9 Write a polemical essay in which you either a) defend the right of speakers of French and German to use English words and phrases whenever they wish or b) make a case for protecting French and German from the use of English words and phrases. Use your essays as the basis for a class discussion on the use of English words and phrases in French and German.

2

Jonathan Lynn and Antony Jay

Party Games – Using Europe in British Politics*

The present prime minister and party leader has decided to resign. There are two main contenders: the chancellor of the exchequer, Eric Jeffries, and the foreign secretary, Duncan Short. Both of them have strong support within the party. Jim Hacker, the head of the Department of Administrative Affairs, has been persuaded to consider running as a compromise candidate. As he is relatively unknown he decides to raise his profile by defending British interests in the European Union. – Transcribed from: Jonathan Lynn, Antony Jay, *The Complete Yes Prime Minister. Series One* (BBC Video BBC V 4790, 1989).

Jim Hacker: By the end of the year we'll be waving goodbye to the good old British sausage and will be forced to accept some foreign muck like salami or bratwurst or something in its place.

Bernard Woolley: But they can't stop us eating the British sausage, can they?

Jim Hacker: They can stop us calling it the sausage, though. Apparently it's got to be called the emulsified high fat offal tube.

Bernard Woolley: And you swallowed it?

Jim Hacker: It's my job to implement EEC regulations. It could finish my career.

Sir Humphrey Appleby, Jim Hacker, Bernard Woolley

Bernard Woolley: What have they got against our sausage?

Jim Hacker: Oh dear, don't you ever read the papers you give me? Apparently there's not enough meat in it. The average British sausage consists of 32.5% fat, 6.5% rind, 20% water, 10% rusk, 5% seasoning, preservatives and colouring, and only 26% meat, which is mostly gristle, head meat, other off cuts and mechanically recovered meat steamed off the carcass ... I don't feel particularly well. I had one for breakfast.

Bernard Woolley: Perhaps the EEC commisioner is right about abolishing it.

In order to try to sort out the problem of the British sausage, Sir Humphrey Appleby arranges a meeting between Maurice, the European Union commissioner responsible for food who happens to be in London at that time, and Jim Hacker.

Sir Humphrey: Maurice! How very nice to see you.

Maurice: Humphrey! Jim! To what do I owe this pleasure?

Jim Hacker: I er ...

Sir Humphrey: Maurice asked me to arrange this little meeting to see if you could ... erm ... help ... erm ... us with a problem.

Jim Hacker: A problem ...

Maurice: Of course.

Sir Humphrey: Now the problem is that the EEC is becoming very unpopular over here. Isn't that so, minister?

Jim Hacker: Very unpopular.

Maurice: And you want me to restore its image?

Jim Hacker: Yes.

Sir Humphrey: No.

Jim Hacker: No.

Sir Humphrey: And the problem is that the minister feels there would be more votes ... he would be better expressing the views of the British people by joining the attack on the EEC rather than leaping to its defence.

Maurice: But ... but your government is committed to support us.

Jim Hacker: Er ...

Sir Humphrey: The minister's point – as I understand it – is that the government's commitment is to the concept and the treaty ...

Jim Hacker: Treaty ...

Sir Humphrey: It's not committed to the institutions, nor to the practices nor to the individual policies. The minister was giving me an example the other day, weren't you minister?

Jim Hacker: [Nods in agreement]

Sir Humphrey: About food production?

Jim Hacker: Oh yes. I've discovered that one of your officials spends all his time paying farmers to produce masses of surplus food while somebody in the next office pays people to destroy the surpluses.

Maurice: That's not true!

Jim Hacker: [Look of surprise] No?

Maurice: He's not in the next office! He's not even on the same floor!

Sir Humphrey: And the minister has hundreds of similar examples, haven't you?

Jim Hacker: Hundreds.

Sir Humphrey: And the nub of the problem is that the minister thinks that some members of the Cabinet ought to start telling the British people about them.

Maurice: That would be intolerable! Not even the Italians would stoop that low.

Jim Hacker: The Italians haven't been asked to redesignate salami as emulsified high-fat offal tubing.

Maurice: Aah! And what are you proposing? After all we are committed to harmonisation. We cannot call it the sausage. What do you suggest?

Sir Humphrey: Well, politics is about presentation. Why don't we call it the British sausage?

Maurice: British sausage? Sausisse anglaise? Britischer [sic] Wurst? Yes, I think we could recommend that to the Commission.

Sir Humphrey: Splendid. The minister's always said that the EEC is a splendid institution, haven't you, minister?

Jim Hacker: Splendid! [Jim Hacker kisses Maurice on the cheek]

Jim Hacker is preparing to meet the newspaper reporters and correspondents of the press lobby at the Department of Administrative Affairs.

Bernard Woolley: The European correspondents are all here now, minister.

Jim Hacker: Good, let them in.

Bernard Woolley: [On the intercom] Will you send them in. Presumably this is to tell them about the Eurosausage problem.

Jim Hacker: That's right, Bernard.

Bernard Woolley: And that you've solved it.

Jim Hacker: Well, no, Bernard. Solved problems aren't news stories. To the press bad news is good news. I'm not going to give them a non-story today. I'm going to give them a disaster today and a triumph tomorrow.

Bernard Woolley: I see ...

Newspaper reporters and correspondents enter Jim Hacker's room.

Jim Hacker: Good morning gentlemen. Come in. Do sit down. So good of you to come. Now look, all of this is on a lobby basis, non-attributable. But we've got some trouble coming up with Brussels. As I suppose somebody's going to tell you about it anyway some time, I'd better tell you about it now myself. The trouble is that Brussels is about to make the British sausage illegal under EEC regulations.

Bernard Woolley: [whispers] They're not making the sausage illegal, just the name.

Jim Hacker: Thank you Bernard. I'll be dealing with that later.

Journalist A: What do you mean, illegal?

Jim Hacker: Well, effectively illegal. The pork sausage will have to contain 75% lean pork. The same for the beef sausage.

Journalist B: 75% pork too?

Jim Hacker: 75% lean beef. Which of course would put it in the luxury food bracket.

Journalist C: When is this being promulgated?

Jim Hacker: Next month probably. They'll deny it of course. Probably they'll say they're just discussing changing its name or something.

Journalist D: What is the government going to do about it?

Jim Hacker: I just don't know. It's a big problem. I won't pretend we've got an answer. All right. Well, I must rush. That's all I've got for now. Is that all? Any more questions?

Journalist E: When can we use this?

Jim Hacker: Tomorrow as far as I'm concerned. Right. Bernard'll give you a drink in the Press Office. Thank you so much for coming.

Bernard Woolley: Minister, you do realise the press will be publishing something that isn't true?

Jim Hacker: Really? How frightful.

Jim Hacker and Bernard Woolley are in their car driving to where Jim Hacker is going to make a speech, apparently on fire and safety regulations in government buildings. They are listening to the news on BBC radio.

Newsreader: Today's big story about the proposed European ban on the British sausage has caused a major political storm. Westminster sources say the sausage could be another banana skin. It adds to the government's problems with the succession. Senior people in the party are increasingly troubled that the two senior candidates represent the extreme wings of the party. Pressure is mounting for them to withdraw in favour of a compromise candidate. None of the other contenders so far seem to have caught the public imagination. Now sport...

Jim Hacker: Turn it off.

Bernard Woolley: Is that true about the compromise candidate?

Jim Hacker: I believe so.

Bernard Woolley: Where do they get their information from?

Jim Hacker: I can't imagine, Bernard. In any case, I never said "compromise", I said "moderate".

Bernard Woolley: Incidentally, minister, why are BBC Television and ITN covering your speech this evening?

Jim Hacker: I can't imagine, Bernard.

Bernard Woolley: I mean, I know that fire and safety policy in government buildings is awfully important, but...

Jim Hacker: Someone suggested I was going to raise other issues as well.

Bernard Woolley: Who?

Jim Hacker: I can't imagine.

Jim Hacker's speech

I'm a good European. I believe in Europe. I believe in the European ideal! Never again shall we repeat the bloodshed of two world wars. Europe is here to stay.

But, this does not mean that we have to bow the knee to every directive from every bureaucratic Bonaparte in Brussels. We are a sovereign nation still and proud of it. (applause)

We have made enough concessions to the European Commissar for agriculture. And when I say Commissar, I use the word advisedly. We have swallowed the wine lake, we have swallowed the butter mountain, we have watched our French 'friends' beating up British lorry drivers carrying good British lamb to the French public.

We have bowed and scraped, doffed our caps, tugged our forelocks and turned the other cheek. But I say enough is enough! (prolonged applause)

The Europeans have gone too far. They are now threatening the British sausage. They want to standardize it – by which they mean they'll force the British people to eat salami and bratwurst and other garlic-ridden greasy foods that are TOTALLY ALIEN to the British way of life. (cries of "hear hear!", "right on", and "you tell 'em Jim!")

Do you want to eat salami for breakfast with your egg and bacon? I don't. And I won't! (massive applause)

GO TO WORK ON A SAUSAGE!

They've turned our pints into litres and our yards into metres. We gave up the tanner and the threepenny bit, the two bob and half crown. But they cannot and will not destroy the British sausage! (applause and cheers)

Not while I'm here. (tumultuous applause)

In the words of Martin Luther: 'Here I stand. I can do no other.'

Jim Hacker's use of anti-European feelings in Britain was successful. His rivals for the leadership of his party withdrew and Jim Hacker gained the leadership of his party unopposed.

Info

The main characters in this episode of *Yes, Prime Minister*

Jim Hacker: Secretary of State for Administrative Affairs, head of the Department of Administrative Affairs
Maurice: (surname not mentioned) European Union (at that time European Economic Community) Commissioner
Bernard Woolley: Principal Private Secretary, a civil servant in the Department of Administrative Affairs
Sir Humphrey Appleby: Permanent Secretary, the senior civil servant in the Department of Administrative Affairs

Vocabulary

Intro: 1 contender (n.): s.o. who is in competition with other people – **4 muck** (n.): s.th. that is unpleasant or of bad quality – **10 emulsified** (adj.): combined with other substances to become a smooth mixture – **11 offal** (n.): the inside parts of an animal – **12 to swallow** (v.): (word play) to make food or drink go down your throat and towards your stomach; to believe s.th. that is not actually true – **21 rind** (n.): /raɪnd/ here: the thick outer skin of some kinds of meat – **22 rusk** (n.): here: hard dry bread – **22 seasoning** (n.): salt, pepper, spices that give food a more interesting flavour – **22 preservative** (n): a chemical substance that is used to prevent food from going bad – **24 gristle** (n.): the part of meat that is not soft enough to eat – **25 off cuts** (n.): here: pieces of meat that are left over after the main pieces have been cut and removed – **62 to be committed to s.th.** (v.): to be willing to work very hard at s.th. – **66 commitment** (n.): being ready to work very hard for s.th. or s.o. – **79 surplus** (adj.): more than what is needed – **89 nub** (n.): the main point – **95 to stoop low** (v.): to do s.th. bad or morally wrong – **97 to redesignate** (v.): to give s.th. a new name – **121 intercom** (n.): a communication system by which people in different parts of a building, aircraft, etc. can speak to each other – **122 presumably** (adj.): used to say that you think s.th. is probably true – **139 non-attributable** (adj.): used when journalists agree not to say who made a statement or comment – **155 lean** (adj.): lean meat does not have much fat on it – **160 bracket** (n.): here: group of products – **161 to promulgate** (v.): (fml.) to make a new law come into effect – **186 proposed** (adj.): suggested as a plan or course of action – **187 ban** (n.): an official order that prevents s.th. being sold, done, etc. – **192 succession** (n.): the act of taking over an official position, here of prime minister – **211 incidentally** (adv.): here: used to introduce a new topic that you have just thought of – **219 to raise an issue** (v.): to introduce a topic that you want to be considered – **225 bloodshed** (n.): the killing of people, usually in war – **230 concession** (n.): s.th. that you allow s.o. to have or to do in order to end an argument – **232 advisedly** (adv.): /əd'vaɪzɪdli/ after careful thought –

236 to bow and scrape (v.): to show too much respect to s.o. – **236 to doff one's cap** (v.): (old-fashioned) to take off the hat you are wearing as a sign of respect – **236 to tug one's forelock** (v.): to show too much respect for s.o. in authority

Explanations

Intro/2 chancellor of the exchequer: the minister in the British government who is responsible for financial matters – **foreign secretary:** the minister in the British government who is responsible for relations with other countries – **13 EEC:** European Economic Community; the first name for what was then named the European Community and is now called the European Union. – **25 mechanically recovered meat:** meat that is taken off bones by machines and used to make sausages and hamburgers – **91 Cabinet:** the politicians with important positions in the government who meet to make decisions – **116 lobby:** a group of journalists and correspondents with privileged access to government information as long as they did not say who gave them the information – **176 Press Office:** this British government office deals with the prime minister's relations with the media. – **185 BBC:** British Broadcasting Corporation; the British radio and television company that is paid for by viewers' and listeners' licence money and not by advertisers. – **190 banana skin:** (humorous) here: used to refer to s.th. that causes problems or difficulties – **227 directive:** an official order or instruction – **231 Commissar:** an official of the Communist Party of the former Soviet Union and of Communist China, responsible for political education and organisation – **Info Box: secretary of state** (n.): chief minister of a department or ministry of the British government – **Department** (n.): usual word for ministry in the British government – **Department of Administrative Affairs:** a fictitious ministry that only occurs in the TV series *Yes Minister* and *Yes Prime Minister* – **Commissioner:** a member of the Commission of the European Union which is headed by the President; it is responsible for administering and implementing the policies and decisions of the members of the European Union – **Principal Private Secretary:** a senior member of the civil service, the British government bureaucracy – **civil servant:** a member of the civil service, the British government bureaucracy

Awareness

1 Why do you think so many British people are sceptical about Britain's membership of the European Union?

Comprehension

2 Why can't the British continue to call a sausage a sausage?
3 Is it true that there is an official in the Commission of the EU who spends his time paying people to destroy food surpluses?
4 How does Maurice solve the problem of the British sausage?
5 Does the EU want to forbid the British from producing the British sausage?
6 Why doesn't Jim Hacker want to tell the journalists that he has solved the problem of the British sausage?
7 Who told the BBC that a compromise candidate for the leadership of the party might be putting himself forward?
8 Why are BBC TV and ITN covering Jim Hacker's speech?

Analysis

9 Analyse the conversation between Sir Humphrey Appleby, Maurice and Jim Hacker. Look at the roles of each of them, the way their language (Reference Library, p. 311) expresses the relationship between them, their aims in the conversation and their rhetorical strategies for achieving those aims.
10 In the conversation between Sir Humphrey Appleby, Maurice and Jim Hacker, Jim Hacker is made to seem rather stupid. Explain what characteristics he has that enable him to achieve such high office in the British government.
11 What is the point of the meeting between Jim Hacker and the journalists? Explain Jim Hacker's strategy at the meeting.
12 Analyse Jim Hacker's speech on "fire and safety regulations in government buildings". Consider what he says, how he says it and why he says it. Discuss the function of the imagery used, the examples cited, rhetorical questions, use of voice, parallelisms and phrases in groups of three (Reference Library, p. 311).

Opinion

13 What is your opinion of the cynicism regarding the European Union displayed by Jim Hacker and Sir Humphrey Appleby?
14 Write a letter (Reference Library, p. 300) to Jim Hacker in response to his speech.

Project

15 Write a report (Reference Library, p. 302) on the advantages and disadvantages for Germany of membership of the European Union.

3 Britain: A Magnet for Migrants*

Britain's booming economy and the open-door policy of the present government (2006) have resulted in the largest influx of immigrants into Britain since the Second World War. Most of these immigrants have come from the new entrants to the European Union: Poland, Slovakia, the Czech Republic and the Baltic states Lithuania, Estonia and Latvia. In this article Ewa Zandman, 22, from Poland, describes her experiences as a migrant in England. - From: Cole Moreton, *The Independent on Sunday*, 27 August 2006, pp. 15f.

Ewa came to do a job nobody else wanted. She flew to England from Poland at the age of 22 to be a carer in a residential home, helping elderly people to bathe, dress, eat and go to the toilet. The hours were long and the pay low. The work was hard, physically and mentally: she saw close up, sickness, dementia and incontinence.

Ewa stuck it out. She wrestled with the language and with the loneliness, finding friends, a flat, and even love with an Englishman – for a while. She made a life for herself that she likes. Ewa loves England. But now, after two years and so much effort, the way much of England seems to feel about immigrants is making people like Ewa want to leave.

"If we are not wanted here, then it makes us want to go," she says quietly, speaking for herself and her sister.

The people she knows are nice, but the headlines are not. The Polish are stealing jobs, living off benefits and sending the country to hell, a raging taxi driver told her. Remembering his anger with a shudder, she says: "If that is how people feel then maybe it is time to go to another country."

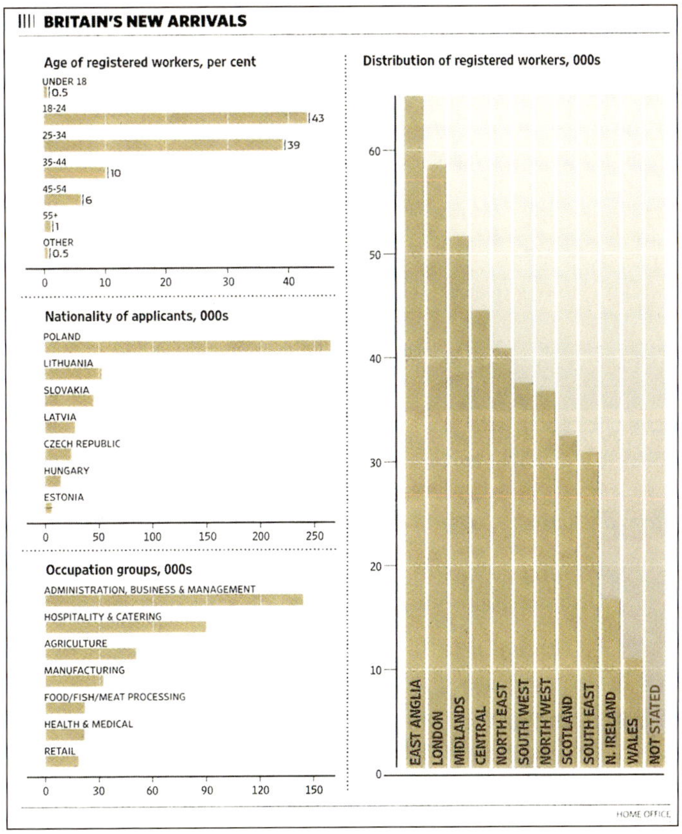

She was afraid this would happen. The first time we met, in the spring of 2004, Ewa was working as a waitress in a vegetarian restaurant in Krakow but preparing to come to England. "Is it dangerous?" she asked then, after seeing angry English people on the television ranting about the "tidal wave" of beggars, criminals and scroungers they feared would flood Britain when eight former eastern bloc countries joined the EU.

Far more people came than was expected – 600,000, it emerged last week – but only a tiny number have claimed benefits. The crime rate has not soared. Those who predicted disaster now say unemployment is being driven up and wages down. But economists and business leaders praise the new Europeans, who contribute about £2.5bn a year to the economy; and research by the Joseph Rowntree Foundation has found that employers prefer hard-working EU migrants to the British, who are perceived to be lazier and unwilling to do low-skilled work.

Ewa did not find it dangerous at all. She has made many friends here. "English people are lovely." But the angry people she saw on the television have a new scare now: the anticipated arrival of Romanians and Bulgarians in January [2007 ed.].

[...]

Now she and her sister, who is teaching here, are discussing what to do. "I do feel guilty because I know there are so many of us here and not everyone is happy with us. I worry that things will get worse."

The Zandman sisters left Poland because they could not find work – Ewa is a physiotherapist but was earning less than £100 a month in Krakow – and they do not want to go back to Poland yet. "It has so many

I stayed with St Helens Town FC for as long as I could. But eventually I was talent-spotted by a scout from Manchester City and signed for them in 1949. I got £10 a week in the playing season and £8 in the closed season. I played two Cup Finals at Wembley, both watched by my mother.

But of course the one that gave her the most worry was the 1956 game against Birmingham City.

With 17 minutes of the match remaining, I dived to snatch the ball from the feet of striker Peter Murphy and was knocked unconscious, still clutching the ball. [...]

Bert Trautmann continued to play to the end of the match, which was won by Manchester City 3–0, in spite of a broken vertebra; substitutes were not allowed at the time. In 1956 he was the first foreign player to gain the title of Footballer of the Year. He ended his playing career in 1964 with a farewell match watched by 60,000 supporters. He became a trainer and then ambassador for German football throughout the world. In 2004 he set up the Trautmann Foundation to further Anglo-British understanding through football. In that year he was awarded the Order of the British Empire by Queen Elizabeth II. He now lives near Valencia in Spain.

Vocabulary

1 chant (n.): words or phrases that are repeated by a group of people – **1 goalie** (n.): (infml.) goalkeeper – **10 innocently** (adv.): being done without intending harm to anyone – **18 paratrooper** (n.): a soldier who is trained to jump out of an aircraft with a parachute – **19 to draft** (v.): here: to order s.o. to go to a place by the armed forces – **20 elation** (n.): a feeling of great happines and excitement – **20 triumphalism** (n.): being too proud of your success and too pleased with the defeat of your enemies – **26 to counter** (v.): to do s.th. in order to prevent s.th. bad from happening – **33 to scale** (v.): to climb to the top of s.th. – **41 release** (n.): when s.o. is officially allowed to go free after being kept s.where – **75 send-off** (n.): (infml.) a party when people meet to say goodbye to s.o. who is leaving – **82 compassion** (n.): a strong feeling of sympathy for s.o. who is suffering and a desire to help them – **83 to appreciate** (v.): here: to understand – **89 to talent-spot** (v.): to look for and find young people who are good at sport, music, etc. – **89 scout** (n.): s.o. whose job is to look for young people who are good at sport, music, etc. – **97 striker** (n.): a player in football whose job is to score goals – **98 to clutch** (v.): to hold s.th. tightly because you do not want to lose it

Explanations

3 Manchester City: the smaller and less famous of the two Manchester football clubs, the other being Manchester United – **6 OBE:** Order of the British Empire – **12 Falcons:** English translation of Falken, the youth organisation of the German Social Democratic Party – **13 Jungvolk:** from 1933–45 the part of the Hitler Youth for boys between the ages of 10 and 14 – **26 D-Day landings:** the invasion of German-occupied Europe by Allied forces in Normandy, starting on 4 June, 1944 – **27 Arnhem:** a town in the eastern Netherlands – **27 Ardennes:** a forested hilly region in south-east Belgium, which was the scene of fierce fighting in December 1944 between German and Allied forces. – **29 GI:** a private soldier in the US army; the term originated in the 1930s when it referred to equipment supplied to US forces and was the abbreviation for government issue.– **39 PoW:** short for prisoner of war – **39 Ashton-in-Makerfield:** small town in northwest England – **64 allied raids:** attacks by British and American bombers – **66 bomb disposal squad:** groups of men who deal with bombs which have not exploded and make them safe – **69 St Helens:** town in the county of Lancashire – **92 Cup Final:** the Football Association Cup Final is the match between the two best English football teams – **92 Wembley:** a sports stadium in northwest London where the Cup Final is played

Awareness

1 Find out about sportsmen and women who have moved from one European country to another and discuss their possible problems and successes.

Comprehension

2 Write a brief chronology of Bert Trautmann's life as presented in the article.
3 Why was Bert Trautmann put in a special section of the prisoner of war camp for Nazis?
4 Why does the writer put the word "education" (l. 42) in inverted commas?
5 Why did Bert Trautmann stay in England rather than return to Germany?

Analysis

6 Write a character study of Bert Trautmann giving your impression of what kind of person he is and how he developed through his life. Base your answer only on what is written in the article.

Opinion

7 Speculate on why the English people he came into contact with treated Bert Trautmann so well.
8 Why do you think Bert Trautmann said that "that gift in a café in St Helens meant more to me than anything else." (ll. 86f.)?

Project

9 Write a letter to the Trautmann Foundation with a concrete suggestion for a project designed to improve Anglo-German relations among young people.

5

Norman Davies

Britain and Europe get closer together*

In this extract the historian Norman Davies outlines those social, economic and political forces that have, over the last hundred years, brought the United Kingdom and continental Europe ever closer together. - Norman Davies, *The Isles: A History* (London: Macmillan, 1999), pp. 1010–1012.

In the course of the twentieth century the Isles [the British Isles ed.] were pulled by stages into a position of ever increasing intimacy with the European mainland. In part, the shift could be explained through far-reaching changes in the patterns of communication and trade. In part, and especially in the second half of the century, it could be attributed to the effects of globalization and the ever-diminishing significance of the old sovereign states. But it must also be seen as the cumulative consequence of three key political decisions – in 1914, in 1939 and in 1972. The end result was not in doubt. In the 1890s the United Kingdom of Great Britain and Ireland was still holding on to its traditional 'semi-detached' stance with regard to the Continent. In the 1990s, both the United Kingdom and the Republic of Ireland were permanently and institutionally engaged in the European Union.

The revolution in communications was there for all to see. If mid-Victorian travellers were thrilled to get from London to Paris in a single day, their mid-century counterparts a hundred years later were accustomed to make the journey in less than an hour. Regular air services round Europe began in the 1920s. Initially, they were very uncomfortable, very expensive, and very exclusive. But from the 1960s commercial jets put air travel within almost everyone's reach. Package holidays boomed. For the first time in history, ordinary British working-class families could take their holidays in Greece, in Italy, or in Spain. On the Mediterranean beaches, and in the *tavernas*, they met millions of other Europeans enjoying themselves in exactly the same way. Their ability to mingle, especially linguistically, was not perfect. But they came back home with the fruits of a learning experience such as no previous generation had been given. They developed a taste for wine; they took a liking to *moussaka*, *pizza*, and *paella*; and they learned the inestimable lesson that the British way of doing things was not necessarily the best. Indeed, if one needed to bag a deckchair and a beach umbrella, the German habit of rising at six o'clock proved rather more effective than the British habit of rising at eight or nine. By the 1990s, a family trip to Corfu or to the Costa del Sol was just as routine as their grandparents' outing to Blackpool or Brighton. What is more, the tavernas of Brighton were matched by the chip shops on Corfu.

Every other form of communication developed at the same dizzy pace. Roll-on, roll-off car ferries replaced cargo ships that had winched tourists' vehicles onto the open deck with a crane. Hovercraft overtook the ferries. Motorways on either side of the Channel put Brussels as close to London as Manchester had been. High-speed rail links – speedier in some countries than others – whisked travellers to and fro with famous despatch. Money-changing, which was once done clumsily with travellers' cheques and suspicious bank clerks, could now be effected instantly at Continental ATMs that accepted British cards. Satellite TV brought Continental programmes into British living rooms. The ultimate step was taken in 1994, when the Channel Tunnel was opened. One could travel from Folkestone to Boulogne by land. Great Britain had ceased to be an island for the first time in seven thousand years.

Globalization drove similar changes in the organizational sphere. All manner of operations once conducted by local or national organizations were now taken over by international bodies that bestrode frontiers and oceans. The phenomenon was by no means limited to Europe. Indeed, its motive force could often be traced to the USA. But it was particularly relevant to a European continent that had hitherto been fragmented by dozens of sovereign states. Indeed, it

"If it weren't for Nelson, we'd all be speaking French... drinking wine... working a 38-hour week, taking August off... bloody Nelson"

promised to give Europe the same economic, transportational and commercial benefits that a huge country like the USA enjoyed. Early steps were taken by international organizations in the postal and transportation spheres. Large multinational firms, like Royal Dutch Shell (1907), were already in existence before the First World War. By the end of the century, there was no important activity in Europe that was not run, regulated, or coordinated by some sort of transnational authority. Britain was locked into the lives of its neighbours as never before.

Changing British trade patterns revealed a growing concentration on export and import with Europe. The trend was in progress several decades before the demise of the British Empire; but it provided a ready-made alternative when 'imperial preference' came to an end in the 1960s. Thanks to the contiguity of the Continent, it developed further and faster than Britain's second line of commercial expansion with the USA. The Confederation of British Industry (CBI) inevitably grew into a fundamental supporter of 'pro-European' sentiment.

Vocabulary

7 to be attributed to (v.): to be believed to be caused by - **13 semi-detached** (adj.): here: not completely believing in s.th. - **14 stance** (n.): opinion - **32 to mingle** (v.): to mix with and meet other people - **37 inestimable** (adj.): (fml.) very great, too much to be calculated - **39 to bag** (v.): (infml.) to reserve s.th. that a lot of people want - **45f. to be matched by** (v.): here: to have s.th. similar or have a similar function - **48 dizzy** (adj.): here: very fast - **48 roll-on roll-off** (adj.): a roll-on roll-off ship is one that vehicles can drive straight on and off - **49 to winch** (v.): to lift s.th. with a machine using a rope or chain - **54 to whisk** (v.): here: to transport s.o. quickly - **55 despatch** (n.): here: speed - **67 to bestride** (v. past tense bestrode): here: to cross easily - **87 demise** (n.): /dɪ'maɪz/ (formal) the end of s.th. that used to exist - **89 contiguity** (n.): the state of being next to s.th. - **94 sentiment** (n.): (fml.) opinion or feeling you have about s.th.

Explanations

10 1914: the decision by the British government to declare war on Germany at the beginning of the First World War because of the German invasion of Belgium - **11 1939:** the decision by the British government to declare war on Germany because of the German invasion of Poland. This started the Second World War. - **11 1972:** the decision by the British government to apply to join the European Community, now the European Union; the law to make Britain a member was signed in 1972 and Britain officially became a member on 1 January 1973. - **19 mid-Victorian** (adj.): in the middle of the reign of Queen Victoria (1837-1901) - **58 ATM:** automated teller machine; a machine outside a bank that you use to get money from your account; also called a cash dispenser, cash machine or cash point - **78 Royal Dutch Shell:** an Anglo-Dutch oil company which was one of the first multinational companies - **88 imperial preference:** a system which gave trading advantages to countries which were members of the British Empire and Commonwealth - **92 Confederation of British Industry:** an employers' organisation which tries to influence the government and promote the interest of its members

Awareness

1 What are some of the ways in which Britain and the rest of Europe have been getting closer together since the beginning of the twentieth century? Bear in mind that the traffic between them is two-way, i.e. from Britain to Europe and from Europe to Britain. Write your ideas down in a mind-map with the following headings: food and drink; music, film, radio and television; clothing; transport and leisure; business, trade and commerce; politics; language.

Comprehension

2 What does Norman Davies mean by "globalization" (l. 7)?
3 Explain what is meant by "old sovereign states" (ll. 8f.).
4 What does Norman Davies mean when he writes that the tavernas of Brighton "were matched by the chip shops on Corfu" (ll. 45f.)?
5 Which operations and organisations do you think Norman Davies is referring to when he writes that "All manner of operations once conducted by local or national organizations were now taken over by international bodies ..." (ll. 65ff.)?
6 In what ways, according to Norman Davies, is Europe becoming similar to the United States?
7 What has been the great transformation in Britain's pattern of trade in the last fifty or sixty years?

Analysis

8 Under keyword headings summarise (Reference Library, pp. 302f.) the effects on Britain that closer links with continental Europe have had.
9 In what ways specifically mentioned in the text and by implication has Britain affected continental Europe over the past one hundred years?
10 In what ways were the "three key political decisions – in 1914, 1939 and in 1972" (ll. 10f.) so decisive for Britain and for Europe (see also question 13)?

OPINION

11 Discuss (Reference Library, p. 299) some of the ways in which Britain can learn from continental Europe and in which continental Europe can learn from Britain.

12 The author states that the motive force for globalisation can be traced to the United States. What do you think these American influences on globalisation might be?

13 Alternative history (see Info Box below) explores what might have happened if at certain crucial moments history had developed differently from the way it actually developed. The cartoon on p. 89, published on the anniversary of Nelson's victory over the French and Spanish fleets at the Battle of Trafalgar in 1804, is a humorous comment on what might have happened had the British been defeated. Write alternative history scenarios for 1914 and 1939 assuming that Britain hat not declared war on Germany, and for 1972, assuming that Britain had not joined the European Economic Community.

PROJECTS

14 Find out and write a report (Reference Library, p. 302) on why Britain adopted a "'semidetached' stance" (ll. 13f.) towards continental Europe up to the 1890s.

15 Choose one of the main British or continental European multinational companies, and write a report on it, giving a brief outline of its history and its activities within and outside Europe.

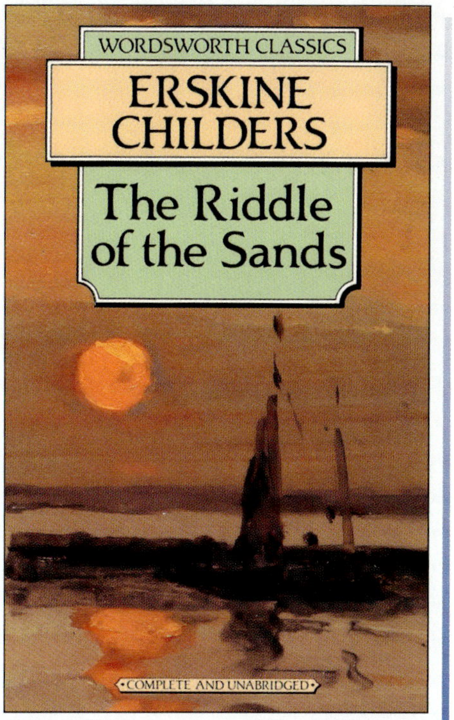

Erskine Childers's spy novel The Riddle of the Sands *is a famous example of alternative history writing*

Alternative history – fiction and non-fiction

The literary genre alternative (or alternate) history is related to and borders on other genres such as fantasy and science fiction but differs from them in that its works are based on real historical events. Writers in alternative history ask themselves the question "What if?": what if a particular historical event had for a number of more or less plausible reasons taken a different turn?

The earliest example of alternative history is probably Book IX, sections 17–19, of Livy's *History of Rome from its Foundation* in which he contemplates the possibility of Alexander the Great expanding his father's empire westward instead of eastward by attacking Rome instead of Persia in the 4th century BC. One of the first alternative novels in English was *The Battle of Dorking*, written by George Chesney in 1871. This was the first of a number of novels inspired by the perceived threat of Imperial Germany to Britain and the British Empire and was followed by Erskine Childers' *The Riddle of the Sands* (1903), *The Invasion of 1910*, by William le Queux (1906), and H. H. Monro's (Saki) *When William Came* (1914). Other notable alternative history novels are Philip K. Dick's *The Man in the High Castle* (1962), in which Nazi Germany and Imperial Japan win the Second World War, Robert Harris's *Fatherland*, in which Nazi Germany wins the Second World War and Philip Roth's *The Plot against America*, in which a United States governed by a fascist regime under President Charles Lindbergh does not enter the Second World War but maintains peaceful relations with Nazi Germany. The most prolific writer of the genre is Harry Turtledove, in one of whose novels, *Ruled Britannia*, the Spanish Armada defeats the English fleet, enabling Spain to successfully invade England.

While some academic historians completely reject speculative history and the asking of the "What if?" question, others, mainly military historians[1], find it a fruitful area of study. The question "What if?" is already implied in the title of Richard Overy's *Why the Allies Won* and in the heading of the first chapter, Unpredictable Victory: Explaining World War II. Overy himself does indeed go on to state: To ask why the Allies won is to presuppose that they might have lost or, for understandable reasons, that they would have accepted an outcome short of total victory.[2]

1) Robert Cowley (ed.), *What If? Military Historians Imagine What Might Have Been*, London: Pan, 2001
2) Richard Overy, *Why the Allies Won, London*: Pimlico, 1996, p. 1

Humour Rules

In real life, comedy and literature

Kate Fox

Kate Fox (b. 1962), a social anthropologist, is a Director of the Social Issues Research Centre (Oxford).

Her work has included research, publications and broadcasts on many aspects of human behaviour and social interaction, including social and cultural aspects of drinking, sex-differences, beauty and body image, aggression, body language, etiquette, gossip, drugs, flirting, celebrations, stress, violence and disorder.

In addition to her work on positive aspects of human interaction, Kate Fox is a respected international consultant on the prevention and management of violence. – *Watching the English: The Hidden Rules of English Behaviour* (London: Hodder and Stoughton, 2004), pp. 61–72.

HUMOUR RULES

This heading can be read both in the straightforward sense of 'rules about humour' and in the graffiti sense of 'humour rules, OK!' The latter is in fact more appropriate, as the most noticeable and important 'rule' about humour in English conversation is its dominance and pervasiveness. Humour rules. Humour governs. Humour is omnipresent and omnipotent. (…)

There is an awful lot of guff talked about the English Sense of Humour, including many patriotic attempts to prove that our sense of humour is somehow unique and superior to everyone else's. Many English people seem to believe that we have some sort of global monopoly, if not on humour itself, then at least on certain 'brands' of humour – the high-class ones such as wit and especially irony. My findings indicate that while there may indeed be something distinctive about English humour, the real 'defining characteristic' is the *value* we put on humour, the central importance of humour in English culture and social interactions.

In other cultures, there is 'a time and a place' for humour; it is a special, separate kind of talk. In English conversation, there is always an undercurrent of humour. We can barely manage to say 'hello' or comment on the weather without somehow contriving to make a bit of a joke out of it, and most English conversations will involve at least some degree of banter, teasing, irony, understatement, humorous self-deprecation, mockery or just silliness. Humour is our 'default mode', if you like: we do not have to switch it on deliberately, and we cannot switch it off. For the English, the rules of humour are the cultural equivalent of natural laws – we obey them automatically, rather in the way that we obey the law of gravity.

THE IMPORTANCE OF BEING EARNEST

At the most basic level, an underlying rule in all English conversation is the proscription of 'earnestness'. Although we may not have a monopoly on humour, or even on irony, the English are probably more acutely sensitive than any other nation to the distinction between 'serious' and 'solemn', between 'sincerity' and 'earnestness'.

Kate Fox's Watching the English *has been her fastest-selling book so far*

This distinction is crucial to any kind of understanding of Englishness. I cannot emphasize this strongly enough: if you are not able to grasp these subtle but vital differences, you will never understand the English – and even if you speak the language fluently, you will never feel or appear entirely at home in conversation with the English. Your English may be impeccable, but your behavioural 'grammar' will be full of glaring errors.

Once you have become sufficiently sensitized to these distinctions, the Importance of Not Being Earnest rule is really quite simple. Seriousness is acceptable, solemnity is prohibited. Sincerity is allowed, earnestness is strictly forbidden. Pomposity and self-importance are outlawed. Serious matters can be spoken of seriously, but one must never take *oneself* too seriously. The ability to laugh at ourselves (…) is one of the more endearing characteristics of the English.

The 'Oh, Come Off It!' Rule

The English ban on earnestness, and specifically on taking oneself too seriously, means that our own politicians and other public figures have a particularly tough time. The sharp-eyed English public is even less tolerant of any breaches of these rules on home ground, and even the smallest lapse – the tiniest sign that a speaker may be overdoing the intensity and crossing the fine line from sincerity to earnestness – will be spotted and picked up on immediately, with scornful cries of 'Oh, come off it!'

And we are just as hard on each other, in ordinary everyday conversation, as we are on those in the public eye. In fact, if a country or culture could be said to have a catchphrase, I would propose 'Oh, come off it!' as a strong candidate for England's national catchphrase. (...) This may be why, as someone once said, the English have satire instead of revolutions. (...)

IRONY RULES

The English are not usually given to patriotic boasting – indeed, both patriotism and boasting are regarded as unseemly, so the combination of these two sins is doubly distasteful. But there is one significant exception to this rule, and that is the patriotic pride we take in our sense of humour, particularly in our expert use of irony. The popular belief is that we have a better, more subtle, more highly developed sense of humour than any other nation, and specifically that other nations are all tediously literal in their thinking and incapable of understanding or appreciating irony. Almost all of the English people I interviewed subscribed to this belief, and many foreigners, rather surprisingly, humbly concurred.

My research suggests that, yet again, the irony issue is a question of degree – a matter of quantity rather than quality. What is unique about English humour is the pervasiveness of irony and the importance we attach to it. Irony is the dominant ingredient in English humour, not just a piquant flavouring. Irony rules.

(...) Like humour in general, irony is a constant, a given, a normal element of ordinary, everyday conversation. The English may not always be joking, but they are always *in a state of readiness* for humour. We do not always say the opposite of what we mean, but we are always alert to the *possibility* of irony. When we ask someone a straightforward question (e.g. 'How are the children?'), we are equally prepared for either a straight-forward response ('Fine, thanks.') or an ironic one ('Oh, they're delightful – charming, helpful, tidy, studious ...' To which the reply is 'Oh dear. Been one of those days, has it?').

The Understatement Rule

Understatement is by no means an exclusively English form of humour, of course: again, we are talking about quantity rather than quality. George Mikes said that the understatement 'is not just a speciality of the English sense of humour; it is a way of life'. The English are rightly renowned for their use of understatement, not because we invented it or because we do it better than anyone else, but because we do it so *much*. (Well, maybe we do do it a little bit better – if only because we get more practice at it.)

The reasons for our prolific understating are not hard to discover: our strict prohibitions on earnestness, gushing, emoting and boasting require almost constant use of understatement. Rather than risk exhibiting any hint of forbidden solemnity, unseemly emotion or excessive zeal, we go to the opposite extreme and feign dry, deadpan indifference. The understatement rule means that a debilitating and painful chronic illness must be described as 'a bit of a nuisance'; (...) an outstanding performance or achievement is 'not bad'; an act of abominable cruelty is 'not very friendly', and an unforgivably stupid misjudgement is 'not very clever'; the Antarctic is 'rather cold' and the Sahara 'a bit too hot for my taste'; and any exceptionally delightful object, person or event, which in other cultures would warrant streams of superlatives, is pretty much covered by 'nice', or, if we wish to express more ardent approval, 'very nice'.

Needless to say, the English understatement is another trait that many foreign visitors find utterly bewildering and infuriating (or, as we English would put it, 'a bit confusing'). (...)

This is the problem with English humour. Much of it, including and perhaps especially the understatement, isn't actually very funny – or at least not obviously funny, not laugh-out-loud funny, and definitely not cross-culturally funny. Even the English, who understand it, are not exactly riotously amused by the understatement. At best, a well-timed, well-turned understatement only raises a slight smirk. But then, this is surely the whole point of the understatement: it is amusing, but only in an understated way. It is humour, but it is a restrained, refined, subtle form of humour.

Vocabulary

4 s.th. rules: (infml.) used to say that the team, school, place etc. mentioned is better than any other; esp. in graffiti, "OK" is added to lend the statement more weight – **7 pervasiveness** (n.): the quality of existing everywhere – **10 guff** (n.): nonsense – **25f. undercurrent** (n.): a feeling that people do not express openly – **28 contrive** (v.): to succeed in doing s.th. in spite of difficulties – **30 banter** (n.): friendly conversation in which people make a lot of jokes with each other – **31 self-deprecation** (n.): making your own abilities or achievements seem unimportant – **40 proscription** (n.): (fml.) saying that s.th. is not allowed to exist or be done – **51 solemn** (adj.): very serious, appropriate for sad or important occasions – **56 crucial** (adj.): /'kruːʃəl/ extremely important – **70 impeccable** (adj.): without any faults, perfect – **91 scornful** (adj.): contemptuous – **102 unseemly** (adj.): not polite or not suitable for a particular occasion – **142 prolific** (adj.): *here:* frequent – **148 feign** (v.): to pretend to have a particular feeling – **148 deadpan** (adj.): sounding and looking completely serious when you are saying or doing s.th. funny – **149 debilitating** (adj.): /-'----/ making someone ill and weak – **159 ardent** (adj.): showing strong positive feelings – **163 bewildering** (adj.): /bɪ'wɪldərɪŋ/ confusing – **163 infuriating** (adj.): very annoying

Monty Python

The surreal TV show 'Monty Python's Flying Circus' (1969 to 1974) broke down the barriers of comedy in dealing not only with such controversial issues as sex and crime, but also putting politics and sheer nonsense into the mix.

Monty Python had its origins in university revues. John Cleese, Graham Chapman and Eric Idle were all members of a comedy troupe, Cambridge Footlights. Terry Jones and Michael Palin were in a similar group at Oxford. They wrote and performed on sixties shows like *The Frost Report* and *The Complete and Utter History of Britain*. The American artist Terry Gilliam joined them later.

BBC bosses objected to some of the show's bad language and accused it of exaggerated sadism. Such criticism was finally the reason why this successful mixture of slapstick, nonsense, absurd drama and sociopolitical satire was abandoned after four series.

Seemingly endless reruns, e.g. on various German television channels, prove, however, that this kind of humour is still very much alive today. "The Pet Shop" is probably the most famous of all Monty Python sketches; the following text is one of the live versions, transcribed from *Monty Python Live At Drury Lane*, Charisma Records CLASS 4, 1974.

The Pet Shop

Customer I wish to register a complaint. – Hello, Miss.

Shopkeeper What do you mean – 'miss'?

Customer I'm sorry, I have a cold. I wish to make a complaint.

Shopkeeper Sorry, we're closed for lunch.

Customer Never mind that, my lad, I wish to complain about this parrot what I purchased not half an hour ago from this very boutique.

Shopkeeper Ah, yes, the Norwegian Blue; what's wrong with it?

Customer I'll tell you what's wrong with it, my lad: he's dead, that's what's wrong with it.

Shopkeeper No, no, he's, uh, he's resting.

Customer But, matey, I know a dead parrot when I see one, and I'm looking at one right now.

Shopkeeper No, no, he's not dead, he's resting, you know. Remarkable bird, the Norwegian Blue, isn't it, eh? Beautiful plumage!

Customer The plumage... don't – wait! He's stone-dead.

Shopkeeper No, no, he's restin'.

Customer All right then, if he's resting I'll wake him up. – Hello, Mister Polly Parrot, I got a nice fresh banana for you! –

Shopkeeper There, he moved!

Customer No he didn't, you hit the cage.

Shopkeeper I never! I never touched that cage – I didn't!

Customer Yes, you did. Hello, Polly!! Wakey, wakey! – This is your nine o'clock alarm call! – Now that's what I call a dead parrot.

Shopkeeper He's stunned.

Customer Stunned?!

Shopkeeper Yeah, you stunned him just as he was waking up. Norwegian Blues stun easily.

Customer Now look; don't play the slippery eel with me. That parrot is definitely deceased. And when I purchased it not half an hour ago, you assured me that its total lack of movement was due to it being tired and shagged out after a long squawk.

Shopkeeper Why, he's probably pining for the fjords.

Customer Pining for the fjords?! What kind of talk is that? And why did he fall flat on his back the moment I got him home?

Shopkeeper The Norwegian Blue prefers klppin' on his back. Remarkable bird, isn't it, eh, Major? Beautiful plumage...

Customer Look, tosh, I took the liberty of examining that bird when I got it home and I discovered that the only reason it had been sitting on its perch in the first place was that it had been nailed there.

Shopkeeper Of course it was nailed there! Listen, moosh, if I hadn't nailed that bird down, it would have muscled up to them bars, bent them apart with its little pecker, and – voom!

Customer Voom? Mate, this parrot wouldn't voom if you put four million volts through it. 'e's bleedin' demised!

Shopkeeper No, no, he's pinin'!

Customer He's not pinin', he's passed on! This parrot is no more. He has ceased to be. He's expired and gone to meet his maker. He's a stiff, bereft of life. He rests in peace. If you hadn't nailed him to the perch he'd been pushin' up the daisies! He's off the twig, he's curled up his tootsies, he's shuffled off this mortal coil, he's rung down the curtain and joined the bleedin' choir invisible. He ***in' snuffed it. These are meta-metabolic processes, he's had his lot. All statements to the effect that this parrot is still a going concern are from now on inoperative. This is an ex-parrot.

Shopkeeper Well ..., I'd better replace it then.

Michael Palin (shopkeeper) – John Cleese (customer)

Customer (If you want to get anything done in this country you got to ...!) – What's the news?
Shopkeeper Well, I've had a look round the back, and we're right out of parrots.
Customer I see, I see, I get the picture.
Shopkeeper I got a slug...
Customer Does it talk?
Shopkeeper Yeah.
Customer Right, I'll have that one then.

Vocabulary

34 what (pron.): (ungramm./sl.) which – **purchase** (v.): (fml.) /'pɛːtʃəs/ buy – **42 matey** (n.): very infml. or disrespectful way of addressing a man (s. also *tosh*, l. 79; *moosh*, l. 85) – **47 plumage** (n.): /'pluːmidʒ/ feathers – **61 stunned** (adj.) knocked senseless, benumbed – **65 don't play the slippery eel with me:** don't evade – **70 shagged out** (v.): (sl.) exhausted – **71 squawk** (n.): /skwɔːk/ a bird's cry – **72 pine** (v.): eagerly long – **76 kip** (v.): (infml.) sleep – **82 perch** (n.): horizontal bar for bird to rest upon – **86 muscle** (v.): force one's way – **87 pecker** (n.): beak – **91 bleedin'** (adj.): (obscene) absolutely – **91 demise** (v.): (fml.) /dɪ'maiz/ die – **96 stiff** (n.): (sl.) corpse – **96 bereft of:** without – **99 curled up** (v.): rolled up – **99f. tootsies** (n.): little feet – **101 rung down** (v.): lowered (as in theatre) – **102f. snuff it:** (to snuff out a candle: to put a candle out) – **103 meta-metabolic processes:** processes that set in after the normal metabolism has stopped (= decomposition) – **105f. going concern** (n.): business in operation – **106 inoperative** (adj.): not working – **113 we're right out of parrots:** we've sold all the parrots we had

Explanations

100 he's shuffled off this mortal coil: quotation from William Shakespeare's *Hamlet* (III.i.67): his soul has left his body and all experiences of mortal life

Tasks and Projects

1 Explain what Kate Fox means by "Humour is our 'default mode'" (ll. 32–33).

2 Is there a German equivalent for "Oh, come off it"? Consult your dictionary or find occurrences of this expression on the Internet, then discuss your findings in your group.

3 "The understatement rule" is something that might cause serious communication problems between German speakers who are not familiar with it, and British people. Think of situations where such problems can arise; you can start with the examples given in ll. 142–160.

4 Make up your own "Monty Python" sketch: imagine you want to return something you are not satisfied with to the shop where you bought it. Plan it carefully (in groups of two or three) before acting it out.

5 Read one of the following books and present them to your course; alternatively, read them just for fun.

Douglas Adams, *The Hitchhiker's Guide to the Galaxy* (1979);
Roald Dahl, *Revolting Rhymes* (1982);
Charles Dickens, *Great Expectations* (1860);
Jasper Fforde, *The Eyre Affair* (2001);
Michael Frayn, *Sweet Dreams* (1973);
Hanif Kureishi, *The Buddha of Suburbia* (1990);
Spike Milligan, *Puckoon* (1963);
Mervyn Peake, *A Book of Nonsense* (1972);
Terry Pratchett, *Guards! Guards!* (1989);
William *Shakespeare, A Midsummer Night's Dream* (1600);
Bernard Shaw, *Pygmalion* (1916);
Meera Syal, *Life Isn't All Ha Ha Hee Hee* (1999);
Oscar Wilde, *The Importance of Being Earnest* (1899);
Victoria Wood, *Mens Sana in Thingummy Doodah* (1990).

6 London

According to the last (2001) census, London as a whole has over 7 million inhabitants, with 2.7 million living in the central areas of inner London. It is obvious that a metropolis of this size will be extremely diverse, and this is indeed the most characteristic quality of London. As Samuel Johnson already said in 1777: "when a man is tired of London, he is tired of life; for there is in London all that life can afford". London went through an extremely varied history, traces of which can still be found today in its architecture. The Romans founded Londinium after the invasion of 43 AD. London was the centre of a flourishing nation during the Elizabethan Era and the British Empire of the 19th century. At the end of the 20th century some parts like the Docklands in east London were restructured dramatically, though with varying success, to express Britain's move into the new millennium.

The Thames in London in 1819

I had neither kith nor kin in England, and was therefore as free as air – or as free as an income of eleven shillings and sixpence a day will permit a man to be. Under such circumstances, I naturally gravitated to London, that great cesspool into which all the loungers and idlers of the Empire are irresistibly drained.
Sir Arthur Conan Doyle, *A Study in Scarlet*

St. James's Park

Diversity and Myth

Notting Hill Carnival

London's inhabitants themselves are as varied as the buildings. There is a very broad social spectrum from the high society which frequents Ascot, the Chelsea Flower Show and exclusive clubs and fashion shops to homeless people selling their magazine *The Big Issue* in the streets. Ethnic origin adds to this diverse picture, as London has traditionally been a very popular place among immigrants to Britain. Nowadays, about 2 million of London's overall population is non-white, with Asian and British Asian people making up the biggest group and black/black British ones following close behind. Geographically, certain areas are particularly favoured by specific ethnic groups as places of residence. In inner London, Asian groups are especially well represented in Newham (east London), while there is a strong black presence in the north-eastern borough of Hackney as well as in Lambeth, Lewisham and Southwark in the south. This vibrant mix of different cultures and traditions has enriched London life throughout the centuries and continues to do so now. Nevertheless, there have also been conflicts with the white majority population and with the state authorities, which have at times (for instance in the Brixton riots of 1981, 1985 and 1995) erupted into open violence.

London, thou art the flower of cities all!
William Dunbar

Info

Notting Hill Carnival

Notting Hill Carnival is a large multicultural arts festival in the heart of London, celebrated on three consecutive days at the end of August. It was started by West Indian immigrants as a small local festivity in the 1960s and has since developed into a Rio-like Caribbean carnival attracting millions of people from all over the world. Five basic elements traditionally belong to the carnival: the masquerade accompanied by Soca, Caribbean carnival music; the Steel Pan, a Caribbean instrument; Afro-Caribbean Calypso-music; and the Sound Systems, which play a wide variety of musical styles, combining the traditional with the new and experimental. In addition, local bands and top international artists perform on three live stages. In 1976, due to tensions between the police and black immigrants, riots broke out and disrupted the so far peaceful carnival celebrations. Today, however, Notting Hill Carnival presents an opportunity for a large number of people to celebrate their cultural heritage and to bring them together in one big, merry event.

Internet Projects

1 Collect information about the people living in London on http://www.london.gov.uk/gla/publications/without_prejudice/without_prejudice1.jsp, http://www.statistics.gov.uk/census/default.asp
2 Find out more about 'Brick Lane' and the Bangladeshi community in London (see section 7) (http://www.cre.gov.uk/diversity/map/london/towerhamlets.html)
3 Collect some information about Queen Elizabeth I and the Elizabethan Era. (http://www.elizabethi.org/)
4 Take a look at the website http://www.britishempire.co.uk/ to find out more about the Empire. In how far might it still be related to London's population today?
5 What is Ascot? (http://www.ascot.co.uk/)
6 Research the Chelsea Flower Show. What is shown there and what kind of audiences does the show attract? (http://www.rhs.org.uk/chelsea/2007/index.asp)
7 Search 'Notting Hill' on the Internet. In which contexts is the area mentioned especially frequently and what might that tell you about its image?
8 Find more information about Margaret Thatcher, her policies and people's reactions to her in the 1980s and later on. (http://www.margaretthatcher.org/, http://www.bbc.co.uk/history/historic_figures/thatcher_margaret.shtml)
9 What was the Scarman Report about? (http://news.bbc.co.uk/1/hi/programmes/bbc_parliament/3631579.stm, http://news.bbc.co.uk/onthisday/hi/dates/stories/november/25/newsid_2546000/2546233.stm)

Info

Brixton Riots (1981, 1985, 1995)

Brixton is an area in the south of London where unemployment, a high crime rate, and bad living conditions caused anger and resentment among the predominantly black population in the 1980s and 90s. Each riot was sparked by encounters between single black persons and the local police which had left the black community feeling unjustly and cruelly treated. Many, especially young people, got together spontaneously directly after the encounters and started protesting violently against their bad treatment. The rioters threw bricks and petrol bombs which destroyed shop windows, set cars and a few public buildings ablaze and injured many people. In the 1985 riot a journalist actually died of his head injuries. Some researchers hold that the riots were a result of Margaret Thatcher's *laissez-faire* politics which created high unemployment and poverty because social welfare spending was cut back. Lord Scarman, who was commissioned to issue a report about the riots, found racial disadvantage and inner city decline to be the main reasons. Nowadays Brixton is experiencing a process of gentrification. It is slowly becoming a fashionable residential area for middle class people and yuppies, with its expensive flats and fancy restaurants.

1

Samuel Pepys

"The Great Fire of London"*

Samuel Pepys /pi:ps/ was born in 1633. Since his parents were not rich he was lucky to receive an education in London. Later he went on to study at Cambridge University and started a successful career in the public service. He was a Member of Parliament, Secretary of the Admiralty, President of the Royal Society and very close to both King Charles II and King James II. Pepys is particularly famous for his diaries written between 1659 and 1669, containing descriptions of his private life as well as colourful accounts of decisive events of the 17th century. The diaries were written in shorthand and had to be deciphered in an arduous process – hence the occasionally strange sentence structure. Samuel Pepys died in 1703. – *The Diary of Samuel Pepys*, ed. by Robert Latham et al. (London: G.Bell and Sons Ltd., 1972), pp. 267–270.

The Great Fire of London

Entry for 2 September 1666

Some of our maids sitting up late last night to get things ready against our feast today, Jane called us up about 3 in the morning, to tell us of a great fire they saw in the City. So I rose, and slipped on my night-gown and went to her window, and thought it to be on the back side of Marklane at the furthest; but, being unused to such fires as followed, I thought it far enough off, and so went to bed again, and to sleep. [...]

By and by Jane comes and tells me that she hears that above 300 houses have been burned down tonight by the fire we saw, and that it was now burning down all Fish Street, by London Bridge. So I made myself ready presently, and walked to the Tower; and there got up upon one of the high places [...]; and there I did see the houses at the end of the bridge all on fire, and an infinite great fire on this and the other side the end of the bridge [...].

So down [I went], with my heart full of trouble, to the Lieutenant of the Tower, who tells me that it began this morning in the King's baker's house in Pudding-lane, and that it hath burned St. Magnus's Church and most part of Fishstreete already. So I [got] down to the waterside and there got a boat and through bridge, and there saw a lamentable fire. [...] Everybody endeavouring to remove their goods, and flinging into the River or bringing them into lighters that lay off. Poor people staying in their houses as long as till the very fire touched them, and then running into boats, or clambering from one pair of stairs by the water-side to another. And among other things, the poor pigeons, I perceive, were loath to leave their houses, but hovered about the windows and balconies, till they were some of them burned, their wings, and fell down.

Having stayed, and in an hour's time seen the fire rage every way, and nobody to my sight endeavouring to quench it, but to remove their goods and leave all to the fire; and having seen it get as far as the Steeleyard, and the wind mighty high and driving it into the city, and everything, after so long a drought, providing combustible, even the very stones of churches [...] – I [went next] to White-hall with a gentleman with me who desired to go off from the Tower to see the fire in my boat – to White-hall, and there up to the King's closet in the chapel, where people came about me and I did give them an account [that] dismayed them all; and the word was carried in to the King, so I was called for and did tell the King and Duke of York what I saw, and that unless His Majesty did command houses to be pulled down, nothing could stop the fire. They seemed much troubled, and the King commanded me to go to my Lord Mayor from him and command him to spare no houses [...].

[I hurried] to [St.] Pauls; and there walked along Watling-street as well as I could, every creature coming away loaden with goods to save – and here and there sick people carried away in beds. Extraordinary goods carried in carts and on backs. At last [I] met my Lord Mayor in Canning Streete, like a man spent, with a [handkerchief] about his neck. To the King's message, he cried like a fainting woman, "Lord, what can I do? I am spent! People will not obey me. I have been pull[ing] down houses. But the fire overtakes us faster than we can do it." [...] So he left me, and I him, and walked home – seeing people all almost distracted and no manner of means used to quench the fire. The houses, too, so very thick thereabouts, and full of matter for burning, as pitch and tar, in Thames-street – and warehouses of oyle and wines and Brandy and other things.

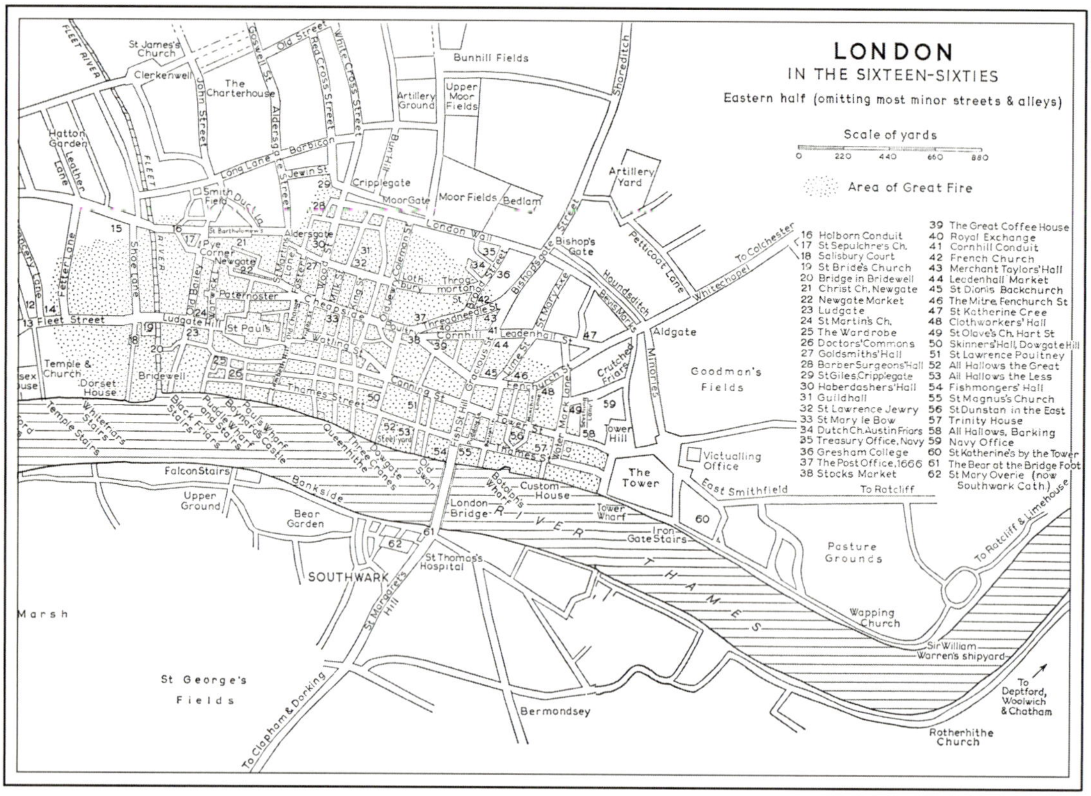

Map: the Great Fire of London

Vocabulary

3 against (prep.): here: for – **5 night-gown** (n.): here: a dressing-gown worn over the night-dress – **10 by and by** (adv., dated): before long, soon – **16 infinite** (adj., here: adv.): having no limits; boundless – **25 lamentable** (adj.): very sad; regrettable – **25 to endeavour** (v.): to try very hard to do s.th. – **26 to fling** (v.): to throw quickly and carelessly – **27 lighter** (n.): a flat-bottomed boat for transporting goods – **27 to lie off** (v.): (of a ship) to stand some distance away from the shore – **31 to be loath to do s.th.** (adj. pred.): to be unwilling to do s.th. – **32 to hover about** (v.): to move closely around s.th. – **35 to rage** (v.): here: to extend forcefully – **36 to quench** (v.): to put out or extinguish a fire – **38 mighty** (adj.): here: very – **39 drought** (n.) /draʊt/: a period without rain – **40 combustible** (n.): any material which catches fire easily – **44 closet** (n.): here: the private apartment of a monarch – **45 to dismay** (v.): to cause great fear, pain and anger – **51 to spare** (v.): to leave out – **58 spent** (adj.) exhausted; having no energy left – **59 handkerchief** (n.): a small square piece of cloth for wiping the face, eyes, or nose – **64 distracted** (adj.): confused and worried – **66 thereabouts** (adv.): in the immediate vicinity – **67 pitch** (n.): a black substance made from oil or coal, used to stop leaks in ships, roofs etc. – **67 tar** (n.): a black substance made from coal, mainly used for building roads – **68 oyle** (n.): archaic spelling of *oil*

Explanations

13 London Bridge: a bridge across the River Thames in London; see p. 103 – **14 The Tower (of London):** a large fortress on the northern bank of the Thames. The original White Tower was founded by William the Conqueror in 1078. It was used as royal residence until 1625 and contained the first observatory, the treasury, a mint, an arsenal and even a zoo. It also functioned as a prison and place for executions. Today the White Tower hosts a weapons museum and the Wakefield Tower the famous Crown Jewels. – **20 lieutenant** /lef'tenənt, AE luː'tenənt/: someone who acts on behalf of a superior; the Lieutenant of the Tower is the acting commandant who works for the Constable (governor) of the Tower – **22 St. Magnus Church:** a church situated on Lower Thames Street at the north end of London Bridge. The original church from 1176 was consumed by the Great Fire. After 1666 it was rebuilt by Sir Christopher Wren. – **37 Steeleyard (Steelyard):** founded in the Middle Ages as a cooperation between Hamburg, Cologne and Lübeck, the Steelyard was the main trading base of the Hanseatic League in London. – **41 White-hall:** (Whitehall): street in Westminster, the government quarter of London; here: the Palace of Whitehall, royal residence from 1530 till 1698 when it was destroyed by a fire – **51 Lord Mayor:** elected head of the council of a city or borough – **53 St. Paul's:** famous cathedral overlooking the City of London. It was designed and built by Sir Christopher Wren after the Great Fire had destroyed the older Cathedral.

Info

The Great Fire of London

The Great Fire of London started in the early hours of 2 September 1666. Thomas Farynor, the king's baker in Pudding Lane near London Bridge, had supposedly forgotten to extinguish the fire in his oven the evening before. By the time this was noticed, the bakery was already ablaze and other buildings in the narrow street had caught fire. In the crammed streets with their thatched-roof houses, people were soon unable to control the flames. The fire spread until London Bridge was burning. Only a part of the Bridge without houses, which the fire could not surmount, prevented it from spreading to the south bank of the Thames. While the Lord Mayor stood helplessly by, the King ordered the houses to be destroyed to create firebreaks. These, however, proved ineffective because the strong east wind allowed the fire to jump the gaps. The west of the City was almost completely burned down. Three days after the fire had started, the wind turned, and the rest of it was blown into the Thames. By the fourth day the fire was completely extinguished. 373 acres of the City with 13,200 houses and 84 churches had been destroyed. Officially only nine people were killed but the real death toll is believed to be much higher. Though the fire seems to have been caused by a fatal combination of unlucky circumstances, blame was mostly laid on the Catholics, who were deeply mistrusted in those times. The inscription on the London monument commemorating the fire which held them responsible for the catastrophe was only removed in 1831.

The Monument to the Fire

Awareness

1 How and why do major catastrophes change the consciousness of people nation- or worldwide?

Comprehension

2 Try to chart the different stages of the fire.

Analysis

3 How does Pepys represent his own role in the events?

Opinion

4 What difference do you think it made to the course of events that the fire occurred in London rather than another city?
5 Why did the fire get out of control?
6 Why may Catholics have been held responsible for the fire in the 17th century?
7 It was widely believed that the Great Fire helped to extinguish the plague that had raged in London for several years before the catastrophe. Why is that unlikely (perhaps consult the *Encyclopaedia Britannica*)? Can you imagine why such rumours were and are so persistent?

Project

6 Use more general maps of London (and / or your own knowledge of the city) to situate the area affected by the fire in the city as a whole. Could that specific location also have played a role in people's responses? (www.bl.uk)

2 London's Burning

London's burning, London's burning
Fetch the engines, fetch the engines
Fire, fire! Fire, fire!
Pour on water, pour on water.

(Old song or nursery rhyme)

Analysis

1 Judging by this example, what is characteristic of the form of traditional or nursery rhymes? Which functions might these formal features have?

Opinion

2 Why might nursery rhymes like this one deal with traumatic events? Might they thereby perform a cultural function?

3 Can you think of any contemporary cultural forms that may fulfil similar functions in society?

Info

"London's Burning" is often defined as either a traditional or a nursery rhyme. *Traditional* is the general term for an English folk song or a certain type of folk dance, while a *nursery rhyme* is a special folk song sung for children in the nursery. Sometimes nursery rhymes are only children's songs on the surface and address complex issues, deal with shocking or threatening events or teach moral lessons. It is unknown when exactly "London's Burning" came into being though the song communicates a rather light-hearted attitude towards the calamity of the Great Fire, which suggests some distance to the actual event. The use of the term 'engines' supports this assumption. At the time of the Great Fire, London certainly did not have organized fire brigades, let alone 'engines' for fire fighting. Fire brigades only began to be formed in the years after the catastrophe. 'Engines' could refer to the first manual pumps used for fire fighting towards the end of the 16th century. Steam-powered fire engines first appeared about two hundred years later.

3 London Bridge Is Falling Down

Old London Bridge

London Bridge as reconstructed in Arizona

London Bridge is falling down,
Falling down, Falling down.
London Bridge is falling down,
My fair lady.

Take a key and lock her up,
Lock her up, Lock her up.
Take a key and lock her up,
My fair lady.

How will we build it up,
Build it up, Build it up?
How will we build it up,
My fair lady?

Build it up with silver and gold,
Silver and gold, Silver and gold.
Build it up with silver and gold,
My fair lady.

Gold and silver I have none,
I have none, I have none.
Gold and silver I have none,
My fair lady.

Build it up with needles and pins,
Needles and pins, Needles and pins.
Build it up with needles and pins,
My fair lady.

Pins and needles bend and break,
Bend and break, Bend and break.
Pins and needles bend and break,
My fair lady.

Build it up with wood and clay,
Wood and clay, Wood and clay.
Build it up with wood and clay,
My fair lady.

Wood and clay will wash away,
Wash away, Wash away.
Wood and clay will wash away,
My fair lady.

Build it up with stone so strong,
Stone so strong, Stone so strong.
Build it up with stone so strong,
My fair lady.

Stone so strong will last so long,
Last so long, Last so long.
Stone so strong will last so long,
My fair lady.

(Old nursery rhyme)

Vocabulary

25 to bend (v.): to become lop-sided and destabilized – **29 clay** (n.): a special type of soil. When mixed with water it can be formed into bricks or pots which are hardened in an oven. – **33 to wash away** (v.): to dissolve in water

Info

London Bridge

"London Bridge is falling down" is a nursery rhyme, the oldest known version of which appeared in the collection *Tommy Thumb's Pretty Song Book* in the 1740s. It refers to the exciting history of London Bridge, which was built, destroyed and rebuilt several times till it obtained its modern appearance. The bridge is famous for being the first and only one for crossing the Thames, until Westminster Bridge was opened in 1750. It was built by the Romans as early as 46 AD. They probably used wood and clay for its construction, thus the reference in the song. In 1013 it was burned down by King Aethelred to divide invading Danish troops. This event might originally have inspired the song. The first stone bridge was started in 1176 and took 33 years to finish. It had 20 arches, a tower, security gates and water wheels used for grinding grain. Several disasters struck the bridge in the decades to follow, most of them serious fires. In the 14th century shops first opened on the bridge, among other things trading silver and gold, to which the song also alludes. The bridge withstood the Great Fire of 1666 but its foundations were weakened. As traffic increased in the 18th century, the houses on the bridge were removed and its arches widened to facilitate traffic on the river. In 1831 a new London Bridge was completed some feet to the west of the original, and the old bridge was destroyed. In the 20th century even the newer bridge proved impractical, and it was rebuilt and reopened in 1973. The 1831 bridge was sold to an American millionaire and reconstructed in Arizona.

Comprehension

1 Is there any kind of narrative logic in the rhyme? (Consult the Info text about London Bridge.)

Opinion

2 Why might the collapse of a bridge have been a shocking experience in London in earlier centuries and thus have merited a similar treatment as the Great Fire?

Internet Projects

3 Try to find out to whom or what the "fair lady", the "pins and needles" and the line "lock her up" might refer. It might be helpful to research King Henry III and his wife Queen Eleanor on the Internet: http://www.historic-uk.com/HistoryUK/England-History/KingsandQueens.htm

4 How is the rhyme sung and acted out by children today? Does that contribute anything to its possible content? (http://www.pitt.edu/~dash/sacrifice.html)

4

Original

Sing a Song of Sixpence

Sing a song of sixpence,
A pocket full of rye;
Four-and-twenty blackbirds
Baked in a pie.

When the pie was opened,
The birds began to sing.
Was not that a dainty dish
To set before the King?

The King was in his countinghouse,
Counting out his money;
The Queen was in the parlour
Eating bread and honey.

The maid was in the garden,
Hanging out the clothes,
When down came a blackbird
And snapped off her nose!

(Old nursery rhyme)

Buckingham Palace: royal splendour

Vocabulary

2 rye (n.): a kind of corn (Roggen) – **3 four and twenty** (dated): twenty-four – **3 blackbird** (n.): a common European bird, the male of which has black feathers (Amsel) – **7 dainty** (adj.): here: opulent and tasty – **9 countinghouse** (n.) (historical): a place where a person's or a company's business accounts and money were kept – **11 parlour** (n.): usually a sitting room reserved for private conversation; here: a room used for dining or eating supper – **16 to snap off** (v.): to cut off; here: to hack off with a sharp beak

Explanations

1 sixpence: a former British silver coin worth six pennies; it went out of use after the decimalization of money in 1971 – **4 pie:** baked food with a pastry shell or covering containing savoury or sweet fillings like meat, vegetables, fruit, chocolate, etc.

Info

"Sing a Song of Sixpence" is another nursery rhyme which was first published in *Tommy Thumb's Pretty Song Book* in the 1740s. It is likely, however, that the song is much older because we find references to it with respect to court jesters in the literature of the late 16th and early 17th centuries. The song's association with jesters or clowns suggests a political significance. Jesters, employed by the king for entertainment, were generally considered fools. Many of them, however, were witty, able to hide critical comments about the monarchy or social problems in funny little songs. The first stanza of "Sing a Song of Sixpence" tells of a very curious culinary custom of medieval Europe. So-called subtlety dishes, spectacular and fantastic meals, were served at royal and upper class banquets to entertain the diners. The song alludes to the custom of baking living birds into pies which would fly out and startle the guests as soon as the pastry was cut. The 'pocket full of rye' could either have been used for feeding those birds or for actually baking the pie. The second stanza describes the king's and queen's jobs as the common people see them. The king is obsessed with money, making sure that none of it is missing so that he can keep on financing his exclusive lifestyle. The queen does nothing but eat bread and honey, food that most of her subjects could not afford. The maid links the two stanzas. The song establishes a contrast between the king and queen and their wasteful lifestyle and ordinary working people like the maid. It is she who suffers from the king's entertainment as her nose gets pecked off by one of the birds, and it was the poor people who suffered from the fact that much of a country's money was spent on the expensive pastimes of the court. The song has a later addition concerning the maid:

They sent for the king's doctor,
Who sewed it on again,
He sewed it on so neatly,
The seam was never seen.

Obviously, at least some people were conscious of the hidden and potentially subversive content of the rhyme.

4a 'Update'

Sing a Song of Esso

Sing a song of Esso
a packet full of lies
and oily greasy dollars
to help the climate fry

when the wallet opened
George Bush began to sing
"the planet may be burning
but I don't see a thing"

The boss is in the counting house
counting out his money
Bush is in the White House while
the weather's going funny

so let us now suggest to you
that when you see their logo,
do something for our planet Earth
and don't go buying Esso

http://www.crypto.com/photos/misc/tube-esso-2003-03-31.html

The poem as published on the London underground, imitating the "Poems on the Underground" posters

Vocabulary

3 greasy (adj.): covered with an oily substance – **4 to fry** (v.): here: (infml.) to overheat – **5 wallet** (n.): small flat case usually kept in the pockets of trousers or jackets for storing cash and credit cards

Explanation

1 Esso: oil firm whose parent company is ExxonMobil, the world's largest oil corporation operating in more than 80 countries

Info

This politically charged poem resembles the style and tone of the nursery rhyme "Sing a Song of Sixpence" which possibly contains a coded attack on medieval authorities. "Sing a Song of Esso" continues this tradition of criticism by rhymes or songs. It became known under very interesting circumstances. A British campaign called "Poems on the Underground" aims at acquainting passengers on the London tube with a variety of poems. Contemporary and older poetry has been displayed in advertising spaces inside trains for twenty years. In 2003, "Sing a Song of Esso" and other political poems appeared in the advertising spaces in almost perfect imitations of the usual "Poems on the Underground" posters. Greenpeace has since claimed responsibility for this artistic protest. The organisation criticises ExxonMobil and its subsidiary Esso for their big share in the world's environmental problems and for investing hardly any money in renewable energy projects. The lines 'when the wallet opened / George Bush began to sing...' hint at the fact that Bush's election campaign was partly financed by ExxonMobil. The company had a high interest in a president supportive of its policies, and George W. Bush and his family have long-standing connections to the oil industry. With Bush as president, the US government, afraid of damaging the American economy, has drawn back from the Kyoto protocol, thereby ensuring continuing and unrestricted sales for oil companies. In 2003 an executive order was signed by Bush which caused indignation because some experts believed that it granted American oil companies immunity from criminal prosecution with respect to the sale of Iraqi oil. Therefore the lines 'when the wallet opened / George Bush began to sing...' additionally accuse ExxonMobil of having bought Bush's support and Bush of being corrupt. 'The boss' in the 'counting house' probably refers to then ExxonMobil boss Lee Raymond, a hardliner on the issues of environmental protection. During his time in office he earned more than 686 million dollars and received compensation of about another 400 million when he retired in 2005. In the same year, ExxonMobil made its highest ever profits of more than 36 billion dollars. The final lines of the song might allude to the "Stop Esso Campaign" launched by Greenpeace and other environmental organisations in several European countries.

Awareness

1 What role does environmental protection play in your life and surroundings?

Comprehension

2 What exactly does "Sing a Song of Sixpence" criticise about the monarchy?
3 For what reasons does Greenpeace specifically attack Esso?

Analysis

4 How is the subversive content concealed in "Sing a Song of Sixpence"?
5 In what ways does the later addition to it try to mitigate this criticism?
6 Compare the Esso song with the original nursery rhyme with regard to both form and content.

Opinion

7 Why do you think Greenpeace chose this particular form and method of distribution for their criticism?
8 Do you consider the issues raised in "Sing a Song of Esso" important? Give reasons for your answer.

Internet Projects

9 Try to find out more about 'subtlety dishes'.
10 Why could "Sing a Song of Sixpence" refer to King Henry VIII, Catherine of Aragon and Anne Boleyn?
11 Find out what the Kyoto protocol is about. (http://www.unfccc.int)
12 What did the 'Stop Esso Campaign' imply? (http://www.greenpeace.org.uk)

5

William Wordsworth

Composed upon Westminster Bridge, Sept. 3, 1802

William Wordsworth is one of the most important poets of the English Romantic movement. He was born in the Lake District in 1770, received a good education and went on to study at Cambridge University. In his youth he sympathised with the ideals of the French Revolution and visited France several times. In 1795 he settled down in England, moved in with his sister and soul-mate Dorothy and met his fellow poet Samuel Taylor Coleridge, with whom he formed a productive partnership. The two poets jointly published their *Lyrical Ballads* in 1798. Some years later, Wordsworth married a childhood friend with whom he had five children. His later works are more conservative, less enthusiastic and more reserved than the early ones. Wordsworth died in 1850. His chief contribution to poetry is his new attitude to nature. In his poems he uses landscape or 'outer nature' to portray his and his characters' 'inner nature'. Good poetry for him is characterised by a 'spontaneous overflow of powerful feelings' on the one hand, but distance from the experience and 'thought long and deep' on the other. "Westminster Bridge" was possibly inspired by one of Dorothy Wordsworth's diary entries. It describes the scene of her and her brother leaving London for France one early morning in July 1802. The poem is now considered a classic and has appeared in the London tube for "Poems on the Underground". – William Wordsworth, *Poetical Works*, ed. by Thomas Hutchinson (London: Oxford University Press, 1936), p. 214.

1 Earth has not anything to show more fair:
Dull would he be of soul who could pass by
A sight so touching in its majesty:
This City now doth, like a garment, wear
The beauty of the morning; silent, bare,
Ships, towers, domes, theatres, and temples lie
Open unto the fields, and to the sky;
All bright and glittering in the smokeless air.
Never did sun more beautifully steep
In his first splendour, valley, rock, or hill;
Ne'er saw I, never felt, a calm so deep!
The river glideth at his own sweet will:
Dear God! the very houses seem asleep;
And all that mighty heart is lying still!

Westminster Bridge in 1871

Vocabulary

2 dull (adj.): boring; here: lacking sensibility or keenness of perception – **4 doth** (v.): (archaic): third person singular present of do – **4 garment** (n.): piece of clothing – **5 bare** (adj.): undisguised, open to view – **6 dome** (n.): here: a stately building, or a cathedral – **9 to steep** (v.): here: of light: to bathe – **10 splendour** (n.): magnificent appearance

Info

The sonnet

Sonnets are poems consisting of fourteen lines and written in a special metre. Scholars distinguish between two different kinds, the Italian or Petrarchan sonnet, introduced into English poetry in the 16th century, and the English or Shakespearean sonnet. In the Petrarchan sonnet, there is usually a break after the eighth line, dividing the poem into an octave and a sestet. The speaker can develop his subject in the octave, and then take a turn and approach a resolution in the sestet. The Shakespearean sonnet is divided into three parts of four lines (quatrains) and a couplet. Often, an idea is introduced in the first quatrain, developed and complicated in the second and third ones and finally resolved in the couplet.

Info

Romanticism

The Romantic era is often placed in the years between the American Declaration of Independence in 1776 and the Great Reform Bill of 1832. However, opinions differ on the exact starting and end points. It was a time of revolutions and of industrialisation, which brought about changes in the political and social order but also in people's minds. On the one hand, English society was future-oriented and there was a widespread belief in progress. Advances in science and technology, for instance the first railways and the telegraph, were embodiments of this positive sentiment. On the other hand, many people felt lost because systems of beliefs and values changed. Some of the Romantic poets, predominantly Lord Byron (1788–1824) and Percy Shelley (1792–1822), were highly critical of their society. Others, like John Keats (1795–1821), withdrew into alternative worlds of the imagination in their poetry. And while the whole country was gripped by a move away from the country and to the cities where people hoped to find employment in factories, the Romantics advocated a return to nature for quiet contemplation and a confrontation with the self.

John Constable, Hampstead Heath with London in the distance

Awareness

1 Are you affected by poetry at all? Why (not)?

Comprehension

2 How does the lyrical I characterise London?

Analysis

3 Which poetic techniques (Reference Library, pp. 309f.) are used to describe London?
4 What can you say about the form of the poem (especially keeping in mind what is written on p. 107 about the sonnet form)?

Opinion

5 Do you think the picture of London in the poem is an adequate representation of the city at that time? Why (not)?
6 Why might Wordsworth (as a Romantic poet) have chosen this particular view of London?

Projects

7 Find out why one sonnet form is called 'Petrarchan' (http://petrarch.petersadlon.com/laura.html).
8 Try to find Dorothy Wordsworth's diary entry on the web and compare it to the poem. How could the relationship between the two texts and the different dates they give relate to the composition of Romantic poetry as described above? (http://www.cie.org.uk/CIE/WebSite/UCLESData/Documents/A%20Level/Other%20Docs/Notes%20on%20AS%20Anthology%20-%20amended%2030-10-2006.pdf)

6 Myth or Reality?

Awareness

1 Compare these images of London (as well as the other postcards reprinted in this chapter) with your own impressions of the city and / or with films about London that you may have seen.

Analysis

2 Which aspects of London do each of the three postcards reprinted here highlight?
3 Why might the producers of the postcards have selected the specific buildings represented there?
4 Do the postcards create a certain 'myth' (or myths) of London?

Opinion

5 Why might someone want to choose these postcards to send home from a trip to London? Would you want to do so?
6 Who would be a suitable target group for the cards?
7 How do you view the relationship between the images of London presented here and the texts discussed so far?

7

Monica Ali

"Nazneen in London"*

Monica Ali was born in Bangladesh in 1967. When she was three years old, her family migrated to England where she has lived ever since. She studied philosophy, political science and economy in Oxford and has worked in PR and marketing. Currently, she lives in London with her family. Brick Lane is a real street in London's East End which hosts about 40,000 immigrants from Bangladesh. Ali's novel, set there, traces the life-story of Nazneen, a young Bangladeshi woman who leaves her home country for an arranged marriage with an older man (Chanu) in London. At first she accepts her role as housewife and mother. Then she gradually begins to emancipate herself, while her husband gets more and more disillusioned. She learns to speak English, finds work, friends and even a lover. When her husband decides to go back to Bangladesh and her lover wants to marry her, Nazneen breaks free from both men and opts for a single life in England with her two daughters. Hasina, also mentioned in the excerpt, is Nazneen's sister. She gets married against her family's will and is turned out. After leaving her abusive husband, she then ends up in the Bangladeshi capital of Dhaka. Nazneen can only keep up a very irregular correspondence with her. (For further texts and information about the topic of ethnic diversity in the UK check chapter 8.) – Monica Ali, *Brick Lane* (London: Black Swan, 2003), pp. 45, 54, 55–56, 57–58, 61, 62–63.

She did not often go out. 'Why should you go out?' said Chanu. 'If you go out, ten people will say, "I saw her walking on the street." And I will look like a fool. Personally, I don't mind if you go out but these people are so ignorant. What can you do?'

She never said anything to this.

'Besides, I get everything for you that you need from the shops. Anything you want, you only have to ask.'

She never said anything to this.

'I don't stop you from doing anything. I am westernized now. It is lucky for you that you married an educated man. That was a stroke of luck.'

She carried on with her chores.

'And anyway, if you were in Bangladesh you would not go out. Coming here you are not missing anything, only broadening your horizons.'

[…]

Behind her a door slammed. She reached the stairwell and cantered down. The overhead light was fierce; she could feel its faint heat even as the concrete cold crept into her toes. The stairs gave off a tang of urine. She bunched the skirts of her sari with one hand and took the steps two at a time until she missed a ledge and came down on her ankle against an unforgiving ridge. She caught the stair rail and did not fall but clung to the side for a moment, then continued down, stamping as if the pain was just a cramp to be marched out.

[…]

Nazneen walked. She walked to the end of Brick Lane and turned right. Four blocks down she crossed the road (she waited next to a woman and stepped out with her, like a calf with its mother) and took a side street. She turned down the first right, and then went left. From there she took every second right and every second left until she realized she was leaving herself a trail. Then she turned off at random, began to run, limped for a while to save her ankle, and thought she had come in a circle. The buildings seemed familiar. She sensed rather than saw, because she had taken care not to notice. But now she slowed down and looked around her. She looked up at a building as she passed. It was constructed almost entirely of glass, with a few thin rivets of steel holding it together. The entrance was like a glass fan, rotating slowly, sucking people in, wafting others out. Inside, on a raised dais, a woman behind a glass desk crossed and uncrossed her thin legs. She wedged a telephone receiver between her ear and shoulder and chewed on a fingernail. Nazneen craned her head back and saw that the glass above became dark as a night pond. The building was without end. Above, somewhere, it crushed the clouds. The next building and the one opposite were white stone palaces. There were steps up to the entrances and colonnades across the front. Men in dark suits trotted briskly up and down the steps, in pairs or in threes. They barked to each other and nodded sombrely. Sometimes one clapped a hand on his companion's shoulder and Nazneen saw that this was not for reassurance, but for emphasis. Every person who brushed past her on the pavement, every back she saw, was on a private, urgent mission to execute a precise and demanding plan: to get a promotion today, to be exactly on time for an appointment, to buy a newspaper with the right coins so that the exchange was swift and seamless, to walk without wasting a second and to reach the roadside just as the lights turned red. Nazneen, hobbling and halting, began to be aware of herself. Without a coat, without a suit, without a white face, without a destination. A leafshake of fear – or was it excitement? – passed through her legs.

[...]

There was a patch of green surrounded by black railings, and in the middle two wooden benches. In this city, a bit of grass was something to be guarded, fenced about, as if there were a sprinkling of emeralds sown in among the blades. Nazneen found the gate and sat alone on the bench. A maharanee in her enclosure. The sun came out from behind a black cloud and shone briefly in her eyes before plunging back under cover, disappointed with what it had seen. She was cold, she was tired, she was in pain, she was hungry and she was lost.

She had got herself lost because Hasina was lost. And only now did she realize how stupid she was. Hasina was in Dhaka. A woman on her own in the city, without a husband, without family, without friends, without protection.

[...]

She got home twenty minutes before her husband, washed the rice and set it to boil, searched through a cupful of lentils for tiny stones that could crack your teeth, put them in a pan on the stove. She removed her shoes and examined her blisters. She put on fresh underclothes and sari and soaped the rain-sodden one. When she had twisted the water out of it, she left it in the bath like a sleeping pink python.

[...]

He dropped to his knees, put his arms around Nazneen's middle and began to sing to her stomach. She held a ladle full of boiling scummy water above his head. She poured it with great care into a bowl.

'You could go there.' The words burst as hot and fast as boils.

'Where?' He pulled down his hood and blinked at her.

'Where? To Dhaka. You could find her.'

[...]

Anything is possible. She wanted to shout it. Do you know what I did today? I went inside a pub. To use the toilet. Did you think I could do that? I walked mile upon mile, probably around the whole of London, although I did not see the edge of it. And to get home again I went to a restaurant. I found a Bangladeshi restaurant and asked directions. See what I can do!

She said, 'It is up to you. I was only suggesting.'

Vocabulary

12 stroke of luck (n.): unexpected and fortunate occurrence – **13 chore** (n.): (household) duty – **19 to canter** (v.): of a horse: to gallop moderately; here: to move briskly – **21 tang** (n.): here: a strong, penetrating smell – **22 to bunch** (v.): here: to gather a dress into folds – **22 sari** (n.): a long, often brightly coloured garment of cloth or silk, worn by Hindu women – **23 ledge** (n.): a narrow shelf projecting from a wall, cliff, etc.; here: a landing – **24 ridge** (n.): an elevation or raised part running along or across a surface – **36 to limp** (v.): to walk lamely – **42 rivet** (n.): pin or bolt holding together the parts of s.th. – **43 fan** (n.): a rotating apparatus with blade-like arms for cooling the air in a room – **44 dais** (n.): low platform; here: a slightly elevated receptionist's desk – **55 sombre** (adj.): darkly serious, gloomy – **62 seamless** (adj.): smooth – **64 to hobble** (v.): to limp – **67 leafshake** (n.): neologism: shaking like a leaf (Zittern wie Espenlaub) – **70 patch** (n.): here: a small area of land or ground – **73 sprinkling** (n.): a small amount – **73 emerald** (n.): bright green precious stone – **74 blade** (n.): long thin leaf of grass – **75 maharanee** (n.): /maː[h]əraːni/: the wife or widow of a maharaja, an Indian ruler – **77 to plunge** (v.): to forcefully move into s.th. – **88 lentil** (n.): small round brownish seed used for making soups (Linse) – **90 blister** (n.): a small bubble on the skin often caused by walking in uncomfortable shoes for too long – **97 ladle** (n.): large, long-handled spoon with a cup-shaped bowl for serving liquid food – **97 scummy** (adj.): covered with foam – **100 boil** (n.): an inflamed swelling on the skin – **101 to blink** (v.): here: to raise the eyelids in surprise

Comprehension

1 Describe the relationship between Nazneen and her husband Chanu.

Analysis

2 How does Hasina's story contribute to the plot in these excerpts?

3 How are London and its (predominantly white) inhabitants seen through Nazneen's eyes?

Opinion

4 Why might the book have evoked some angry criticism from the Bangladeshi community in Britain?

Projects

5 Find out more about multi-ethnic London. What are important positive and negative developments currently taking place in the field of ethnic relations in London? (http://www.runnymedetrust.org/projects/meb/report.html, http://www.cre.gov.uk/, http://www.cre.gov.uk/diversity/map.html)

6 In the summer of 2006, *Brick Lane* was filmed by Sarah Gavron (Ruby Films). Research the making of the film and the problems encountered in it on the Internet. (http://books.guardian.co.uk/news/articles/0,,1831046,00.html)

7 Ireland – A Story of Beauty

But why Ireland? Because Ireland is different! Often, if talk centres on this small island at the periphery of Europe, people from abroad shake their heads indicating they do not understand the place and the people. Of course, what they have in mind is in most cases the so-called 'Troubles', i.e. the conflict in Northern Ireland which is, indeed, so difficult for a foreigner to understand.

But Ireland is not only Northern Ireland and the 'Troubles'. Once you meet people who have experienced that difference, it will probably now be your turn to shake your head, as many of them will have their own stories to tell about the Emerald Isle. To some people it is the island's unspoilt nature and beautiful scenery, to others it is the fascinating spectacle of sun and rain, of light and colour that immerses the Emerald Isle in "forty shades of green", as an old ballad claims. Others come for the easy-going way of life, the music and the friendliness of the people or Ireland's omnipresent signs of history and its rich culture. Many visitors from abroad have fallen under its spell, among them, as we can read from his *Irisches Tagebuch* (1957), the German writer Heinrich Böll. The book became a secret travel guide to an island that, in its secludedness, simplicity, scenic beauty and cultural richness, seemed the ideal place for Europeans tired of civilization's achievements.

Hands across the divide

and Hope

There is, however, more to Ireland than most people are aware of. As Irish pop singer Sinéad O'Connor puts it in her song "Famine": "I see the Irish as a race like a child that got itself bashed in the face." And what she means is Ireland's history of subjugation and exploitation through its powerful neighbour England, natural disasters and self-inflicted violence that has left the country in a state of traumatic stagnation living its past through its songs and traditions again and again.

But the Republic of Ireland is changing. A formerly all-powerful Catholic Church has to admit that its influence is fading, while an astonishing economic success story has taken the Republic of Ireland into the top ranks of the EU member states. And what about Northern Ireland? The situation in Northern Ireland is changing, too. Almost unnoticed by the world, committed women and men have worked hard to keep the hope alive that the Belfast Agreement of 1998 raised – that lasting peace may have a chance in the troubled province for the first time.

1

Makki Marseilles

"Impressions of Ireland"

Whatever gateway the visitor to Ireland may choose, he or she will be greeted with the words "céad míle fáilte" ("a hundred thousand welcomes"). This is the Irish way of inviting every traveller to discover this 'Treasure Island'. For many people their first visit to Ireland is the beginning of a life-long 'love affair'. Makki Marseilles describes the people and the country he loves best. – Makki Marseilles, "Impressions of Ireland", in: *Practical English Teaching*, June 1993 (London: Mary Glasgow, 1993), pp. 32f.

Landscape in Co. Galway

Seductive Powers

As early as the 15th century, English settlers in Ireland noticed the country's extraordinary ability to assimilate visitors. A century later, Edmund Spenser, Queen Elizabeth's hagiographer, lamented Ireland's seductive powers, which frustrated the process of Anglicization. Today it is thought that Ireland exerted a stronger influence on its conquerors than they ever did on her.

Impressions reviewed

A stranger to Ireland might be forgiven if he formed the opinion that Ireland was a wild and distant country wrapped in the misty vapours of North Europe and constantly lashed by the fury of the Atlantic. Moreover, anyone who has not visited the island may easily get the impression that Ireland is an economically and politically struggling country ...

[...]

I suspect that not even the most ardent Irish nationalist would support the idea that all the problems besetting Irish society have been solved, but the image of a poor, under-developed country, made up mostly of uneducated and untrained people with a fatal attraction to a Latin American-type church, only good enough to swell the ranks of unemployment or support Britain's construction industry ('McAlpine's fusiliers' as they were aptly described) is, I think, over.

Stereotypes on demand

Stories about Ireland and the Irish, as everyone knows, are legion. Most of these are indeed concocted by the Irish themselves, who talk like other people breathe, confirming the genius of the race by playing to an audience that demands stereotypes and then claiming the applause. Brendan Behan, hardly a 'word slouch' himself, once said that 'the Irish spend words like sailors spend money'; and they tell stories with the same facility with which nuns say their prayers.

Dublin for the Irish is the omphalos of the world, and justifiably so. Once the second city of the British Empire, it is now the beneficiary of a great architectural tradition, the recipient of a building largesse which gives it the good fortune to change personalities faster than an actor changes makeup. [...]

Famous names

Strolling around Dublin, the visitor cannot help but fall under the city's magic spell and has difficulty choosing what to admire first: the Gothic bulk of Trinity College; the width of O'Connell Bridge, reputedly exceeding its length, the Greek Temple-style Post Office, scene of the 1916 Irish rising; the Doric portico of the Pro-Cathedral with its Renaissance interior and white marble altar; the Gate Theatre, Michael MacLiammoir's former home, where actor Orson Welles made his debut; or Moore

Living culture on Dublin pavement

Street, Dublin's answer to Covent Garden, where fish-mongers, flower-sellers and costermongers might have jumped out of the pages of James Joyce's or Brendan Behan's stories.

Sitting or standing you will never be too far away from the mythical, historical and literary Ireland: at the entrance to Grafton Street, Dublin's most fashionable area, Molly Malone, whose name is sung on many an English course, will confront you in brazen defiance. The surrounding pubs and cafés are still haunted by the spirits of Oscar Wilde, W. B. Yeats, [...] James Joyce, George Bernard Shaw, Samuel Beckett, [...] Sean O'Casey, Brendan Behan, perhaps in endless metaphysical argument with the likes of Jonathan Swift, Oliver Goldsmith, or Richard Brinsley Sheridan, [...]. At the Abbey Theatre, the portraits of those who created the Celtic Dawn (W. B. Yeats, Lady Gregory, Maude Gonne, Anne Horniman, painted by Yeats senior) will furnish you with an instant passport to history; and if you enter a pub and talk to any of the customers, you'll go away believing in miracles.

Beyond Dublin

But Ireland is not only Dublin. On the west coast of the banks of the river Corrib stands Galway City, Ireland's Venice, gateway to Connemara, county Mayo, Sligo and Donegal to the north, Clare, Kerry and Cork to the south, a stone's throw from Blarney country, where, if you are brave enough to climb to the top of a gutted medieval castle and slide backwards from the ramparts to kiss a slightly discoloured stone, you may deservedly acquire "the gift of the gab", something all Irish people possess as a right of birth. [...]

Essence of Irishness

To become Irish however takes a lifetime of an irreverent, illogical, irresponsible, incomprehensible, inconsistent attitude to life and history, mixed with liberal quantities of love, indulgence and humour – humour that insists on sustaining a distorted image of a race that has excelled in every aspect of human endeavour. [...]

Great returns

Notwithstanding history, Ireland today has a modern look about it. With one of the youngest populations in the whole of Europe, it leads in a whole range of products and services: finance, computers, high technology, food and drink; moreover, as a result of its membership of the EEC it has been able to make dramatic changes in infrastructure: build roads, bridges and improve telecommunications and industry, modernise agriculture and fisheries. As a result [...] the Irish are coming back to Ireland in increasingly large numbers.

Of course, not all problems have been solved – far from it – but right now Ireland, with a high standard of living and very low inflation, appears to be a good-looking proposition for its young people who have to look no longer towards London, New York, Christchurch, Montreal, Sydney, or Melbourne for their future, but right here, in the Emerald Isle, in Ireland, their own home.

Modern Ireland

What's what called?

Ireland: name of the island; historical name for the whole of Ireland; today common name for the Republic of Ireland

Republic of Ireland: official name for the southern part of Ireland

Éire: Gaelic name for the Republic of Ireland

Erin, Emerald Isle: poetic names for Ireland

Northern Ireland: official name of that part of the United Kingdom

Ulster: an area in the North of Ireland; traditional name of the province of Ulster; three of its nine counties now lie in the republic (County Cavan, County Monaghan, and County Donegal); the other six define the boundaries of Northern Ireland, often referred to as, simply, Ulster

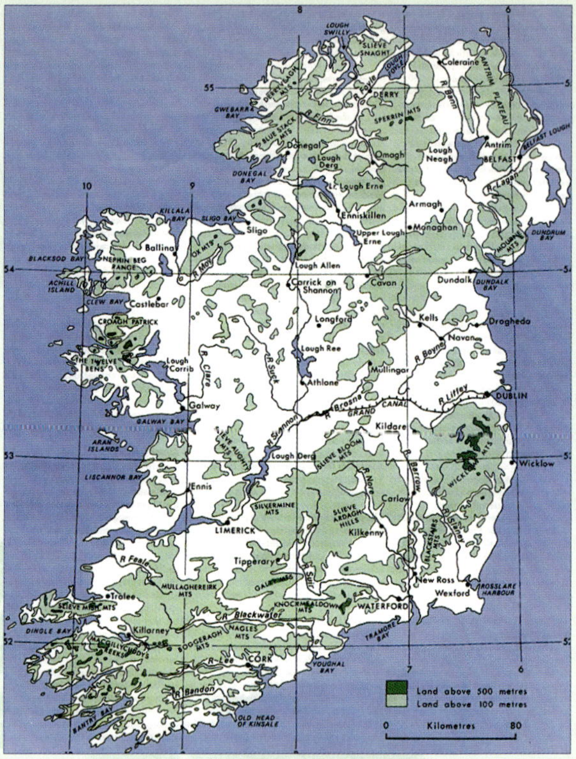

Ireland meets industrialisation

Irish Stew

Use a deep casserole to hold the layers of meat and vegetables, and allow for long slow cooking so that the liquid is thickened and enriched. Use a firm potato such as the Romano or Maris Piper varieties. (Serves 4)

- *700 g (1 1/2 lb) middle neck of lamb, cut into cutlets and trimmed*
- *2 medium onions, skinned and sliced*
- *450 g (1 lb) old potatoes, thinly sliced*
- *15 ml (1 tbsp) chopped fresh parsley*
- *5 ml (1 tsp) dried thyme*
- *salt and pepper*
- *chopped fresh parsley to garnish*

1. *Make layers of meat, vegetables, herbs and salt and pepper in a deep casserole, ending with a top layer of potato to make neat 'lid.'*
2. *Pour in 300 ml (1/2 pint) water and cover with greaseproof paper or foil and then the casserole lid. Bake at 170°C (325°F) mark 3 for about 2 hours or until the meat and vegetable are tender. Serve hot, garnished with parsley.*

Éire

A Singing Pub

President: Mary McAleese (1997)
Taoiseach (Prime Minister): Bertie Ahern (1997)
Area: 27,135 sq mi (70,280 sq km)
Population (2006 est.): 4,2 m (growth rate: 1.2%) [...] density per sq mi: 146
Capital (2003 est.): Dublin, 1,018,500
Other large cities: Cork, 193,400; Limerick, 84,900; Galway, 67,200
Monetary units: Euro (formerly Irish pound [punt])

A modern industrial estate

Languages: English, Irish Gaelic
Ethnicity/race: Celtic, English, Vikings, Scots
Religions: Roman Catholic 91.6%, Anglican 2.5%, other 5.9%
Literacy rate: 98% (1981 est.)
Economic summary: (2005 est.): GDP $167,9 bn; PPP per capita $34,100. Real growth rate: 2.1%. **Inflation:** 3.7%. **Unemployment:** 5%. **Arable land:** 19%. **Agriculture:** turnips, barley, potatoes, sugar beets, wheat; beef, dairy products. **Labor force:** 1.8 million (2001); agriculture 8%, industry 29%, services 64% (2002 est.).

Seamus Heaney

"Digging"

Between my finger and my thumb
The squat pen rests; snug as a gun.

Under my window, a clean rasping sound
When the spade sinks into gravelly ground:
My father, digging. I look down

Till his straining rump among the flowerbeds
Bends low, comes up twenty years away
Stooping in rhythm through potato drills
Where he was digging.

The coarse boot nestled on the lug, the shaft
Against the inside knee was levered firmly.
He rooted out tall tops, buried the bright edge deep
To scatter new potatoes that we picked
Loving their cool hardness in our hands.

By God, the old man could handle a spade.
Just like his old man.

My grandfather cut more turf in a day
Than any other man on Toner's bog.
Once I carried him milk in a bottle
Corked sloppily with paper. He straightened up
To drink it, then fell to right away
Nicking and slicing neatly, heaving sods
Over his shoulder, going down and down
For the good turf. Digging.

The cold smell of potato mould, the squelch and slap
Of soggy peat, the curt cuts of an edge
Through living roots awaken in my head.
But I've no spade to follow men like them.

Between my finger and my thumb
The squat pen rests.
I'll dig with it.

An Irishman's approach to a problem: Where the rest of the world would say – this problem is very serious, but not impossible... – the Irishman would say: "This is impossible but not very serious."

St. Kevin's Church (Glendalough)

"Here in Ireland we would have the best weather in the world – if the climate didn't spoil it."

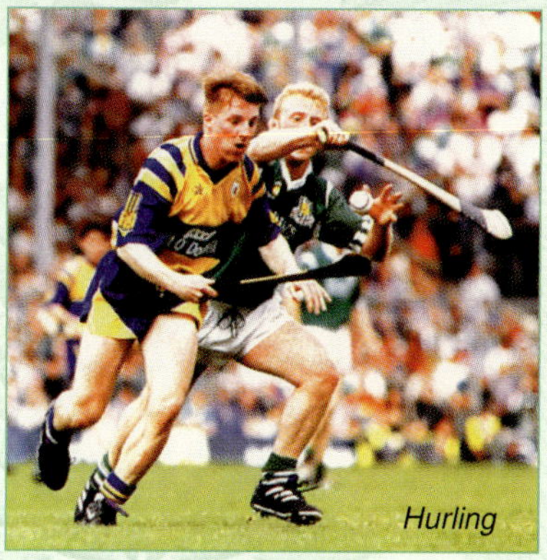
Hurling

YOU'LL NEVER PLOUGH A FIELD BY TURNING IT OVER IN YOUR MIND.

Cross of Muiredach

Makki Marseilles is an educational journalist in Athens, Greece. He was born in France in 1947, educated in Britain (Kingston College; London University; University of Birmingham) and started his career as an actor there. Later he turned to directing and to managing five regional theatres and the Astoria in London, before setting up his own company, Abbey Laird, at the Edinburgh Fringe Festival. Although he dabbled in journalism and public relations, his main love remained the theatre in all its forms. In 1985 Makki Marseilles went to Greece where he worked for *Athens News*; later he set up and for eight years edited *ELT News*, an English language newspaper. Today he is the Greek correspondent for the *Times Educational Supplement* and artistic director of the Rainbow Theatre in Athens. Makki Marseilles is married to Dublin-born Kim O'Neill, hence his deep love for Ireland and the Irish.

Vocabulary

5 hagiographer (n.): /ˌhægiˈɒgrəfə(r)‖hag- / a biographer who is too admiring or favourable towards his subject – **5 to lament** (v.): to express feelings of great sadness about s.th. – **5 seductive** (adj.): s.th. that is very interesting or attractive to you, in a way that persuades you to do s.th. you would not usually do – **12 vapour** (n.): a mass of small drops of a liquid which float in the air, for example because the liquid has been heated – **13 to lash** (v.): to hit against s.th. with violent force – **19 to beset** (v.): to make s.o. experience serious problems or dangers – **22 Latin American** (adj.): of the Spanish - or Portuguese-speaking countries of South and Central America (known as Latin America) – **23 to swell the ranks of s.th.** (v.): to increase the number of people in a particular situation – **25 aptly** (adv.): named, described, etc. in a way that seems very suitable – **29 legion** (adj.): very many – **29 to concoct** (v.): to invent a clever story, excuse or plan – **33 word slouch** (n.): /slaʊtʃ/ s.b. who does not say very much – **35 facility** (n.): a natural ability to do s.th. easily and well – **37 omphalos** (n.): /ˈɒmfəlɒs/ a rounded stone in Apollo's temple at Delphi, considered the centre of the world by the ancients – **39 beneficiary** (n.): /ˌbenəˈfɪʃəri‖-ˈfɪʃieri/ s.o. who gets advantages from an action or change – **40 recipient** (n.): s.o. who receives s.th. – **40 largesse** (n.): /lɑːˈʒes/ the quality or act of being generous and giving money or gifts to people who have less than you – **46 bulk** (n.): a big mass of s.th. – **47 reputedly** (adv.): according to what most people say or think – **49 portico** (n.): a covered entrance to a building, consisting of a roof supported by pillars – **54 costermonger** (n.): /ˈkɒstəˌmʌŋgə‖ˈkɑːstərˌmɑŋər/ s.o. who sells fruit and vegetables in the street – **66 metaphysical** (adj.): used to describe a complicated arrangement of words and ideas – **80 to gut** (v.): to completely destroy the inside of a building, esp. by fire – **83 the gift of the gab**: an ability to speak confidently and to persuade people to do what you want – **86 irreverent** (adj.): having a lack of respect for organizations, customs, beliefs, etc. – **90 to sustain** (v.): to make s.th. continue to exist over a period of time – **90 to distort** (v.): to explain a fact, statement, idea, etc. in a way that changes its real meaning – **91 endeavour** (n.): an attempt or effort, esp. to do s.th. new or difficult

Explanations

Intro/1 céad míle fáilte: /ˈkeɪd miːl ˈfɔːltɪ/ Irish for "a hundred thousand welcomes" – **Intro/2 *Treasure Island***: a novel written by Robert Louis Stevenson (1850–94) – **4 Edmund Spenser**: (?1552–99) an English poet, famous for his epic poem *The Faerie Queene*, which he never finished – **4 Queen Elizabeth I**: (1533–1603) a queen of England, daughter of Henry VIII. She never married, and is thought of as a very strong woman. While she was Queen, Catholics were persecuted and Protestants looked on favourably, the Spanish Armada was defeated, and Mary Queen of Scots was executed; England became very powerful under her control. – **25 McAlpine's fusiliers**: /məˈkælpaɪnz ˈfjuːzəlɪəz/ McAlpine is one of the largest construction firms in Britain and Europe; as many Irish have worked for that company, Dominic Behan has written a song with the above title about the Irish men on the building sites. – **33 Brendan Behan**: /ˈbiːən/ (1923–64) an Irish writer who wrote about his experience of being in prison for IRA activities in plays such as *The Quare Fellow* and in his autobiography *Borstal Boy* – **46 Gothic**: of or in a style of building common in Western Europe between the 12th and 16th centuries, with pointed arches, tall pillars, and windows with tall thin coloured glass in them – **46 Trinity College**: founded by Elizabeth I in 1591 as a Protestant university – **47 O'Connell Bridge**: Daniel O'Connell (1775–1847) was an Irish politician who forced the government to give rights to Roman Catholics. – **49 1916 Irish rising**: on 24 April 1916 armed fighting broke out in Dublin against British rule in Ireland. After six days the revolutionaries had to surrender. – **49 Doric**: in the oldest and most simple of the Greek building styles – **49 Pro-Cathedral**: St. Mary's Pro-Cathedral was built between 1815 and 1825 modelled after the Theseus temple in Athens. – **50 Renaissance**: the period between the 14th and 17th centuries, when the art, literature, and ideas of ancient Greece were discovered again and widely studied, causing a rebirth of interest and activity in Europe – **51 Gate Theatre**: shows mainly contemporary theatre plays – **51 Michael MacLiammoir**: /mkˈliːmɔː/ manager and main actor of the Gate Theatre during the 1960s, 70s, and 80s – **52 Orson Welles**: (1915–85) an American actor, director, and producer, whose famous works include his radio production of *The War of the Worlds* and his film *Citizen Kane* – **53 Covent Garden**: an area of London once famous for its fruit and vegetable market, now replaced by expensive but popular shops, eating places, etc. – **55 James Joyce**: (1882–1941) an Irish writer who greatly influenced the way English novels were written, with his use of unusual and invented words and different styles of writing and narrative perspective. His novels include *Ulysses* and *Finnegan's Wake*. – **60 Molly Malone**: a famous Dublin character, well-known from the song *In Dublin's Fair City* – **63 Oscar Wilde**: (1854–1900) an Irish writer best known for his play *The Impor-*

tance of Being Earnest and his novel *The Picture of Dorian Gray.* Many of the clever and funny things he said in conversations are still famous. He was sent to prison for two years because he was a homosexual and this was not allowed in Britain at that time. – **63 W. B. Yeats**: /jeɪts/ (1865–1939) an Irish poet, considered to be one of the most important Irish writers. He also wrote stories and plays and was active in Irish politics. – **64 George Bernard Shaw**: (1856–1950) an Irish writer and critic, famous for his writings on Socialism and for his clever plays which point out faults in moral attitudes and in society. His best-known play is *Pygmalion.* – **64 Samuel Beckett**: (1906–89) an Irish writer of plays, books and poetry, who lived in France and is best known for his play *Waiting for Godot.* – **64 Sean O'Casey**: /ʃɔːn əʊ'keisi/ (1880–1964) an Irish playwright. His plays *The Shadow of a Gunman, Juno and the Paycock* and *The Plough and the Stars* all convey the tense atmosphere of the armed fighting and the revolutionary times of the Dublin in which he lived at the beginning of the 20th century. – **66 Jonathan Swift**: (1667–1745) an Irish satirical writer and cleric, who wrote *Gulliver's Travels* as well as many shorter works attacking corruption in religion and education – **67 Oliver Goldsmith**: (1728–74) an Irish poet and writer of books and plays. His works include the book *The Vicar of Wakefield* and the play *She Stoops to Conquer.* – **67 Richard Brinsley Sheridan**: (1751–1816) an English politician and writer of plays, born in Dublin. He is famous for his comedies *The Rivals* and *The School for Scandal,* which gently criticize the society of his time. – **68 Abbey Theatre**: a theatre situated in Dublin's Abbey Street, the centre of the Irish dramatic movement initiated by Lady Gregory and W. B. Yeats. Best known for its productions of Synge and of the early plays of O'Casey, the Abbey was a major theatrical venue throughout the first 30 years of the 20th century. The present theatre was opened in 1966, after the earlier building had burnt down in 1951. – **69 Celtic Dawn**: also Celtic Revival or Irish Literary Renaissance, a literary movement in Ireland during the 19th century that drew inspiration from Celtic-Irish sources – **69 Lady Gregory**: (1852–1932) an Irish dramatist, folklorist, and translator – **69 Maude Gonne**: /'mɔːd 'gʌn/ (1866–1953) a woman whom W. B. Yeats was in love with for many years. Yeats wrote his drama *The Countess Cathleen* for her. – **70 Anne Horniman**: (1860–1937) the founding patron of the Abbey Theatre – **77 Connemara**: /kɒnə'mɑːrə/ a mountainous region in West Galway county, famous for its rocky coastline, the so-called Twelve Bens, its peat bogs and numerous lakes – **77–78 Mayo** /'meɪəʊ/, **Sligo** /'slaɪgəʊ/, **Donegal** /dɒnə'gɔːl/, **Clare**, **Kerry**: counties in the West of the Republic of Ireland – **78 Cork**: the largest county in the South of the Irish Republic – **82 Blarney Stone**: a stone in the wall of Blarney Castle, near Blarney, a small village in Cork county, which is supposed to bring good luck and skill in flattery to people who kiss it – **98 EEC**: former name of EU – **109 Emerald Isle**: Ireland, so called because of the greenness of its countryside

Collage – What's what called?

Éire: /'eərə/ Irish (Gaelic) for "Ireland"

Gaelic: /'geɪlɪk/ any of the Celtic languages, esp. that of Scotland, or those of Ireland and the Isle of Man. Gaelic is still spoken in some parts of Scotland and Ireland but by fewer and fewer people.

Irish Stew

stew (n.): a dish consisting usually of meat and vegetables cooked together in liquid – **herb** (n.): any of several kinds of small plant which are used to improve the taste of food or to make medicine – **ingredient** (n.): any of the things that are formed into a mixture when making s.th., esp. in cooking – **casserole** (n.): a deep usually covered dish in which food can be cooked and served – **lb**: pound, equal to 453,6 g – **to trim** (v.): to make neat, even, or tidy by cutting or removing unwanted parts – **to chop** (v.): to cut into small pieces – **parsley** (n.): a small plant (herb) with curly strong-tasting leaves, grown in gardens and used in cooking or as a decoration on food – **thyme** (n.): /taim/ a plant used for giving food a special taste – **to garnish** (v.): to decorate food – **greaseproof paper** (n.): waxed paper; a type of paper which grease or oil cannot pass through – **foil** (n.): metal beaten or rolled into very thin paperlike sheets – **tender** (adj.): easy to bite through; soft

Éire

Celtic (adj.): relating to the Celts or their languages – **Anglican** (n.): a Christian who is a member of the Church of England or related churches – **literacy** (n.): the state of being able to read and write – **GDP** (gross domestic product): the total value of all goods and services produced in a country, in one year, except for income received from abroad – **PPP per capita** is a way of expressing income per head in a country in order to make fair comparisons between standards of living in different countries possible. PPP (Purchasing Power Parity) does this by eliminating differences in price levels between countries in the process of currency conversion. – **billion** (AE): thousand millions (BE) – **per capita**: used to describe the average amount of something in a particular place, calculated according to the number of people who live there – **arable** (adj.): relating to growing crops – **turnip** (n.): a large round pale yellow vegetable that grows under the ground, or the plant that produces it – **barley** (n.): a plant that produces a grain used for making food or alcohol

Seamus Heaney, "Digging"

Seamus Heaney: /'ʃeiməs hiːni/ (1939–) an Irish poet; his collections of poems include *Death of a Naturalist* and *North,* in which he reflects upon the troubles in Northern Ireland. In 1995 he was awarded the Nobel Prize for Literature. – **2 squat** (adj.): unattractively short and thick or low and wide – **2 snug** (adj.): usually s.th. small, warm, and comfortable that makes you feel protected – **3 to rasp** (v.): to make a rough unpleasant sound, like that of two surfaces rubbing together – **4 gravelly** (adj.): covered with or containing a mixture of small stones with sand – **6 rump** (n.): (humor.) the part of your body that you sit on – **8 to stoop** (v.): to bend your body forwards and down – **8 potato drills** (n.): rows of potatoes – **10 to nestle** (v.): to move into a comfortable position – **10 lug** (n.): a part of s.th. that sticks out and can be used as a support; here: where you put your foot on when using a spade - **12 top** (n.): the leaves of a plant whose root you can eat - **18 bog** (n.): an area of wet muddy ground that you can sink into - **21 to fall to doing s.th.**: to start doing s.th. - **22 to nick** (v.): to make a small cut in the surface or edge of s.th. - **22 sod** (n.): a piece of earth or the layer of earth with grass and roots growing in it - **25 mould** (n.): loose, soft, easily worked soil, esp. good for growing plants - **25 squelch** (n.): the sucking sound made by walking in soft wet mud - **25 slap** (n.): a sound like s.o. being slapped in the face - **26 soggy** (adj.): unpleasantly wet and soft - **26 peat** (n.): a substance formed from decaying plants which can be burned instead of coal - **26 curt** (adj.): short or brusque

Irish Writers

The writers on the paintings are: W. B. Yeats, George Bernard Shaw, James Joyce, Seamus Heaney

Glendalough /'glendəlɒk/, Co. Wicklow

founded in the 6th century; most important religious centre in Ireland in the 8th century. The most prominent sight, the Round Tower, was built for the protection of the monks.

The Cross of Muiredach /'mjuːrdək/

in Monasterboice /ˌmɒnəstə'bɔɪs/, Co. Louth /'kaʊntɪ 'laʊð/, 9th century A.D.; Ireland's most beautiful High Cross. It shows 22 biblical scenes.

Rock of Cashel

Co. Tipperary, a fine example of Irish Romanesque architecture; centre of religious and secular power

Awareness

1 Look at the photos in the collage. What do you associate with them?
2 Ireland is often poetically called the Emerald Isle. What does that bring to mind? Do the photos convey this idea?

Comprehension

3 What is a common misconception about Ireland? What does the author say about this?
4 Why is Dublin a city with a "magic spell" (l. 45)?
5 Why would young people in Ireland formerly have looked "towards London, New York, Christchurch", etc. (l. 107) and what might keep them in their own country today?

Analysis

6 Analyse Marseilles' definition of the "essence of Irishness" (l. 85) and consider its implications critically.
7 What attitude does the author assume towards Ireland and how does he convey it to his readers? Consider, for example, the choice of words (Reference Library, p. 311) or his technique of including the reader.
8 Look at the collage and read Nobel Prize winner Seamus Heaney's poem "Digging" carefully.
a) Analyse the imagery (Reference Library, p. 311) that appears in the poem. What is its effect on the reader?
b) List and group the stylistic means such as diction, syntax or rhetorical devices the poet employs (Reference Library, p. 311). What is their function?
c) Explain the poet's choice of title.
d) How does Seamus Heaney see his position as a writer within the Irish tradition?
9 On the basis of the information given in the text, the photos and the collage, try to give a general picture of Ireland. You can use these headings: landscape, people, history, art/literature.

Opinion

10 Compile a list of arguments why or why not you prefer Ireland to other European countries.
11 What kind of food do you like? Do you prefer simple but wholesome food or are you more of a gourmet? What arguments can be put for or against either of these ways of enjoying food? Would you give Irish Stew a try? What typical dishes are there in your country?

Projects

12 Find out from suitable sources what the harp, the shamrock and the colours of the tricolour (the Irish national flag) have to do with Ireland (see illustration on p. 114).
13 Collect information about Ireland in general and about special places like Dublin or the West coast counties, and prepare a classroom exhibition about Ireland.

Internet Projects

14 Form groups and, via the Internet, try to "visit" the places mentioned in the text to find out more about them. Use any international search engine, preferably www.searchboxland.com/Ireland-search/. In the same way collect information about the people mentioned in the text. Reorganize your findings and make an information bazaar in your classroom.

2 Cragie Hills

The Great Famine forced millions of people to leave their homeland and emigrate, mainly to the United States. Because of the death toll of the famine years and emigration, the years between 1845 and 1858 saw a decline in the Irish population from eight million to four million. Emigration is an on-going process in Ireland and there are by far more people of Irish origin living elsewhere in the world than in Ireland itself. In many emigration songs this fate has been deplored, often combined with the promise to come back to "Paddy's Green Shamrock Shore". – The song is taken from Dolores Keane's CD *Farewell to Eirinn* (Ebergötzen: Wundertüte Musik, 1988).

It being in spring when the small birds were singing,
Down by the shady harbour I carelessly did stray,
Where the trushes they were warbling, the violets were charming,
To hear the fond lovers talking while I did delay.

She said, my dear, don't leave me for another season,
If fortune does seem pleasing, I'll go along with you,
I'll forsake friends and relations, I'll quit this Irish nation,
And to the bonny Bann Isles forever I'll bid adieu.

He said my dear don't grieve me, or you'll annoy my patience,
You know I love you dearly the more I'm going away,
I'm going to a foreign nation, to purchace a plantation,
To comfort us hereafter all in Amerikay.

Then after a short while if fortune does seem pleasing,
T'will cause you for to smile at our late going away,
We'll be happy as Queen Victoria all in her greatest glory,
We'll be drinking wine and porter all in Amerikay.

The landlords and their agents, their books and their bailifs,
the lands of our forefathers were forced for to give o'er,
Now we're sailing on the ocean, for honour and promotion,
And parting with our sweethearts its them we do adore.

If you were in your bed lying and thinking upon dying,
One sight of bonny Bann banks, your sorrow would give o'er,
Or if you were one hour down in yon shady bower,
Pleasure would surround you, you'd think on death no more.

Then fare-you-well sweet Cragie Hills where often times I roved,
I never thought in my youthful days, I'd part you any more,
Now we're sailing on the ocean, for honour and promotion,
While the bonny boats are sailing, down by Doon's shore.

It is in their songs and ballads that the Irish have kept their history alive. In general, singing and dancing can be heard and seen all over the country at music festivals and in so-called 'singing pubs'. Walking through the streets of Dublin, you may happen to hear the lively sound of the tin-whistle just around the next corner. All this is a strong reminder of Ireland's Celtic heritage, which is also symbolised in the heraldic harp found in the coat of arms of the Republic of Ireland. To a large extent, Irish music is folk music, but Irish rock-music has also been made world-famous by, e.g., U2 or Sinéad O'Connor. *Cragie Hills* is a traditional folk song arranged and adapted by **Dolores Keane**, an Irish folksinger specialising in emigration songs. Her singing style comes from her family who are from Caherlistrane in Co. Galway. She learned many of her songs from her aunts, Rita and Sarah Keane.

Info

Eviction

In 1847, at the height of the famine, the British government under Lord John Russell passed the Poor Law Extension Act which was intended to reduce government expenditure on famine relief. It put the burden of paying for relief on to the Irish landlords. Apart from other aggravating changes to the worse for the poor Irish peasantry under the new legislation, rising poverty among Irish tenants made it more and more impossible for them to pay their rent to the landlords. Faced with the prospect of paying local property taxes for hundreds of impoverished tenants and, in the end, ruin, many landowners turned to the expulsion of smaller tenants in order to consolidate their land and to make it profitable. These evictions, as they came to be known, often went along with the destruction of the former tenants' cottages to keep other impoverished people from occupying them. Perhaps the most well-known because most aggravating case was reported from the village of Mullaroghe on the peninsula of Belmullet, where 102 families were evicted by their landlord, a certain Mr Walshe, shortly before Christmas and their cottages pulled down.

Vocabulary

Intro: death toll (n.): the total number of people who die in a particular accident, war, etc. – **2 to stray** (v.): to wander away, esp. from the right path or place – **3 trush** (n.): (BrE) thrush (n.): a singing bird with a brownish back and spotted breast – **3 to warble** (v.): /ˈwɔːbəl‖wɔːr-/ (esp. of a bird) to sing with a clear, continuous, yet varied note – **3 violet** (n.): a small plant with sweet-smelling dark purplish-blue flowers – **4 to delay** (v.): to move or take action slowly, esp. on purpose – **7 to forsake** (v.): to desert; leave forever – **8 bonny** (adj.): (esp. Scottish) pretty and healthy – **9 to grieve s.b.** (v.): to cause grief; to make very unhappy – **9 to annoy one's patience**: to make s.b. lose his patience – **9 patience** (n.): the ability to accept pain, trouble, or anything that causes annoyance, without complaining or losing one's self-control – **11 to purchace** (v.): to purchase: to buy – **11 plantation** (n.): a large piece of land, on which crops such as tea, cotton, sugar, or rubber are grown – **14 T'will**: It will – **17 landlord** (n.): a man from whom s.b. rents a room, a building, or land – **17 bailif** (n.): bailiff: 1. (in British law) an official who takes possession of goods or property when money is owed; 2. a person who looks after a farm or land for the owner – **19 promotion** (n.): advancement in rank or position – **20 its**: it is – **25 to rove** (v.): to wander; move continually (around)

Explanations

Title: Cragie Hills: geographical name: Cregagh /ˈkreɪɡɪ/ Hills, south of Belfast Lough /lɒk‖lɒx/, a long narrow bay east of Belfast in Northern Ireland – **Intro: "Paddy's Green Shamrock Shore"**: a traditional Irish emigration folk song – **8 Bann**: main river in Northern Ireland – **15 Queen Victoria**: (1819–1901) queen of Great Britain and Ireland, empress of India. Her rule was the longest in British history. It saw the expansion of the British Empire and also the Industrial Revolution. She was married to Prince Albert and had nine children. – **16 porter**: a dark brown bitter beer – **28 Doon**: /duːn/ the Co. Down in Northern Ireland

Info

Emigration

Because of the poverty of the land and for political reasons the Irish started very early to leave their country for a better life. Large-scale emigration began in the 17th century, when America promised the fulfilment of this wish. The Great Famine of the 1840s caused emigration to increase rapidly. In those years about 1 million people are believed to have left Ireland, most of them for America. Emigration, not only to the U.S.A., continued throughout the rest of the century at a high rate. Today, many millions of Americans claim Irish descent.

Emigrants leaving Cobh for America

Awareness

1 What kind of music do you like? Does it include folk music? Say why it does or does not.

2 Have you ever been to an Irish or a Scottish folk festival? If so, tell your group or class about it. Together compare it with a folk festival in your own country. Explain the differences between them.

Comprehension

3 Why does the singer suddenly "delay" (l. 4)?

4 Where does the event take place?

5 What, briefly, do the two lovers talk about?

6 What promises does the "He" make to win the girl over?

7 Explain the girl's situation.

Analysis

8 Examine the use of tenses (Reference Library, pp. 314f.) in the part of the "He". What do these tenses express?

9 What background information do we get about the time in which the two lovers live? Look at the extra information on eviction (p. 122) to find out what the "He" is referring to in the first two lines of the fifth stanza.

Opinion

10 Emigration, especially to the United States, has always been an option for the Irish. Why might someone want to leave their country? Name some reasons the Irish might have had. What feelings might they have had?

11 If you were faced with a lack of job opportunities, pollution problems or an increase in population density in your country, would you decide to emigrate? Why? Why not?

12 Irish history is kept alive in Irish folksongs. Should music-making only be good entertainment or should it convey a message? Give reasons for your answer. Consider the following statement by Irish singer Sinéad O'Connor: "As artists [...] I believe that our function is to express the feelings of the human race – always to speak the truth, and never to keep it hidden, even though we are operating in a world which does not like the sound of truth. I believe that our purpose is to inspire and in some way guide and heal the human race of which we are all equal members." Sinéad O'Connor in *Newsweek*, 25 February 1991, p. 46.

Projects

13 Take a sad or wonderful event in your life and write a song or poem about it, putting your feelings into it.

14 Find out about the fate of Irish immigrants in the New World, for example from other Irish folk songs (like "Edward Connors" sung by Andy Irvine).

Internet Projects

15 Find out via the Internet about the so-called "Irish Diaspora". What is its purpose and what do the people involved in it have to do with Ireland?

16 Use any American search engine such as altavista.com, yahoo.com or northernlight.com and collect information about Irish influence in Boston, Mass. or New York City. How or where does it show?

3 "No More Terror?"

The news of 31 August 1994, the day of the IRA ceasefire statement, lifted the spirits of everyone in Northern Ireland and raised the hopes of the world that another trouble spot might at last find peace. – *Belfast Telegraph,* 31 August 1994, p. 10.

Sixth

Belfast Telegraph

Wednesday, August 31, 1994 124th Year *The National Newspaper of Nothern Ireland* Price 26p (36p Eire)

COUNTDOWN TO CEASEFIRE **Special Section inside**

After 3,168 deaths and 25 years of terror, the IRA says...

IT'S OVER

No more terror?

Looking ahead: *The hope we must all cling to*

Today could be one of the most significant days in the history of Northern Ireland – if not the island of Ireland. It could be the day when the Provisional IRA announced that after nearly 25 years they were abandoning politically-motivated murder and mayhem in favour of politics, pure and simple. Or it could be another false dawn, to add to all the rest. [...]

Belfast Telegraph, "Viewpoint", 31 August 1994, p.10.

Vocabulary

Intro: ceasefire (n.): an agreement to stop fighting for a period of time, esp. so that a more permanent agreement can be made - **6 to abandon** (v.): to decide that you no longer believe in a particular idea or principle - **7 mayhem** (n.): an extremely confused situation in which people are very frightened or excited; chaos - **8 a false dawn**: s.th. that seems positive or hopeful but really is not

Explanations

Intro: *Belfast Telegraph*: a Belfast daily newspaper - **5 Provisional IRA**: a group within the IRA that uses violence and terrorism to achieve its aim of a united Ireland. It is separate from the official IRA.

Awareness

1 Imagine you are a non-militant/ militant/ Protestant/ Catholic citizen of Belfast. Describe your feelings after reading this headline from the *Belfast Telegraph*.

Analysis

2 How did the *Belfast Telegraph* news staff manage to capture the historical importance of the event on their front page?

3 What is the author's position as expressed in the "Viewpoint" section?

Opinion

4 a) Is there any justification for the use of violence as a means of achieving political ends? What makes people use violence?

b) It is often stated that the history of humankind is the history of battles and bloodshed. Do you agree (Reference Library, p. 306) with this statement? Justify your answer.

5 Attack and counterattack, hopes raised and hopes dashed – what do you think prevents people from leaving Belfast or Northern Ireland or what motivates them to stay? What would you do if you lived in a troubled area like this?

Project

6 Try to establish contact with a school in Northern Ireland either via an Internet home page or email or write to the Belfast school authorities to help you with an address. Carry out together a project about living in a Northern Irish and a German community. This may include the exchange of information and its analysis by comparing the personal situation of the students and also the political, social, economic and cultural background of the two communities. If possible, exchange ideas about how things may be changed in Northern Ireland.

Internet Project

7 Collect information on the Internet about the situation in Northern Ireland in the aftermath of the ceasefire the IRA announced in 1994. What has happened since then? Make a timeline to show the various steps in the Irish Peace Process.

4 A Farewell to Arms? From Long War to Uncertain Peace in Northern Ireland*

The Agreement of 1998 has sparked hope that a lasting peace might finally come to Northern Ireland. Yet, doubts, objections, manoeuvring, delaying, evasiveness, misinterpretations of the Agreement by the different parties involved in it and above all the tentative decommissioning of IRA weapons have been formidable obstacles on the road to peace. The bestselling book which refers in its title to the famous Hemingway novel *A Farewell to Arms* gives the reader a profound insight into the after-Agreement situation and is an excellent in depth study of the highly complex Northern Ireland peace process. The extract has been taken from the Introduction. - Michael Cox, Adrian Guelke and Fiona Stephen (eds.), *A farewell to arms? From 'long war' to long peace in Northern Ireland* (Manchester: Manchester University Press, 2000), pp. 1f.

All wars, we are told, must one day come to an end. However, the pace at which they do so may be agonisingly slow, especially when there is no obvious winner or loser, and particularly so in a society as deeply divided as Northern Ireland where the quarrel, to paraphrase Winston Churchill, appears to have lost none of its original integrity. And there has been no peace process so long in gestation as the one in Northern Ireland. Indeed, so tentative has the process been at times, that the more cynical might conclude that many within the North either did not care for the peace or had become so used to the conflict that they preferred its certainties to the uncertainty of the new world order awaiting them round the corner. This might seem unfair, and no doubt some of those on the ground would argue that the real obstacle to peace was not the people of Ireland but certain politicians and parties at Westminster. There is some truth in this, but there is still something we should never forget about the struggle for peace in the North: it happened not because the different protagonists were necessarily convinced that harmony was preferable to conflict, but rather because they were finally impelled to the rather unpalatable conclusion that they could no longer go on pursuing their mutually incompatible objectives by means of armed violence or by repeating the time-honoured slogan of 'no surrender'. It would be comforting to report that there had been a meeting of minds; that peace was the natural result of a rapid growth of that most valuable piece of scarce political real estate – the middle ground. But it did not happen like that and it would be dishonest to assume that it did. There was no Road to Damascus conversion to the other side's point of view, no sudden outbreak of moderation, but a long and very painful, and as yet incomplete, recognition that the old means of achieving desired ends either would not work or were no longer acceptable to those upon whom the opposing camps depended for support. This is why the various parts of the jigsaw puzzle called the Irish peace process have taken so long to fit into place, and why many still feel that the process itself is either an illusion or a mere interlude – an inter-war period if you like – that will one day give way to yet another cycle of hostilities until one of the two sides finally triumphs and the other concedes defeat.

This rather tough-minded assessment will no doubt shock liberal sensibilities and those who feel that peace is somehow more natural than war, discussion more productive than the threat of violence, and intransigence less likely to achieve one's aims and objectives than accommodation. However, the Irish Question has never been one with which liberal moderates have ever felt particularly comfortable, or to which they have ever provided particularly insightful answers – or at least answers to which the different peoples of Ireland have ever listened with very much interest or enthusiasm. This is no criticism of the people or even of liberals. It is simply a statement of the obvious, and a recognition that when peace did finally come to Ireland it did so for perhaps the least idealistic of motives. Moreover, when it came, it surprised nearly all of the so-called experts. In fact, most seasoned observers of the Irish scene believed there would never be a peace process in the first place, not because it was wrong in principle, but because there was little if any chance of it happening. It is easy to forget now, but we do need to remind ourselves, that back in the early 1990s the wise money was not on peace but a on a continuation of what the IRA had come to term the 'long war'. The idea that within a few years there would be a cessation of serious military violence, that some time on there would be an agreed settlement, and that within eighteen months of that Unionists might even contemplate the idea of sitting around the same table with republicans, would have been regarded as mere fantasy. That there remained obstacles to peace was obvious: but we should not forget how far the process has come and how few had earlier anticipated it.

Vocabulary

Intro/1 to spark (v.): to make someone feel interested, hopeful etc. – **Intro/2 evasiveness** (n.): not willing to answer questions directly – **Intro/3 tentative** (adj.): not definite or certain, and may be changed later – **to decommission** (v.): to stop using a ship, weapon, or nuclear reactor and to take it to pieces – **Intro/4 formidable** (adj.): very powerful or impressive, and often frightening – **Intro/6 in-depth** (adj.): thorough, complete, and considering all the details – **3 agonising** (adj.): extremely painful – **7 integrity** (n.): the quality of being honest and strong about what you believe to be right – **8 gestation** (n.): the process by which a new idea, piece of work etc. is developed, or the period of time when this happens – **23 unpalatable** (adj.): an unpalatable fact or idea is very unpleasant and difficult to accept – **30 real estate** (n.): property in the form of land or houses – **32 conversion** (n.): when someone changes from one religion or belief to a different one – **39 jigsaw puzzle** (n.): a picture cut up into many pieces that you try to fit together – **45 to concede** (v.): to admit that you are not going to win a game, argument, battle etc. – **46 assessment** (n.): a process in which you make a judgment about a person or situation, or the judgment you make – **49 intransigence** (n.): state of being unwilling to change your ideas or behaviour, in a way that seems unreasonable – **51 accommodation** (n.): an agreement between people or groups who have different views or opinions, that satisfies everyone – **62 seasoned** (adj.): used to describe someone who has a lot of experience of a particular thing

Explanations

Intro/5 Ernest Hemingway: (1899–1961) one of the great US writers of the 20th century, who won the Nobel prize for literature in 1954. He wrote many novels and short stories in a simple and direct style. His novels include *A Farewell to Arms, For Whom the Bell Tolls*, and *The Old Man and the Sea*. He died by shooting himself. – **32 Road to Damascus**: a situation in which someone experiences a sudden and complete change in their opinions or beliefs. The phrase is based on the story in the New Testament, in which St Paul, a soldier trying to prevent Christianity from spreading, saw a blinding light and heard God's voice while he was travelling on the road to Damascus. He immediately became a Christian.

Awareness

1 Have you ever asked yourself why people cannot live peacefully together? List ten reasons why people may be hostile to others. You may look at your family, neighbours or at world politics.

Comprehension

2 What did the different protagonists have to accept about the struggle for peace?
3 What was the "wise money" on in the early 1990s and what has happened since?

Analysis

4 Why can the Irish peace process be compared to a "jigsaw puzzle"?
5 Explain the sceptical attitude of many people towards the peace process (end 2nd paragraph).
6 Put down the main ideas of this article in a flow chart.
7 Analyse the style (Reference Library, p. 311) and tone (Reference Library, p. 312) used by the authors. What type of reader does the extract address?

Opinion

8 After reading this extract do you think that peace will have a chance in Northern Ireland?

Project

9 Study Ernest Hemingway's novel *A Farewell to Arms* and compare the situation depicted there to the situation in Northern Ireland. Why have the authors referred to this title?

Internet Project

10 Go to the Bloody Sunday Inquiry website www.bloody-sunday-inquiry.org and study their work. Do you consider this investigation to be a step forward in the peace process or not? Give reasons.

8 Ethnic Diversity in the UK

At Uphall primary school in Ilford, East London, pupils speak 52 different home languages. The 28 children in the picture speak 23 different languages. "It's like a micro world," says head teacher Andrew Morrish. "We have got children from all corners of the globe." One in three of the children at the school come from a Pakistani background, but the cultures represented also include eastern European, Chinese, Afro-Caribbean, Russian and African. Despite these varied ethnic backgrounds, the school has recently been praised by the school inspectors: "The inspectors judge this to be an outstanding school ... Standards are rising and pupils achieve well, in spite of the fact that almost all have English as an additional language." (reported in *The Independent*, 26 July 2006)

Ashim Rehman, 11, has attended Uphall primary school for seven years. "I've got lots of friends there. We speak Urdu at home all the time, but I was born here and don't need any special help with English."

Irma Kliucininkaite, 11, was born in Lithuania and came to Britain aged three with her parents and baby brother. "When I first started at the school they took me into a class with other children who spoke all different languages and who couldn't speak English. Once I could speak a bit more I went back to the general class and got books that helped me learn English as well."

Eliana Jesus, 11, speaks Portuguese, French and English. She was born in Portugal to a Portuguese mother and an African father but the family came to Britain when she was a toddler. "My friends at school come from lots of different countries in Africa and India."

Pranav Patel, 10, speaks fluent Gujurati and English. His parents came from India but Pranav was born in the UK. "All the children in my class speak English but lots speak other languages at home. I speak Gujurati if I'm talking to my auntie or my grandma but when I talk to my sisters or my mum and dad I speak English. I'm from India – well, I was born here, I'm English – but I'm from India as well."

Difference and Identity

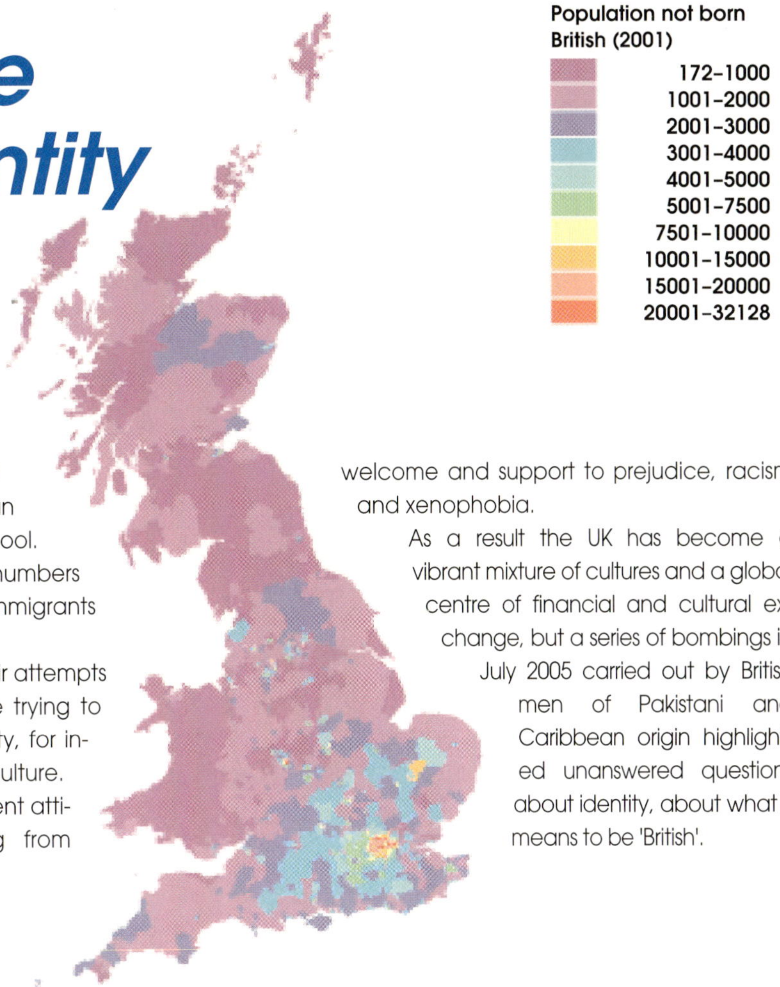

The United Kingdom is a country of increasing ethnic diversity, as can be seen from the example of this school. Since the Second World War large numbers of people have entered the UK as immigrants or to seek asylum.

They have faced challenges in their attempts to integrate into British society while trying to preserve aspects of their own identity, for instance their language, religion and culture.

They have also experienced different attitudes from British society ranging from welcome and support to prejudice, racism and xenophobia.

As a result the UK has become a vibrant mixture of cultures and a global centre of financial and cultural exchange, but a series of bombings in July 2005 carried out by British men of Pakistani and Caribbean origin highlighted unanswered questions about identity, about what it means to be 'British'.

I want my children to go to a school where at our summer fair today the International Food Stall will sell, at a modest guess, the cuisine of 20 different countries. London can and does hold within it a diversity which astounds even visiting Americans – that melting-pot nation of immigrants ... And since our children will grow up in a global economy, it is better they get used to it now.

(Janice Turner, The Times, *9 July 2005)*

1

Sam Selvon

"Moses in London"*

Sam Selvon (1923–1994) was born in Trinidad, but his ancestors had been brought to the Caribbean from India by the British to work on the sugar plantations after the abolition of slavery. He lived in London from 1950 until 1978. In his novel *The Lonely Londoners* he describes the experiences of the West Indian immigrants to Britain in the 1950s, who responded to British requests for labour from its former colonies. The narrator's use of West Indian dialect adds an element of authenticity to his story. – Sam Selvon, *The Lonely Londoners* (London: Alan Wingate, 1956), pp. 7ff.

One grim winter evening, when it had a kind of unrealness about London, with a fog sleeping restlessly over the city and the lights showing in the blur as if is not London at all but some strange place on another planet, Moses Aloetta hop on a number 46 bus at the corner of Chepstow Road and Westbourne Grove to go to Waterloo to meet a fellar who was coming from Trinidad on the boat-train.

When Moses sit down and pay his fare he take out a white handkerchief and blow his nose. The handkerchief turn black and Moses watch it and curse the fog. He wasn't in a good mood and the fog wasn't doing anything to help the situation. He had to get up from a nice warm bed and dress and come out in this nasty weather to go and meet a fellar that he didn't even know. That was the hurtful part of it – is not as if this fellar is his brother or cousin or even friend; he don't know the man from Adam. But he get a letter from a friend in Trinidad who say that this fellar coming by the ss Hildebrand, and if he could please meet him at the station in London, and help him until he get settled. The fellar name Henry Oliver, but the friend tell Moses not to worry that he describe Moses to Henry, and all he have to do is to be at the station when the boat-train pull in and this fellar Henry would find him. So for old time sake Moses find himself on the bus going to Waterloo, vex with himself that his heart so soft that he always doing something for somebody and nobody ever doing anything for him.

Because it look to Moses that he hardly have time to settle in the old Brit'n before all sorts of fellars start coming straight to his room in the Water when they land up in London from the West Indies, saying that so and so tell them that Moses is a good fellar to contact, that he would help them to get place to stay and work to do.

"Jesus Christ," Moses tell Harris, a friend he have, "I never see thing so. I don't know these people at all, yet they coming to me as if I is some liaison officer, and I catching my arse as it is, how I could help them out?"

And this sort of thing was happening at a time when the English people starting to make rab about how too much West Indians coming to the country: this was a time, when any corner you turn, is ten to one you bound to bounce up a spade.

In fact, the boys all over London, it ain't have a place where you wouldn't find them, and big discussion going on in Parliament about the situation, though the old Brit'n too diplomatic to clamp down on the boys or to do anything drastic like stop them coming to the Mother Country. But big headlines in the papers every day, and whatever the newspaper and the radio say in this country, that is the people Bible. Like one time when the newspapers say that the West Indians think that the streets of London paved with gold a Jamaican fellar went to the income tax office to find out something and first thing the clerk tell him is "You people think the streets of London are paved with gold?" Newspaper and radio rule this country.

Now the position have Moses uneasy, because to tell truth most of the fellars who coming now are real hustlers, desperate; it not like long time when forty or fifty straggling in, they invading the country by the hundreds. And when them fellars who here a long time see people running from the West Indies, is only logic for them to say it would be damn foolishness to go back. So what Moses could do when these fellars land up hopeless on the doorstep with one set of luggage, no place to sleep, no place to go?

Early West Indian immigrants

Vocabulary

3 blur (n.): s.th. whose shape is not clearly seen – **7 fellar** (n.): (CarE) fellow, man – **17f. he don't know the man from Adam:** he doesn't know the man at all – **20 ss:** abbreviation for 'steamship' – **27 vex** (adj.): (CarE) angry (vexed) – **38 liaison officer** (n.): an official who works with two or more different groups to establish contacts between them and help both sides – **38f. I catching my arse as it is:** (CarE sl.) I'm getting enough trouble in any case – **41 rab** (n.): (CarE) a fuss, trouble – **43 ten to one:** very likely, you could bet on it – **44 bounce up a spade:** (sl.) meet a black person – **48 to clamp down on** (v.): to be more strict with (prevent them immigrating) – **61 hustler** (n.): a person prepared to use any method to sell s.th. or obtain s.th.

Explanations

Intro: The West Indies: the English-speaking Caribbean countries – **6 Chepstow Road and Westbourne Grove:** an area of London in Notting Hill, just North and West of Hyde Park – **7 Waterloo:** Waterloo Station, south of the Thames, is the terminus for trains arriving from the port at Southampton – **8 Trinidad:** island in the West Indies – **32 the Water:** the Bayswater area of London, North of Hyde Park, between Edgeware Road and Notting Hill – **50 the Mother Country:** Trinidad was a British colony from 1797–1962, other West Indian islands for even longer. Britain was therefore seen as the 'mother country' and often portrayed in this way. Empire and Commonwealth citizens had free right of entry to Britain until 1961.

Awareness

1 What do you know about the 'West Indies', who lives there, and their connections with Britain?

Comprehension

2 Why is Moses going to Waterloo Station to meet someone he does not know?
3 What attitudes does Moses observe in Britain with so many new immigrants arriving?
4 What reason do older immigrants give for not returning to the West Indies?

Analysis

5 'Translate' parts of it into standard English, noting what elements of Caribbean dialect are used.
6 a) Distinguish between author, narrator and protagonist (Reference Library, pp. 320f.). b) Comment on the 'voice' of the narrator, as it appears in the descriptions (e.g. of London, Moses blowing his nose, sources of racial tension etc.).
7 What does the text reveal about why immigrants came to Britain from the West Indies, and how they might have been disappointed?

Opinion

8 Moses thinks what the media say is 'the people Bible' (l. 52). How do the media influence what people think and say about immigrants?
9 Comment on the significance of the choice of name for the protagonist.

Internet Projects

10 Find out more about the Caribbean immigrants to Britain ('the Windrush generation').
11 The other main sources of immigration in the 1950s were the Indian subcontinent and West Africa. What sort of people came from those countries, and where did they settle?
12 Where did the people not born in Britain come from? What is the situation in your own country?

Info

Us and Them

'Foreigner', meaning a person from another country, usually refers to tourists or visitors.
If a person comes to live in a country, that person is called an **'immigrant'**. People who have been living there for longer, but are identified as belonging to a particular group, are **members of ethnic groups.**
African, Afro-Caribbean, Asian, Australian, German, Polish, etc. are used to describe these minorities.
People escaping persecution or oppression in other countries are **refugees** or **asylum-seekers**.
People who are not recognized as genuine refugees are sometimes called **bogus asylum-seekers** or **economic migrants**. **Illegal immigrants** are brought in by **people traffickers**.
People who come for a limited period to work are called **migrant workers**.
Xenophobia is a dislike of foreigners. People with this prejudice are **'xenophobic'**. It may express itself in **racial** or **colour prejudice**, or even a whole philosophy of **racism**. A **racist** attitude leads people to **discriminate against** others, or subject them to **racist attacks** or **abuse**.
The aim of the UK government, as expressed through the Race Relations Act 1976, is a just society which gives everyone an equal chance to learn, work and live free from discrimination and prejudice and from the fear of racial harassment and violence.

2 Enoch Powell

"The Birmingham Speech"*

In the 1950s and 1960s immigrants arrived in Britain in considerable numbers from the Caribbean, the Indian subcontinent and Africa, and congregated in particular areas of the country. They encountered racial prejudice from some British people. When Enoch Powell (1912–1968), a Midlands MP and former government minister, warned against the consequences of immigration in a notorious speech in 1968, he claimed to be expressing public opinion, but his views were also widely condemned. – Enoch Powell, "The Birmingham Speech", reprinted in Brian MacArthur (ed.), *The Penguin Book of Twentieth Century Speeches* (London: Penguin, 1993), pp. 377f., 383.

Giles, Daily Express, *27 February 1968*

In fifteen or twenty years, on present trends, there will be in this country three and a half million Commonwealth immigrants and their descendants. That is not my figure. That is the official figure given to parliament by the spokesman of the Registrar General's office. There is no comparable official figure for the year 2000; but it must be in the region of five to seven million, approximately one-tenth of the whole population, and approaching that of Greater London. Of course, it will not be evenly distributed from Margate to Aberystwyth and from Penzance to Aberdeen. Whole areas, towns and parts of towns across England will be occupied by different sections of the immigrant and immigrant-descended population. [...]

It almost passes belief that at this moment twenty or thirty additional immigrant children are arriving from overseas in Wolverhampton alone every week – and that means fifteen or twenty additional families of a decade or two hence. Those whom the gods wish to destroy they first make mad. We must be mad, literally mad, as a nation to be permitting the annual inflow of some fifty thousand dependants, who are for the most part the material of the future growth of the immigrant-descended population. It is like watching a nation busily engaged in heaping up its own funeral pyre. So insane are we that we actually permit unmarried persons to immigrate for the purpose of founding a family with spouses and fiancées whom they have never seen. Let no one suppose that the flow of dependants will automatically tail off. On the contrary, even at the present admissions rate of only five thousand a year by voucher, there is sufficient for a further twenty-five thousand dependants per annum *ad infinitum*, without taking into account the huge reservoir of existing relations in this country – and I am making no allowance at all for fraudulent entry. In these circumstances nothing will suffice but that the total inflow for settlement should be reduced at once to negligible proportions, and that the necessary legislative and administrative measures be taken without delay. [...]

As I look ahead I am filled with foreboding. Like the Roman, I seem to see 'the River Tiber foaming with much blood'. That tragic and intractable phenomenon which we watch with horror on the other side of the Atlantic but which there is interwoven with the history and existence of the States itself, is coming upon us here by our own volition and our own neglect. Indeed, it has all but come. In numerical terms, it will be of American proportions long before the end of the century. Only resolute and urgent action will avert it even now. Whether there will be the public will to demand and obtain that action, I do not know. All I know is that to see, and not to speak, would be the great betrayal.

Vocabulary

38 funeral pyre (n.): a pile of wood for the ceremonial burning of a (dead) body – **41 spouse** (n.): /spaʊs/ a wife or husband – **41 fiancé** (n.) (fem. fiancée): /fɪˈɒnseɪ/ the person to whom one is engaged (to be married) – **45 voucher** (n.): (BrE) a kind of ticket for a special purpose, (here) quota – **48 ad infinitum** (adv.): (Latin) /ˌæd ɪnfɪˈnaɪtəm/ without end – **50 reservoir** (n.):

a large supply - **53 fraudulent** (adj.): done by fraud, illegally - **59 negligible** (adj.): too small to be worth any attention - **65 foreboding** (n.): a feeling of coming evil - **69 intractable** (adj.): (formal) very difficult to deal with - **73 volition** (n.): choice, without being forced

Explanations

4 Commonwealth: states formerly ruled by Britain. Here Powell means the 'New Commonwealth', i.e. countries whose citizens were mostly black or Asian, who had special rights to enter the UK before it joined the EU. - **10 Registrar General's Office:** government department in charge of compiling population statistics - **21 Margate, Aberystwyth, Penzance, Aberdeen:** towns in, respectively, the southeast of England, West Wales, southwest England and northeast Scotland - **30 Wolverhampton:** town in the West Midlands, northwest of Birmingham. Enoch Powell was MP for a Wolverhampton constituency. - **32 Those whom ... make mad:** "Whom Fortune wishes to destroy she first makes mad." Publius Syrus, *Moral Sayings*, 1st century B.C. - **67 the River Tiber foaming with much blood:** "Bella, horrida bella, et Thybrim multo spumantem sanguine cerno." (I see wars, horrible wars, and the Tiber foaming with much blood) Virgil, *Aeneid*, VI, 86. This quote ensured immediate notoriety for Powell's speech.

Awareness

1 Why are *individual* immigrants often welcomed, while *numbers* of immigrants cause concern?

Comprehension

2 How does Powell arrive at his figures for the year 2000?
3 What sort of immigrants is Powell most concerned about, and why?
4 What dangers does he warn against, and what is his solution?

Analysis

5 Look up the word 'occupy' (l. 25) in the dictionary. What meaning(s) does Powell expect his listeners to associate with it? Find examples where language is used in an emotive rather than factual way.
6 What exactly does Powell mean by 'that tragic and intractable phenomenon' (ll. 68ff.) when talking about the US? What assumptions is he making?
7 Analyse what features of the text are typical of a speech and why they are effective for that purpose.

Opinion

8 Comment on Powell's conclusion that 'to see, and not to speak, would be the great betrayal' (ll. 89f.). What do you see as the advantages and disadvantages of expressing an opinion in this way?
9 Compose a letter (Reference Library, p. 300) to a newspaper giving your opinion about immigration to your country.
10 Powell's speech implies that dependants should not be allowed entry. What do you think about treating families in this way?

Project

11 Look carefully at the cartoon, noticing its date. Explain the cartoon and comment on its ironies.

3

Linton Kwesi Johnson

"Mekkin Histri"

In 1981 the frustrations felt by black immigrants in the face of prejudice, bad housing, poor job prospects and what they saw as police harassment came to a head. The resulting riots, of which the most important was in Brixton in April, were seen by the Jamaican-born 'dub' poet Linton Kwesi Johnson as an expression of black resistance and pride. "Blacks aren't helpless victims who need the white left to organise our struggles for us." - Linton Kwesi Johnson, "Mekkin Histri" from *Tings an Times* (Newcastle upon Tyne: Bloodaxe Books, 1991), pp. 45f.

now tell mi someting
mistah govahment man
tell mi someting

how lang yu really feel
yu coulda keep wi andah heel

wen di trute done reveal
bout how yu grab an steal
bout how yu mek yu crooked deal

well doun in Soutall
where Peach did get fall

di Asians dem faam-up a human wall
gense di fashist an dem police sheil
an dem show dat di Asians gat plenty zeal

it is noh mistri
wi mekkin histri
it is noh mistri
wi winnin victri

now tell mi someting
mistah police spokesman
tell mi someting

how lang yu really tink
wi woulda tek yu batn lick
yu jackboot kick
yu dutty bag a tricks
an yu racist pallyticks

well doun in Bristal
dey ad noh pistal
but dem chase di babylan away
man yu shoulda si yu babylan
how dem really run away
yu shoulda si yu babylan dem dig-up dat day

it is no mistri ...

now tell mi someting
mistah ritewing man
tell mi someting

how lang yu really feel
wi woulda grovel an squeal
wen so much murdah canceal
wen wi woun cyaan heal
wen wi feel di way wi feel

well dere woz Toxteth
an dere woz Moss Side
an a lat a addah places
whey di police ad to hide
well dare woz Brixtan
an dere woz Chapeltoun
an a lat a addah place dat woz burnt to di groun

it is noh mistri...

Linton Kwesi Johnson in concert

Vocabulary

Intro/2 harassment (n): making life difficult by being insulting, aggressive, unfair etc. – **Intro/3 dub** (n. & adj.): speaking poetry accompanied by reggae music – **5 to keep under heel (v.):** to keep s.o. in a position of subjection and powerlessness – **8 to make a crooked deal:** to have a criminal agreement – **13 zeal** (n.): (usually formal) keenness, energy, courage – **22 baton lick** (n): (CarE) beatings with sticks carried by the police – **23 jackboot** (n): military boot associated with Hitler's armies; the instrument of cruel or Fascist behaviour – **24 bag of tricks** (n): equipment or techniques used by experts, here: secret or illegal activities performed for a government or other organisation – **37 to grovel** (v): to lie on the ground, showing extreme respect to s.o. powerful

Explanations

Intro/3 Brixton: an area of South London with a large Caribbean population where crowds attacked the police in 1981, drawing national attention to their problems – **9 Southall:** This predominantly Indian suburb of West London was the scene of disturbances when residents and sympathizers opposed the extremist National Front holding a rally in 1979. – **10 Peach:** Blair Peach, a visiting teacher from New Zealand, died during the Southall disturbances after being hit by a police baton. – **26 Bristol:** city in South-West England, where riots began in 1980–81 – **28 Babylon:** Rastafarian word for Western society and the police in particular – **34 right-wing man:** Traditionally, those on the right wing in politics have opposed immigration most strongly. – **41 Toxteth:** Toxteth in Liverpool, Moss Side in Manchester and Chapeltown in Leeds saw serious disturbances in 1981.

Awareness

1 What do you know about reggae music, Bob Marley and Rastafari?

Comprehension

2 Listen to the poem/song (Viewfinder Special Audio CD) first without the text, then with it.
3 Try to 'translate' the poem into standard English.
4 Who are the three people the poem addresses? What does the poet accuse them of?

Analysis

5 Explain what the poet is celebrating in each verse.
6 Explain why the poet claims "wi mekkin histri" in the chorus (l. 15 etc.).

Opinion

7 After 1981 the opinions of black people were taken more seriously. The text suggests that resistance – even violent resistance – is sometimes necessary. Would you agree (Reference Library, p. 306)? Explain your view.

Projects

8 Find out more about fusions of music/poetry/politics in reggae or rap in the work of Linton Kwesi Johnson, Benjamin Zephaniah, or American rappers. Try to write and perform a rap or dub poem (Reference Library, p. 310) of your own.

4 "From Riot to Racial Harmony"*

The 'Insurrection' of the 1980s led to important changes in public attitudes towards ethnic minorities. The Stephen Lawrence affair, in which the 1993 racist murder of a black teenager and the dignified struggle over the next 10 years by his parents to obtain justice revealed 'institutionalized racism' in the police force, was another important milestone on the road to ending discrimination. There was also a recognition that some simple changes could produce surprisingly positive results, as on the Broadwater Farm estate. - Cahal Milmo, *The Independent*, 5 October, 2005.

Broadwater Farm today, with green spaces between the concrete blocks

Twenty years ago today, Clasford Sterling awoke to the sound of breaking glass and screaming sirens outside his home on the Broadwater Farm estate. He then witnessed from his balcony the riot which within 48 hours turned 12 low-rise housing blocks in Tottenham, north London, into a byword for urban decay, crime and racial tension in Britain's inner cities.

The youth worker, then 26, had his nose broken by a police truncheon as he tried to calm the rioters amid flying petrol bombs and burning barricades in gloomy car parks that had become the private domains of drug dealers and street robbers.

Today Broadwater Farm – the one-time no-go estate which entered infamy after PC Keith Blakelock was hacked to death during the riot on 6 October 1985 – could hardly be more different. [...]

The transformation of the 21-acre estate, completed in 1970 and currently home to 3,000 people, is on one level purely physical. Gone are the concrete walkways that linked each of the 12 housing blocks above ground in what designers hoped would be a master stroke of social engineering by lifting inhabitants away from cars and roads.

The reality by the early 1980s was less utopian. The walkways formed a warren that could not be policed while the car parks underneath were stalked by crack dealers. Now, each of the housing blocks has a secure entrance hall with a concierge service. Green spaces and play areas punctuate the blocks, renovated at a cost of £33m.

But it is only when its inhabitants talk that the true nature of Broadwater Farm 2005 becomes apparent. Yesterday, a £1m Children's Centre was opened next to its existing community centre and primary school. Jennifer Kamara, 35, a mother-of-four who has lived on the estate for 12 years since coming to Britain from the civil war in Sierra Leone, said: "This is not paradise on earth, we still have the same problems as anywhere else, but people have been given back their purpose and dignity. The kids have their free time occupied and we enjoy the fact that so many different cultures are here. My neighbours are Turkish, my kids walk to school with their Bangladeshi friends. We are one big family on Broadwater."

The statistics prove her point. In 1985, the population of the estate was 49 per cent white, 42 per cent Afro-Caribbean, and 9 per cent from the Indian subcontinent and other areas. Today it is 30 per cent white, 27 per cent west African, principally Ghanaian, 24 per cent Afro-Caribbean and 15 per cent Turkish or Turkish Kurd. A sign at the entrance to the estate says "welcome" in 14 different languages. [...]

Less than a mile from the estate stands the 1,220-pupil White Hart Lane School. Its former pupils include Trevor Phillips. Its former headteacher said it was time to celebrate diversity, not try to quash it. Under multicultural policies such as teaching science in Turkish and implementing special lessons for Caribbean pupils, David Daniels and his team were able to increase the number of pupils passing five or more GCSEs from 10 per cent in 2001 to an expected 50 per cent next year.

He said: "Far from being something which impacts upon UK life I see [diversity] as something that revitalises us and makes us powerful economically."

The extent to which the tensions that sparked events of 20 years ago have eased was demonstrated last month when police raided a suspected drugs den. Chief Superintendent Stephen Bloomfield, the Haringey commander, said: "There was a time when an operation like that would have caused us concern but afterwards the residents came out of their houses and applauded the officers. Broadwater Farm is no longer a place we would consider to be out of the ordinary."

Many outside the Farm do not share his view. Residents complain that taxi drivers refuse to visit the estate after dark and some say they use friends' addresses when applying for jobs.

So it fell to one the estate's oldest residents to explain its new allure. Mary Kemp, 82, has lived on the estate with her husband, Bill, since it was opened. She said: "We moved here from a house with no bathroom. It was like a holiday camp and that remains the case. We are pure English and do you know what that means? It means being tolerant of people, regardless of colour or creed. It means embracing people who are different from you. That's why we stayed here."

Marley, Gandhi and Lennon united on a mural in Broadwater Farm

Vocabulary

Intro/6 estate (n.): a group of buildings planned and built as a unit - **15 low-rise** (adj.): not very tall (opposite of high-rise or tower block) - **18 to be a byword for:** be known as typical of - **18 urban decay** (n.): gradual deterioration of buildings and facilities in part of a town - **26 PC, P.C.:** abbreviation for Police Constable - **31 walkway** (n.): a path to walk along above the ground - **33 master stroke** (n.): a very clever and successful action - **34 social engineering** (n.): changing social behaviour by changing the environment - **36 utopian** (adj.): designed for a perfect world - **38 to stalk** (v.): here: to walk through, causing danger - **38 crack dealer** (n.): a person selling the drug crack cocaine - **40 concierge** (n.): s.o. who looks after a building and checks on people entering and leaving - **68 to quash** (v.): to stop s.th. existing - **75 to impact upon** (v.): have an effect on (here negative) - **92 allure** (n.): attractiveness

Explanations

67 Trevor Phillips: a black politician and writer of Guyanese origin; he was Chairman of the Commission for Racial Equality. - **73 GCSEs:** exams in a range of subjects usually taken by pupils at the age of 15 or 16

Awareness

1 Describe any district near where you live which has a large proportion of immigrants.

Comprehension

2 In what ways has the Broadwater Farm estate changed since 1985?

Analysis

3 Why was the Broadwater Farm estate built as is was, what unexpected problems did it have, and what concrete measures were taken to improve things.
4 What does the text reveal about changes in relations between the police and the community?
5 "This is not paradise on earth." (ll. 49f.) – What sort of problems do you think residents still face?

Opinion

6 Comment on what Mary Kemp says.

Internet Project

7 Use the Internet to find out more about the murders of PC Keith Blakelock, Stephen Lawrence and Damilola Taylor.

5

Gurinder Chadha

"Going for Goal"*

Jesminder (Jessie) Bhamra is a passionate footballer, whose greatest ambition is to play as a professional with skills like her idol, David Beckham, renowned for bending the ball past defenders. However, as a girl, and as a Sikh, whose families have strict ideas about their daughters' upbringing, this is a problem. Her parents want her to study to be a lawyer or a doctor, and forbid her to continue playing in her local Hounslow team. Gurinder Chadha, who wrote and directed the movie *Bend It Like Beckham*, has not always found it easy to be a Punjabi woman film-maker. - *Bend It Like Beckham* (film released in 2002).

"I played in the final today, and we won!"

Jesminder: How am I going to tell them, Tony? I'll have to now or I'll end up a solicitor, bored out of my mind.

Tony: Come with me. (*They go into the living-room*) Mum, Uncleji, Auntieji, we've got something we want to tell you.

Aunt Biji: Why is he holding her hand?

Tony: We've been good friends for a long time now. We'd like to ask for your blessings. (*All look puzzled*) We'd like to get engaged.

(*Exclamations in Punjabi*)

But look, there's one condition: I want Jesminder to go to college first, anywhere that she wants.

Mr Bhamra: Of course, putar. (*He congratulates Tony*)

Mrs Bhamra: Well, we have relatives all the way, in Glasgow, in Portsmouth ...

(*Embraces*)

Jesminder: Mum, Dad ... Tony's lying.

Voice: Lying?

Jesminder: We're not getting married. Tony only said that to help me, but I'm not lying any more. I played in the final today, and we won!

Mrs Bhamra: How? When?

Jesminder I wasn't going to go, but Dad let me. And it was brilliant! I played the best ever! And I was happy because I wasn't sneaking off and lying to you! I didn't ask to be good at football. Guru Nanak must have blessed me. Anyway, there was a scout from America there today, and he's offered me a place at a top university with a free scholarship and a chance to play football professionally, and I really want to go, and if I can't tell you what I want now, then I'll never be happy, whatever I do.

Mrs Bhamra: You let her leave her sister's wedding to go to a football match?!

Mr Bhamra: Maybe you could handle her long face; I could not. I didn't have the heart to stop her. (*gets up and moves towards the bar*)

Mrs Bhamra: And that's why she's ready to go all the way to America now!

Bubbly: (*whispering and gesturing*) She's dead, man.

Tony: (*to his mother*) It's allright, Mum, just leave it.

Mr Bhamra: (*pouring himself a glass of whisky*) When those bloody English cricket players threw me out of their club, like a dog, I never complained. On the contrary, I vowed that I will never play again. Who suffered? Me. But I don't want Jessie to suffer. (*Jesminder sheds a tear*) I don't want her to make the same mistakes that her father made of accepting life, accepting situations. I want her to fight. And I want her to win... because I've seen her play and she's, she's brilliant! I don't think anybody has the right of stopping her. (*Jesminder embraces him*) Two daughters made happy in one day. What else can a father ask for?

Mrs Bhamra: At least I've taught her full Indian dinner. The rest is up to God. (*Laughter*)

Vocabulary

2 solicitor (n.): a lawyer who gives legal advice to people – **15 putar** (n.): Hindi / Punjabi word meaning son (or daughter)

Explanations

5 uncleji: In Indian English the parents of friends are often called 'aunt' and 'uncle'. The suffix -ji is added as a sign of respect and affection. – **29 Guru Nanak:** Guru Nanak Dev (1469–1539) was the founder of the Sikh religion. A picture representing him hangs on the wall in the Bhamras' house. – **50 those bloody English cricket players:** Mr Bhamra explained earlier in the film how he had been a good cricketer in East Africa, where he used to live, but in England the local cricket club refused to admit a non-white player.

Awareness

1 Do you know any cases where parents quarrelled with their children about what they wanted them to do or be?

2 Find out from the internet about the main principles of the Sikh religion, in particular the teachings of the gurus and the '5 Ks'. You could start at www.sikhs.org.

Comprehension

3 Why does Tony announce that he and Jesminder are engaged?

4 What two other things have happened on this day?

5 Why does Bubbly (a friend of Jesminder's sister's, also grown up in a Sikh family) say what she does?

Analysis

6 How do Mrs Bhamra's words reveal the attitudes of traditionalist Sikh women?

7 What differences in speech can be observed between the older and younger generations?

8 In what ways is Mr Bhamra not a good Sikh?

Opinion

9 Is Mr Bhamra's agreement a decision to reject his traditional values? Explain your opinion.

Internet Projects

10 Use the Internet to find out more about the part of London near Heathrow airport (where the film is set) and the ethnic groups that live there.

11 Compare this with another film on similar themes, like *East is East,* or *What's Cooking*?

12 Gurinder Chadha is a successful film director. Find out about other successful Indians in the UK.

6

Gautam Malkani

"Names"*

In the 1970s white racist 'skinhead' gangs regularly went 'Paki-bashing': insulting and beating up Asians (people from the Indian subcontinent), because they thought they would not fight back. In the novel *Londonstani*, set in contemporary Hounslow, the situation is very different. Gautam Malkani, its author, was born in 1976, grew up near Heathrow Airport and works as a journalist, - Gautam Malkani, *Londonstani* (London: Fourth Estate, 2006), pp. 3ff.

– Serve him right he got his muthafuckin face fuck'd, shudn't b callin me a Paki, innit.

After spittin his words out Hardjit stopped for a second, like he expected us to write em down or someshit. Then he sticks in an exclamation mark by kickin the white kid in the face again. – Shudn't b callin us Pakis, innit, u dirrty gora.

Again, punctuation came with a kick, but with his left foot this time so it was more like a semicolon. – Call me or any a ma bredrens a Paki again an I'ma mash u an yo family. In't dat da truth, Pakis? – Dat's right, Amit, Ravi an I go, – dat be da truth.

The three a us spoke in sync like we belonged to some tutty boy band, the kind who sing the chorus like it's some blonde American cheerleader routine. Hardjit, Hardjit, he's our man, if he can't bruckup goras, no one can. Ravi then delivers his standard solo routine: – Yeh, blud, safe, innit.

– Hear wat my bredren b sayin, sala kutta? Come out wid dat shit again n I'ma knock u so hard u'll b shittin out yo mouth 4 real, innit, goes Hardjit, with an eloquence an conviction that made me green with envy. Amit always liked to point out that brown people don't actually go green: – We don't go red when we been shamed an we don't go blue when we dead, he'd said to me one time. – We don't even go purple when we been bruised, jus a darker brown. An still goras got da front to call us coloured.

It was an old joke but, green or not, I in't shamed to admit I'm envious a Hardjit. Most bredren round Hounslow were jealous a his designer desiness, with his perfectly built body, his perfectly shaped facial hair an his perfectly groomed garms that made it look like he went shopping with P Diddy. Me, I was jealous a his front – what someone like Mr Ashwood'd call a person's linguistic prowess or his debating dexterity or someshit. Hardjit always knew exactly how to tell others that it just weren't right to describe all desi boys as Pakis. [...] People're always tryin to stick a label on our scene. That's the problem with havin a fuckin scene. First we was rudeboys, then we be Indian niggas, then rajamuffins, then raggastanis, Britasians, fuckin Indobrits. These days we try an use our own word for homeboy an so we just call ourselves desis but I still remember when we were happy with the word rudeboy.

"Designer desiness": Sacha Baron Cohen, as 'Ali G', made fun of urban youth culture in various media shows and films

Vocabulary

2 innit: (isn't it?): (urban sl.) all-purpose question tag - **7 gora** (n.): Hindi / Punjabi for a white person - **10 bredren** (n.): Jamaican English / Rastafarian word for brother - **11 to mash** (v.): (CarE) to squash, beat up - **14 tutty** (adj.): (urban sl.) low-quality, dirty - **16 bruckup** (v.): (CarE) beat up - **18 blud** (n.): (urban sl.) mate, friend (from Jamaican and US usage) - **18 safe** (adj.): (urban sl.) all right - **19 sala kutta:** Hindi / Punjabi insult: stupid dog or stupid ox - **19 front** (n.): (urban sl.) effrontery, cheek - **31 desiness** (n.): /'deɪsɪ'nɪs/ being a 'desi' (from Sanskrit 'from the Mother Country') - **33 garms** (n.): (urban sl.) clothes (from garments)

Explanations

3 Hardjit: The narrator's friend Harjit has changed his name to express his hardness - **34 P Diddy:** American record-producer and rapper Sean John Combs, born 1969, previously known as Puff Daddy, is also a clothing designer. - **35 Mr Ashwood:** the narrator's favourite teacher at college

Awareness

1 Give some examples of how young people use language that older people might not understand or approve of.

Comprehension

2 What is Hardjit doing, and why?

Analysis

3 Investigate and comment on the use of language and try to 'translate' it into standard English.
4 In what ways does the narrator (Reference Library, pp. 310f.) seem to use language differently? What might this suggest about him?
5 What different cultural ingredients can be found in this passage?

Opinion

6 What is ironic (Reference Library, p. 311) about Hardjit's actions?
7 What do you think makes a person 'cool'?

Projects

8 Find out about the meanings and origins of the terms rudeboys, niggas, rajamuffins, raggastanis, Britasians, Indobrits and desis.
9 Explore the dictionary of urban slang at www.urbandictionary.com.
10 Compare this scene with either Anthony Burgess's *A Clockwork Orange* or Irvine Walsh's *Trainspotting*.

Info

The Role of Humour

Being able to laugh at oneself has always been valued highly in British culture. In the 1990s Sanjeev Bhaskar, Nina Wadia, Kulvinder Ghir, and the film-maker and novelist Meera Syal (*Bhaji on the Beach, Anita and Me*) created a sketch show whose title alluded to the stereotype image of Indians portrayed by Peter Sellers in his famous duet with Sophia Loren, "Goodness Gracious Me"; it helped make everything Indian part of mainstream culture, and questioned all sorts of prejudices and assumptions which communities have about themselves and others, thus preparing the way for the even more irreverent humour of Ali G. – BBC TV, *Goodness Gracious Me.*

An Indian father and his son are watching television.

Son: Ah, Trooping of the Colour! Great! The Queen looks nice, doesn't she?
Father: Nice? Of course nice! Because she's Indian!
Son: Not the Queen!
Father: All of them, the whole Royal family, Indian!
Son: What'ya talking about?
Father: Uh? Think about it, yaar. Descended from Queen Victoria, Empress of India, so Indian!
Son: Rubbish!
Father: Not rubbish. Look at them. They all live in the same family house together. Indian! All work in the family business. Indian! All have arranged marriages. Indian! They all have sons. Daughters no good. Indian!
Son: But Dad ...
Father: Children live with their parents until they're married. Indian!
Son: Dad, Dad ...
Father: What more do you want? Do you want them to put on turbans and charm snakes out of baskets?
Son: But Dad, Harry, Wills, Fergie ...
Father: All Indian! All except Prince Charles. He's African.
Son: What?
Father: If he was Indian, he'd have smaller ears!

7 Europe's Tarnished Golden Door?

After the EU enlargement of 2004, citizens of the new member states were allowed to enter the UK freely to live and work. As a result, Britain experienced its biggest post-war influx of immigrants from Poland, the Czech Republic and the Baltic states. In this extract from a BBC radio documentary, the presenter Quentin Peel gathers views from experts Sir Digby Jones, representing industry, John Monks, a trade-unionist, Sir Andrew Green, a critic of immigration, Sarah Spencer and Danny Sriskandarajah, who are academics, about the effects of immigration and the prospects for the future. – BBC Radio 4: *Europe's Tarnished Golden Door?*, broadcast 30 March & 2 April 2006

PEEL: Just look around you. Migrants from the east are changing the face of immigration in Britain and western Europe. Workers from the ten new member states of the European Union are taking advantage of free labour movement. Strange Slavonic tongues can be heard from the construction sites of Camberwell to the mushroom farms of Monaghan. But who's benefiting? Sir Digby Jones is director general of the Confederation of British Industry.

JONES: Oh, it's excellent for business! We haven't got enough skilled people. We've made the leap to a re-structured economic society far more quickly and certainly more recently than France or Germany, and we actually need more and better skilled people, and, frankly, we ain't growing enough of our own.

GREEN: He would say that, wouldn't he? Employers are laughing all the way to the bank. What they can do is to get skilled workers off the shelf – no training costs, un-unionized and quite possibly at a lower level of pay. It's lovely!

PEEL: Sir Andrew Green, chairman of MigrationWatch UK.

GREEN: In a welfare state, there is no such thing as cheap labour. It's simply that the other costs, the costs of infrastructure and so on, are met by the taxpayer. So if you're an employer, you're very happy; if you're a worker, you've got reason for concern.

PEEL: Job-seekers from central and eastern Europe are the latest contributors to an upsurge in net migration into Britain over the past decade. They're young, bright and hard-working, and they're taking jobs everywhere from cafes to care work. [...] Sir Andrew Green's think-tank, MigrationWatch UK, is worried about Britain's capacity to take in so many people.

GREEN: Our problem with the present scale of immigration is that it is having a major impact on our infrastructure and on our community relations. Foreign immigration is running now at a third of a million every year. We simply don't think that's sensible, we don't think we can absorb that number of people. [...] British emigration is of the order of one hundred and twenty thousand a year. I see no reason why we should not have inward migration of a similar level. That should be quite enough.

PEEL: That sounds neat and tidy. But is it? Sarah Spencer is associate director of the Centre on Migration Policy and Society at Oxford University, and a member of the Commission for Racial Equality.

SPENCER: There has been an increase. It's not very meaningful as a total figure because we're talking about such very different people. There are people who are coming for family reunion; there are people coming for asylum who may or may not stay in the long-term; there are students who come for a short or longer period to study – and indeed to work; and then there are labour migrants. [...] I think it is important to recognize that migration isn't something that you can turn on and off like a tap – and also governments are anxious to reassure the public that immigration is under control. In fact, it is enormously difficult to control because we're talking about complex pull factors – not least the fact that employers very much want people to come and work here – and also a range of push factors, not least for people fleeing and wanting to claim asylum. The danger of trying to close a gate – for instance, saying we won't have any more low-skilled workers – is that if the demand is still there for them, then those jobs are going to be filled; and if they're not filled by legal workers coming in through a legal channel then somebody else is going to take those jobs.

PEEL: In other words, on the black market. It's not just the huddled masses that are knocking at the door. The number of asylum seekers has dropped significantly, but now our own economic growth is pulling would-be workers in. [...] Does John Monks, the British general secretary of the European Trade Union Confederation, see a threat to his members from these new eastern invaders?

MONKS: Free movement of labour – and now it's the twenty-five countries, plus one or two others actually – is what the EU is all about, and we recognize that if you're in favour of the European Union, you've got to be in favour of that as well. Its value, though, is, I think, proven, although there are many difficulties. The fact is that with an ageing population in many of Western European countries, it's important that migration is encouraged. It's done a lot for the British economy and it'll do a lot for a lot of other economies as well.

PEEL: Can you be a bit more specific about how economic migration would actually benefit, for example, workers in Britain then?

MONKS: Well, at the moment, the migrants tend to be doing jobs that it's quite hard to find the British ready to do. Although we've got alarming pockets of high unemployment, there's still major problems in finding people who'll go picking in the fields and serving in the cafés and working unsocial hours in hotels. And these migrant workers have done those jobs. They've been doing it since the war. West Indians and others came in. Now the main thrust has switched to central and eastern Europe. But I'm astonished and delighted by the absence of tensions. Of course, if it was ten per cent unemployment – as it is in Germany – it would be rather different. [...]

PEEL: In 1999, for the first time, the largest group of immigrants came from non-Commonwealth and non-EU countries. What does Danny Sriskandarajah, head of migration studies at the Institute for Public Policy Research in London, think are the implications?

SRISKANDARAJAH: Britain's multiculturalist policies have been about broad categories, defining people, almost a tick-a-box approach to multiculturalism – you're black, you're white, you're Asian. The reality is much, much more complex; that even within a group such as black Africans, we're seeing incredible diversity, for example, in socio-economic outcomes. Nigerians and Somalis will both tick the black African box. But in socio-economic terms they are at different ends of the profile – they have incredibly different rates of employment, incredibly different average incomes – and so unless we come to terms with that diversity policy interventions just won't be effective. On the ground, I think we also need to think about how public service delivery comes to terms with something like super-diversity. For far too long our public service provision, when it comes to education or healthcare, has been about targeting the needs of a particular minority. That might work if you have fifteen per cent of a population which consists of one ethnic minority. It might not work when there are fifteen different groups, each making up one per cent of the community. It's that challenge of tackling super-diversity that we need to be aware of.

PEEL: Britain's more super-diverse in its immigrant population than the rest of Europe; partly because the English language is such a magnet. [...] Our prosperous European continent acts as a fatal attraction, especially to its near abroad. Well managed, immigration can be of great mutual benefit: providing skills to the developed economies when they need them, remittances for migrant workers to send to their families and training – as well as seed capital – for those who want to return home.

Trying to close the golden door will only create a miserable buffer zone, where impoverished migrants clamour for admittance. We shouldn't close the door, even if we could. Instead, we should export our prosperity and seek to close the income gap. We should encourage more two-way movement. It may not ease Europe's economic pull, but it would alleviate the push of the huddled masses.

Vocabulary

Title: to tarnish (v.): become less bright and attractive - **17 to benefit** (v.): to gain or give an advantage - **22f. to restructure** (v.): to change the economy (i.e. to more modern industries) - **26 frankly ... ain't:** used as a humorous catch-phrase with a dialect short form of 'are not' - **29 off the shelf:** immediately available - **30 un-unionized** (adj.): not part of a trade union - **36 infrastructure** (n.): the organizational systems of a country, e.g. providing housing, health care, education, pensions, etc. - **40 net** (adj.): overall amount (here: how many more come in than go out) - **48 community relations** (n.): relations between different sections of the population, particularly those different in race or origin - **63 family reunion** (n.): bringing dependents to join family members - **115 tick-a-box approach** (n.): way of dealing with something by making simple choices - **125 intervention** (n.): here: measures, taking action - **142 its near abroad** (n.): foreign countries not far away from it - **143 of great mutual benefit:** good for both sides - **145 remittance** (n.): money sent to s.o. - **146 seed capital** (n.): money to start a new business - **149 miserable** (adj.): sad, poor - **149 buffer zone** (n.): area outside a state, designed to protect it - **154 to alleviate** (v.): to make s.th. less bad

Explanations

14 Camberwell: part of South London - **16 Monaghan:** a county in the northern part of Eire - **19f. Confederation of British Industry:** organization of employers, representing companies - **27 He would say that, wouldn't he?:** well-known humorous catch-phrase to dismiss someone's statement, made famous by Mandy Rice-Davies in a 1963 trial when a lord denied having an affair with her - **32f. MigrationWatch UK:** an 'independent and non-political' organization which opposes immigration - **59 Commission for Racial Equality:** an organization set up by law in 1976 to improve relations between races and prevent discrimination - **111f. Institute for Public Policy Research:** an organization set up to discuss social issues, which investigated immigration from a positive point of view

Awareness

1 Should people be able to live and work where they want? If not, why not?

Comprehension

2 What differences in immigration to the UK have been seen in recent years?
3 What is meant by 'push' and 'pull' factors?
4 Why does the text suggest that a particularly large quantity of immigrants want to come to the UK?
5 What is Peel's conclusion about how Europe should act in future?

Analysis

6 Use the views expressed in the programme to list the advantages and disadvantages of immigration.
7 Explain the allusion to the 'huddled masses' (ll. 84 and 155).
8 How does Danny Sriskandarajah think priorities in dealing with immigrants will have to change?
9 Show how the presenter uses provocative questions or opinions as cues for his interviewees.
10 Analyse the language used by the presenter and his interviewees. For instance, look particularly at the register (formal or informal), rhetorical devices, idiomatic phrases and ways of expressing number, amount or degree (Reference Library, p. 311, p. 322).

Opinion

11 Organize a debate about immigration.
12 In an age of globalization, what is the effect of restricting the movement of people?

Projects

13 Find out more about migration within the EU, and immigration to the EU, and what different EU countries are doing about it. What happens to people who apply to enter, or try to enter illegally?

Special Feature 4

Civil Rights

"Today we'll learn about segregation in America."

Civil Rights Movement: In the US, the attempt from 1954 onwards to get equal rights for black people, and people of any race or colour, through non-violent actions, was led especially by Dr Martin Luther King, Jr. Several cases involving civil rights went to the US Supreme Court; the most important was "Brown v. Board of Education of Topeka". In 1964 a Civil Rights Act was passed making unequal treatment of races illegal, and in 1965, the government banned the last tests and restrictions which some states had used to stop black people from voting; this gave all adults the right to vote, regardless of colour.

"Civil Rights" vs. "Civil Liberties"

It is important to note the difference between "civil rights" and "civil liberties." The legal area known as "civil rights" has traditionally revolved around the basic right to be free from unequal treatment based on certain protected characteristics (race, gender, disability, etc.) in settings such as employment and housing. "Civil liberties" concern basic rights and freedoms that are guaranteed – either explicitly identified in the Bill of Rights and the Constitution, or interpreted through the years by courts and lawmakers. Civil liberties include:

- Freedom of speech
- The right to privacy
- The right to be free from unreasonable searches of your home
- The right to a fair court trial
- The right to marry
- The right to vote

One way to consider the difference between "civil rights" and "civil liberties" is to look at (1) what right is affected, and (2) whose right is affected. For example, as an employee, you do not have the legal right to a promotion, mainly because getting a promotion is not a guaranteed "civil liberty." But, as a *female* employee you *do* have the legal right to be free from discrimination in being considered for that promotion – you cannot legally be denied the promotion based on your gender (or race, or disability, etc.). By choos-

Tasks and Project

1. Look at the cartoon at the top ("History/Black History"). What is ironic about it?
2. The cover illustration above shows one of the main ways of expression which the Civil Rights Movement used: a demonstration march. – Would you join such a march if your rights were concerned? Would you take part for reasons of solidarity with other people?
3. Find out about the four people mentioned on the book cover on the right.

During his signing of the landmark Civil Rights Act of 1964, President Lyndon B. Johnson shook hands with the Rev. Martin Luther King Jr. (United Press International/ File 1964)

ing not to promote a female worker solely because of the employee's gender, the employer has committed a civil rights violation and has engaged in unlawful employment discrimination based on sex or gender.

Discrimination
The act, practice, or an instance of discriminating categorically rather than individually; prejudiced or prejudicial outlook, action, or treatment.

Hate crime
Any of various crimes (as assault or defacement of property) when motivated by hostility to the victim as a member of a group (as one based on color, creed, gender, or sexual orientation).

Poll tax
A tax of a fixed amount per person levied on adults. – The poll tax was a voting fee charged to reduce the number of blacks that were eligible to vote.

Segregation
The separation or isolation of a race, class, or ethnic group by enforced or voluntary residence in a restricted area, by barriers to social intercourse, by separate educational facilities, or by other discriminatory means.

The "Jim Crow" figure was a fixture of the minstrel shows that toured the South; a white man made up as a black man sang and mimicked stereotypical behavior in the name of comedy. – Soon this name came to stand for black people in general, especially if treated unfairly. Laws that enforced segregation were called "Jim Crow laws". The time between the 1870s and the 1950s are labeled "Jim Crow era".

"It is never too late to give up our prejudices."
Henry David Thoreau (1817–1862)

"Equality ... is the result of human organization. We are not born equal."
Hannah Arendt (1906–1975)

"There are those who say we can stop now, America is a color-blind society. But it isn't there yet. There are those who say we have a level playing field, but we don't yet. There are those who say that all you need is to climb up on your bootstraps, but there are too many Americans who don't have boots, much less bootstraps."
Colin Powell, 25 May 1996

Colin L. Powell was nominated by President Bush on December 16, 2000 as Secretary of State. After being unanimously confirmed by the U.S. Senate, he was sworn in as the 65th Secretary of State on January 20, 2001.

Prior to his appointment, Secretary Powell was the chairman of America's Promise – The Alliance for Youth, a national nonprofit organization dedicated to mobilizing people from every sector of American life to build the character and competence of young people.

Secretary Powell was a professional soldier for 35 years, during which time he held myriad command and staff positions and rose to the rank of 4-star General. He was Assistant to the President for National Security Affairs from December 1987 to January 1989. His last assignment, from October 1, 1989 to September 30, 1993, was as the 12th Chairman of the Joint Chiefs of Staff, the highest military position in the Department of Defense. During this time, he oversaw 28 crises, including Operation Desert Storm in the victorious 1991 Persian Gulf war.

Powell was born in New York City on 5 April 1937 and was raised in the South Bronx. His parents, Luther and Maud Powell, immigrated to the United States from Jamaica. Secretary Powell was educated in the New York City public schools, graduating from the City College of New York (CCNY), where he earned a bachelor's degree in geology. His further academic achievements include a Master of Business Administration degree from George Washington University.

Tasks and Projects

1. Find out more about the "Jim Crow era" at this website: http://www.pbs.org/jazz/time/time_jim_crow.htm
2. What do the two quotations (left) have in common? – Do you agree with them?
3. The success of the minstrel shows clearly proves what attitude towards black people their audiences had. How would you characterize this attitude? – Get more information there: http://en.wikipedia.org./wiki/Minstrel_show
4. What significance did Colin Powell's career have for the self-esteem of non-white Americans? – Also find out about his successor in office, Condoleezza Rice. You might start at this website: http://www.state.gov/secretary/

9 THE POSTCOLONIAL EXPERIENCE

In the past, talk of 'The British Empire' or 'The Commonwealth' centred on Britain, and relationships Britain formed with the world. Britain, the Metropolis, was the 'hub of empire', and its language, literature and culture were regarded as superior to that of the 'Periphery'. At its greatest extent, in 1922, the British Empire spanned the globe, with over 450 million people. But it was already an empire in decline, the "winds of change" were blowing, and by 1970 almost all Britain's former colonies were politically independent. But their people, whose lives had been shaped by the colonial experience, faced the harder task of achieving economic and cultural freedom and adapting the values and language they had inherited to express their own individuality.

This Canadian stamp boasts: "We hold a vaster empire than has been".

What important historical empires do you know about?
Try to identify the modern names of the countries marked in red on the map.

Now that Britain has ceased to be a colonial power the roles have changed. The important new voices, the literary prizewinners, the masters of the English language are now to be found outside Britain. As Salman Rushdie put it, "The Empire writes back to the Centre – with a vengeance." The 'new literatures in English' and the societies they represent, using a variety of 'Englishes' with a new, equal status, have come of age.

Metropolis and Periphery

Globalization – with easy air travel, instant communication, worldwide information link-ups, multinational corporations – may seem to bring the world together, but often it emphasizes the growing gulf between rich and poor, inequalities in military and economic power, and threats to individual culture and identity. That is why the experiences of people who have emerged from colonialism are now so relevant. From their attempts to overcome the influence of a dominant culture, and then to express themselves on equal terms with it, we can learn valuable lessons about how we might try to live together more harmoniously and face the challenges of the new century.

When the British began to build their empire, at the beginning of the 17th century, William Shakespeare wrote his last major play, *The Tempest*. The exiled duke Prospero, who is a magician, lands on a strange island with his daughter Miranda. He makes the original owner of the island, Caliban, his slave. The relationship between Prospero and Caliban can be compared to the relationships of colonialism between the Metropolis and the Periphery, affecting postcolonial developments in widely differing parts of the world such as India, Africa, Australia and the Caribbean.

How can Caliban redefine his relationship with Prospero? Must he accept an inferior status? Will he reject Prospero's culture entirely? Will he take revenge on Prospero for his previous suffering? Will he demand that everything that was stolen should be returned? Are these solutions even possible?

Or can he repossess the culture in an extraordinary feat of the imagination?

2

Derek Walcott

Pantomime

The poet and dramatist Derek Walcott comes from St Lucia, one of the islands in the Caribbean, often called the West Indies. He shares the concern of other postcolonial authors to find a way to achieve cultural independence. Is it possible simply to reverse the colonial relationship? Daniel Defoe's *Robinson Crusoe*, like Shakespeare's *The Tempest*, has a connection with the Caribbean. Tobago is believed to be where the shipwreck occurred which inspired Defoe's story. In the play *Pantomime* Harry Trewe, a retired English comedian, runs a guest house on Tobago where he employs Jackson Philip, a black calypso singer, to be his 'factotum'. Their decision to attract customers with some light entertainment based on the Crusoe story with the roles reversed puts Harry's intention of treating Jackson as an equal under some strain. - Derek Walcott, *Remembrance* and *Pantomime* (New York: Farrar, Straus & Giroux, 1980), pp. 125ff.

HARRY: Look, I'm sorry to interrupt you again, Jackson, but as I – you know – was watching you, I realized it's much more profound than that; that it could get offensive. We're trying to do something light, just a little pantomime, a little satire, a little picong. But if you take this thing seriously, we might commit Art, which is a kind of crime in this society ... I mean, there'd be a lot of things there that people ... well, it would make them think too much, and well, we don't want that ... we just want a little ... entertainment.

JACKSON: How do you mean, Mr Trewe?

HARRY: Well, I mean if you ... well, I mean. If you did the whole thing in reverse ... I mean, okay, well, all right ... you've got this black man ... no, no ... all right. You've got this man who is black, Robinson Crusoe, and he discovers this island on which there is this white cannibal, all right?

JACKSON: Yes. That is, after he has killed the goat ...

HARRY: Yes, I know, I know. After he has killed the goat and made a ... the hat, the parasol, and all of that ... and, anyway, he comes across this man called Friday.

JACKSON: How do you know I mightn't choose to call him Thursday? Do I have to copy every ... I mean, are we improvising?

Scene from the 1954 fim The Adventures of Robinson Crusoe *directed by Luis Buñuel*

HARRY: All right, so it's Thursday. He comes across this naked white cannibal called Thursday, you know. And then look at what would happen. He would have to start to ... well, he'd have to, sorry ... This cannibal, who is a Christian, would have to start unlearning his Christianity. He would have to be taught ... I mean ... he'd have to be taught by this – African – that everything was wrong, that what he was doing ... I mean, for nearly two thousand years ... was wrong. That his civilization, his culture, his whatever, was ... horrible. Was all ... wrong. Barbarous, I mean, you know. And Crusoe would then have to teach him things like, you know, about Africa, his gods, patamba, and so on ... and it would get very, very complicated, and I suppose ultimately it would be very boring, and what we'd have on our hands would be ... would be a play, and not a little pantomime ...

JACKSON: I'm too ambitious?

HARRY: No, no, the whole thing would have to be reversed; white would become black, you know ...

JACKSON [*smiling*]: You see, Mr Trewe, I don't see anything wrong with that, up to now.

HARRY: Well, I do. It's not the sort of thing I want, and I think you'd better clean up, and I'm going inside, and when I come back I'd like this whole place just as it was, I mean, just before everything started.

JACKSON: You mean you'd like it returned to its primal state? Natural? Before Crusoe finds Thursday? But, you see, that is not history. That is not the world.

HARRY: No, no. I don't give an Eskimo's fart about the world, Jackson. I just want this little place here *cleaned up*, and I'd like you to get back to fixing the sun deck. Let's forget the whole matter. Righto. Excuse me.

Vocabulary

Intro/6 pantomime (n.): (BrE) a kind of British play (usu. for children) performed around Christmas, with music, jokes, songs etc. – **Intro/7 calypso** (n.): /kə'lipsəʊ/ a West Indian song based on a subject of interest in the news – **Intro/7 factotum** (n.): /fæk'təʊtəm/ a servant who has to do all kinds of work – **5 picong** (n.): /pɪ'kɒŋ/ (CarE – from French piquant) humorously critical comment – **20 parasol** (n.): a sunshade – **54 I don't give an Eskimo's fart**: I don't care at all

Explanations

37 patamba (n.): Harry's idea of what the name of an African god should be

Beachside tourist hotel in St Lucia

Awareness

1 In the Robinson Crusoe story, does the reader identify more with Friday or with Crusoe? What is the effect of this, for example, on a black Caribbean citizen?

Comprehension

2 What is Jackson intending to do?
3 Which things would be 'reversed' in Jackson's version? Make a list.
4 What are Harry's objections?
5 How does Harry finally try to solve the problem?

Analysis

6 Point out the parallels with the colonial and postcolonial situation here.
7 Comment on Harry's point that "white would become black" (l. 44).
8 Analyse the power relations between the two men. (Look, for instance, at how they use language; see Reference Library, p. 311.)

Opinion

9 Comment on Harry's point about "committing Art" (l. 6). What does he mean? Does his remark apply in our society?
10 For a postcolonial culture, is there any alternative to rejecting the culture of the colonists in order to achieve true independence?
11 What is the importance of the two men's previous careers?
12 Look at the notes on intertextuality (see below). Comment on how intertextuality is used here.

Project

13 Try to write a sketch putting Jackson's idea into practice: a 'reversed' Robinson Crusoe, or another reversed situation where slavery, or mission, or other European relationships with native or black peoples are parodied, and perform it in the group.

Info

Intertextuality

One of the ways writers have used to change the relationship between metropolis and periphery is intertextuality. This means that they refer to or use one of the great works of European or American literature, but alter it or show different aspects of it, so that it becomes a living part of a new tradition that is relevant to the experience the writer is describing. A good example of this strategy, sometimes called 'writing back', is the novel *Wide Sargasso Sea* by the Caribbean author Jean Rhys. She used the famous 19th century novel *Jane Eyre* by Charlotte Brontë, in which there is a marginalized character, a madwoman who is locked in the attic of the house belonging to Jane's employer, Mr Rochester. Jane's hopes of marrying Mr Rochester are dashed when it is revealed that this woman, who comes from the Caribbean, is actually Mr Rochester's wife. Rhys takes this character and makes her the central figure of her own novel. Intertextuality depends on the combination of familiarity with a well-known story and the sense of alienation at seeing it in a new context.

3

R. K. Narayan

"The Story Machine"*

In this extract from the novel *The Vendor of Sweets* by R. K. Narayan, which is set in the imaginary Indian town of Malgudi in the 1950s, Jagan, the confectioner, is talking to his son Mali. Mali has disappointed Jagan by not showing an interest in any profession, but then he returns home from a visit to America with a machine which can write stories. – R. K. Narayan, *The Vendor of Sweets* (first published as *The Sweet-Vendor*) (London: The Bodley Head, 1967), pp. 82ff.

Jagan took the visitor's chair, looked for a moment at his son and plunged into the subject straight away. "How exactly does the story-machine operate?"

"I explained it to you yesterday," said Mali.

"There were some points which I did not quite grasp, but I was in a hurry."

The son looked pityingly at him, rose, opened a packing case, pushed aside a lot of brown paper and thread and lifted out a small object which looked like a radio cabinet and placed it on the table. "I was only waiting for this to arrive; yesterday I had to clear it from the railway office. What a lot of time is wasted here! I have never seen a more wasteful country than this." Jagan refrained from retorting, "We find it quite adequate for our purpose." Now Mali stood beside the cabinet in the attitude of a lecturer, he patted it fondly and said, "With this machine anyone can write a story. Come nearer, and you will see it working." Jagan obediently pushed his chair back, rose and stood beside his son, who seemed to tower above him. He felt proud of him. "God knows what he eats out of those tins; he looks tired, no doubt, but how well grown he is!" he reflected as Mali explained, "You see these four knobs? One is for characters, one for plot situations, one for climax, and the fourth is built on the basis that a story is made up of character, situations, emotion and climax, and by the right combination ..." He interrupted his oration for a moment to pull a drawer out and glance at a cyclostyled sheet of paper; he shut the drawer and came back to say, "You can work on it like a typewriter. You make up your mind about the number of characters. It works on a transistor and ordinary valves. Absolutely fool-proof. Ultimately we are going to add a little fixture, by which any existing story could be split up into components and analysed; the next model will incorporate it."

Jagan asked, "Do you want to use this for writing stories?"

"Yes, I am also going to manufacture and sell it in this country. An American company is offering to collaborate. In course of time, every home in the country will possess one and we will produce more stories than any other nation in the world. Now we are a little backward. Except for *Ramayana* and *Mahabharata*, those old stories, there is no modern writing, whereas in America alone every publishing season ten thousand books are published." He rushed back to his desk-drawer and gazed on the cyclostyled sheet again before repeating, "Yes, ten thousand titles. It is a 'must' for every home; all a writer will have to do is own one and press the keys, and he will get the formula in a moment, on a roll of paper, from which he can build up the rest ..."

Jagan left his seat and went over to examine the machine as if it were something from another planet. He approached it so cautiously that Mali said, "Touch it and see for yourself." Jagan peered at the apparatus closely and read the headings: "Characters: good, bad, neutral. Emotions: love, hate, revenge, devotion, pity. Complexities: characters, incidents, accidents. Climax: placement and disposal and conclusion." It looked pretty, its mahogany veneer was grained, its keys were green, red and yellow to indicate the different categories. "How can one write a story with it?" Jagan asked.

"Exactly as one does with a typewriter," Mali answered, and Jagan admired him for the fund of information he had gathered on the subject.

R. K. Narayan (1906–2001) grew up in Madras, where his father was a teacher. His family later moved to Mysore, where he qualified as a teacher and began to write. The death of his wife (from typhoid) in 1939 inspired the autobiographical novel *The English Teacher* (1945). From then until 1983 novels appeared at regular intervals, mostly concerning the events in a fictitious Southern Indian town called Malgudi. His editions of the Indian epics *Ramayana* and *Mahabharata* were published in the 1970s.

Vocabulary

Intro: confectioner (n.): a person who makes and sells sweets – **14 to refrain** (from) (v.): (fml.) to hold oneself back from – **14 to retort** (v.): to reply, answer (disagreeing) – **27 oration** (n.): a formal or public speech – **28 cyclostyled** (adj.): /ˈsaɪkləstaɪld/ copied on a machine from a stencil – **32 valve** (n.): a closed glass tube to control the flow of electricity, formerly used in a radio, television etc. – **58 complexity** (n.): s.th. which makes things more complicated and difficult to deal with – **60 veneer** (n.): /vəˈnɪə/ a thin covering of good quality wood – **60 grained** (adj.): covered with the pattern of lines in wood

Explanations

43 *Ramayana, Mahabharata*: /rəˈmaɪən, məˌhɑːˈbɑːrət/ the two great Sanskrit epics of ancient India, probably composed between the 5th and 2nd centuries BC. The *Ramayana* concerns a hero-king of Ayodhya, Rama-Chandra. The *Mahabharata*, which is eight times as long as the Iliad and Odyssey together, deals with the conflict between good and evil.

Awareness

1 Where do stories come from? Are there important differences between the 'old stories' like the *Odyssey*, the *Nibelungenlied* or the *Ramayana* and stories today?
2 What do American products represent for us, or for people in poorer countries?

Comprehension

3 Explain what Mali aims to do.
4 Where in the text is there a contrast between the 'old India' and America? What do the characters think about it?

Analysis

5 Comment on the way father and son behave towards each other. To what extent can this extract be seen as exemplifying a conflict between different generations?
6 Analyse the narrative perspective (Reference Library, pp. 310f.). What effect does it have?
7 Comment carefully on the appearance of the machine.
8 What might the 'story machine' represent? Discuss its implications.

Opinion

9 Are stories really written in the way suggested here? If so, what sort of stories? Could stories be analysed in the same way?
10 Salman Rushdie describes the relationship between the USA and the rest of the world as 'Coca-colanisation'. Comment on this, in the light of this extract.

Suggested Further Reading

11 Read one of R. K. Narayan's Malgudi books (e.g. *The Vendor of Sweets, The Bachelor of Arts, The Maneater of Malgudi*).
12 Look at other authors dealing with the theme of Anglo-American culture (e.g. Anita Desai, Ruth Jabhvala, or Suniti Namjoshi). Note also its importance in contemporary works like Michael Ondaatje's *The English Patient*, Zadie Smith's *White Teeth*, or Monica Ali's *Brick Lane*.

Internet Project

13 Remembering that Narayan published The *Vendor of Sweets* in 1967, find out about the computer program Dramatica Pro.

4

Felix Mnthali

"Neocolonialism"

The poet Felix Mnthali, born in 1933 in Zimbabwe of Malawian parents, was educated in Zimbabwe, Lesotho and Canada. He has been Professor of English at the University of Malawi, and more recently at the University of Botswana. In this poem he expresses the frustration felt by many black Africans that independence has not brought the economic and cultural freedoms they dreamed of. – Felix Mnthali, *When Sunset Comes to Sapitwa* (Harlow: Longman, 1982), pp. 10f.

Above all, define standards
prescribe values
set limits; impose boundaries

and even if you have no satellites
in space
and no weapons of any value
you will rule the world

Whatever tune you sing
they will dance
whatever bilge you spill
they will lick
and you may well pick
and choose
their rare minerals
and their rich forests

They will come to you
in fear and trembling
for the game will be played
according to your rules
and therefore the game will be played
only when you can win

Above all,
prescribe values
and define standards
and then sit back
to allow the third world
to fall into your lap.

Vocabulary

2 to prescribe (v.): say what must be done, what must exist - **10 bilge** (n.): the bottom of a ship or the dirty water in it; foolish talk (rubbish)

Awareness

1 Why do you think poor nations in the 'Third World' are poor?

Comprehension

2 Who do the words "you" and "they" in the poem refer to?
3 What is the poem's recipe for achieving power in comparison with other methods?

Analysis

4 Explain what the poet might mean by "values" and "standards" (ll. 1f., 23f.).
5 Relate the poem to the cartoons.
6 What seems to be the central image of the poem?
7 Show how language (Reference Library, p. 311) is used to help convey the meaning of the poem.

Opinion

8 Discuss some of the problems involved with aid to the Third World; are food aid, loans, educational programmes etc. always in developing countries' best interests?
9 Is the situation of Third World countries only the fault of the old colonialist powers, or do other countries like the US and Germany have something to do with it?

Project

10 Use the central message and the ideas in the poem and cartoons as the basis for a project: what is our relationship with the Third World?

Internet Project

11 Use the Internet to find out more about the word 'globalization'. What does it mean, and what are its effects on international trade and the relationships between richer and poorer countries?

5

"Tourists Follow in Mandela's Footsteps"

Tourists can now visit the prison near Cape Town where Nelson Mandela, South Africa's first black president, spent many years as a prisoner of the apartheid regime. He, and other important figures in the ANC (African National Congress) imprisoned with him, had been a focus for the opposition against apartheid. After his release, Mandela laid special emphasis on the importance of reconciliation and co-operation between the different races in the new South Africa. – Joanna Coles, *Guardian Weekly*, 12 January 1997, p.7.

The theme music to *Good Morning Vietnam* was blasting from the row of pizzerias as the good tug Proteus, on its maiden voyage, manoeuvred away from Cape Town's waterfront shopping complex.

"Right," shouted the captain, "we'll be travelling at a rate of 20 knots, so hold on to your babies." The swell in Table Bay was compensated only by the spellbinding view behind us of Table Mountain flanked by the Lion's Head and Devil's Peak.

It takes 40 minutes by boat from Cape Town to Robben Island, and this was the first boat to take ordinary South Africans on a tour of the island where their president spent a third of his life in prison.

"I wanted to come and understand it first hand, for myself," said Elizabeth Matheka, with her husband, a legal consultant from Johannesburg.

In the ultimate gesture of reconciliation, our guides turned out to be former prisoners and ex-prison officers, indistinguishable in their uniform of guinea fowl-patterned shirts.

As the boat docked they herded us on two old charabancs and the trip took on the nature of a surreal school outing, with passengers hurling questions.

"Was it true that sharks were fed from the island to prevent prisoners from swimming?" demanded a small Indian boy. "No," said Neil Fourie, a former "correctional officer". "But can you still see sharks?" the boy persisted.

"What about the leper colony?" asked Lynda Robinson. "The lepers were here from 1845 to 1935," said Mr Fourie, pointing to a tidal pool where the lepers had bathed, hoping the salt water would ease their terrible disease.

Past the wreck of a yacht called Song of Love, past a Taiwanese fishing vessel and the colony of 10,000 penguins, the bus circled the island, juddering to an abrupt halt in another quarry, this time of bright white stone.

'This is where President Mandela worked," Mr Fourie said, and the bus broke into spontaneous wolf whistles. "Take off your sunglasses and imagine working in this glare five days a week. The dust blocked the tear ducts – no wonder our president has trouble with his eyes."

"Shame," called out Mrs Matheka, to more whooping. "Were the prisoners shackled?" inquired the Indian boy. Lionel Davids, a former political prisoner, shook his head.

It was here in the white glare that the prisoners would swap stories and information from their correspondence courses, educating each other in the process.

The highlight of the trip is the prison itself, which still bears its notorious motto, "We Serve With Pride", over the entrance.

"Aren't you scared he'll lock you up?" the Indian boy asked Mr Davids as he and Mr Fourie counted us through the prison door. "But I'm used to staying here," grinned Mr Davids, adding that the political prisoners were never actually allowed a view of Cape Town.

"They didn't want us to orientate ourselves," retorted Lizo, another ex-prisoner, sharply, as he led us down the corridor to Nelson Mandela's old cell.

"Was he treated any differently to the others?" asked Ms Robinson, eyeing the grim bed, grey blanket and six bars on the window of the two-by-three-metre cell.

"Fear," said Mr Davids slowly, shepherding us back to the bus. "Fear ... The prison officers were all scared of him, you know."

Vocabulary

6 knot (n.): /nɒt/ a measure of the speed of a ship (about 1853 metres per hour) – **6 swell** (n.): the movement of the sea up and down – **16 legal consultant** (n.): a person who gives professional advice about the law – **22 charabanc** (n.): (BrE) an old-fashioned word for a coach, a bus used for a special trip – **28 leper colony** (n.): a place where people with the disease leprosy, which attacks the extremities of the body, were kept away from contact with healthy people – **39 wolf whistle** (n.): a loud, penetrating whistle, here used to express disapproval – **41 tear duct** (n.): a vessel which carries tears into the eye – **48 correspondence course** (n.): a set of lessons, often leading to a degree, in which the student receives material and sends in work by mail

Explanations

1 ***Good Morning Vietnam***: an American film and television series about a disc jockey in Vietnam – **10 Robben Island**: a small island just off the coast near Cape Town, famous for its prison. The island was named by Dutch settlers from the seals they found there. – **38 Nelson Mandela**: Born in 1918, he was one of the leaders of the resistance against Apartheid and was sentenced to life imprisonment by the white government in 1964. He was released in 1990, conducted negotiations with the government, and won the resulting free elections to become the country's first black president in 1994.

A poor township ...

and a prosperous suburb

Awareness

1 If someone has treated you very badly, and you have a chance to get your own back, do you do it, or can you forgive the person and be friends with him or her?

Comprehension

2 What makes Robben Island a tourist attraction?
3 What are tourists to Robben Island shown?
4 Why was Robben Island a good place to site a leper colony and a prison?

Analysis

5 Characterize the different sorts of tourists described in this article. Why do you think the author has chosen these particular people to describe?
6 In what ways were conditions difficult for prisoners on Robben Island?
7 How does the text suggest the prisoners also profited from their time in prison?
8 Explain the meaning(s) of the prison motto. Why do you think it is described as 'notorious'?
9 What signs are there in the text that reconciliation is taking place?
10 What can be deduced about life in Cape Town from the first part of the text?

Opinion

11 Why do you think the prison officers were scared of Mandela?
12 If you were visiting Cape Town, would you want to go to Robben Island? Give reasons for your answer.

Projects

13 Find out about the workings of Apartheid and the struggle against it. You could watch the film *Cry Freedom* (1987).
14 Think of somewhere near you which is an unlikely place to be a tourist attraction. How could you turn it into one? Write a brochure to try to 'sell' it.

Internet Project

15 Find out as much as you can from the Internet about the life and career of Nelson Mandela and his importance for South Africa and the world, then turn it into a PowerPoint presentation for the learning group.

6

Bruce Chatwin

"The Dreamtime"*

Bruce Chatwin (1940-89) was born and brought up in England. In 1960 he began a study of nomads, travelling widely to different parts of the world. His first book *In Patagonia* was a mixture of travel writing and fiction, and this was a form he always preferred, using fictional characters to report real occurrences or to illustrate things he had observed, so as to bring them to life in a way that a scientific anthropological study could not. *The Songlines* is one of these 'novels based on fact', and introduces a wider readership to the culture of the Australian Aborigine and the 'Dreamtime', which few people had previously shown interest in. In this conversation, the author is talking to Arkady, a white Australian who knows Aborigines well and is advising a railway company on where they should build to avoid conflicts with the Aborigines about their sacred sites. – Bruce Chatwin, *The Songlines* (London: Picador, 1987), pp. 14ff.

To get to grips with the concept of the Dreamtime, he said, you had to understand it as an Aboriginal equivalent of the first two chapters of Genesis – with one significant difference.

In Genesis, God first created the 'living things' and then fashioned Father Adam from clay. Here in Australia, the Ancestors created themselves from clay, hundreds and thousands of them, one for each totemic species.

"So when an Aboriginal tells you, 'I have a Wallaby Dreaming,' he means, 'My totem is Wallaby. I am a member of the Wallaby Clan.'"

"So a Dreaming is a clan emblem? A badge to distinguish 'us' from 'them'? 'Our country' from 'their country'?"

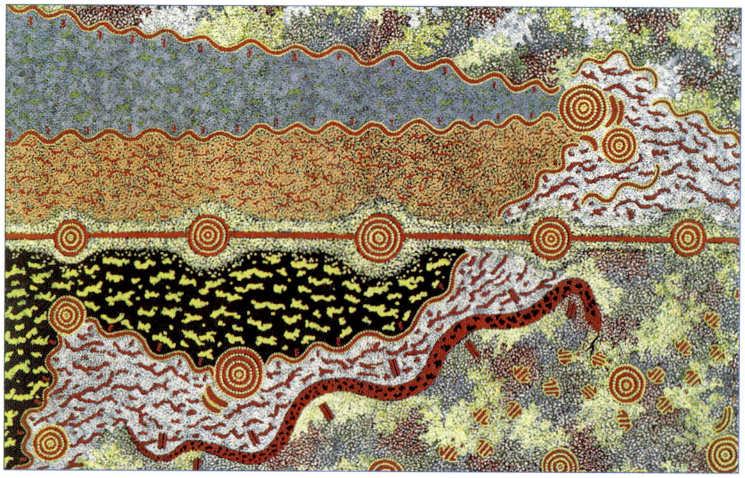

Michael Nelson Tjakamarra: Five Tjukurrpas (Dreamings), 1984 (Gabrielle Pizzi Collection, Melbourne). The painting shows the tracks of the flying ant, possum and rock wallaby ancestors between sacred sites near Vaughan Springs.

"Much more than that," he said.

Every Wallaby Man believed he was descended from a universal Wallaby Father, who was the ancestor of all other Wallaby Men and all living wallabies. Wallabies, therefore, were his brothers. To kill one for food was both fratricide and cannibalism.

"Yet," I persisted, "the man was no more wallaby than the British are lions, the Russians bears, or the Americans bald eagles?"

"Any species," he said "can be a Dreaming." [...]

He went on to explain how each totemic ancestor, while travelling through the country, was thought to have scattered a trail of words and musical notes along the line of his footprints, and how these Dreaming-tracks lay over the land as 'ways' of communication between the most far-flung tribes.

"A song," he said, "was both map and direction-finder. Providing you knew the song, you could always find your way across country."

"And would a man on 'Walkabout' always be travelling down one of the Songlines?

"In the old days, yes," he agreed. "Nowadays, they go by train or car."

"Suppose a man strayed from his Songline?"

"He was trespassing. He might get speared for it."

"But as long as he stuck to the track, he'd always find people who shared his Dreaming? Who were, in fact, his brothers?"

"Yes."

"From whom he could expect hospitality?"

"And vice versa."

"So song is a kind of passport and meal-ticket?"

"Again, it's more complicated."

In theory, at least, the whole of Australia could be read as a musical score. There was hardly a rock or creek in the country that could not or had not been sung. One should perhaps visualize the Songlines as a spaghetti of Iliads and Odysseys, writhing this way and that, in which every 'episode' was readable in terms of geology.

"By episode," I asked, "you mean 'sacred site'?"

"I do."

"The kind of site you're surveying for the railway?"

"Put it this way," he said. "Anywhere in the bush you can point to some feature of the landscape and ask the Aboriginal with you, 'What's the story there?' or 'Who's that?' The chances are he'll answer 'Kangeroo' or 'Budgerigar' or 'Jew Lizard', depending on which ancestor walked that way."

"And the distance between two such sites can be measured as a stretch of song?"

"That," said Arkady, "is the cause of all my troubles with the railway people."

It was one thing to persuade a surveyor that a heap of boulders were the eggs of the Rainbow Snake, or a lump of reddish sandstone was the liver of a speared kangaroo. It was something else to convince him that a featureless stretch of gravel was the musical equivalent of Beethoven's Opus 111.

By singing the world into existence, he said, the Ancestors had been poets in the original sense of *poesis*, meaning 'creation'. No Aboriginal could conceive that the created world was in any way imperfect. His religious life had a single aim: to keep the land the way it was and should be. The man who went 'Walkabout' was making a ritual journey. He trod in the footprints of his Ancestor. He sang the Ancestor's stanzas without changing a word or note – and so recreated the Creation.

Vocabulary

4 Genesis: /'dʒenəsɪs/ the first part of the Bible, in which the creation is described - **11 totemic** (adj.): /təʊ'temɪk/ having a close relation to a tribal group; used as a sign of that tribe - **13 wallaby** (n.): a small Australian animal related to the kangaroo - **24 fratricide** (n.): the act of murdering one's brother or sister - **42 to stray** (v.): to wander away from the right path - **43 to trespass** (v.): /'trespəs/ to walk over land without permission - **48 hospitality** (n.): food and a place to sleep given to a guest - **49 vice versa** (adv.): /ˌvaɪs 'vɜːsə/ and the other way round - **50 meal-ticket** (n.): (infml.) help and support given without having to provide anything in return - **53 score** (n.): a written copy of a piece of music - **53 creek** (n.): a stream - **56 to writhe** (v.): /raɪð/ to twist (like a snake) - **75 gravel** (n.): small stones and sand

Explanations

38 Walkabout: a period spent travelling about on foot through the country. Australian Aborigines regularly disappear from their homes and jobs for a time to go on 'Walkabout'. - **56 Iliad and Odyssey**: ancient Greek epic poems by Homer about the Trojan War and the return of Odysseus (Ulysses) to his home - **76 Beethoven's Opus 111**: Piano Sonata No 32 in C Minor, Beethoven's last sonata, composed in 1822 and widely regarded as one of the greatest works of classical music

Awareness

1 Collect images of Australia from television, film, travel brochures etc. What identity does the country seem to convey of itself?

2 Read the first two chapters of Genesis in the Bible, and compare the story with other creation myths you know (e.g. Norse, North American etc.)

Comprehension

3 What are the main differences between the Aborigenes' idea of Creation and that described in the book of Genesis in the Bible?

4 What is meant here by "totemic species" (l. 11), "Dreaming" (l. 13) and "Songline" (l. 39)? Explain in your own words.

5 Why is it so difficult for the railway company to avoid sacred sites?

6 What does the Aborigine see as the importance of going "Walkabout" (l. 38)?

Analysis

7 What are the consequences for the lifestyle of people who share beliefs such as those described here?

8 Comment on the form the author has chosen to explain the idea of the songlines to his readers.

Opinion

9 Do you believe we have anything to learn from the Aborigines about a successful relationship with the land?

Projects

10 Relate the text to the painting on p. 160.

11 Imagine a dispute between the railway company and the Aborigines. Write about it in two different ways: as Arkady might describe it to Chatwin, and as it might be reported in a newspaper.

7

"Born in a Hurricane"*

The slums of Kingston, Jamaica, are as dangerous as any in the US. From them emerged one of the most influential forms of music in the last decades: reggae. Millions of people in Europe and America still buy and love reggae music, though its style and lyrics are completely alien to their cultural references. For most of them Bob Marley was the king of reggae. – *The Independent Review*, 5 September, 2003, p. 20.

Many people think Bob Marley stole his crown. But it was Jimmy Cliff who gave reggae to the world, when he starred in and wrote half the music for Perry Henzell's *The Harder They Come* (1972). As Ivan, a country boy new to Kingston who is hustled out of a sure-fire hit by corrupt producers, and ends as a murderous ghetto legend, Cliff's unpredictable, brooding charisma powered one of the greatest pop movies. Filmed guerrilla-style on violent streets and burning with raw energy, it was a simmering underground smash across a globe till then indifferent to reggae. Cliff's soulful "rude bwoy" rebel character then became the model for Chris Blackwell at Island, when he met Marley soon afterwards, and marketed him into international immortality. From Peter Tosh recording with The Rolling Stones to Sean Paul in the Top 10, reggae as a global phenomenon started with Cliff.

But it was his music, on perhaps the best soundtrack album ever, that ensured *The Harder They Come*'s success. Songs like the title track and "You Can Get It If You Really Want" summed up his musical personality: indomitability, tempered by harsh realism, and a spiritual yearning to get past worldly cares. The high purity of his voice on "Many Rivers to Cross", especially, is as transcendent as anything in pop. I know friends whose lives have literally been saved by its mix of hurt and healing. But until recently, I wasn't sure if its maker was even alive.[...]

"I grew up hard," he says simply. "Everybody comes into this planet in some kind of way - it has something to do with how we are. I was born in a hurricane."

Cliff's voice had made him a star singer at his local church aged only 6. Hearing Jamaican music on the radio, as its 1962 independence neared, showed him how to reach a wider world. Aged 12, he moved by himself to Kingston, and the anarchic music scene later exposed in *The Harder They Come*, where rival producers routinely and violently ripped artists off. Cliff plunged in before his voice had broken.

"Kingston was rough," he admits, "because in the city you know no one. You can't go to your neighbour like in country and say, 'I'm hungry, give me something.' But by the time I got there, I was prepared to face whatever came. Even that young, I knew what I wanted to do. I had songs I had written, and I wanted them recorded. I had no consciousness about money. It was about getting my art exposed."

Typically, Cliff seized hold of the situation himself, cajoling local entrepreneur Leslie Kong to produce him, and having his first local hit aged 13. The spirituality which would define his great work was also beginning to build, as he met Kingston's despised Rastafari minority. Having grown up in demeaning poverty, in a colony owned by British whites, little more than a century after slavery, the themes of black power and African roots in Rasta were essential in giving Cliff, and his generation, strength.

"I remember the first dreadlock Rastaman I met, as a child," Cliff says. "Everybody except my father shunned him. But I was attracted to how he spoke, about Africa, in a deep, raspy voice. Then in Kingston I went to the heart of Rastafari. They call it Tivoli Gardens now, but it was then Backawall, where there were killers, criminals – and Rasta. I went there, and learnt more." He adds: "It made me want to fight. Because racism existed even in my district. We felt downtrodden, and our music expressed that. In the ska era, we were expressing the fact of independence, so music was fast and upbeat. Music slowed down through rocksteady, and then after that [in the mid-Sixties, when Jamaica's corrupt economy crashed] people were looking for something to hold on to, so it was slower still. And Rasta really took over, because it was the essence of roots."

Vocabulary

Intro/3 cultural references (n.): the things normally understood as part of the customs, beliefs, art, music, etc. of a particular group of people at a particular time – **7 to hustle out of** (v.): to trick out of – **7 sure-fire hit** (n.): a song that is certain to be a success – **10 brooding** (adj.): mysterious and dangerous – **13 simmering underground smash** (n.): a film that is very successful among particular groups of fans – **13 rude bwoy**: (CarE) an often violent criminal **21 soundtrack album** (n.): a collection of songs and music from a film – **25 to temper** (v.): to make stronger – **42 to rip off** (v.): to exploit, trick – **55 to cajole** (v.): to persuade using any method possible – **64 dreadlock Rastaman** (n.): a Rastafarian with long hair matted in dreadlocks – **80 essence** (n.): the true nature of s.th. – **80 roots** (n.): a style of music connected with cultural traditions

There are few ways to escape the poverty of Trenchtown's yards

Explanations

Intro/1 Kingston: the capital of Jamaica (pop. 600 000) – **Intro/4 Bob Marley**: (1945–81) Born in the hills of central Jamaica, he grew up and started playing music in Trenchtown. He formed a group called the Wailing Wailers with Bunny Livingston and Peter Mackintosh (later Bunny Wailer and Peter Tosh). First successes came at the end of the 1960s, and by 1975 they were known around the world. In spite of an assassination attempt on him in 1976, he returned to Jamaica in 1978 to try to bring peace between the political parties, who were killing each other at election time. Marley died of cancer in Miami. – **5 *The Harder They Come***: a film, set in Jamaica, about a boy who wants to be a singer but gets into trouble with the police and dies in a Western-style shoot-out. The title alludes to the proverb: 'The bigger they come, the harder they fall'. – **16 Island:** Island Records, the company Marley made his great recordings with – **19 Sean Paul:** a popular Jamaican performer when the article was written – **34 hurricane:** Jamaica is periodically subject to devastating hurricanes. The 'government yards in Trenchtown' in Marley's song 'No Woman No Cry' were built after a hurricane destroyed to district – **58 Rastafari, Rasta (Rastafarianism):** a religion originating in Jamaica which involves a belief in the return of black people to Africa (spiritually if not in fact) and lays down strict rules of behaviour. More controversially, it makes religious use of 'the healing of the nations' (cannabis). – **68 Tivoli Gardens:** a slum district in West Kingston next to Trenchtown, where Marley spent his youth. In the 1980s and 1990s there was a war between the two communities.

Awareness

1 What do you associate with reggae music and Jamaica?
2 What image do you have of the Caribbean (in advertising, music, films or travel brochures)?

Comprehension

3 Explain what part Jimmy Cliff played in the making of *The Harder They Come*.
4 What does the text suggest were the influences on Cliff?

Analysis

5 What does the text imply about the reasons Marley 'stole Cliff's crown'?
6 What does the text say is special about Cliff's music?
7 Explain how Rastafarians were originally seen in Jamaica, and what Rastafari meant to Cliff.
8 How, according to Cliff, did Jamaican music develop, and why?

Opinion

9 From the introduction and text, discuss why reggae is such a significant phenomenon as part of the postcolonial experience.

Projects

10 Listen to the song 'Exodus' by Bob Marley and try to analyse it. Compare it with Jimmy Cliff's 'Many Rivers to Cross'.
11 Look at the author's description of Cliff's music in ll. 21–31. Try to describe music that has had a powerful effect on you.
12 Watch the film *Cool Runnings* and compare what it says about Jamaica with this text, or with *The Harder They Come.*

Internet projects

13 Find out more about Rastafari.
14 Look up the website of the Trenchtown Reading Centre (www.trenchtownreadingcentre.com) about a project that helps people in the area of Kingston where Bob Marley wrote his early songs. See how the project has developed and, if you would like to, try to get actively involved in it or a similar project.

10

Australia –

A cattle station

When you are celebrating Christmas or New Year's Eve in the middle of summer, when the water runs down the sink the other way round, and it's not the North Star but the Southern Cross that points the way at night you know you are "Down Under", where things are not upside down but, nevertheless, quite different.

Australia is 24 times larger than the British Isles or Germany. Remote cattle farms in the Outback are so vast that helicopters are used to round up the herds. One ranch is the size of Belgium.

Ayers Rock – Uluru

The "Three Sisters" rock formation in the Blue Mountains

Uluru (or Ayers Rock) is sacred to the Australian Aborigines. It is about 550 million years old. The Aborigines have lived in Australia for at least 40,000 years. The first white settlers arrived in 1788.

Eleven of the world's most poisonous snakes live in Australia and 3,000 people are bitten by snakes every year.

Eighty per cent of Australia's 18 million people (including the 200,000 Aborigines) live in cities mainly along the fertile coast between Brisbane and Adelaide.

Down Under on Top

Sydney Opera House

Bondi Beach, Sydney

The Great Barrier Reef

Australia is flat. The highest peak, Mount Kosciousko, is only 7,310 feet (2,230 metres) high. In the deserts temperatures can reach a blistering 175 degrees F. Over 2,000 kms of coral make the Great Barrier Reef the world's largest living phenomenon. It is so big that it can be seen from outer space.

Waltzing Matilda

The unofficial Australian national anthem

Once a jolly swagman camped by a billabong
Under the shade of a coolibah tree.
And he sang as he watched and waited till his billy boiled
"Who'll come a-waltzing Matilda with me?"

Chorus: Waltzing Matilda, waltzing Matilda,
You'll come a-waltzing Matilda with me.

Down came a jumbuck to drink at the billabong.
Up jumped the swagman and grabbed him with glee.
And he sang as he put that jumbuck in his tucker-bag
"You'll come a-waltzing Matilda with me!"
Chorus

Up came the squatter riding on his thoroughbred.
Up came the troopers, one, two, three.
"Where's that jolly jumbuck, you've got in your tucker-bag?
You'll come a-waltzing Matilda with me!"
Chorus

Up jumped the swagman and sprang into the billabong.
"You'll never take me alive!" said he.
And his ghost may be heard as you pass by that billabong
"Who'll come a-waltzing Matilda with me!"
Chorus

1

Kate Grenville

"First Encounters"*

Kate Grenville was born in Sydney in 1950. Her books have won several awards, including the Orange Prize and the Commonwealth Writers' Prize, awarded to her novel *The Secret River* in 2006. This extract deals with an imagined encounter between Australian Aborigines and a British convict, William Thornhill. Thornhill, sentenced to be 'transported for life' to New South Wales in 1806 for stealing wood in London, has settled with his family (like the novelist's ancestors) on what he thinks is empty land on the banks of the Hawkesbury River near Sydney. - Kate Grenville, *The Secret River* (Edinburgh: Canongate Books, 2006), pp. 201-204

Something made him turn. Behind him was a group of men standing together watching. They had arrived so quietly they might have risen up out of the ground. There were six of them, or perhaps eight, or ten. Something about the way their skins were shadows among the shadows of the trees made it hard to see them straight.

In London William Thornhill counted as a big man, but these men made him feel small. They were as tall as he was, their shoulders sinewy but powerful, their chests defined with pads of muscle. Each held a few spears, the lengths of wood shifting like insects' feelers.

He stood legs apart, his heavy new boots planted on the ground. He imagined the way he looked to them: his mysterious clothes, his face shadowed under his hat.

An Aborigine family as seen by a 19th century painter

It seemed important to act the part of host. That way, they were his guests. He made himself hail them in a jovial way, looking them right in the face, as if they were dogs that would bite if they caught the scent of fear.

Good-day to you gentlemen, he called. *How are you this fine day?*

He heard his words evaporate, thin and silly, into the air, and was glad that Ned and Dan were not with him to hear. He felt something hot in his chest: anger? Or was it fear?

He wished he had the gun.

A bird began a long tweetling somewhere in the trees and the humming in the grass swelled and faded, swelled and faded. A stick fell in the fire with a soft collapsing sound.

A haze of steam was starting to come up from the place in the coals where the snake was cooking, and a good greasy smell was wafting over to him, like nothing so much as a nice fat mutton chop. He found himself wondering if a yard of serpent might not be such a bad dinner.

Cat got your tongues, he said. *You black buggers?* As if this was a signal, they came towards him, moving in that loose-kneed way they had, the spears easy in their hands. One – the same greybeard he had slapped the first day – separated himself from the others and came right up to Thornhill, reaching out and placing a long black hand on his forearm. Authority radiated from this naked old man like heat off a fire. A stream of words began to come out of his mouth.

Thornhill forced himself to break the spell. *Very good, you old bugger*, he said, his voice harsh, cutting across the flow. *Now you listen.* He bent down and with a twig drew marks on the dust: a curving line that was the river, and a tidy square representing his own hundred acres. *This mine now. Thornhill's place.*

The man stared at him.

You got all the rest, Thornhill said. He could hear his voice getting louder. *You got the whole blessed rest of it, mate, and welcome to it.* But his words seemed to flow past the man as if they mattered as little as a current of air. He had not noticed before how white the white part of the man's eyes were. He wondered if it was that, the darkness of the skin against the whiteness of the eyes, that made his eyes seem to be lit from within.

The old man took a step towards the fire and from one of the bark dishes picked something up: a cluster of the daisy-roots, six or eight narrow tubers dangling from the stem. He pointed at the roots and spoke again. Finally he took a bite of one of them. Chewed, swallowed, nodded.

Even with the words as meaningless to Thornhill as the cry of a bird, he understood. The man snapped off a finger of root and held it out to Thornhill. The flesh was translucent, glassy, crisp-looking, something in the nature of a radish.

But Thornhill did not intend to eat. *Kind of you, old boy.* That was a joke that had not lost its savour. *But you can keep your radishes.* He looked again at the thing on the man's brown-seamed pink palm. *Monkey food, I would call that, mate, but good luck to you.*

The man was vehement now. He was explaining something in detail. He turned and pointed towards the river-flats, holding up the bundle of roots. There seemed to be a question in his voice now, a phrase repeated, as if he wanted agreement.

Yes, mate, Thornhill said. *You can keep your monkey's balls that you like so much.* The old man said something, loud and sharp, and Thornhill recognised the same phrase.

He longed for words.

It seemed that the old man was ready to wait all day for an answer.

We'll stick to our victuals, mate, you stick to yours, Thornhill said. He met the man's eyes and nodded. The old man gave a curt nod back.

A conversation had taken place. There had been an inquiry and an answer. But what inquiry, which answer?

They stared at each other, their words between them like a wall.

Info

Who are the Aborigines?

Aborigines are Australia's indigenous people. They came originally from somewhere in Asia and have been in Australia for at least 40,000 years. The first came at a time when the sea level was lower and there was an almost continuous land bridge between Asia and Australia. Traditionally the Aborigines were hunter-gatherers who grew no crops and did not domesticate animals, so they were completely dependent on their natural environment.

In 1770 there were about 300,000 (estimates differ) Aborigines who occupied the entire continent, divided into 500–600 distinct groups. 200 different languages were spoken and we may assume that most Aborigines were bilingual or multilingual.

Most of the year people lived dispersed into small nomadic groups or bands, a band consisting of several families, and moved about a well defined territory or "estate" in search of food and water. They were intimately acquainted with all the country within their range of movement and could read the ground like a map.

Vocabulary

16 sinewy (adj.): /'sɪnjuːi/ thin and muscular – **36 tweetling** (n.): noise made by a small bird – **42 to waft** (v.): move through the air (said esp. of smells) – **44 mutton** (n.): meat of a (mature) sheep – **45f. yard of serpent** (n.): a snake about 90 cm long – **48 cat got your tongues:** (have you) lost your tongues? Used to ask s.o. why they are not talking – **49 buggers** (n.): here: rather humorous, infml. term for these men – **63 spell** (n.): magical power – **71 blessed** (adj.): here: used to express annoyance – **79 bark** (n.): outer covering of a tree – **80 tuber** (n.): fleshy underground stem of a plant (such as the potato) – **89 savour** (n.): here: the power to cause pleasure

Explanations

32 Ned, Dan: Thornhill's servants; as a free man Thornhill was allowed to pick some men from the convict newcomers who had to serve him as farmhands. – **53 greybeard:** Thornhill had slapped this elderly Aborigine (with a grey beard) when he had tried to take Thornhill's spade.

Awareness

1 Use the Internet to find the meanings of the following words and say which come from Australian Aboriginal languages.

barramundi	*billabong*	*boomerang*	*cockatoo*	*coolibah*	*corroborree*
didgeridoo	*dugong*	*kangaroo*	*koala*	*wallaby*	*wombat*

Comprehension

2 Who are the two main figures dominating the scene? Describe them and explain the problem they have.

3 What is Thornhill trying to do in this passage?

4 Why does he refuse to eat?

Analysis

5 Describe the setting of the scene (Reference Library, p. 309) and explain how the writer creates an uneasy atmosphere.

6 Show that Thornhill's attitude towards the Aborigines is ambivalent.

7 At the end of the text the narrator says: "They stared at each other, their words between them like a wall." Explain the meaning of this simile (Reference Library, p. 311).

8 What is the effect of the author's notation of direct speech?

Opinion

9 Do you think the men would have come to an agreement if they had spoken the same language? Give reasons for your view. You may also consider the present relationship between white Australians and Aborigines.

10 Why do you think is it so important for Thornhill to own a piece of land?

Projects

11 Gather information about the concept of *terra nullius*. Explain its meaning and the consequences it had for the history of Australia.

12 Find out about early European explorers of Australia and why some of them starved to death.

Scene near the river Darling (1835)

2

Oodgeroo Noonuccal

No More Boomerang

Oodegeroo Noonuccal (1920–1993) was the first of the modern Aboriginal protest writers, being known for most of her life as Kath Walker, but then reverting to the tribal name in 1988 to dissociate herself from the Bicentenary celebrations of the conquest of Australia that appeared to be pure hypocrisy for a person who had had to work as a domestic servant from the age of 13, and who was not allowed to become a nurse because of her Aboriginal origin. She became involved in the Aboriginal activist movement, seeking to generate cultural pride. – Oodgeroo Noonuccal, *My People* (1970; Milton: Queensland, 1981), pp. 32f. Originally published in: *The Dawn is at Hand* (Brisbane: The Jacaranda Press, 1966), pp.26f.

No more boomerang
No more spear;
Now all civilized -
colour bar and beer.

No more corroboree,
Gay dance and din.
Now we got movies,
And pay to go in.

No more sharing
What the hunter brings.
Now we work for money,
Then pay it back for things.

Now we track bosses
To catch a few bob,
Now we go walkabout
On bus to the job.

One time naked,
Who never knew shame;
Now we put clothes on
To hide whatsaname.

No more gunya,
Now bungalow,
Paid by hire purchase
in twenty year or so.

Lay down the stone axe,
Take up the steel,
And work like a nigger
For a white man meal.

No more firesticks
That made the whites scoff.
Now all electric,
And no better off.

Bunyip he finish,
Now got instead
White fella Bunyip,
Call him Red.

Abstract picture now -
What they coming at?
Cripes, in our caves we
Did better than that.

Black hunted wallaby,
White hunt dollar;
White fella witch-doctor
Wear dog-collar.

No more message-stick;
Lubras and lads
Got television now,
Mostly ads.

Lay down the woomera,
Lay down the waddy.
Now we got atom-bomb,
End everybody.

Vocabulary

4 colour bar (n.): social barrier separating people of different colour – **6 din** (n.): loud noise – **13 to track** (v.): to follow – **14 a few bob** (n.): some money (originally: shillings) – **15 walkabout** (n.): an Aborigine's period of nomadic wandering – **29 firestick** (n.): smouldering stick used for carrying fire from camp to camp – **30 to scoff** (v.): to mock – **39 cripes** (n.): interj., coll. (an expression of amazement, disgust, or the like), euphemistic for: Christ – **41 wallaby** (n.): /'wɑləbi/ animal with large hind feet and a long tail, smaller than a kangaroo – **43 witch-doctor** (n.): person who possesses magical powers – **44 dog-collar** (n.): here: a stiff collar, worn by members of the clergy

Explanations

Intro/3 Bicentenary celebrations: The Bicentenary celebrations were held in 1988 in order to commemorate the 200th anniversary of European settlement in Australia. They mark the events of 26 January 1788, when the eleven ships of Captain Arthur Phillip's First Fleet arrived from Britain and gathered in Port Jackson to found the colony of New South Wales. – **Intro/6 Aboriginal activist movement:** movement for the advancement of Aboriginal rights – **5 corroboree** (n.): Aboriginal assembly of festive, sacred or warlike character – **21 gunya** (n.): Aboriginal hut – **33 bunyip** (n.): an imaginary creature of Aboriginal legend, said to haunt swamps and waterholes – **36 Red** (n.): Noonuccal was a member of the Communist party – **45 message-stick** (n.): a short wooden stick used by Aborigines to convey messages, also a kind of permit for sb passing through alien territory – **46 lubra** (n.): young Aboriginal woman – **49 woomera** (n.): a throwing stick, used to propel a spear. It gave its name to the Woomera rocket range, where nuclear weapons were tested in the 1950s and 60s. More recently it was a controversial detention centre for illegal immigrants. – **50 waddy** (n.): Aboriginal heavy wooden war-club

Awareness

1 In class: Read the poem silently. Choose one stanza which you learn by heart. Recite the poem from memory together with twelve other students, each speaking one stanza aloud.

Comprehension

2 Give a rough idea of what you think the poem is about.

3 Write down in your own words what each stanza says. In class the task can be divided up and each student can choose the stanza he/she has learned by heart.

Analysis

4 Explain the basic principle according to which the poem is structured (Reference Library, pp. 309f.).

5 Make a list contrasting the aspects of Aboriginal life with those of white civilisation.

6 Stanza five may be seen to be of central importance. Explain its meaning in the context of our Christian culture (cf. Genesis 1).

7 Identify the rhetorical devices (Reference Library, pp. 309f.) in the poem and explain what effect they have.

8 Consider the improvements technological and economic progress has brought to the Aborigines and explain what point the author is making about them.

Opinion

9 Do you think that the poem is successful? Give reasons for your view.

10 Is there anything which our western civilisation could learn from Aboriginal culture? Support your opinion.

Project

11 Try to turn the poem into a rap song:
Find a suitable rhythm to accompany the reading.
The students can form different groups and take turns reading the stanzas. They can also choose one speaker/singer who speaks/sings the first part of each stanza or each line and the "chorus" shouts the rest. Present the "song" to an audience.

3

Midnight Oil

Beds are Burning

On Sunday, 28 May 2000, more than 150,000 people walked across Sydney Harbour Bridge in an expression of support for reconciliation between indigenous people and the wider (mainly white) community of Australia. According to the *Sydney Morning Herald* the walk "put meaning back into the near exhausted public dialogue on a great unresolved question for all Australians, the relationship between black and white."[1] The day before 1600 people had attended the Corroboree 200 ceremony at the Sydney Opera House to celebrate national reconciliation. The white rock group Midnight Oil has always taken an interest in the Aborigines' struggle for their rights. Since the release of their first album in 1978 Midnight Oil have become one of the most famous, most political and probably most Australian of all Australian bands. Their catchy hit single *Beds Are Burning* (1987) even reached the American top charts and brought global attention to the problems of the Aborigines. It was played by the "Oils" in the closing ceremony of the Sydney Olympics. – The song was first released on the album Midnight Oil, *Diesel and Dust* (1987), Columbia Records (Sony Music), CDM 02-460005-10.

Out where the river broke
The bloodwood and the desert oak
Holden wrecks and boiling diesels
Steam in forty five degrees

The time has come
To say fair's fair
To pay the rent
To pay our share
The time has come
A fact's a fact
It belongs to them
Let's give it back

How can we dance when our earth is turning
How do we sleep when our beds are burning

Four wheels scare the cockatoos
From Kintore East to Yuendemu
The western desert lives and breathes
In forty five degrees

The time has come
A fact's a fact
It belongs to us all
Let's give it back

A public apology?

[1] *The Sydney Morning Herald*, 29 May 2000

Vocabulary

2 bloodwood (n.): *(Brosimum Rubescens)* a eucalyptus tree that has reddish timber and yields a dark red gum – **2 desert oak** (n.): *(Allocasuarina decaisneana)* tree with feathery leaves found in the dry desert region around Central Australia, a young tree being tall and thin, an old tree full and bushy – **15 cockatoo** (n.): *(Cacatua)* a bird:

Explanations

3 Holden wreck (n.): broken down car; in 1948 Australia began to produce its own car, the Holden – **16 Kintore, Yuendemu:** settlements in the Northern Territory, in the Alice Springs area, in the desert, where the highest recorded temperature is 53 degrees Celsius

Awareness

1 Can you imagine what the problems between white Australians and Aborigines which this song alludes to may be?

Comprehension

2 Consider ll. 1–4 and 15–18. Describe what the singer sees, feels and hears.

3 Who is the singer? What group of the Australian people does he belong to? Whom does he address?

Analysis

4 The singer repeats the phrase "The time has come" (ll. 5, 9, 19). What time does he mean? Explain what stylistic means (Reference Library, pp. 309f.) he uses to illustrate his statements.

5 Comment on the phrase "fair's fair" in l. 6.

6 Examine the questions of the song in ll. 13f. and explain what they might imply.

Opinion

7 What is the attitude of the singer towards the problem addressed in the song? Would you share his opinion if you were a white Australian? Explain why you think so.

8 What is meant by "it", and can you "give it back"?

9 Why do you think the song was chosen to be performed at the closing ceremony of the 2000 Sydney Olympics?

Project

10 What similarities and what differences can be found in the way European settlers and native peoples treated each other in Australia, North America, the Caribbean, New Zealand and Southern Africa?

Info

Midnight Oil – a band with a conscience

Having fronted the band for 25 years Peter Garret, lead singer of Midnight Oil, quit the band in December 2002 in order to concentrate fully on environmental activism. Until then the band had probably shown more environmental and social awareness than any other rock group in the history of music. They had always been concerned with the problem of reconciliation and as the first white group started on a tour together with an Aboriginal group, the Warumpi band. After this famous Black Fella/White Fella tour of indigenous communities they were asked by the Aborigines to write a song that would accompany the handover of Uluru (Ayers Rock) back to the Aboriginal people. The song they wrote, *The Dead Heart*, perfectly suited the occasion and helped to put the problem of Aboriginal land rights on the political agenda.

But it was not only Aboriginal problems that the band was concerned with. Their record *Blue Skye Mine*, e.g., was a song about asbestos miners in the Australian outback who had developed a range of cancers and respiratory diseases and frequently died at an early age. The same song was used to draw attention to one of the world's largest pollution incidents, the *Exxon Valdez* oil spill before the Alaskan coast. The Oils went to New York and, although forbidden to do so, played a gig outside *Exxon's* headquarters causing a traffic jam that brought areas of the city to a standstill.

After the split-up in 2002 the band only reunited once to perform at a concert on January 29, 2005, to raise funds for the tsunami victims. Lead singer Peter Garret joined the Australian Labor Party and in the 2004 General Elections won a seat in the House of Representatives which he still holds.

4

John Everingham

"Children of the First Fleet"

Punishment by banishment and transportation had been a legal practice in England since the 16th century. After the new-born American state resolved not to accept any more convicts, the jails of England became overcrowded. Since Australia was distant, the escape of convicts difficult and their return improbable, the Australian coast became a suitable replacement and was consequently turned into a penal settlement (convict colony). As the ship-merchants profited from the transport, they overcrowded their ships and cut supplies in order to leave more room for freight, and often kept the convicts in irons or in quarters below decks. When they arrived, many were first in hulks, which were ships made into floating prisons, and some of them never touched land. Convict transportation continued well into the 19th century until, finally, over 150,000 convicts had been brought to Australia. – John Everingham, "Children of the First Fleet," *National Geographic Australia*, 173,2 (February 1988), pp. 236f.

Gentlemen convicts at work, Port Arthur, 1836

"A CONVICT? THAT'S TERRIBLE!" My friend's face contorted with a mix of sympathy and suppressed horror. I'd just mentioned, over the noise of a dinner party, that my ancestor had been a convict – mentioned it my Australian way, with a tinge of First Fleet pride. But he missed that, for this was Bangkok, Thailand, a royal land where rank and pride are one. – "You should dig deeper," he said. 'With a name like Everingham, surely you could find a lord back there."

Maybe, but Australians do like their convicts.

It was July 1784, trial number 775 in London's Old Bailey court. Judge Rose passed a stern, crime-calloused look over the trembling lad of 14 or 15, charged with stealing two lawbooks.

"The prisoner's defense?" demanded the judge. The boy could scarcely brave a glance up through his matted, dirty hair.

"I was in great distress ..., " whispered Matthew James Everingham, my ancestor and founder of a small dynasty on a far face of the earth.

"Guilty!"

"In great distress" described a large portion of Georgian London's population. England shuddered with social turmoil. The industrial revolution had created a new class of urban poor, hungry and bitter in their back-alley hovels. Crime flourished, and the elite's reprisal – the iron fist of law – was severe to the extreme.

The court transcript recorded young Matthew Everingham's penalty succinctly: 'Transported for seven years."

Transported. Discarded from his motherland, crammed into the dark, airless hold of a tiny sailing vessel, *Scarborough*, Matthew and 775 other petty criminals spent eight months as cargo carcasses exported to the unimaginable, farthest edge of the world.

That distant shore had seen only one other English vessel, James Cook's *Endeavour* in 1770. No land survey had been made. It was quite a shock when that First Fleet of 11 little vessels finally arrived and found the rich soil and open grassy lands of their expectations to be thin, rocky hills dense with wiry, inhospitable bush.

The convicts cut the rocky surface, but crops didn't grow. Seven of the colony's eight cattle escaped. Aborigines, though often friendly, would occasionally spear an unwary colonist. The fleet had brought two years of supplies, but more than two years later neither supply ship nor news had arrived from England. When five ships finally rounded Sydney Harbour's heads, Matthew may have been one of the jubilant rushing to greet them. While one carried some stores, others brought only convicts – another 739 pitiful mouths to feed!

The tiny settlement was stunned by the battered, starving women disgorged like listless sacks from the stinking holds of the hell ship *Neptune*, one of the Second Fleet. The dead and the near dead were dumped ashore. Some 160 had been disposed of at sea.

Among the 341 survivors of *Neptune*, Matthew Everingham found Elizabeth Rimes, about 17, whom he would marry within a year. Of our family's convict ancestress, transported for stealing a blanket and sheet, Matthew later wrote: "A most excellent woman ... hard indeed to be found in this Colony for the generallity of them ... disgrace the very name of Woman." The violence of Australia's birth left thousands more dead until the last of 162,000 transported convicts were landed in 1868.

Vocabulary

24 calloused (adj.): /kæləst/ hardened – **37 hovel** (n.): a small dirty dwelling – **70 to round** (v.): to go round – **75 to stun** (v.): to overcome with astonishment – **76 to disgorge** (v.): to discharge, to empty – **76 listless** (adj.): without energy

Explanations

Intro/4 penal settlement: The most severe 'secondary' punishment (short of execution) inflicted on the convicts was transportation to a penal settlement, of which the most important were Newcastle, Port Arthur, Maria Island in Van Diemen's Land and Norfolk Island. At times discipline in these settlements was, as prisoners used to say, 'worse than death'. – **Intro/9 John Everingham** (author): journalist and contributor to magazines like the *National Geographic* – **22 Old Bailey:** the Central Criminal Court in the West of the City of London – **34 Georgian** (adj.): belonging to the time of the reigns of George I to George III (appr. 1714–1811) – **58 James Cook's *Endeavour*:** On Captain Cook's voyage round the world in 1770 he became the first Englishman to see and map the coast of South-eastern Australia. – **66 Aborigines:** the dark-skinned people who were the first people to live in Australia – **picture: Port Arthur:** a small settlement on the Tasman Peninsula in south-eastern Tasmania, which, named after Lieutenant-Governor Arthur, became the most infamous of the penal stations on the island in the 19th century; it is now a museum.

Awareness

1 How might the revelation that one's forebears were convicts change one's identity?

Comprehension

2 What, according to the writer, is the difference between Thailand and Australia?
3 How were the convicts treated?
4 What may have led to an increase in the crime rate at the end of the 18th century in Britain?
5 How did the majority of the female convicts supposedly disgrace the "very name of Woman" (l. 82)?

Analysis

6 What words and phrases are used to arouse sympathy with the early convict settlers?

Opinion

7 White Australians are proud if they can trace their ancestry back to convicts. Why? What sort of ancestors would you feel proud of?

Projects

8 Find out how many percent of the present Australian population trace their origin back to convicts.
9 Find out what proportion of present-day Australians have German ancestry and why those Germans emigrated to Australia. You might write a letter to the Australian embassy asking for relevant statistical material.

5

Greenpeace

Faking It

The greenhouse effect, where industrial gases such as carbon dioxide trap the sun's heat in the upper atmosphere, is now seen as the principle cause of global warming. As a result weather conditions will become more extreme. Deserts will grow and there will be severe storms and disastrous floods. Global warming affects the whole world but it is mainly caused by the industrialised West including Australia, where over recent years droughts and floods have increased. Greenpeace takes a critical look at what Australia does to tackle this problem. – Taken from the Internet: Greenpeace Australia Pacific, Australian Conservation Foundation, Friends Of The Earth, *Faking It* (ISBN 1 876221 11 9).

As concern grows over the environmental and economic threats posed by human-induced climate change, the Australian Government has intensified its attempts to create an image of a progressive country with a comprehensive range of climate change policies. In truth, as this report shows, Australia's greenhouse performance is shameful.

Not satisfied with bullying the rest of the world into allowing Australia an 8% increase in emissions under the Kyoto Protocol, the Australian Government is failing to take serious action to tackle climate change.

According to figures submitted to the Intergovernmental Panel on Climate Change (IPCC), Australia is among the highest per capita greenhouse emitters in the world. Per capita emissions are almost twice the industrialised country average of 13.4 tonnes. In 1998 emissions excluding landclearing increased to 116.9% of 1990 levels – well beyond Australia's +8% Kyoto target.

Congested traffic pollutes the air in Sydney.

This contrasts sharply with countries like Germany, which has reduced emissions by 17%. In the last two years the United Kingdom, Denmark, India and China have all achieved reductions. Denmark and the United Kingdom have already achieved reductions equal to their Kyoto targets.

Despite the government trumpeting that it has spent $1 billion on greenhouse, action in Australia amounts to an elaborate smoke-and-mirrors exercise. Rather than confronting the problem head-on, the government relies on voluntary initiatives that have failed to move the nation beyond business as usual. Emissions rates from transport and electricity consumption have accelerated since Australia signed the Kyoto Protocol and the government has admitted, that even with measures already introduced, it expects emissions in the first commitment period to be 18–20% above 1990 levels.

Unwilling to take any serious action, the Australian Government is relying on loopholes in the Kyoto Protocol to meet its target. Risky sinks schemes, deceptive 'renewable' energy proposals and dubious technology transfers to the developing world could potentially allow Australia to meet its Kyoto commitments 'on paper' while industrial pollution continues to rise.

This report, a joint analysis by Greenpeace Australia, Friends of the Earth and the Australian Conservation Foundation shows that, contrary to the honest broker image the government attempts to portray, when it comes to genuine action on climate change, Australia is faking it.

Conclusion

It is a short-sighted agenda. The cost to Australia of not taking serious action to tackle climate change is high. Recent modelling shows the impacts of climate change on Australia include:

- increased intensity and frequency of coral bleaching leading to annual bleaching events on the Great Barrier Reef by 2030–2070, threatening the survival of the reef itself and a tourism industry worth $2 billion a year
- significant changes to rainfall patterns, exacerbating both floods and droughts;
- insufficient snow for viable operations at most ski resorts by 2070;
- the loss of up to 20% of all species in south-eastern Australia;
- major negative impacts on agriculture, including reduced milk yields, a 138% increase in heat stress on beef cattle and rapidly declining wheat yields resulting from temperature increases and decreased rainfall.

Vocabulary

Title: to be faking it (v.): to pretend to be doing s.th. one is not – **2 to pose a threat** (v.): to be a danger – **10 to bully** (v.): to use unfair means to make s.o. do s.th. **22 per capita:** for each person – **26 landclearing** (n.): the destruction of native vegetation, e.g. the bulldozing of native bushlands, forests, savannah woodlands and grasslands – **36 smoke-and-mirrors exercise** (n.): s.th. intended to disguise or draw attention away from s.th. (esp. from s.th. embarrassing) – **43f. first commitment period** (n.): 2008–2012, time by which a number of promised goals (of reduction) must be achieved – **46 loophole** (n.): possibility of avoiding s.th. because the words of a contract are not clear – **47 sinks** (n., pl.): processes which remove greenhouse gases from the atmosphere, e.g. growing forests – **60f. honest broker:** a person who tries to get other people to reach an agreement – **76 to exacerbate** (v.): /ɪg'zæsəbeɪt/ to make worse, aggravate – **78 viable** (adj.): possible – **83 milk yields** (n.): the amount of milk that is produced

Explanations

14 Kyoto Protocol: The United Nations Framework Convention on Climate Change, or Global Warming Convention, was one of the main documents agreed upon at the EARTH SUMMIT, a conference held at Rio de Janeiro, Brazil (14 June 1992). The Kyoto Protocol is an amendment to this treaty on climate change. The countries which signed this protocol have agreed to reduce their greenhouse gas emissions. – **21 IPCC:** The Intergovernmental Panel on Climate Change was established by the United Nations Environmental Programme (UNEP) in 1988 to assess the information relevant for the understanding of human induced climate change and its potential impacts on the environment. – **57f. Friends of the Earth:** a worldwide federation of environmental organisations from 66 countries (2002) – **58 Australian Conservation Foundation (AFC):** a democratic, membership-based organisation that works towards a society which protects, sustains and restores the environment, a society that changes our relationship to the Earth to one of harmony with the environment. Since its beginnings in the mid-1960s, ACF has successfully worked together with governments, industry groups and the general community. Peter Garrett, front man of the world famous, politically active rock group *Midnight Oil* (see pp. 171f.), is a former director of AFC. – **71 coral bleaching** (n.): the dying of corals because of changes in the reef environment. Even slight changes in water temperature (1–2 degrees C) make certain (coloured) parts of reef-building corals vulnerable to damage by light. When these parts die, the corals lose their colour and will eventually die themselves. In recent years small increases in sea temperature have led to bleaching events in coral reefs all over the world. These rises of temperature are said to be the result of climate change.

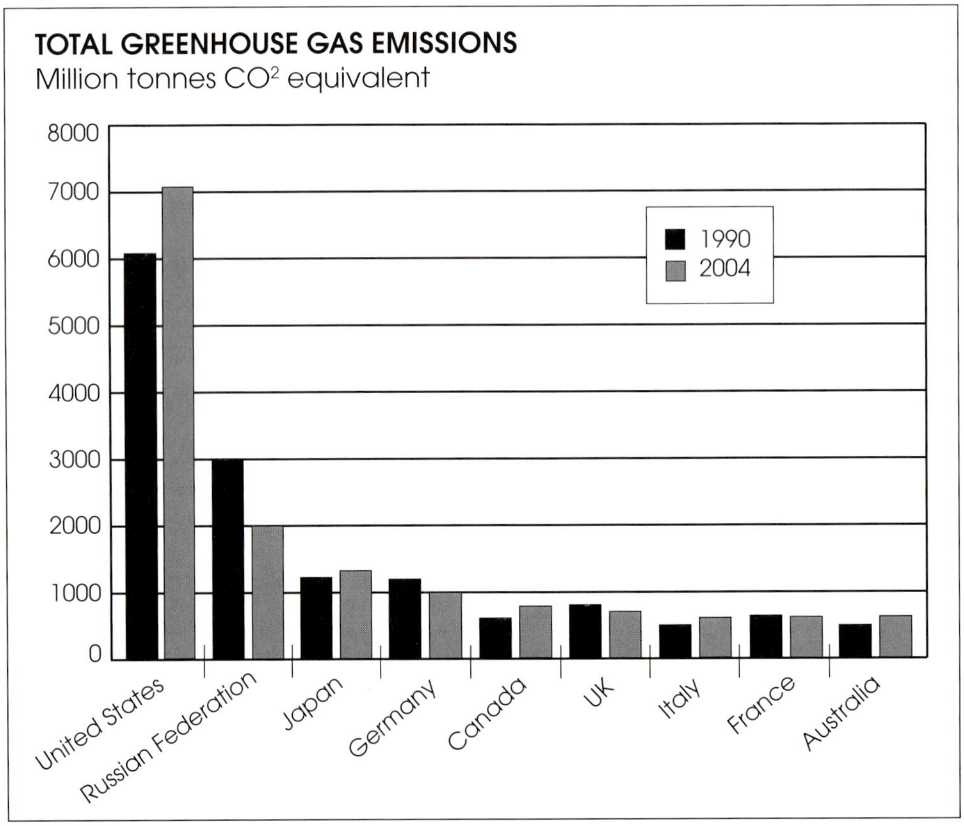

Source: US Department of Energy

AWARENESS

1 What are the most serious environmental problems Germany has to deal with at present?
2 What is the "greenhouse effect?"
3 Explain what is meant by 'carbon footprint' and how it could be reduced.

COMPREHENSION

4 Why does Greenpeace think the Australian government is not doing enough to tackle global warming?

ANALYSIS

5 Explain what consequences the following problems have on the people living in the areas affected:
   - coral bleaching
   - changing rainfall patterns
   - insufficient snow in ski resorts
   - loss of animal species

6 Compare the greenhouse gas emissions of Australia, the United States and Germany. Calculate the per capita emission and the percentage of change for each year. With the help of your findings prove or disprove what Greenpeace says in the text.
7 Present your figures in form of a graph or diagram in order to illustrate their meaning.
8 Distinguish between objective scientific terminology used in the text and emotive words and phrases.

OPINION

9 Write a letter (Reference Library, p. 300) to the editor of a newspaper suggesting what Australians should do to achieve sustainable development

PROJECTS

10 Collect information on changes may be linked to global warming. Put them together in a brochure which you may present to other groups at your school.
11 An environmentalist from Greenpeace and a politician representing people in an industrial area are invited to give their opinions (Reference Library, p. 306) on a radio programme. Write down or improvise what they say.
12 Search the Internet for a class at an Australian school with which you may discuss environmental concerns of Germany and Australia. The following address may help you: http://www.edunet.ie/links/aus.html

6

Jennifer Buckingham

"Modern perils in a lucky country"

Jennifer Buckingham is a Research Fellow and Policy Analyst at the Centre for Independent Studies. She has published policy monographs on school choice, boys' education and school performance reporting and edited the CIS' State of the Nation series. Her article "Modern perils in a lucky country" was published in *The Daily Telegraph*, currently the newspaper with the largest circulation in Sydney. – *The Daily Telegraph*, August 31, 2001.

What is the state of our nation? For the most part, Australians are better off than they have ever been before. On average, the people of Australia are healthier, wealthier, more educated and more active than at any other time this century. Yet the picture is not entirely rosy. Where things have changed for the worse, the changes have been dramatic and unrelenting.

On the positive front, life expectancy reached a new high in 2000, and death rates reached a new low. Even male youth suicide rates, which have increased markedly over the last three decades with little sign of abatement, have shown a significant decrease in the most recent statistics. The 1999 suicide rates for 15–19 and 20–24 year old males are the lowest in twelve years.

Educational attainment is on the rise. The proportion of the working age population with a bachelor degree or higher doubled between 1984 and 2000. This more highly educated workforce is reflected in the changing nature of occupations. Managerial, professional and administrative occupations now comprise 36% of the workforce compared to 17% in 1966.

With the increase in skilled workers has come an increase in Gross Domestic Product. Australia is one of the top ten richest nations in the world. Analyses by

One of the many beautiful landscapes in a lucky country: sunset at Broken Bay, Sydney

overseas think-tanks have shown a direct relationship between economic freedom and per capita income, and Australia rates well on all measures of economic freedom except labour market regulation.

One of the more surprising trends, given recent talk of Australia's lack of commitment to research and development, is that total expenditure on R&D has increased by almost 50% in real terms since the late 1960s. This increase has been primarily fuelled by business investment in R&D, demonstrating the importance of considering all funding sources, not just taxpayers.

Government expenditure quadrupled in the last four decades, with the biggest increases in spending going to education, health and social security. Such massive investment in public services attests to the fact that Australia is, despite statements to the contrary, a compassionate country. Welfare payments in excess of the poverty line bear this out.

Health care has also been a major beneficiary of increases in public spending. Although numbers of nurses have declined over the last decade, there were still three times as many doctors and nurses per capita in 1999 than at the beginning of the century.

Growing government expenditure is necessarily accompanied by increasing taxation. If taxation revenue as a proportion of gross national income is converted into days of the year, it is possible to calculate 'Tax Freedom Day' – the symbolic day on which people stop working to pay off the national tax bill and start working for their own benefit. In 2000, 'Tax Freedom Day' was April 21st – the 111th day of the year. In 1901/02, it was January 23rd.

Offsetting the tax burden over recent years have been decreases in the cost of many goods and services. For example, the average cost of long distance and international telephone calls dropped by 25% and 50% respectively between 1997 and 2000. Home loan interest rates are the lowest in thirty years. So, in reviewing our nation's progress, there are many positive stories. But there are also trends that do not bode well for the future. At the heart of these are crime, drug use and the wellbeing of children.

Taking the last of these first, statistics on child abuse and neglect show that children in non-intact families, that is living apart from one of their natural parents, are statistically eight to ten times at greater risk of child abuse and neglect than children living with both of their natural parents. They are also twice as likely to suffer a mental health problem. These statistics are troubling enough alone, but given that there are a growing number of children living apart from a natural parent, this is serious cause for concern.

Like all developed countries, Australia has seen a rise in the use of prescribed, legal and illicit drugs, at least over the last several decades. Use of antidepressants increased by 250%, while prescriptions of medication used to treat Attention Deficit Hyperactivity Disorder increased by a massive 1400% over the 1990s. Tobacco smoking, especially by men, has continued a fifty year decline, but there is a tendency toward heavier drinking in recent years.

Between 1985 and 1998, the proportion of teenagers aged 14–19 who had used an illicit drug rose by 55% to become a majority. The statistics on opioid (usually heroin) overdoses show a steep and steady rise in death rates over the last thirty years, with the biggest increase in the most recent twelve month period. A perhaps related trend is the escalation of crime rates, particularly violent crimes, in the last few decades of the twentieth century. The rise in violent crime rates was driven primarily by assaults, which increased by a factor of forty between 1964 and 2000, and by almost 50% between 1993 and 2000. While it is possible that more people are reporting crimes, rather than more crimes being committed, it is reasonable to argue that the opposite may be the case.

All in all, Australia is a nation in the midst of profound social and economic change. Taking stock of our progress over a long period of time is important, so that we can more reliably assess trends and make predictions about the future. It is not enough, however, to congratulate ourselves on our successes and make excuses for our failures. It is necessary to examine what has led to the changes we have witnessed, both positive and negative, and to act accordingly.

Vocabulary

7 unrelenting: continuously unpleasant – **42 to bear out:** to prove – **50 revenue:** money that a business or organization receives over a certain period of time – **57 to offset** (v.): compensate for – **66 to bode well** (v.): be a good sign

Explanations

23 Gross Domestic Product (GDP): The GDP is one of the ways for measuring the size of its economy. It is defined as the market value of all final goods and services produced within a country in a given period of time. The most common approach to measuring and understanding GDP is the expenditure method: GDP = consumption + investment + government spending + (exports – imports) – **31 R&D:** Research & Development – it normally refers to future-oriented, longer-term activities in science or technology. It expresses the state of an industry, the degree of competition or the lure of progress – **42 the poverty line:** the minimum level of income deemed necessary to achieve an adequate standard of living. In practice, like the definition of poverty, the official or common understanding of the poverty line is significantly higher in developed nations than in developing countries. – **87 Attention Deficit Hyperactivity Disorder:** a condition found in children and some adults whose symptoms are not being able to concentrate on things and constantly needing to be active

Awareness

1 What is there about Australia that makes people call it "the lucky country"?
2 The epithet "The Lucky Country" was coined by Professor Donald Horne in 1964. Use the Culture and Recreational Portal website of the Australian Government in order to find out in which context the phrase was used and what Horne intended it to mean.

Comprehension

3 List the positive changes that have occurred in modern Australia in order of importance.
4 In 2000 "Tax Freedom Day" (l. 52) was April 21. Explain what this day symbolizes. What does it tell us about a country's economy and its welfare system?
5 Two major problems Australia has to cope with are drug use and crime. Describe what developments have taken place in this area in recent decades. How are the two problems linked?

Analysis

6 Examine how Buckingham has arranged her ideas:
- Subdivide the text into parts and find headings for them.
- What hypothesis is she putting forward, and what evidence does she offer to support it?
- What is her conclusion?

7 Explain how the structure of the article is reflected in the headline.
8 Analyse the language (Reference Library, p. 311) used and – considering what you have already found out about the structure – determine what kind of text this is.
9 Examine the way in which the writer makes use of statistics. Do her figures allow the reader to make an objective judgement about recent trends in Australian society?

Opinion

10 Do you think Buckingham has left out important aspects in writing her article?
11 Do you share the view that the wealth of a nation can be measured in terms of the "Gross Domestic Product" (l. 23)?
12 From reading this article, do you conclude that Australia is a better or worse place to live than Germany?

Projects

13 Tax Freedom Day reports are currently being published in eight countries. Find out when this "Tax Freedom Day" is in Australia, Germany and the US. Explain what it reveals about the economies of these countries. Find out what differences there are between direct and indirect taxation. What are the effects of raising or lowering taxes?
14 Compare Australia, The US, Germany and one developing country in Africa or Asia with respect to their
- GDP,
- Government expenditure,
- expenditure on R&D,
- welfare system,
- health care system,
- drug use
- and crime rates.

Illustrate your findings with the help of charts, diagrams and graphs.

11 India

Facts and Figures

With 1,103,371,000 people, India is not only the second largest country in the world in terms of population, it is also one of the most diverse. In India, there are 23 official languages, and eight major religions exist side by side.

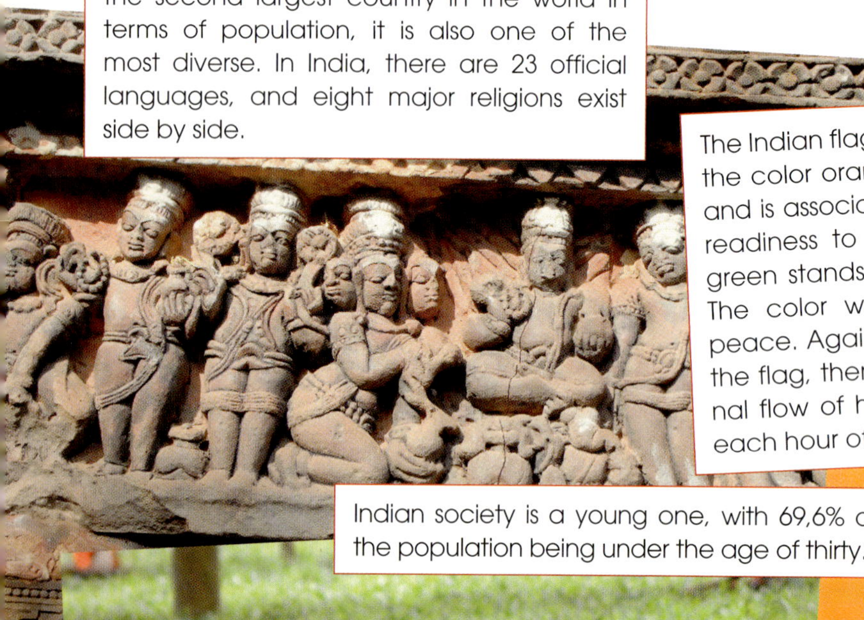

The Indian flag symbolizes the unity of all religious groups: the color orange represents Hinduism as well as Sikhism, and is associated with the qualities of courage and the readiness to give oneself up to the common cause; green stands for Islam as well as for faith and chivalry The color white represents the hoped-for unity anc peace. Against the white background, at the center o the flag, there is a spinning wheel, symbolizing the eter nal flow of human life, with twenty-four spikes, one fc each hour of the day.

Indian society is a young one, with 69,6% of the population being under the age of thirty.

The Taj Mahal, built in the 17th century by Emperor Shahjahan for his beloved wife Mumtaz, is one of the Seven Wonders.

Despite its megacities such as Bombay and Delhi, India is still a largely rural country. Only 28,3% of its population live in urban areas, with 71,7% living in the countryside.

Model Democracy or Many-Headed Giant?

Despite India's immense economic growth, especially in the service sector, 25% of the population continue to live below the poverty line.

Northeastern India gets the most rainfall in the world. Monsoon season lasts from June to September; it is dry the rest of the year.

The name 'India' is a term originally used by Europeans and is derived from the river 'Indus.' Contemporary India dates back to the Indus Valley Civilization, which, at around 3300 BC, possessed both an elaborate literary tradition and a complex political system. The Indian name for the country is 'Bharat.'

Did you know that our numerals originate in India, as does chess? Or that many English words – among them bungalow, punch, and pyjama – are derived from Indian languages? Or that "yoga" simply translates as "plus" (and is also used in mathematical equations), meaning the link between man and God?

1

Camellia Panjabi

"Curries of India"

Perhaps more than many other countries, India is known all over the world for its foods, especially for the intricacy of its spices. More than just nourishment, food in India is a marker of regional, religious, and ethnic identity. The diversity of India as a nation can hence be traced through its food. The following excerpt addresses not only this "unity in diversity" that is Indian cuisine, but it also engages with the idea that food, too, is always subject to historical change. Camellia Panjabi, *The Great Curries of India* (New York: Simon and Schuster, 1995), pp. 8f.

Rich in color as well as in taste, there is no end to Indian spices

Ever since I can remember I have loved and been passionately involved in food. From the age of five I wanted to be consulted at home on the menu that my mother discussed with the cook every evening for the following day. Lunch at school (Queen Mary's in Bombay) arrived from home in a tiffin carrier, as it did for everyone else, and a large, warehouse-like hall with four long rows of benches housed the 300-plus girls who mouthed their way through lovingly cooked meals from home, brought by *ayahs* and drivers. I often walked between the benches eyeing the plates, taking in the color, texture and aroma of everyone's lunch, which always seemed more interesting than my own. Then in the evening I would explain to my mother in great detail what the dishes that I coveted looked like, and entreat her to make them for me. As I grew older I began to tell her the names of the recipients, hoping she would recognize the communities they belonged to, and hence the dishes that I was raving about. But knowledge of the cuisine of communities other than one's own was very limited in those days. Strangely, it is only recently that I managed to track down the particular favorite (appearance-wise at least) of my childhood memories: a bright golden sunset-colored curry that a Parsee girl sitting behind me often ate; known simply as 'fish curry' to the Parsees, this was a homestyle dish, never encountered since in any cook-book, or at dinner parties in Parsee homes, in restaurants or even at the famous Parsee wedding and *navjote* (thread ceremony) feasts.

A few years later, due to domestic reasons, my sister Namita and I signed up for 'school lunch', cooked and provided in a separate dining room for those children whose parents could not arrange for delivery of lunch to the school every midday. Our meal now consisted of 'English food' (Queen Mary's was run by Scottish missionaries): baked fish, baked mince (cottage pie), *dhol* (English and Anglo-Indian for lentil, *dal*) and yellow rice, mutton curry and rice, coconut pancakes, and Malabar sago pudding, the taste of which I had never encountered before. Later I searched for years for the exact replica of the mutton curry – once, in the mid-sixties, I found it accidentally on the buffet table of the old-world West End Hotel in Bangalore, only to return in the seventies to find that the cooks of the old brigade had retired, leaving no recipes.

When I went to university in England, I was astonished to find at college dinner that the dishes had none of the spices and seasonings that we had experienced as children in 'English food' in India. It was then that I realized that 'Indian English food' was a sort of hybrid-cuisine in its own right, and was fairly widespread, being popularly eaten in India in clubs, where masala liver on toast was a favorite, on the railways which had to cater for British and Indian tastes alike, with the cooking done in cramped conditions by local cooks, and in *dak* government bungalows where masala omelette must have been and still is the number one seller, as well as popular restaurants like Gourdon and the Wayside Inn in Bombay, Koshy's in Bangalore and Flury's in Calcutta where cutlets were staple fare. (Incidentally, in India cutlets are patties made of a mash of anything – meat, fish, vegetables or chicken.)

Vocabulary

15 to covet (v.): to wish for earnestly, to desire – **15 to entreat** (v.): to make an earnest request – **17 recipient** (n.): one who receives (here: the schoolgirls receiving their lunch) – **19 to rave about** (v.): here: to talk with extreme enthusiasm – **36 mince** (n.): chopped bits of food, e.g. minced meat – **50 hybrid** (n.): s.th. heterogeneous in origin or composition, here: adj. – **55 cramped** (adj.): confined, restrained – **60 cutlet** (n.): small flat piece of meat on a bone – **60 staple fare** (n.): main traditional dish, also: main topic – **61 patty** (n.): little pie (from French pâté)

Explanations

Title: curry (n.): European appellation for what is actually a mixture of spices. Contrary to the European idea that one spice ("curry") can be used for every Indian dish, spice mixtures (called "masalas" in India) vary with each particular dish, each region and even each household. – **6 tiffin carrier** (n.): portable lunch box – **10 ayah** (n.): nurse, governess, nanny – **24 Parsee** (n.): In India Parsees/Parsis are a community of Zoroastrians who emigrated to the Indian subcontinent over 1000 years ago to escape religious persecution. Zoroastrianism is a religious system, commonly known as *fire-worship*. – **28 navjote** (n.): thread ceremony feast, a Zoroastrian initiation rite, similar to confirmation for Christians – **37 dal/dhol** (n.): lentil – **52 masala/massala** (n.): a special mixture of spices – **56 dak bungalows** (n.): dak or dawk bungalows are government rest-houses established at intervals for the use of travellers on the high roads of India.

Awareness

1 Imagine an Indian restaurant. What do you consider "typical"?

Comprehension

2 Describe in your words why eating at Queen Mary's School was so special for Camellia Panjabi. What does this imply about India?

3 Which role do the tiffin carriers play?

Analysis

4 Divide the text into its constituent parts (Reference Library, pp. 312f.).

5 What message is Camellia Panjabi trying to get across to her reader?

6 How do you explain the changing attitude towards food in India?

7 What does she want her book to do?

Opinion

8 A famous publishing house asks you – an expert on the subject – to write a book on German foods. Write an email to the chief editor explaining your ideas/opinion.

Project

9 Collect material on the definition, origin and history of a) curry and b) tea. Search the web at pages like those listed below. Illustrate the important points of your presentation with the help of pictures, maps etc.
http://www.kurma.net/essays/e8.html.
http://en.wikipedia.org/wiki/Curry.
http://www.curryhouse.co.uk/faq/define.htm.

2 Bachi Karkaria

"The Dabba Connection"

Especially in a mega-metropolis like Bombay (the name was officially changed to Mumbai in 1995, but the use of the former name is still widely spread), India's ability to negotiate between tradition and modernity is much in evidence. The "institution" of the dabbawalla exemplifies, first, India's need to maintain religious identities marked by dietary laws and, second, the intersection between high tech and a food infrastructure which functions by altogether different means. Bachi Karkaria, one of India's most incisive humorous writers, here describes the dabbawalla culture of Bombay which keeps half of the city's office-goers fed with home-cooked meals at lunch time. – "The Dabba Connection," www.uppercrustindia.com/11crust/eleven/mumbai3.html.

What most symbolises Bombay? Not the historic Gateway of India immortalised on a million postcards or even the Gothic, gargoyled Victoria Terminus (now known as Chhatrapati Shivaji Terminus). For me, Bombay is the dabbawalla, the doughty little man in distinctive white Gandhi cap, who delivers thousands of hungry lunches to officer-goers every afternoon. The dabbawalla gets his name from the dabba, the aluminium containers fitted one above the other, held in place by a wire grip and lowered into an outer tin case, which serves the double purpose of keeping the food warm and preventing it from splashing out during the dabbawalla's rushed and jostling journey.

He carries about 39 of these dabbas on an unwieldy,

The Gateway of India in Bombay (Mumbai)

long tray, a combined weight of more than 50 kilograms, on his head as he moves speedily through sweaty miles and cramped trains. His world is one of rush, rush, run, propelled only by a single thought: whatever happens, get the lunches delivered in time.

The fact that makes Bombay's dabbawalla system unique and incredible is the complexity of the task and the simplicity of its operation. It is not a set-up where an individual man delivers one or even five lunches. It is a gargantuan service in which some 2,000 men carry over a hundred thousand dabbas every day across the city's 60-kilometre sprawl in an inter-woven relay with each dabba changing hands at least four times.

Yet, for all its intricacy and size, it is unerringly run by a group of simple, illiterate, one-time peasants using nothing more than a handful of symbols crudely painted on the lunch boxes – that, and their own intuition and team work.

Eight out of ten white-collar workers in Bombay live too far from their office to go home for lunch. A restaurant meal costs five to fifteen times more than home-food. To them, the dabbawalla brings the security of a cheap, clean, tasty and often still-warm, home-cooked meal.

Come rain or shine, the dabbawalla service does not stop. The doughty little men deliver on time. Let us tail the dabba of Ram Mohile, a typist with the Bombay Municipal Corporation, on its daily adventure from kitchen to office canteen. Mrs. Mohile starts cooking at 7 a.m. to prepare her husband's mutton curry, rice, vegetables and chapati. She packs them in the dabba.

The outer case of Mohile's dabba is marked with a black swastika, a red dot, a yellow stroke. Each symbol marks a different stage of the dabba's odyssey from Mohile's flat to his office and back. The dabbawalla reads the hieroglyphics like a sentence. But as one man on the beat said, "We often recognise a dabba by its feel, like we would a familiar slipper."

Mohile's dabbawalla knocks precisely at 10 and he isn't wearing a watch. He grabs the dabba from Mrs. Mohile and sprints down the three flights. His daily beat covers 35 boxes spread over 20 square kilometres. Each box has different marking as each is bound for different destinations. At exactly 10.20, he has a rendezvous with dabbawalla No. 2 who takes over all the swastika-marked boxes he has collected from other couriers, pedals off to the suburban rail head of Dadar. Dabbawalla No. 1 continues picking up dabbas meant for other pick-up men. [...]

With the sheer size of the operation and the nerve-racking rush, surely, the dabbas get mixed up. In a country with rigid food taboos, this could be disastrous. Krishnan, a staunch vegetarian South Indian brahmin, recalls how he opened his dabba one day hoping to see fluffy, snow white rice and instead found half a fried fish staring back at him. "I couldn't look at food for a week without that wretched fish head swimming up before my eyes," he remembers with a shudder. But such instances are rare.

Not so infrequent is the loss of dabbas, about 10 to 15 every day. Some have merely gone astray and are soon traced. But some are stolen. In this case, the owner is paid back half the price of a new lunch pail. In a dabbawalla's tray, a brahmin's rice jostles along with a low-caste chapati; a Hindu's vegetable curry with a Muslim's mutton korma – thus, in a way, the dabba system dissolves the barriers of class, caste and community which haven't been entirely demolished from Indian society.

The man who carries the dabba is not his own master. He is the "servant" employed by one of the city's 635 mukadams or contractors, ex-dabbawallas themselves or even still plying the beat. It is they who orchestrate the whole system. They in turn are answerable to their guild, The Bombay Tiffinbox Suppliers Association.

Apart from the daily hardship, the dabbawalla is exposed to constant hazards: a slip from the doorway of a crowded, speeding train, juggernaut buses elbowing his fragile bicycle into the gutter in a bid to prove that might is right, a car not caring that he cannot cross the road too fast with his cumbersome headload.

Some months ago, a dabbawalla waiting on his bicycle at a traffic light was hurled off the road by a lorry gone berserk and was smashed to death. Yet, even in such an extreme situation, his quota of dabbas was delivered. News travels fast on the network. The mukadam got to hear of the accident within minutes and contracted the secretary of the Association (who patrols the city for just this kind of emergency), asked him to look after the police formalities, collected the dead man's dabbas, and being familiar with the symbols, got them to their destination – just 30 minutes late. Bombay's salute to its dabbawalla's, as you see, is well deserved.

The job, never a cushy one, gets even worse during the city's notorious monsoon when rains lash the metropolis for days without let-up, flooding railway tracks, paralysing the trains – and thus the dabbawallas. A contractor proudly tells of how his "boys" think nothing of getting down on the flooded tracks and walking a few extra kilometres in the lashing rain.

Tiffin carrier or "dabba"

Vocabulary

5 doughty (adj.): tough, feisty, determined - **14 unwieldy** (adj.): not easily managed, handled, or used (because of bulk, weight, complexity, or awkwardness) - **33 gargantuan** (adj.): enormous - **73 staunch** (adj.): /stɔːntʃ/ standing firm and true to one's principles or purpose, determined - **83 pail:** bucket, container for food - **84 to jostle** (v.): to come into collision with, also: to push one against another as in a crowd - **92 to ply** (v.): to use, handle, or wield vigourously or diligently; to apply oneself to, work at (one's business, and industry, a task, etc.) - **92 beat** (n.): daily route, city space covered by the dabbawallas - **97 juggernaut** (n.): /ˈdʒʌgənɔːt/ a massive inexorable force, campaign, movement, or object that crushes whatever is in its path; from Hindi "Jagannath," lit. lord of the world, title of the god Vishnu - **98 gutter** (n.) here: a low area (as at the edge of a street) to carry off surface water (as to a sewer) - **100 cumbersome** (adj.): unwieldy because of heaviness or bulk - **102 to hurl** (v.): to dash - **103 to go berserk** (v): to go insane; to go off the rails - **113 cushy** (adj.): entailing little hardship or difficulty; from Hindi "khush," pleasant - **116 to lash** (v.): to strike violently

Explanations

Intro: dabbawalla (n.): lit. one who carries a box (dabba = box) - **53 swastika** (n.): /ˈswɒstɪkə/ an ancient symbol in the form of an equal-armed cross with each arm continued at a right angle, used (in clockwise form) as the emblem of the German Nazi party - origin: Sanskrit word meaning 'well-being' - **74 Brahmin** (n.): Hindu of the highest caste traditionally assigned to the priesthood, etymology: Sanskrit "brahmana" - of the Brahman caste - **94 tiffinbox** (n.): a container used widely in India to conveniently carry homemade food to work, school or a picnic; British equivalent of "dabba"

Chhatrapati Shivaji Terminus (the former Victoria Terminus) is one of the busiest railway stations in India

Awareness

1 What do you associate with the German "Henkelmann"? Why has it disappeared from German everyday life?

Comprehension

2 What is a 'dabba'? What constitutes the dabbawalla's job?
3 What makes the dabbawalla system remarkable?
4 Why would a dabba mix-up be disastrous?
5 Who cooks the food delivered by the dabbawallas, and what does this imply?

Analysis

6 What role does the text ascribe to the contractors?
7 What is the author's attitude towards the dabbawalla?
8 Why is no dabbawalla mentioned by name? Whom does the article provide with a name? What effect does this have?
9 What aspects of the dabbawalla's job could the text be said to leave out?

Opinion

10 Why could the dabbawalla be compared to monuments such as the Victoria Terminus (see picture above) or even the Taj Mahal? What do these monuments and the dabbawalla have in common?
11 Why do the dabbawallas continue to be necessary even for contemporary India?

Project

12 Write a text from the perspective of a dabbawalla, talking to his son about his job. What would he tell him?

3 Arundhati Roy

The God Of Small Things

The following passage of Arundhati Roy's novel *The God of Small Things*, a literary criticism of caste prejudice, is especially remarkable because it emphasizes that caste barriers are being upheld not only by the Hindu community, but by Christians as well. – Arundhati Roy, *The God of Small Things* (London: Flamingo, 1997), pp. 73-77.

Summary

The God of Small Things is set in Ayemenem, in the state of Kerala, southern India. The story is told from the perspective of seven-year-old twins, Estha and Rahel, and it derives much of its power from this perspective. Innocent as yet of social laws and codes, the children are surrounded by emotions they cannot comprehend: the powerful influence of their grandmother Mammachi, the family patriarch and founder of the family's pickle factory; the bitterness of their great-aunt, Baby Kochamma, whose hopeless love for a priest has turned her into a hateful woman; and the longing of their divorced mother, Ammu, for a love against all odds. Ammu's love for Velutha, the son of the family servant, Vellya Paapen, becomes the twin's tragic initiation. Because society, as Estha and Rahel have to find out, has laid down the "love laws" (laws laying down "who should be loved and how. And how much"), Ammu's love affair with an untouchable is a shocking breach of social taboo. To the twins, however, Velutha is their "god of small things," who can make their life – and their mother's – magic. Yet, because society punishes those who break its rules, Estha and Rahel eventually find their hero dead, murdered by the local police force.

[…] As a young boy, Velutha would come with Vellya Paapen to the back entrance of the Ayemenem House to deliver the coconuts they had plucked from the trees in the compound. Pappachi would not allow Paravans into the house. Nobody would. They were not allowed to touch anything that Touchables touched. Caste Hindus and Caste Christians. Mammachi told Estha and Rahel that she could remember a time, in her girlhood, when Paravans were expected to crawl backwards with a broom, sweeping away their footprints so that Brahmins or Syrian Christians would not defile themselves by accidentally stepping into a Paravan's footprint. In Mammachi's time, Paravans, like other Untouchables, were not allowed to walk on public roads, not allowed to cover their upper bodies, not allowed to carry umbrellas. They had to put their hands over their mouths when they spoke, to divert their polluted breath away from those whom they addressed.

When the British came to Malabar, a number of Paravans, Pelayas and Pulayas (among them Velutha's grandfather, Kelan) converted to Christianity and joined the Anglican Church to escape the scourge of untouchability. As added incentive they were given a little food and money. They were known as the Rice-Christians. It didn't take them long to realize that they had jumped from the frying pan into the fire. They were made to have separate churches, with separate services, and separate priests. As a special favour they were even given their own separate Pariah Bishop. After Independence they found they were not entitled to any Government benefits like job reservations or bank loans at low interest rates, because officially, on paper, they were Christians, and therefore casteless. It was a little like having to sweep away your footprints without a broom. Or worse, not being *allowed* to leave footprints at all. […]

When he returned to Ayemenem after his years away from home, Velutha still had about him the same quickness. The sureness. And Vellya Paapen feared for him now more than ever. But this time he held his peace. He said nothing.

At least not until the Terror took hold of him. Not until he saw, night after night, a little boat being rowed across the river. Not until he saw it return at dawn. Not until he saw what his Untouchable son had touched. More than touched.

Entered.

Loved.

When the Terror took hold of him, Vellya Paapen went to Mammachi. He stared straight ahead with his mortgaged eye. He wept with his own one. One cheek glistened with tears. The other stayed dry. He shook his own head from side to side to side till Mammachi ordered him to stop. He trembled his own body like a man with malaria. Mammachi ordered him to stop it but he couldn't, because you can't order fear around. Not even a Paravan's. Vellya Paapen told Mammachi what he had seen. He asked God's forgiveness for having spawned a monster. He offered to kill his son with his own bare hands. To destroy what he had created.

In the next room Baby Kochamma heard the noise and came to find out what it was all about. She saw

Grief and Trouble ahead, and secretly, in her heart of hearts, she exulted.

She said (among other things) – *'How could she stand the smell? Haven't you noticed, they have a particular smell, these Paravans?'*

And she shuddered theatrically, like a child being force-fed spinach. She preferred an Irish Jesuit smell to a particular Paravan smell.

By far. By far. [...]

Arundhati Roy was born in 1961 to a Syrian Christian mother and a Bengali Hindu father. She is originally an architect by training; her semi-autobiographical debut novel, *The God of Small Things,* won the Booker Prize in 1997. The book is famed for its lyricism as much for its political stand against caste barrieres. Roy has recently reconsidered her decision to fight for her political causes only in non-fiction. Realizing that a novel can reach a much wider audience than non-fiction, Roy has recently started work on her long-awaited second novel, this time about Kashmir.

Vocabulary

4 compound (n.): fenced area – **11 to defile** (v.): to make s.th. less pure and good, esp. by showing no respect – **22 scourge** (n.): /skɜːdʒ/ plague – **23 incentive** (n.): motivation, impulse – **59 to spawn** (v.): create – **64 to exult** (v.): rejoice exceedingly, triumph

Explanations

9 Paravan (n.): subdivision or caste of Hinduism, member of the lowest social class, also referred to as "untouchable." Paravans were assigned to the task of picking coconuts, which was considered a lowly occupation. – **10 Brahmin** (n.): Brahman, a member of the highest or priestly caste among the Hindus; see Info Box below – **19 Malabar:** region in Southern India which includes the northern part of the state of Kerala. Historically, the Malabar coast (with port cities such as Calicut and Cochin), was the center of Indian ocean trade. It is these port towns, also, which were among the centers of foreign colonization, esp. for the Portuguese, but also – as this excerpt indicates – for the British. – **20 Pelayas, Pulayas:** members of the caste of the untouchables; term used in Kerala as well as Tamilnadu – **21 Kelan:** Vellya Paapen's father, Velutha's grandfather – **29 Pariah:** s.o. who is considered an outcast of society – **50 chi, ji:** syllable added in many Indian languages as an expression of respect. Mammachi (the name used in the novel for Ammu's mother) would hence translate as "venerable mother." – **51 to mortgage** (v.): to give s.b. a claim on property as a security for payment of a debt or loan; context here: Mammachi paid for Vellya Paapen's glass eye, under the condition that he stay in his place and obey the roles connected with his social status as an untouchable

Info

Caste System

The Vedic texts, written in old Sanskrit by Aryan invaders of Indogermanic descent, who began settling the Indus valley around 1,500 b.C., specify the existence of four castes: the priests and teachers (*brahmana*), the rulers and warriors (*kshatriya*), the merchants and cultivators (*vaiśya*) and those who were destined to serve (*śūkdra*). The so-called untouchables (those who performed labors such as sweeping which were considered "unclean") were considered as being outside the caste hierarchy, as being classless altogether. The caste system was originally based on a specialization of labor: all castes were necessary for the social system as a whole to function efficiently. Yet, as members of the higher castes were anxious to preserve their privileges, the system evolved into a *social* division, a division which, because caste membership is inherited, has been highly difficult to overcome.
The term "untouchable" is a highly problematic one in that it implies the "looking down" of a high caste Hindu on a person literally outside society. Untouchables are considered "unclean" by higher caste Indians, as it is believed that touching them would render these members of higher castes "unclean" as well. Mahatma Gandhi changed the term "untouchable" to "Harijan," children of God, thus implying that the members of the lowest caste were worthy and legitimate members of Indian society. This terminology in turn has been replaced, in more recent years, with the community's self-description as being "dalits," meaning those who are "ground down" by society. Today, there is a quota system which is aimed at overcoming caste discrimination and at enabling dalit participation in all spheres of Indian political, cultural and social life. The quota system and other government measures are key to an understanding of India as a secular state aiming at overcoming social divisions based on religious prejudice.

Awareness

1 What do you know about the caste system in India?
2 What does the term "untouchable", denoting a particular social group, imply?

Comprehension

3 Sketch the constellation of characters, depicting family relationship and social status.
4 How are the characters described (Reference Library, p. 309)?
5 Sum up the first paragraph on p. 186 in your own words.

Analysis

6 Examine the different reactions presented in ll. 42–71.
   a) How does Vellya Paapen react to his son's love affair? How does the narrator present his reaction? Why does Vellya react like that?
   b) What is Mammachi's reaction?
   c) What is Baby Kochamma's response and its religious implication?
   d) Which role does the narrator (Reference Library, pp. 310f.) play in this context? Give proof, quoting from the text.
7 Analyze the image (Reference Library, p. 311) of broom and footprints as it is presented in the text. What does this suggest about the changing role of untouchability in society?
8 The metaphor (Reference Library, p. 311) of the frying pan and the fire illustrates an attempted escape from the predicament of untouchability. Explain.
9 In what way is Velutha's attitude, as expressed in his movements and manner, symbolic of a transformation of social order? Find other passages illustrating this transformation.

Opinion

10 Why do you think the caste system has proved so resilient to historical change?
11 Imagine measures which could be taken by the state for abolishing the caste system.
12 Give a two minute speech (Reference Library, p. 301) on why the caste system should or should not be abolished.

Projects

13 What is the situation of untouchables like today?
14 Read Roy's novel, focusing on its political implications. Work in groups and specialize on topics such as caste system, Marxism, and the role of the English in India.

4

Meenakshi Shedde

"Switzerland Is a Disneyland of Love"

Bollywood's very name spells out its declared goal to rival Hollywood's global status. With over 900 films made each year, Bollywood's film production, based in Bombay, has come to exceed the number of films made in Hollywood each year. These movies, shot in Hindi, are often marked by an intricate structure of parody and the "Indianization" of Hollywood motifs, as in Bollywood's own version of E.T., *Koi Mil Gaya*; mega-star Shah Rukh Khan is hailed as Bollywood's Brad Pitt. The signature scenes of these movies are elaborately choreographed song-and-dance sequences; the songs sung by the filmic protagonists – in playback – feature India's most famous singers, such as Lata Mangeshkar, known as the "voice of India". Bollywood films are being shot in Switzerland, New Zealand, Australia, and, more recently, Germany as well. Their content is decidedly Indian; yet, their scope and outlook is nevertheless profoundly transnational. From: *Bollywood – The Indian Cinema and Switzerland*, ed. Alexandra Schneider (Zürich: Edition Museum für Gestaltung Zürich, 2002), pp. 4-6.

"You came into my life, the way you smiled, you don't know what dreams you showed me. Now my heart can neither wake nor sleep, something happens in the heart." This song, hugely popular in India, is from the Bollywood superhit film *Kuch Kuch Hota Hai* ("Something Happens", Karan Johar, 1997). In the public mind, the song picturisation is the epitome of how ordinary, banal life in India can be transformed into a state of happy delirium, with a little help from Switzerland.

In fact, the song was shot in Scotland, but the public is not unduly concerned with such petty geographic details. As far as they are concerned, it is set in the

A scene from the Bollywood film Paheli *featuring India's favorite romantic hero, Shah Rukh Khan, and Rani Mukherjee*

mythical, romantic landscape of Switzerland that they have relished in scores of films before.

Switzerland has for decades enjoyed a near monopoly when it comes to providing images for a romantic paradise in Bollywood cinema. Its snow-capped mountains seem exotic, as the tropical Indian sub-continent has no snow to offer, except in the Himalayas in the extreme north and north-east. Part of its enduring popularity can be ascribed to a pretty unromantic set of circumstances dating back to the 1960s, when colour processing came to India. The social realism of our black and white films went out of the window as directors vied for more excuses to show off the colour, cramming songs shot in several lush Indian locations into the film. Kashmir was a popular 'song stop', for its snow and natural beauty, but because of continuing militancy in this state, which borders Pakistan, since the 1980s, it came to be replaced by safer foreign locations, primarily Switzerland. The idea was to give the viewer a free foreign tour for the price of a cinema ticket. [...]

Bollywood's sexual fantasies are pure visual Viagra. The couple may leap on each other, rhythmically slither about, get soaked together in pouring rain, and imaginatively generate heat while sliding down glaciers. Bollywood's favoured erotic images – the wet sari, the heaving bosom – effortlessly blur the distinction between sexual fantasy and obscenity. The iconic wet sari nymphs include Zeenat Aman in *Satyam, Shivam, Sundaram* ("Truth, God, Beauty", Raj Kapoor, 1978), Mandakini in *Ram Teri Ganga Maili* ("Ram, Your Ganga Is Dirty", Raj Kapoor, 1985) and Dimple Kapadia in *Saagar* ("The Sea", Ramesh Sippy, 1985). The bosom-heaving oomph gals include Madhuri Dixit in the famous song *Choli ke peeche kya hai* ("What is behind the blouse?!") in *Khalnayak* ("The Villain", Subhash Ghai, 1993) and Urmila Matondkar scorching the beach in *Rangeela* ("Flamboyant", Ram Gopal Varma, 1985).

Despite a formidable armoury of these heat-seeking missiles, and notwithstanding all its software genius exports and other appurtenances of the 21st century, India remains a fairly conservative society. Even in a modern city like Mumbai (the new name for Bombay), where I live, couples can barely hold hands. The city authorities have actually broken down park benches into individual seats to prevent lovers holding hands, and the police are on the alert to prevent canoodling in public. No wonder romantic Bollywood song fantasies, in which all your dreams come true, have a special place in the heart of this romantic, movie-mad, music-mad nation. [...]

Indeed, underlining traditional values by painting Westerners as decadent and corrupt is a hoary tradition in Indian and many other film cultures. The classic East-West clash of values was again showcased in a recent film, *Ajnabee* ("Stranger", Abbas and Mustan Alibhai Burnwalla, 2001), written by Shyam Goel, which explores the madly daring idea (for India) of wife-swapping. Exceptionally, the film is almost entirely shot in Switzerland, rather than just its songs. Says Goel "For the Swiss, adultery is like having a cup of tea. It's nothing. But for the Indians, there is a lot of excitement and curiosity about it. We wanted to show how the Swiss, representing Western values, are materialistic and selfish. Even Bipasha Basu (the Indian heroine who plays a Swiss-based bar dancer), has no use for love – she wants to live in style and splurge in Swiss shopping malls." Yet in the end, a film that promised much sexual excitement didn't dare to carry out its promise, and audiences felt cheated.

So it is hardly surprising that many Bollywood films of the 1990s show the heroines in Western tights and plunging necklines while courting the hero in India and abroad, but slipping into demure Indian saris the minute there's talk of marriage. Says Nasreen Munni Kabir; filmmaker and author of *Bollywood: The Indian Cinema Story*, "The idyllic helps to emphasize the escape from reality. In *Dilwale Dulhaniya Le Jayenge* ("Braveheart Wins the Bride", Aditya Chopra, 1995), Shah Rukh Khan and Kajol, who share a room together in Europe, would never have found themselves in such a situation in India. So travel is seen as akin to freedom from the Indian family and society, and a certain sexual

Hugely proportioned advertisements for upcoming movies have become an essential part of the cityscape

freedom. The clothes match the image of freedom: the little black dress versus the elegant but defining sari. The foreign settings encourage closeness between two people who can normally be that close only after marriage in India. Often love in Hindi films isn't addressed through sexuality, but is seen as an ideal that doesn't really exist in real life. So Switzerland is like a Disneyland of love. Everything is perfect." [...]

Vocabulary

7 epitome (n.): here: typical or ideal example – **19 to relish** (v.): to be pleased or gratified by – **30 to vie for** (v.): to exchange in rivalry – **31 lush** (adj.): of plants, esp. of grass: succulent, and luxuriant in growth – **42 glacier** (n.): /ˈglæsiə/ a large body of ice moving slowly down a slope or valley or spreading outward on a land surface – **45 icon** (n.): idol – **51 oomph** (n.): /ʊmf/ (infml.) the quality of being exciting, energetic, or sexually attractive; here used as an adjective – **51 gal** (n.): Am sl. girl – **54 to scorch** (v.): to burn or discolor the surface of s.th. by dry heat; here: allusion to the actress' sex appeal – **57 armoury** (n.): supply of arms – **59 appurtenance** (n.): /əˈpɜːtɪnəns/ accessory object – **65 to canoodle** (v.): to pet, to fondle – **71 hoary** (adj.): /ˈhɔːrɪ/ extremely old – **85 to splurge** (v.): to indulge o.s. extravagantly – **91 to plunge** (v.): to descend or dip suddenly – **92 demure** (adj.): reserved, modest – **100 akin to** (adj.): of the same kind, related

Explanations

92 sari (n.): Length of material (often silk) wrapped around the body, main garment of Hindu women. Traditionally worn by married women, the sari is worn by Indian women generally on festive occasions; also spelled 'saree'

Awareness

1 What does the term "Bollywood" suggest?
2 Do you know any Bollywood movies? What is their trademark? In how far are they different from Hollywood or even German movies?

Comprehension

3 Why do Indian directors choose Switzerland as a fitting location?
4 How is Bollywood's eroticism described in the text?
5 How is the West portrayed in these Bollywood movies?
6 What impression do we get of the Indian authorities?
7 According to the text, what are typical features of a Bollywood movie?

Analysis

8 Why couldn't the films mentioned be shot in Kashmir? What does this imply about the link between history and entertainment?
9 What role does Switzerland play for Bollywood's eroticism? How are heroines transformed by Switzerland?
10 What does the author mean by the expression "the classic East-West clash of values"? In how far do the movies transform, for instance, "colonial" stereotypes of India?
11 Explain the sentence "So Switzerland is like a Disneyland of love" in your own words.

Opinion

12 The article continues with a statement by film critic Maithili Rao: "There is an in-built ambivalence in the expression of repressed sexuality in the freedom offered by the West." Explain this sentence in your own words and comment on it.
13 Do you think Bollywood movies will be increasingly popular in Europe, too? Give reasons for your estimation.

Projects

14 Divide the class and watch a different Bollywood film in each group (for instance, *Kal Ho Naa Ho – Indian Love Story; Kabhi Khushi Kabhie Gham – Sometimes Happy, Sometimes Sad;* or *Svadesh – Home*). Analyse the movies (Reference Library, pp. 323ff.) with regard to their locations, the function of songs, the role and representation of men and women, the representation of sexuality, and the representations of moral codes and values. Then compare your results. Which conclusions can you draw about Bollywood's India?
15 Find out where Bollywood films are shot. Are local actors being cast as well? What effect does this have on Indian diasporic communities in these locations?

5

Inderpal Grewal

"Traveling Barbie"

"Barbie" is known across the world as a symbol of feminine beauty. Given the fact that she is manufactured by an American company, Mattel, however, Barbie has also been associated with the United States – even its "cultural imperialism" – more specifically. Responding to pressures calling for a diversification of beauty standards, Mattel was quick to add to its line of dolls not only Ken, Barbie's male companion, but also a number of "ethnic" Barbie dolls. It may be news to some, however, that the company has recently also started manufacturing Indian Barbie dolls, complete with national, even regional dress. The following article investigates the politics of consumption associated with this new line of Barbie dolls. What is happening in Mattel's targeting of yet another "transnational" market? And who buys, for instance, a Bengali Barbie? Inderpal Grewal, "Traveling Barbie: Indian Transnationality and New Consumer Subjects", *positions* 7.3 (1999), pp. 653–66.

In the extensive field of cultural studies of Barbie, there are only some cursory references to international dimensions. Mostly written from the feminist viewpoint, scholarly work on Barbie continues to grow in the direction of U.S.-based race and queer studies. However, very little in this area of U.S. feminist and cultural studies concerns the matter of Barbie in the world. This essay examines the globalization of Barbie and her limited marketing success in India through the theoretical perspective of transnational feminist cultural studies. By focusing on consumers as active participants in the construction of national, gendered, and classed subjectivities through consumption, this essay analyzes the new subjects of consumption created as a result of economic liberalization policies in India and their transnational contexts.

These subjects may not be wholly resistant to the spread of global brands such as Barbie but may certainly subvert the project because they are not hailed by it. The failure of new products on the market certainly suggests such possibilities; people do not buy indiscriminately. Why some products sell and some do not suggests important issues of culture, identity and subjectivity. Resistance to multinationals in India comes from different locations and cannot be seen as always subversive to dominant formations; such resistances are also recuperated by the multinational companies. Whereas parties on the left have been organizing opposition to multinationals, so that it is clear that the Indian central government's support of open markets is opposed at many levels, resistance also comes from religious fundamentalist groups such as the RSS (the Rashtriya Swayamsevak Sangh, the Hindu right-wing party), who in the struggle for political power use the example of multinationals as the "American" threat to national sovereignty. Other kinds of resistance appear in the obsession with ethnic chic, for instance, or the recuperations of "tradition" by various entities. My analysis of the marketing of Barbie in India suggests both the subversion and the recuperations that occur in the formation of new consumer subjects.

The "traditional" Hindu Barbie in a gold-trimmed sari

In a context of localization through transnational formations, it is important to note that a Barbie in a sari being sold in India is not an Indian or South Asian Barbie.

She is what Mattel calls the traditional Barbie, a white, American Barbie, but one who travels, she has, in one version, blond hair, the standard face, the ideal female Euro-American body, a shiny sari, and a red *bindi* on her forehead. The side panel on the box reads, "Dressing in an *all-seasons* classic saree with exotic borders, Barbie is totally at home in India." This reconfiguration of Euro-American fashion discourse uses the term *all-seasons* to differentiate the sari from the fashion industry in the West, which is organized around seasonal clothes. The term *exotic* resonates in reference to colonialism, tourism, and the eroticization of the female Asian body that depends on the misrecognition of socioeconomic realities and changes. Barbie in a sari is material evidence of the movements of transnational capital to India. The doll suggests that difference, as homogenized national stereotype, could be recovered by multinational corporations, that the national could exist in this global economy.

The impact of India's process of economic liberalization, which began in the 1980s with increased incentives for foreign investment and multinationals and a more open market policy, has been important not only in changing the nature of consumption and new consumer subjects in India, but also in connecting such subjects to patterns of globalized consumption, production, and circulation. One aspect of the economic liberalization process has been the Indian government's focus on Indian diasporics' as potential investors, such that tax breaks and special investment incentives for the category of persons termed *non-resident Indian* (NRI) have been created. This incorporation of the diaspora has turned the national imaginary into a transnational imaginary, in which diasporic cultural formations create new forms of community under conditions of globalization. Diaspora and home have become connected in new ways in this new economic climate, such that NRIs have become integrated into the political, cultural, and economic practices of the Indian nation-state. [...]

Mattel in India: The Production of New Consumer Subjects

In any toy store in India's urban centers catering to the children of the middle and upper classes, one can find not only the whole array of Masters of the Universe dolls (where the idea of conquest, war, and power, not only within the world but of space as imperial quest, is implicit), but also a large range of Barbie dolls. This range includes the blonde Barbie, the brunette, and the bride ("standard", of course) as well as one refinement for the South Asian market: the Barbie in a sari.

When Mattel began manufacturing for the Indian market in 1986–1987, Barbie was only known to the affluent section of the urban population, to those who travelled to the United States for various reasons, or to Indian immigrants living in the West. In 1991, after the standard Barbie did not sell very well, Barbie emerged with an Indian look, complete with sari, bangles, bindi, and black hair. While the Indian affiliate, Leo Mattel, based in Nagpur, produces the dolls, the marketing also is now done by an Indian company, Blowplast Inc., presumably to find more locally specific ways to sell the product by using the services of a company that knows the Indian market. Early advertising strategies included print ads, TV ads, and other promotions such as Barbie Friends Club (now defunct) and a Barbie magazine that encouraged a greener world and health issues. The club sent out cards and "I Love Barbie" badges and had a database of about fourteen or fifteen thousand names, a relatively small number in India. Since then, five categories of Barbies have emerged: (1) the penetration Barbie, which is a marketing term denoting that his is the low-end, most accessible Barbie, with shoulder-length hair and Western clothes, (2) Activity Barbie, which includes both black-haired and blonde, long-haired Barbies in a sari; (3) Theme Barbie, such as Best Friend Barbie and Birthday Barbie; (4) Glamour Barbie, such as Happy Holidays Barbie; and (5) Collector Barbie, or Limited Edition

Some "Indian" Barbies sport quasi-traditional garments which no "traditional" Indian woman would wear in public

Barbie, such as the Expression of India series, which includes Barbie in Indian costumes from various states (Rajasthan, Panjab, etc.), this array presents diversity in an Indian context. Though Ken does appear in Indian clothes, sales of Ken are small compared with those of Barbie.

Mattel targets the middle and upper classes in India as well as the overseas and diaspora markets, as it creates Barbie in a sari and the new series of Barbies in various authentic and ethnic costumes. While the bottom-line, Western-dress Barbie sells for about Rs. 99 (approx. $2), the travelling Barbie in Indian dress (which did penetrate the market) sells for about Rs. 250 (approx. $6) and the Expression of India Barbie sells for Rs. 600 (approx. $15). The availability of different Barbies varies with location. The most expensive Barbies, the Collector and Glamour dolls, are available only in the big cities. These expensive Barbies, with depictions of ethnic and regional diversity, are targeted to NRIs and tourists from the West, and Mattel has started to sell these in five-star hotels, airports and other tourist areas. These versions are priced far above what most people would spend in India and are targeted at the very rich and buyers with dollars, pounds, currency more powerful that the rupee. With economic liberalization, as Arvind Rajagopal argues, consumption patterns have changed and become more fluid. As a result, Mattel's segmented products are participating in the creation of new and more segmented subjects of consumption. [...]

Vocabulary

2 cursory (adj.): /ˈkɜːsərɪ/ running or passing rapidly over a thing or subject, so as to take no note of details - **5 queer studies** (n.): area of academic research relating to homosexuality - **10 transnational** (adj.): extending or going beyond national boundaries - **18 brand** (n.): a trade-mark - **38 to recuperate** (v.): to recover, to restore - **53 entity** (n.): here: an organization (as a business or governmental unit) - **57 localization** (n.): here: adapting to local demands - **65 panel** (n.): here: a part, a division - **67 reconfiguration** (n.): new arrangement of parts, reshaping - **68 discourse** (n.): verbal interchange of ideas - **72 eroticization** (n.): the process of making s.th. erotic - **82 incentive** (n.): stimulus, encouragement - **94 diaspora/diasporic** (n./adj.): people settled far from their ancestral homelands - **107 quest** (n.): an act or instance of seeking, pursuit - **114 affluent** (adj.): here: having a generously sufficient and typically increasing supply of material possessions - **118 bangle** (n.): ornamental rigid band worn around the ankle - **119 affiliate** (n.): here: subsidiary company - **126 defunct** (adj.): no longer living, existing, or functioning - **132 penetration** (n.): here: the extent to which a commercial product or agency is able to enter a new market - **142 array** (n.): arrangement in line or ranks - **166 fluid** (adj.): a situation that is fluid is likely to change

Explanations

118 bindi (n.): (Hindi, coll.) dot, red dot on a Hindu woman's forehead, traditionally worn by married women, but also (often in other colors) worn generally by way of fashion

Awareness

1 What do you associate with a Barbie doll? What influence does the Barbie have on (global) beauty standards?

Comprehension

2 Find out what "localization through transnational formations" means (ll. 57f.).
3 How does Grewal describe the "Indian Barbie"? Why does she revise the term?
4 Explain in your own words what the author describes as the "reconfiguration of Euro-American fashion discourse".
5 Give a short account of the economic liberalization process in India.

Analysis

6 Which image of India does Mattel sell? How is the sari significant here?
7 Which role does localization play in the process of economic liberalization? What does Mattel's status as a transnational organization mean in this context?
8 Who buys "Indian Barbies" and where are they sold? What does this imply about Indian society? What is the role of urban India, or of Indians living abroad?
9 Who benefits from the sale of Indian Barbies? What role do Mattel's Indian affiliates play?

Opinion

10 Why do you imagine did the "standard" Barbie (l. 63) not sell well in India? What are Grewal's implications in using this term?
11 Suggest a global sales strategy for Mattel. Should they produce "ethnic Barbies" for each nation or ethnic group? What would this mean, for instance, for Germany or South Africa respectively? Consider aspects such as profitability and cost-effectiveness.

Projects

12 Find out which other markets Mattel has targeted with its Barbie dolls (especially with the "Dolls of the World" series). Consult the following links:
http://barbie.everythinggirl.com/catalog/,
http://www.mattel.com/our_toys/ot_barb.asp,
http://www.barbiecollector.com/.

6

Subir Bhaumik

"Calcutta Plans Ban on Rickshaws"

Across the world, Indian transportation has traditionally been associated with the rickshaw – hand-drawn by barefoot "drivers," or, in its more fancy version, drawn by a driver on bicycle, the rickshaw is the cheapest form of transportation. In an Indian metropolis such as Bombay or Calcutta, where one is likely to spend hours stuck in traffic, the rickshaw also seems to be the most efficient form of moving from one part of the city to another: often in highly dangerous manoeuvres, rickshaws can be seen to weave effortlessly through even the most congested streets. While scooter rickshaws have now become the most common, hand-pulled rickshaws have by no means disappeared. Yet, these rickshaws also pose a dilemma. While they may be considered "quaint" by Western tourists, rickshaw pulling has recently come under attack as being an inhuman form of human labor. The following article by journalist Subir Bhaumik discusses a recent government measure taken in West Bengal, which seeks to ban rickshaws altogether. – BBC News, Calcutta (online).

Calcutta's famous hand-pulled rickshaws will soon be banned, according to the chief minister of the Indian state of West Bengal.

The rickshaws had long been considered "inhuman" and did not exist anywhere else, Buddhadev Bhattacharya said. The rickshaw, immortalised as a living symbol of Calcutta in films such as *City of Joy*, will be phased out in four to five months. The hand-pulled rickshaw came from China in the 19th century. Mr Bhattacharya said: "We have taken a policy decision to take the hand-drawn rickshaw off the roads of Calcutta on humanitarian grounds."

"Nowhere else in the world does this practice exist and we think it should also cease to exist in Calcutta," he said. The chief minister said the authorities were thinking of alternative modes of transport so that the transition did not affect either the pullers or the riders.

"This involves money and training. It will be about the end of this year when the rickshaws are finally gone," he said.

Uncertain future

A recent study by a non-governmental organisation, ActionAid India, put the number of hand-rickshaw pullers at 18,000 with more than 1,800 joining the pool every year. Many Calcuttans are uncertain whether they will be able to move around the city's old lanes without the hand-pulled rickshaws – particularly during the monsoon. "When we have to wade in chest-deep water during rains, no other transport works but you can still find the hand-pulled rickshaws taking people from one place to another," says Dipali Nath, a housewife in north Calcutta.

Some trade unions are demanding adequate compensation and an alternate livelihood for all the pullers before their licences are cancelled and the mode of transport banned.

"We expect the government will not throw them into the streets and leave them an empty stomach," said Mohammed Nizamuddin, a communist party leader who is involved with the rickshaw pullers union in Calcutta.

In India's major cities, bicycle rickshaws exist side by side with scooter rickshaws and hand-drawn ones

Vocabulary

Intro/6 congested (adj.): /kən'dʒɛstɪd/ overcrowded – **Intro/6 scooter** (n.): a low two-wheeled or three-wheeled automotive vehicle having a seat so that the rider does not straddle the engine – **Intro/8 quaint** (adj.): pleasingly or strikingly old-fashioned or unfamiliar – **6 to immortalize** (v.) to make immortal, eternal – **8 to phase out** (v.): to diminish gradually and put to an end, to discontinue – **14 to cease** (v.): to stop – **17 transition** (n.): a passing or passage from one condition to another; change – **34 trade union** (n.): an association of the workers in any trade for the protection of their interests in regard to wages, hours, and conditions of labour etc.

Awareness

1 Read up on the history of rickshaws on Wikipedia. Where does the name come from? In which countries was it first introduced? Why were these countries especially well suited for the introduction of the rickshaw?

Comprehension

2 Explain the sentence "We have taken a policy decision ... on humanitarian grounds" in ll. 10ff. in your own words.

Analysis

3 Why did the rickshaw puller union in Calcutta resist the prohibition?

4 Why would the rickshaw be a symbol especially of Calcutta? What is Calcutta's economic situation?

5 The banning of rickshaws has been considered a "facelift" for Calcutta as a global city in the age of globalization. Prime Minister Buddhadev Bhattacharya has justified his measure by the fact that rickshaws have already been banned from Tokyo. What role does globalization play here?

6 Buddhadev Bhattacharya (also sometimes spelled as Buddhadeb Bhattacharya) has been the Chief Minister of West Bengal since November 6, 2000. He is a member of the Communist Party of India (Marxist) or CPI (M).
Is it significant that rickshaws are being banned by a communist government? What does this imply?

Opinion

7 Should rickshaws be banned? Form two parties: one party made up of rickshaw drivers, another by political supporters of Bhattacharya's government measure.

Projects

8 Watch the film *City of Joy*. What does the rickshaw symbolize?

9 Write a fictitious account of an Indian rickshaw puller's life.

10 Why would rickshaws be introduced in Western cities today? As a customer, why would you take a rickshaw? What would you associate with the ride in a rickshaw? What would you consider the main difference between rickshaws in London and Calcutta?

11 Visit the website of "Velotaxi Frankfurt," Frankfurt's bicycle rickshaw operator and answer the following questions.
How does Velotaxi describe itself?
How has the image of the rickshaw changed?
What role does advertising play?
How is the drivers' motivation described?
What is their background?
Compare their motivation to that of Indian rickshaw drivers. Is this really the same rickshaw?
Give reasons for your decision.

12

Canada

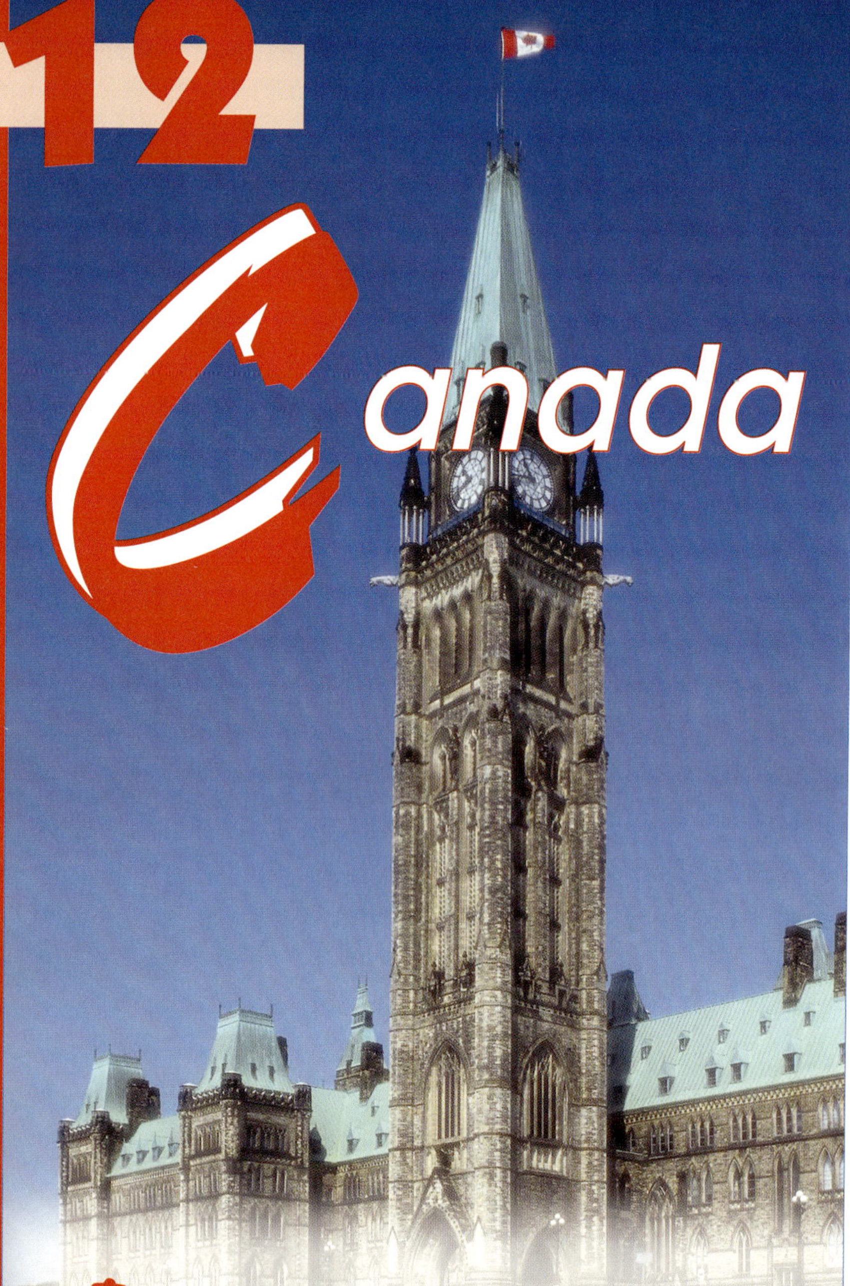

In Ottawa, Ontario, the federal government and the Parliament buildings are located. Ottawa became the **national capital** of Canada in 1857, chosen by Queen Victoria as a compromise. The Canadian government and the Queen feared it would be politically dangerous to choose one of the fiercely competing candidates Toronto, Kingston, Montréal and Québec City. Ottawa back then was a lumber town of 10,000 people which had been incorporated as a city only two years before.

The red and white **Canadian flag** was officially raised for the first time over Parliament Hill, Ottawa, on February 15th, 1965. It contains the two traditional colors of Canada, which in heraldry and in history are red and white. Many people claim that the two red blocks on its sides symbolize the Atlantic and the Pacific Ocean. In the centre you can see the maple leaf which was used as a symbol of Canada as early as 1700. It can also be found on the Canadian penny, where its design has hardly changed since 1937.

The **name Canada** probably derived from the word "Kanata", a term the Huron and Iroquois, Native American people of the East coast, used for "village" or "community". On his second voyage to this part of the world, Jacques Cartier noted his entrance to the St Lawrence River with the words: "The (...) Indians have assured us that this is the way to and the beginning of (...) the route to Canada."

Long before Cartier, who is often said to have "discovered" Canada, first explored the St Lawrence region (nowadays Eastern Canada) in 1534, many **aboriginal societies** had spread across every region of North America. In the country known as Canada today, there were more than 50 languages, many of which were as different as Japanese and German. Only three of them proved strong enough to survive (Cree, Ojibwa and Innuktitut); entire nations have vanished and cultures have been lost. In addition to Jacques Cartier, John Cabot and Samuel de Champlain were the other two most important white explorers in early Canadian history.

Unity in Diversity from Sea to Sea

Canada is over 7,000 kilometres from **east to west**. It takes seven days to drive from Halifax, Nova Scotia, on the East Coast, to Vancouver, British Columbia, in the far West. By airplane, the same trip would take about seven hours. The nation's only neighbor is the USA, including Alaska in the North. In relation to its physical size, Canada has a rather small population, about 31 million people, most of whom live in the southern parts of Canada close to the US borders.

Canada's borders are lined by three **oceans**: the Pacific Ocean on the west, the Atlantic Ocean on the east, and the Arctic Ocean to the north.

On July 1, 1867, the provinces now known as Ontario, Quebec, New Brunswick and Nova Scotia joined together to create the new country of Canada. This is known as **Confederation**, made official by the British North America Act of 1867. As time passed, other provinces and territories joined the Confederation and became part of Canada. Today, Canada has ten provinces and three territories. Canada became truly politically independent from Britain with the passing of the Constitution Act of 1982. However, the British Crown is formally still the head of the Canadian state.

The **Constitution Act of 1982** was proclaimed by Queen Elizabeth II and also signed by Pierre Trudeau, the Canadian Prime Minister and Jean Chrétien, the Canadian Minister of Justice.

This Act meant that the Canadian Constitution was no longer under British jurisdiction and thus marked the true moment of Canada's political independence. It also added the **Charter of Rights and Freedoms** to the Constitution which recognized fundamental freedoms as the basis of Canadian society, for example, the freedom of religion, the freedom of expression (including freedom of the press) and the freedom of peaceful assembly.

All Canadian citizens are united by the Charter in a moral and legal sense.

Provinces and territories (source: www.cic.gc.ca)

Region	Province/Territory	Capital
Atlantic Region	Newfoundland and Labrador	St. John's
	Prince Edward Island	Charlottetown
	Nova Scotia	Halifax
	New Brunswick	Fredericton
Central Canada	Quebec	Québec
	Ontario	Toronto
Prairie Provinces	Manitoba	Winnipeg
	Saskatchewan	Regina
	Alberta	Edmonton
West Coast	British Columbia	Victoria
North	Nunavut	Iqaluit
	Northwest Territories	Yellowknife
	Yukon Territory	Whitehorse

Vocabulary

lumber (n.): wood that is prepared for use in building etc. – **to incorporate** (v.): to include s.th. so that it forms a part of s.th. – **heraldry** (n.): the history of old families and their special symbols

1

Duke Redbird

"Building a Nation: From Confederation to the 21st Century"*

Duke Redbird, born 1939, is a member of the Chippewa (or Ojiba), an important First Nations tribe whose ancestors are often called the "Romans of the north woods". The Chippewa once were the primary middlemen in the aboriginal fur trade and they controlled the widest Native territory north of Mexico. Duke Redbird is one of the leading political Métis people in the country. He has worked with all levels of government and the private sector to meet the needs of Indians and fight their problems in the fields of education, alcohol and drug abuso, oconomic development, housing, tourism, culture, the arts, and health care. Duke Redbird is also a respected scholar, artist, writer, journalist and story-teller. – Duke Redbird, "I am a Canadian", in: Daniel David Moses / Terry Goldie (eds.), *An Anthology of Canadian Native Literature in English.* Second Edition (Oxford et al.: OUP, 1998), pp. 120f.

I am a Canadian
I'm a lobster fisherman in Newfoundland
I'm a clambake in P.E.I.
I'm a picnic, I'm a banquet
I'm mother's homemade pie
I'm a few drafts in a Legion hall in Fredericton
I'm a kite-flyer in a field in Moncton
I'm a nap on the porch after a hard day's work is done
I'm a snowball fight in Truro, Nova Scotia
I'm small kids playing jacks and skipping rope
I'm a mother who lost a son in the last great war
And I'm a bride with a brand new ring
And a chest of hope
I'm an Easterner
I'm a Westerner
I'm from the North
And I'm from the South
I've swum in two big oceans
And I've loved them both
[…]
I'm Sir John A. MacDonald
I'm Alexander Graham Bell
I'm a pow-wow dancer
And I'm Louis Riel
I'm the Calgary Stampede
I'm a feathered Sarcee
I'm Edmonton at night
I'm a bar-room fight
[…]
I am French
I am English
And I am Métis
But more than this
Above all this
I am a Canadian and proud to be free.

John A. MacDonald

Vocabulary

3 clambake (n.): an outdoor party, esp. for eating seafood – **6 draft** (n.): the practice of ordering people by law to serve in the armed forces – **11 jacks** (n.): a children's game in which players bounce a small ball and pick up small metal objects – **14 chest** (n.): here: a large strong box, usually made of wood – **24 pow-wow** (n.): /ˈpaʊwaʊ/ a meeting of Native Americans

Explanations

Intro: Métis: members of the Canadian population with mixed aboriginal and European ancestry. Collectively with the Native Indians and the Inuit (i.e. the Eskimo people) they are called Native Canadians or First Nations. – **3 P.E.I.**: Prince Edward Island, Canada's smallest and most densely populated province. It is one of the Maritime Provinces in Eastern Canada and entered Confederation in 1873. – **25 Louis Riel:** A Canadian politician (1844-1885) and leader of the Métis people of the Canadian prairies. He led two resistance movements against the Canadian government; they sought to preserve Métis rights and culture as their homelands in the Northwest Territories came progressively under Canadian influence. He is often called the Father of Manitoba. – **26 the Calgary Stampede**: a big 10-day festival with shows, exhibitions, concerts, dancing and eating that takes places in Stampede Park, Calgary (Alberta), starting in the second week of July with a huge parade – **27 Sarcee**: a people of the First Nations who nowadays live on an Indian reservation near Calgary, Alberta. They call themselves *Tsuu T'ina* which can mean "beaver people" or "many people".

Info

John A. MacDonald

can be called the "author" of modern Canada. In October 1864 delegates from the different provinces met in Québec City and the Canadians discussed the specifics of a possible union which were called the 72 resolutions. These were based on a federal system and were mainly written by John A. MacDonald, a conservative Scot who distrusted the English. In Québec City the structure of the union, the division of power between national and provincial governments and other details were hammered out. John A. MacDonald was asked to form an interim government until 1867 when Queen Victoria signed the British North America Act (BNA Act) that came into effect on July 1st. On that day, a new nation was born, Canada, consisting of 3.5 million people and of the first four provinces, which had agreed to the revised version of the resolutions (Nova Scotia, New Brunswick, Quebec and Ontario). The BNA Act did not grant Canada full independence: it was still part of the Empire, Canadians were still British citizens. Nevertheless, John A. MacDonald and the 35 delegates in Québec City had paved the way for a giant step forward.

Awareness

1 Name aspects (e.g. people, experiences, events) that constitute a nation's "culture". To what extent is the present day culture defined by the history of a country, in your opinion? What role do different cultures play in a world that is called a global village?

Comprehension

2 Look at a map of Canada and try to find the place names and other locations the author mentions. Can you find possible reasons for his choice?

3 Put the metaphors (Reference Library, p. 311) in the poem into certain categories (e.g. people, places, experiences etc.). How can you characterize the different categories?

Analysis

4 Describe the tone (Reference Library, p. 312) of the poem and how it is created by the author.

5 The author, Duke Redbird, is a Métis. Explain the additional dimension this adds to the poem.

6 According to the author, what role does history play for the present face of a country?

7 Some of the metaphors (Reference Library, p. 311) point to conflicts within Canada. Explain them and the author's attitude towards them.

8 What is the author's underlying message about his home country, Canada?

Creative Writing

9 Try to write a similar poem about your home country.

Internet Project

10 Research the other Fathers of Confederation under www.collectionscanada.ca. Write two or three short bios and try to characterize important differences but also similarities these men shared.

2

Margaret Atwood

"Early Pioneers: The Story of Susanna Moodie"*

Susanna Moodie (1803-1885) was a writer of children's tales, a poet and an essayist and an early immigrant to Canada. Many of her works show that immigration and life in the backwoods of Canada in the middle of the 19th century were a tough experience, especially for women. In 1970 Margaret Atwood, one of Canada's best-known contemporary authors, published *The Journals of Susanna Moodie*, a collection of poems based on the pioneer's work *Roughing It in the Bush* (1852). Atwood recreated Moodie's meditations on pioneer life, on nature's relationship with animal and human inhabitants, and on human dislocation. In her work, Atwood brought Susanna Moodie, one of Canada's earliest and best-known pioneers, back to life. – Margaret Atwood, "The Double Voice", in: Margaret Atwood / Charles Pachter, *The Journals of Susanna Moodie*. With a memoir by Charles Pachter and a foreword by David Staines (Boston and New York: Houghton Mifflin Company, 1997).

The Double Voice

Two voices
took turns using my eyes:
One had manners,
painted in watercolours,
used hushed tones when speaking
of mountains or Niagara Falls,
composed uplifting verse
and expended sentiment upon the poor.

The other voice
had other knowledge:
that men sweat
always and drink often,
that pigs are pigs
but must be eaten
anyway, that unborn babies
fester like wounds in the body,
that there is nothing to be done
about mosquitos;

One saw through my
bleared and gradually
bleaching eyes, red leaves,
the rituals of seasons and rivers

The other found a dead dog
jubilant with maggots
half-buried among the sweet peas.

Margaret Atwood was born in Ottawa in 1939 and spent the summers of her childhood in northern Ontario and Quebec. She later attended the University of Toronto, Radcliffe, and Harvard. Up to the present day she is one of Canada's best-known authors – at home and abroad; she has served as the chairperson of *The Writers' Union of Canada* and has actively supported *Amnesty International* and *PEN Canada*. Thus far, Atwood has written more than 30 literary works and has been translated into more than 25 languages. Although she has written non-fiction and children's literature, she is best known for her novels, like, for example, *The Edible Woman* (1969), *The Handmaid's Tale* (1985), and *The Robber Bride* (1993), in addition to her numerous collections of poetry and short stories.

Vocabulary

6 hushed (adj.): here: speaking very quietly – **9 to expend** (v.): to spend or use a lot of energy, time, money etc. – **17 to fester** (v.): to become badly infected; to become much worse – **21 bleared** (adj., of eyes): not able to see clearly, especially because of tiredness – **22 to bleach** (v.): to become white or pale by a chemical process or the effect of the sunlight – **25 jubilant** (adj.): /ˈdʒuːbɪlənt/ feeling or showing great happiness because of a success – **25 maggot** (n.): a creature that looks like a small short worm and is often found in decaying meat and other food – **26 sweet pea** (n.): a climbing garden plant with a sweet smell and pale flowers

Susanna Moodie

Info

Susanna Moodie

On the first of July 1832, Susanna, her husband and first child embarked on a ship from Leith, Scotland, to Canada. Their ship arrived at the end of August at Grosse Isle, north of Québec City. Ten days later, the family reached their final destination, Cobourg, a small Lake Ontario town seventy miles east of Toronto, where they settled on a farm. Eighteen months later, the Moodies moved to a backwoods area further north where they lived until 1840.

For a respectable woman like Susanna, raised in a well-off family in Southern England, life as a pioneer in Canada was far from easy. She reflected on her experiences in a series of sketches published in 1852. Her best-known book was *Roughing It in the Bush: Or, Life in Canada*, which included the Moodies' responses to the culture shock, the ordeals and the pleasures of immigration and pioneer life, from their arrival at the quarantine station of Grosse Isle in 1832, to their departure from the backwoods in 1840.

Awareness

1 Susanna Moodie, who came to Canada with her family in 1832 and later became one of the best-known early pioneers, wrote a book entitled *Roughing It in the Bush* (1852) about the first years in her new home country. According to the title of the book, what do you assume her "Canadian experience" was like?

Comprehension

2 Try to paraphrase the first two lines of the poem.
3 Compare in your own words the feelings and the behaviour of Susanna 1 (with "manners", l. 4) and of Susanna 2 (with "other knowledge", l. 11).
4 In what way do both Susannas perceive their surroundings?

Analysis

5 Explain the title of the poem. To do so, make a list of Susanna's positive and negative experiences which are described in the poem.
6 Describe Susanna's mood reflected in the poem in your own words. How does she feel?
7 How does the author intensify the "Double Voice" on a formal level?
8 Explain to what extent and in what ways Susanna Moodie's inner feelings and her perception of the outer world correspond. Pay particular attention to the last three lines of the poem in this context.

Opinion

9 Which of the two voices in Susanna is stronger? Give reasons and evidence from the text for your opinion.
10 Do contemporary authors like Margaret Atwood have the right to speak in the voice of a person who died a long time ago? Discuss (Reference Library, pp. 306f.) the advantages and possible dangers of this device/technique and its effects.
11 Compare Susanna's situation to a modern-day immigrant who has recently arrived in Canada. Take into account similarities as well as differences. In your opinion, has life as a pioneer (or immigrant) become easier these days?

Creative Writing

12 You are Susanna's best friend who stayed back home in England. You got a letter from her that contains the information given in the poem "The Double Voice" and in which the same mood is also reflected. Write a reply to your friend.

Project

13 Many of Margaret Atwood's novels also deal with heroines and their often gender-related struggles in everyday life.
a) Read one of these novels (e.g. *The Edible Woman* or *Lady Oracle*) or watch one of the respective movies (e.g. *The Handmaid's Tale*) and present it to the class.
b) Compare the situation of the central female characters to that of Susanna Moodie. As a whole class you could create a collage comparing the different characters as a result.

3

René Lévesque

My Quebec

René Lévesque was one of the key figures of the *Québec Liberal Party* and an important strategist of the so-called Quiet Revolution which transformed Quebec from an anachronistic Northern American province into a modern energetic entity in the first half of the 1960s. One of the driving forces behind this movement was a new sense of nationalism. For Lévesque who had, for example, brought together eleven private power companies to form the publicly owned *Hydro Québec*, the *Liberal Party* soon became too federalist. By 1968, he had brought together several smaller separatist groups to form a larger political union known as the *Parti Québécois*. In November 1976, in an election that shocked the nation, Lévesque defeated the Liberals and put the province's first openly separatist government into power. – René Lévesque, *My Quebec* (Toronto: Methuen, 1979), pp. 156-160.

René Lévesque (1922–1987)

Imagine that the entire continent of North America ought to have been French instead of … Neo-Roman. For indeed our beginnings were incredible. From Hudson Bay and Labrador in the north to the Gulf of Mexico in the south, from the Gaspé near the Atlantic to the Rockies, from which one can almost see the Pacific, there we were – and there you were – as the discoverers and the first European settlers. When Champlain built his home in Quebec and Nouvelle France was born, the Mayflower pilgrims had not even raised anchor on their journey to found New England. And so, for a hundred and fifty years soldiers and missionaries and colonists […] wrote a good number of the most extraordinary, if not the most famous, pages of the history of the seventeenth and eighteenth centuries. […]

However, this history, for a century and a half, was ours – and also yours. And I remember that when we arrived at the last chapter, the one which ended with defeat and conquest, we lost the desire to know what followed, and instead returned indefatigably to the beginning; because what followed, with due respect to our British compatriots, seemed in some way to have become the history of another people.

This is not a nostalgic idealization of a tiny society of some tens of thousands of poor people who, in 1760 in the Saint Lawrence Valley, had to submit to a foreign domination which was destined to remain for a long time. As with all the other colonies of the time, this was as yet nothing more than a modest outgrowth of a metropolis which was both natural and distant, and whose power, once its job was done, should have ended with us as it did elsewhere had its continuity not been broken. Already in fact, distance, the climate, contact with the Indian population, the continental experience had fashioned a mentality and a way of life which were becoming more and more different from that of the mother country. This was a nation, and a French nation certainly, but a nation which was just as able to live its own life and to be a presence in the world as any other.

This is what defeat broke up, but it did not manage to dispel the dream. It was a dream which, though normally unacknowledged, was strong enough to nourish, even today, a national identity and a national idea that only numerical weakness and total isolation prevented us from realizing. […]

[To our] rapid awakening, which we were ourselves the first to find astonishing, we have given the name the "quiet revolution," which was not ill-founded. Revolutionary it certainly was, if one accepts that a fundamental change can happen without killings and ruins. Quiet, and in consequence marked by a continuity in change, even in the most radical change, which is one of the characteristics of our people. Quietly therefore, but on all levels we saw a liberation which was as sudden as is the breaking of the icepacks on our rivers in the spring. And the ground began to flower and to produce like never before: reform as profound as it was late in the field of education; the initiation of a modern administration [...] – but also a jump in social awareness which on several major points moved rapidly from the back to the foreground; and an increasingly keen consciousness of responsibilities such as the essentials of economic life. [...]

Inevitably this metamorphosis owed it to itself to create an instrument for its political expression and to try to conduct it to its logical conclusion. This instrument is the Parti Québécois. We were just a few hundred, then a few thousand, to bring it into being in 1967–68, with two objectives which have remained coupled since then: sovereignty and association. This means a sovereign State of Quebec which will accept, or rather offer in advance, new links of interdependence with Canada, but links which will this time be negotiated between equal peoples, as a function of their geographic and other unquestionable common interests. [...]

This, briefly, is the national option, inscribed from the beginning in the heart of a political program in which each paragraph, each word, has been rigorously exposed to the attention of every Quebecer. But like anyone else, certainly, over and above these existential but not very day-to-day questions which we are resolving – for a while – in the Constitution, our people are also experiencing all the problems, the frustrations and the hopes of the men and women of their time. This is why, on the way, we must also try to respond the best we can, with the power the federal regime deigns to give us, to these requirements of our citizens.

Vocabulary

21 indefatigably (adv.): never giving up or getting tired of doing s.th. - **37 domination** (n.): control - **42 outgrowth** (n.): a natural result of s.th. - **54 to dispel** (v.): to make s.th. go away or disappear - **55 unacknowledged** (adj.): ignored or not noticed - **99 to deign** (v.): /'deɪn/ to do s.th. in a way that shows your are feeling too important to do it

Info

The October Crisis

The Quiet Revolution did not remain quiet for long. By 1963, a terrorist group calling themselves the *Front de liberation du Québec* (FLQ) had begun calling publicly for an end to "Anglo-Saxon colonization" and backed up their statements by setting off bombs in Montréal. Over the next seven years the FLQ, who consisted mainly of separatist and would-be revolutionaries, staged more than 30 armed robberies and set off more than 200 bombs, killing six people and injuring more than 40. On October 10th, armed men from an FLQ group abducted Quebec's minister of Labour and Immigration, Pierre Laporte. As public panic started to grow, Prime Minister Pierre Trudeau ordered the army into Ottawa in order to show force and protect government officials. Furthermore, he passed the War Measures Act in the House of Commons (with an overwhelming majority of 190 to 16), which gave the Canadian government dictatorial powers for a limited time, for example, the right to ban the FLQ and to suspend civil liberties. The day after the War Measurements Act was passed, Pierre Laporte was found strangled in the trunk of a car. He had become the FLQ's seventh and final victim. To this day, historians are arguing about whether the government's actions were justified. In any case, Trudeau managed to break the power of the terrorist separatist movement. In Quebec there has never been a resurgence of political terrorism after 1970.

Explanations

2 Neo-Roman: In using the term "Neo-Roman" for the English, Lévesque implies that the English like the Romans in earlier times took over control in other countries (in this case North America), usually after defeating them in a war. This system is also called imperialism. – **8 Champlain**: Samuel de Champlain (1567–1635) was a Frenchman who began further explorations of New France in the early 1600s; he settled in Québec City and Montréal was founded soon after in 1642 as a missionary outpost. Champlain is often called the Father of New France since his activities, contrary to those of his predecessor, Jacques Cartier, marked the shift from exploration to permanent settlement.

Info

The Seven Years' War and the End of New France

New France had strived as a royal colony in the 17th century mainly in the part of Canada which is Quebec today. The fall of New France, however, had begun at the turn of the century and was finally marked by the Seven Years' War (1756-1763), the last in a series of wars, in which Quebec was taken and the British captured the French fortress of Louisburg. In the Treaty of Paris, signed Februrary 10th, 1763, France ceded all its territories in North America, except for a pair of small islands off Newfoundland. It marked the end of New France and more than 150 years of conflict between Britain and France for control of North America.

Awareness

1 "In history, the past conditional explains nothing." Think about this statement by Gérard Pelletier, who was Canadian Secretary of State in the 1970s. What could be meant by it? Can you think of historical events to which it could be applied?

Comprehension

2 Who is speaking in the text and to whom?
3 What happened to the French-Canadians after New France was defeated?
4 What is the dream Lévesque is talking about in l. 54 and why has it not been realized?
5 What was the so-called "quiet revolution" (l. 61)?
6 What are the two main objectives of the *Parti Québécois*?
7 What is the party's main task before these objectives can be realized?

Analysis

8 Describe the tone (Reference Library, p. 312) of the text. Give evidence from the text in your analysis.
9 Find out why, according to Lévesque, the whole continent of North America should have been French and why, on the other hand, this did not happen.
10 Explain in what ways the Quiet Revolution was a special revolution and what the effects for the people living in Quebec were, according to the author.

Opinion

11 Lévesque does not mention the FLQ (see Info Box on "The October Crisis") in his text. Explain why, in your opinion.

Project

12 Whereas Canada is a bilingual country on a federal level, by the 1970s Quebec became more or less unilingual. Bill 22 (1974) made French the only official language of Quebec which affected, for example, businesses which operated in English or children attending English schools. Bill 101 (1978) banned English on commercial signs and severely restricted access to English-language education.
In a role play with three partners, one of you is a politician from Quebec who wants to pass new bills enforcing the already existing laws on the use of French as the only language of the province. The other one is a family mother/father from Quebec who want their children to be educated in English. You are interviewed by a journalist from the national broadcast corporation, CBC. Apply your knowledge from the text and the Info Boxes to collect arguments, prepare questions and answers. In a last step, conduct the interview and record it on tape or videotape.

4

Douglas Coupland

"Where Civilization Ends"*

Vancouver with 2.1 million inhabitants is the biggest city of Canada's westernmost province, British Columbia (BC). The province contains some of the world's most spectacular scenery, from the Canadian Rocky Mountains in the southeast to the Pacific coastal areas with rainforests and countless islands bordering in the west. Lifestyle and culture in BC, especially in the southwest corner where Vancouver is situated in a magnificent location between the sea and the mountains, are often called typically "West Coast". The lifestyle and culture there differ from that in the rest of Canada. Douglas Coupland, one of Canada's most successful contemporary authors, has very special feelings about his home town which many people, Vancouver-born or not, consider one of the most beautiful cities in the world. - Douglas Coupland, "Lions Gate Bridge, Vancouver, B.C., Canada", in: Douglas Coupland, *Polaroids from the Dead* (New York: Regan Books, 1996), pp. 69–76.

Lions Gate Bridge, Vancouver, connecting North Vancouver and Stanley Park

View of Vancouver, BC, with BC Place on the right and False Creek on the left

Perhaps in your city there is a structure so potent and glorious that its existence in your mind becomes the actual architecture of your mind – a structure through which all of your dreams and ideas and hopes are funneled. In my city, Vancouver, there is one such structure, a fairy-tale bridge called Lions Gate Bridge. Its three delicate spans link the city of Vancouver with the suburbs of the North Shore, where I grew up, and with the mountains and wilderness of British Columbia beyond those suburbs. [...]

Lions Gate Bridge is by no means a practical bridge – it looks to be spun from liquid sugar [...]. By urban planning and engineering standards it borders on being a disaster, but then isn't it true of life in general that nothing is more seductive than the dying starlet? The lost cowboy? The self-destructive jazz musician? The bridge has three harrowingly narrow lanes. Depending on the time of day, commuters on the Lions Gate may have either one or two of these lanes apportioned to them. [...] But enough about the bridge's technicalities. We tolerate goodness knows how much from the people we love; the same goes for objects we love, too. I figure I have driven across the bridge maybe five or six thousand times in my life – that's all the way from Vancouver to Halifax and back – and never in all these miles have I once tired of the view, endlessly renewing, endlessly glorious. Some of my happiest memories of Vancouver, or my life, for that matter, have been simple memories of driving across Lions Gate Bridge. [...] Maybe I am headed to my parents' house or maybe I am off to the airport – the bridge's very existence is a metaphor for journey.

[...] I have always noticed that traffic headed cityward mysteriously slows to a crawl once it hits the bridge's first [...] span. It then shortly resumes its normal speed. I ascribe this predictable slowdown to people who are not from Vancouver. When they suddenly encounter the beauty that surrounds them from mid-bridge – the quartz of the city to the south; the freighters below, plump with wheat and ore; the cruise liners tramping away off in the distance; as well as the swoop of the bridge above them – the out-of-towners are overwhelmed. They respond by jamming on their brakes. In an odd way this makes me proud of my city – proud to live here. I never begrudge this inevitable slowdown. [...]

In late 1986 I arrived back in Vancouver after living abroad for a year. On that first evening back I looked down at the bridge and saw that it garlanded with brilliant pearls of light along its thin parabolic lines. I was shocked – it was so beautiful it made me lose my breath. I asked my father about these lights and he told me they were called "Gracie's Necklace" after a local politician. [...] Now, whenever I fly back to Vancouver, it is Gracie's Necklace I look for from my seat, the sight I need to see in order to make myself feel I am home again. We often forget, living here in Vancouver, that we live in the youngest city on earth, a city almost entirely of, and *only* of, the twentieth century – and that this is Vancouver's greatest blessing. It is the delicacy of Gracie's Necklace that reminds me we live, not so much in a city but in a dream of a city. [...]

I want you to imagine you are driving north, across the Lions Gate Bridge, and the sky is steely gray and the sugar-dusted mountains loom blackly in the distance. Imagine what lies behind those mountains – realize that there are only more mountains – mountains until the North Pole, mountains until the end of the world, mountains taller than a thousand me's, mountains taller than a thousand you's.

Here is where civilization ends; here is where time ends and where eternity begins. Here is what Lions Gate Bridge is: one last grand gesture of beauty, of charm, and of grace before we enter the hinterlands, before the air becomes too brittle and too cold to breathe, before we enter that place where life becomes harsh, where we must become animals in order to survive.

Info

Vancouver – Short History of a City

The area which is known as Vancouver today was first settled in by a Native American tribe, the Salish people. The first Europeans who set foot there were Spanish explorers in the late 18th century. In order to convince BC to join the Canadian confederation, Ottawa promised BC in 1870 to build a transcontinental railroad. The capital of British Columbia, Victoria, was on an island, but the Canadian Pacific Railway (CPR) which was to link Canada's east and west had to build a mainland coastal terminus. Railroad engineers chose a site on one of the south-westernmost sheltered Pacific shore inlets, Burrard Inlet, which at that time was a collection of saloons, farms and lumber mills. In 1886, the first train arrived from Montréal in the brand-new settlement called Vancouver. Only four years later, the transportation and trading centre had already outpaced Victoria in population. Today, Vancouver is considered to be one of the Pacific Rim's economic and cultural capitals.

Vocabulary

5 to funnel (v.): to move or make s.th. move through a narrow space - **7 span** (n): here: the part of a bridge between one vertical support and another - **12 to spin** (v.): to make thread from wool, cotton, silk etc. by twisting it - **17 harrowing** (adj.): /ˈhærəʊɪŋ/ very frightening and / or shocking, making you feel upset - **19 to apportion** (v.): to give a share of s.th. to s.b. - **35 to resume** (v.): to begin again or continue after an interruption - **39 quartz** (n.): a hard mineral, often used to make clocks and watches - **40 freighter** (n.): /ˈfreɪtə/ here: a large ship carrying goods - **40 ore** (n.): /ɔː/ rock, earth etc. from which metal can be obtained - **41 to tramp** (v.): to walk with heavy or noisy steps - **42 swoop** (n.): a sudden and quick move through the air in a downward direction, as birds often do - **43 to jam** (v.): to push s.th. somewhere with a lot of force - **45 to begrudge** (v.): to feel unhappy about having to do s.th. - **50 parabolic** (adj.): moving in a curve similar to the path of an object thrown into the air and falling back to earth - **61 delicacy** (n.): the quality of being, or appearing to be, easy to damage or break - **75 brittle** (adj.): here: hard and sharp (usually used with sounds)

Awareness

1 Think about what or who best symbolizes your home village, town, city or country to you (this can be a feeling, an experience, a monument, a text, a person or whatever else comes to your mind). Give reasons for your choice.

Comprehension

2 Describe the location of Lions Gate Bridge and its appearance in your own words.
3 Why is Lions Gate Bridge not a practical bridge? Why is it nevertheless tolerated by many people, including the author?
4 Why does the traffic moving towards the city always slow down in the middle of the bridge?
5 Explain what "Gracie's necklace" is and where the name comes from.
6 What can you see when driving north on Lions Gate Bridge on a clear day?

Analysis

7 Explain what is so special about Vancouver as a city and as a place to live in, according to the author.
8 Coupland claims that Lions Gate Bridge is "where civilization ends". Explain this image in more detail, taking into account the physical location of the bridge.
9 Explain what else the bridge symbolizes to the author. Concentrate on two major aspects, starting with descriptions, comparisons and metaphors (Reference Library, p. 311) he uses in order to develop a clear analysis of your own.

Opinion

10 "Home is where the heart is." Discuss (Reference Library, pp. 306f.) this statement and give reasons for your opinion.

Project

11 Put your suggestions from task 1 (awareness) into words. You can also use drawings, illustrations and other types of visual support to express your ideas about what symbolizes home to you and where home actually is. Collect the material from the whole class to produce a collage.

Internet Project

12 Imagine that you have decided to take part in this year's competition "Discover Vancouver and Vancouver Island", which is funded every year by the City of Vancouver for pupils from all over the world. The prize is a 14-day round trip to Vancouver and Vancouver Island. To take part in the competition you have to hand in a detailed description of your planned trip which has to impress the jury. The categories they pay special attention to are: interest, fun, variety and efficiency. The overall aim of the trip is that you, as a group of pupils from abroad, get a good impression of the city and the island. Your task now is to produce a detailed and convincing plan for a 14-day trip according to the jury's categories and attach it to a short letter of application to the committee. The maximum amount of money paid for your flights, transportation (e.g. bus and train tickets) and overnight stays is 6,000 Canadian Dollars for the whole group. There will be extra money for food and for activities like, for example, visits to museums, provided your suggestions are convincing. A good website to start from is www.hellobc.com.

5

Roche Carrier

"Don't Say It's Just a Game"*

Hockey is *the* national game and Canada's most important contribution to the world of sports. Interest has always been particularly high in Quebec where hockey originated; the first game with rules was played in Montréal in 1879. An annual competition for the top Canadian team has existed since 1892 and was named The National Hockey League (NHL) in 1917. Today, the best 30 Northern American teams, some of them from the USA, take part in this annual competition whose winner takes home the Stanley Cup. Up to the present day, Hockey has remained a favourite topic of national discussion. This is reflected in one of the most famous Canadian books for children in which a little boy who grew up in Quebec in the 1940s relates one of his most important childhood memories. The story was originally written in French but has become equally popular in the English version all over the country. – Roche Carrier, *Le Chandail de Hockey / The Hockey Sweater* (Montréal: Tundra Books, 1979).

The winters of my childhood were long, long seasons. We lived in three places – the school, the church and the skating-rink – but our real life was on the skating-rink. Real battles were won on the skating-rink. Real strength appeared on the skating-rink. The real leaders showed themselves on the skating-rink. [...]

As for church, we found there the tranquillity of God: there we forgot school and dreamed about the next hockey game. Through our daydreams it might happen that we would recite a prayer: we would ask God to help us play as well as Maurice Richard.

I remember very well the winter of 1946. We all wore the same uniform as Maurice Richard, the red, white and blue uniform of the Montréal Canadiens, the best hockey team in the world. [...] We cut his pictures out of all the newspapers. Truly, we knew everything there was to know about him. On the ice, when the referee blew his whistle, the two teams would rush at the puck: we were five Maurice Richards against five other Maurice Richards, throwing themselves on the puck. [...]

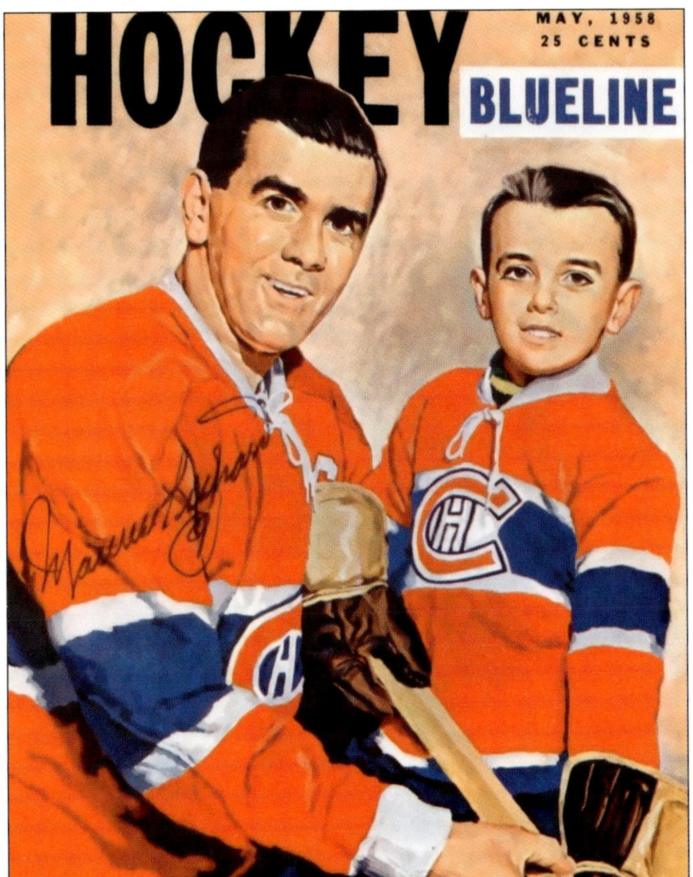

Maurice "Rocket" Richard ("Mr. Hockey") with a little boy, both wearing Montréal Canadiens sweaters

One day, my Montréal Canadiens sweater was too small for me; and it was ripped in several places. My mother said: "If you wear that old sweater, people are going to think we are poor!" Then she did what she did whenever we needed new clothes. She started to look through the catalogue that the Eaton company in Montréal sent us in the mail every year. [...] My mother did not like the order forms included in the catalogue. They were written in English and she did not understand a single word of it. To order my hockey sweater, she did what she always did. She took out her writing pad and wrote in her fine schoolteacher's hand: "Dear Monsieur Eaton, Would you be so kind as to send me a Canadiens' hockey sweater for my son, Roche, who is ten years old and a little bit tall for his age? [...] I am sending you three dollars. Please send me the change if there is any. I hope your packing will be better than it was last time."

[...] Two weeks later we received the sweater. That day I had one of the greatest disappointments of my life! Instead of the red, white and blue Montréal Canadiens sweater, Monsieur Eaton had sent the blue and white sweater of the Toronto Maple

Leafs. I had always worn the red, white and blue sweater of the Montréal Canadiens. [...] Besides, the Toronto team was always being beaten by the Canadiens.

With tears in my eyes, I found the strength to say: "I'll never wear that uniform." "My boy," said my mother, "first you're going to try it on! If you make up your mind about something before you try it, you won't go very far in this life." [...] "Maurice Richard would never wear it." "You're not Maurice Richard! Besides it's not what you put on your back that matters, it's what you put inside your head." [...] My mother sighed in despair and explained to me: "If you don't keep this sweater which fits you perfectly I'll have to write to Monsieur Eaton and explain that you don't want to wear the Toronto sweater. Monsieur Eaton understands French perfectly, but he's English and he's going to be insulted because he likes the Maple Leafs. If he's insulted, do you think he'll be in a hurry to answer us? Spring will come before you play a single game [...]." So, I had to wear the Toronto Maple Leafs sweater.

When I arrived at the skating rink in my blue sweater, all the Maurice Richards in red, white and blue came, one by one, and looked at me. The referee blew his whistle and I went to take my usual position. The coach came over and told me I would be on the second line. A few minutes later the second line was called; I jumped onto the ice. The Maple Leafs sweater weighed on my shoulders like a mountain. The captain came and told me to wait; he'd need me later, on defense. By the third period I had still not played.

Then one of the defensemen was hit on the nose with a stick and it started to bleed. I jumped onto the ice. My moment had come! The referee blew his whistle and gave me a penalty. He said there were already five players on the ice. That was too much! It was too unfair! "This is persecution!" I shouted. "It's just because of my blue sweater!" I crashed my stick against the ice so hard that it broke. I bent down to pick up the pieces. When I got up, the young curate, on skates, was standing in front of me. "My child," he said, "just because you're wearing a new Toronto Maple Leaf sweater, it doesn't mean you're going to make the laws around here. A good boy never loses his temper. Take off your skates and go to the church and ask God to forgive you."

Wearing my Maple Leafs sweater I went to the church, where I prayed to God. I asked God to send me right away a hundred million moths that would eat up my Toronto Maple Leafs sweater.

Info

Maurice Richard (Joseph Henri Maurice Richard, *Montréal August 4th, 1921, † May 27th, 2000) was one of the most famous Canadian hockey players ever. "The Rocket", as he was called by his fans, played his entire career (1942–1960) with the team of the Montréal Canadiens. During this time he became not only a hockey star but also a French-Canadian icon. Maurice Richard established many National Hockey League records; for example, he was the first to score 50 goals in a regular season (which was then 50 games).

Vocabulary

3 skating-rink (n.): a specially prepared flat surface where you can ice-skate and play hockey - **17 referee** (n.): the official who controls the game in some sports, such as soccer, basketball or hockey - **88 persecution** (n.): the cruel and unfair treatment of s.b. especially because of their race, religious or political beliefs - **91 curate** (n.): /'kjʊərɪt/ an assistant to the priest - **99 moth** (n.): a flying insect with a long thin body; moths mostly fly at night, are attracted to bright lights and can destroy cloth and garments

Explanations

14 Montréal Canadiens: a hockey legend and one of the most consistently successful professional sports teams in Canadian history. A high percentage of the team's fans has traditionally been catholic and spoke French as their mother tongue. - **49 Toronto Maple Leafs**: one of the most famous competing Canadian Toronto-based hockey teams

Awareness

1 Hockey is to Canadians what baseball is to Americans and football (soccer) to Germans. Can you identify any more "national sports"? What do you know about their traditions and the role they play in the respective countries nowadays?

Comprehension

2 Name the factors that have shaped the main character's youth (in order of the priority he assigns to them).

3 Why does the boy refuse to wear his new hockey sweater? What are his mother's arguments against it?

4 What are the reasons why his mother does not send the sweater back and ask for a new one?

5 Why is he sent off from the hockey game by the curate?

6 Describe in your own words what happened during the first hockey game which the boy took part in with his new sweater.

Analysis

7 In which Canadian province did the main character grow up? In what way did this shape the hobbies and interests of his childhood?

8 Define the role Maurice Richard plays in the boy's and his friends' youth.

Opinion

9 There is a misunderstanding between the mother and the Eaton company about what a Canadian hockey sweater (in this case a hockey sweater of the leading Canadian team) is. This leads to the wrong sweater being sent to the main character. Explain this misunderstanding in more detail and discuss in which ways it could be considered "typically" Canadian. Can you imagine a similar misunderstanding happening in Germany?

10 Gerald Friesen, history professor from the University of Manitoba, Canada, claims that hockey defines Canada's culture just like examples of high art, for example, the art of famous painters or musicians. He says that "hockey is an art form. [...] It is the glue that helps hold the country together." Discuss (Reference Library, pp. 306f.) the pros and cons of this position and express your opinion in a letter to Prof. Friesen.

Creative Writing

11 Describe the hockey game in the story from the point of view of the main character's best friend and team mate who keeps a diary. Also include a second diary entry dated two weeks later that shows what happened to the boy and his new sweater.

The USA, the World

EU-US: The Indispensable Partnership

Speech by The Rt. Hon. Christopher Patten, External Relations Commissioner of the European Union, at the Westdeutscher Rundfunk ARD Europa Forum, 3 December 2002

Christopher Patten (b. 1944) has had a successful and varied political and academic career. Among other things, he was the British Minister for Overseas Development (1986–89), the Governor of Hong Kong (1992–97), External Relations Commissioner of the EU (1999–2003); since 2003, he has been Chancellor Elect of Oxford University. Patten is married, with three children.

I want to begin with a remark that the last American Secretary of State, Madelaine Albright, made during the years of the Clinton Administration. She described the United States as 'the indispensable nation' and I think that that is unarguably true. But it is my case today that the relationship between the United States and Europe should be seen as the indispensable *partnership*. I think, the United States is more likely to accomplish its objectives when it is working in partnership with Europe and I think it is even more likely that Europe is likely to achieve what we want internationally if we do so with the United States which is the natural leader of the institutions of global governance which Americans more than anybody else created.

Of course, the United States today is spectacularly powerful. Some people say that the United States is today's only superpower. A friend of mine, a very distinguished American diplomat and Ambassador in London, Ray Seitz, said 'no, America is not a superpower, it is a super-duper-power.' And it is, economically, militarily, technologically, in terms of its cultural reach (...). But however strong the United States are, it cannot do everything on its own. And it seems to me that one of the lessons of the appalling atrocities of the 11th September is to underline the case for international co-operation.

What is interesting is when you look at the surveys of American public opinion, there appears to be the view which American voters themselves take. There has just been a very interesting survey done by the Chicago Council on Foreign Relations and the German Marshall Fund which demonstrated how similar American and European attitudes are to international threats and which underline the extent to which mainstreet America understands how vital international co-operation is in order for America to play as legitimately and credibly as possible its role as the leader of the international community.

I think the United States has always been at its best, at its most influential, at its strongest, when it has done that. American international policy for over a (decade) after the Second World War, was based on principles associated with the names of two great statesmen, Truman and Marshall. Containment on the one hand and on the other the establishment of a global rule book which everyone, including the United States, was subject to, with international institutions which implemented the rules and provided – as generously as possible – assistance to those who shared the values of democratic capitalism. (... The other day) I read a number of General Marshall's speeches, including the historic address that he made at Harvard in 1947, described by European statesmen at the time as the most generous single act – Marshall Aid – that any country had offered to others. And what was remarkable about what General Marshall said was how relevant his remarks in the 1940s and early 1950s are to our problems today. Nobody, he argued, should confuse a security policy with a war policy. Our enemy, he said, is not this or that country but desperation and chaos and poverty. It is very difficult, he argued, to give people lectures on democracy, if they have got empty stomachs. And above all, he argued the case passionately for international co-operation. I think all those arguments are equally valid today and if American citizens want – as they do – to live in a prosperous and secure world, then I think it is very important that they continue to recognise that international co-operation is essential in order to achieve those aims. (...)

Vocabulary

2 indispensable (adj.): so important that it is impossible to manage without – **3 unarguably** (adv.): /ʌn'ɑːgjuəbli/ definitely – **12 atrocity** (n.): an extremely cruel and violent action, esp. during a war – **18 vital** (adj.): extremely important and necessary for s.th. to succeed – **22 containment** (n.): keeping s.th under control

Explanations

13 11th September: 11 September 2001, when terrorists used planes to attack New York and Washington – **22 Truman:** Harry S. Truman (1884–1972), 33rd President of the US (1945–53), set up the Marshall Plan – **22 Marshall:** George C. Marshall (1880–1959), chief of the US army during World War II, organized the "Marshall Plan".

and Europe

A special relationship that's not just Jack and Condi

Sunday 2 April 2006 / The Observer

The most powerful woman in the world does not drop into Blackburn for want of anything better to do. Her visit is testimony to the special relationship between the US Secretary of State and the UK Foreign Secretary, Jack Straw.

While Presidents and Prime Ministers come and go, the axis between London and Washington remains the most stable and strongest alliance in the world. Maintaining it has rightly been a foreign policy priority for every British government since the Second World War.

That does not mean that our relationship with the rest of Europe comes second. Britain plays a central role in the European Union; geography, trade, and security considerations mean it could not be otherwise. Labour has reversed the confrontational approach to EU diplomacy run by its Tory predecessor – a shift that survives differences within the union over Iraq. Besides, it is false to talk of a dichotomy between a pro-US Britain and an anti-American continent. The new EU members from the former communist bloc – Europe's best hope for an injection of economic dynamism – are better disposed to the Atlantic alliance than France or Germany.

The tectonic plates of world power are shifting. As economic superpower, the US will soon be challenged by China and India. In this new world, Britain's special relationship with the world's most powerful democracy is a prized strategic asset, not just for us but for Europe as a whole.

Vocabulary

4 testimony (n.): a fact or situation that shows or proves very clearly that something exists or is true – **16 dichotomy** (n.): /daɪˈkɒtəmi/ complete contrast – **21 prized** (adj.): extremely important or valuable to s.o. – **21 asset** (n.): s.th. that is useful because it helps you succeed or deal with problems

Explanations

1 Jack and Condi: Jack Straw (born 1946), British foreign secretary since 2001, and Condoleezza Rice (born 1954), US secretary of state during George W. Bush's second term of office (since 2005) – **2 Blackburn:** a town near Manchester, in the north of England, center of Jack Straw's constituency

Tasks and Projects

1. What does it mean if America is a "super-duper power"? – For further study, refer to: http://www.telegraph.co.uk/news/main.jhtml?xml=/news/2003/06/18/turner/turner1606.xml
2. Which of General Marshall's statements does Chris Patten find particularly applicable to "our problems today"?
3. What is special about the "special relationship" between Great Britain and the US?
4. Some people say that the war against Iraq has damaged this relationship. Look at this article to learn more about it: http://www.telegraph.co.uk/news/main.jhtml?xml=/news/2006/11/30/wusuk30.xml

13 The American Dream

Humankind's Second Chance?

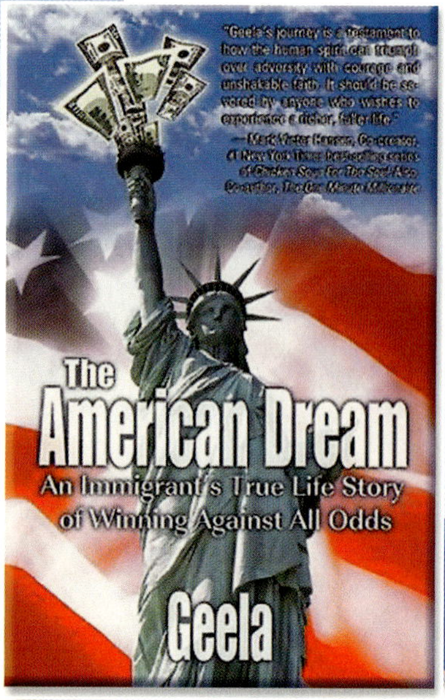

In 1931, the American historian James Truslow Adams first coined the phrase "the American Dream" to describe the complex beliefs, religious promises, and political and social expectations of his nation.

This enduring notion which, in 2001, Dan Rather could praise as "one of the most powerful ideas in the history of human achievement," came into being when the religious, political, and social expectations of European immigrants met with the actual realities of the New World and when the concept of 'America' took on mythic proportions for the millions of immigrants flocking there: a new promised land, a land flowing with milk and honey, an El Dorado where the Fountain of Youth bubbled forth in a pastoral landscape; the site of the New Jerusalem and the City upon the Hill where Christ's Second Coming would establish a new paradise on earth; and a new and ideal nation where the tyrannical restraints of the Old World would be replaced by human equality, liberty and brotherhood for all.

The concept has endured to this day, but no one as yet has succeeded in providing a universally acceptable definition of "the American Dream," which Adams called "the dream of a land in which life should be better and richer and fuller for every man, with opportunity for each according to his ability or achievement." However, the "Dream" can be said to be made up of the following major elements:

- the future-oriented belief in a steady improvement of individual, communal and societal conditions of existence, that is, the belief in progress;
- the conviction that everybody can realize his highest ambitions by means of their own endeavors, that is, the belief in the general attainability of success;

- the certainty that God has singled out America as his chosen country and has appointed the Americans to convert the rest of the world to true American-style democracy, that is, the belief in manifest destiny;
- the assurance that, in the context of civilization's irresistible westward movement, ever new borderlines are to be crossed and ever new obstacles are to be surmounted, that is, the idea of the continual challenge of respective frontiers;[1]
- the belief in the American form of government of the people, by the people and for the people as the sole guarantor of liberty and equality; and
- the idea that immigrants of different nationalities, different ethnic stock and different religious affiliations can be fused into a new nation, that is, the conviction expressed in the notion of the melting pot; or the hope that they can live peacefully together without abandoning their diverse cultures, that is, the belief in cultural pluralism, multi-ethnicity, or multiculturalism.[2]

The "American Dream" is a highly controversial concept – especially at the beginning of this new millennium. For some it is a fascinating object of hopes and beliefs, for others a hollow ideal belied by reality. Thus, Dan Rather could praise the "Dream" as an enduring influence which has "made us a nation of idealists, pointing us toward tomorrow and teaching us to struggle toward social justice" in his 2001 book on *The American Dream: Stories from the Heart of Our Nation*. And thus, Michael Moore could ironically ask: "Remember the American Dream? For those of you too young to have experienced it, this is what it used to be: If you work hard, and your company prospers, you, too, shall prosper. That dream has gone up in smoke. It has been turned into the American Bad Dream" in his 1996 book *Downsize This: Random Threats from an Unarmed America*.

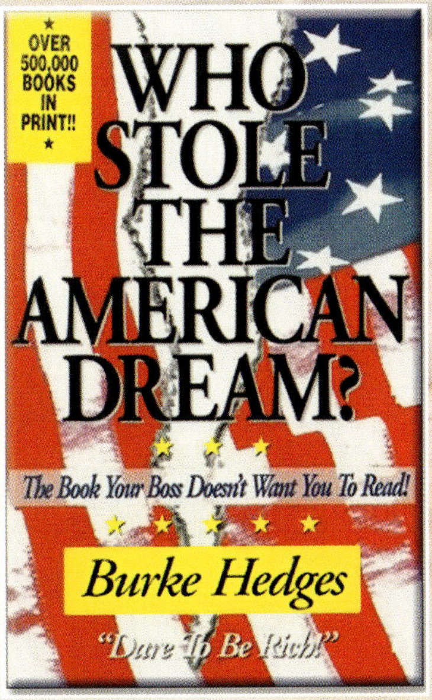

[1] *Dealt with in detail in the VIEWFINDER Topic: Michael Porsche, ed.,* The American Frontier: "Go West, Young Man!" *1997ff.*
[2] *Dealt with in detail in the VIEWFINDER Topic New Edition: Peter Freese, ed.,* From Melting Pot to Multiculturalism: "E pluribus unum"? *2005ff.*

1

James Truslow Adams

"The American Dream"*

In the midst of the Great Depression an American historian published a voluminous study, in which he dealt with what he called "the American dream." He thus coined a term which has since become the widely used and hotly contested catchphrase for the basic lure and promise of America. Since nobody has yet been able to come up with a generally accepted definition of "the American dream," it seems only logical that any consideration of this charged concept should begin with Adams' text. - James Truslow Adams, *The Epic of America* (New York: Blue Ribbon Books, 1931), pp. 404, 405, 411, 412, and 416.

Margaret Bourke-White, "Bread-Line during the Louisville Flood, Kentucky"

If [...] the things already listed were all we had had to contribute, America would have made no distinctive and unique gift to mankind. But there has been also the *American dream*, the dream of a land in which life should be better and richer and fuller for every man, with opportunity for each according to his ability or achievement. It is a difficult dream for the European upper classes to interpret adequately, and too many of us ourselves have grown weary and mistrustful of it. It is not a dream of motor cars and high wages merely, but a dream of a social order in which each man and each woman shall be able to attain to the fullest stature of which they are innately capable, and be recognized by others for what they are, regardless of the fortuitous circumstances of birth or position.

[...]

No, the American dream that has lured tens of millions of all nations to our shores in the past century has not been a dream of merely material plenty, though that has doubtless counted heavily. It has been much more than that. It has been a dream of being able to grow to fullest development as man and woman, unhampered by the barriers which had slowly been erected in older civilizations, unrepressed by social orders which had developed for the benefit of classes rather than for the simple human being of any and every class. And that dream has been realized more fully in actual life here than anywhere else, though very imperfectly even among ourselves.

[...]

The point is that if we are to have a rich and full life in which all are to share and play their parts, if the American dream is to be a reality, our communal spiritual and intellectual life must be distinctly higher than elsewhere, where classes and groups have their separate interests, habits, markets, arts, and lives. If the dream is not to prove possible of fulfillment, we might as well become stark realists, become once more class-conscious, and struggle as individuals or classes against one another. If it is to come true, those on top, financially, intellectually, or otherwise, have got to devote themselves to the "Great Society," and those who are below in the scale have got to strive to rise, not merely economically, but culturally. We cannot become a great democracy by giving ourselves up as individuals to selfishness, physical comfort, and cheap amusement. The very foundation of the American dream of a better and richer life for all is that all, in varying degrees, shall be capable of wanting to share in it. It can never be wrought into a reality by cheap people or by "keeping up with the Joneses." There is nothing whatever in a fortune merely in itself or in a man merely in himself. It all depends on what is made of each.

[...]

If we are to make the dream come true we must all work together, no longer to build bigger, but to build better. [...] In a country as big as America it is as impossible to prophesy as it is to generalize, without being tripped up, but it seems to me that there is room for hope as well as mistrust. The epic loses all its glory without the dream. The statistics of size, population, and wealth would mean nothing to me unless I could still believe in the dream.

[...]

We have a long and arduous road to travel if we are to realize our American dream in the life of our nation, but if we fail, there is nothing left but the old eternal round. The alternative is the failure of self-government, the failure of the common man to rise to full stature, the failure of all that the American dream has held of hope and promise for mankind.

Vocabulary

Intro/1 voluminous (adj.): producing or containing much writing – **Intro/2 to coin a term** (v.): to invent (a word or phrase) – **Intro/3 catchphrase** (n.): a phrase, often with little meaning, which becomes popular for a time so that everyone uses it – **Intro/3 lure** (n.): s.th. that attracts by promising pleasure – **9 weary** (adj.): /'wɪəri/ very tired – **9 mistrustful** (adj.): having or showing lack of trust – **12 to attain** (v.): to succeed in arriving at, esp. after an effort – **12 stature** (n.): /'stætʃə(r)/ the quality or position gained by development or proved worth – **13 innate** (adj.): (of qualities) which s.o. was born with – **14 fortuitous** (adj.): /fɔː(r)'tjuːətəs/ happening by chance, accidental; fortunate, lucky – **22 unhampered** (adj.): without difficulty in movement or activity – **23 to erect** (v.): to build or establish (a solid thing which was not there before) – **38 stark** (adj.): hard, bare, or severe in appearance; pure, complete – **41 to devote** (v.): to set apart for; to give wholly or completely to – **43 scale** (n.): a set of numbers or standards for measuring or comparing – **43 to strive** (v.): to struggle hard; to make a great effort, esp. to gain s.th. – **49 wrought**: old past tense and past part. of to work – **50 to keep up with the Joneses**: (derog.) to compete with one's neighbors socially, esp. by buying the same expensive new things that they buy – **59 to trip up** (v.): to (cause to) make a mistake as in a statement or behavior – **65 arduous** (adj.): needing much effort – **67 the old eternal round**: the accustomed procedure that repeats itself for ever

James Truslow Adams (1878–1949) was educated at Brooklyn Polytechnic Institute and Yale and spent thirteen years in business in New York before he devoted himself full-time to historical research. In 1921 he won a Pulitzer Prize for *The Founding of New England,* the first volume of a trilogy which reinterprets the ideals and achievements of the Puritans and their descendants and which was followed by *Revolutionary New England* (1923) and *New England in the Republic* (1926). Adams' other books include *Provincial Society, 1690–1763* (1927), *The March of Democracy* (1932/33), *The American: The Making of a New Man* (1943), *Frontiers of American Culture* (1944), and *Big Business in a Democracy* (1945).

Explanations

Intro/1 Great Depression: The stock-market crash of 1929 set off an economic crisis, which was unprecedented with regard to its length and the poverty and tragedy it inflicted upon American society. At its depth in 1933, about one third of the labor force was without employment. Although the economic, agricultural and relief policies of President Franklin Delano Roosevelt's New Deal administration did a great deal to mitigate the effects of the depression, it was not until the government began to spend heavily for defense in the early 1940s that complete business recovery and the end of unemployment were reached.

Awareness

1 Think about, and verbalize, the contradictions expressed by the illustration on p. 216.

Comprehension

2 What does Adams warn against when he stresses that the 'Dream' is "not a dream of motor cars and high wages merely" (l. 10)?

3 What, according to Adams, must be done and what must be avoided in order to make the 'Dream' a "reality" (l. 33)? Make two lists.

4 What are the major elements of the 'American Dream' as described by Adams?

ANALYSIS

5 Analyze the implications of Adams' vision of a "better and richer and fuller [life] for every man, with opportunity for each according to his ability or achievement" (ll. 5ff.).

6 Collect and systematize the arguments which Adams offers in order to show that the 'Dream' is more than just the promise of material success.

OPINION

7 Is America today closer to the attainment of the 'Dream' than it was in 1931, or has the 'Dream' been lost or even turned into a 'Nightmare'? Give reasons for your answer.

INTERNET PROJECT

8 Collect information about the famous photograph by Margaret Bourke-White and the situation it shows. Use www.photo-seminars.com/Fame/MargaretWhite.htm to start with.

2 The 'American Dream' in Political Rhetoric

Since James Truslow Adams, the notion of the 'American Dream' has come to stand for a complex combination of enduring beliefs and convictions, which cannot be precisely defined. But despite its changes with time the Dream has endured, and if one looks at selected instances of political rhetoric, it becomes obvious how easily its fundamental values and promises can be made to fit the respective requirements of a given historical situation.

Jimmy Carter *in his Inaugural Address on 20 January 1977:*

Two centuries ago our nation's birth was a mile-stone in the long quest for freedom, but the bold and brilliant dream which excited the founders of this nation still awaits its consummation. I have no new dream to set forth today, but rather urge a fresh faith in the old dream. […] The American dream endures. We must once again have full faith in our country – and in one another. I believe America can be better. We can be even stronger than before. […]

These are not just my goals. And they will not be my accomplishments, but the affirmation of our nation's continuing moral strength and our belief in an undiminished, ever-expanding American dream.

Ronald Reagan *in his First Inaugural Address on 20 January 1981:*

If we look to the answer as to why for so many years we achieved so much, prospered as no other people on Earth, it was because here in this land we unleashed the energy and individual genius of man to a greater extent than has ever been done before. […]

It is no coincidence that our present troubles parallel and are proportionate to the intervention and intrusion in our lives that result from unnecessary and excessive growth of government. It is time for us to realize that we're too great a nation to limit ourselves to small dreams. We're not, as some would have us believe, doomed to an inevitable decline. I do not believe in a fate that will fall on us no matter what we do. I do believe in a fate that will fall on us if we do nothing. So, with all the creative energy at our command, let us begin an era of national renewal. Let us renew our determination, our courage, and our strength. And let us renew our faith and our hope.

We have every right to dream heroic dreams.

Your dreams, your hopes, your goals are going to be the dreams, the hopes, and the goals of this administration, so help me God.

***Michael S. Dukakis** in his nomination acceptance speech at the Democratic National Convention in Atlanta on 21 July 1988:*

We're going to win because we are the party that believes in the American dream.

A dream so powerful that no distance of ground, no expanse of ocean, no barrier of language, no distinction of race or creed or color can weaken its hold on the human heart.

And I know, because my friends, I'm a product of that dream and I'm proud of it. A dream that brought my father to this country 76 years ago, that brought my mother and her family here one year later – poor, unable to speak English but with a burning desire to succeed in their new land of opportunity.

And tonight in the presence of that marvelous woman who is my mother and who came here 75 years ago; with the memory in my heart of the young man who arrived at Ellis Island with only $25 in his pocket, but with a deep and abiding faith in the promise of America – [...]

My friends, the dream that carried me to this platform is alive tonight in every part of the country – and it's what the Democratic Party is all about.

[...] to every American, you are a full shareholder in our dream.

And my friends, if anyone tells you that the American dream belongs to the privileged few and not to all of us, you tell them that the Reagan era is over and that a new era is about to begin. [...]

It's time to meet the challenge of the next American frontier – the challenge of building an economic future for our country that will create good jobs at good wages for every citizen in this land [...]

[...] we believe that there are no limits to what America can do. [...]

But my friends, maintaining the status quo – running in place – standing still – isn't good enough for America. Opportunity for some isn't good enough for America. Because working together, we're going to forge a new era of greatness for America. [...]

My friends, the dream that began in Philadelphia 200 years ago; the spirit that survived that terrible winter at Valley Forge and triumphed on the beaches at Normandy; the courage that looked Khrushchev in the eye during the Cuban missile crisis – is as strong and as vibrant today as it has ever been. [...]

A new era of greatness for America.

And when we leave here tonight, we will leave to build that future together.

To build the future so that when our children and our grand-children look back in their time on what we did in our time; they will say that we had the wisdom to carry on the dreams of those who came before us; the courage to make our own dreams come true; and the foresight to blaze a trail for generations yet to come.

***William Jefferson (Bill) Clinton** in his Second Inaugural Address on 20 January 1997:*

The promise of America was born in the 18th century out of the bold conviction that we are all created equal. It was extended and preserved in the 19th century, when our nation spread across the continent, saved the union, and abolished the awful scourge of slavery.

Then, in turmoil and triumph, that promise exploded onto the world stage to make this the American Century.

We,- the American people, we are the solution. Our founders understood that well and gave us a democracy strong enough to endure for centuries, flexible enough to face our common challenges and advance our common dreams in each new day.

Thirty-four years ago, the man whose life we celebrate today spoke to us down there, at the other end of this Mall, in words that moved the conscience of a nation. Like a prophet of old, he told of his dream that one day America would rise up and treat all its citizens as equals

The Immigrant's Dream

before the law and in the heart. Martin Luther King's dream was the American Dream. His quest is our quest: the ceaseless striving to live out our true creed. Our history has been built on such dreams and labors. And by our dreams and labors we will redeem the promise of America in the 21st century.

Yes, let us build our bridge. A bridge wide enough and strong enough for every American to cross over to a blessed land of new promise.

May those generations whose faces we cannot yet see, whose names we may never know, say of us here that we led our beloved land into a new century with the American Dream alive for all her children; with the American promise of a more perfect union a reality for all her people; with America's bright flame of freedom spreading throughout all the world.

***George W. Bush** on Homeownership for All on 18 June 2002:*

We also have got to understand, in this land of plenty, there are pockets of hopelessness and despair. You know, I mentioned the word American Dream in Atlanta. I also recognize that some people aren't sure that dream extends to them. Some people don't even know what the dream means. And our job – our jobs, our collective jobs, is to make sure that notion of the American Dream extends into every single neighborhood around this country.

I know this isn't the right department when I talk about education, but education, making sure every child is educated and no child is left behind, is part of making sure the American Dream extends to every single neighborhood in America. And we're making progress in a practical way when it comes to educating children, because, you know what, for the first time the federal government says, if you receive money, you need to let us know whether the children are learning to read and write and add and subtract. And if they are, we'll praise the teachers and praise the parents and praise the administrators.

But if not, if our children can't read and write and add and subtract, instead of just hoping something changes, we're going to use the accountability system to insist upon change, so every child has a chance to realize the dream in America.

And so what are the barriers that we can deal with here in Washington? Well, probably the single barrier to first-time homeownership is high down payments. People take a look at the down payment, they say that's too high, I'm not buying. They may have the desire to buy, but they don't have the wherewithal to handle the down payment. We can deal with that. And so I've asked Congress to fully fund an American Dream down payment fund which will help a low-income family to qualify to buy, to buy.

We believe when this fund is fully funded and properly administered, which it will be under the Bush administration, that over 40,000 families a year – 40,000 families a year – will be able to realize the dream we want them to be able to realize, and that's owning their own home.

But I also want people to see the deep compassion of America, as well. I want the world to see the other side of our character, which is the soft side, the decent side, the loving side. I want people to know that when we talk about dreams, we mean big dreams. And when we talk about a free society, we want a society in which every citizen has the chance to advance, not just a few.

Vocabulary

Intro/5 requirement (n.): s.th. needed or demanded – **7 quest** (n.): a search, an attempt to find – **8 bold** (adj.): (of a person or behavior) brave, confident, not afraid to take risks – **12 consummation** (n.): the point at which s.th. is made complete or perfect – **20 accomplishment** (n.): s.th. completely and successfully done – **20 affirmation** (n.): declaration (usu. as made again or in answer to a question) – **22 to diminish** (v.): to (cause to) become or seem smaller – **28 to prosper** (v.): to become successful and rich – **31 to unleash** (v.): to set free from control (feelings, forces, etc.) – **35 coincidence** (n.): a combination of events, happening by chance, but in such a way that it seems planned or arranged – **36 proportionate** (adj.): in proportion, that is, in the correct relationship between the size, position, and shape of the different parts of a whole – **36 intervention** (n.): the act of intervening, that is, of interrupting, esp. in order to prevent s.th. from happening – **36 intrusion** (n.): the act of intruding, that is, of entering unwanted or unasked or of bringing in, esp. without good reason or permission – **40 to doom** (v.): to cause to experience or suffer s.th. unavoidable and unpleasant, such as death or destruction – **49 administration** (n.): (esp. AmE) the (period of) government, esp. of a particular president or ruling party – **62 creed** (n.): a system of beliefs or principles – **74 abiding** (adj.): without end; lasting – **78 shareholder** (n.): (AmE) an owner of one or more shares in a business; here used figuratively – **93 to forge** (v.): to form by heating and hammering; to form or bring into being, esp. by an effort – **100 vibrant** (adj.): alive; forceful; powerful and exciting – **109 foresight** (n.): the ability to imagine what will probably happen, allowing one to act to help or prevent developments – **109 to blaze a trail** (v.): to make marks along a path for others to follow; to be the first in some direction or activity – **120 scourge** (n.): s.th. that causes a lot of harm or suffering

(+ of) - **121 turmoil** (n.): a state of confusion, excitement, or
205 anxiety - **134 quest** (n.): see l. 7 - **137 to redeem** (v.): to do what you promised to do

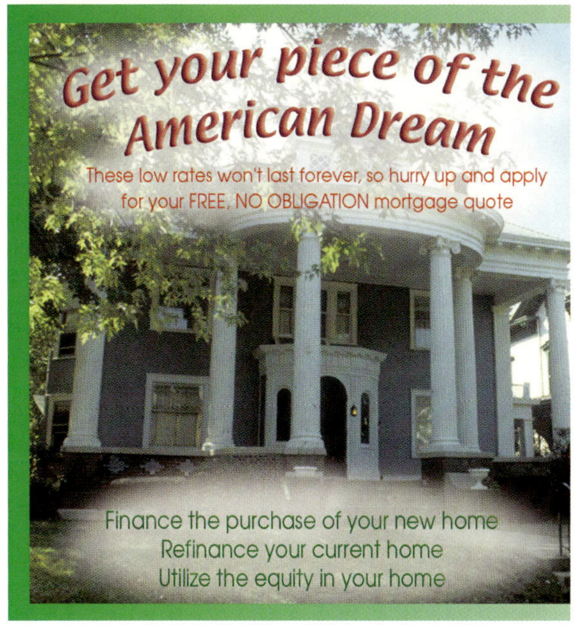

Explanations

1 inaugural address (n.): the formal speech given by the newly elected president at the special ceremony during which he is introduced into office - **73 Ellis Island**: an island in Upper New York Bay southwest of Manhattan, which was long the site of an arsenal and a fort, but became famous when it replaced Castle Garden as the chief immigration station of the country in 1892. Today the island, which sometimes received as many as 15,000 immigrants in one day, is a museum. - **97 Valley Forge**: a site on the Schuylkill River, about twenty miles northwest of Philadelphia. General Washington's army wintered there in 1777/78, following the defeats at Brandywine and Germantown. The severe suffering and persistent patriotism of most of the soldiers have made the locality a national shrine. - **97 the beaches at Normandy**: Operation Overlord, the Allied invasion of the European continent during World War II began on 6 June 1944 (D day) on "the beaches at Normandy." - **98 Nikita Sergeyevich Khrushchev**: (1894-1971) a communist leader who emerged from the power struggle after the death of Stalin as the first secretary of the Communist Party (1953-64) and the premier of the U.S.S.R. (1958-64) - **99 Cuban missile crisis**: a major cold war confrontation between the U.S. and the Soviet Union. After the Bay of Pigs Invasion, the USSR increased its support of Castro's Cuban regime, and in the summer of 1962, Khrushchev secretly decided to install ballistic missiles in Cuba. When the U.S. discovered the missile launching sites, President Kennedy publicly denounced the Soviet actions on 22 October 1962, imposed a naval blockade on Cuba, and declared that any missile launched from Cuba would warrant a full-scale retaliatory attack. For a few days the threat of thermonuclear war cast its shadow, but on 24 October, Russian ships carrying missiles to Cuba turned back, and when Khrushchev agreed on 28 October to withdraw the missiles and dismantle the sites, the crisis ended as suddenly as it had begun. - **130 Mall**: a kind of park in Washington, D.C., surrounded by the Washington Monument and several famous museums, esp. the Smithsonian Institution.

Awareness

1 Consider the circumstances under which convention speeches, nomination acceptance speeches and inaugural addresses are given and discuss the degree to which such speeches are believable.

Comprehension

2 Name the major elements of 'The Immigrant's Dream' as conjured up by Dukakis, and relate them to the poster with that title.
3 What is the "American Dream down payment fund" (ll. 188f.) mentioned by Bush Jr.?
4 Collect the decisive words and phrases which express each politician's idea of the 'American Dream.'

Analysis

5 Establish the meaning which each politician ascribes to the 'Dream'; collect and analyze the rhetorical means (Reference Library, p. 311) which each politician employs to make his promises convincing.
6 In what way do the speakers employ references to persons and events of earlier American history in order to strengthen and enhance their claims and promises?
7 What does Clinton mean when he speaks of "the American Century" (l. 122).

Opinion

8 Consider the relation between the material and the spiritual implications of the 'Dream' in the light of the cartoon on p. 221.
9 Comment on Reagan's claim that "we're too great a nation to limit ourselves to small dreams" (l. 39).
10 Discuss (Reference Library, p. 299) in how far Dukakis' promise to make every American "a full shareholder in our dream" (ll. 78f.) is a contradiction in terms.
11 Do you think that owning a house is a crucial part of the 'American Dream'? Explain your opinion (Reference Library, p. 306).
12 Try to identify the common denominator which links all speeches. Could that be a valid definition of the 'American Dream'?

Projects

13 Relate the various meanings of the 'Dream' to the historical situation in which each speech is delivered. Use relevant biographical and historical background material.
14 Connect what the politicians say about the 'Dream' to its ingredients as given in the Introduction.

Internet Project

15 Use the speeches archive www.americanrhetoric.com to find other speeches that deal with the topic of the 'American Dream' and compare them with the ones shown in this chapter.

The complete text of Dukakis' speech can be found under http://www.4president.org/speeches/mikedukakis1988acceptance.htm; the complete text of George W. Bush's speech can be found under http://www.georgebush.com/Agenda/Chapter.aspx?ID=4; the complete texts of all the other speeches are available under http://www.americanrhetoric.com.

3 The 'American Dream' as Seen by American Citizens

In 1980, Studs Terkel published a bestselling collection of interviews with about one hundred Americans from all realms of life. He found that "the old dream is still dreamt" and that "we've always managed, despite our worst, unbelievably nativist actions to rejuvenate ourselves, to bring in new people. Every new group comes in believing more firmly in the American Dream than the one that came a few years before." In 1988, Terkel continued his investigation of the 'Dream' in yet another collection of interviews, and this time he encountered a widespread loss of belief and a "deepening chasm between the haves – and have-somewhats – and the have-nots." Here are some of the definitions of the 'Dream' which he was offered by the people he interviewed. – Studs Terkel, *American Dreams Lost and Found* (New York: Ballantine Books, 1981), pp. 42; 96; 73; 137; 56; 316f.; 63; 178; and *The Great Divide: Second Thoughts on the American Dream* (New York: Avon Books, 1989), p. 70.

The middle-aged president of a corporation

The American Dream is to be better off than you are. How much money is 'enough money'? 'Enough money' is always a little bit more than you have.

An African American newspaper columnist from Chicago

My dreams have not expired entirely. There are moments when I waver between despair and hopelessness and flashes of inspiration. Years ago, when we were in trouble, we thought we could one day go north. Well, we are north now. We are at that Promised Land. The Promised Land has less hope now than it had when we were not in the Promised Land. We used to say: "We're being abused now, but one day we'll have the ballot. One of these days we're not gonna have presidents and governors who abuse us. One of these days the Ku Klux Klan is not gonna be around lynching us." All that has happened. But we didn't realize that there were some basic corrections that haven't yet been made.

A historian from New England

The American Dream always has a greater force when you don't already have it. People who grew up without it are told if you can only work long enough and hard enough, you can get that pot of gold at the end of the rainbow. When you already have the pot of gold, the dream loses its force. You can't aspire after anything material if, in fact, you're trying to get rid of the material things, [...] You need some alternative way of giving meaning to your life.

A twenty-five-year-old Hollywood actor

I guess I'm still looking for the American Dream. To me, it's people having control over their lives.

The Native American author Vine Deloria

You have to ask yourself: What kind of people were these that came here? They must have been absolutely frantic to set down roots. It was more than subduing the land. I mean, that's a hell of a toll to pay for the right to live on a piece of land.

Maybe the American Dream is in the past, understanding who you are instead of looking to the future: What are you going to be? 'Cause we've kind of reached the future. I'm not just talking about nostalgia. I'm talking about finding familiar guideposts.

A radio commentator from California

I worry about our young people. Do they have the dreams, the guts, the sinews, the red-blooded ability, to preserve our way of life? The thing our grandparents came over here to find. They found a nation founded, if you'll pardon the expression, under God and a Divine Constitution. Every youngster should have the dream of becoming president of the United States. Of course, I believe in Horatio Alger, and I love it.

A Businesswoman from Lancashire

I think the American dream for most people today is just survival. When people came here from the old country, it was for a better life, not just survival. I see that people that come over today seem to prosper faster than the ones who were born here. Maybe it's because they know what it is to do without. They scrimp and save and live meagerly, where the American person, no matter what color, is spoiled. They're more docile, where the new people seem to stick together and help one another. But the average American is just out to help himself, to survive.

A Japanese-American from Seattle

The American Dream? I think: for whites only.

Vocabulary

Intro/2 realm (n.): a world; an area – **Intro/3 nativist** (adj.): believing in nativism, that is, a policy defined by hate or fear of foreigners that favors native inhabitants as opposed to immigrants – **Intro/3 to rejuvenate** (v.): to make or become young again – **4 columnist** (n.): a person who writes a regular article for a newspaper or magazine – **5 to waver** (v.): to be uncertain or unsteady in movement or decision – **8 to abuse** (v.): to put to wrong use, use badly; to handle without care; treat badly – **8 ballot** (n.): the right to vote – **9 gonna**: coll. for 'going to' – **15 to aspire** (v.): to direct one's hopes and efforts to some great or important aim – **21 frantic** (adj.): in an uncontrolled state of feeling; wildly anxious, afraid, happy – **21 to subdue** (v.): to conquer or control the actions of – **21 toll** (n.): /təʊl/ here the cost in health, life, etc., from illness, an accident, etc. – **27 guts** (n. pl.): (infml.) bravery, determination; value, force – **27 sinews** (n. pl.): /'sɪnjuːz/ means of strength and support – **27 red-blooded** (adj.): (of a person's behavior, etc.) bold, strong – **34 to scrimp** (v.) to try to save as much money as you can even though you have very little – **35 meager** (adj.): (BrE **re**) having much less than you need – **35 docile** (adj.): quiet and easily controlled

Explanations

7 Promised Land: (in the Bible) the land of Canaan promised by God to Abraham and his people; hence metaphorically a place or condition not yet experienced, which one hopes or believes will bring happiness or success (for many blacks from the slave-holding South the North seemed to be the 'promised land') – **9 Ku Klux Klan**: the name of two secret terrorist societies. The original Klan, organized in 1865 as an instrument against reconstructionism, was composed of local committees and intended to keep the newly freed blacks in a subservient condition. It used various methods of instilling fear, such as masks, flowing white robes, horseback parades and raids by night, whippings, and tarring and feathering. The first general organization of local Klans took place in 1867, with the election of N. B. Forrest, an ex-Confederate general, as Grand Wizard, and it remained powerful in Southern politics and local affairs into the 1870s. The more recent Ku Klux Klan movement has been nation-wide, originating in Georgia in 1915, but spreading to many Northern regions. Based on a program of white supremacy, nativism, fundamentalism, anti-Semitism, and anti-Catholicism, it has had considerable political influence. – **19 Vine Deloria**: a Sioux who was born in 1933 and came to public attention with the publication of his book *Custer Died for Your Sins: An Indian Manifesto* (1969). He writes about the situation of Native Americans in the U.S. with ironic wit and destroys the stereotypes and myths which white society has built up about the 'red man.' – **30 Horatio Alger**: /'ældʒə(r)/ (1834–99), an erstwhile Unitarian minister and the enormously successful author of nearly 130 popular books for boys, all based on the principle that a struggle against poverty and temptation inevitably leads a boy to wealth and fame. His most noted hero was the central figure in the Ragged Dick series, and it is estimated that more than twenty million copies of his novels were published. Consequently, his name became a byword for the American myth of success

Comprehension

1 What does the black newspaper columnist from Chicago imply when he says "Well, we are north now" (ll. 6f.)?

2 What does Vine Deloria mean by speculating that "maybe the American Dream is in the past" (l. 23)?

Analysis

3 For which reasons do certain groups of Americans think they are excluded from the 'Dream'?

Opinion

4 What do you think of the New England historian's observation that the 'Dream' is only attractive as long as it remains unfulfilled?

4

John Gast

American Progress

In 1872, John Gast completed his famous painting *American Progress* to the specifications of the New York firm of George A. Crofutt. Crofutt, who would later use Gast's painting as a frontispiece for his travel guidebooks, had the painting reproduced as a 12 x 16 chromolithograph, which sold for $10 and bore a detailed explanation of the painting's symbolism on the reverse side.

American Progress! Subject, The United States of America

This rich and wonderful country - the progress of which at the present time, is the wonder of the old world - was, until recently, inhabited exclusively by the lurking savage and wild beasts of prey. If the rapid progress of the "Great West" has surprised our people, what will those of other countries think of the "Far West," which is destined, at an early day, to be the vast granary, as it is now the great treasure chamber of our country? How this change has been wrought, and by whom is illustrated by our Chromo, "American Progress."

Purely National in design, this beautiful painting represents the United States' portion of the American continent in its beauty and variety, from the Atlantic to the Pacific Ocean, illustrating at a glance the grand drama of Progress in the civilization, settlement and history of our own happy land.

In the foreground the central and principal figure, a beautiful and charming Female, is floating Westward through the air bearing on her forehead the "Star of Empire." She has left the cities of the East far behind, crossed the Alleghanies and the "Father of Waters," and still her march is Westward. In her right hand she carries a book - Common schools - the emblem of Education and the testimonial of our National enlightenment, while with the left hand she unfolds and stretches the slender wires of the Telegraph, that are to flash intelligence throughout the land. On the right of the picture is a city, steamships, manufactories, schools and churches, over which beams of light are streaming and filling the air - indicative of civilization. The general tone of the picture on the left declares darkness, waste and confusion. From the city proceed the three great continental lines of railway, passing the frontier settler's rude cabin, and extending toward the Western Ocean. Next to these are the transportation wagons, overland stage, hunters, gold seekers, pony express, the pioneer emigrant and the war dance of the "noble red man." Fleeing from "Progress," and towards the blue waters of the Pacific, which shows itself on the left of the picture beyond the snow-capped summits of the Sierra Nevadas, are the Indians, buffaloes, wild horses, bears and other game, moving Westward, ever Westward the Indians with their squaws, papooses, and "pony lodges," turn their despairing faces towards, as they flee from the presence of, the wonderous vision. The "Star" is too much for them.

What American man, woman or child does not feel a heartthrob of exultation as they think of the glorious achievements of Progress since the landing of the Pilgrim Fathers, on staunch old Plymouth Rock! What home, from the miner's humble cabin to the stately marble mansion of the capitalist, should be without this Great National Picture, which illustrates in the most artistic manner all the gigantic results of American Brains and Hands! Who would not have such a beautiful token to remind them of our country's grandeur and enterprise which have caused the mighty wilderness to blossom like the rose!!! One of the best art critics has pronounced this picture "one of the grandest conceptions of the age."

Vocabulary

3 to lurk (v.): to wait somewhere quietly and secretly, usu. because you are going to do s.th. wrong – **3 beast of prey** (n.): a bird or animal which lives by killing and eating other animals – **3 rapid** (adj.): fast, quick – **5 granary** (n.): a place where grain, esp. wheat, is stored – **13 testimonial** (n.): s.th. that is given or done to s.o. to thank or praise them, or show admiration for them – **14 slender** (adj.): thin in an attractive or graceful way – **16 indicative** (adj.): to be a clear sign that a particular situation exists or that s.th. is likely to be true – **22 game** (n.): wild animals, birds, and fish that are hunted for food, esp. as a sport – **23 papoose** (n.) a young child of Native American parents; a sort of bag fixed to a frame, used for carrying a baby on a person's back – **25 heartthrob** (n.) a specific type of heartbeat that occurs when feeling strong emotions – **29 token** (n.): s.th. that represents a feeling, fact, event, etc.

Explanations

6 Chromo: short for chromolithograph, an image printed in colors by lithography and produced by hand separation of the colors – **12 Alleghanies**: a range of mountains which go from Virginia to Pennsylvania in the eastern U.S., and are part of the Appalachians – **12 Father of Waters**: a poetic term for the Mississippi River – **13 Common Schools**: The Common School movement, ensuring that every child could receive a basic education funded by local taxes, was spearheaded by Horace Mann (1796–1859), the 'Father of the Common School', who, as the Secretary of the newly created Massachusetts Board of Education, worked for his belief that political stability and social harmony depended on education. – **21 Sierra Nevada**: a mountain range in California – **23 Pony Lodge**: a small hut in which horses are kept

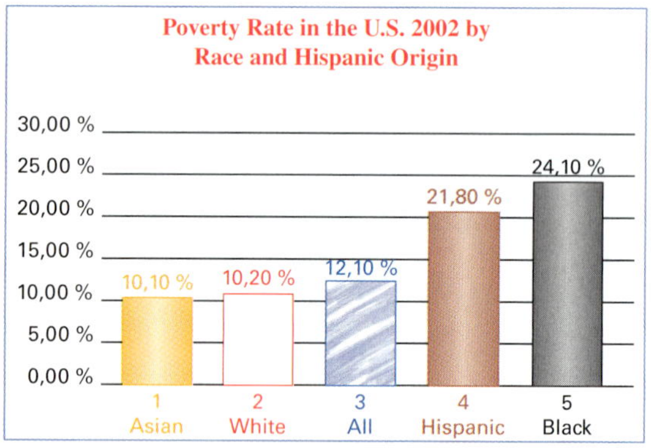

5

"Arnold Schwarzenegger: From Body Builder to Governor"*

Born in Graz, Austria, in 1947, Arnold Schwarzenegger emigrated to the U.S. in 1968 where he became the world's most successful body builder. In 1983 he attained U.S. citizenship. In the 80s he starred in action movies like *The Terminator* and by the 90s he was listed as one of the most successful Hollywood stars. Being a moderate Republican, Schwarzenegger was chosen by George Bush, Sr. as chairman of the President's Council on Physical Fitness and Sports. He is married to John F. Kennedy's niece Maria Shriver and lives in California where he was elected Governor in 2003 and re-elected in 2006. – In 1980 Studs Terkel published a collection of interviews which includes the following statement by Arnold Schwarzenegger. – Studs Terkel, *American Dreams Lost and Found* (New York: Pantheon, 1980), pp. 129ff.

Call me Arnold.

I was born in a little Austrian town, outside Graz. It was a 300-year-old house.

When I was ten years old, I had the dream of being the best in the world in something. When I was fifteen, I had a dream that I wanted to be the best body builder in the world and the most muscular man. It was not only a dream I dreamed at night. It was also a daydream. It was so much in my mind that I felt it had to become a reality. It took me five years of hard work. Five years later, I turned this dream into reality and became Mr. Universe, the best-built man in the world.

"Winning" is a very important word. There is one that achieves what he wanted to achieve and there are hundreds of thousands that failed. It singles you out: the winner.

I came out second three times, but that is not what I call losing. The bottom line for me was: Arnold has to be the winner. I have to win more often the Mr. Universe title than anybody else. I won it five times consecutively. I hold the record as Mr. Olympia, the top professional body-building championship. I won it six times. That's why I retired. There was nobody even close to me. Everybody gave up competing against me. That's what I call a winner.

When I was a small boy, my dream was not to be big physically, but big in a way that everybody listens to me when I talk, that I'm a very important person, that people recognize me and see me as something special. I had a big need for being singled out.

Also my dream was to end up in America. When I was ten years old, I dreamed of being an American. At the time I didn't know much about America, just that it was a wonderful country. I felt it was where I belonged. I didn't like being in a little country like Austria. I did everything possible to get out. I did so in 1968, when I was twenty-one years old.

If I would believe in life after death, I would say my before-life I was living in America. That's why I feel so good here. It is the country where you can turn your dream into reality. Other countries don't have those things. When I came over here to America, I felt I was in heaven. In America, we don't have an obstacle. Nobody's holding you back.

Number One in America pretty much takes care of the rest of the world. You kind of run through the rest of the world like nothing. I'm trying to make people in America aware that they should appreciate what they have here. You have the best tax advantages here and the best prices here and the best products here.

One of the things I always had was a business mind. When I was in high school, a majority of my classes were business classes. Economics and accounting and mathematics. When I came over here to this country, I really didn't speak English almost at all. I learned English and then started taking business courses, because that's what America is best known for: business. Turning one dollar into a million dollars in a short period of time. Also when you make money, how do you keep it?

That's one of the most important things when you have money in your hand, how can you keep it? Real estate is one of the best ways of doing that. I own apartment buildings, office buildings, and raw land. That's my love, real estate.

I have emotions. But what you do, you keep them cold or you store them away for a time. You must control your emotions, you must have command over yourself. Three, four months before a competition, I could not be interfered by other people's problems. This is sometimes called selfish. It's the only way you can be if you want to achieve something. Any emotional things inside me, I try to keep cold so it doesn't interfere with my training.

Many times things really touched me. I felt them and I felt sensitive about them. But I had to talk myself out of it. I had to suppress those feelings in order to go on. Sport is one of those activities where you really have to concentrate. You must pay attention a hundred percent to the particular thing you're doing. There must be nothing else on your mind. Emotions must not interfere. Otherwise, you're thinking about your girlfriend. You're in love, your positive energies get channelled into another direction rather than going into your weight room or making money.

You have to choose at a very early date what you want: a normal life or to achieve things you want to achieve. I never wanted to win a popularity contest in doing things the way people want me to do it. I went the road I thought was best for me. A few people thought I was cold, selfish. Later they found out that's not the case. After I achieve my goal, I can be Mr. Nice Guy. You know what I mean?

California is to me a dreamland. It is the absolute combination of everything I was always looking for. It has all the money in the world there, show business there, wonderful weather there, beautiful country, ocean is there. Snow skiing in the winter, you can go in the desert the same day. You have beautiful-looking people there. They all have a tan.

I believe very strongly in the philosophy of staying hungry. If you have a dream and it becomes a reality, don't stay satisfied with it too long. Make up a new dream and hunt after that one and turn it into reality. When you have that dream achieved, make up a new dream.

I am a strong believer in Western philosophy, the philosophy of success, of progress, of getting rich. The Eastern philosophy is passive, which I believe in maybe three percent of the times, and the ninety-seven percent is Western, conquering and going on. It's a beautiful philosophy, and America should keep it up.

Arnold Schwarzenegger's Acceptance Speech

[...]

I want to [...] thank the people of California. From the time I came over to this country, you've opened up your arms to me. You've received me. You've given me opportunities, endless amount of opportunities. Everything that I have is because of California. I came over – that's right. I came here with absolutely nothing. And California has given me absolutely everything. And today, and today, California has given me the greatest gift of all. You've given me your trust by voting for me.

Thank you very much to all the people of California for giving me their great trust [...]

Gov. Arnold Schwarzenegger's Inaugural Address

To the thousands of you who came here today, I took this oath to serve you. To others all across this state – Democrats, Republicans, Independents – it makes no difference. I took this oath to serve you. To those who have no power, to those who have dropped out – too weary or disappointed with politics as usual – I took the oath to serve you. I say to everyone here today and to all Californians, I will not forget my oath and I will not forget you. [...]

But for guidance, let's look back in history to a period I studied when I became a citizen. The summer of 1787. Delegates of the original 13 states were meeting in Philadelphia.

The dream of a new nation was falling apart. Events were spiraling downward. Divisions were deep. Merchant against farmer. Big states against small. North against South.

Our founding fathers knew that the fate of the union was in their hands, just as the fate of California is in our hands.

What happened in that summer of 1787 is that they put their differences aside – and produced the blueprint for our government; our Constitution. Their coming together has been called "the Miracle of Philadelphia." Now, the members of the Legislation and I must bring about the "Miracle of Sacramento" – a miracle based on cooperation, good will, new ideas – and devotion to the long-term good of California.

What we face may look insurmountable. But I learned something from all those years of training and competing.

What I learned is that we are always stronger than we know. And California is like that, too.

We are stronger than we know. [...]

Ladies and gentlemen, I have an immigrant's optimism that what I have learned in citizen class is true: The system does work.

And I believe that with all of my heart.

I have big hopes for California. President Reagan spoke of America as "the shining city on the hill." I see California as the golden dream by the sea.

Perhaps some think this is fanciful or poetic, but to an immigrant like me, who, as a boy, saw Soviet tanks rolling through the streets of Austria, to someone like me who came here with absolutely nothing and gained absolutely everything, it is not fanciful to see this state as a golden dream.

For millions of people around the world, California has always glimmered with hope and glowed with opportunity. Millions of people around the world send their dreams to California with the hope their lives will follow.

My fellow citizens.

I have taken the oath to uphold the Constitution of California. Now, with your help and God's, I will also uphold the dream that is California.

Vocabulary

18 bottom line (n.): used to tell s.o. what is the most important part of a situation or the most important thing to consider – **43 obstacle** (n.): s.th. that makes it difficult to achieve s.th. – **53 accounting** (n.): the profession or work of keeping or checking financial accounts, calculating taxes, etc. – **61 real estate** (n.): the business of selling houses or land – **69 to interfere** (v.): to deliberately get involved in a situation where you are not wanted or needed – **81 to channel** (v.): to control s.th. such as money or energy towards a particular purpose.

Explanations

11 Mr. Universe: a body building title – **21 Mr. Olympia**: another body building title – **63 raw land**: a piece of land without any buildings on it – **91 Mr. Nice Guy** – s.o. who behaves honestly and fairly

Awareness

1 What is the "Western Philosophy" (l. 110) Schwarzenegger talks about in the first text?

Comprehension

2 Explain the term 'California as "the golden dream by the sea"' (l. 171).

3 Find and name the differences in the two texts regarding Schwarzenegger's image of the 'American Dream.'

Opinion

4 Collect your images (Reference Library, p. 311) of California. Do you think that California stands out in terms of its possibilities to fulfill the 'American Dream'?

5 Do you see Schwarzenegger's career as an example of an American Dream realized?

Internet Projects

6 Use the Internet Movie Database www.imdb.com or Schwarzenegger's official site http://www.schwarzenegger.com/en/index.asp to gather information about the movies Schwarzenegger starred in. Examine the content of these films and Schwarzenegger's roles, compare them to his 'real-life' career, and discuss (Reference Library, p. 299) a possible connection.

7 Research and discuss Schwarzenegger's 'discovery' of environmentalist concerns, which led to his 2006 re-election.

14 Politics in the U.S.A.

In 1982, Klaus Harpprecht published a book on the United States of America based on his experience as a film-producer and journalist in this country. Its title was: *Der fremde Freund*, which expresses in a nutshell why it is important and rewarding to analyze and understand U.S.-American politics.

Since the end of World War II, the relationship, based on shared values, has been very firm between the Federal Republic of Germany and the United States of America. Yet, it has always been dynamic. In spite of the fact that Germany has been one of the country's most loyal allies for a long time, there have been periods of misunderstanding, minor tensions and discord. Chancellor Schröder's (1998 – 2005) clear stance against the military intervention in Iraq in 2003 caused the most recent strain on the German-American relationship.

However, it should not be forgotten that Germany has been participating in *Operation Enduring Freedom*, the U.S. military operation launched in 2001, against the Taliban regime in Afghanistan. In January 2006, Angela Merkel made her first visit to Washington, D.C., as the new Chancellor of the Federal Republic. The exchange of opinions – despite some differences with President George W. Bush on crucial issues – was unanimously evaluated as the beginning of a new chapter in U.S.-American / German post-war relations. Gaining insight into American politics helps to pave the way for intercultural understanding. Presenting developments, issues, and mechanisms of U.S. society and its political institutions in a cultural and historical context may help to prevent naive anti-Americanism as well as an uncritical admiration of American ways.

The following outline aims to give an introduction to the main features of *Politics in the U.S.A.*:

• Firstly, the genesis and the content of the **Constitution** emphasize the philosophical ideas of the Age of Enlightenment as the main source of the U.S.-American democracy as a model for modern democracies. The *Constitution*, based on the principles of *Separation of Powers* and *Checks and Balances*, and its *Amendments* (with the first ten amendments constituting *The Bill of Rights*), guarantee the system and spirit of a workable and adaptable **Democracy in Action**.

• Secondly, the importance of **Religion** in the United States of America, the ostentatious demonstration of piety, the religious and moral attitudes frequently expressed in political speeches and determining decisions and – at the same time – the emphasis on the constitutionally established dividing line between Church and State, the exact definition of which has repeatedly been the central issue of numerous Supreme Court cases, seems to be a paradox to many European observers. These phenomena have to be explained in a wider historical and social context to understand certain facets of U.S. domestic and foreign policies.

• Thirdly, current problems in such fields as **Social Policy**, **Education**, and the relationship between **Ecology** and **Economy** are normally not so thoroughly covered by the media as other political topics, but information on these issues is necessary to complete our understanding of the political landscape of the U.S.A. However short-lived some of the dates and figures offered may be (they can easily be updated with the help of official

We the people ...

websites, e.g. www.usembassy.de) – the issues allow insights into the more lasting principles of pragmatic political thought. Besides, the current topics of home affairs invite comparison with current problems and issues in Germany and other countries within the European Union at a time in which economic and social reforms are urgently needed.

- Fourthly, throughout history, America has perceived itself as a nation of **Immigrants**. This has led to challenges and controversies concerning the structure of American society up to the present day. The never-ending debates on assimilation versus diversity, the current socio-economic issue of the status of illegal immigrants and the development of new legislation on immigration prove this fact.
- Fifthly, **Terrorism**, above all, the atrocities of 9/11, brought about a paradigmatic change in U.S.-American politics. Apart from such reactions as shock, fear, and measures dictated by the priority of home security, the terrorist attacks initiated fundamental reflections on U.S.-American identity and values. Famous scholars re-examined and reaffirmed the validity of the United States' values and human rights in a style reminiscent of classical political writing in the Age of Enlightenment before they justified *the War on Terrorism*. The justification of defense measures went hand in hand with self-critical explanations why something like 9/11 had happened. More radical self-criticism of the American way of life and the nation's foreign policy blend in with the general criticism of the globalization process. For outside observers of politics in the United States, it is important to see that much of their own critical reactions to the U.S.-American administration's decisions are expressed in open, controversial debates within the United States of America itself. This also holds true for the assessment and reassessment of America's military commitments – such as the Vietnam War and the military operation in Iraq of 2003 – due to its changing **Global Role** as a leading superpower.

1 "WE THE PEOPLE OF THE UNITED STATES"

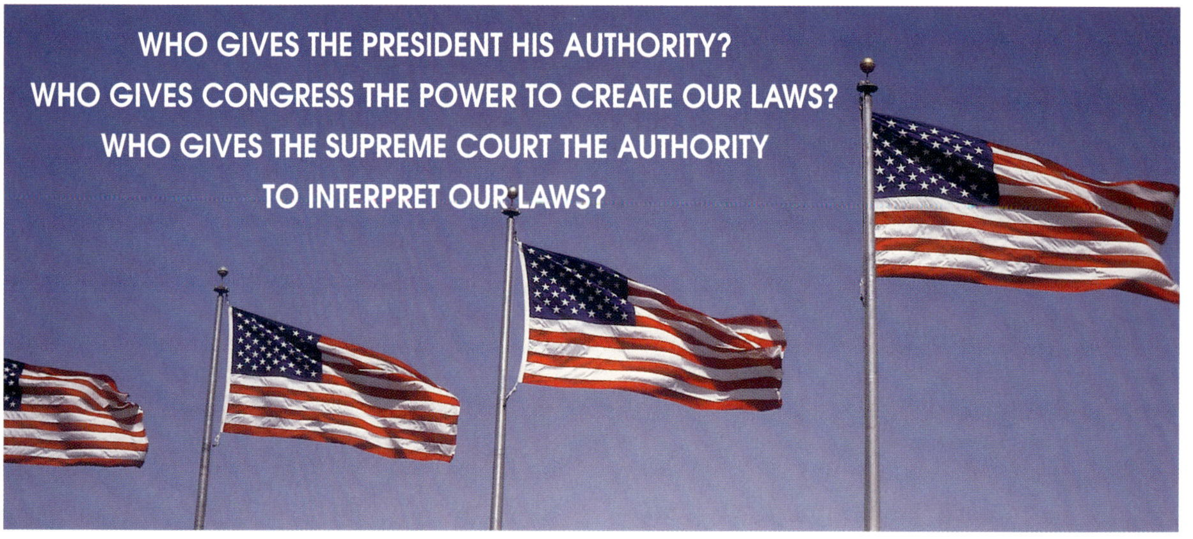

"The Constitution does not solve our problems.
It gives people freedom and opportunity to solve their own problems.
It gives representatives of the people authority to help solve problems.
It provides an executive to enforce the laws and administer the government.
It provides a judicial branch to say what the law means.
From there on it is up to the people."

Warren E. Burger,
Chairman of the Commission, Chief Justice of the United States (1969–1986)

Supreme Court Justices

The U.S. Constitution – celebrating 200 years of successful government by the people.

Two hundred years ago, a document was drafted establishing the American system of government. No other people had ever written such a document. And the government it created has successfully endured longer than any of its kind in history.

Washington

In 1787, there was a need for a strong national government.

After the Continental Congress voted for independence from England in 1776, the "Articles of Confederation" were drafted, granting limited federal power. But the government could not levy taxes or regulate trade between the states or with foreign countries.

In America's early years, disputes often arose among the states. Locked into a clumsy structure, the U.S. government was too weak to enforce treaties or settle differences.

A decade after independence, it was apparent that the articles were ineffective. To survive, the national government needed a stronger foundation.

55 experienced delegates met to decide how the American government should function.

Madison

In May, 1787, the Constitutional Convention opened in Philadelphia. Its purpose was to strengthen the Articles of Confederation. But after some debate, it was agreed that a completely new government should be created.

The Convention delegates were a distinguished group comprised of some of the best educated, most respected men in the United States. They were men who had studied law, government, political theory, and history. Some of the delegates are familiar to you – George Washington, James Madison, Alexander Hamilton, and Benjamin Franklin.

The executive, legislative and judicial branches – a careful "separation of powers".

Many obstacles were faced and overcome during the course of the Convention. With some skilful compromise, a structure for the new government finally emerged.

There would be three equal branches of government. The Executive Branch, led by the President, who would administer the government.

The Legislative Branch, comprised of the Senate and the House of Representatives, would make the nation's laws.

And the Judicial Branch, consisting of our federal court judges, would interpret the laws for particular cases.

The Constitution grants power, limits power, and protects against abuses of power.

The Constitution assigned responsibilities and powers to each of these three branches and the government. At the same time, it provided for a system of "checks and balances" to ensure that no one branch could abuse its power.

Hamilton

To ratify or not to ratify – a long, hard struggle.

In September of 1787, the new Constitution was presented to the states for ratification. Supporters and opponents took up their positions, and a rich dialogue ensued which lasted for almost nine months.

The Federalists supported the Constitution. They believed a strong national government would help America prosper and compete with foreign countries. Since the government was responsible directly to America's citizens, they believed the rights of the people would be safe.

The Anti-Federalists felt differently. They argued that the Revolution had been fought to overcome excessive government power. They feared the new Constitution granted too much strength to the federal government, and would interfere with individual rights.

In the end, an addition – The Bill of Rights.

Franklin

To guard against the loss of liberties, the first Congress agreed that a Bill of Rights should be added to the Constitution. The Bill of Rights, the first ten amendments, was ratified by the states and became part of the Constitution on December 15, 1791.

Amendments let the Constitution reflect change.

Through the years, other amendments have been added to the Constitution. There are now 26. The most recent was added in 1971, granting the vote to eighteen-year-olds.*)

Most of the amendments have either altered governmental structure or strengthened the Constitution's guarantee of equality and justice.

The ability to add amendments ensures the Constitution's vitality and effectiveness through changing times.

The basic principle – all political power rests with the people.

If there is one guiding principle of the U.S. Constitution, it is that power is granted to the government by those who are governed – We the people of the United States.

We the people are the foundation of our representative government.

As Americans, we have rights and we have responsibilities.

Each person has the right to participate or not to participate in government.

However, an informed, involved citizenry is the best insurance for a continued free and representative government. Be involved in your community.

The Constitution is the foundation of the American way of life. Learn more about it.

Your public library is full of information on the history of the Constitution, the men who drafted it, and the functioning of the American government. To celebrate the birthday of the U.S. Constitution, learn about the illustrious document that has guaranteed our rights and kept the nation free for the past 200 years.

U.S. GOVERNMENT PRINTING OFFICE, The Constitution (Washington, D.C., 1990).

*) At present, there are 27 amendments.

Separation of Powers and Checks and Balances

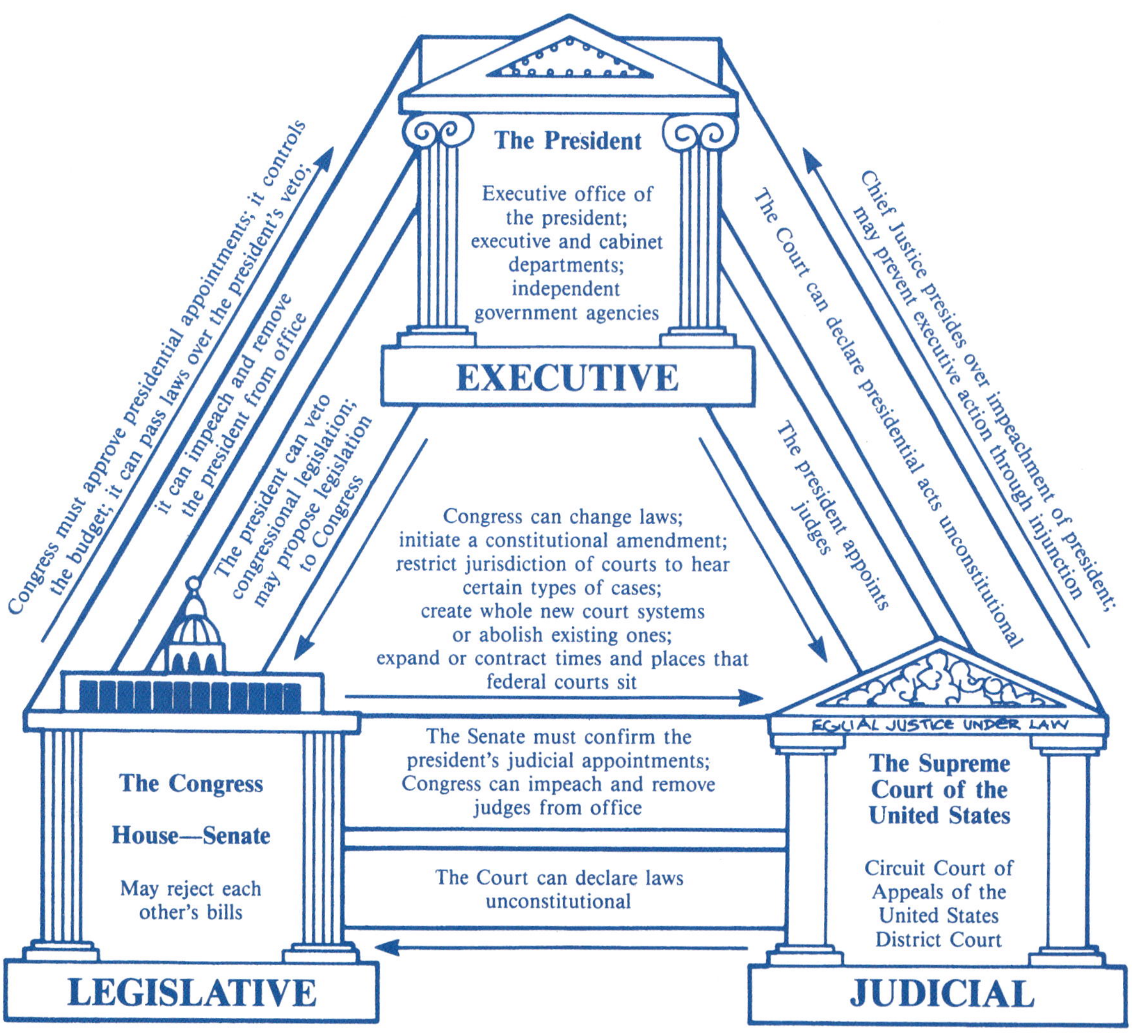

Vocabulary

9 executive (n.): s.o. who is part of a governing body – **9 to enforce** (v.): to apply – **10 to administer** (v.): to carry out – **21 to draft** (v.): to write down one's ideas – **24 to endure** (v.): to last – **33 to grant** (v.): to give – **35 to levy** (taxes) (v.): to demand or collect officially – **39 locked into** (adj.): – bound by; restricted by – **40 treaty** (n.): an agreement made between countries and formally signed by their representatives – **42 decade** (n.): ten years – **43 ineffective** (adj.): of no great use; of poor result – **57 distinguished** (adj.): /dɪ'stɪŋgwɪʃt/ outstandingly able; famous – **58 comprised** (adj.) (of): consisting of – **68 to emerge** (v.): to be the result of – **79 abuse** (n.): wrong or not authorized use – **80 to assign** (v.): to give to – **85 to ratify** (v.): to make a written agreement official by signing it – **93 to ensue** (v.): /ɪn'sjuː ‖ ɪn'suː/ to be the consequence of – **97 to prosper** (v.): to become wealthy and powerful – **97 to compete** (v.): to measure one's forces with – **105 to interfere (with)** (v.): to enter into or take part in a matter in which one is not wanted – **114 amendment** (n.): an improvement made in or suggested for a rule, law, etc. – **124 to alter** (v.): to make or to become different – **127 to ensure** (v.): to make sure – **140 involved** (adj.): closely connected in relationship and activities with others – **140 citizenry** (n.) : /'sɪtɪzənri/ all the citizens of a state

Explanations

29 Continental Congress: the law-making body that governed the thirteen colonies that later formed the U.S. It passed the Declaration of Independence. – **49 Constitutional Convention**: (also Philadelphia Convention) the meeting of representatives in Philadelphia in 1787 that led to the writing of the Constitution of the U.S.A. – **52 Articles of Confederation**: the agreement drawn up in 1781 by the 13 original colonies of the U.S. which served as the basic law for the government until the U.S. Constitution was agreed upon in 1788 – **62 George Washington** (1732–1799): commander in chief of the army of the thirteen colonies, after the War of Independence first president of the United States (1789-97) – **62 James Madison** (1751–1836): 4th president of the U.S. (1809–17) and leading statesman during the War of Independence, one of the authors of the Declaration of Independence – **62 Alexander Hamilton** (1757–1804): leading federalist and main advocate of the Constitution of 1787 – **63 Benjamin Franklin** (1706–1790): diplomat and inventor (Franklin-stove, a new kind of clock, lightning rod), was ambassador in France, negotiated with England and became the first secretary of state (=foreign minister) under President George Washington – **95 Federalist**: a member of a political party (founded in 1787) which was in favor of a strong federal government

Awareness

1 Working in groups, gather information about the German Constitution (Fundamental Law). As a useful Internet source you can use www.datenschutz-berlin.de/recht/de/gg/.
  a) When was it drafted and why?
  b) Who were the authors?

Comprehension

2 Why did 55 experienced delegates meet in Philadelphia in May 1787?
3 What was the main structure of the new Constitution of September 1787?
4 What does the term "checks and balances" mean?
5 How can the American Constitution be modernized to react to changes in society?
6 What was the first major modification of the new Constitution and why had it become necessary?

Internet Project

7 Working in groups, find out major similarities and differences between the American and German constitutions:
  a) the U.S. Senate and the Bundesrat
  b) the U.S. House of Representatives and the Bundestag
  c) the U.S. President and the Bundespräsident
  d) the U.S. Government and the Bundesregierung

As starting points, use the following Internet sources:
http:thomas.loc.gov/home/legbranch/ legbranch.html;
http:bensguide.gpo.gov/9-12/index.html;
http://de.wikipedia.org./wiki/wahlrecht;
www.bundesregierung.de/;
www.bundestag.de/htdocs_e/index.html.

2

Dirk Johnson

"A Nation Bound by Faith"

A fascinating phenomenon is the importance of religion in American society. Church attendance, publicly demonstrated affiliations to Bible, God, and religious institutions appear strange to a lot of Europeans who are used to more secularized forms of society. - Dirk Johnson, "A Nation Bound by Faith," in: *Newsweek* (February 24, 2003), pp.17-21.

George W. Bush and the Power of Religion

Of all its national traits, America's religiosity is probably the most baffling – and infuriating – for the rest of the world. Where does it come from? Why do Americans think they're on the side of right? And why it will not go away.

With her nation at the brink of war, Anne Summers is searching for answers. The 35-year-old software engineer follows the debate over Iraq. But like a lot of Americans, she also does something else. She prays. So it was, on a frigid Wednesday night, that she trudged out to a prayer service at Willow Creek Community Church in the affluent Chicago suburb of South Barrington. One of the nondenominational "megachurches" that have proliferated in American suburbs in recent years, Willow Creek looks like a corporate conference center. No crosses, no stained-glass windows, no pews. Willow Creek holds its services in a 4,500-seat, theater-style auditorium. There is even a video café, where congregants sip coffee and watch services on closed-circuit television.

This day, 3,000 people turn out, most of them white, well-educated and suburban. A giant video screen displays the words OUR FATHER. Summers had prayed it would not come to this, but she supports the war even so. "Bush and Powell and all those guys are Christian," she says. "I do believe that God has blessed this country."

When it comes to matters of might and right, Americans look to the heavens in a way that bewilders much of the rest of the world – especially Europe. A majority of Americans say religion shapes their lives and it clearly shapes politics. Regular churchgoers are far more likely to vote Republican than Democratic, according to polls, and it's well known that the religious right is the Bush administration's political base. The president himself sometimes sounds like the nation's commander in the pulpit. His State of the Union address last month repeatedly invoked divine power, declaring confidence in the "loving God behind all of life and all of history." "May He guide us now," George W. Bush beseeched.

The president has never shied from talking about his own embrace of born-again Christianity, at 39, a transformation, that he says helped him kick a drinking problem. Bush attends regular Bible-study sessions in the White House. Others around him do the same; Attorney General John Ashcroft begins every business day with a prayer meeting. After a California court ruled the Pledge of Allegiance violated the constitutional separation of church and state for declaring "one nation under God," indignant politicians filed out of the Capitol and loudly recited the pledge.

Invoking the Almighty is common among American politicians, who know well that voters in the United States prefer leaders who side with the angels. But with Bush, religious conservatives can for the first time fully claim one of their own in the White House. What detractors – at home as well as abroad – find most alarming is the president's tendency to blur the lines between personal faith and policy. In fact, the White House often deliberately infuses its message with Biblical overtones. Bush's famous denunciation of the Axis of Evil – Iraq, Iran and North Korea – was originally penned as the "Axis of Hatred." The change came about, according to former speechwriter David Frum, when senior White House staff opted for a more "theological" formulation. "If people want to know me," Bush said during his campaign for president, "they've got to know that's an integral part of my life – my acceptance of Christ."

Faith increasingly seems to affect the administration's decisions. Just last week the president named a doctrinaire Christian, Dr. W. David Hager, as head of

an advisory committee on reproductive-health issues for the Food and Drug Administration. Hager, who describes himself as pro-life, refuses to prescribe contraceptives to unmarried women and has written that women should treat premenstrual syndrome by reading the Bible and praying. In the Congress, the House Republican whip, Tom DeLay, refers to disputed Middle East territories as Judea and Samaria, as they were known in the Bible. Last year House Majority Leader Dick Armey suggested that Israel is entitled to the West Bank, on Biblical grounds, and that "Palestinians should leave," a claim he later tried to qualify.

Such religious rhetoric is not as out of step as it may seem. According to polls, 80 percent of Americans say a belief in God shapes their views. Conservative, evangelical churches have seen strong growth across the country in recent years, while more liberal denominations struggle to fill their pews. A popular wristband reads WWJD, or "What would Jesus do?" Many Americans today want prayer in schools and sex-education campaigns to consist solely of teaching abstinence. The Boy Scouts of America excludes gays and atheists. Pro-football players point to heavens in gratitude for scoring a touchdown, then praise Jesus in postgame television interviews.

From across the sea, it might seem that the United States is a nation of religious zealots, united in crusade. The truth is that America itself is divided. Fewer than half of all Americans attend church regularly. Much of the country, like Europe, is growing more secular, especially on the coasts and in the metropolitan centers of the upper Midwest. These are the regions where Al Gore prevailed in the 2000 presidential election – and which in fact gave him a plurality of votes. Even among the faithful, religion scarcely speaks with a single voice, especially when it comes to war. Polls show the nation is largely split on attacking Bagdhad, and opponents of war, too, often draw on faith.

And in the shaping of American values, there is more than God in the details. Capitalism, like sports – a sort of secular religion in America – takes as an article of faith that competition is the fairest arbiter, a way to yield winners and losers. Americans may see war as a last resort, but it is a resort - a decisive way to settle a contest. As Robert Cagan, of the Carnegie Endowment for International Peace, has noted, Americans see the military as a perfectly acceptable tool of foreign policy.

Europeans may cringe at the "cowboy ways" of President Bush. But in America, the cowboy is sacred in the nation's mythology, a symbol of youth, strength and self-reliance. Capital punishment, seen as barbaric in most other Western societies, derives from the time-honored code of frontier justice. Bad people – including leaders like Saddam Hussein – need to be hunted down and dealt with harshly. It is not a matter of might for its own sake, or even necessarily for narrow self-interest. Americans tend to see their country as being on the side of mercy and righteousness. What is good for America, the thinking goes, is good for the rest of the world, whether it realizes it or not.

This notion of American exceptionalism was the underpinning of Manifest Destiny, the mid-19th-century idea that America had a right and duty to extend its reach of power. The self-image of benevolence, with regard to international affairs, was burnished by America's role in the two world wars of the 20th century. Given that Americans sent millions of men to fight tyranny in Europe, and then helped rebuild war-ravaged nations, the voices of pacifism coming from the Continent ring painfully hollow.

Many Americans agree with the White House that the looming war with Iraq is a battle against tyranny, a righteous act of liberating an oppressed people. "When Americans see a picture of a woman who is suffering, they say simply, 'I want to help'," says Zainab Salbi, a 33-year-old Iraqi immigrant who founded Women for Women in Washington. "This is not something I see in the rest of the world." The flip side of that generosity, she adds, is the sometimes naive view that America "can fix everything – and always knows best." Benevolent or arrogant, perhaps some of both, Americans are praying for peace in the eleventh hour. But their faith may also bring them war.

Info

The Relationship between Church and State

"There is no country in the world where the Christian religion retains a greater influence over the souls of men than in America."
Alexis de Tocqueville (1831)

The inscription on the dollar bill: "In God we Trust"

The President swears his oath on the Holy Bible.

As strange as it may seem - considering the above quotations and examples - there is a clear-cut separation of church and state in the US, also called the "Wall of Separation," which is based on the First Amendment.

"Congress shall make no law respecting an establishment of religion, or prohibiting the free exercise thereof; or abridging the freedom of speech, or of the press; or the right of the people peaceably to assemble, and to petition the Government for a redress of grievances."
First Amendment

This First Amendment to the American Constitution - also referred to as the "Establishment Clause" – was interpreted by Justice Hugo Black.

"Neither a state nor the Federal Government can set up a church. Neither can pass laws which aid one religion, aid all religions, or prefer one religion over another. Neither can force nor influence a person to go to or to remain away from church against his will or force him to profess a belief or disbelief in any religion. No person can be punished for professing religious beliefs, for church attendance or non-attendance. [...] Neither a state nor the Federal Government can participate in the affairs of any religious organizations or groups and vice versa. In the words of Jefferson, the clause against establishment of religion by laws was intended to erect 'a wall of separation' between Church and State."

The intention of the "establishment clause" was to separate religious activity and civil authority completely and permanently. Even if a religious group is considered dangerous by whoever, it will be protected by this constitutional right.
The Supreme Court has repeatedly ruled that a person's faith is no concern of the state.

Vocabulary

13 nondenominational (adj.): not relating to one particular religion or religious group – **14 to proliferate** (v.): to increase and spread quickly – **16 pew** (n.): a long wooden seat in a church – **19 congregants** (n.): people coming together for worship – **19 closed-circuit television**: a system of cameras and television used in public buildings usually for safety reasons – **37 pulpit** (n.): a raised structure inside a church at the front that a priest or minister stands on giving a sermon – **38 to invoke divine power:** to refer to God to justify your views, to ask for God's support – **41 to beseech**, besought, besought or beseeched, beseeched (v.):(lit.)to eagerly and anxiously ask s.o. for s.th., to beg – **51 indignant** (adj.): angry and surprised because you feel insulted or unfairly treated – **58 detractor** (n.): s.o. who says bad things about s.o.; harsh critic – **59 to blur** (v.): to make the difference less clear – **73 doctrinaire** (adj.): /ˌdɒktrᵻˈneə ‖ - ˌdɑːktrᵻˈner/ certain that your beliefs are absolutely true and unwilling to change them or to make compromises – **74 advisory committee** (n.): advice-giving group of experts – **100 zealot** (n.): /ˈzelət/ s.o. who has extremely strong beliefs and is extremely eager to make other people share them – **101 crusade** (n.): a strong attempt to change s.th. because you think you are morally right; campaign – **104 secular** (adj.): not connected with or controlled by a church or religious authority – **106 to prevail** (v.): to be successful, win the upper hand – **116 arbiter** (n.): judge, referee – **117 to yield** (v.): to help to find out, to produce a result, answer – **123 to cringe** (v.): to feel very uncomfortable about s.th. – **133 righteousness** (n.): quality of being morally good and fair (Rechtschaffenheit) – **137 underpinning** (n.): foundation – **139 benevolence** (n.): /bᵻˈnevələns/ kindness, generosity – **140 to burnish** (v.): to polish s.th. until it shines – **143 war-ravaged** (adj.): very badly damaged by war – **147 to loom** (v.): to happen almost certainly and very soon

Info

Pledge of Allegiance

The American citizens' promise to respect the U.S.A. and be loyal to it. It is made each morning at American schools and often on formal public occasions. People look at the flag and put their right hands over their hearts while proclaiming: "I pledge allegiance to the flag of the United States of America, and to the republic for which it stands, one nation under God, indivisible, with liberty and justice for all."

The phrase "under God" has become a legal issue since in June 2002, a divided three-judge panel of the U.S. Circuit Court of Appeals for the Ninth Circuit, a regional court, ruled in Newdow vs. U.S. Congress that the inclusion of these words violated the First Amendment to the Constitution. This ruling caused spontaneous protests and Congress reaffirmed the words as part of the Pledge. In June 2004, the Supreme Court left the traditional Pledge intact. In September 2005, a federal judge, however, decided that school children attending public schools should not be obliged to articulate the disputed phrase, a ruling that ignited further protest and litigation.

Explanations

74 reproductive-health issues: medical fields relating to sexuality, family-planning, pregnancy – **75 Food and Drug Administration**: Consumer Protection and Health Agency – **76 pro-life** (adj.): opposed to abortion, (opposite:) pro-choice – **80 House Republican whip**: the Republican member of the House of Representatives who is responsible for making sure that the members of the party attend and vote – **119 The Carnegie Endowment for International Peace**: founded in 1910, private, nonprofit, nonpartisan organization dedicated to advancing cooperation between nations, promoting international engagement by the United States.

Awareness

1 What role has religion played in your upbringing and what does it mean to you now?

Comprehension

2 Skim through the article and say what the American attitude toward war is like.
3 Outline the different examples given in the text which show the close relation between everyday life and religion.
4 Describe President Bush's attitude toward religion and church.
5 What is meant by "... the President's tendency to blur the lines between personal faith and policy"?
6 What does the cowboy image of G. W. Bush have to do with S. Hussein?
7 What political consequences of the U.S.-American attitude toward religion are described in the text?

Analysis

8 Examine George Bush's connection to religion and church and find out in how far it influences the political life in the U.S.A.. Use your findings from above (task 5).
9 What does the description of the church Anne Summers attends evoke?
10 In how far does the text present an ambivalent picture of religion in the U.S.? Refer to the Info Box on p. 238.

Opinion

11 Comment on the attitudes and concepts of Dr. W. David Hager, Tom DeLay, and Dick Armey.

Project

12 There has been a new religious wave in Europe, especially since the death of Pope John Paul II. Try to explore if there is anything like a new religious youth culture in Germany.
13 Write a newspaper article (Reference Library, p. 298) in which you explain the relationship of state and church in Germany to an American audience.

3

Jennifer Washburn

"The Tuition Crunch"

Frequently German educators and politicians refer to the U.S.-American university system with its inbuilt competition, based on evaluation and ranking, and its tradition of demanding tuition fees as a model. Financial problems - due to sometimes very high fees - have been met by a complex web of public and private grant and scholarship schemes. However, it has become increasingly difficult to make ends meet as a student at a college or university. - Jennifer Washburn, "The Tuition Crunch," in: *The Atlantic Monthly* (Boston, January 20, 2004), p.140.

For low-income students college is increasingly out of reach

A four-year college degree has become all but a necessity for getting ahead in the information age. Since the 1980s the average real income of workers with only a high school diploma has fallen, while salaries among those with at least a college degree have risen: they now earn 75 percent more than high school graduates. At the national level, having a highly educated work force is critical in order to sustain our technological edge in the global economy.

College Graduates in the U.S.A.

America's higher-education system ranks among its greatest achievements. But in the past two decades our commitment to equal opportunity in post-secondary education has deteriorated markedly. In 1979 students from the richest 25 percent of American homes were four times as likely to attend college as those from the poorest 25 percent; by 1994 they were ten times as likely.

Part of the problem is the skyrocketing cost of college. Since 1980 tuition and related charges have increased at more than twice the rate of inflation, rising by nearly 40 percent in real terms in the past decade alone. Public attention has focused largely on the $35,000-plus annual cost of elite schools like Harvard and Brown. The bigger problem rests with the public colleges and universities that serve 80 percent of the nation's students. In 2003 the University of Arizona's average annual tuition rose by 39 percent, to $3,604, and Iowa State's rose by 22 percent, to $5,028. For many low-income families increases like these are difficult to absorb. Indeed, the cost for such families of sending a child to a four-year public institution shot from 13 percent of family income in 1980 to 25 percent in 2000 (for middle- and high-income families the percentage barely increased).

Congressional Republicans, led by Representative Howard McKeon, of California, contend that universities are largely to blame for these tuition hikes. However, most experts agree that fluctuations in state spending are the principal cause of tuition increases at public institutions, which depend heavily on appropriations to subsidize their operations. As Arthur Hauptman, an expert on college financing, explains, in each of the past three economic recessions – in the mid-1970s, the early 1980s, and the early 1990s – state higher-education spending per student declined, forcing students and their families to shoulder more of the cost in the form of double-digit percentage hikes in tuition. Increases during the recent recession reflect the same pattern.

The tuition spiral is not the only impediment to equality of opportunity. More significant perhaps is the nation's backsliding on need-based financial aid. In 1975–1976 the maximum federal Pell Grant award (for low-income students) covered 84 percent of the cost of attendance at a public four-year college; by 1999–2000 it covered only 39 percent. This is part of a broader shift to a system dominated by loans, which has left a generation of students struggling to finance heavy debt.

Hardest hit are low-income students, whose numbers are expected to increase dramatically over the next decade. From 1989 to 1999 the average cumulative debt of the poorest 25 percent of public-college seniors grew from $7,629 to $12,888 (in constant 1999 dollars). Studies find that when financial-aid packages inadequately cover expenses, students work long hours, attend school part time, and opt for two-year as opposed to four-year programs – all of which reduce their chances of acquiring a bachelor's degree.

Federal efforts during the past decade or so to address rising tuition have done little to help low-income families. Both the Clinton and the George W. Bush administrations promoted tax breaks and saving incentives encouraging families to set aside money for college. These programs largely benefited middle- and upper-income families, who have both taxable income and resources to save. With the Higher Education Act up for renewal this year, Congress should focus on aiding those students unlikely to complete – or attend – college without greater financial support, and should encourage universities to do the same. To begin with, it should restore the purchasing power of Pell Grants by raising the maximum award from the current $4,050 to $8,000. Many will argue that the cost – roughly $15 billion in additional annual spending – is unrealistic. Historically, however, our nation's investments in expanding access to higher education have paid off many times over. And the money required, according to a new Century Foundation publication, is roughly equivalent to the annual revenue lost to the Treasury from tax and savings benefits that currently help those higher on the income ladder. To relieve the extraordinary debt burden that many students face, Congress should also put the college-loan system under federal administration, and let every student consolidate loans and pay them off on an income-contingent basis, as one federal loan program already allows.

Broadening access to higher education has never been the answer to inequality, but it *is* the way to ensure that every young person has a chance to move upward in society. Either we can continue to ignore the persistent disparities in post-secondary training and rely increasingly on foreign students to fill our graduate-level science and engineering programs, or we can renew our commitment to educating the young people who are already here.

Vocabulary

Title/crunch (n.): a difficult situation caused by a lack of money – **2 college degree** (n.): the qualifications and the academic title a student gets after successfully attending an institution of higher learning – **7 graduate** (n.): s.o. who has finished an educational course – **9 critical** (adj.): important, decisive – **9 to sustain** (v.): to keep up, make s.th. continue – **10 edge** (n.): here: advantage – **14 to deteriorate** (v.): /dɪ'tɪəriəreɪt ‖ -'tɪr-/ to become worse – **18 to skyrocket** (v.): to go up, rise very fast – **36 to contend** (v.): to maintain, to state, to argue – **38 hike** (n.): rise – **42 appropriation** (n.): /ə,prəʊpri'eɪʃən ‖ ə,proʊ-/ money to be used for a specific purpose – **43 to subsidize** (v.): to support financially – **52 double-digit** (adj).; (only before noun, esp. AmE): numbers between 10 to 99 (BrE: double-figure) – **55 impediment** (n.): hindrance, s.th. that makes it difficult to reach a goal – **57 backsliding** (n.): falling back into a former undesirable situation or behavior – **62 loan** (n.): money borrowed from a bank – **63 debt** (n.): /det/ a sum of money that a person or organization owes – **66 cumulative** (adj.): /'kjuːmjʊlətɪv ‖ -leɪtɪv/ increasing gradually as more of s.th. is added – **77 tax break** (n.): a special reduction in taxes – **77 incentive** (n.): motivation, encouragement to do s.th. – **93 revenue, revenues** (n., uncountable): /'revɪnjuː, -z ‖ -nuː, -nuːz/ money received from selling goods or services or from tax or fees – **99 income-contingent** (adj.): depending on the future income – **105 persistent** (adj.): ongoing, continuing – **105 disparity** (n.): (unfair) difference

Explanations

Title/tuition (n., especially AmE): the money you pay for being taught; BrE: tuition fees – **13 post-secondary education**: here: used in the sense of higher education after the high school diploma at a community college, college or university for a first degree, usually the bachelor's degree – **58 Pell Grant award**: a federal Pell Grant can be awarded to financially eligible undergraduate students on application and – by contrast to a loan – does not have to be paid back.

Awareness

1 How do students in Germany finance their studies? What about your personal plans?

Comprehension

2 What does the text say about the development of average annual tuition costs and what does it say about family incomes in the last two decades?
3 What reasons for the current financial situation of students does the author give?
4 What are the consequences of this development?
5 What is proposed to improve the difficult situation for students?

and even very few people who speak the language," said Obersdorfer, who now teaches at Johns Hopkins University. This lack of understanding helps explain why the coalition has so consistently underestimated the challenges of occupation. Obersdorfer remembers when U.S. officials helped write a constitution and stage elections in South Vietnam, resulting in a government "with absolutely no legitimacy, because we never figured out what people wanted." [...]

Although it is hard to imagine the people of Iraq opposing U.S. occupation as strongly as did the peasants of South Vietnam, the tide seems to be turning. Even in the supposedly peaceful Shiite areas of southern Iraq, many local leaders oppose the occupation and yearn for an alliance with Iran. [...]

In a Gallup Poll conducted before the Ramadan offensive and released after it began, 54 percent of Americans disapproved of the job President Bush was doing in Iraq, up from a low 21 percent at the war's start. It was the first time that Bush's disapproval ratings on Iraq had exceeded 50 percent. Just as demoralizing for the White House, perhaps, was Gallup's observation that the polling resembles no other wartime experience more than that of "the war recent presidents have avoided repeating – Vietnam." In February 1968, in the last poll before Lyndon Johnson announced he wouldn't run for re-election, 57 percent of the public disapproved of his handling of Vietnam. The next poll may show Bush beyond this mark.

The most apparent and significant similarity between Iraq and Vietnam is the difficulty of convincing Americans that the fight is worthwhile. First by asserting an unsubstantiated link to the war on terror and then by soft-pedaling problems in Iraq, Bush, like Johnson, has created a "credibility gap," said Stanley Karnow, "by giving the impression that he is not leveling with the

American people." When Bush said on October 27 that the increased violence in Iraq was a sign of progress, he reminded many of the doublespeak of Vietnam.

His unshakably positive rhetoric, the premature declaration of "Mission Accomplished," the multiple and sometimes questionable justifications for war have all shaken faith in a hugely popular president. Perhaps Iraq's strongest resemblance to Vietnam lies in the unmistakable signs that Bush has heeded his shift of opinion, and is responding to recent setbacks in Iraq with the dubious claim that the schedule for withdrawal should be accelerated.

In the opinion of one Vietnam veteran, this hastening would only assure a repeat of Vietnam, where the U.S. hurriedly turned security over to an ill-prepared South Vietnam, withdrew U.S. troops, and then watched the regime fall a few years later. "Iraq is not Vietnam," said Sen. John McCain, R-Ariz., but "when our Secretary of Defense says that it's up to the Iraqi people to defeat the Baathists and terrorists, we send a message that America's exit from Iraq is ultimately more important than the achievement of American goals."

Vocabulary

8 yearning (n.): a strong desire for s.th. - **13 to tote up** (v.): to add up - **18 lost cause** (n.): s.th. that has no chance of succeeding - **22 defeatism** (n.): believing or expecting that one will not succeed - **35 verge** (n.): to be on the verge of s.th. is to be at the point where s.th. is about to happen - **36 to deploy** (v.): to organize or move soldiers, military equipment, etc., so that they are in the right place and ready to be used - **45 to badger** (v.): to put pressure on s.o.; to harass - **66 deterioration** (n.): /dɪˌtɪəriəˈreɪʃən || -ˌtɪr-/ becoming worse - **71 to stave off** (v.): to keep s.o. or s.th. from reaching you or affecting you for a period of time - **74 shooting gallery** (n.): place where people shoot guns at objects to win prizes - **82 testament** (n.): to be a testament to s.th. = proving or showing very clearly that s.th. exists or is true - **83 to dismiss** (v.): to refuse to consider s.o.'s idea, opinion, etc., because you think it is not serious, true or important - **83 insurgent** (n.): one of a group of people fighting against the government of their own country, or against authority - **85 to topple** (v.): to take power away from a leader or government, esp. by force - **91 overarching** (adj.): including or influencing every part of s.th. - **106 tide** (n.): here: the way in which events or people's opinions are developing - **126 to assert** (v.): /əˈsɜːt || -ɜːrt/ to state firmly that s.th. is true - **127 unsubstantiated** (adj.): /ˌʌnsəbˈstænʃieɪtɪd/ not proved to be true - **128 to soft-pedal** (v.): to make s.th. seem less important or less urgent than it really is - **129 credibility gap** (n.): the difference between what s.o. says and what they do - **130 to level with** (v.): to speak honestly to s.o., after hiding some unpleasant facts from them - **133 doublespeak** (n.): speech that is complicated and can have more than one meaning, sometimes used deliberately to deceive or confuse people - **139 to heed** (v.): to pay attention to s.o.'s advice or warning

Explanations

23 Panglossiamism: The term refers to Pangloss, a character in Voltaire's novel *Candide*. Panglossianism stands for baseless optimism. – **39 Lyndon Baines Johnson**: (1908–1973) the 36th president of the U.S. (1963–1969), a Democrat. As John F. Kennedy's vice president, Johnson became president when Kennedy was killed. He was re-elected in 1964 and helped start many social programs in his plans for a Great Society, but he became unpopular after increasing U.S. involvement in Vietnam. – **41 Gulf of Tonkin Resolution of 1964**: The distorted account of a minor naval engagement in the Gulf of Tonkin was used by President Johnson to justify the escalation of U.S. military action in Vietnam. (cf.: www.fair.org/index.php?page=2261) – **90 The Washington Post**: a serious American newspaper, printed in Washington, D.C., famous for uncovering the Watergate Scandal – **96 Johns Hopkins University**: The university in Baltimore, Maryland, opened Feb. 22, 1876. It is one of America's leading universities in both teaching and research. (cf.: www.jhu. edu/) – **107 Shiite**: a member of the second-largest branch of the Muslim religion, which is based on the teachings and acts of Muhammed's cousin Ali and of the teachers who came after him – **110 Gallup Poll**: a special count of opinions in a country, done esp. in order to try to say what the result of a politi-cal election will be, by questioning a number of people chosen to represent the whole population. They are named after the American statistician George Horace Gallup, who invented them. – **110 Ramadan**: the ninth month of the Muslim year, during which no food or drink may be taken between sunrise and sunset. – **115 White House (the)**: the official Washington, D.C., residence of the President of the United States – **129 Stanley Karnow**: author of "Vietnam: A History" – **135 "Mission Accomplished"**: On May 2, 2003, President Bush declared the end of major combat in Iraq aboard the aircraft carrier USS Abraham Lincoln under a banner which read "Mission Accomplished". The "Mission Accomplished" claim has been criticized and ridiculed because of the unsuccessful search for weapons of mass destruction and the continuing violence in Iraq. – **150 Baathist**: a member of a socialist political party, esp. active in Syria and Iraq

Awareness

1 Since the end of World War II, U.S. troops have been deployed in Germany. What do you know about the military goals that have kept American forces stationed in Germany in the course of the past 60 years?

Comprehension

2 What are the main differences between the U.S. occupation of Iraq and the Vietnam War?
3 Why does the author think that significant parallels between Iraq and Vietnam may be less in what is happening on the battlefield than at home?
4 What is the international support for both campaigns like?
5 Why are historical experience, familiarity with the culture, and speaking the language of a foreign country so important in military commitments like Vietnam and Iraq?
6 What do opinion polls show about the American people's attitudes toward both conflicts?

Analysis

7 Make a list of all the technical terms used in this text which are related to military aspects.
8 Analyze the cartoon (p. 244). Explain the message and relate it to the statements made in the article.

Opinion

9 Should the United States as the only remaining superpower after the end of the Cold War expand its military effort to defeat terrorism, prevent the development of weapons of mass destruction and/or establish democracies overseas?
10 Military force, diplomacy, international organizations like the United Nations, trade policies and economic programs could be used to achieve foreign policy goals. Discuss the efficiency and justification of the different approaches to solving international problems.

Internet Project

11 Working in groups, find out about the widespread global U.S. troop deployment at present. As a starting point, use the material offered under www.globalsecurity.org/military/ops/global-deployments.htm.

15

New York City

In 1626 Peter Minuit bought Manhattan for goods valued at the legendary sum of $24 and founded Niew *Amsterdam*. In 1664 the British conquered the town and renamed it *New York*. In 1898 New York merged with Brooklyn, itself the third-largest city in America, and with 38 towns and villages in Queens, Staten Island, and the Bronx, to create the five-borough metropolis of *Greater New York*. For the past two centuries, New York has been the largest and wealthiest American city, and its ethnic diversity, religious variety, and commercial success have made it the most attractive urban center in the country with the most famous skyline in the world.

Aerial view of Midtown Manhattan

There are more Jews in New York than in Tel Aviv, more Italians than in Naples, more Irish than in Dublin, and more Puerto Ricans than in San Juan. And many parts of the city have become emblems that are known throughout the world: *Wall Street* stands for finance, *Broadway* for theater, *Fifth Avenue* for shopping, *Seventh Avenue* for fashion, *Madison Avenue* for advertising, *Greenwich Village* for bohemian lifestyles, *Harlem* for African American

The pre-9/11-skyline from Ellis Island

The 'Tip' from the Staten Island Ferry

culture, the *U.N. Headquarters* for international politics, and the *Metropolitan* or the *Guggenheim* for world-class museums. The 'Big Apple' is a city of contradictions, and while visitors may experience it as a bewildering place of hustle and bustle, for its residents it is a mosaic of local neighborhoods with distinct customs and values.

Here are some essential figures:

In 2005, New York City had a population of 8,143,197 with a density of 10,316 people per square kilometer. The population of the Metropolitan Area was 18,747,320.

In 2005, 42.6 million visitors spent $22.8 billion in New York, slept in one of the city's 71,000 hotel rooms (at an average room rate of $243), and ate in one of New York's 18,696 restaurants (at an average dinner price of $37.61). Most of them came through one of the three airports: John F. Kennedy International (JFK), LaGuardia (LGA), and Newark Liberty International (EWR), which in 2005 serviced 99.8 million passengers with 1.19 million flights.

On an average weekday in 2005, the Metropolitan Transit Authority (MTA) transported 4.5 million people in its 6,200 subway cars, 2.4 million people in its 4,489 buses, and 65,000 people on the Staten Island Ferry. The number of passengers transported per day by the total system (subway, buses, commuter rail) was 7,785,174.

New York City has 12,778 licensed taxis, and according to the 2000 Census it is the only locality in the U.S. where more than half of all households do not own a car (the Manhattan figure is even over 75%, with the national rate being 8%).

the Big Apple

Columbia University

New York is a different country. Maybe it ought to have a separate government. Everybody thinks differently, acts differently. They just don't know what the hell the rest of the United States is.
Henry Ford

New York City has
- 34 universities and colleges
- 42 Broadway theaters (which, in the 2003/04 season, drew more than 11 million visitors)
- about 90 Off-Broadway theaters
- 25 concert halls
- 375 movie theaters
- about 120 museums and 600 art galleries

Times Square at night

New York City has
- about 6,400 miles of streets
- 578 miles of waterfront
- about 720 miles of subway track
- 26,138 acres of parks, with the Central Park alone comprising 843 acres

According to the Census 2000, New York City's ethnic makeup was as follows:

White	44.7%
Hispanic or Latino	27,0%
African American	26.6%
Asian	9,8%
American Indian and Alaska native	0,4%
Other races	13.4%
Persons reporting two or more races	4.9%
Foreign-born persons	35.9%
Language other than English spoken at home at age 5+	47.6%

[Hispanics may be of any race, so they are also included in other categories.]

Brooklyn Bridge

New York City produces
- about 11,000 tons per day of residential waste
- about 10,000 tons per day of commercial waste
- about 26,000 tons per day of construction and demolition debris.

Since the Fresh Kills landfill has been closed, New York City no longer has any operating waste disposal facilities (landfills or incinerators) within its borders. As a result, the Department of Sanitation (DSNY) must export all waste produced in New York that is not recycled or composted, to disposal facilities located outside of the city.

You will have heard of our taking of New Amsterdam ... 'Tis a place of great importance to trade. It did belong to England heretofore, but the Dutch by degrees did drive our people out and built a very good town, but we have got the better of it and now 'tis called New York.
King Charles II

1

Fred Ebb; Edward Field

"New York, New York"; "New York"

There are countless poems and songs about New York City. The best known song is the theme song from Martin Scorcese's 1977 film *New York, New York*, with music by John Kander and lyrics by Fred Ebb, sung in the film by Liza Minelli. Two years later, this song was most famously recorded by Frank Sinatra, and it has become a highly popular celebration of New York, played at many social events. – Among the poems, Edward Field's "New York," which appeared in the same year as Scorcese's film as the opening text of his collection *A Full Heart* (1977), evokes a much more complex image of "the city that never sleeps." – "New York, New York," from http://www.brave.com/bo/lyrics/nyny.htm; "New York" from *New York Observed: Artists and Writers Look at the City, 1650 to the Present*, ed. by Barbara Cohen, Seymour Chwast and Steven Heller (New York: Harry M. Abrams, 1987), p. 116.

"New York, New York"

Start spreading the news
I'm leaving today
I want to be a part of it, New York, New York
These vagabond shoes
Are longing to stray
And make a brand new start of it
New York, New York
I want to wake up in the city that never sleeps
To find I'm king of the hill, top of the heap
These little town blues
Are melting away
I'll make a brand new start of it
In old New York
If I can make it there
I'll make it anywhere
It's up to you, New York, New York.
I want to wake up in the city that never sleeps
To find I'm king of the hill, top of the heap
These little town blues
Are melting away
I'll make a brand new start of it
In old New York
If I can make it there
I'll make it anywhere
It's up to you, New York, New York.

Inside the Trump Tower

"New York"

I live in a beautiful place, a city
people claim to be astonished
when you say you live there.
They talk of junkies, muggings, dirt, and noise,
missing the point completely.

I tell them where they live it is hell,
a land of frozen people.
They never think of people.

Home, I am astonished by this environment
that is also a form of nature
like those paradises of trees and grass
but this is a people paradise
where we are the creatures mostly
though thank God for dogs, cats, sparrows, and
roaches.

This vertical place is no more an accident
than the Himalayas are.
The city needs all those tall buildings
to contain the tremendous energy here.
The landscape is in a state of balance.
We do God's will whether we know it or not:
Where I live the streets end in a river of sunlight.

Nowhere else in the country do people
show just what they feel –
we don't put on any act.
Look at the way New Yorkers
walk down the street. It says,
I don't care. What nerve,
to dare to live their dreams, or nightmares,
and no one bothers to look.

True, you have to be an expert to live here.
Part of the trick is not to go anywhere, lounge about,
go slowly in the midst of the rush for novelty.
Anyway, beside the eats the big event here
is the streets which are full of love –
we hug and kiss a lot. You can't say that
for anywhere else around. For some
it is the sex part they care about and get –
there's all the opportunity in the world if you want it.

For me it is different:
Out walking, my soul seeks its food.
It knows what it wants.
Instantly it recognizes its mate, our eyes meet,
and our beings exchange a vital energy,
the universe goes on Charge
and we pass by without holding.

The Woolworth Building (1913; 241 meters)

Vocabulary

Song: 10 little town blues: blues, i.e. low spirits, melancholy bred by living in a boring little town – **Poem: 4 mugging** (n.): an attack on s.o. in which they are robbed in a public place – **15 roach** (n.): (AmE infm. for) **cockroach**, a large black insect often found in old or dirty houses – **25 to put on an act:** to play a role – **32 to lounge about** (v.): to spend time doing nothing – **34 the eats** (n. pl.): (infml.) food, esp. for a party – **45 to go on charge:** to take in a charge of electricity, here used metaphorically

Explanations

4 junkie (n.): (sl.) a person who habitually takes a drug such as heroin and is dependent on it. Attempts to end the sale and use of drugs through law enforcement began in 1973, when a new law was enacted which mandated minimum prison terms for offenses that earlier had been punishable only by probation. This law greatly increased the number of drug offenders in prison, but it did not diminish the use of drugs. During the 1970s cocaine regained popularity, and when in the mid-1980s there surfaced a smokable form of cocaine known as 'crack,' it was generally realized that cocaine was a dangerous drug leading to violence and paranoia. The fear of the effects of crack triggered an increased emphasis on law enforcements, which filled the courts and prisons with drug offenders. When in the 1980s it became clear that AIDS was being spread rapidly by shared hypodermic needles, attention shifted again to intravenous drug users. In the mid-1990s it was estimated that there were 500,000 drug addicts in New York, including 200,000 heroin addicts.

AWARENESS

1 Imagine a young person from Germany preparing to move to New York to make "a brand new start of it." Sketch her/his feelings, expectations, fears, etc.

COMPREHENSION

2 What are the implications of ll. 14f. and 23f. of the song?
3 What does Field mean when he maintains that one has to be "an expert" (l. 31) to live in New York City?

OPINION

4 Is the song just a sentimental variation of the myth of a new beginning, or is it confirmed by reality? Give reasons for your position.

ANALYSIS

5 Analyze the form of Field's poem.
6 Sum up the major steps of Field's arguments in prose.

PROJECT

7 Get hold of the text of 50 Cent's "Rotten Apple" and compare his image of New York with that of Sinatra's song and Field's poem (http://www.azlyrics.com/lyrics/50cent/rotten-apple.html).

A back alley in the Lower East Side

2

E. B. White

"Here is New York"

No one has captured New York City as efficiently as the humorist, essayist, and children's writer E. B. White (1899–1985). His famous essay was written in two days in a hot hotel room in the summer of 1948 and first published in 1949. Its often quoted opening sentence introduces a brilliant portrait that describes New York's contradictory components in a convincing way. – The excerpt is taken from *Writing New York: A Literary Anthology*, ed. by Phillip Lopate (New York: Literary Classics of the United States, 1998), pp. 693, 696f., and 699.

On any person who desires such queer prizes, New York will bestow the gift of loneliness and the gift of privacy. It is this largess that accounts for the presence within the city's walls of a considerable section of the population; for the residents of Manhattan are to a large extent strangers who have pulled up stakes somewhere and come to town, seeking sanctuary or fulfillment or some greater or lesser grail. The capacity to make such dubious gifts is a mysterious quality of New York. It can destroy an individual or it can fulfill him, depending a good deal on luck. No one should come to New York to live unless he is willing to be lucky.

The Stock Exchange

New York is the concentrate of art and commerce and sport and religion and entertainment and finance, bringing to a single compact arena the gladiator, the evangelist, the promoter, the actor, the trader and the merchant. It carries on its lapel the unexpungeable odor of the long past, so that no matter where you sit in New York you feel the vibrations of great times and tall deeds, of queer people and events and undertakings.

[…]

There are roughly three New Yorks. There is, first, the New York of the man or woman who was born here, who takes the city for granted and accepts its size and its turbulence as natural and inevitable. Second, there is the New York of the commuter – the city that is devoured by locusts each day and spat out each night. Third, there is the New York of the person who was born somewhere else and came to New York in quest of something. Of these three trembling cities the greatest is the last – the city of final destination, the city that is a goal. It is this third city that accounts for New York's high-strung disposition, its poetical deportment, its dedication to the arts, and its incomparable achievements. Commuters give the city its tidal restlessness; natives give it solidity and continuity; but the settlers give it passion. And whether it is a farmer arriving from Italy to set up a small grocery store in a slum, or a young girl arriving from a small town in Mississippi to escape the indignity of being observed by her neighbors, or a boy arriving from the Corn Belt with a manuscript in his suitcase and a pain in his heart, it makes no difference: each embraces New York with the intense excitement of first love, each absorbs New York with the fresh eyes of an adventurer, each generates heat and light to dwarf the Consolidated Edison Company.

[…]

Manhattan has been compelled to expand skyward because of the absence of any other direction in which to grow. This, more than any other thing, is responsible for its physical majesty. It is to the nation what the white church spire is to the village – the visible symbol of aspiration and faith, the white plume saying that the way is up.

[…]

South Street Seaport

Vocabulary

1 queer (adj.): (old-fash.) strange or difficult to explain – **3 largess(e)** /lɑːˈʒes/ (n.): generosity – **6 to pull up stakes:** (infml.) to leave your job or home – **7 sanctuary** (n.): a peaceful place that is safe and provides protection, esp. for people who are in danger – **8 grail** (n.): s.th. that people want very much, but which is very difficult or impossible to achieve – **8 dubious** (adj.): probably not good or not of good quality – **23 unexpungeable** (adj.): s.th. that cannot be expunged, i.e., removed or made forgotten – **24 odor** BrE **odour** (n.): a smell, esp. an unpleasant one – **35 locust** (n.): an insect that lives mainly in Asia and Africa and flies in a very large group, eating and destroying crops – **37 quest** (n.): (lit.) a long search for s.th. that is difficult to find (in connection with "grail" it refers to the Quest for the Holy Grail) – **41 high-strung**; BrE **highly strung** (adj.): nervous and easily upset or excited – **41 deportment** (n.): (old-fash., esp. AmE) the way that s.o. behaves in public – **43 tidal** (adj.): relating to the regular rising and falling of the sea – **54 to dwarf** (v.): to be so big that other things are made to seem very small – **61 aspiration** (n.): a strong desire to have or achieve s.th. – **61 plume** /pluːm/ (n.): a cloud of smoke, dust, etc. which rises up into the air; a large feather or bunch of feathers, esp. one used as a decoration on a hat

The Flatiron Building, one of New York's earliest skyscrapers (1902, 91 meters) on 175 Fifth Avenue

When an American stays away from New York too long, something happens to him. Perhaps he becomes a little provincial, a little dead, a little afraid.
Sherwood Anderson

Explanations

49 Corn Belt: the area of the middle west US in which most corn (BE maize) is grown, esp. Iowa, Illinois, and Indiana as well as parts of other states – **54 Consolidated Edison Company:** the electric utility that provides gas and electricity to most of New York City, formed in 1884. In the mid 1990s Con Edison had over $10,000 million in assets and 19,000 employees, and sold nearly 40,000 million kilowatt-hours of electricity to about three million customers.

Awareness

1 Since you have certainly seen reports about or films taking place in New York City or perhaps even been there yourself, make (a) a list of the places you know about and (b) a list of associations you have when you hear the name of the city.

Comprehension

2 What does White mean when he maintains that one of the most crowded cities can provide "the gift of loneliness and [...] privacy" (l. 2)?
3 Which are the "three New Yorks" (l. 30) that White distinguishes in his essay?
4 What, according to White, is responsible for New York's "physical majesty" (l. 59)?

Internet Project

5 Form four groups and use the data provided on pp. 246f. and facts collected from relevant Internet addresses to assemble information about such central aspects of New York as (a) transportation, (b) ethnic diversity, (c) sanitation, and (d) crime. Relevant material for (a) is provided in the MTA Annual Reports (http://www.mta.nyc.ny.us/), for (b) in the US Census data for New York City (http://quickfacts.census.gov/qfd/states/36/3651000.html), for (c) by the New York Department of Sanitation (http://www.nyc.gov/html/dsny/html/home/home.shtml) and for (d) by the New York City Police Department (http://www.nyc.gov/html/nypd/).

3

Abraham Cahan

"The Meeting"*

Cahan's short novel *Yekl* (1896) deals with the life of East European Jewish immigrants around 1890. Yekl is a young Russian Jew, who has been living in the U.S. for three years while his wife Gitl and their son stayed behind in Povodye in Russia. The excerpt depicts the family's reunion on Ellis Island, where a nervous Yekl, who has Americanized his name to Jake, meets his wife and son. – Abraham Cahan, *Yekl and the Imported Bridegroom and Other Stories of Yiddish New York* (New York: Dover Publications, 1970), pp. 33–38.

A few weeks later, on a Saturday morning, Jake, with an unfolded telegram in his hand, stood in front of one of the desks at the Immigration Bureau of Ellis Island. He was freshly shaven and clipped, smartly dressed in his best clothes and ball shoes, and in spite of the sickly expression of shamefacedness and anxiety which distorted his features, he looked younger than usual.

All the way to the island he had been in a flurry of joyous anticipation. The prospect of meeting his dear wife and child, and, incidentally, of showing off his swell attire to her, had thrown him into a fever of impatience. But on entering the big shed he had caught a distant glimpse of Gitl and Yosselé through the railing separating the detained immigrants from their visitors, and his heart had sunk at the sight of his wife's uncouth and un-American appearance. She was slovenly dressed in a brown jacket and skirt of grotesque cut, and her hair was concealed under a voluminous wig of a pitch-black hue. This she had put on just before leaving the steamer, both "in honor of the Sabbath" and by way of sprucing herself up for the great event. Since Yekl had left home she had gained considerably in the measurement of her waist. The wig, however, made her seem stouter and shorter than she would have appeared without it. It also added at least five years to her looks. But she was aware neither of this nor of the fact that in New York even a Jewess of her station and orthodox breeding is accustomed to blink at the wickedness of displaying her natural hair, and that none but an elderly matron may wear a wig without being the occasional target for snowballs or stones. She was naturally dark of complexion, and the nine or ten days at sea had covered her face with a deep bronze, which combined with her prominent cheek bones, inky little eyes, and, above all, the smooth black wig, to lend her resemblance to a squaw.

The Great Hall on Ellis Island filled with newly arrived immigrants

Hester Street in 1890

Jake had no sooner caught sight of her than he had averted his face, as if loth to rest his eyes on her, in the presence of the surging crowd around him, before it was inevitable. He dared not even survey that crowd to see whether it contained any acquaintance of his, and he vaguely wished that her release were delayed indefinitely.

Presently the officer behind the desk took the telegram from him, and in another little while Gitl, hugging Yosselé with one arm and a bulging parcel with the other, emerged from a side door.

Orchard Street

"Yekl!" she screamed out in a piteous high key, as if crying for mercy.

"Dot'sh alla right!" he returned in English, with a wan smile and unconscious of what she was saying. His wandering eyes and dazed mind were striving to fix themselves upon the stern functionary and the questions he bethought himself of asking before finally releasing his prisoners. The contrast between Gitl and Jake was so striking that the officer wanted to make sure – partly as a matter of official duty and partly for the fun of the thing – that the two were actually man and wife.

"*Oi* a lamentation upon me! He shaves his beard!" Gitl ejaculated to herself as she scrutinized her husband. "Yosselé, look! Here is *taté*!"

But Yosselé did not care to look at taté. Instead, he turned his frightened little eyes – precise copies of Jake's – and buried them in his mother's cheek.

When Gitl was finally discharged she made to fling herself on Jake. But he checked her by seizing both loads from her arms. He started for a distant and deserted corner of the room, bidding her to follow. For a moment the boy looked stunned, then he burst out crying and fell to kicking his father's chest with might and main, his reddened little face appealingly turned to Gitl. Jake continuing his way tried to kiss his son into toleration, but the little fellow proved too nimble for him, it was in vain that Gitl, scurrying behind, kept expostulating with Yosselé: "Why, it is taté!" Taté was forced to capitulate before the march was brought to its end.

At length when the secluded corner had been reached, and Jake and Gitl had set down their burdens, husband and wife flew into mutual embrace and fell to kissing each other. The performance had an effect of something done to order, which, it must be owned, was far from being belied by the state of their minds at the moment. Their kisses imparted the taste of mutual estrangement to both. In Jake's case the sensation was quickened by the strong steerage odors which were emitted by Gitl's person, and he involuntarily recoiled.

"You look like a *poritz*," she said shyly.

"How are you? How is mother?"

"How should she be? So, so. She sends you her love," Gitl mumbled out.

"How long was father ill?"

"Maybe a month. He cost us health enough."

He proceeded to make advances to Yosselé, she appealing to the child in his behalf. For a moment the sight of her, as they were both crouching before the boy, precipitated a wave of thrilling memories on Jake and made him feel in his own environment. Presently, however, the illusion took wing and here he was, Jake the Yankee, with this bonnetless, wigged, dowdyish little greenhorn by his side! That she was his wife, nay, that he was married at all, seemed incredible to him. The sturdy, thriving urchin had at first inspired him with pride; but as he now cast another side glance at Gitl's wig he lost all interest in him, and began to regard him, together with his mother, as one great obstacle dropped from heaven, as it were, in his way.

Gitl on her part, was overcome by a feeling akin to awe. She, too, could not get herself to realize that this stylish young man – shaved and dressed as in Povodye is only some young nobleman – was Yekl, her own Yekl, who had all these three years never been absent from her mind. And while she was once more examining Jake's blue diagonal cutaway, glossy stand-up collar, the white four-in-hand necktie, coquettishly tucked away in the bosom of his starched shirt, and, above all, his patent leather shoes, she was at the same time mentally scanning the Yekl of three years before. The latter alone was hers, and she felt like crying to the image to come back to her and let her be *his* wife.

Presently, when they had got up and Jake was plying her with perfunctory questions, she chanced to recognize a certain movement of his upper lip – an old trick of his. It was as is she had suddenly discovered her own Yekl in an apparent stranger, and, with another pitiful outcry she fell on his breast.

"Don't!" he said, with patient gentleness, pushing away her arms. "Here everything is so different."

She colored deeply.

"They don't wear wigs here," he ventured to add.

"What then?" she asked perplexedly.

"You will see. It is quite another world."

"Shall I take it off then? I have a nice Saturday kerchief," she faltered. "It is of silk – I bought it at Kalmen's for a bargain. It is still brand new."

"Here one does not wear even a kerchief."

"How then? Do they go about with their own hair?" she queried in ill-disguised bewilderment.

"*Vell, alla right*, put it on, quick!"

As she set about undoing her parcel, she bade him face about and screen her, so that neither he nor any stranger could see her bareheaded while she was replacing the wig by the kerchief. He obeyed. All the while the operation lasted he stood with his gaze on the floor, gnashing his teeth with disgust and shame, or hissing some Bowery oath.

A Lower East Side store for "Hebrew Religious Articles"

"Is this better?" she asked bashfully, when her hair and part of her forehead were hidden under a kerchief of flaming blue and yellow, whose end dangled off her back.

The kerchief had a rejuvenating effect. But Jake thought that it made her look like an Italian woman of Mulberry Street on Sunday.

"*Alla right*, leave it be for the present," he said in despair, reflecting that the wig would have been the lesser evil of the two.

When they reached the city Gitl was shocked to see him lead the way to a horse car.

"*Oi* woe is me! Why, it is Sabbath!" she gasped.

He irately essayed to explain that a car, being an uncommon sort of vehicle, riding in it implied no violation of the holy day. But this she sturdily met by reference to railroads. Besides, she had seen horse cars while stopping in Hamburg, and knew that no orthodox Jew would use them on the seventh day. At length Jake, losing all self-control, fiercely commanded her not to make him the laughingstock of the people on the street and to get in without further ado. As to the sin of the matter he was willing to take it all upon himself. Completely dismayed by his stern manner, amid the strange, uproarious, forbidding surroundings, Gitl yielded.

As the horses started she uttered a groan of consternation and remained looking aghast and with a violently throbbing heart. If she had been a culprit on the way to the gallows she could not have been more terrified than she was now at this her first ride on the day of rest.

The conductor came up for their fares. Jake handed him a ten-cent piece, and raising two fingers, he roared out: "Two! He ain' no maur as tree years, de liddle feller!" And so great was the impression which his dashing manner and his English produced on Gitl, that for some time it relieved her mind and she even forgot to be shocked by the sight of her husband handling coin on the Sabbath.

Having thus paraded before his wife, Jake all at once grew kindly disposed toward her.

"You must be hungry?" he asked.

"Not at all! Where do you get your *varimess*?"

"Don't say varimess," he corrected her complaisantly; "here it is called *dinner*."

"*Dinner*? And if one becomes fatter?" she confusedly ventured an irresistible pun.

This was the way in which Gitl came to receive her first lesson in the five or six score English words and phrases which the omnivorous Jewish jargon has absorbed in the Ghettos of English-speaking countries.

Vocabulary

4 clipped (adj.): with short cut hair – **8 flurry** (n.): sudden confusion or excitement – **11 swell:** (adj.): AmE very good, excellent – **11 attire** (n.): clothes, dress – **14 to detain** (v.): to prevent from leaving for a certain time – **16 uncouth** /ʌn'kuːθ/ (adj.): not having good manners, awkward and impolite in speech and behavior – **17 slovenly** /'slʊvənlɪ/ (adj.): (of habits) not neat, clean or orderly; untidy – **19 wig** (n.): artificial hair, used to hide one's real hair or lack of hair – **21 to spruce o.s. up** (v.): to make o.s. clean and tidy – **24 stout** (adj.): fairly fat and heavy, or having a thick body – **28 breeding** (n.): here: education – **29 to blink** (v.): here: to seem not at all surprised – **29 wickedness** (n.): here: sin – **36 squaw** (n.): (old use, now considered offensive) a Native American woman – **38 to avert your eyes, gaze, etc.** (v.): to look away from s.th. so that you do not see it – **38 loth** /ləʊθ/ (adj.): unwilling – **47 piteous** /'pɪtiəs/ (adj.): (lit.) expressing suffering and sadness in a way that makes you feel pity – **49 wan** /wɒn, wɑːn/ (adj.): ill, weak, and tired – **52 functionary** (n.): s.o. who has a job doing unimportant or boring official duties – **58 *oi*:** a Yiddish ejaculation expressing a.th. from ecstasy to horror – **59 to scrutinize** (v.): to examine s.o. or s.th. very carefully – **60 *taté*:** Yiddish for "dad" or "papa" – **68 stunned** (adj.): shocked, surprised – **72 nimble** (adj.): quick and light in movement – **73 to scurry** (v.): to move hastily, esp. with short quick steps – **73 to expostulate** (v.): (fml.) to express strong disapproval, disagreement, or annoyance with s.o. – **81 to belie** (v.): to give a false idea of; to show (hopes, promises) to be false or mistaken - **84 steerage** (n.): the part of a passenger ship where people who had the cheapest tickets used to travel in the past - **85 to recoil** (v.): to move back suddenly and quickly - **86** ***poritz***: Yiddish for "nobleman" - **95 to precipitate** (v.): to make happen sooner, to hasten - **98 dowdy(ish)** (adj.): (esp. of a woman) dressed in a dull and unattractive way - **101 sturdy** (adj.): strong and firm - **101 urchin** (n.): (old-fash.) a small dirty and untidy child - **106 akin** (adj.): having the same appearance, character or nature; similar - **112 cutaway** (n.): tailcoat; a man's coat with a long back divided into two below the waist - **113 four-in-hand necktie** (n.): a necktie tied in a simple slipknot - **114 starched** (adj.): stiffened with starch (*Stärke*) - **119 to ply s.o. with s.th.** (phr. v.): to keep supplying s.o. with s.th. - **120 perfunctory** (adj.): done hastily and without thought, interest or care - **120 to chance to do s.th.** (v.): (lit.) to happen in a way which is not expected and not planned - **131 kerchief** (n.): scarf - **132 to falter** (v.): to say in a weak and broken manner - **136 to query** (v.): to express doubt or uncertainty about - **143 to gnash one's teeth** (v.): to strike one's teeth together - **148 rejuvenating** (adj.): making s.o. feel or look young and strong again - **157 irately** (adv.): in a very angry way because one's moral feelings have been offended - **164 laughingstock** (n.): s.o. or s.th. that is regarded as foolish and causes unkind laughter - **172 uproarious** (adj.): very noisy - **178 aghast** (adj.): suddenly filled with great surprise, fear, and shock - **181 culprit** (n.): a person guilty of a crime or responsible for a problem - **189 dashing** (adj.): wearing nice clothes and being attractive and confident - **196** ***varimess***: Yiddish for "dinner," whereas *dinner* = Yiddish for "thinner" - **202 score** (n.): a group of twenty, or about twenty, people or things - **203 omnivorous** /ɒm'nɪvərəs/ (adj.): (esp. of animals) eating everything, both plant and animal food

Explanations

3 Ellis Island: an island of about eleven hectares in Upper New York Bay southwest of Manhattan, which was long the site of an arsenal and a fort, but became famous when it replaced Castle Garden as the country's chief immigration station in 1892. Today the island, which sometimes received as many as 15,000 immigrants in one day, is an outstanding museum. - **21 Sabbath:** Hebrew for "rest" or "cessation of labor," the Jews' day of rest and worship. The Sabbath begins just before sunset on Friday and ends at sundown on Saturday. Strict rules as to cleanliness, meals, and the abstention from work have to be observed on the Sabbath. - **144 Bowery:** a street in lower Manhattan that stretches for about one mile from Chatham Square to Cooper Square and derives its name from Dutch *bowerij* = farm. For a time it was an elegant entertainment area with many theaters, but after the Civil War it turned into a site of cheap lodging houses, missions and late-night saloons, and 'Bowery' became synonymous with homeless derelicts and tramps. - **150 Mulberry Street:** In Yekl's days, Mulberry Bend was a mainly Italian area with wretched tenements and liquor stores, known for some of the worst overcrowding in New York. Today, Mulberry Street is the center of New York's shrinking Little Italy, leading into Chinatown.

Awareness

1 By the end of the 19th century, many immigrants who had found jobs and earned some money in the U.S. paid for the passage of their families, who had stayed behind in the old countries, and met them on Ellis Island. Imagine their meeting, after a long separation, and try to reconstruct the emotions and expectations of the (assimilated) father and the ("greenhorn") mother and child(ren).

Comprehension

2 What is the significance of (a) Gitl's wig and (b) her unwillingness to board a car.

3 What is the meaning of the "irresistible pun" (l. 200)?

Analysis

4 Analyze the cultural, the social, and the metaphorical implications of the meeting between "Jake the Yankee" (ll. 97f.) and Gitl, the Eastern European Jewish woman.

Opinion

5 How do you assess Jake's behavior? State your reasons.

6 What do you think about the family's future?

7 Do you think one can draw parallels between the USA immigrants at the end of the 19th century and the immigrants coming to Germany today? Discuss (Reference Library, p. 299).

Internet Projects

8 Use the excellent material provided under http://www.ellisisland.org to prepare reports on the immigration experience of different nationalities.

9 Use the hypertext edition of Jacob Riis' famous book *How the Other Half Lives* (http://www.yale.edu/amstud/inforev/riis) and some of his photos available under http://www.masters-of-photography.com//R/riis/riis.html to research (a) the distribution of the different nationalities on the Lower East Side, (b) the conditions of life in the tenement houses, (c) the sanitary problems in the ghetto, and (d) the problem of crime.

4

Paul Auster

Moon Palace

In his novel *Moon Palace* (1989), Paul Auster tells the story of Marco Stanley Fogg, whose life is slowly running down to a penniless and hopeless existence. When he finally even loses his rooms, he makes Central Park his home. – Paul Auster, *Moon Palace* (London: Faber and Faber, 1990), pp. 56-58.

Info

Central Park

A public park in Manhattan, covering 340 hectares, bounded to the north by 110th Street, to the east by 5th Avenue, to the south by 59th Street (Central Park South), and to the west by Central Park West. It was the first landscaped public park in the U.S. Advocates of its construction were mostly wealthy merchants and landowners who wanted New York to have public grounds similar to those of London and Paris and who also believed that a park would provide workers with a healthful alternative to the saloon. The 1857 contest for a suitable design was won by Frederick Law Olmsted and Calvert Vaux, and it called for a combination of the pastoral (open rolling meadows), the picturesque (the Ramble), and the formal (the Promenade and Bethesda Terrace). The construction of the park was one of the most extensive public works projects. About 20,000 workers removed 2.3 million cubic meters of soil, planted more than 270,000 trees, and built a large reservoir. The park opened to the public in the winter of 1859, and by 1865 it had more than seven million visitors a year. Later, ever new facilities (a carousel, tennis, bicycling, a zoo, etc.) were added; during the sixties the park became a symbol of both urban revival and the counter-culture (with rock concerts and be-ins), during the seventies lack of money led to severe problems, but meanwhile a private fund-raising body, the Central Park Conservancy, sees to it that the park is well kept and functions as the green lung of the metropolis.

Central Park South from the Lake

1 I slept in the park every night after that. It became a sanctuary for me, a refuge of inwardness against the grinding demands of the streets. There were eight hundred and forty acres to roam in, and unlike the massive gridwork of buildings and towers that loomed outside the perimeter, the park offered me the possibility of solitude, of separating myself from the rest of the world. In the streets, everything is bodies and commotion, and like it or not, you cannot enter them without adhering to a rigid protocol of behavior. To walk among the crowd means never going faster than anyone else, never lagging behind your neighbor, never doing anything to disrupt the flow of human traffic. If you play by the rules of this game, people will tend to ignore you. There is a particular glaze that comes over the eyes of New Yorkers when they walk through the streets, a natural and perhaps necessary form of indifference to others. It doesn't matter how you look, for example. Outrageous costumes, bizarre hairdos, T-shirts with obscene slogans printed across them – no one pays attention to such things. On the other hand, the way you act inside your clothes is of utmost importance. Odd gestures of any kind are automatically taken as a threat. Talking out loud to yourself, scratching your body, looking someone directly in the eye: these deviations can trigger off hostile and sometimes violent reactions from those around you. You must not stagger or swoon, you must not clutch the walls, you must not sing, for all forms of spontaneous or involuntary behavior are sure to elicit stares, caustic remarks, and even an occasional shove or kick in the shins. I was not so far gone that I received any treatment of that sort, but I saw it happen to others, and I knew that a

The Great Lawn

Spring in Central Park

day might eventually come when I wouldn't be able to control myself anymore. By contrast, life in Central Park allowed for a much broader range of variables. No one thought twice if you stretched out on the grass and went to sleep in the middle of the day. No one blinked if you sat under a tree and did nothing, if you played your clarinet, if you howled at the top of your lungs. Except for the office workers who lurked around the fringes of the park at lunch hour, the majority of people who came in there acted as if they were on holiday. The same things that would have alarmed them in the streets were dismissed as casual amusements. People smiled at each other and held hands, bent their bodies into unusual shapes, kissed. It was live and let live, as long as you did not actively interfere with what others were doing, you were free to do what you liked.

There is no question that the park did me a world of good. It gave me privacy, but more than that, it allowed me to pretend that I was not as bad off as I really was. The grass and the trees were democratic, and as I loafed in the sunshine of a late afternoon, or climbed among the rocks in the early evening to look for a place to sleep, I felt that I was blending into the environment, that even to a practiced eye I could have passed for one of the picnickers or strollers around me. The streets did not allow for such delusions. Whenever I walked out among the crowds, I was quickly shamed into an awareness of myself. I felt like a speck, a vagabond, a pox of failure on the skin of mankind. Each day, I became a little dirtier than I had been the day before, a little more ragged and confused, a little more different from everyone else. In the park, I did not have to carry around this burden of self-consciousness. It gave me a threshold, a boundary, a way to distinguish between the inside and the outside. If the streets forced me to see myself as others saw me, the park gave me a chance to return to my inner life, to hold on to myself purely in terms of what was happening inside me. It is possible to survive without a roof over your head, I discovered, but you cannot live without establishing an equilibrium between the inner and outer. The park did that for me. It was not quite a home, perhaps, but for want of any other shelter, it came very close.

Unexpected things keep happening to me in there, things that seem almost impossible to me as I remember them now. Once, for example, a young woman with bright red hair walked up to me and put a five-dollar bill in my hand – just like that, without any explanation at all. Another time, a group of people invited me to join them on the grass for a picnic lunch. A few days after that, I spent the whole afternoon playing in a softball game. Considering my physical condition at the time, I turned in a creditable performance (two or three singles, a diving catch in the left field), and whenever my team was at bat, the other players kept offering me things to eat and drink and smoke: sandwiches and pretzels, cans of beer, cigars, cigarettes. Those were happy moments for me, and they helped to carry me through some of the darker stretches when my luck seemed to have run out. Perhaps that was all I had set out to prove in the first place: that once you throw your life to the winds, you will discover things you had never known before, things that cannot be learned under any other circumstances. I was half-dead from hunger, but whenever something good happened to me, I did not attribute this to chance so much as to a special state of mind. If I was able to maintain a proper balance between desire and indifference, I felt that I could somehow will the universe to respond to me. How else was I to judge the extraordinary acts of generosity that I experienced in Central Park? I never asked anyone for anything, I never budged from my spot, and yet strangers were continually coming up to me and giving me help.

Sunday morning cyclists in the Park

Vocabulary

2 sanctuary (n.): a peaceful place that is safe and provides protection, esp. for people who are in danger – **2 refuge** (n.): a place that provides protection or shelter from danger – **3 grinding** (adj.): making your life very difficult and unhappy, and never seeming to improve – **5 grid(work)** (n.): a pattern of straight lines that cross each other and form squares – **5 to loom** (v.): to come into sight without a clear form, esp. as to seem very large and threatening – **6 perimeter** /pəˈrɪmɪtə(r) (n.): the border around any enclosed space or special area of ground – **8 commotion** (n.): sudden noisy activity – **12 to lag behind** (v.): to move or develop more slowly than others – **15 glaze** (n.): an expression showing that you are not interested or tired – **19 outrageous** (adj.): extremely unusual and slightly amusing or shocking – **26 deviation** (n.): noticeable difference from what is expected, esp. from accepted standards of behavior – **28 to swoon** (v.): to faint; to lose consciousness – **30 to elicit** (v.): to succeed in drawing out (facts, information, etc.) from s.o., esp. after much effort – **30 caustic** (adj.): showing strong dislike or disapproval, and intended to hurt – **42 fringe** (n.): the part farthest from the center, edge – **55 to loaf** (v.): to waste time, esp. by not working when one should – **64 speck** (n.): a very small piece, spot, or colored mark – **64 pox** (n.): here: the marks left by the disease – **95 to be at bat** (v.): (in baseball) to be the person or team who is trying to hit the ball

The San Remo Apartments from the Lake

Paul Auster (*1947) was born in Newark, New Jersey, and is best known for his successful *New York Trilogy*, in which he turned the American detective novel into an experimental and innovative kind of narrative. Among his other books are *The Invention of Solitude* (1982); the science-fiction novel *In the Country of Last Things* (1987); the modern bildungsroman *Moon Palace* (1989), which plays with the American myths of success and the West; *The Music of Chance* (1990), an absurdist novel about a meaningless universe; *Leviathan* (1992), a kind of anti-establishment novel; *Mr. Vertigo* (1994), the story of an orphan who learns to levitate; *Timbuktu* (1999), a tale told by a dog; *The Book of Illusions* (2002), yet another investigation of the role of chance in human life; *Oracle Night* (2002), a kind of postmodern ghost story; and *The Brooklyn Follies* (2005), a typical Auster book about loneliness, sudden reversals and coincidences. Auster, who is more famous in Europe than he is at home, has also written autobiographies and essay collections ranging from *The Art of Hunger* (1982) to *Hand to Mouth* (1997) and screenplays for several films from *Smoke* (1995) to *The Inner Life of Martin Frost* (2006). He is the Vice-President of PEN American Center, and is married to Siri Hustvedt, who is herself a successful writer.

The Tavern on the Green

Comprehension

1 What, according to Fogg, are the differences between life in the streets and life in the park?
2 What does Fogg mean by "rigid protocol of behavior" (l. 10)?

Analysis

3 What could Fogg mean by saying that "the grass and the trees were democratic" (l. 54)?
4 What is the effect of the narrative point of view (Reference Library, pp. 310f.), chosen by Auster?
5 What does the Central Park come to symbolize in Fogg's experience?

Internet Projects

6 Collect additional information about the Central Park. Start with the Central Park Conservancy's official website http://www.centralparknyc.org/.
7 Reconstruct the history of the Central Park by using relevant Internet sources.
8 Fogg's living in the park represents a major New York problem: homelessness. In August 2006 some 33,000 homeless men, women, and children were sleeping each night in the New York City shelter system, and thousands more slept on park benches and in subway trains. Collect information about this problem, starting with the material provided by the Coalition for the Homeless (http://www.coalitionforthehomeless.org/advocacy/basic_facts.html).

5

Encyclopaedia Britannica; Mary Gonzalez

The September 11 Attacks

The 9/11 attacks on the Twin Towers of New York's World Trade Center mark a crucial event not only in the history of the Big Apple, but also in that of the United States at large. The first of the following texts, taken from the *Encyclopædia Britannica 2007 Ultimate Reference Suite* (Chicago: Encyclopædia Britannica, 2006), s.v. "September 11 attacks," sums up what happened; the second, taken from the Internet (http://www.coping.org/911/memory/marypoetry.htm), is one of countless amateur poems trying to come to terms with the shock of the attack.

The Twin Towers of the World Trade Center (1974, 420 meters)

… series of airline hijackings and suicide attacks committed by 19 militants associated with the Islamic extremist group al-Qaeda against targets in the United States. The attacks caused extensive death and destruction and triggered an enormous U.S. effort to combat terrorism.

The hijackers, most of whom were from Saudi Arabia, established themselves in the United States, many well in advance of the attacks. They traveled in small groups, and some of them received commercial flight training. On September 11, 2001, groups of attackers boarded four domestic aircraft (a 20th suspected militant had been detained by U.S. authorities) at three East Coast airports and soon after takeoff disabled the crews and took control of the planes. The aircraft, all large and bound for the West Coast, had full loads of fuel.

At 8:46 AM (local time) the terrorists piloted the first plane, which had originated from Boston, into the north tower of the World Trade Center in New York City. A second plane, also from Boston, struck the south tower roughly 15 minutes later. Each structure was badly damaged by the impact and erupted into flames. A third plane, from the Washington, D.C., area, struck the southwest side of the Pentagon just outside the city at 9:40, touching off a fire in that section of the structure. Within the next hour the fourth aircraft (from Newark, New Jersey) crashed in the Pennsylvania countryside after its passengers – informed of events via cellular phone – attempted to overpower their assailants.

At 9:59 the World Trade Center's heavily damaged south tower collapsed; the north tower fell about a half hour later. A number of other buildings adjacent to the twin towers suffered serious damage, and several subsequently fell. Fires at the World Trade Center site smoldered for more than three months.

Rescue operations began almost immediately, as the country and the world sought to come to grips with the enormity of the losses. Some 2,750 people were killed in New York, 184 at the Pentagon, and 40 in Pennsylvania; all 19 terrorists died. Police and fire departments in New York were especially hard hit: hundreds had rushed to the scene of the attacks, and more than 400 police officers and firefighters were killed.

The emotional distress caused by the attacks – particularly the collapse of the twin towers, New York City's most visible landmark – was overwhelming. Unlike the relatively isolated site of the Pearl Harbor attack of 1941, to which the September 11 events were soon compared, the World Trade Center lay at the heart of one of the world's largest cities. Hundreds of thousands of people witnessed the attacks firsthand (many onlookers photographed events or recorded them with video cameras), and millions watched the tragedy unfold live on television. In the days that followed September 11, the footage of the attacks was replayed in the media countless times, as were the scenes of throngs of people, stricken with grief, gathering at "ground zero" – as the site where the towers once stood came to be known – some with photos of missing loved ones, seeking some hint of their fate.

Moreover, world markets were badly shaken; the towers were at the heart of New York's financial district, and damage to Lower Manhattan's infrastructure, combined with fears of stock market panic, kept New York markets closed for four trading days. Markets afterward suffered record losses.

Countries allied with the United States rallied to its support. Evidence gathered by the United States soon convinced most governments that the Islamic militant group al-Qaeda was responsible for the attacks. The group had been implicated in previous terrorist strikes against Americans, and its leader, Osama bin Laden, had made numerous anti-American statements. Al-Qaeda was headquartered in Afghanistan and had forged a close relationship with that country's ruling Taliban militia, which subsequently refused U.S. demands to extradite bin Laden and to terminate al-Qaeda activity there. In early October, U.S. and allied military forces launched an attack that, within months, killed or captured thousands of militants and drove Taliban and al-Qaeda leaders into hiding.

After September 11 the U.S. government exerted great effort to track down other al-Qaeda agents and sympathizers throughout the world, and it made combating terrorism the focus of U.S. foreign policy. Meanwhile, security measures within the country were tightened considerably at such places as airports, government buildings, and sports venues.

Vocabulary

1 hijacking (n.): the use of violence or threats to take control of a plane - **5 to trigger** (v.): to make s.th. happen very quickly; to initiate - **5 to combat** (v.): to fight against - **12 suspected** (adj.): s.o. who is thought to be guilty of a crime - **13 to detain** (v.): to officially prevent s.o. from leaving a place - **14 to disable** (v.): to make s.o. unable to act - **22 to erupt** (v.): to break out - **29 cellular phone** (n.): (esp. AmE) a telephone that you can carry with you and use in any place - **30 assailant** (n.): (fml.) s.o. who attacks another person - **33 adjacent** /ə'dʒeisənt/ (adj.): next to - **36 to smolder**, BrE **ou** (v.): to burn slowly without a flame - **38 to come to grips with** (v.): to understand or deal with s.th. difficult - **45 distress** (n.): a feeling of great unhappiness and pain - **55 to unfold** (v.): if a story unfolds, it is told; if events unfold, they happen - **56 footage** (n.): film material - **58 throng** (n.): crowd - **68 to rally** (v.): to come together, join - **72 to be implicated in** (v.): (usu. pass., fml.) to be the cause of, be involved in - **76 to forge** (v.): to develop s.th., esp. a relationship - **78 to extradite** /'ekstrədaɪt/ (v.): to use a legal process to send s.o. who may be guilty of a crime back to the country where the crime happened in order to judge them in a court of law - **80 to launch** (v.): to start - **89 venue** (n.): a place where an organized meeting, concert, etc. takes place

Explanations

19 World Trade Center: a complex of seven buildings, mostly designed by the Japanese-American architect Minoru Yamasaki and developed by the Port Authority of New York and New Jersey. Located in the heart of New York's downtown financial district, the complex contained 1.24 million m^2 of office space. All of the original buildings in the complex were destroyed in the 9/11 attacks: 1 WTC, 2 WTC (the North and South Towers) and 7 WTC collapsed; 3 WTC (the Marriott Hotel) was crushed by the collapse of the Twin Towers; and 4 WTC, 5 WTC, and 6 WTC were damaged beyond repair and later demolished. - **24 Pentagon:** the large five-sided building near Washington D.C. which contains the main offices of the U.S. Department of Defense, and from which the armed forces of the U.S. are directed

Ground Zero

Mary Gonzalez
"New York At Christmas"

There is a somber yet festive tone in the air,
Down at Ground zero;
Voices of despair
And the memories of loved ones and the heroes
Are silenced and soothed as the snowflakes fall;
In the distance voices like angels
rise in silent hymns and prayers,
To remember the fallen with love and Carols
People united together,
With one voice ... one heart, united …
Offering love and peace
To the dearly departed.
There is a different drum beat in the City.
The Big Apple dresses in red and green.
Picking up the pieces of 911 with as much dignity …
Everywhere you turn love, unity and charity can be
seen …
As never before …
Christmas in New York City
Reigns down once more …
Shining the light of love and brotherhood
Through Manhattan, Brooklyn and every single
neighborhood …
The enemy, like some wretched grinch thought that
it could
steal Christmas from us this year.
But they have failed …
Everywhere you turn there is still laughter, love and
cheer …
Christmas is here again … Love prevailed
To restore the peace and unity we once knew …
Christmas reigns in the City that never sleeps
and it spreads a healing balsam that will renew
The Spirit of generosity, love and fortitude!

Vocabulary

1 somber, BrE **sombre** (adj.): sad and serious – **5 to soothe** /suːð/ (v.): to make s.o. calmer and less anxious, upset, or angry – **30 to prevail** (v.): (fml.) here: to be successful in the end – **34 generosity** (n.): a generous attitude or behavior

Explanations

24 the Grinch: a popular cartoon character created by Dr. Seuss. He first appeared in the children's book, *How the Grinch Stole Christmas!* (1957) and then, in response to the success of the book, in a 1966 television special and in further prize-winning TV plays. Having become a cultural icon, the Grinch is referred to by the media when holiday displays are ruined by vandals or holiday burglaries are committed. Outside Christmas, "grinch" means "grouch" (s.o. who is always complaining).

Fritz König's sculpture "The Sphere," which stood on the World Trade Center Plaza and was meant to symbolize world peace through world trade

Awareness

1 Certain historical events leave a lasting impression, and the terrorist attacks on New York and Washington on 11 September 2001 certainly belong to this category. Try to remember what you were doing when you learned about these events, and how you reacted to the news.

Opinion

2 Many commentators have said that the events of 9/11 have changed the world. Do you agree or disagree (Reference Library, p. 306)? Give reasons for your position.

Analysis

3 Analyze Mary Gonzalez' poem with regard to its form (Reference Library, pp. 309f.) and its message.

Projects

4 Collect poems and songs from the many memorial Internet sites such as http://www.9-11heroes.us/victims-world-trade-center.php or http://fp.sherwoodparkbiz.com/Ricon/wtcpoems.htm or http://www.coping.org/911/memory/content.htm#Poetry, arrange them in a collage, select two poems that appeal to you, and explain why.

5 Find out about the plans for erecting a new Freedom Tower on ground zero (see http://www.lowermanhattan.info/construction/project_updates/freedom_tower_26204.aspx). Prepare a presentation stating the reasons for the project, its cost, and how and when it is to be done.

6 Check http://www.heise.de/tp/r4/special/wtc.html, report (Reference Library, p. 302) on the conspiracy theories concerning the events of 9/11, and discuss (Reference Library, p. 299) their credibility.

16

From Melting Pot

A Zuni parade group at the famous Indian Ceremonial in Gallup

From the Native 'Indians' who came from Asia many thousand years ago to the new arrivals who now daily stream into the 'promised land' of America, the United States has been a nation of immigrants.

While many came on their own volition in search of a better life, others were deported to the New World by force, and from 1619 onwards, when a first shipload of black slaves was brought to Virginia, an estimated 15 million Africans survived the brutal 'middle passage' and were pressed into slavery. Today their descendants constitute about 12% of the overall population.

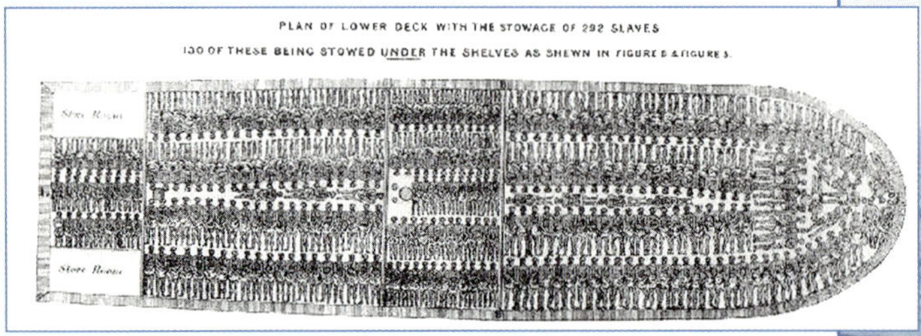

The loading plan of a slave ship

to Multiculturalism

E pluribus unum?

The Concord, *which, in 1683, brought a group of Mennonites from the Rhineland to what became Germantown, Pennsylvania*

Between 1820 and 1975 more than eighty percent of all the arrivals who were 'pushed' out of their home countries by poverty, religious persecution and other pressures and 'pulled' to America by their hope for a better life, came from only ten countries, with Germany, Italy, Britain, Ireland, and Austro-Hungary being the top five. Recent years, however, have seen a dramatic change.

Among the almost ten million immigrants who entered the U.S. in the last decade, about 80% came from non-European countries, with Mexico, the Caribbean and Central America contributing 27.1%, 10.7% and 6.9% respectively and Asian countries adding another 26.7%.

A replica of the Mayflower, *which, in 1620, brought 102 'Pilgrims' to Plymouth, Massachusetts*

Thus, the ethnic makeup of the population is undergoing a crucial change, and ethnographers predict that by the middle of the 21st century the 'Browning of America' will have reduced 'whites' to a minority and made the long dominant WASPs (White Anglo-Saxon Protestants) a small segment in a 'multicultural' society.

CENSUS 2004

total population	**293.6 million**	
Non-Hispanic Whites	197.8 million	75 %
Hispanics	41.3 million	12.5%
Blacks	37.5 million	12.3%
Asians	12.3 million	3.6%
American Indians + Alaska Natives	2.8 million	0.9%
Others	4.9 million	1.7%

The sum of the populations is larger than the total because some people belong to more than one race (Hispanic and Black, American Indian and White, etc.).

A collage of neon signs advertising ethnic cuisine

The unique 'Sky City' of Acoma in New Mexico, which has been continuously inhabited since around 1300 A.D.

The influential metaphor which has long stood in the center of the American immigration discourse is that of the 'melting pot,' which Israel Zangwill popularized in his influential play *The Melting Pot* of 1908, and Arthur M. Schlesinger, Sr. counted among America's ten greatest contributions to civilization.

By now, however, the concept of the 'melting pot' and the idea that immigrants from different ethnic stock and with different languages, religions, values, and customs would 'melt' into what Zangwill's hero called "the fusion of all races, perhaps the coming superman," has been revealed as an untenable myth. And in 1963 Glazer and Moynihan could laconically observe that "the point about the melting pot [...] is that it did not happen."

Although the members of all immigrant groups adopt certain shared values and customs which help to constitute their 'American' identity, each of these groups keeps their own ethnic heritage alive. Thus they celebrate their particular holidays and stick to their traditional cuisine, and often they also live in separate places such as the 'Chinatowns' of many large cities, the 'Little Italy' of New York or the former 'Germantown' near Philadelphia, the more recent 'Japantowns' and 'Koreatowns,' the major black ghettos, and the numerous reservations of the Indian nations.

In the ongoing multiculturalism controversy, ethnicity has become a major issue, and while the universalists argue that the nation needs a shared core of values and customs as well as English as a shared language, the particularists insist that the long cherished position of *e pluribus unum* be replaced by *e pluribus plures*.

1

Emma Lazarus

The New Colossus

In the early 1880s, Emma Lazarus, the daughter of a wealthy Jewish family in New York, began to work for the relief of the poor Jewish immigrants from Eastern Europe who were coming to America in ever-increasing waves. When the Statue of Liberty was dedicated in 1886 as a monument to the concept of liberty as both a timeless ideal and a force in history, Lazarus' sonnet of 1883 was almost completely unknown. Later, however, it began to win recognition as an American classic, in 1903 it was engraved on a plate which was mounted on the base of the statue, and today it is one of the best-known American poems of all times. – Emma Lazarus, *The Poems* (Boston and New York: Houghton Mifflin, 1888), vol. I, pp. 202f.

Not like the brazen giant of Greek fame,
With conquering limbs astride from land to land;
Here at our sea-washed, sunset gates shall stand
A mighty woman with a torch, whose flame
Is the imprisoned lightning, and her name
Mother of Exiles. From her beacon-hand
Glows world-wide welcome; her mild eyes command
The air-bridged harbor that twin cities frame.
"Keep, ancient lands, your storied pomp!" cries she
With silent lips. "Give me your tired, your poor,
Your huddled masses yearning to breathe free,
The wretched refuse of your teeming shore.
Send these, the homeless, tempest-tost to me,
I lift my lamp beside the golden door!"

Joseph Keppler, "Welcome to All!" (Puck, 1880)

2 Thomas Bailey Aldrich

Unguarded Gates

Not all of Lazarus' contemporaries shared her belief that America should be the "Mother of Exiles," and Thomas Bailey Aldrich spoke for many Americans when, in a poem which first appeared in the *Atlantic Monthly* in the same year as Keppler's cartoon, he demanded that the gates to the new world should be closed and unwanted foreigners should be kept out. – *The Writings of Thomas Bailey Aldrich* (Boston and New York: Houghton Mifflin, 1907), vol. II, pp. 71f.

Wide open and unguarded stand our gates,
Named of the four winds, North, South, East, and West;
Portals that lead to an enchanted land
Of cities, forests, fields of living gold,
Vast prairies, lordly summits touched with snow,
Majestic rivers sweeping proudly past
The Arab's date-palm and the Norseman's pine –
A realm wherein are fruits of every zone,
Airs of all climes, for lo! throughout the year
The red rose blossoms somewhere – a rich land,
A later Eden planted in the wilds,
With not an inch of earth within its bound
But if a slave's foot press it sets him free.
Here, it is written, Toil shall have its wage,
And Honor honor, and the humblest man
Stand level with the highest in the law.
Of such a land have men in dungeons dreamed,
And with the vision brightening in their eyes
Gone smiling to the fagot and the sword.

Wide open and unguarded stand our gates,
And through them presses a wild motley throng –
Men from the Volga and the Tartar steppes,
Featureless figures of the Hoang-Ho,
Malayan, Scythian, Teuton, Kelt, and Slav,
Flying the Old World's poverty and scorn;
These bringing with them unknown gods and rites,
Those, tiger passions, here to stretch their claws.
In street and alley what strange tongues are loud,
Accents of menace alien to our air,
Voices that once the Tower of Babel knew!

O Liberty, white Goddess! is it well
To leave the gates unguarded? On thy breast
Fold Sorrow's children, soothe the hurts of fate,
Lift the down-trodden, but with hand of steel
Stay those who to thy sacred portals come
To waste the gifts of freedom. Have a care
Lest from thy brow the clustered stars be torn
And trampled in the dust. For so of old
The thronging Goth and Vandal trampled Rome,
And where the temples of the Caesars stood
The lean wolf unmolested made her lair.

Joseph Keppler, "Looking Backwards" (Puck, 1893). This cartoon mocks successful Americans who call for immigration restriction, forgetting their own humble origins.

Emma Lazarus (1849–1887) was born in New York City, the descendant of Sephardic Jews who had immigrated from Portugal in the seventeenth century. She began to write poems as a young girl, and her *Poems and Translations: Written Between the Ages of Fourteen and Sixteen* (1866) were praised by the leading writers of her day. The wave of pogroms against Jews in Russia and the onset of the mass migration of Eastern European Jews to America awakened her Jewish consciousness, and her widely acclaimed *Songs of a Semite* (1882) made her the first avowedly Jewish-American poet to receive literary recognition. She died at the early age of thirty-eight, and her collected poems were published posthumously in 1889. Her sonnet to the Statue of Liberty is the best-known expression of her love for the United States as a refuge for the oppressed.

Vocabulary

1 brazen (adj.): of or like brass (a hard bright yellow metal, a mixture of copper and zinc); without shame, immodest – **2 limb** (n.): a leg or arm of a person or animal – **4 torch** (n.): a mass of burning material tied to a stick and carried by hand to give light – **6 beacon** (n.): a tall object or a light on or near the shore, acting as a guide or warning to sailors – **12 to teem with** (v.): (of a place) to be full of (esp. a certain type of creature) – **13 tempest** (n.): a violent storm – **13 to toss** (v.): to throw, pitch, or fling about; 'tost' is an archaic form of the past part. 'tossed'

Explanations

1 the brazen giant of Greek fame: an allusion to the Colossus of Rhodes, a large bronze (or "brazen") statue of Helios, the sun god, in the harbor of Rhodes, which was one of the seven wonders of the ancient world – **8 twin cities**: When Lazarus wrote her poem, New York (Manhattan) and Brooklyn were still separate cities, since Greater New York, including Manhattan, Brooklyn, the Bronx, Queens, and Staten Island, was not formed until 1898.

Thomas Bailey Aldrich (1836–1907) was born in Portsmouth, New Hampshire, and later lived in New Orleans, New York, and Boston. He had planned to enter Harvard, but had to go into business when his father died in 1852. Soon he began to write poetry for magazines, and after various posts on diverse journals and magazines, he took up permanent residence in Boston in 1865, the home of the New England group of authors whom he deeply admired. While he was the editor of *Every Saturday*, he published his successful semi-autobiographical novel *The Story of a Bad Boy* (1870) and such accomplished short stories as "Marjorie Daw" (1873). His best-known stories were collected in *Marjorie Daw and Other People* (1873) and *Two Bites at a Cherry, with Other Tales* (1894). As editor of the *Atlantic Monthly* (1881–90) he was known for his conservative policy and his adherence to New-England traditions.

Vocabulary

3 to enchant (v.): to use magic on s.b. or s.th. – **6 to sweep** (v.): to move (over or past s.th.) – **7 date** (n.): a small brown sweet fruit with a long stone, from hot dry countries – **7 date-palm** (n.): the tree that produces this fruit – **7 pine** (n.): any of several types of tall tree with thin sharp leaves that do not drop off in winter, found esp. in colder parts of the world – **9 clime** (n.): poet. for 'climate' – **14 toil** (n.): hard or continuous work – **19 fagot** (n.): here a heap of sticks set afire for burning a person; a stake – **21 motley** (adj.): of different kinds, esp. having a mixture of good and bad, of higher and lower worth, class, etc. – **21 throng** (n.): a large crowd of people or things – **23 featureless** (adj.): uninteresting, because of having no noticeable features – **25 scorn** (n.): strong and sometimes angry disrespect towards a person or thing that is regarded as worthless; contempt – **28 alley** (n.): a narrow street or path between buildings in a town – **29 menace** (n.): s.th. which suggests threat or brings danger – **34 to tread** (v.): /tred/ to walk on, over, or along (trod, trodden) – **37 lest** (conj.): in order that ... not; in case – **37 clustered** (adj.): being close together – **41 unmolested** (adj.): not troubled, not bothered – **41 lair** (n.): the place where a wild animal hides, rests, and sleeps

Explanations

7 Norseman: a Scandinavian of Viking times – **22 Volga**: the principal river of the former Soviet Union in the Great Russian Plains – **22 Tartar**: a member of a Mongol tribe that settled in eastern Mongolia and western Manchuria; in informal usage a fierce person with a violent temper – **23 Hoang-Ho**: the second-longest river in China, flowing 2,900 miles east from the Tibetan highlands across northern China to the Gulf of Chihli – **24 Scythian**: /'sɪðɪən/ a member of a group of loosely related tribes that lived in a region of southeastern Europe in ancient times – **24 Teuton**: /'tjuːtən || 'tuːtən/ one of the tribes that comprised the ancient Germanic peoples of northwestern Europe – **24 Kelt**: a person of Celtic linguistic stock, now represented by the Irish, Welsh, Highland Scots, Manx, Cornish, and Bretons, formerly by the ancient Gauls and Britons – **24 Slav**: any of the East European peoples speaking Slavic languages – **39 Goth**: a member of the people who spread from their homeland in Scandinavia over much of the Roman world from the 3rd to the 6th centuries A.D. – **39 Vandal**: a member of the people related to the Goths who lived in northern Germany at the beginning of the Christian era; in modern usage a person who intentionally damages or destroys public property or things belonging to other people

Ms. Liberty

Awareness

1 What made people want to immigrate into America in the last century? Would you have gone, too? Why / Why not?

Comprehension

2 What are the differences between "the brazen giant" (l. 1) and the Statue of Liberty as seen by Lazarus?
3 What message does the Statue of Liberty send out into the world? (In your own words.)
4 How does Aldrich describe America?
5 To whom does he compare the immigrants?
6 What warning does he give?

Analysis

7 What means does Lazarus use to create the contrast between the old world and the new world?
8 How does Aldrich build up his argument (Reference Library, pp. 312f.)?
9 Work out the metaphorical (Reference Library, p. 311) implications of such ethnic groups as the Tartars, Teutons, Goths, Vandals, etc. and discuss how Aldrich manipulates his readers by referring to these particular groups of immigrants only.
10 Compare the pictures drawn of the Statue of Liberty by Lazarus and Aldrich.

Opinion

11 Modern research thinks of migration as a push-and-pull phenomenon and explains it by distinguishing between the forces which push people into emigrating from their home country and the forces which pull them towards the target country into which they immigrate. Consider the groups of asylum seekers and *Aussiedler* whom you know about in present-day Germany and examine the threats that pushed them out of their respective home countries and the promises which pulled them into the Federal Republic of Germany.
12 Describe the two cartoons (pp. 265 and 266) and compare their respective messages.
13 Discuss (Reference Library, p. 299) the arguments for and against unlimited immigration.

Haig Whisky

Internet Projects

14 Use appropriate Internet sources (http://www.nps.gov/stli/prod02.htm and/or http://www.endex.com/gf/buildings/liberty/liberty.html might be a good starting point) to research the history of the Statue of Liberty.
15 Use the facts and figures offered under http://www.jwa.org/exhibits/lazarus/e/1.html to compose a report (Reference Library, p. 302) on the life and work of Emma Lazarus.
16 Do the same for Thomas Bailey Aldrich by using http://seacoastnh.com/Famous_People/Thomas_Bailey_Aldrich/Portsmouth%27s_Bad_Boy_Tom/.
17 Use http://www.spartacus.schoolnet.co.uk/ARTkeppler.htm to do some research on the life and work of Joseph Keppler. Select some of his political cartoons and present them to your course in a Powerpoint presentation.

3

Madison Grant

The Passing of the Great Race

In 1916 Madison Grant combined romantic notions of national glory with biological hypotheses about the different values of different racial stock in his controversial book *The Passing of the Great Race*. This militant pseudo-scientific treatise, which is an example of so-called Anglo-Saxon Racialism, rejects the concept of the melting pot as suicidal - "If the Melting Pot is allowed to boil without control, the native American of colonial descent will become as extinct as the Athenian of the age of Pericles and the Viking of the days of Rollo" - and demands strong measures against 'undesirable' immigrants. - Madison Grant, *The Passing of the Great Race* (New York: Scribner, rev. ed., 1918), pp. 89ff.

The transportation lines advertised America as a land flowing with milk and honey and the European governments took the opportunity to unload upon careless, wealthy and hospitable America the sweepings of their jails and asylums. The result was that the new immigration, while it still included many strong elements from the north of Europe, contained a large and increasing number of the weak, the broken and the mentally crippled of all races drawn from the lowest stratum of the Mediterranean basin and the Balkans, together with hordes of the wretched, submerged populations of the Polish Ghettos. Our jails, insane asylums and almshouses are filled with this human flotsam and the whole tone of American life, social, moral and political has been lowered and vulgarized by them.

With a pathetic and fatuous belief in the efficacy of American institutions and environment to reverse or obliterate immemorial hereditary tendencies, these newcomers were welcomed and given a share in our land and prosperity. The American taxed himself to sanitate and educate these poor helots and as soon as they could speak English, encouraged them to enter into the political life, first of municipalities and then of the nation [...].

These immigrants adopt the language of the native American, they wear his clothes, they steal his name and they are beginning to take his women, but they seldom adopt his religion or understand his ideals and while he is being elbowed out of his own home the American looks calmly abroad and urges on others the suicidal ethics which are exterminating his own race.

In this cartoon from Judge, *22 March 1890, Miss Liberty tells Treasury Secretary William Windom: "If you're going to turn this island into a garbage dump, I'm going back to France."*

This cartoon, entitled "Unrestricted Immigration and Its Results – A Possible Curiosity of the Twentieth Century. The Last Yankee," appeared on 8 September 1882 in Frank Leslie's Illustrated Newspaper.

An advertisement for celluloid cuffs, collars and bosoms meant to make Chinese laundries superfluous

Awareness

1 What do you think is the message of the cartoon "The Last Yankee" (p. 269)?

Comprehension

2 How does Grant distinguish between 'old' and 'new' immigrants and what are his 'biological' premises?

Analysis

3 How does Madison Grant try to persuade his readers? Are his arguments convincing, does he tell the truth?

4 Relate Grant's description of the European governments "unload [ing] the sweepings of their jails and asylums" (ll. 3–5) upon a careless America to the cartoon from *Judge* (p. 269).

5 Describe the sorry figures around the tall Yankee in the cartoon and see whether you can detect national stereotypes.

Opinion

6 Imagine you had a chance to talk to Madison Grant. What would you tell him?

7 Comment on the sequence described in Grant's final paragraph.

Projects

8 The Yankee of the cartoon from *Frank Leslie's Illustrated Newspaper* is obviously a variation of 'Uncle Sam.' Find out about the concept of the 'Yankee' and research both the origin and the meaning of the 'Uncle Sam' figure.

9 Lazarus, Aldrich and Grant embody opposite ideas of America (unlimited immigration vs. nativism). What role does the time factor or do historical events play for their respective position? What are the races they mention which melt/do not melt?

Internet Projects

10 Use the material offered under http://www.amren.com/9712issue/9712issue.html for a more detailed discussion of Grant's ideas.

11 Use excerpts from Grant's book, the complete text of which is available under http://www.africa2000.com/XNDX/madgrant intro. html, to discuss Grant's questionable attempt "to elucidate the meaning of history in terms of race."

Vocabulary

Intro/3 treatise (n.): a serious book or article that examines a particular subject – **10 stratum** (n.): a level of people in society; social class – **13 almshouse** (n.): a house provided in former times by a rich person, in which old or poor people could live without paying rent – **14 flotsam** (and jetsam): people without homes or work, who move helplessly through life – **16 to vulgarize** (v.): (derog.) to spoil the quality of; to lower the standard of (s.th. that is good) – **17 fatuous** (adj.): very silly without seeming to know it – **17 efficacy** (n.): the state or quality of being effective – **19 to obliterate** (v.): to remove all signs of; to destroy – **19 immemorial** (adj.): going back to ancient times – **19 hereditary** (adj.): which can be passed down from an older to a younger person, esp. in the same family – **22 to sanitate** (v.): to apply sanitary measures, i.e., measures concerning human health, esp. the treatment of human waste substances – **24 municipality** (n.): /mjuːˌnɪsɪˈpælətɪ ‖ mjʊ-/ a town, city, or other small area having its own government for local affairs – **32 to exterminate** (v.): to kill all the creatures or people in a place, or all those of a certain kind or race

Explanations

Intro/5 Pericles: Athenian statesman of the 5th century B.C., whose name is closely associated with the great age of Athenian democracy and culture, the Athenian Empire, and the Peloponnesian War – **Intro/6 Viking:** a designation of the adventurous people of the North and a collective name for the Norwegians, Swedes, and Danes in the 8th to 10th centuries – **Intro/6 Rollo**: a Norse conqueror of Normandy who lived from about 860 to about 930 – **22 helot** (n.): orig. a member of the state slaves in Sparta, in a figurative sense a member of any social group which is not respected

4

Art Buchwald

"Look West, Miss Liberty, and Shine Your Light ..."

James Baldwin once rightly observed that "the past is all that makes the present coherent," and the following article by a leading American humorist, which appeared in *The Washington Post* of 6 May 1975 and deals, in a satirical fashion, with the influx of 130,000 Vietnamese fleeing from their defeated country, illustrates Baldwin's insight by measuring the widespread unwillingness to admit Asian immigrants against the old promise of providing asylum for everyone.

"What happened to the one we used to have?"

"The only way to handle it!"

The Statue of Liberty was gazing toward Europe when I tapped her on her shoulder. "Ma'am," I said, "if you look the other way, we have about 130,000 Vietnamese refugees coming in from Guam and the Philippines. I thought you might hold your torch high and light the way for them."

The statue seemed irritated. "We have too many people in this country now. What am I going to do with Orientals?"

"The same thing you did with everybody else. Welcome them. They're tired and they're poor and they are yearning to breathe free."

"And what about jobs? Who is going to support them?" she said petulantly.

"You never worried about that before," I said. "Whoever came to this country eventually found jobs, and almost all of them made very good citizens. There is no reason to think the Vietnamese will be different. After all, you are the mother of exiles."

"Times have changed," she growled. "The American people are not that thrilled about having a bunch of refugees dumped on them. Who is going to feed them? How many will go on welfare? How do we know their kids won't get in trouble in the streets? We have enough problems in this country without asking for more."

"But," I pleaded, "we're responsible for them being refugees. We screwed up a country like it's never been screwed up before. We supported their corrupt governments, loaded them down with weapons they couldn't use, defoliated their rice paddies and wrecked their families."

"We left the country in a mess. The least we can do is take in whatever huddled masses escaped to our teeming shore."

"That's easy for you to say," the Statue of Liberty replied, "but we have to think of Americans first. They don't want any more foreigners in this country."

"But most of our fathers and grandfathers and greatgrandfathers were foreigners. You've welcomed them all. Tell me the truth. Do you have anything against Orientals?"

"I don't personally. But you know how some people

are. The Vietnamese have different habits, and they're from another culture. They just don't fit in. Besides I'm supposed to welcome the homeless from Europe. That's why I'm looking in that direction."

"These people need refuge," I protested. "Their lives are in ruins. Remember a few weeks ago when they flew in orphans from Vietnam and Cambodia. Nobody seemed to object to that."

"It's not the same thing," the statue said. "You can adopt orphans. But what can you do with refugees?"

"Help them find homes, jobs, make them citizens."

"It's out of the question. It isn't our fault they lost the war. Look, no one minds one or two Vietnamese in a community. But you're talking about thousands. They'll stick out like a sore thumb. The unions would never stand for it."

"Please don't turn your back on them," I begged. "If somebody just said, 'Welcome. We're glad you came,' most Americans would go along with it. The American people gripe a lot, but they'll do the right thing if somebody leads them. If you could shine your torch toward the Golden Gate bridge, perhaps the people will be ashamed of the way they've behaved."

The Statue of Liberty turned slowly. There was a tear in her eye. "I've been here so long I almost forgot why I was holding this lamp. Where did you say I should shine my torch?"

"Over here. Hold it as high as you can and point it toward the West so every American can see it. That's it. Now repeat after me, 'Send these, the homeless, tempest-tost to me, I lift my lamp beside the golden door.'"

Jean Lagarrigue, Liberté-Cola *(1974)*

Vocabulary

14 petulant (adj.): /ˈpetʃʊlənt/ showing childish bad temper over unimportant things, or for no reason at all – **21 bunch** (n.): a number of things (usu. small and of the same kind) fastened, held, or growing together at one point – **27 to screw s.th. up** (v.): infml. for to ruin, to cause to fail – **30 to defoliate** (v.): to use a chemical substance on plants in order to cause their leaves to drop off too soon – **57 to stick out like a sore thumb**: to be very clearly seen and look very unsuitable – **62 to gripe** (v.): to complain continually

Art Buchwald (1925–2007) was born in Mount Vernon, New York. He left high school without a diploma to join the Marines, and later left college without a degree to live in Paris. There he got his first job as a correspondent for *Variety* in 1948 and then joined the editorial staff of the Paris edition of the *New York Herald Tribune*. After writing such highly successful columns as "Paris After Dark," "Mostly About People," and "Europe's Lighter Side" from Paris and other European points for fourteen years, Buchwald switched to Washington, D.C., in 1962, and his column, usually published just as "Art Buchwald," was syndicated to 550 newspapers throughout the world. Buchwald increasingly adopted the stance of the shrewd humorist reminiscent of Mark Twain, and he was probably the most successful humorous columnist in the United States. He was awarded a Pulitzer Prize in 1982 and elected to the American Academy and Institute of Arts and Letters in 1986. His texts are collected in more than thirty books ranging from *Art Buchwald's Paris* (1953) to *Too Soon to Say Goodbye* (2006).

Awareness

1 Consider James Baldwin's famous statement that "the past is all that makes the present coherent" and relate it to the German notion of *unbewältigte Vergangenheit.*

2 Reconsider the promise of America as expressed in Emma Lazarus' poem and establish the background which is necessary for an understanding of Buchwald's article.

Comprehension

3 The Vietnamese immigrants entered the country under a special refugee act. How does the "I" substantiate his claim that the U.S. is responsible for these people?

4 Why is the Statue especially skeptical about "Orientals" (l. 9)?

5 Why does the Statue say that "times have changed" (l. 20)?

6 What does the I-narrator ask her to do?

Analysis

7 The article unfolds as an imaginary dialogue between a narrating "I" and the Statue of Liberty. Define the positions of each speaker and the ideals expressed by the narrator (Reference Library, pp. 310f.).

8 Describe the tension between promise and reality, 'dream' and 'nightmare,' which becomes obvious in Buchwald's article.

9 Examine the stylistic means (Reference Library, p. 311) which make this essay so 'ironic.'

Opinion

10 What did the Statue of Liberty embody and what in your view does it embody today?

11 Work out the implications of Lagarrigue's painting (p. 272) and relate them to the frequently heard notion of America's 'cultural imperialism.' Is this your image of America?

12 Use Lagarrigue's painting as the starting point for an investigation of the degree to which you and your friends are 'Americanized.' Consider the 'Americanisms' in your everyday language, your favorite pieces of clothing and your cuisine, the music you like to hear, the films and TV serials you like to see, the sports you like to engage in, the video games you play, the popular idols you admire, etc.

Project

13 Investigate, in a weekly television guide of your choice, (a) the cinema films shown by major German TV stations during prime-time, (b) the TV serials broadcast by the same stations in the *Vorabendprogramm*, and (c) the pop songs listed in the charts. Figure out the respective percentage of American products in all three categories.

Richard Rodriguez went to Sacramento's parochial schools, studied at Stanford and Columbia Universities, and did graduate work at the Warburg Institute, London, and the University of California at Berkeley. His autobiography *Hunger of Memory: An Autobiography* (1982) is a searching account of a journey from being a "socially disadvantaged child" to a fully assimilated American. It was both widely acclaimed and strongly criticized, and because of his stand against affirmative action and bilingual education Rodriguez was even accused of being a traitor. In his second book, *Days of Obligation: An Argument with My Mexican Father* (1993), he explores the dilemma of ethnicity even more directly, and in his most recent book, *Brown: The Last Discovery of America* (2000), he deals once more with the issue of race in America and argues that Hispanic is not a race but a culture.

Good business relies on clear communication. Unless each party knows what the other means, there is the danger of ambiguity, the probability of its attendant loss of faith, and the real chance of failure.

So it is essential for Latinos dealing with Anglo businesses to speak the same language. By this I don't mean just being fluent in the language of business – English. I mean understanding those subtleties that are part of any communication, things that are implied or left unsaid, a kind of code that can be learned only by acute observation and practice.

Most Latinos living in the United States are bilingual and bicultural, great assets in a world where more and more corporations are becoming committed to doing business with Latin America. (...)

Most Anglos, by contrast, speak only English and have difficulty with foreign languages. In fact, many times Anglo Americans actually expect the rest of the world to learn English, so they don't have to bother with other languages. Many also have difficulties with foreign cultures. So it makes sense that they will rely on Latinos more and more to be part of their team when it comes to doing business with Latin countries and – by extension – for doing business, period. We are therefore a vital link in a new world economy.

Lionel Sosa, *The Americano Dream: How Latinos Can Achieve Success in Business and in Life* (New York: Plume Books, 1999 (first 1998)), pp. 105f.

When **Lionel Sosa** published his bestseller *The Americano Dream*, he was Chief Executive Officer of KjS, a multicultural advertising agency that helps Fortune 500 companies expand their businesses into the Latino, Asian, and African American markets. Sosa, who lives in San Antonio, Texas, was the founder of the largest Hispanic ad agency in the U.S., Sosa, Bromley, Aguilar, Nobel & Associates, and was later chairman of DMB&B Americas, a network of twenty ad agencies specializing in Latin America. He was the winner of *Adweek's* Advertising Executive of the Year Award, and *Texas Monthly* named him one of the "most impressive, intriguing, and influential Texans of 1996."

Analysis

1 Analyze the Cisneros vignette with regard to narrative perspective (Reference Library, pp. 310f.), imagery, and style (Reference Library, p. 311).

Opinion

2 Study the statements by Rodriguez and Sosa and write a short paper (Reference Library, p. 301) in which you express and substantiate your position with regard to bilingual education.

Project

3 Read Francisco Jiménez' story "The Circuit" (available in *Growing up in a Multicultural Society: Nine American Short Stories*, ed. by Peter Freese [München: Langenscheidt, 1994 and ff.], pp. 68–80) and discuss it as yet another exploration of the problems of biculturalism and bilingualism.

Internet Project

4 In June 1998 and in November 2000 respectively the citizens of California and Arizona voted for laws abolishing bilingual schooling as a wasteful educational experiment which had demonstrably failed. In California "Proposition 227" was accepted with 61%, and in Arizona "Proposition 203" was accepted with 63%. Research the hotly debated pros and cons of these decisions by using the material offered under http://www.onenation.org as a starting point.

7 America 2000: A Map of the Mix

As the country becomes more and more diverse, three states and the capital city have nonwhites gain majority status. *Newsweek*, 18 September 2000, p. 66. – Meanwhile, California, too, has less than 50% non-Hispanic Whites.

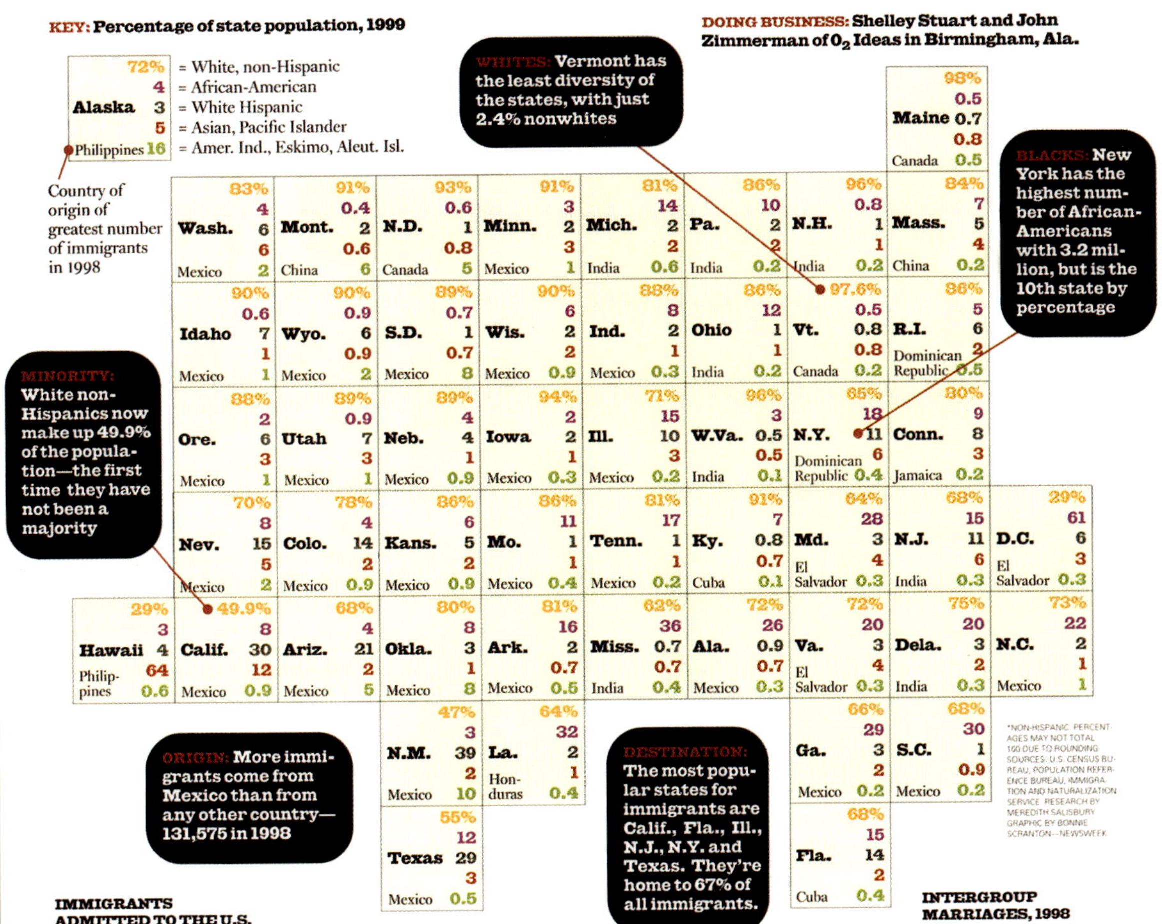

IMMIGRANTS ADMITTED TO THE U.S.

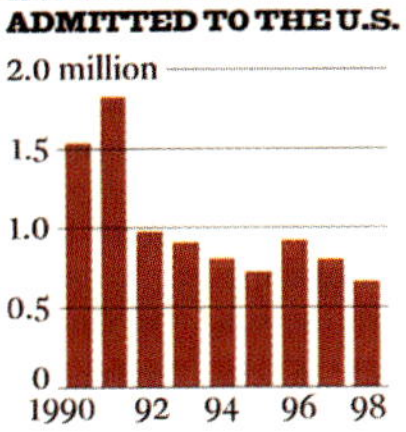

U.S. POPULATION, IN THOUSANDS AND PERCENT CHANGE

	1990	2000	% change '90–'00	2050	% change '00–'50
White, non-Hispanic	188,315	196,659	+4%	207,901	+6%
Black, non-Hispanic	29,304	33,476	+14%	53,555	+60%
Hispanic (of any race)	22,379	32,440	+45%	96,508	+197%
Asian and Pacific Islander*	6,996	10,504	+50%	32,432	+209%
Amer. Ind., Eskimo, Aleut. Isl.*	1,797	2,050	+14%	3,534	+72%

INTERGROUP MARRIAGES, 1998

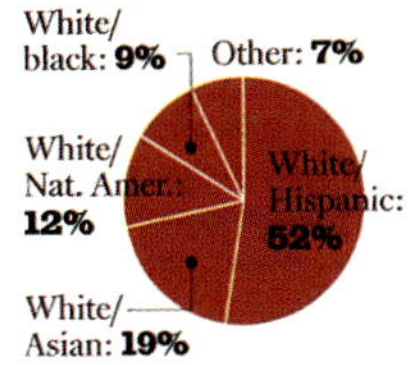

Projects

1. Find the four states (including the District of Columbia) in which 'white, non-Hispanic' citizens do not form the majority and work out the respective (historical) reasons for this situation.
2. According to the graph, only six out of fifty states, namely California, Florida, Illinois, New Jersey, New York, and Texas, accommodate 67% of all immigrants. Use the detailed data provided by the Census 2000 (available under http://www.census.gov/main/www/cen2000.html) to find explanations for such an uneven distribution.
3. Look for the states with the lowest number of 'non-whites.' Try to explain why in these states there are so few 'minority' groups.

Language

Stuart Waters

"2B or not 2B: Why Shakespeare is Doomed"*

Natural linguistic evolution, politics and technology will have an effect on the development of English, according to linguists, and may lead to the language of Shakespeare being lost entirely while English is spoken everywhere. Australian journalist Stuart Waters explains why in this online article. – Stuart Waters, "Why Shakespeare is Doomed", ABC online (www.abc.net.au/science/slab/futures2002), 20 November 2002.

"Macbeth, Act 1, Scene 1" (The cartoon alludes to the superstition among actors that Macbeth *is unlucky. Actors avoid using the name, and call it "The Scottish Play".)*

This is not a high-tech crime involving time travelling assassins. Shakespeare's death is a long, slow, silent decline that began even as he put quill to paper. And while we hold the knives now, the mortal blow will be dealt in the future. He will then be buried, and then forgotten and the world at large will no longer know of one of the greatest exponents of human genius. That is my prediction.

There is no motive in this crime of the future, just an inevitability based on one undeniable fact. Language changes, and ironically, Shakespeare was himself perhaps the greatest ever at introducing new terms, concepts and metaphors into the language. The very craft he mastered will eventually consign his works to history.

How do I know this? Let me count the ways. (...)

It is easy to see how the romance languages – French, Spanish, Italian, Sardinian, Romanian, Catalan and Portuguese – all emerged from Latin. But further delving has shown that the Germanic family – English, German, Danish – evolved from an unknown Proto-Germanic language. Latin, Proto-Germanic and Proto-Slavic (Russian, Polish, Serbo-Croatian) are among the Indo-European family of languages, and they in turn share more ancient roots with other language groups.

If language evolves there must be some mechanism for change, and linguists have a good idea of what that mechanism is. Dr Cynthia Allen from the School of Languages at the Australian National University suggests that language changes with each generation. When we are born, we have no language and must learn it from scratch, and while virtually all babies are told things like 'dog', 'cat', 'Mummy' and 'Daddy', most of our language skills are simply picked up on the run. The more abstract the concept, the less is the likelihood that it will be described to us in detail. We must simply make a guess based on the context. This process works very well, but it is not flawless. (...)

But the slightly imperfect transmission of meaning from one generation to the next is far from the only influence on language evolution. Geopolitical events can catalyse enormous and rapid developments, as the English found in the years after the Norman invasion in 1066. After William conquered, says Dr Allen, his language became the language of government and state and we are left with words such as bureaucracy that tell of a time when speakers of French ruled Britain. (...)

"The future of a language is closely bound up with the influence and prestige of its speakers", says Professor David Crystal, a leading international expert in linguistics. He suggests that English, being the language of the most powerful state on Earth, has a rosy future.

"The role of English has developed to such an extent, unprecedented in world history, that it is difficult to see how it can be dislodged". However, as Professor Crystal goes on to caution, people must once have thought that about Latin.

One of the more bizarre potential future scenarios for the English language is that all English speakers, wherever they are in the world, will need to be bilingual in English. That is, they will speak their own local English, and also another English David Crystal calls "World Standard Spoken English".

Bilingualism will be necessary because a language separated by geography or culture – even if it is the same language – will evolve in different directions, until it becomes a series of mutually unintelligible regional dialects. North American English will be very different to British English, which will differ from Australian, South African, Indian and Caribbean English.

These 'new Englishes' will diverge over time in the same way that different languages have always evolved from common roots. At the same time, the theory goes, a World Standard Spoken English will be maintained so that all speakers of English can communicate effectively with each other. Though it sounds unlikely, a similar situation currently exists in China where the several spoken dialects are mutually unintelligible, but written Chinese is understood by all.

But making predictions about the future of the English language is particularly difficult because it stands at a threshold beyond which we cannot see. The threshold is both demographic and technical.

In terms of demography, David Crystal predicts that in just a few years there will be more speakers of English as a second language than native born English speakers, at which point the language will become "open to the winds of linguistic change in totally unpredictable ways". English is fast becoming a truly global language and what that means, nobody can predict with confidence.

Technologically, the very nature of communication is changing on a daily basis and we are only at the beginning of this revolution. The internet, email and text messaging are tremendously fertile fields for the growth of new words and concepts and because this type of technology changes so quickly it is very difficult to see where it will take the language. On the one hand communication technology exerts pressure for language evolution, but on the other hand, it puts everyone in touch with everyone else, breaking down the barriers of distance and culture which traditionally fuel language change. What will be the outcome? Who can say.

In yet another twist, David Crystal describes the possible impact of instant translation technology. Perhaps in a few years or decades we will all wear the equivalent of Douglas Adams' babel fish, which translates all languages instantaneously. What impact will this have on the evolution of language? There will no longer be a need for an international lingua franca and people will be free to speak in whatever tongue they choose. World Standard English may not be necessary after all.

Vocabulary

Title: doomed (adj.): certain to die – **7 quill** (n.): a pen made from a feather – **9 mortal** (adj.): leading to death – **15 exponent** (n.): (here) best example – **19 undeniable** (adj.): certain – **23 craft** (n.): skill, ability to do s.th. difficult – **24 to consign to history** (v.): to make s.th. out of date – **29 delving** (n.): digging, (here) investigation – **42 from scratch** (adv.): starting with nothing – **45 on the run** (adv.): while something is being done, (here) while it is being used – **56 geopolitical** (adj.): connected with geography and politics – **57 to catalyze** (v.): be a catalyst for, cause to happen – **75 to dislodge** (v.): to force s.th. out of its position – **78 bizarre** (adj.): very strange – **78 scenario** (n.): a situation that might happen – **102 threshold** (n.): the beginning of a new development – **103 demographic** (adj.): concerning numbers of people – **115 fertile** (adj.): able to produce a lot – **123 to fuel** (v.): drive forward – **132 lingua franca** (n.): (from Latin) language used to communicate by people who speak different languages – **133 tongue** (n.): language

Explanations

61 William: William of Normandy conquered England in 1066, becoming William I, or William the Conqueror – **128 Douglas Adams' babel fish:** In *The Hitch-Hiker's Guide to the Galaxy*, a science-fiction parody by Douglas Adams, a fish can live in ears, eating brainwaves in any language around and excreting them in its host's, thus providing instant translation. It is called Babel fish because of the story in the Bible about languages being created during the building of the Tower of Babel.

Tasks and Projects

1. Talk about how often you have needed English to speak to or understand native speakers of English or speakers of other languages.
2. What professions or fields of study do you think require a good command of English?
3. Why, according to the author, is Shakespeare 'doomed'?
4. What exactly are 'Englishes'? Can you imagine 'German English'? What might it be like?
5. Draw up a 'family tree' of European languages.
6. What effect may the Internet have on the development of English?
7. Get a 'machine translation' of a web page from your search engine. What are the problems of translation?
8. In Douglas Adams' *The Hitch-Hiker's Guide to the Galaxy* it says "... the poor Babel fish, by effectively removing all barriers to communication between different races and cultures, has caused more and bloodier wars than anything else in the history of creation." Do we really want a global language?

Lisa Jardine

"A Lingua Franca"*

The European Union was founded as a multilingual community with shared values and mutual respect among members. It has 23 official languages. Travelling to a conference, Professor Lisa Jardine of Oxford University notices how well the Belgians and Dutch speak English. British people have never liked learning other languages, and the number doing so in schools is falling. - Lisa Jardine, "A Point of View", BBC News (bbc.co.uk), 9 May 2006

Britons believe that there is really no need for them to learn any other European language, when in the end everyone aspires to speak theirs.

Mind you, although the average British teenager seems confident that English will enable them to get by anywhere, the EU administration is equally clear that no one language ought to be allowed to dominate. European Union documentation still refuses to acknowledge the fact that English has become Europe's lingua franca, insisting that the languages of all the member states weigh equally.

To the obvious question, "Why not adopt a single language for business?", posed on an official website, the answer given is categorical: There is no obvious language to choose. The EU language with the largest number of native speakers is German; the languages with the largest number of native speakers worldwide are Spanish and Portuguese; French is one of the official languages of three Member States (France, Belgium and Luxembourg).

As for English: "Although it is the most widely known language, recent surveys show that fewer than half the EU population have any usable knowledge of it." Wishful thinking, I'm afraid. For ease of communication among the enlarged membership, for everyday business and exchange of information, English will inevitably be used.

This is not the first time that Europe has embraced a lingua franca. At the beginning of the 16th Century, Latin was the language of choice for educated Europeans, who reserved their national vernaculars for commerce and the domestic sphere. The great linguist, theologian, author and educator Erasmus of Rotterdam - a favourite Renaissance figure of mine - presided over a pan-European educational system designed to instil good, elegant Latin into all citizens.

Erasmus of Rotterdam

In classroom textbooks and scholarly editions he argued that the language of ancient Rome contained within it the seeds of universal human values and an international ethic of compassion and tolerance. Erasmus's textbook, *On Copious Speaking and Writing*, which went into dozens of editions, taught the student how to say "thank you for your letter" in 150 different, equally elegant ways. By mastering Latin, Erasmus maintained, anyone could become a European.

But around 1515 Erasmus began to identify himself, in the prefaces and introductions to his works, as a Dutchman - as someone whose ideas and values were rooted in the northern Netherlands. And he did so because he had begun to realise that it is not enough to identify with the shared values of Europe as a whole. Each individual still needed a sense of belonging to a smaller group, with whose customs and way of life they could identify. We cannot be sure what changed Erasmus's mind, but it marked the beginning of the rise of the European vernaculars, the emergence of the modern nation state, and the demise of Latin.

Watching the easy mingling of the young British, Belgian and Dutch at my conference this week it was clear to me that they are all now confidently European in their habits and outlook. So perhaps I have reluctantly to concede that it may not be necessary for the British, who have the good fortune to speak the European lingua franca as their mother tongue, to be made to learn a second language. They can do alright without it, and after all, they can learn any specified language later, as the need arises.

But if that is the case, then the pressure on English as our mother tongue becomes intense. Unlike our Belgian and Dutch neighbours, it is the only language we have in which to learn to understand ourselves and others. If (as Erasmus thought) our emotional bearings are rooted locally, in the language of the place we call "home", then we are going to have to turn our attention fully and energetically towards English as the source and historical origin of understanding for the British Isles.

In its rich literature and history, in the nuanced subtleties of its meaning, must lie our own peculiar sense of belonging. For us, English is far more than the 21st Century European lingua franca. It is the bedrock upon which our sense of what it is to be British is built.

Vocabulary

3 to aspire to (v.): to desire to, have the ambition to - **4 mind you:** however - **6 administration** (n.): people governing a country - **14 categorical** (adj.): not open to discussion - **27 to embrace** (v.): to accept enthusiastically - **31 vernacular** (n.): ordinary people's language - **66 demise** (n.): the end of s.th.'s importance - **67 mingling** (n.): mixing with and talking to other people - **71 to concede** (v.): to admit that a different opinion is right - **82 bearings** (n.): a sense of where and what you are - **87 nuanced** (adj.): using slight differences to express things - **90 bedrock** (n.): basis, foundation

Explanations

36 Erasmus of Rotterdam: Desiderius Erasmus (c. 1466–1536), one of the best-known intellectuals of his time, was a friend of Thomas More (the author of *Utopia*). He criticized the Church, but remained a Catholic after the Reformation. Born in Rotterdam, he lived for much of his life in Basel. A programme of co-operation between European universities is named after him.

Facade of the European Parliament, Strasbourg

Tasks and Projects

1 Do you think one country should have one official language? What about the EU? What is the situation in multilingual countries like India, Nigeria, South Africa, or Switzerland?

2 What was the lingua franca in Europe until the 16th Century? Why did Erasmus think it so important?

3 What happened to it after the 16th Century?

4 Would it be a good idea to make the language of instruction in universities and/or secondary schools in your country English?

5 Find out what the EU's multilingual policy is and how much it costs. Debate whether it is worth it, or whether the money could be spent better.

Gautam Malkani

"Proper Words"*

Belonging to a group means being able to use their linguistic code. This may be a long way from standard English and show some of the characteristics mentioned in Text 1. This example is taken from a novel about a boy – the narrator – who spends his time with friends of Punjabi origin in West London (although he himself is white English). – Gautam Malkani, *Londonstani* (London: Fourth Estate, 2006), pp. 45f.

– I'ma take da short cut back to college, goes Ravi, – othawise we b headed for traffic, innit, Hardj?

– Nah, man, it gettin late an we gots twenty fuckin fones in da bag. Fuck college, let's take em straight 2 my yard.

Rudeboy Rule #4:

According to Hardjit, it don't matter if the proper word for something sounds fuckin ridiculous. If it's the proper word then it's the proper word.

Yard is one a them words. If it was me who was the American hiphop G or whoever the fuck it was who invented all this proper speak, no way the proper word for house'd be yard. That's the garden, for fuck's sake. I in't feelin the word crib either cos that's what American babies sleep in. Also, I wouldn't decide that the proper word for wood is heavy. Why they decided that The Shit should mean The Greatest I got no idea, maybe cos bad's always meant good. But more than all a this, if I was the Proper Word Inventor I'd do two things differently. I wouldn't decide that the proper word for a dickless poncey sap is a gay batty boy or that the proper word for women is bitches. That shit in't right. I know what other poncey words like homophobic an misogynist mean an I know that shit in't right. But what am I s'posed to do bout it? If I don't speak proply using the proper words then these guys'd say I was actin like a batty boy or a woman or a woman actin like a batty boy. One good thing though: now that I use all these proper words I'm hardly ever stuck for words. I just chuck in a bit a proper speak an I sound like I'm talkin proper, talkin like Hardjit. I just wish I was the Proper Word Inventor so I could pick different proper words, that's all. But, seeing as how I in't that person, we were cruisin to Hardjit's yard in Ravi's ride, checkin out the bitches round the high street.

Vocabulary

2 innit?: (youth slang) an all-purpose question-tag – **6 rudeboy** (n.): (CarE) cool gangster – **12 G** (n.): abbrev. for gangster – **16 to feel** (v.) (urban sl.) agree with, like – **16 crib** (n.) (urban sl.) home – **18 wood** (n.): (sl.) erection – **23 dickless** (adj.): (sl.) with no penis (cowardly) – **23 poncey** (adj.): (sl.) pompous, thinking a lot of oneself – **23 sap** (n.): s.o. who is Sad And Pathetic – **23 batty boy** (n.): (CarE) homosexual (from bottom boy) – **24 bitch** (n.): (urban sl.) woman (originally female dog) – **26 homophobic** (adj.): hating homosexuals – **26 misogynist** (n.): a person who despises women – **32 stuck for:** unable to find – **37 ride** (n.): (urban sl.) car – **37 to check out** (v.): to look at

Task

In groups, decide what questions to ask about this text and then give the answers.

17 The Global

• Playing bridge with Siberia

In the summer of 1998 my then seventy-nine-year-old mother, Margaret Friedman, who lives in Minneapolis, called me sounding very upset. "What's wrong, Mom?" I asked. "Well," she said, "I've been playing bridge on the Internet with three Frenchmen and they keep speaking French to each other and I can't understand them." When I chuckled at the thought of my card-shark mom playing bridge with three Frenchmen on the Net, she took a little umbrage. "Don't laugh," she said, "I was playing bridge with someone in Siberia the other day."

(Thomas L. Friedman in his book The Lexus and the Olive Tree, *p. xix)*

• Globalization wears Mickey Mouse ears

Today, globalization often wears Mickey Mouse ears, eats Big Macs, drinks Coke or Pepsi and does its computing on an IBM PC, using Windows 98, with an Intel Pentium II processor and a network link from Cisco Systems. Therefore, while the distinction between what is globalization and what is Americanization may be clear to most Americans, it is not – unfortunately – to many others around the world.

(Friedman, The Lexus and the Olive Tree, *p. 382)*

• Hopes of the Pepsi-Generation of Russia

Once upon a time in Russia, there really was a carefree, youthful generation that smiled in joy at the summer, the sea and the sun, and chose Pepsi. (...) No matter which way it was, as the children lounged on the seashore in the summer, gazing endlessly at a cloudless blue horizon, they drank warm Pepsi-Cola decanted into glass bottles in the city of Novorossiisk and dreamed that some day the distant forbidden world on the far side of the sea would be part of their own lives.

(Victor Pelevin in his novel Babylon, *translated from the Russian in 1999, p. 3)*

Vocabulary

upset (adj.): unhappy and angry – **take umbrage**: /ˈʌmbrɪdʒ/ be offended by s.th. that s.o. has done or said, often without good reason – **chuckle** (v.): /ˈtʃʌkl/ laugh quietly – **card-shark** (n.): (humorous usage) someone who uses their skill at cards to cheat other players out of money – **distinction** (n.): a clear difference or separation between two similar things – **lounge** (v.): stand, sit, or lie in a lazy or relaxed way – **gaze** (v.): look at s.o. or s.th. for a long time, giving it all your attention, often without realizing you are doing so – **Novorossiisk**: a harbour by the Black Sea, an industrial city of the Ukraine – **on the far side**: on the other side – **inevitable** (adj.): /ɪnˈevɪtəbl/ certain to happen and

Village

Progress or Disaster?

• The forces of history?

Globalization is inevitable and irreversible.

(Tony Blair, British Prime Minister, in a speech, 2003, qtd. in New York Times *(international ed.), May 2, 2005, p. 2)*

• Global media

Turkish guest workers in Germany watch Turkish films in their German flats, Koreans in Philadelphia watch the 1988 Olympics in Seoul through satellite feeds from Korea, and Pakistani cabdrivers in Chicago listen to cassettes of sermons in mosques in Pakistan or Iran.

(Arjun Appadurai, Modernity at Large: Cultural Dimensions of Globalization, *1996, p. 4)*

• Global terror

For most Americans, the age of globalization or interdependence has brought enormous benefits. (...) Though it worked for us, interdependence is not by definition good or bad. It can be either or; it can be both. On September 11th, 2001, the Al Quaeda terrorists used the forces of interdependence – they used the open borders, easy travel, easy immigration, easy access to information and technology, to turn a jet airplane full of fuel into a weapon of mass destruction to kill 3100 people in the United States, including hundreds of people from 70 foreign countries who were in America looking for positive interdependence. Over 200 of the people they killed were Muslims, indicating the racial and religious diversity of the positive side of this equation.

(Bill Clinton, former President of the USA, in a speech, 2003)

• The information age

According to a recent study from October 2000 by the American EMC(2) data storage corporation and the university of California at Berkeley, the total amount of accumulated information in the world has doubled in just the last three years.

(Brendan Dooley, Professor of History, International University of Bremen, 2003, blueprint 4/2003, *p. 5)*

impossible to avoid – **irreversible** (adj.): /ˌɪrɪˈvɜːsəbl/ a change is so serious or so great that you cannot change things back to how they were before – **interdependence** (n.): a situation in which people or things depend on each other – **Al Quaeda**: an international terrorist network, held responsible for the 9 / 11 attacks – **access** (v.): find information, esp. on a computer – **diversity** (n.): a range of different people, things, or ideas – **equation** (n.): /ɪˈkweɪʒən/ the set of different facts, ideas, or people that all affect a situation and must be considered together – **sermon** (n.): here: prayer

1 The Shrinking Map of the World

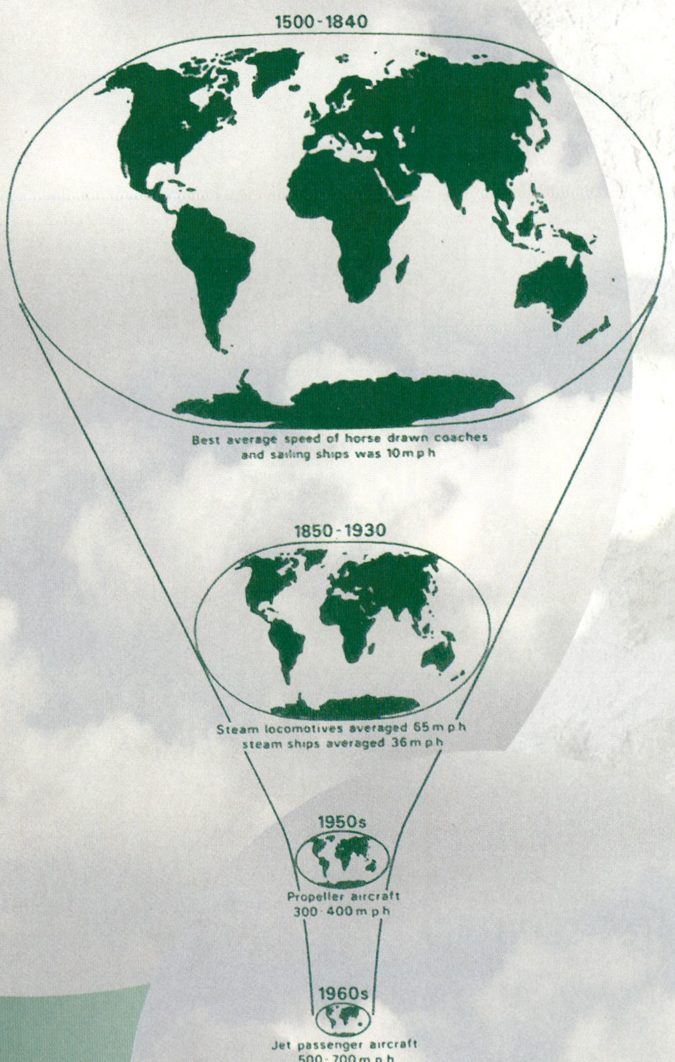

The shrinking map of the world through innovations in transport which 'annihilate space through time' (Source: David Harvey, The Condition of Postmodernity. *Cambridge MA: Blackwell, 1996, 245).*

Awareness

1 The term "global village" was introduced by the Canadian media specialist and philosopher Marshall McLuhan. What exactly does the term signify? Has this world become a village to you?

Comprehension

2 Look at the excerpts and quotes on the preceding pages. Then describe how they contribute to an understanding of globalization.

3 Describe the idea behind the diagram "the shrinking map of the world". What does it illustrate?

Analysis

4 Take a second look at the excerpts and quotes on the preceding pages. Then assess how they express feelings of hope or fear.

5 The diagram "The shrinking map of the world" ends in the 1960s. Find a way to describe how recent innovations have furthered the "shrinking of the world".

Opinion

6 Which quote characterizes the process of globalization best? Why?

7 Give some examples how the world has shrunk for you. What are the advantages, what are the disadvantages (for you)?

Project

8 Write a short paragraph or statement giving an instance from your life which could characterize the global village. Use all the statements from your class/group and make a collage of them. Discuss what they have in common.

data storage: the way how or a place where information is kept on a computer – **accumulate** (v.): /ə'kjuːmjʊleɪt/ gradually get more and more

Vocabulary

shrink (v.): become smaller – **annihilate** (v.): /ə'naɪəleɪt/ cause to disappear

2

B. B. Kachru; David Crystal

The Family Tree of English – Three Circles of English

English is increasingly becoming the *lingua franca* – the language of international communication – in the global village. Historically, English has attained its privileged status primarily as the result of two factors: the expansion of British colonial power, which peaked towards the end of the nineteenth century, and the emergence of the United States as the leading economic power of the 20th century. It is the latter factor which continues to explain the world position of the English language today.

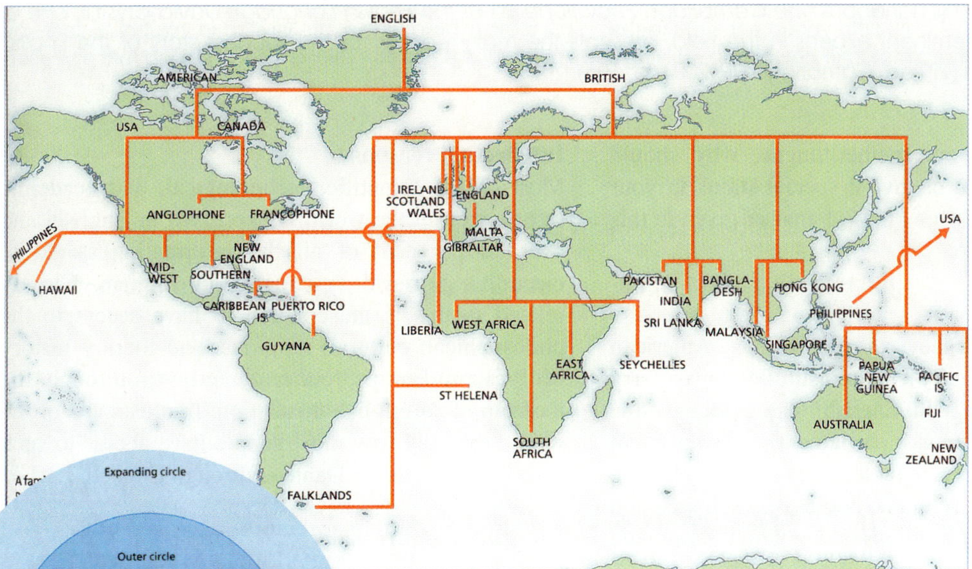

Family Tree of English

A family tree representation of the way English has spread around the world, showing the influence of the two main branches of American and British English.

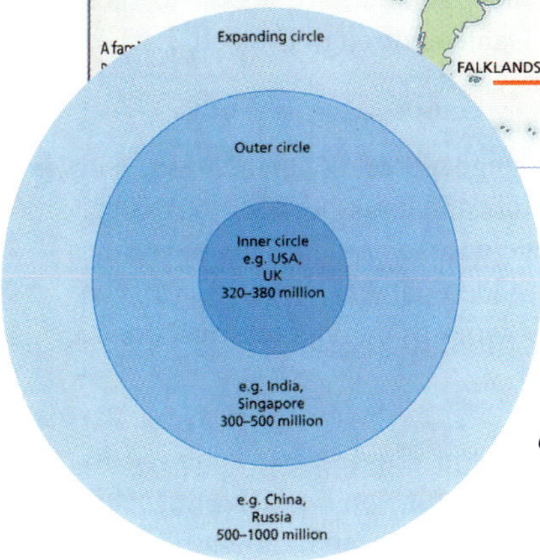

Three Circles

The spread of English can be visualized as three concentric circles, representing different ways in which the language has been acquired and is currently used. (1) The inner circle refers to the traditional bases of English – English is the primary language. (2) In the outer or extended circle English has become part of the country's chief institutions; it fulfils an important "second language role" in multilingual settings. (3) In the expanding circle or extending circle the importance of English is recognized as an international language.

Awareness

1 How many varieties of English do you know? Can you describe how they differ from each other?

Comprehension

2 Describe the spread of English, using your own words.

Analysis

3 Discuss the problems of Kachru's model of the concentric circles as far as language skills are concerned.

Opinion

4 Are native speakers automatically the best speakers of English?
5 Which English has the most prestige and authority? Is this changing? Are there Englishes which have little prestige? Why?

4

Thomas L. Friedman

"The Five Gas Stations of the World"

The journalist Thomas L. Friedman was born in Minneapolis in 1953, educated at Brandeis University and St. Anthony's College, Oxford. For his first book, *From Beirut to Jerusalem*, he was awarded the National Book Award in the US. He has also won two prestigious Pulitzer Prizes for reporting for *The New York Times*. Living in Bethesda, Maryland, he is today one of the most prominent supporters of globalization. His main publication on the issue is the book *The Lexus and the Olive Tree*. In its title, the contradictions of the age of globalization are symbolized. The Lexus, a large, high-tech luxury car made by the "global player" Toyota, is one aspect of this process; the olive tree as the product of traditional farming and production methods is its complementary symbol. – Thomas L. Friedman, *The Lexus and the Olive Tree: Understanding Globalization* (New York: Anchor Books, 2000), pp. 379–381.

I believe in the five gas stations theory of the world. That's right: I believe you can reduce the world's economies today to basically five different gas stations. First there is the Japanese gas station. Gas is $5 a gallon. Four men in uniforms and white gloves, with lifetime employment contracts, wait on you. They pump your gas. They change your oil. They wash your windows, and they wave at you with a friendly smile as you drive away in peace. Second is the American gas station. Gas costs only $1 a gallon, but you pump it yourself. You wash your own windows. You fill your own tires. And when you drive around the corner four homeless people try to steal your hubcaps. Third is the Western European gas station. Gas there also costs $5 a gallon. There is only one man on duty. He grudgingly pumps your gas and unsmilingly changes your oil, reminding you all the time that his union contract says he only has to pump gas and change oil. He doesn't do windows. He works only thirty-five hours a week, with ninety minutes off each day for lunch, during which time the gas station is closed. He also has six weeks' vacation every summer in the south of France. Across the street, his two brothers and uncle, who have not worked in ten years because their state unemployment insurance pays more than their last job, are playing boccie ball. Fourth is the developing-country gas station. Fifteen people work there and they are all cousins. When you drive in, no one pays any attention to you because they all are busy talking to each other. Gas is only 35 cents a gallon because it is subsidized by the government, but only one of the six gas pumps actually works. The others are broken and they are waiting for the replacement parts to be flown in from Europe. The gas station is rather run-down because the absentee owner lives in Zurich and takes all the profits out of the country. The owner doesn't know that half his employees actually sleep in the repair shop at night and use the car wash equipment to shower. Most of the customers at the developing-country gas station either drive the latest-model Mercedes or a motor scooter – nothing in between. The place is always busy, though, because so many people stop in to use the air pump to fill their bicycle tires. Lastly there is the communist gas station. Gas there is only 50 cents a gallon – but there is none, because the four guys working there have sold it all on the black market for $5 a gallon. Just one of the four guys who is employed at the communist gas station is actually there. The other three are working at second jobs in the underground economy and only come around once a week to collect their paychecks.

What is going on in the world today, in the very broadest sense, is that through the process of globalization everyone is being forced toward America's gas station. If you are not an American and don't know how to pump your own gas, I suggest you learn. With the end of the Cold War, globalization is globalizing Anglo-American-style capitalism and the Golden Straitjacket. It is globalizing American culture and cultural icons. It is globalizing the best of America and the worst of America. It is globalizing the American Revolution and it is globalizing the American gas station.

But not everyone likes the American gas station and what it stands for, and you can understand why. Embedded in the Japanese, Western European and communist gas stations are social contracts very different from the American one, as well as very different attitudes about how markets should operate and be controlled. The Europeans and the Japanese believe in the state exercising power over the people and over markets, while Americans tend to believe more in empowering the people and letting markets be as free as possible to sort out who wins and who loses.

Because the Japanese, Western Europeans and communists are uncomfortable with totally unfettered markets and the unequal benefits and punishments they distribute, their gas stations are designed to cushion such inequalities and to equalize rewards. Their gas stations also pay more attention to the distinctive traditions and value preferences of their communities. The Western Europeans do this by employing fewer people, but paying them higher wages and collecting higher taxes to generously support the unemployed and to underwrite a goody bag of other welfare-state handouts. The Japanese do it by paying people a little less but guaranteeing them a lifetime employment, and then protecting those lifetime jobs and benefits by restricting foreign competitors from entering the Japanese market. The American gas station, by contrast, is a much more efficient place to drive through: the customer is the king; the gas station has no social function; its only purpose is to provide the most gas at the cheapest price. If that can be done with no employees at all – well, all the better. A flexible labor market will find them work somewhere else. Too cruel, you say? Maybe so. But, ready or not, this is the model that the rest of the world is increasingly being pressured to emulate.

Vocabulary

5 gallon (n.): a unit for measuring liquids, equal to eight pints; in the US it is 3.79 litres – **6 lifetime employment contract:** a written statement by the state or a company granting you a job for life – **13 hubcap** (n.): a round metal cover for the centre of a wheel on a vehicle – **15 grudgingly** (adv.): showing a feeling of dislike – **17 union contract:** official agreement with an organization representing workers – **24 state unemployment insurance:** money you get from the state when you are out of work – **26 boccie ball:** a game similar to lawn bowling played on a long narrow usually dirt court – **30 subsidize** (v.): the government pays part of the cost of a company – **35 absentee owner:** the owner is somewhere else – **64 embedded** (adj.): to be put firmly and deeply into s.th. – **77 unfettered** (adj.): /ʌn'fetəd/ not restricted by laws or rules – **82 cushion** (v.): to protect s.o. from an unpleasant situation – **84 reward** (n.): s.th. that you get because you have done s.th. good or helpful or have worked hard – **83 equalize rewards:** give the same reward to everybody – **97 underwrite** (v.): here: support s.th. with money – **97 goody bag:** s.th. which is full of pleasant and desirable things – **107 labor market:** the people looking for work and the jobs that are available at that time – **110 emulate** (v.): /'emjʊleɪt/ do s.th. or behave in the same way as s.o. else, esp. because you admire them

Explanation

57 Golden Straitjacket: a central metaphor used by Friedman for the condition most economically advanced states are in. The usual image is that of a golden cage (straitjacket: AmE; BrE: straightjacket: /'streɪtˌdʒæk·ɪt/ 1. a special piece of clothing that prevents s.o. from moving their arms, used to control s.o. who is being violent or, in the past, s.o. who was mentally ill. 2. s.th. such as a law or set of ideas that puts very strict or unfair limits on s.o.

Awareness

1 How do attitudes towards work and the economy differ worldwide? Remember impressions you gained when abroad. Also think about some of the clichés that exist about the work ethic in other countries.
2 What is the common image of American, African, Asian, etc. attitudes towards work?
3 How does the process of globalization influence work, especially job perspectives, in your country?
4 Think of globalization as a process of many conflicts and contradictions. Friedman uses the pair of the Lexus and the olive tree. Make a list of similar contradictory couples that could symbolize the global village.

Comprehension

5 Divide the text into sections (Reference Library, pp. 312f.).
6 Look at the first part of the text dealing with the five gas stations. Describe in your own words the particularities of each station. How do the gas stations reflect on the countries' respective mentality?
7 What, according to the text, becomes clear about the differences between the world economies?
8 Make a list of all the negative sides of non-American gas stations as mentioned in the text, beginning with lifetime employment contracts, state subsidies, etc.
9 Then make a list of all the positive aspects of American gas stations.
10 Why, according to the author, is the American gas station possibly the only solution to the world's problems?
11 Look at the last part of the text. What are the conclusions the author draws from his comparisons? Do you agree?

Analysis

12 Comment on the author's description of the gas stations. What peculiarities does he choose in each case and why? Does he exaggerate? If yes, is there some truth in his descriptions?
13 Comment in detail on the author's summing up of the disadvantages of non-American gas stations and the recipe he offers to the rest of the world.
14 Why are more and more countries "pressured" to follow the American model? Give some suggestions (Reference Library, p. 306).
15 Explain the "Golden Straitjacket" image.
16 Explain the term "lifetime employment contract" and comment on its usage in the text (l. 6). What, on the contrary, is meant and implied by the term "flexible labor market" (l. 107)?
17 Why, according to the author, are state subsidies negative for the economy?
18 Why is the term "efficiency" so important in the context of globalization? Give some suggestions (Reference Library, p. 306).

Opinion

19 "The customer is king" – discuss (Reference Library, p. 299) this term, referring to experiences in your own country.
20 What consequences might follow if we all were to imitate the model of the American gas station?
21 Comment on the author's pro-American attitude.
22 Why does globalization equal Americanization for many people?
23 Do you think that Americanization has its advantages?
24 To what degree has everyday life in your country become Americanized?

Projects

25 Read more passages from *The Lexus and the Olive Tree*, a book with a wealth of information on what effects globalization has on everyday lives everywhere on this planet. Write a book review, commenting on Friedman's optimistic view on globalization as Americanization.
26 Imagine being a politician who has to introduce a new economic model, less social than the existing one because of severe cuts to adapt to the international market situation. Make a list of the arguments which might come up in favour of or against this model.
27 The American gas station, according to Friedman, has "no social function; its only purpose is to provide". What do you know about the economic system in your country? Which implications does its concept have? Is it a good idea to abandon it completely in favour of an American-style economy as described by Friedman?

5

Bill Gates

The Road Ahead

William "Bill" Gates (born 1955) is chairman and chief software architect of Microsoft Corporation, one of the world's leading companies. He is not only (at the moment) the richest man in the world, but also a living example of the American success story. His unbounded optimism and belief in the personal computer, the Internet and information technology (=IT) in general are expressed in his bestselling book *The Road Ahead*. In it he develops his vision of a world in which everybody is interconnected globally by interactive computer networks. For Bill Gates, the spread of the Information Age will transform all our lives for the better. In the following excerpt from the book he writes about the need to adapt to the Information Age – and its benefits. – Bill Gates, *The Road Ahead: Completely Revised and Updated* (Harmondsworth: Penguin, 1996), pp. 294, 298.

The younger you are, the more important it is that you adapt. If you're fifty or older today, you may be out of the workforce before you'll need to use a computer – although I think that if you don't learn you'll be missing out on the chance for some meaningful experiences. But if you're twenty-five today and not comfortable with computers, you risk being ineffective in almost any kind of work you pursue.

Ultimately, the interactive network isn't for my generation or the one before me. It's for future generations. The kids who have grown up with PCs in the last decade, and the kids who will grow up with the network in the next, will push the technology to its limits.

We have to pay particular attention to correcting the gender imbalance. When I was young, it seemed that only boys were encouraged to mess around with computers. Girls are far more active with computers today than they were two decades ago, but there are still many fewer women than men in technical careers. By making sure that girls as well as boys get comfortable with computers at an early age, we can ensure that both sexes enjoy their rightful share of the good jobs that are available to people with computer expertise.

My own experience as a child and the experience of my friends raising children today is that, once a child is exposed to computing, he or she is hooked. But we have to create the opportunity for that exposure. Schools should have low-cost access to computers connected to the interactive network, and teachers need to become comfortable with the new tools. One of the wonderful things about the interactive network is that virtual equity can be achieved much more easily than real-world equity. It would take a massive amount of money to give every grammar school in every poor area the same library resources as the good schools in Beverly Hills. But when you put schools online, they all get the same access to information, wherever it might be stored. We are all created equal in the virtual world, and we can use this equality to help address some of the sociological problems that society has yet to solve in the physical world. The network won't eliminate barriers of inequality and prejudice, but it will be a powerful force in that direction. […]

The presence of advanced communications systems promises to make countries more alike and reduce the importance of national boundaries. The fax machine, the portable video camera, and Cable News Network are among the forces that brought about the end of communist regimes and the Cold War because they enabled news to pass both ways through the Iron Curtain. […]

The new access to information can draw people together by increasing their understanding of other cultures. But commercial satellite broadcasts to countries such as China and Iran offer citizens glimpses of the outside world that are not necessarily sanctioned by their governments. Some governments are afraid that such exposure will cause discontent and worse, a "revolution of expectations" when disenfranchised people get enough information about another lifestyle to contrast it with their own. Within individual societies, the balance between traditional and modern experiences is bound to shift as people use the network to expose themselves to a greater range of possibilities. Some cultures may feel under assault as people pay greater attention to global issues and cultures and less to their traditional local ones.

Vocabulary

13 pursue (v.): /pə'sjuː/ wish to have - **23 gender imbalance** (n.): uneven chances and different interests depending on whether you are male or female - **24 mess around with** (v.): toy with - **31 expertise** (n.): /ˌekspə'tiːz/ special skills or knowledge in a particular subject - **34 expose to** (v.): show s.th. that is usually covered or hidden - **34 hooked** (adj.): caught, addicted - **39 equity** (n.): /'ekwɪti/ a situation in which all people are treated equally and no one has an unfair advantage - **55 eliminate** (v.): /ɪ'lɪmɪneɪt/ to completely get rid of s.th. - **70 broadcast** (v.): to send out radio or television programmes - **71 glimpse** (n.): a look at - **72 sanction** (v.): to officially accept or allow something - **74 exposure** (n.): experience of new things - **74 discontent** (n.): a feeling of being unhappy and not satisfied with the situation you are in - **75 disenfranchised** (adj.): /ˌdɪsɪn'fræntʃaɪzd/ not having any rights, especially the right to vote, and not feeling part of society - **78 is bound to**: will certainly - **81 assault** (n.): attack

Explanations

14 interactive network: computer systems or computer games which allow you to communicate directly with them - **64 Cable News Network**: a US news network on television, paid for by the person watching it - **66 Cold War**: the unfriendly relationship between the US and the Soviet Union after the Second World War - **67 Iron Curtain**: the name that was used for the border between the Communist countries of Eastern Europe and the rest of Europe

The growing number of Internet users

Worldwide number of Internet users (in million)

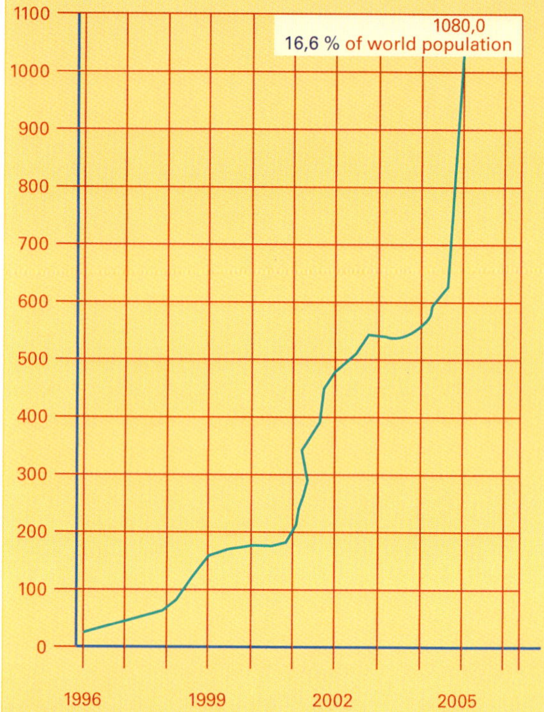

Sources: IDC Research, Killen and Associates, MIDAS, MIDS, Nua. Internet Surveys (http://www.nua.ie/surveys/)

Awareness

1 How is your life formed by the tools of the Information Age? Could you "survive" without your mobile phone, your PC, the Internet, e-mail access, etc.?

Comprehension

2 Make a list of all the technical terms used in the article. Do you understand them all? If not, does that make you "IT-illiterate" and therefore unfit for the Information Age?
3 What, according to Gates, are the IT challenges for the young generation? Can you meet them?
4 Make a list of all the advantages of IT – past and future – Gates enumerates in this text.
5 What are the reasons Gates gives for his optimism?

Analysis

6 Provide a summary (Reference Library, p. 307) of Gates' line of argument.
7 "The younger you are, the more important it is that you adapt" (ll. 1f.). Adapt to what and why? Base your answer on quotations from the text.
8 What does the term "gender imbalance" (l. 23) express?
9 Explain the term "virtual equity" (l. 39).
10 Why and how would private corporations finance school networks? Consider the problems of such ventures.

Opinion

11 How is worldwide equality via information technology achieved? Discuss Gates' vision and develop counter-arguments.
12 Do you agree that the fax machine contributed to the end of Communism? Or that new technologies in general brought about the fall of the Wall? Is this an exaggeration?
13 Does easier exchange of information lead to less intercultural misunderstanding, as suggested by Gates? Think about examples from your own life.

6

Pico Iyer

"The Nowhere Man"

Born in England to Indian parents, Pico Iyer was educated at Eton, Oxford and Harvard. Currently dividing his life between California and Japan, Iyer is a renowned regular contributor to international magazines and a writer of non-fiction. His articles explore how our world is shaped by the way cultures interact, collide and coexist. Drawing on his personal experiences, he relates in his writings extraordinary insights into the way the global and the local meet. - Pico Iyer, "The Nowhere Man", *Observer*, February 16, 1997.

By the time I was nine, I was already used to going to school by transatlantic plane, to sleeping in airports, to shuttling back and forth three times a year, between my parents' Indian home in California and my boarding school in England. While I was growing up, I was never within 6,000 miles of the nearest relative. From the time I was a teenager, I took it for granted that I could take my budget vacations in Bolivia and Tibet, China and Morocco. It never seemed strange to me that a girlfriend might be ten hours flying time away, that my closest friends might be on the other side of a continent.

It was only recently that I realised that all these habits of mind and life would scarcely have been imaginable in my parents' youth; that the very facts and facilities that shape my world are all distinctly new developments, and mark me as a modern type. It was only recently, in fact, that I realised that I am an example, perhaps, of an entirely new breed of people, a transcontinental tribe of wanderers that is multiplying as fast as international telephone lines and frequent flyer programmes. We are the transit loungers, forever heading to the departure gate. We buy our interests duty-free, we eat our food on plastic plates, we watch the world through borrowed headphones. We pass through countries as through revolving doors, impermanent residents of nowhere. Nothing is strange to us, and nowhere is foreign. We are visitors even in our own homes. [...]

This kind of life offers an unprecedented sense of freedom and mobility: tied down nowhere, we can pick and choose among locations. Ours is the first generation that can go off to visit Tibet for a week, or meet Tibetans down the street. At a superficial level, this new internationalism means that I can meet, in the Hilton coffee shop, an Indonesian businessman who is as conversant as I am with Magic Johnson and Madonna. At a deeper level, it means that I need never feel estranged. If all the world is alien to us, all the world is home.

I have learned to love foreignness. In any place I visit, I have the privileges of an outsider: I am an object of interest, and even fascination; I am a person set apart, able to enjoy the benefits of the place without paying the taxes. And the places themselves seem glamourous to me – romantic – as seen through foreign eyes: distance on both sides lends enchantment. Policemen let me off speeding tickets, girls want to hear the story of my life, pedestrians will gladly point me to the nearest golden arches. Perpetual foreigners in the transit lounge, we enjoy a kind of diplomatic immunity; and, living off room service in our hotel rooms, we are never obliged to grow up, or even, really, to be ourselves.

And yet, sometimes, I stop myself and think. What kind of heart is being produced by these new changes? Must I always be a None of the Above? When the stewardess presents me with disembarkation forms, what do I fill in? My passport says one thing, my face another. My accent contradicts my eyes. Place of residence, final destination, even marital status are not much easier to fill in; usually, I just tick "other".

Beneath all the boxes, where do we place ourselves? How does one fix a moving object on a map? I am not an exile, really, nor an immigrant; not deracinated, I think, any more than I am rooted. I have not felt the oppression of war, nor found ostracism in the places where I do alight; I scarcely feel severed from a home I have scarcely known. Yet is "citizen of the world" enough to comfort me?

Alienation, we are taught from kindergarten onwards, is the condition of our time. This is the century of exiles and refugees, of boat people and statelessness; the time when traditions have been abolished, and men become closer to machines. This is the century of estrangement: one third of all Afghans live outside of Afghanistan; the second city of the Khmers is a refugee camp; the second tongue of Beverly Hills is Farsi. [...]

We airport hoppers can, in fact, go through the world as through a house of wonders, picking up something at every stop, and taking the whole globe as our playpen. And we can mix and match as the situation demands. "Nobody's history is my history," Kazuo Ishiguro, a great spokesman for the privileged homeless, once said to me, and went on, "Whenever it was convenient for me to become very Japanese, I could become very Japanese, and then, when I wanted to drop it, I would just become this ordinary Englishman." Instantly, I felt a shock of recognition: I have a wardrobe of selves from which to choose, and I savour the luxury of being able to be an Indian in Cuba (where people are starving for Yoga and Rabindranath Tagore), an American in Thailand or an Englishman in New York. [...]

Unable to get stirred by the raising of a flag, we are sometimes unable to see how *anyone* could be stirred. I sometimes think that this is how Salman Rushdie, the great analyst of this condition, somehow became its victim. He had juggled homes for so long, that he forgot how the world looks to someone who is rooted – in country or belief. He had chosen to live so far from affiliation that he could no longer see why people choose affiliation in the first place. Besides, being part of no society means one is accountable to no one, and need respect no laws outside one's own. If single nation people can be fanatical as terrorists, we can end up ineffectual as peace keepers.

We become, in fact, strangers to belief itself, unable to comprehend many of the rages and dogmas that animate (and unite) people. Conflict itself seems inexplicable to us, because partisanship is; we have the agnostic's inability to retrace the steps of faith. I could not begin to fathom why some Muslims would think of murder after hearing about *The Satanic Verses*: yet sometimes I force myself to recall that it is we, in our floating scepticism, who are the exceptions, that in China or Iran, Korea or Peru, it is not so strange to give up one's life for a cause.

We end up, then, a little like non-aligned nations, comfirming our reservations at every step. We tell ourselves, self-servingly, that nationalism breeds monsters, and choose to ignore the fact that internationalism breeds them too. Ours is the culpability not of the assassin, but of the bystander who takes a snapshot of the murder. Or, when the revolution catches fire, hops on the next plane out.

Sometimes though, just sometimes, I am brought up short by symptoms of my condition. I have never bought a house of any kind, and my ideal domestic environment, I sometimes tell my friends, is a hotel room. I have never voted, or ever wanted to vote, and I eat in restaurants three times a day. I have never supported any nation (in the Olympic games, say) or represented "my country" in anything. Even my name is weirdly international, because my "real name" is one that makes sense only in the home where I have never lived. [...]

If I have any deeper home, it is, I suppose, in English. My language is the house I carry around with me as a snail his shell; and in my lesser moments I try to forget that mine is not the language spoken in America, or even, really, by any member of my family.

Yet even here, I find, I cannot place my accent, or reproduce it as I can the tones of others. And I am so used to modifying my English inflections according to whom I'm talking to – an American, an Englishman, a villager in Nepal, a receptionist in Paris – that I scarcely know what kind of voice I have.

I wonder, sometimes, if this new kind of non-affiliation may not be alien to something fundamental in the human state. The refugee at least harbours passionate feelings about the world he has left – and generally seeks to return there; the exile at least is propelled by some kind of strong emotion away from the old country towards the new – indifference is not an exile emotion. But what does the transit lounger feel? What are the issues that we would die for? What are the passions that we would live for?

Vocabulary

4 boarding school (n.): a school where students live as well as study – **8 budget** (adj.): very low in price – **13 scarcely** (adj.): almost not or almost none at all – **18 breed** (n.): a particular kind of person or type – **18 transcontinental** (adj.): crossing a continent – **18 tribe** (n.): a social group consisting of people of the same race – **21 transit lounge** (n.): airport lounge for people who use the airport to switch directly to another flight without leaving the airport – **25 revolving door** (n.): a type of door in the entrance of a large building, which goes around and around as people go through it – **25 impermanent** (adj.): /ɪm'pɜːmənənt/ not staying the same for ever – **28 unprecedented** (adj.): /ʌn'presɪdəntɪd/ never having happened before – **33 internationalism** (n.): the belief that nations should work together and help each other – **46 enchantment** (n.): the quality of being very pleasant or attractive – **56 disembarkation form**: form to be filled out before getting off a ship or airplane – **59 marital status** (n.): /'mærɪtl/ whether s.o. is married – used especially on official forms – **63 deracinated** (adj.): /dɪ'ræsəneitɪd/ with one's (cultural) roots removed – **65 ostracism** (n.): /'ɒstrəsɪzəm/ if a group of people ostracize s.o., they refuse to accept them as a member of the group – **66 alight** (v.): to step out of a vehicle after a journey – **66 severed** (adj.): /'sevəʳd/ cut off – **67 citizen** (n.): someone who lives in a particular town, country, or state – **69 alienation** (n.): the feeling of not being part of society or a group – **70 exile** (n.): a person who is forced to leave his or her country and live in another country, especially for political reasons – **71 refugee** (n.): s.o. who has been forced to leave their country, esp. during a war, or for political or religious reasons – **80 playpen** (n.): an enclosed area in which a very small child can play safely, that is like an open box with sides made of bars or a net – **88 savour** (v.): to fully enjoy a time or experience – **92 stirred** (adj.): if a feeling stirs in you, you begin to feel it – **96 juggle** (v.): here: to try to fit two or more jobs, activities etc. into your life, especially with difficulty – **99 affiliation** (n.): the connection or involvement that s.o. or s.th. has with a political, religious etc. organization – **101 accountable** (adj.): responsible for the effects of your actions and willing to explain or be criticized for them – **106 dogma** (n.): a set of firm beliefs held by a group of people who expect other people to accept these beliefs without thinking about them – **108 inexplicable** (adj.): too unusual or strange to be explained or understood – **109 agnostic** (n.): s.o. who believes that people cannot know whether God exists or not – **108 partisanship** (n.): strongly supporting a particular political party, plan or leader, usually without considering the other choices carefully - **110 fathom** (v.): to understand what s.th. means after thinking about it carefully - **116 non-aligned** (adj.): a non-aligned country does not support, or is not dependent on, any of the powerful countries in the world - **118 self-serving** (adj.): showing that you will only do s.th. if it will gain you an advantage - used to show disapproval - **118 nationalism** (n.): exaggerated love for your own country and the belief that it is better than any other country - **118 breed** (v.): produce - **120 culpability** (n.): deserving blame - **121 bystander** (n.): s.o. who watches what is happening without taking part - **126 domestic environment** (n.): relating to family relationships and life at home - **136 snail** (n.): a small soft creature that moves very slowly and has a hard shell on its back - **141 inflection** (n.): the way in which a word changes its form to show a difference in its meaning or use - **143 receptionist** (n.): s.o. whose job is to welcome and deal with people arriving in a hotel or office building, visiting a doctor etc. - **150 propel** (v.): to move, drive, or push s.th. forward

Explanations

48 golden arches: synonym for McDonald's (the yellow M-sign of McDonald's looks like two golden arches) - **55 None of the Above**: Option to be filled out on forms if no other answer fits - **75 Khmer**: tribe of Cambodia - **75 Farsi**: the language of Iran - **81 Kazuo Ishiguro**: (1954-) novelist, born in Nagasaki but came to England in 1960. Well-known for novels such as *The Artist of the Floating World* (1986) and *The Remains of the Day* (1989) - **89 Rabindranath Tagore**: (1861-1941) a Bengali Indian writer, one of the most important Indian writers of the 20th century. His works include *Gitanjali* and *Chitra*, a play which he translated into English - **94 Salman Rushdie**: (1947-) a British writer born in India, who won the Booker Prize for his novel *Midnight's Children*. In 1988 his novel *The Satanic Verses* offended Muslims because they said that it was insulting to their religion, with the result that Ayatollah Khomeini in Iran gave a *fatwa*, an order that Rushdie should be killed. He had to live in a secret place for many years.

Awareness

1 "Mobility" is much in demand in today's job market. Make a list of the advantages and disadvantages of an international career.
2 Would you be willing and able to move around the world for a large part of your (future) career?

Comprehension

3 Describe Iyer's life as a "global player". What makes it so different from the life of the average person?
4 What advantages of his lifestyle does Iyer mention? Make a list.
5 What disadvantages and problems does he mention? Again, make a list.
6 In Iyer's opinion, do the advantages outweigh the disadvantages?

Analysis

7 Sum up the line of Iyer's article in a short précis.
8 Describe and define the position Iyer has towards globalization.
9 Can you define what it means to be a "nowhere man"?
10 Find synonyms in the text to describe this sort of person. Then decide whether they carry positive or negative connotations for you.
11 With regard to the text, does this sort of person belong to a certain class or social group? Give reasons for your answer.
12 Examine the style (Reference Library, p. 311) which makes this article very deep and reflective.
13 "If all the world is alien to us, all the world is home." Discuss the paradox.
14 Iyer does not "get stirred by the raising of a flag" – what does the author imply here? Do more and more people feel like him?
15 Explain the significance and meaning of the phrase "nationalism breeds monsters, [...] internationalism breeds them too" (ll. 118f.). What, specifically, are these "monsters"?
16 "My language is the house I carry around with me as a snail his shell." Explain the effects of these words (ll. 135f.). Would you agree (Reference Library, p. 306)?

Opinion

17 Consider Iyer's description of the life of a cosmopolitan. Does it look attractive to you?
18 What are the limits to Iyer's lifestyle? You may want to consider values or things that are important to you, which are not mentioned in the text.

Projects

19 Imagine you had a chance to talk to Iyer. What sort of questions would you ask him?
20 What will your life look like, say, twenty years from now? Write an essay (Reference Library, pp. 299f.) describing your way of life.

7

Polly Toynbee

"Who's Afraid of Global Culture?"

Polly Toynbee is a journalist, broadcaster and columnist for the British quality newspaper *The Guardian*. In the following excerpt from her article "Who's Afraid of Global Culture?" she tackles three of the major issues of globalization: Globalization as Americanization, globalization as the spread of Western cultural values, and, finally, the spread of an American-style free market system throughout the world. – The article was published in Will Hutton, Anthony Giddens (eds.), *Global Capitalism*. New York: The New Press, 2000, 191–222 (here 195f., 201).

There may be a great conspiracy to Americanise the planet, a Coca-Cola push into remotest corners, but there's no doubt it is often greeted with a warm welcome, creating just as strong a pull to suck more of it in. (Remember trips behind the Iron Curtain and how everyone begged for jeans or any artefact that symbolised the West.) For them the clash of cultures is a draw, but for Westerners it can make us ashamed. Visit a popular holiday resort in the Gambia or in Kenya and you find yourself staying in enclaves that are perfect little replicas of life in Florida plonked down in the midst of such poverty that the schoolchildren, carrying water home for miles, stop to beg for old biros outside the heavily guarded hotel compound gates. The hotel probably uses more electricity than the whole surrounding district. No holiday is better designed to make Westerners feel their own lives to be greedy, idle, rich and wasteful in comparison, though infinitely desirable to those denied it.

Naturally they want more of what we have got. Cultural globalisation for them means seizing the opportunity to have our wealthy life-style, even if, sadly, a baseball cap is as much as they can get their hands on. It may be relatively easy for the Taliban or the Iranians at their strictest to stop this Western filth crossing their borders, to ban television and every outward sign of decadence. But they know the real battle is in the hearts and minds of their own people: unless ruthlessly suppressed by culture police, people can't be trusted to watch Western television.

Why? Is it just the cry of poverty for more wealth? Often no doubt it is, though something more important may lie beneath. In the artefacts of the West they glimpse not just a world of plenty, but of freedom and opportunity – the American dream symbolised in the baseball cap. It may be dangerous folly for we know how savage Western society is and what the West has done to exploit and destroy native and alien cultures everywhere. Western 'freedom' traditionally tends to arrive as it does to the Yanomami in the rain forest – in the form of hired killers and bulldozers. Some dream.

But for many others the dream is real enough: opportunity lies in the West even if you have to swim there. Those harmonious village communities can be stifling with their rigid hierarchies and an immutable social predestination for every baby born. Getting away may be dangerous and lead to much worse, but the wide world still beckons seductively, every ancient fairy story starting with boys setting out to seek their fortune.

We are selective in our feelings about global culture. We may regret the Coca-Cola bottles but we will strive with missionary fervour to spread our most important values. In our political and social culture we have a democratic way of life which we know, without any doubt at all, is far better than any other in the history of humanity.

Deeply flawed maybe, but the best so far, Western liberal democracy is the only system yet devised that maximises freedom for the many. We preach and struggle to practise a doctrine of freedom for women and multicultural optimism – by no means perfect, but probably the best there is. Modern urban society may sometimes be frighteningly free, alienating and lonely,

"Another Starbucks on Venus."

but (for those above abject poverty) it offers a welcome escape from social pressure, superstition, patriarchy and hierarchy. […]

However, there are aspects of cultural globalisation that we should and can resist. Proud though we may be of freedom and democracy, too often it comes linked to a culture of the rampant free market and economic theories entirely predicated on insatiable greed. We deliberately encourage the greed ethos everywhere in order to create new markets, only lending money to those who profess to share our belief in it. Western economies only know how to grow or die, overproducing and over-consuming without any concept of satiety.

With shameless triumphalism at the end of the Cold War the West sent in nothing but the hard culture of Thatcherism which has brought the former USSR to its knees, allowing privateering banditry to run riot. Worse still, it has risked the reputation of liberal capitalism and democracy with a disillusioned people. The unfettered market is not the best ambassador of freedom, unmitigated by real human rights ideals or softened by the policies with which we ourselves regulate and tame it at home. The communist world discovered you can't have a thriving competitive economy without political freedom – but the West knows it is also difficult to control the worst savagery of the free market within a politically free system.

Vocabulary

6 artefact (n.): an object such as a tool, weapon etc. that was made in the past and is historically important – **8 draw** (n.): a fight ends in a draw if neither party has won – **10 enclave** (n.): /ˈenkleɪv/ a small area that is within a larger area where people of a different kind or nationality live – **11 replica** (n.): /ˈreplɪka/ an exact copy of something, especially a building, a gun, or a work of art – **11 plonk down** (v.): put s.th. down somewhere, especially in a noisy and careless way – **14 compound** (n.): an area that contains a group of buildings and is surrounded by a fence or wall – **45 stifling** (adj.): /ˈstaɪflɪŋ/ a situation that is stifling stops you from developing your own ideas and character – **45 immutable social predestination**: society has prearranged the individual's course of life right from his or her birth – **48 beckon** (n.): call – **53 fervour** (n.): /ˈfɜːvə/ very strong belief or feeling – **61 doctrine** (n.): a set of beliefs that form an important part of a religion or system of ideas – **66 patriarchy** (n.): social system in which men have all the power – **71 rampant** (adj.): if s.th. bad, such as crime or disease, is rampant, there is a lot of it and it is very difficult to control – **72 predicated on insatiable greed**: based on greed which will never be satisfied – **79 satiety** (n.): (rare) having satisfied a desire or need for s.th. such as food or sex, esp. so that you feel you have had too much – **80 triumphalism** (n.): behaviour which shows that s.o. is too proud of their success and too pleased about the defeat of their opponents; used to show disapproval – **83 allowing privateering banditry to run riot**: allowing rampant and brutal capitalism to spread without any checks – **86 unfettered** (adj.) not restricted by laws or rules – **87 unmitigated** (adj.): s.th. that is completely bad or good – **89 tame** (v.): reduce the power or strength of s.th. and prevent it from causing trouble – **90 thriving** (adj.): /ˈθraɪvɪŋ/ a thriving company, business etc. is very successful

Explanations

Cartoon: Starbucks: a global chain of coffee shops – **82 Thatcherism:** The general principles on which Margaret Thatcher's government was based when she was Prime Minister of the UK, esp. her ideas about economic management. Her ideas have also influenced politicians in other countries. She reduced taxes, took away power from trade unions, and started a programme of privatization (= selling state-owned services such as electricity, gas, and the telephone service, so that they became private companies). Similar terms are Reaganomics (referring to the former US president Ronald Regan), laissez-faire capitalism, neo-liberalism, etc.

Awareness

1 Mahatma Gandhi, a great Indian politician, once stated: "Western civilization? I think it would be a good idea." What did he imply by this remark?

Comprehension

2 Why, according to the author, is Westernization "greeted with a warm welcome" (l. 3) in many developing countries?
3 Why, according to the author, do we feel uneasy about this?
4 What is the best the West "exports" to other countries?
5 What, on the contrary, is the worst the West spreads across the globe?

Analysis

6 Divide the text into sections (Reference Library, pp. 312f.) and write down a key phrase for each section.
7 Outline the main argument of the article in a summary of about five to six sentences.

Opinion

8 Comment on the author's attitude towards what the West has to offer for other countries. Do you find her opinion convincing?
9 Are there alternatives to the spread of free market economies? If yes, describe them.

Viewfinder Special Reference Library

This section of **Viewfinder Special** aims to help you acquire the language, knowledge, and skills that you need in order to work on the texts, exercises and assignments in this book. It is meant as a reference section; in other words, when you are given a task like analysing a text or answering some questions on language, you can look up the relevant topic in this section and you will find helpful information and advice.

Section One – Tasks and Study Skills

This section explains the kind of tasks and assignments which you are expected to perform in connection with the texts, and gives you practical advice on how to carry them out.

Section Two – How to Communicate

This section contains phrases and expressions you will need in order to improve your communicative skills (for example, in a discussion or debate).

Section Three – How to Analyse Texts

This section explains the terminology and techniques you require to analyse literary and non-literary texts.

Section Four – Language Workshop

This section contains the information you need to answer any questions on language in the main chapters of the book, and gives extra information on many other aspects of English grammar.

Section Five – How to Read a Film

This section explains the terminology you need in order to analyse and understand the techniques of film-making.

www **Section Six – How to Use the Internet**

This section will help you to use the Internet more effectively when doing research.

Section One - Tasks and Study Skills

Tasks

Article

An **article** is a text which is written for a newspaper, journal or a magazine. It may be scientific (scholarly) and serious, or popular and entertaining. The aim of an article is to present ideas or facts in an interesting way. Serious articles in scholarly magazines are very similar to essays (see below). Popular articles in newspapers and magazines will normally use some eye-catching device to attract a reader's attention. This device might be: a picture (photograph), an interesting or unusual heading. Popular articles in newspapers frequently begin with a quotation or a report of an exciting or outrageous incident or anecdote.

When you write an article, make sure you:
- organise your facts and ideas logically
- keep to the point and do not digress too much
- think of a way to catch your reader's attention.

You find further useful information under **essay** below.

Brainstorming

In a **brainstorming** session, the class spontaneously tries to find a solution to a problem or an answer to a question.

1 The problem or question is stated simply and clearly (for example, "How can we make our school more attractive to work in?").

2 Working together in groups of four or five, the students give single sentence ideas for about five minutes. One or two students are responsible for writing the ideas down (on the board, perhaps) as they come.
Only single sentences may be used.
There must be no explanations, no discussion, no reactions at this stage.

3 The class goes through the list of ideas, each person explaining what he/she meant by his/her sentence.

4 Now the suggestions are open for general discussion.
The advantage of brainstorming is that, because it is spontaneous, ideas are put forward which might otherwise not be mentioned. Many of the ideas will be absurd, irrelevant, beside the point, but usually there are some which are very useful indeed. For brainstorming to succeed it is essential that no one is afraid to say what he/she thinks. All points are of value in some way to begin with.

Debate

A **debate** is a discussion with very fixed procedures:

1 It always begins with a **motion**: the subject of the debate is read out by the chairperson, who is neutral and does not express any views on the subject. It is his/her job to make sure the rules are kept to and the debate is fair. The motion is usually formulated like this: "This House believes that ..."

2 Four designated speakers then put forward their views and arguments. Two speak in favour of the motion and two speak against it. They usually have prepared speeches and stand up to deliver them. The first speaker supports the motion, the second speaker is against, the third supports, the fourth is against. The most important speakers are the first speakers for and against the motion.

3 When the official speeches are finished, the motion is "open to the floor", i.e. the chairperson calls upon the other people present at the debate to put forward their views.

4 When this is finished, the chairperson calls upon the proposer of the motion (the first speaker in favour) to sum up his/her points, which he/she does quickly and precisely. Now the chairperson takes a vote asking who is for the motion and who is against it. Everyone except the chairperson is allowed to vote. The votes are counted and the winning side is announced. If both sides get equal votes, the chairperson can now cast his/her deciding vote.

Discussion

The aim of a **discussion** is to give people the chance to air their views on a particular subject, to listen to what other people have to say, to criticise other views, to defend or change one's own views. A final conclusion may be arrived at but this is not the main aim. It is not the result of the discussion which is of greatest importance but the process of exchanging ideas.
A discussion can be quite informal but for it to succeed some basic rules must be kept to:

1 There should be a discussion leader, i.e. someone who decides whose turn it is to speak, to make sure that the rules are kept to. It is a good idea if this discussion leader occasionally summarises what has been said so far, so that those discussing remember what they are actually talking about. It is very easy to get off the track and forget the original subject. The discussion leader need not always be the class teacher, in fact it is very useful when he/she isn't!

2 The discussion can either be a class discussion or can take place in groups.

3 If you are a participant in a discussion, it is a good idea to write down in note form beforehand what you want to say. This will give you greater confidence when speaking in public.

Essay

An **essay** is a formal written discussion of a topic.

Introduction

Start your essay with an introduction. Here you can tell the reader what you are going to discuss. Phrases that you can use are: *This essay will be about ... . In this essay I shall discuss ... . In the following I shall be concerned with the problem/subject of ...*
An alternative is to give an illustration of what you want to discuss, perhaps in the form of a story or anecdote or an experience that you have had.

Main Part

Here you discuss/deal with the topic you mentioned in your introduction. It is very important that your main part should have a suitable form to it, in other words that it does not consist of just a collection of any ideas that occurred to you. The structure of your main part depends very much on the type of essay that you are writing. Is it argumentative (discussing the pros and cons of a certain idea, suggestion, etc.) or illustrative (giving information on a particular subject)? Here are some suggestions for structuring your main part:

Argumentative: If you want to argue for and against a particular idea (for example, "Is it a good idea to keep pets?"), one way you can do this is to present the arguments *in favour* in the first part and the arguments *against* in the second.
Alternatively, you can discuss the pros and cons of each point at a time – first discussing whether keeping a pet teaches a person responsibility or not; next, to what extent pets provide company or not; then, whether pets are a health hazard or not, and so on.
Illustrative: If you want to give information about a particular subject, make sure you do not end up with a kind of shopping list. Arrange your facts into sections. For example, if you are asked to characterise a person in a story, first of all present all the information you have about his/her appearance; next, about his/her behaviour; then about his/her feelings/attitudes, and so on.
It is a good idea in such illustrative essays to show your reader how the information is connected; for example, you might have arranged your facts in order of importance – if so, you could indicate this by introducing them together with expressions like: *first of all; next; then; finally,* etc. If you are giving examples, use phrases like: *for example; for instance.* If you are pointing out similarities, show this with expressions like: *similarly; likewise.* If your facts refer to contrasts, use phrases like: *on the one hand ..., on the other hand ...* . For a more complete list of linking expressions see p. 307 below.

Conclusion

When you have finished discussing your theme or illustrating your topic, end your essay with a conclusion. Here you can sum up your main points again; give your own opinion (particularly important in an argumentative essay); refer back to your introduction; mention aspects of the subject you did not discuss in detail. It is also a good idea to show your reader that he/she has reached the conclusion by using certain concluding phrases like: *to sum up; all in all; in conclusion; to conclude,* and so on.

Now some general 'Dos and Donts:
1 Always collect your facts before you start writing. Do this in note form (see p. 304 below).
2 Always write down an essay plan, so that you know what you are going to write before you start.
3 Always read through your essay carefully afterwards to check for mistakes.
4 Never write your essay in German first and then translate it into English. You will only make lots of mistakes in expression and grammar.
5 Always use a learner's dictionary to see how words and phrases are properly used (see pp. 304f. below for information on using a dictionary).
6 Try to use words and phrases that you have actually seen or used before.

Letter

There are basically two types of **letter** that you might want to write – the personal letter and the formal letter. For personal letters, there are no standard rules that you must follow, but formal letters are a different matter. You might be applying for a job, asking for information, complaining about something, and so on. The impression that your letter makes, therefore, is very important. Here are some tips that will help you to write personal and formal letters:
1 Write your own address, without your name, in the top right-hand corner.
2 In a formal letter, write the receiver's address, with his/her name, below your address but on the left-hand side.
3 Write the date below this on the right-hand side.
4 In a formal letter, write the subject of your letter below the date on the left-hand side. Introduce it with *Re*:.
5 Begin your personal letter with *Dear* + name; begin your formal letter with *Dear + Sir/Madam* or *Dear Mr/Mrs/Ms* + name.
6 Finish your personal letter with *Love* + your Christian name; finish your formal letter with *Yours sincerely/faithfully* + your full name. It is a good idea to use a closing phrase like *I'm looking forward to hearing from you soon* or *Thank you very much in advance for your help.*

Mind Map and Topic Web

Mind maps and **topic webs** are used to discover in an interesting way what you know (or don't know!) and feel about a topic, subject, idea, etc. They both start off with a main idea which is presented in the form of a sentence, word, concept, picture, etc. in the middle of a page. This forms the starting-point for your map or web. Then any questions, thoughts or associations that you might have about the subject you write down, using lines which branch off from the original idea. Any further ideas that occur can also be attached at any place at which they are relevant. Don't forget that branches can be attached to other branches. There are differences between a mind map and a topic web.
A **mind map** is subjective and reveals what you personally associate with and how you react to a particular subject.
A **topic web** is objective and aims to reveal the structure of your knowledge about a particular subject.
Mind maps and topic webs can be carried out individually or in groups. The illustrations below show how mind maps and topic webs work.

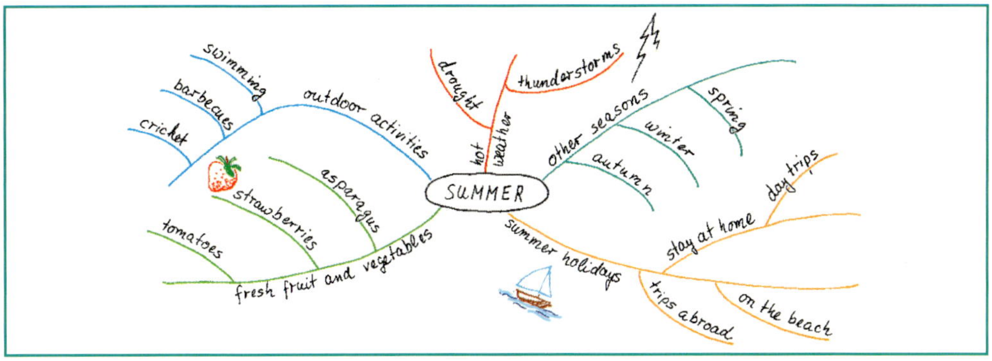

A mind map on 'summer'

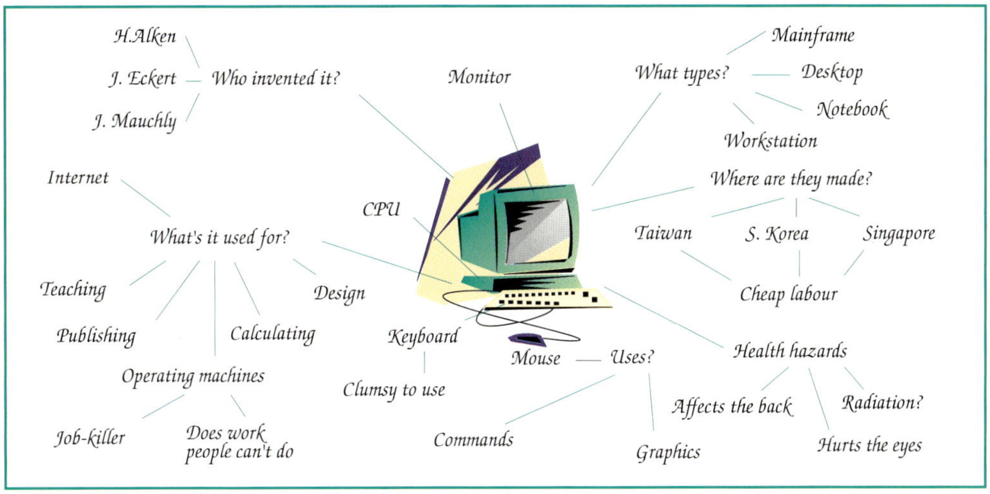

A topic web on 'computers'

Paper and Speech

Giving a **paper** and making a **speech** are both forms of public speaking. When you give a paper, you present information or your ideas/views to your listeners in an academic way, often illustrating what you say with examples, proving your points, etc. When you make a speech, you are normally trying to persuade people to accept your views. These two forms of speaking, however, share one important feature: your paper/speech will only be heard and not read, so you have to be particularly careful about the way in which you present your information. Listening requires more attention and concentration than reading, and as very few people can concentrate for longer than ten minutes at a time, the presenter of a paper has to give the listener some help. Here are a few suggestions:

1 Don't simply read out your paper/speech and forget your audience. The best thing is to try to speak freely, just using your written paper or notes to remind you of what you want to say.
2 Don't be afraid to repeat yourself and summarise your points every few minutes or so. The more often you say something, the more likely it is to be remembered. That doesn't mean, of course, that you must repeat every sentence ten times.
3 Look at your audience frequently to see if they are following you. Their faces will tell you this. If they're not all following, it may be that you are speaking too fast, so slow down a bit.
4 It is helpful for the listener to know what to expect from a paper, so you should state at the beginning what it is you will be talking about. Don't forget to summarise your main points at the end. For further information on this, see the section on writing an essay, pp. 299f., above.

Special techniques for giving a paper:

1 If possible, illustrate what you are saying with diagrams, maps, etc. If you don't give a Power Point presentation you might write down your main points on the blackboard or on a transparency on the overhead projector. It is even better if you prepare a handout with your main points and give it to your fellow students.
2 You might want to give people the chance to ask questions while you are delivering your paper. If not, you should allow questions at the end.

Project

One of the most complex tasks you have to do in this book is the **project.** The idea behind a project is that you both take up and develop the knowledge, insights and skills that you have gained by working on a text or collection of texts. The project can have different forms, but every project requires careful planning.

1 If you are working on a group project, delegate responsibilities and set deadlines for when certain tasks should be completed.

2 Collect information and materials, etc., using the Internet (see p. 326) and/or your school or local library. Some information can be found in encyclopaedias such as *Encyclopaedia Britannica*, which is in English, other information must be looked up in specialist books. Other important sources of information are the British Council, the *Amerikahaus* and other government agencies in the USA or the UK.

3 When making notes on information you have found, always write down the source carefully in case you wish to quote from it – include information about: the author, the title, the publisher, the place and date of publication, relevant page and line numbers.

4 Make sure that any written text has a presentable form.

5 Check your work through for errors of content and language.

6 Give the work you have produced to others for critical comment.

Report

You are probably familiar with writing a **report** from your mother-tongue classes, but here, just to remind you, are a few points for you to bear in mind:

1 A report is supposed to present important information in a direct way. The information should be relatively easy for the reader to understand.

2 A report often answers the reader's questions about: when, where, why and how something happened and who did what to whom.

3 A report is objective both in style and in content. This means that the writer should use language which is not too colloquial and familiar – for example, if you are reporting about a crime which has been committed by someone, then refer to the person as "the man", "the young woman", possibly "the accused", but not "the guy". At the same time you should avoid expressing your own feelings and thoughts, because you should be concentrating on the facts. You might, however, give your own thoughts or views at the end.

4 Sometimes it is a good idea to illustrate your report with diagrams or pictures, if they make it easier for the reader to understand the information.

The following is a good example of a typical newspaper report:

Witness denies army claim on Ulster shoot-out

Soldiers had 'no reason' to open fire on unarmed brothers at checkpoint

by Liam Clarke

Belfast: A key witness who saw two Irish brothers shot by Royal Marines after they passed an Ulster checkpoint last week has contradicted army accounts that they drove into soldiers.

Pat Martin, a publican who was waiting in a queue of traffic at the same checkpoint in South Armagh, has given a detailed statement to detectives in which he says the army patrol opened fire without warning. Fergal Caraher was killed and his brother was seriously injured.

Who? When? Who? Where? What happened? How? What happened? How?

Role Play

In a **role play** you are expected to act out a scene in which you and your fellow students represent a particular character in a certain situation. The situation and the characters are normally described to you and you have to develop a scene based on the information given. Role plays can be performed spontaneously or they can be prepared beforehand and then acted out. If they are prepared, it is not usually a good idea to perform the scene on the basis of a finished text. Such scenes often make a rather stiff and stilted impression on the spectator. If you wish to prepare your role play in advance (normally a good idea) you can do this by writing role cards. A role card will inform a character:

who she/he is
in which situation she/he finds her/himself
how the situation will probably develop
what kind of things the character will be likely to say.

When preparing a role play, do this in a group. Don't forget to think about the kind of language (vocabulary, phrases etc.) you will probably want to use. Sometimes you can increase the difficulty (and the excitement) of a role play by writing role cards not for your own group but for another one.

Summary

Being able to give a **summary** is an important skill that you need when you have to report information to other people. Very often you are asked to give a summary of a written text. Here are some suggestions how to do it:

1 Concentrate on basic facts and arguments and leave out information which is not essential: for example, anecdotes, explanations, and minor details.

2 Read the text through to the end at least twice to find out what is important.
3 During the second or third reading make notes on the important details (see p. 304 below).
4 Use your notes as the basis for your summary.
5 Think carefully about the tenses you use. Generally the Present Simple is used to summarise literature.
6 Aim to write a summary which is about one third of the original length.
7 Finally, read through your text and check if there are still any words which are not absolutely necessary, e.g. phrases like "The author mentions ...", "The author points out ...".

Survey

Carrying out a **survey** means finding out what other people think, do, etc. It is supposed to provide objective statistical information in cases where usually we only have subjective impressions. A survey can be conducted in the written or the spoken form. Both have their advantages and disadvantages: the written survey ensures that all respondents receive exactly the same questions; with the spoken survey misunderstandings can be clarified on the spot.

The **written** survey is conducted using a **questionnaire**. If you decide to use this form:

1 Make sure the questions are straightforward and can be easily answered, (for example, by multiple choice).
2 Give the respondents enough space to answer questions.
3 Give proper attention to presentation and layout – the respondent should get a favourable impression.

The **spoken** survey takes the form of an **interview**. If you decide to use this form:

1 Record your interview on a cassette or tape recorder (make sure that it functions properly beforehand).
2 Help your respondent to feel at ease.
3 Make sure that your important questions have been formulated before you start the interview.

General points:

1 Assure your respondents of the anonymity of the survey (use numbers rather than names on questionnaires).
2 Try as far as possible to present your findings in the form of statistics.
3 Use diagrams to make your findings more easily comprehensible.

Translation

Translating from a foreign language into your mother tongue is a difficult task but these suggestions might help you:

1 Read through the whole of the original text carefully, making sure you have understood its basic meaning. Note down any good ideas for translating certain phrases that occur to you.
2 Read the text again, this time looking up any words or expressions that you do not understand either in a monolingual English dictionary or in a bilingual dictionary (see pp. 304f.).
3 Go through the original text again and this time translate it into your own language. In this first version of the translation it does not matter if the expression is a bit clumsy. The main thing is to get the basic meaning.
4 Go back to the beginning and read your 'raw' translation through again. This time make sure that what you have written makes sense and reads fluently. If a phrase or sentence sounds unusual, reformulate it so that it fits in with the rest of the sentence or text.
5 Read through your translation again, this time paying attention to the style (see p. 311). If the original text is colloquial and familiar, for example, then the translation must be in a style which is colloquial or familiar.
6 Keep as close to the original text as possible, but if this makes the translation in your own language sound strange, then alter the expressions until they sound acceptable.
7 Pay particular attention to the following aspects:
   a) Avoid using 'false friends' – words which look very similar in English and German but have different meanings. 'Eventually' translates as *schließlich* not *eventuell*; 'biscuit' as *Keks*, not *Biskuit*; 'chips' as *Pommes Frites* and not *Chips*; 'gymnasium' as *Turnhalle* and not *Gymnasium*; 'become' as *werden*, not *bekommen*, and so on.
   b) Do not simply try to translate idioms (expressions whose meanings cannot be understood from the individual words) and collocations (set phrases) word for word, but look for corresponding expressions in your own language. For example, the idioms 'to beat about the bush' and 'to kill two birds with one stone' can be translated as *um den heißen Brei herumreden* and *zwei Fliegen mit einer Klappe schlagen* respectively. The collocations 'to go <u>on foot</u>' and 'to go <u>by car</u>' are translated as *<u>zu Fuß</u> gehen* and *<u>mit dem Auto</u> fahren*, for example. Phrasal verbs are often idiomatic in English and you will need to look them up in a dictionary: 'to set out' – *sich auf den Weg machen*; 'to turn down' – *ablehnen*; 'to give over' – *aufhören* are just some examples from among hundreds.
   c) You cannot usually translate English present participles (p. 320) with German participles. Normally you have to paraphrase the sentences in which they appear. For example, '<u>Being</u> very tired, the students fell asleep' could be translated as *<u>Da</u> sie sehr müde <u>waren</u>, schliefen die Studenten ein.* Sometimes there is a similar problem with gerunds (p. 320): 'You open a parachute <u>by pulling</u> a cord' – *Man öffnet einen Fallschirm, <u>indem man</u> an einer Schnur <u>zieht</u>.*
   d) Think very carefully about the tenses (pp. 314f.) and modal verbs (pp. 316f.) that you use in your German translations. An English Past Simple can be translated with either a German *Perfekt* or a German *Präteritum*, depending on the context. "John, I saw your girlfriend yesterday" will be translated as *"John,*

ich habe gestern deine Freundin getroffen" (colloquial, spoken German), but 'When Columbus first saw America, he thought that he was in India' would be translated as *Als Kolumbus das erste Mal Amerika sah, glaubte er in Indien zu sein* (formal, written German). The tenses in Reported Speech (pp. 318f.) also need some thought: 'He said that he was ill' – *Er sagte, er sei krank.* Back-shift (see p. 318) is used in English, *Konjunktiv* in German. Some English modal verbs can lead to misunderstandings too: 'You must not do what he says' – *Du darfst nicht machen, was er dir sagt* and not *Du musst nicht machen, ...* (see pp. 316f.).

Study Skills

Note-Making and Note-Taking

Making notes means writing down in short form information which you have got from a written source (essay, article, etc.). **Taking notes** means doing the same with a spoken source (paper, speech, lecture, etc.). Being able to make/take notes is an essential skill which will enable you to cope with many of the tasks in this book and generally at school and university. Here are some tips to help you improve your note-making/taking skills:

1 Only write down essential information. Do not attempt to 'get' everything.
2 Make sure your notes are legible.
3 Only write down important nouns, verbs, adjectives and adverbs. Avoid using pronouns, articles, auxiliary verbs, prepositions.
4 Use abbreviations for names or concepts that you have already mentioned once. Some abbreviations are standard: e.g. for 'for example'; i.e. for 'that is'.
5 Develop symbols to stand for certain relationships (for example, = for 'is/are/were', etc.; ≠ for 'is not'; → for 'became').
6 Quotations should be given in full.

Using a Dictionary

Foreign language **dictionaries** fulfil three main purposes:
1 they tell you the meaning of a word;
2 they help you to find a word you do not know;
3 they tell you how to use a word.

There are generally two kinds of dictionary which are used: a **monolingual dictionary**, which explains the meanings of English words in English and gives example sentences to show how words are used, and a **bilingual dictionary**, which gives translations of English words into another language, and from another language into English.
We shall concentrate here on using a monolingual learner's dictionary. The following extract is typical of the kind of entry you will find:

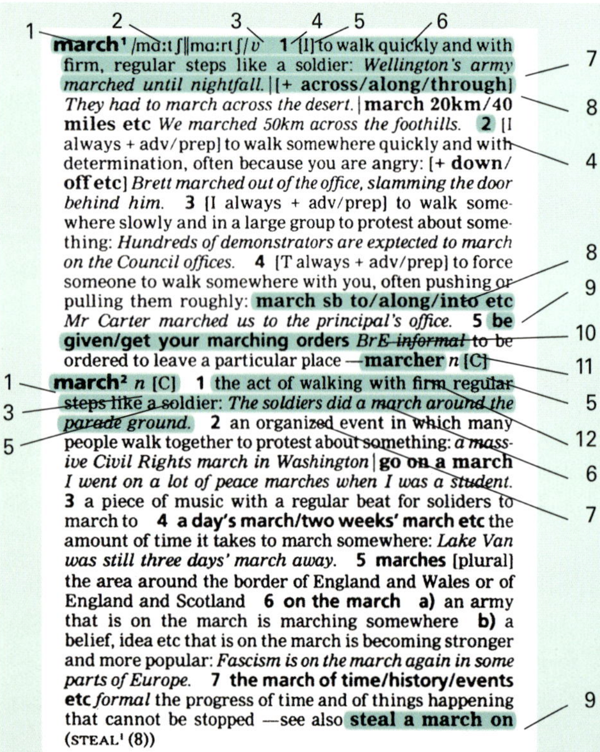

march¹ /mɑːtʃ‖mɑːrtʃ/ *v* **1** [I] to walk quickly and with firm, regular steps like a soldier: *Wellington's army marched until nightfall.* | [+ **across/along/through**] *They had to march across the desert.* | **march 20km/40 miles etc** *We marched 50km across the foothills.* **2** [I always + adv/prep] to walk somewhere quickly and with determination, often because you are angry: [+ **down/off etc**] *Brett marched out of the office, slamming the door behind him.* **3** [I always + adv/prep] to walk somewhere slowly and in a large group to protest about something: *Hundreds of demonstrators are exptected to march on the Council offices.* **4** [T always + adv/prep] to force someone to walk somewhere with you, often pushing or pulling them roughly: **march sb to/along/into etc** *Mr Carter marched us to the principal's office.* **5 be given/get your marching orders** *BrE informal* to be ordered to leave a particular place —**marcher** *n* [C]
march² *n* [C] **1** the act of walking with firm regular steps like a soldier: *The soldiers did a march around the parade ground.* **2** an organized event in which many people walk together to protest about something: *a massive Civil Rights march in Washington* | **go on a march** *I went on a lot of peace marches when I was a student.* **3** a piece of music with a regular beat for soliders to march to **4 a day's march/two weeks' march etc** the amount of time it takes to march somewhere: *Lake Van was still three days' march away.* **5 marches** [plural] the area around the border of England and Wales or of England and Scotland **6 on the march a)** an army that is on the march is marching somewhere **b)** a belief, idea etc that is on the march is becoming stronger and more popular: *Fascism is on the march again in some parts of Europe.* **7 the march of time/history/events etc** *formal* the progress of time and of things happening that cannot be stopped —see also **steal a march on** (STEAL¹ (8))

A dictionary gives you the following information:

1 The two main uses of the word: as a noun and as a verb, for example.
2 The British and the American pronunciation.
3 The word class that the word belongs to: noun (*n.*), verb (*v.*), etc.
4 The number of different meanings that the word has (1, 2, 3 ...).
5 Grammatical information about the word. With a verb, whether it is transitive (T) or intransitive (I); with a noun, whether it is countable (C) or uncountable (U).
6 The explanation(s)/meaning(s) of the word.
7 How the word is used (in example sentences).
8 Other words (prepositions, adverbs, adjectives, etc.) that can be used together with it.
9 Set expressions or idioms.
10 Special British (BrE) or American (AmE) usage.
11 The style (formal, informal, etc.) that the word belongs to. If there is no information about this, then the word does not belong to any specific style but can be used in most contexts.
12 Other words belonging to the word family.

Suggestions for using a **monolingual dictionary**:

1 Check to see which word class your word is. If it is a verb, you do not need to look at the information about its use as a noun, for example.
2 Look quickly through the different meanings given. Choose the one that fits your context best. The first meaning given is not necessarily the one you want.
3 Look at the grammatical information given (countable noun, intransitive verb, etc.) so you know how to use the word.
4 Read through the example sentence(s) so that you can see how the word is used in context.
5 Write down in your vocab. book any useful words or phrases that you find.

Suggestions for using a **bilingual dictionary**:

1 The first word offered as a translation is not necessarily the one you want, so look at the others too before you decide.
2 Think of the context in which you wish to use the word.
3 Try to find a translation word which is the same style as the original word (colloquial, formal, etc.).
4 Find out how your translation word is used. Look in the English section of your bilingual dictionary and/or in a monolingual dictionary to do this.

Language Acquisition Techniques

When we have progressed from being language learning beginners and moved on to being intermediate or advanced learners, we find that it is no longer only the teacher or the textbook that are responsible for improving our knowledge of the foreign language. We are now responsible ourselves. So what can we do to make sure that we improve our knowledge and skills? Here are some suggestions:

1 Read, watch and listen to as much English as possible. **Read** anything in English which catches your eye – thrillers, comics, newspapers, magazines, food wrappers, etc. Note down any words, expressions that you find interesting, or useful in your own personal private notebook. Look up new words in the dictionary. Try occasionally to paraphrase what you have read. Is there any other way of saying the same thing? For example, you might read: "The way we speak reveals just about as much about ourselves as the clothes we wear." You could also say: "Our accent tells other people what kind of person we are."
Watch English language films on video, DVD or TV. Some TV channels (like ARD and ZDF in Germany) occasionally show dual language broadcasts, which means you can usually listen either to the dubbed version or the original, if you have a stereo receiver (TV or video recorder). If you have cable or satellite TV, in most countries you can receive CNN, Super Channel, or Sky Movies, which broadcast in English. Particularly news programmes, discussions, and films will be useful for you. If possible, record films and TV programmes. Many videotheques also have DVDs and videos in English. Watch them several times. The first time concentrate on the basic theme or the story (if it's a film). Afterwards try to work out everything which is said. Do this by replaying the DVD over and over again until you get (almost) every word. Many DVDs showing British or American films also have subtitles in English. Begin by viewing with subtitles then without.
Listen to English language broadcasts (for example, the World Service of the BBC, which can be picked up in most parts of Europe on the medium wave band). Listen to English-language pop and rock music (you probably do so already). Don't just listen to the beat. Note down as much of the text as possible. This will not only increase your vocabulary (of course, you'll look up all the words you don't know!), but also train your listening comprehension. If possible, get hold of the texts of your favourite songs.
2 Plan and reflect on your day in English. You might even want to keep an English diary.
3 Practise and extend your vocabulary by putting together **word fields** (groups of words with related meanings) and **word families** (groups of words derived from a specific word) in your vocabulary book. For example, using a word field, you might think of all the verbs that you know that express the idea of 'movement': for example, 'to crawl', 'to creep', 'to dawdle', 'to go', 'to march', 'to run', 'to rush', 'to stroll', 'to walk', 'to wander', 'to hop', 'to skip', 'to jump', 'to fly', 'to drive', 'to ride', 'to swim', and so on. Sometimes it is useful to try to think of **synonyms** (words of the same meaning) and **antonyms** (opposites). Synonyms are, for example, 'rich', 'wealthy', 'affluent', 'well-off', but you have to be careful with their different uses, so look them up in a dictionary before you use them. Antonyms are, for example, 'patient – impatient', 'just – unjust', 'mean – generous', 'sweet – sour/bitter', 'deep – shallow', and so on. Working on word families, take a word that you know, the verb 'to work', for example, and now think of all the words and expressions that contain it: 'work', 'worker', 'workman', 'workshop', 'workshy', 'workaholic', 'workbasket', 'workbook', 'workforce', 'workstation', 'homework', etc. Another word-building technique is to try to change the meaning of a word by adding **prefixes** (syllables added to the front of a word) or **suffixes** (syllables added to the end of a word) attached to it. In this way 'do' can become 'redo', 'undo' and 'doable'. Check up the words you have thought of in a dictionary to see if they exist, what they mean and how they are used.

Making verbs from nouns and adjectives: *-ify, -ise*
(e.g. glory – glorify, modern – modernise)

Making nouns from verbs: *-ence, -er/-ess, -ment, -tion/-sion*
(e.g. refer – reference, teach – teacher, pay – payment, examine – examination)

Making nouns from adjectives: *-(i)ty, -ness*
(e.g. cruel – cruelty, happy – happiness)

Making adjectives from nouns: *-ful, -less, -y*
(e.g. hope – hopeful – hopeless, dirt – dirty)

Making adjectives from verbs: *-able*
(e.g. love – lovable)

Forming opposites: *dis-, im-, in-, un-*
(e.g. agree – disagree, possible – impossible, direct – indirect, happy – unhappy)

Section Two – How to Communicate

This section is concerned with the phrases and expressions you will need in order to participate in a discussion or a debate. Many of the phrases you will know already, but it's a good idea to remind yourself of them before beginning a conversation, discussion or debate.
Don't forget that these lists of expressions are only suggestions and that their use depends very much on the context.

Expressing Agreement and Disagreement

Complete Agreement:

- *You're absolutely right.*
- *I completely agree with you on that point.*
- *Precisely. / Exactly.*
- *So do I* (agreement with a positive statement).
- *Nor do I* (agreement with a negative statement).
- *That's what I think, too.*

Partial Agreement:

- *You're right up to a point.*
- *That might be the case.*
- *You could be right.*
- *You've got a point.*
- *Maybe that is true.*
- *That's true enough.*

Partial Disagreement:

- *Do you really think so?*
- *Are you sure?*
- *That's an exaggeration.*
- *That's not necessarily the case.*
- *It's not as simple as that.*
- *I wouldn't quite say that.*
- *I can't imagine that.*

Complete Disagreement (careful with this one! You don't want to make enemies, do you?):

- *It certainly isn't.*
- *It certainly is* (disagreement with a negative statement).
- *That's not true at all.*
- *You're quite wrong there.*

Note that when we disagree with someone, we often begin with a partial agreement: for example, "You could be right, **but** ..."

Giving an Opinion

- *In my view ...*
- *In my opinion ...*
- *As I see it ...*
- *To my mind ...*
- *If you ask me ...*

Making Suggestions/Recommendations

- *If I were you, I would ...*
- *The best thing would be to ...*
- *You'd better ...*
- *Why don't you ...?*
- *How about ...?*
- *Have you tried ...* (+ gerund)?
- *You should ...*
- *You could ...*

Beginning a Discussion

It is not a very good idea to start a discussion without any kind of introduction. Here are a few suggestions for getting started:

- *I saw an interesting programme on TV last night. / I read a fascinating article in the newspaper yesterday about ... . What do you think about that?*
- *Have you ever thought about ... / what it would be like if ...?*
- *I was really surprised to find out that ... .*
- *Did you know that ...?*

Bringing in your Partner

Sometimes in a discussion you find that you are monopolising the conversation, and you would like to know what your partner thinks. Here are some expressions for doing this:

- *So what do you think,* (+ name)?
- *How do you feel about that?*
- *What is your view on this (matter)?*

Interrupting your Partner

Sometimes it's the other way round. Your partner is monopolising the discussion and you want to have your say:

- *Can I come in there?*
- *Can I just make a point?*
- *Perhaps I can interrupt you there.*
- *I'd like to come in on that if I may.*
- *Do you mind if I say something on that point?*

Holding the Floor

Sometimes you notice that someone is trying to interrupt you but you haven't finished what you want to say, so you try to carry on (we call this "holding the floor"):

- *If I might just say this.*
- *Do you mind if I just finish this?*
- *I'd just like to finish making this point and then over to you.*
- *Let me just say this.*
- *This is my final point.*

Defending Yourself

If someone attacks you in a discussion or debate, you need some phrases to defend yourself:

- *That's not what I said/meant at all. I was merely pointing out that ...*
- *You've got that wrong. What I said was ...*
- *You're putting words in my mouth.*
- *You are distorting what I actually said.*

Ending a Discussion

When you feel that you've effectively finished your discussion, or that the conversation is not getting anywhere or that you have exhausted the topic, you have to finish off:

- *We'll just have to agree to disagree on that point.*
- *Further discussion is pointless, so let's end there.*
- *We've heard some interesting points / some new ideas, so let's stop there and go away and think about them.*
- *I can understand you better now, even though I don't completely agree with you.*

Linking Words for Essays, Reports, Papers, etc.

Listing: *first, second, third ...; firstly, secondly, thirdly ...; one, two, three* (esp. in academic and technical use); *a, b, c,* (esp. in academic and technical use); *for one thing ... (and) for another (thing); to begin with; to start with; in the first place, in the second place; next; then; finally; last(ly); to conclude; last but not least*

Adding/Reinforcing: *also; too; furthermore; moreover; then; in addition; above all; what is more*

Comparison/Similarity: *equally; likewise; similarly; in the same way*

Summary/Conclusion: *then; all in all; in conclusion; to sum up*

Exemplification: *namely; for example (e.g.); for instance; that is (i.e.); that is to say*

Result: *consequently; hence; so; therefore; thus; as a result*

Reformulation: *or rather; to put it another way; in other words*

Alternative: *alternatively; on the other hand*

Contrast: *on the contrary; in contrast; by contrast; on the one hand ..., on the other (hand)*

Concession: *besides; however; nevertheless; still; though; in spite of that; on the other hand*

Section Three – How to Analyse Texts

This section gives you some help about how to analyse literary and non-literary texts.

Literary texts are texts whose purpose is primarily artistic, imaginative and creative rather than to convey information. Literary texts include: poems, dramas, novels and short stories.

Non-literary texts are texts the purpose of which is mainly to convey information, ideas and arguments. Non-literary texts include: newspaper/magazine articles, letters, brochures, advertisements, reports, and so on.

When analysing **literary texts** you might want to consider the following aspects:
- Genre (Is the text a poem, a drama, a novel or a short story, for example?)
- Theme (What is the text about, what ideas is it discussing/presenting/conveying/evoking?)
- Character and characterisation (What are the characters like and how are they presented to us?)
- Setting and atmosphere (Where and when do the events take place and what kind of sensations are aroused in the reader/spectator?)
- Structure and other formal aspects (How has the text been put together? What poetic devices, like rhyme and rhythm, has the poet used? What narrative perspective has the author chosen?)
- Style (What kind of language has the author used?)
- Tone (What is the apparent attitude of the poet, dramatist or writer of fiction to what he/she is writing about?)

When analysing **non-literary texts** you might want to consider the following aspects:
- Text type (Is the text a newspaper article, advertisement, etc.?)
- Content (What kind of information does the text convey?)
- Structure and form (How is the text organised and how is it presented?)
- Function (Why has the text possibly been written and what does the author probably want to achieve with it?)
- Style
- Tone

In addition, both literary and non-literary texts may be in themselves or may contain one or more passages which are:
- argumentative = the author puts forward his/her opinions and/or discusses other people's ideas.
- descriptive = the author describes a place, a person or an atmosphere.
- dialogue = the author reports what people/characters say directly (as in a play).
- didactic or instructive = the author tells the reader what to think or how to behave.
- expository = the author explains some matter or topic to the reader.
- narrative = the author tells a story.

Literary Texts

Genre

When we talk about **genre** in connection with literary texts, we are referring to different text types. The main genres are: poetry, drama and fiction.

Poetry is frequently (although not always) characterised by rhyme and rhythm, which may be regular or irregular.

Drama is normally meant to be acted (on the stage, radio, etc.) and is characterised by dialogue and stage directions (which describe the scenery and tell the actors what to do). It may be written in poetry or prose.

Fiction, which may be a short story or a novel, is characterised by having a narrator, i.e. a figure/voice who tells the story. It is written in prose.

Of course, you will find poetic elements in drama and fiction, dialogue in fiction and poetry, but these will usually not be determining features of the work you are considering.

Cutting across the broad categories of poetry, drama and fiction, we also have types of genre which relate to the way the subject matter of a text is treated or presented. Such categories are, for example, **satire, realism, fantasy** and **allegory** (also comedy and tragedy).

In a **satire** an author will expose vice or stupidity by making them look ridiculous or contemptible. **Realistic** texts present the real world as the author actually sees it, while in a **fantasy** text the author actually creates a world that exists only in his/her imagination. An **allegory** operates on at least two levels of meaning. There is first of all the surface level of the characters, events and places etc. But the characters, events and places also stand for or symbolise abstract concepts like, for example, beauty or truth, sin or evil. Sometimes stories, novels, plays and poems are characterised by a combination of these categories.

Theme

Possible **themes** of literary texts are countless in number: a poem might deal with the themes of love or loneliness, a drama with the themes of personal relationships or conflicts in society, a novel with the theme of nature and industrialism, conflicts between ethnic groups, and so on. Discovering the theme(s) of a work of literature is one of

the main purposes of interpretation. In order to discover the theme(s):
- in a drama look, for example, at what the characters say, the way they interact, the language they use,
- in a work of fiction look, for example, at the characters, the setting, the symbols and the comments of the narrator,
- in a poem look, for example, at the comments of the "I" of the poem, the language, images and symbols used.

Character and Characterisation

By the term **character** we mean the kind of people presented by the text, looked at as though they were real living persons. A character may be shy, self-confident, ambitious, kind, ruthless, and so on. The impression of character that the reader or spectator receives is determined by the means of **characterisation** used by the author; in other words the techniques that he/she employs.

In drama, characters might be shown by means of their **appearance** (what they look like), **actions** (what they do), **language** (what they say and the way that they say it), **thoughts** (if they express them in some way in the form of a monologue, for example), **interaction** (the way that they behave towards other characters and *vice versa*), or **hearsay** (what other characters say about them).

In fiction, an author has more subtle ways of presenting character than in drama, since he/she can make use of a narrator, which you do not normally have in a play. The means of characterisation he/she may use are of two main kinds: **showing techniques** and **telling techniques**. Showing techniques are almost the same as those used by a dramatist (appearance, actions, language, thoughts, interaction). With telling techniques the author informs the reader more directly about what characters are like, analysing and summarising their characteristics, usually by means of the **narrator**. In addition, in both drama and fiction a character's **name** often gives an indication of the kind of person he/she is.

Another important aspect we have to consider with respect to character regards the function of the character in a story or play; in other words, is he/she the **protagonist** (the main character) or a **minor character**? The protagonist is often a very **complex** character with a number of different characteristics. Minor characters are frequently **flat**, having only one or two basic characteristics. If a flat character is in some way very typical of a class, gender, race or nation, etc., he/she may be referred to as a **stereotype**.

Setting and Atmosphere

By **setting** we mean the time, place and social background against which the action of a story/novel or drama takes place. **Time** might refer to the time of day, the time of year or time in the future (as in science fiction, for example) or the past (as in the historical novel). **Place** refers to the country, the city or the countryside, inside or outside a house or building. With the term **social setting**, we refer to the social class or the ethnic group to which the characters perhaps belong. It is important to be able to analyse the setting in order to be able to understand the context of a literary work. The setting affects the way we see the characters and understand the meaning of a story/drama.

In a work of fiction the place is frequently described by the narrator while in a drama it is conveyed by the scenery (often described by the dramatist in the **stage directions**, including the stage properties or "props" – tables, chairs, etc.). Frequently the setting will help to create an atmosphere.

By **atmosphere** we mean the feelings and moods created within the reader and/or the characters by means of certain techniques. The atmosphere may be melancholic, threatening, depressing, optimistic, joyful, and so on. Atmosphere is created by such means as setting, interaction and the use of language.

Structure and Other Formal Aspects

As it is in their structure and forms that they differ most, poetry, drama and fiction will be dealt with separately here.

Poetry

In considering a poem, the structural and formal aspects you might want to analyse are:

Stanza: How are the lines of poetry grouped together: in threes, fours, fives, sixes, and so on? Traditionally all of these stanza types have individual names, the most common one is the **quatrain** for stanzas of four lines.

Rhyme: Do the lines rhyme at the end, and if so is there any pattern? Common **rhyme schemes** are *aabb, ccdd,* etc. or *abab, cdcd*, and so on.

Sound patterns: One of the most obvious characteristics of poetry is the use of distinctive sound patterns. The most common pattern is **rhyme**; in other words, lines ending with the same sound. Common **rhyme schemes** are *aabb*, *ccdd* or *abab*, *cdcd*, and so on. Other patterns of sound are **alliteration** – a string of words in a line beginning with the same sound; **internal rhyme** – words rhyming within a line rather than at the end; and **assonance** – a pattern of similar vowel sounds.

Rhythm: By rhythm we mean the pattern of stress in a line of poetry. More traditional poems tend to have a regular stress pattern, while many modern poems have irregular stress. If a line of poetry has a regular rhythm, we can divide it into groups of syllables, which are called **feet** (singular: **foot**). Common patterns of feet are the **iamb** (x/ x/ x/) = one unstressed syllable followed by a stressed one – as in "I wandered lonely as a cloud"); the **trochee** (/x /x /x) = one stressed syllable followed by an unstressed one – as in "Lay your sleeping head my love"); the **dactyl** (/xx /xx /xx) = one stressed syllable followed by two unstressed ones – as in "Woman much kissed, how you call to me, call to me"). A line of poetry will frequently consist of a regular number of feet – ranging from one to about eight. One, two or eight feet are rare; the most common numbers are three (known as a **trimeter**), four (**tetrameter**), five (**pentameter**), six (**hexameter**) and seven (**heptameter**). Thus, in order to describe the regular rhythm of a poem, we combine the name of the type of foot with the number of feet in a line (e.g. iambic pentameter, or dactylic hexameter). When we have such regular patterns of stress, we refer to this as **metre**. Sometimes, a poet will break out of a regular metre and introduce irregular elements – for example, a line of poetry might be incomplete in its sense and run on to the next line (**'run on' line**). This technique is called **enjambement**. Some poems make use of a regular number of stressed syllables and an irregular number of unstressed ones in each line.

Modern poetry is sometimes characterised by an irregularity of rhythm and a lack of rhyme. This kind of poetry is referred to as **free verse**. It is important, however, not only to be able to determine the rhythm of a poem but also the effect of the rhythm. The effect of a regular metre might be to convey a sense of motion, for example; the effect of an irregular rhythm might be to suggest chaos, riot, violence or disorder.

Some poems conform to set conventions with respect to form, subject matter or tone. The following are fairly common types of poem:

The **ode** is a traditional type of lyric poem (i.e. it expresses the poet's "personal" feelings). It is characterised by its length, intricate form, grandeur of style and seriousness of purpose. Many odes are addressed to a particular person or object.

The **sonnet** is also a traditional kind of lyric poem but with a set poetic form. It has fourteen lines, it rhymes and has a set rhythm (iambic pentameters – see above).

The **dub poem** is a modern form of verse which originated in Jamaica in the 1970's. It is characterised by the speech idioms and strongly marked rhythms of West Indian English. Dub poems are meant to be performed.

Drama

The structure of a drama can be looked at from different points of view. Usually the dramatist will have given some indication of the structure by dividing a play into **acts** (one-act, two-act, three-act and five-act plays are the most common). Each act is divided into **scenes**, in which a particular set of characters interact with one another.

The division of the play into acts also gives some idea of its internal structure. In the traditional five-act play, the first act is the **exposition**, where the characters, setting and conflict are presented. The second act contains the **rising action**, whereby a latent conflict starts to make itself felt and problems, relationships and tensions begin to develop. The third act provides the **climax**, when a conflict reaches its highest point of tension. In the fourth act, a **falling action** is presented, when the tension begins to decrease and it seems as if a catastrophe or a major conflict has been avoided. The fifth act presents the **catastrophe** (in a tragedy), when the protagonist usually dies and some kind of destructive event occurs, or a **denouement** (in a comedy), when misunderstandings are sorted out or mistaken identities are cleared up and we have a happy ending. Modern plays mostly break with this traditional structure but some elements can be found: there may be some expository information presented, there may be a climax. On the other hand, the dramatist may present an open beginning or an open ending, when the spectators themselves must speculate about the context of the situation or the later development of the events.

Another aspect of structure concerns **conflict**. By conflict, we mean the quarrels, arguments, rivalry, animosity and strife between characters, groups of characters, social classes, ethnic groups, and so on. Frequently a conflict develops by stages or phases which can be described and analysed. For example, a conflict may have its starting point in an incompatibility between characters. Gradually a conflict arises, intensifies and reaches a climax, after which it may be resolved. In this context it will be important to define the causes of the conflict, its development and the extent to which a solution is found.

Fiction

The term 'fiction' is used to refer jointly to novels and (short) stories. A **novel** is usually a longer work of fiction with a complicated plot, a large number of characters and different settings. A **short story**, as the name suggests, is shorter, usually with a simple plot, a limited number of characters and one or, at the most, two settings. In between the novel and the short story, there is a grey area that contains short novels and long short stories.

One of the most important structural aspects of a work of fiction is the question: Who is telling the story? Or to use the technical term: Who is the **narrator**? It might be a character within the story, in this case the author uses a **first person narrator** (because he/she will refer to himself/herself as "I"). Or it might be a figure (possibly only a voice) who is not a character in the story but exists quite independently outside it; in this case the author will have used a **third person narrator** (because the narrator will refer to all of the characters as "he"/"she"/"they"). A third person narrator can be one of two main types. He/She may portray the events and the characters from the outside, show the feelings and thoughts of the characters from the inside, and comment on the events and the characters – in this case he/she is referred to as an **omniscient third person narrator**. Or alternatively he/she may show the events through the eyes of one (or maybe more) characters, so that we, the readers, only see what they see and the way that they see it, usually by means of their thoughts and feelings – in this case we talk of a **limited third person narrator**. Sometimes the action of the story is conveyed to the reader more or less only by means of the thoughts of a character, almost as if he/she were thinking out loud. This technique is referred to as **interior monologue**. If an interior monologue is fairly extensively used by the author, then we talk of the **stream of consciousness** technique. This structural aspect of fiction is usually referred to as the **point of view** or the **narrative perspective** used by the author. We must be careful not to

confuse the narrator with the author: the author is the real person who wrote the story; the narrator is the figure, voice or character that tells the story. Sometimes, of course, the narrator is very similar to the author and expresses some of the author's own thoughts and ideas.
As in drama, works of fiction can also be analysed with regard to the way they have been put together or constructed. If a drama consists of acts and scenes, a novel will be made up of **chapters**, and a short story of **parts** or **sections**. Some of the structural elements of drama can also be found in fiction: many stories and novels have an exposition, or a climax, although we talk of the 'ending' of a novel rather than its denouement or catastrophe.
Short stories particularly can have an almost dramatic structure with a rising action, climax and falling action. Modern stories, however, almost systematically do without an exposition and a solution, employing an open beginning and open ending technique. The readers themselves can decide how the situation came about and speculate how it might end.
One structural element shared by all three genres – poetry, drama and fiction – is the use of **symbols**. By symbols we mean the concrete objects or actions in a literary work which stand for something abstract (an idea or a feeling perhaps). For example, the sun might stand for life and happiness, night for death and fear, white for purity and red for danger, passion, and so on. Sometimes a work contains a number of symbols that form a pattern and give the reader an idea of what the theme of the work is. For example, a story might begin in a small room (perhaps a symbol for the fact that the main character is trapped in his/her everyday life of work and family) but end in the open countryside (a symbol for his/her having gained freedom).

Style

The term **style** has a variety of different meanings but in general one can say that it refers to the kind of language the author employs. In order to analyse the style of a text, look at the following aspects:

Register

Is the language formal, familiar, colloquial (the style of everyday speech) or neutral? For example, does the author refer to a character as "gentleman", "man" or "guy"?

Diction

What kind of words are used? Are they taken from any particular word field – e.g. religion (like 'sermon', 'awe', 'devotion', 'pious'), or business (like 'credit', 'investment', 'deal', 'contract', 'firm', 'partner', 'profit')? Does the author use a lot of descriptive adjectives and adverbs (like 'sweet', 'glowing', 'humid', 'tightly', 'shyly') or verbs of motion (like 'jump', 'hobble', 'hop', 'rush')?

Syntax

What is the sentence structure like? Are simple sentences or complex sentences (with main clauses and sub-clauses) used? Does the author use predominantly active or passive sentences? To what effect? To suggest objectivity or neutrality perhaps?

Rhetorical Devices

Does the writer use language in a non-literal sense or in an unusual way? For example:

Alliteration – a string of words beginning with the same sound, e.g. "Round the ragged rock the ragged rascal ran."

Assonance – a certain similarity between the sounds of words used, without there being proper rhyme, e.g. "The murmuring of innumerable bees."

Contrast – opposite or strongly contrasting forms of words, e.g. "I am going north by train; she is coming south by car."

Ellipsis – leaving out words to avoid repetition, e.g. "Caesar came, saw and conquered" instead of "Caesar came, then he saw and then he conquered."

Hyperbole /haɪˈpɜːbəlɪ/ – a form of exaggeration, e.g. "The chair weighs a ton."

Imagery – sometimes writers want to create a special effect by comparing different things with each other. If he/she uses a metaphor or a simile to do this (see below), the comparative object is an **image** (or word picture). For example, in "My love is like a red, red rose" (simile), the rose functions as an image. If an author uses a number of images that are somehow connected – for example, there are references to different flowers – then we talk of the **imagery** in a text.

Irony /ˈaɪərənɪ/ – to say one thing but mean another. Irony can usually only be detected from the context. If we say "What charming behaviour" when someone has been rude, this may be called irony, but is more usually referred to as **sarcasm**.

Metaphor – an expression used to describe s.th. or s.o. by comparing it/them directly with s.th. else (without 'like' or 'as'; also see 'simile'), e.g. "Transportation was hell for the slaves going to America."

Onomatopoeia /ˌɒnəmætəˈpiːə/ – words that sound like the thing they refer to, e.g. "The chain clanked and clanged along the path."

Parallelism – a string of sentences, clauses or phrases all with more or less the same structure; for example, "the barons tyrannised the knights, the knights tyrannised the peasants and the peasants tyrannised their wives." In this quotation there is an example of repetition, when the same word is used a number of times.

Personification – a non-living thing is described as though it were a living being, e.g. "The sun is smiling on us today."

Rhetorical question – a question which expects no answer, e.g. "Who knows how long the war will last?"

Simile /ˈsɪməlɪ/ – a comparison between two things with similar qualities, using "like" or "as if", e.g. "Transportation was like hell for the slaves going to America."

Understatement – the opposite of hyperbole, when we play down rather than exaggerate a matter, e.g. "He was quite upset" for "He went into a terrible rage".

Tone

Tone refers to the apparent attitude of an author, poet, narrator or character towards the information or message that he/she is conveying to the reader. Typical tones are: ironic, serious, humorous, witty, pompous, sentimental. The tone of a work is sometimes difficult to detect, but can usually be discovered by looking at the language the author uses and the rhetorical devices that he/she employs. Particularly hyperbole, understatement and irony are important in this connection.

Non-Literary Texts

Text Type

As with literary texts, the first thing we have to determine with **non-literary texts** is the text type. Possible non-literary text types are: newspaper/magazine articles, letters to the editor, brochures, advertisements, recipes, instructions, speeches, reports, and editorials. Normally it is not difficult to decide which type of text we are analysing; we have to look at the kind of information conveyed and the format in which it is presented. Typical features of:

Newspaper/magazine articles – headlines, photographs, human interest stories, (frequently) colloquial or idiomatic language.

Letters to the editor – praise about a good article; criticisms of opinions expressed by the newspaper; suggestions for improving the newspaper; criticisms or praise of politicians.

Brochures – information about a product or service; glossy format; photographs and illustrations.

Advertisements – eye-catching pictures, illustrations or cartoons; humorous or witty remarks with a play on words; exaggerated praise of the product or service offered.

Instructions – advice on how to operate machines, construct devices etc. Instructions for cooking are called **recipes**. Instructions are supposed to be as simple and straightforward as possible. They often make use of imperatives or constructions based on the second person (you).

Speeches – formal addresses to an audience, normally for political purposes. The aim of a speech is more often than not to convince the audience of the speaker's ideas on a particular subject. Sometimes speeches are given to praise a certain person. Speakers very often include some humorous remarks in their speech to get the audience on their side.

Reports – factual information; objective style; diagrams or photographs to illustrate points.

Editorials – the opinion of the newspaper on a particular subject; rhetorical devices like metaphors, hyperbole, irony (see above).

Content

Here we are interested in determining what kind of information the text conveys or what subject-matter it contains. Does it contain facts or does it express an opinion, for example? Is the text anecdotal (telling interesting illustrative stories) or is it analytical (presenting causes, reasons and effects)? What role does any visual material play? What is the relationship between the text and the visual material?

Structure and Form

As with literary texts, it is important to define the structure of a non-literary text. Many formal, non-literary texts will follow the pattern described for essays (see pp. 299f.) with an introduction, main part and conclusion. It is a good idea to determine these main sections first. Sometimes it is difficult to say exactly where the introduction ends and the main part begins, so you will need to point out transitions that link the sections of the text together.

Once you have determined the main sections, look at each section in greater detail.

Introduction

1 Does the author tell the reader what the text will be about?
2 Does he/she begin with an example or anecdote?

Main Part

This section is usually more complex than the others. Try to find answers to the following questions:

1 What kind of information is presented – facts, arguments, opinions?
2 How are the facts/arguments/opinions arranged – as a numbered list, as examples, as pros and cons?

For this purpose it is a good idea to look at the individual **paragraphs** which make up the section that you are examining, since the author himself/herself will have already arranged his/her ideas in paragraphs. Generally, each paragraph will contain one important idea, normally expressed in a **topic sentence** (which says what the paragraph is about) and illustrated by **developers** (which usually give examples). So try to summarise in perhaps one sentence what each paragraph expresses. If you then look at your list of sentences, you should get a fairly clear idea of the internal structure of the text.

If the text presents **facts**, try to determine how the facts are arranged as:

1 A list?
2 A selection of examples?
3 Contrasts?
4 Comparisons?

You will find the information in **Section One** of the **Reference Library** on linking words helpful here.

If the text presents **arguments**, try to discover how the arguments relate to each other:

1 All of the pro-arguments, followed by all of the con-arguments, followed by a conclusion?
2 The pro-arguments and the con-arguments for each individual point, followed by a final conclusion?

Does the author try to take account of other opinions apart from his/her own? If so, where?

Conclusion

1 Does the author give his/her own opinion?
2 Does he/she refer back to the introduction?
3 Does he/she draw a conclusion on the basis of the facts presented? If so, he/she will probably have used an **inductive** approach (presentation of facts from which a conclusion is drawn).
4 How do the text and headline or title go together?

In non-literary texts formal aspects of presentation can play a very important role. Here it might be useful to look at the kind of graphic techniques which are employed – type of script, size of print, colour of text, black and white or coloured illustrations, etc.

Function

For what purposes might a text have been written? Any conclusions that we draw are normally speculative, as we can never be entirely sure about an author's intentions. Possible functions are:

1 to inform
2 to amuse
3 to criticise
4 to satirise
5 to persuade
6 to praise

A text may also have as its purpose any combination of these functions.

Style and Tone

Just as with literary texts it is important to analyse the style and tone of a non-literary text. For information about style and tone see pp. 311f.

Visual Texts

One special kind of non-literary text is also a non-linguistic one, namely the **visual text**. Visual texts can have a variety of functions: to illustrate an idea, to comment on an idea or form of behaviour etc., to decorate a text or another visual element, to attract a potential reader's / spectator's attention, to suggest ideas without explicitly explaining them, to create positive or negative emotions in a spectator/viewer. Common visual texts are: illustrations, photographs, films, advertisements, drawings, paintings, cartoons, sketches, engravings. When analysing a visual text answers to the following questions might be important:
Is it:

- a portrait, a landscape, an illustration?
- in colour, black and white?
- still, in motion?
- realistic, non-realistic, allegorical, satirical?
- What size does it have?
- How are the visual elements (e.g. people, places, objects etc.) arranged?
- Does it have any written or spoken text incorporated?
- What is its function? Does it help the spectator to understand something? Does it comment on a person, idea etc.? Is it meant to persuade or to entertain, or both?

Section Four – Language Workshop

The Tenses

Tense	Meaning	Examples	Comment
Present Simple	1 General truth 2 Permanent habit 3 Permanent state 4 Commentary	Americans drive larger cars than Europeans. On average they move house every five years. She lives on her own. In the story, Jack leaves his mother.	The Present Simple refers generally to things which are true at the present time. It describes events, habits or states which are not limited to a specific period or which are somehow 'timeless'. It can be used to refer to a work of literature or a film, etc. in order to describe a sequence of events or to comment on the work.
Present Progressive	1 Event in progress 2 Limited habit 3 Limited state	I'm writing a letter at the moment. We're taking the bus this week because our car has broken down. They're living with her parents till their own flat is ready.	The Present Progressive describes events which are in progress at the moment of speaking, or states and habits which are going on now and are of limited duration.
Past Simple	1 Past event 2 Past events in a sequence 3 Past habit	Columbus discovered America in 1492. Frances took her money and left home. She always drove to college by motorbike.	The Past Simple refers to events, habits, or states in the past (i.e. last week, last year, three years ago, etc.), in other words at a time which is not connected with the present.
Past Progressive	Incomplete event, habit or state in the past	He was having a bath when she rang him up at two o'clock.	The Past Progressive refers to events, habits or states which were in progress at the time being talked about.
Present Perfect Simple	1 Resultative meaning 2 Experiential meaning 3 Permanent state or habit up to now	Frances has left her parents. She has travelled to N.Y. before. She has always obeyed her parents.	The Present Perfect Simple is used to refer to events which 1 have had an effect on the present (resultative = you can still see the results); or 2 happened at some uncertain time between the past and now (experiential = at some time in a person's life); or 3 have happened over a period of time up to and including the present (permanent habit/state up to now). Expressions with 'for' and 'since' are common. The Present Perfect Simple is used in contrast to the Past Simple.
Present Perfect Progressive	Temporary events, habits or states up to now	We have been cleaning the house all morning.	The Present Perfect Progressive describes events, habits and states that have been taking place over a limited period of time up to now (and are often still continuing). Very often it is used to explain how s.th. unpleasant came about. In this example meaning: "And that is why we're tired and dirty."

Tense	Meaning	Examples	Comment
Past Perfect Simple			The Past Perfect Simple refers to events that happened in the past. We see these events, however, not from the point of view of the present but from the point of view of the past.
	1 Resultative meaning	The goalkeeper had injured his leg, and so he couldn't play.	1 In some cases we want to express the idea that one event in the past had an effect on another event in the past (resultative).
	2 The past in the past (Pre-past)	She took him to a Korean restaurant. He had been there twice before.	2 In other cases we want to refer to past events that happened in the pre-past (i.e. before the time we originally referred to).

Ways of Referring to the Future

English has the following ways of referring to the future:

Form	Meaning	Examples	Comment
Present Simple	Fixed events in the future	The lesson begins tomorrow at 8.30. The match ends at four o'clock. The plane arrives at 6 pm.	The Present Simple can refer to future events that are fixed and cannot normally be rearranged, as in timetables, schedules and fixtures.
Present Progressive	Arrangements	Jane and Jack are visiting their parents next weekend.	The Present Progressive is used to refer to arrangements that have been made in advance. In this example, Jane and Jack have actually talked to their parents and arranged their visit with them.
To be going to			'To be going to' can be used
	1 Intention	Frances is going to marry Paul after all.	1 to express the idea that we intend to do s.th. but have not yet taken any concrete steps; or
	2 Prediction	It is going to rain in a couple of minutes.	2 to make a prediction based on concrete evidence available at the moment of speaking. In this example, a few drops of rain have probably just fallen and the sky is very dark.
Will			'Will' can indicate
	1 Spontaneous decision	He's here now, is he? O.K. Well, I'll tell him right away.	1 that the speaker has decided to do s.th. at the very moment of speaking. Compare this with "I'm going to tell him", which means that the speaker had decided before speaking; or
	2 Objective prediction or forecast	There will be snow all over England and Wales tomorrow.	2 that an objective prediction has been made, based upon scientific evidence. Compare this with "It's going to snow", which is subjective and based upon an impression.

Modal Verbs

Modal verbs like 'can', 'must', and 'may' are used to talk about possibilities, speculations, abilities, obligations, and so on. They refer not to the world as it actually is but as it might be. They can be looked at from the point of view of speech intentions, in other words what a speaker wishes to express by using them. Note particularly that some modal verbs have different past forms, depending on their meaning (e.g. 'must' – 'had to' – 'must have'). When the negative form of a modal verb has a special meaning (for example, 'can't'), it is included in the table under its own heading.

Modal Verb		**Concept**	**Examples**	**Comment / Speech Intention / Alternative Expressions**
Present / Future	**Past**			
Can	Could Was/Were able to	Ability	She can drive.	The speaker discusses whether s.o. is able to do s.th.
Can		Suggestion	You can give it to me and I'll post it for you.	A very straight-forward and not particularly polite form.
Can't	Can't have	Logical necessity (negative)	She can't possibly be in love with him.	On the basis of evidence the speaker thinks that s.th. is not true or likely. Surprise about an apparent situation is also expressed in this way.
Could	Could have	Possibility	It could be quite useful.	The speaker is not completely sure, but thinks that it may be the case.
Could	Could have	Careful suggestion	You could ask the headmaster.	More polite than 'can'.
Couldn't	Couldn't have	Uncertain logical necessity (negative)	It couldn't be the video recorder that's not working because we've only just bought it!	On the basis of evidence the speaker thinks that s.th. is not true or likely. However, he/she is a bit uncertain.
May	May have	Possibility	She may come, she may not.	Similar in meaning to 'perhaps' and 'maybe'.
May	Was/Were allowed to (Might)	Permission	You may smoke, if you wish.	A polite way to give permission. Note in the past: s.o. was allowed to do s.th. 'Might' is possible but not very common.
Might	Might have	Uncertain possibility	She might be there. Who knows?	The speaker is less certain than with 'may'.
Must Have to Have got to	Had to Had got to	Obligation	I must do the garden tomorrow.	'Must' expresses the idea that the obligation comes either from the speaker or from s.o. else. 'Have / Have got to' express the idea that the speaker is merely reporting an obligation. 'Have got to' is more colloquial.
Must Have to Have got to	Must have	Logical necessity	You must be mad!	The speaker assumes that s.th. is true on the basis of evidence, or is expressing surprise. The opposite of 'can't possibly'.

Modal Verb Present / Future	Modal Verb Past	Concept	Examples	Comment / Speech Intention / Alternative Expressions
Mustn't	Was/Were not allowed to	Negative obligation (prohibition)	You mustn't tell her, whatever happens.	The opposite of 'must' (= *nicht dürfen*).
Not have to Haven't got to	Didn't have to (Hadn't got to)	Absence of obligation	You don't have to do what he says.	No one says that the action must be carried out.
Not need to	Didn't need to	Absence of necessity	You needn't do it today. Tomorrow will be fine.	There is no need for the action to be carried out.
Ought to	Ought to have	Moral obligation / advice	You ought to do it now, since you have time.	The speaker feels that it would be good if the action was carried out but he/she does not insist.
Ought to	Ought to have	Uncertain logical necessity	He ought to be finished by now.	The speaker thinks that s.th. is true but is not certain.
Shall		Insistence	You shall do as I say!	The speaker demands that s.o. else does s.th.
Should	Should have	Moral obligation / advice	You should try harder.	An alternative to 'ought to' (moral obligation / advice).
Should	Should have	Uncertain logical necessity	She should be here by now.	An alternative to 'ought to' (uncertain logical necessity).
Will	Would	Insistence	I will do it!	The speaker demands to be allowed to do s.th. himself/herself.
Will	Would	Characteristic behaviour	He would come round to their place day after day as if it was his own home.	This special use of 'will/would' refers to typical, characteristic or habitual behaviour.

If-Clauses

***If*-Clauses** are used to speculate on what might happen / have happened under certain circumstances. They are not particularly difficult, but you have to bear in mind the sequence of tenses in the **main clause** and the ***if*-clause**. Notice that the order of the clauses can be: main clause + *if*-clause or *if*-clause + main clause, depending on the emphasis the speaker wants to give. The second item is emphasised more than the first. 'Will' and 'would' should not be used in *if*-clauses.

Main Clause	*If*-Clause	Comment
Future with *will* I'll tell her	**Present Simple** if I see her.	Used when there is a real possibility in the future that these things might happen.
Conditional I I would tell her	**Past Simple** if I saw her.	Speculating about the present/future but whether these events will happen or not remains an open question.
Conditional II I would have told her	**Past Perfect** if I had seen her.	Speculating about past events, which, of course, cannot now be changed.

Reported Speech

When we wish to tell a person what someone has said, we can either express word for word what the other person said (Alice said, "I'm coming to see you next week") which is called **direct speech**, or we can use **reported speech** (Alice said that she was coming to see me the following week). The difficulties in using reported speech are connected with the changes that need to be made when converting direct speech into reported speech. These changes affect the use of tenses, pronouns and adverbials of time and place.

Type of Utterance	Reporting Verbs (in Past Tense)	Examples Direct Speech	Reported Speech	Comment
State-ments	believed, claimed, denied, felt, remarked, said, shouted, stated, thought, told s.o., whispered, etc. or said + adverb of manner (They said politely that ...)	"I like Joan." "I've never met her." "We lived in Spain."	He said that he liked Joan. He said that he had never met her. She said that they had lived in Spain.	Usually when reporting what s.o. said, we use back-shift rules. In other words, the verb in reported speech is one step further back in the past than the verb in direct speech. The following table will help you to use back-shift: **Direct Speech** → **Reported Speech** Present Tense → Past Tense Present Perfect → Past Perfect Past Tense → Past Perfect will / shall → would / should can → could must → had to, etc.
Questions	asked, inquired, wanted to know, wondered, etc. (+ adverb of manner)	1 "Where do you live?" 2 "Are you going?"	She asked him where he lived. He wanted to know if she was going.	Back-shift is also used in reported questions. Pay particular attention to the following: 1 A reported question is a statement and not a question, so use the statement form not the question form: He asked her where she lived. Not: He asked her where did she live.* 2 Use 'if' or 'whether' when reporting yes/no questions.
Com-mands / Requests	asked s.o. to, ordered s.o. to, persuaded s.o. to, requested s.o. to, told s.o. to, etc. (+ adverb of manner)	"Go home!" "Please be quiet!"	They told him to go home. She asked him to be quiet.	To report commands, orders and requests, do not use back-shift rules. Instead use the following pattern: reporting vb + object + to + infinitive

Note

When we report indirectly what someone said, asked or commanded we often have to change pronouns and adverbials of time and place.

Pronouns

The changes depend on who is talking to whom.

Direct Speech: John said, "**I**'ll tell **you** when **I** know."

Reported Speech: John said that **he** would tell **me** when **he** knew.

Adverbials of Time and Place

Because we normally report speech in a different time and place from when and where we originally heard it, the reported speech normally has different adverbials of time and place from the direct speech.

Direct Speech: John said, "I'll meet you **here tomorrow**"

Reported Speech: John said that he would meet me **there the next day**.

Here is a rough guide on how to change the adverbials:

Dir. Speech		Rep. Speech	Dir. Speech		Rep. Speech	Dir. Speech		Rep. Speech
now	→	then	yesterday	→	the day before	here	→	there
tomorrow	→	the next day	last week	→	the week before			

Back-Shift Rules with Reporting Verbs in the Present Tense

Back-shift rules only apply when the reporting verb is in the Past Tense. If the Present Tense is used, the tenses remain unchanged: "Are you coming?" – He wants to know if you are coming.

Would

As you can see from this table, 'would' has a number of different meanings:

Examples	Comment
He said that he **would** come.	In reported speech, it is the Past Tense form of 'will'.
She **would** do it if she could.	Together with an *if*-clause, it is the auxiliary verb in a conditional sentence.
They **would** spend their holiday lying in the sun.	It can be used to express the idea of insistence (they insisted on spending their holiday lying in the sun; nobody could stop them).
They **would** get up at five o'clock every morning, go for a long walk and then come home in time for breakfast.	It can be used to refer to a regular habit in the past. This is what they did regularly.
They **would** like to visit Montana one day.	It is used to refer to wishes or desires.

The Passive

When we want to report an action and we do not know who did it, or the person who did it is somehow less important than the action itself, then we can use the **Passive Voice**. The **Passive** is frequently used in formal or official texts, in order to suggest objectivity. Here is some information on how to form passive sentences:

Subject	Auxiliary (Form of 'to be')		Past Participle	By-Agent
I	**Present Simple**	am, are, is	watched	by the police, the teacher, etc. The person who carried out the action is sometimes mentioned by means of 'by' + agent (noun phrase).
You	**Present Progressive**	am/are/is being	taught	
He	**Present Perfect Simple**	have/has been	told	
She	**Past Simple**	was, were	given	
Mrs Brown	**Past Progressive**	was/were being	etc.	
etc.	**Past Perfect**	had been		
	Future with *will*	will be		

Participle and Gerund Constructions

Although you are more than familiar with participles (going, done, etc.) in English because they are used to form various tenses. (Present Progressive, Present Perfect Simple, etc.), you might not be too sure about their other uses. Here is a survey. Notice that participle constructions can often (but not always) be reformulated using other forms:

Uses of Participles	Participle	Reformulation / Alternative Constructions	Comment
As Post-modifiers (Shortened Relative Clauses)	**Present Participle** The people **living** next door are very friendly. **Past Participle** The man **injured** in the accident was John's uncle.	The people **who live/ are living** next door ... The man **who was injured** in the accident ...	A participle appearing after a noun is normally a kind of post-modifier (a word changing/limiting the meaning of another word). Usually such a participle construction can be reformulated using a relative clause.
As Participial Adverbial Clauses (Shortened Adverbial Clauses)	**Present Participle** **Entering** the room, she discovered that he had gone. **Having** more than enough money, she bought him a new car. **Past Participle** **Cleared**, the land was worth millions. **Cleared**, the land would be worth millions.	**When/As she entered** the room, she ... **Because she had** more than enough money, she ... **After it had been cleared**, the land ... **If it was cleared**, the land ...	A participle can introduce an adverbial clause. This clause normally refers to time, manner, reason or condition (depending on the context). The clause can usually be reformulated as an adverbial clause with a conjunction, like: 'after', 'when', 'while', 'as', 'since', 'because', or 'if'. Sometimes it is difficult to say exactly what kind of adverbial is meant: two events happen at the same time. Here we talk of **attendant circumstance**; for example, "Feeling that she had made a terrible mistake, she left the room."
As Pre-modifiers (Like Adjectives)	**Present Participle** They bought a **talking** parrot. He was pushed out of a **moving** train. They met the **following** week. **Past Participle** They lived in a partly **demolished** house. He lived in a **semi-detached** house.	... a parrot **that could talk**. ... a train **that was moving**. ... a house **that had been partly demolished**.	A participle can be used as pre-modifier of a noun, like an adjective. Participles in English, however, can only be used in this way under certain conditions : 1 if they refer to a permanent characteristic – as in "talking parrot" and "demolished house"; or 2 if they are derived from verbs of motion – as in "moving train" (only present participles); or 3 if they have become adjectives in their own right – "following", "semi-detached" – and appear as such in a dictionary.
After Verbs of Perception	**Present Participle** He watched her **leaving** the house.	He watched her **as she was leaving the house.**	After verbs of perception (see, watch, notice, observe, feel, sense, hear, etc.) + object, a present participle is frequently used to express the idea of an action in progress.

Gerunds are very similar to present participles in that they are also *-ing*-forms. But whereas a participle has mainly the function of a verb, the gerund is more like a noun. It can:
1 follow a preposition: "Without knowing it, she had succeeded in her task."
2 function as the subject of a verb: "Walking is healthier than driving."
3 function as the object of a verb: "They didn't like walking."

Expressing Concepts

When we want to describe or comment on an event, we often need to refer to when, how often, where, why, etc. the event took place, in other words to refer to the time, place and other circumstances of the event. Ideas like time, place, reason, and so on are referred to in grammar as **concepts**. One of the most important types of grammatical construction used to refer to concepts is the **adverbial**. The **adverbial** can be constructed in different ways. The following will give you some ideas about how to refer to important concepts, using adverbial constructions:

	Adverbial				
Concept	**Noun Phrase**	**Adverb**	**Prepositional Phrase**	**Adverbial Clause**	**Comment**
Time	the day before yesterday, two years ago	now, then, tomorrow	in two weeks' time, after the match, before lunch, during the meal	when he comes, after she has left, while he was there, after seeing her home	The time **when** an event happened.
Frequency	every day	never, sometimes, occasionally, frequently, always	from time to time, on occasions	whenever she was home	**How often** an event happened. Certain adjectives can also indicate frequency, e.g. 'daily', 'weekly' and 'yearly'.
Manner		quickly, violently, softly	in a friendly manner, in a disrespectful way	falling on his knees	**How** or **in what way** an event happened. Notice that the adverbial clause has the form of a present participle construction.
Place		here, there, everywhere, home	in the house, by the field, over the road, next to the church, across the river	wherever she went	**Where** an event happened.
Reason			because of the noise, owing to the weather, due to the frost	because he had to, believing that it was their duty, since it was so cold, as it was rainy	**Why** an event happened. Notice that a present participle construction can be used.
Purpose			(He went to the butcher's) for some meat	in order to buy some bread, to buy some bread, so that she would be able to see better	**Why** s.o. did s.th. in the sense of the aim or intention.

Concept / Adverbial	Noun Phrase	Adverb	Prepositional Phrase	Adverbial Clause	Comment
Result				so (cold) that they couldn't leave the house	One event gives rise to another.
Contrast / Concession			despite the weather, in spite of her request	whereas she is ..., (he is ...), while Britain has a monarch, (the USA has a president), although he was hurt, though she was injured	Two events or sets of circumstances are contrasted with each other (**contrast** = while; whereas), or a surprising event or fact is referred to (**concession** = despite; although).

Quantifiers

We use **quantifiers** (like 'some', 'much', 'many', 'a lot of', etc.) to refer to **amounts**. In order to use quantifiers correctly, however, we must pay regard to the type of noun to which they refer. Depending on whether the noun is **countable** or **uncountable (mass)**, different sets of quantifiers will be used. Countable nouns are nouns that can be used in the plural and can appear together with **numerals** (1, 2, 3, ...) – for example, cars, tables, chairs, roads, trains, kisses, and so on. Uncountable (mass) nouns refer to things which are not made up of definable units; they cannot be counted and, therefore, do not usually occur in the plural form – things like water, tea, coffee and other liquids and foodstuffs, iron, copper, wood and other substances, love, pity, hatred and many other feelings and abstract concepts. A learner's dictionary will tell you if a noun is countable or uncountable, if you are not sure (see pp. 304f. above).

Countable	Uncountable (Mass)
Not a (sound) No (cars) Not any (cars)	No (money) Not any (money)
Few (bicycles)	Little (love)
Some (apples)	Some (time)
A few (people)	A little (milk)
(Not) many (books)	(Not) much (interest)
A lot of (friends)	A lot of (happiness)
All (the) (teams) Every (member) Each (student)	All (the) (responsibility)

Note the Comparative / Superlative Forms:

Few – Fewer – Fewest (Least) Many – More – Most	Little – Less – Least Much – More – Most

Section Five – How to Read a Film

Film is one of the most popular and widespread sources of entertainment. The film industry is a global conglomerate of capital as well as a cultural influence and power. For these reasons films have for a long time been the subject of media studies. But is it really necessary to learn how to analyse, "to read" a film given the assumption that the average cinema-goer is able to grasp the basic content of a film without any special training? Precisely because the media in general and the film in particular exert such as strong influence on our everyday lives, it is necessary to understand the different ways in which they influence the way we perceive the world. Therefore it is important to understand the complex artistic and technical means by which filmmakers and production crews work together to create a film.
The following ideas are intended to help you to "read" a film and to identify its meaning.

The historical, social and cultural context of a film

One step on an approach to interpreting film should consider some questions of the different dimensions of the context of a film:

- When was the film made?
- To what contemporary events does the film refer?
- What is the significance of the temporal setting?
- Which economic, social or political factors conditioned the production of the film?
- What does the film show about the society in which the characters find themselves?
- What is the role of phenomena like race, religion, nationality, culture, ethnicity, gender?

The basic ingredients of a film story: plot – narrative – theme

Plot = *what happens in the story*

The plot of a film is the element that is the easiest to grasp. In most cases it is a sequence of events with a beginning, a middle part and an ending unfolding over a period of time. Sometimes there are sub-plots which reveal more about certain aspects of the film.

Narrative = *how the story is told*

The narrative of a film is the way its story is told. Narrative film and narrative literature contain similar elements of fictional story telling, e.g. plot, character, theme setting, point of view. The basic difference, however, is the fact that the dominant mode of film is presentational (= visual showing) rather than the mode of telling in literature.
Film stories can be told

- in a linear way
- with flashbacks/flashforwards
- episodically

In some films you can find a narrator who has the function of a commentator, which is achieved by the technical device of voice-over.

Theme = *what the story is about*

The theme of a film is revealed through its plot and its narrative, through symbols, the characters in the film and their interaction. It is a generalization about life, humanity, human relationships, etc. The themes of science fiction stories often focus on human triumph over an extra-terrestrial enemy. Films can, of course, have more than one theme.

The film crew

The production of a film requires a large number of people who deal with different aspects of the making of a film, of whom only some are listed here:

Director
The director has the overall creative responsibility for turning a screenplay into a visual motion picture. His/her main tasks are preparing and positioning actors/actresses for a shot, supervising the production (camera positioning, lightning, etc.) and completing the postproduction work (editing, soundtrack, etc.)

Scriptwriter
The Scriptwriter is responsible for the screenplay or the script, which is the written text of a film prepared before production. It includes, e.g., the dialogues, the shot, scene descriptions or specific camera directions.

Producer
The Producer is in charge of financial and logistical aspects of the production of a film including budgeting, scheduling and set construction.

Director of photography
The director of photography is responsible for setting up the camera and lighting on a shot

Production designer
The production designer coordinates and implements the elements of the film's visual style, such as a set construc-

tion design, the costumes, decor, the placement/movement of the camera, in short, everything that appears before the camera.

Editor
The editor assembles the individual shots of the film into a visual continuity, i.e. the structuring and linking of shots and sequences in a film.

Sound designer
The sound designer is in charge of the film's soundtrack, i.e. sound effects, music, narration.

Gaffer
The gaffer is the chief electrician.

The "language" of the film

Just like texts do, the language of film communicates meaning in two different ways: denotatively and connotatively.
A film image (or sound) has, just like other images or words, a *denotative meaning*, which refers to its literal, descriptive meaning (=what the image really shows). But images or films are also "texts" with encodes, *connotative meanings* which can be read above, beyond or behind the literal meaning. Meaning is conveyed through the use of *iconic, indexical* and *symbolic* devices which can be identified by the audience of a film.

Icon
The iconic signifier always resembles what it signifies, e.g. there is a similarity between a photo of a daffodil and most people's experiences of these flowers.

Index
The indexical signifier is used as a kind of evidence, e.g. smoke of a fire, sweat of effort, spots of measles.

Symbol
The symbolic signifier is an object, a person or an event that represents a more general quality or situation, e.g. the diamond-studded headgear often worn by monarchs is called a crown an symbolizes monarchy; the cross symbolises Christianity.

The making of a film

"Mise-en-scene"
Mise-en-scene is the placing into the setting of all the elements to be filmed such as props, lighting, figures, make-up, and anything else that is in the frame of the camera lens at the time of filming.
Example: A typical Dracula horror film might include graveyards, moonlight and lightning-filled night skies.

Set/setting: refers to the location of the plot, e.g. a contemporary or a historical setting. Filming 'on location' means filming away from the studio. The setting is the major element in establishing what the genre of a film is.

Lighting: refers to the illumination of a camera subject being filmed. The lighting may be natural or artificial, very bright (high-key lighting) or dark (low-key lighting). 'Backlighting' lights the subject from behind, creating a silhouette effect while leaving, e.g., a face in the shadow.

Acting/choreography: the effect actors/actresses have on the audience, including their appearance, movements, gestures, facial expressions, voice. Acting (together with the choreography or scheme of movements) attract and guide the viewer's attention in a certain way or even manipulate his/her sympathies. They might also create tension or wrong clues.

Costume/make-up: as a consequence of costume and make-up a realistic or stylized/abstract impression can be achieved. Costumes can signify status wealth, foreignness, etc.

Cinematic codes
All films are assembled from four basic building blocks:

The *Frame* is the individual picture.

The *Shot* is the basic unit of the film's image-meaning system. There are basically three categories of shots: distance (e.g. long shot, medium shot, close-up), angle (e.g. low angle, flat angle, high angle), movement (e.g. pan, tracking shot, zoom).

The *Scene* is a group of interrelated shots in a location.

The *Sequence* is a group of interrelated scenes forming a natural unit of the story.

These basic elements have to be edited together to make a coherent final whole.

Editing
The process of editing concerns the deliberate placement of separate shots or sequences in relation to each other. Special editing techniques are used to place the narrative in sequence and also to shape time and space.
Example: the scene of a boxing match in a film has to be filmed first and is then edited to make the viewer feel he is in the ring with the fighters as well as to include the spectators' point of view.
Some editing techniques are:

Real time editing: the time taken by the sequences is equal to the time of the performance.

Dissolves: include alternating from one scene to another, e.g., to show that time has passed in the same place.

Wipes: enable a narrative transition from one place to another, e.g. to move from a scene in London to one in New York.

Cuts: are the direct changes from one shot to another to help both action and narrative move quickly and sharply.

Fades: fading in or fading out create emerging or disappearing scenes, and are common techniques to show the passage of time.

The sound and music

Although the sound and the music are often given less attention than the visual dimension of a film, they are important for the viewer's ability to follow the narrative line an to make sense of the story.

Dialogue: the characters may employ different kinds of language (e.g. slang, dialect), but characters can also communicate through their silence.

Music: the music can create the expressive, emotional mood of a scene: There are different kinds of music like classical or popular music: The music can be typical of the period that is presented in the film: it may comment on (foreshadow or contradict) the action, thereby directing the viewer's attention within the film.

Sound effects: can be based on a natural (rain, wind) or artificial sound.

Voice-over: this technique consists of a narration or dialogue coming from a time or space other than that of the screen image. It explains what is not shown in the scene or comments on what is only implied by the action, the setting or the characters.

Synchronisation: the technique of matching the sound with the image. The sound may not be simultaneous with the picture, e.g. in the case of a reminiscing narrator or when the sound from the next scene begins while the images of the last one are still in the screen (= 'sound bridge').

Film genre

When similar types of films are grouped together they are referred to as 'genre', i.e. they are thought to have common codes and conventions. The word 'genre' was originally used to define works of literature into different categories such as romance, gothic or comedy. When applied to films the word 'genre' also means 'type' or 'category'.

Modern films often combine genres and create their own unique labels and categories, e.g. *Frankenstein* (1994) combines horror, adventure, romance and period costume drama.

The following list includes examples of some basic film genres: action film, adventure film, comedy, crime story, drama, fantasy film, horror, mystery, romance, science fiction, thriller, Western film.

Audiences find genres satisfying because they know that certain expectations may be fulfilled and they enjoy predicting what will happen next. Viewers know what to expect from a genre, but at the same time they want to find something they do not expect as it would otherwise be boring. Thus any film in any genre is a combination of the familiar and the unexpected.

Each genre has a recipe, which is comprised of a number of accepted ingredients that will allow the audience to recognise the product as a particular genre.

The key components are:

Stock characters
Genres nearly always have some key lead and supporting characters. e.g. a chief cop and his side kick in cop dramas.

Stock plots, situations, issues, themes
Certain plots are expected within genres, e.g. plots in Western films are often concerned with a search for a particular character or characters.

Stock *situations* can be found in most genres, e.g. the car chase in police series or detective stories.

Recurring *issues* also appear in certain genres, e.g. teenage pregnancy, divorce or infidelity in soap operas.

Themes should not be confused with plot. Greed and power are themes that underline the plots of many gangster films. The good versus the evil, jealousy, loyalty, etc., are important themes in a variety of genres.

Stock locations
The craterous landscape in science fiction films, the pub and the café in soap operas, the mean streets in cop thrillers are all locations that are recognisable to the audience and will communicate the type of genre.

Stock props and signifiers
These are often small items that sometimes hold a great deal of significance, e.g. the ray gun is a stock prop in science fiction. Certain sounds are also signifiers such as the creak of a door in a horror film.

Section Six – How to Use the Internet

Until quite recently if you wanted to find out some information the usual method was to consult a book. If you didn't own such a book yourself then you went to a library and tried to find it there. It is still possible to do research in this way, and often even necessary, but the real library of books, encyclopaedias and articles etc. has been supplemented by a kind of virtual library known as the Internet. When doing research the Internet has some great advantages over the traditional library but also some serious disadvantages. To help you tap into the advantages and avoid the disadvantages the following tips have been included in this reference library.

Searching

When looking for information on the Internet you generally need what is called a "search engine". There are several of them available, the most popular being Google and Yahoo, but there are others, of course. When you start the search engine you are required to type in keywords like "nanotechnology" or "gender" depending on the topic you are interested in. After you have done this the search engine will report how many "hits" it has made. Google comes up with about 26,800,000 for nanotechnology, which is not very helpful. By the time you have looked through all the websites listed nanotechnology would probably no longer exist and neither would you! The problem is that you probably didn't really know what exactly you were looking for. So before beginning your search, you need to have a fairly clear idea of what it is you want find out about. Maybe it is the possible dangers of nanotechnology. In this case you refine your enquiry by increasing the number of keywords for the search. If you type in dangers + nanotechnology the hits are reduced to 427,000, still not ideal but more manageable. Notice that keywords are usually added using the + sign. A further limitation might be the restriction to "dangers to health" (79 hits) or "health hazards" (81,400 hits). Notice here that complete phrases like "health hazards" are placed in quotation marks "...". If you don't do this you get all the websites that include health, hazards and nanotechnology irrespective of the phrase you're looking for. Most search engines also have advanced settings that enable you to choose websites in a specific language, in a specific format (e.g. html, pdf), produced after a certain date or excluding certain words, etc. Normally you have to proceed by a process of trial and error until you get the results you want. Be patient and take your time!

Finding

One of the main difficulties of using the Internet for research is making sure you find or select good quality information. As there is no real restriction on who may place texts in the public domain so, in contrast to books and articles, there is no real quality control. The Internet is a very democratic place! But there are some tests you can do to at least partly guarantee that you are making use of reliable sources.

Ask yourself the following questions

Who is the author? Have you heard of him/her before? Have they published books and articles that you have heard of or that are referred to in the text? Is this person an acknowledged expert? Is the text anonymous? Is an e-mail address provided? If the answer is "yes", then it is more than likely that you have found some reliable source.

Whose website is it published on? Is it one the website of a known university or a public organization with a recognized reputation?

Is the information factual? And are any opinions supported by evidence? Sometimes an Internet text is made up purely of opinion; this is usually the sign that someone is inexperienced or has a special agenda that they want to get across. Avoid such articles.

Are there references to other sources? If there are, you can cross-check for reliability.

How up-to-date is the information? When was the text originally published? Has it recently been updated? Obviously the more up-to-date the text is, the better.

If you continually ask yourself these questions and find satisfactory answers to them you should avoid making too many errors of judgement when selecting Internet materials as sources of information.

Index

Abbreviations

n.	=	noun	infml.	=	informal
v.	=	verb	coll.	=	colloquial
adj.	=	adjective	derog.	=	derogatory
adv.	=	adverb	sl.	=	slang
prep.	=	preposition	dial.	=	dialect
conj.	=	conjunction	s.o.	=	someone
sing.	=	singular	s.th.	=	something
pl.	=	plural	o.s.	=	oneself
BrE	=	British English	i.e.	=	that is
AmE	=	American English	l./ll.	=	line/lines
CarE	=	Caribbean English	p./pp.	=	page/pages
esp.	=	especially	f.	=	and the following (page, line etc.)
usu.	=	usually	ff.	=	and the following (pages, lines etc.)
interj.	=	interjection	e.g.	=	for example
fml.	=	formal	vol.	=	volume

The phonetic transcriptions follow the *Longman Dictionary of Contemporary English (DCE).*